History Through the Black Experience

Simon Hudson

Published by New Generation Publishing in 2022

Copyright © Simon Hudson 2022

First Edition

The author asserts the moral right under the Copyright, Designs and Patents Act 1988 to be identified as the author of this work.

All Rights reserved. No part of this publication may be reproduced, stored in a retrieval system or transmitted, in any form or by any means without the prior consent of the author, nor be otherwise circulated in any form of binding or cover other than that which it is published and without a similar condition being imposed on the subsequent purchaser.

ISBN: 978-1-80369-092-6

www.newgeneration-publishing.com

New Generation Publishing

Introduction:

If you are reading this I would expect that you are already familiar with volume one of "History Through The Black Experience" which showcases events and characters linking January through to June. Volume two, July through to December, has numerous connections to the previous book.

In telling and cataloguing these stories the aim is for the reader to recognise how the Black community has been present and represented at every level throughout wider society. The Black narrative is rich and diverse but all too often it has been affected by misrepresentation; be it stereotyping, pigeon holing, distortion, redaction, being ignored in parts, or as a whole, or even appropriation.

This work comes from personal experiences. Growing up in the late 1960's and 70's I lost count of the times I was told to go back to Africa or simply to return to the jungle. Although born in England, for some, it was clear that I was not welcome. When Clive Lloyd's all conquering West Indies cricket team beat the world, in the one day form of the game, in 1975, the pride within me could not be contained. As Bob Marley and reggae music permeated the airwaves I identified with a sound that reflected my heritage. Attending a Black Pentecostal Church I felt comfortable and secure surrounded by a dynamic extended family of Brothers and Sisters. Still I existed in a false bubble, a fragile bubble, that could and would frequently burst punctured by persistent racist attacks and a lack of self awareness fostering self doubt.

It was a time that followed Enoch Powel's 'Rivers of Blood' speech in 1968. We were witnesses to the rise of the far right represented by The National Front. Few people of colour escaped the daily epithets directed at a visible minority. Race relations legislation introduced by Harold Wilson's Labour government attempted, but failed, to secure equal and fair treatment in employment, in housing and the legal system. As a young Black male I had to navigate an often hostile environment. It became accepted advise for parents to instruct their Black children to work twice as hard as their White counterparts. I inhabited a world where White culture and norms dominated. Tarzan ruled in the African jungle. Cowboys and the white heroes of the US Cavalry saved the day massacring, those scalping savages, the 'red' skinned Indians. The actor Sidney Poitier allowed us to see a Black character on TV. Shaft was a welcome, but brief, break from traditional images at the cinema. Both were exceptions to the rule. Black representation on the box, on the big screen, in literature and in the historical context was rare or limited to slavery, humiliation in movies such as King Kong were common. There was representation of singers and in sport. It was not until the rise and rise of Michael Jackson that the community had someone to challenge the supremacy of Sinatra, Elvis or the Beatles. Muhammad Ali became an icon able to champion the Black story.

This book is written to offer the Black community the opportunity to embrace our history; achievements, successes, failings and weaknesses. We do not have to be ignorant of our past. We do not have to feel limited or behind the curve searching for heroes and sheroes. We were there, that is why we are here, we have always been present. Our story is not about the select few permitted to make it through by the gatekeepers. Entries do not have to be apologetically positive. We do not need to defend ourselves. We were sinned against through colonialism, empire and slavery. We do need to explain, putting records straight, and providing context. The Black narrative should be as common place in the wider (White) society as the stories of Henry VIII, Shakespeare, Queen Victoria, Hitler, Churchill and Kennedy are to the Black community.

Having a past with stories to tell provides one with a sense of pride, direction and relevance. Having a narrative breaks down stereotypes and limitations. Others can no-longer claim ignorance and should see a whole person, one that is fully rounded. As a people we go beyond the one dimension to a three dimensional complex character. This book will not end the evils of racism and prejudice. I do hope that for many eyes, minds and doors will be opened, and that all ethnic groups, white and those of colour, will bathe in and share in this part of the Human story.

July 1st:

On this day in 1863 **slavery became illegal in Surinam and the Antilles** in the Dutch East Indies. The Dutch were amongst the last European powers to end the practice. Although illegal enslaved people were required to work for their 'masters' for a further ten years. The slave owners were compensated by the state 300 guilders for every individual freed.

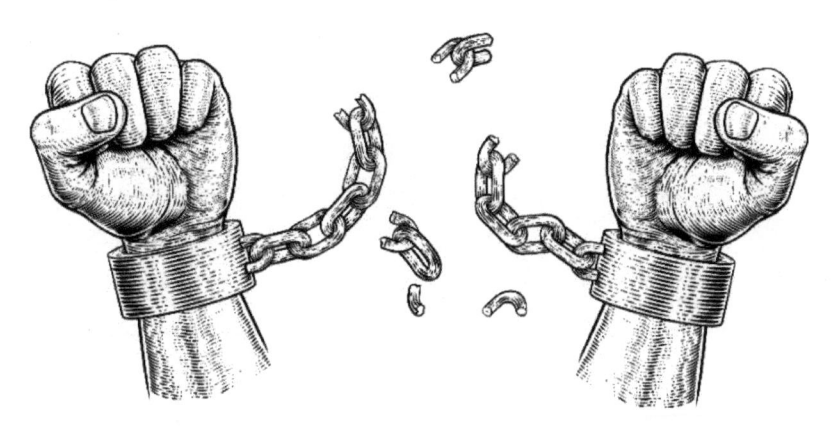

Walter White, born on this day in 1893, joined the National Association for the Advancement of Colored People (NAACP) as an investigator in 1918. He could pass as a white person so was able to infiltrate areas that would have been life threatening for someone who looked black.

Walter White, the Civil Rights champion, led the NAACP from 1929–1955. He died March 21st in 1955, aged sixty-one.

To grasp the true brutal senseless horror of what started **on this day** 1917, and continued for a total of three days, I suggest that the reader go online to read a copy of the account: **The Massacre of East St Louis** found in the NAACP paper 'The Crisis' an account written by W. E. B. Du Bois, Vol 14, No 5, September 1917.

The narrative is all too sickeningly familiar; official records write of thirty-nine blacks and nine whites dead. Unofficial accounts estimate between 100 and 200 black men, women and children murdered. $400,000 ($7 m in 2020) worth of damage to property leaving 6,000 black people homeless. A local reporter (witness) writing for the *St Louis Post Dispatch*, wrote of well dressed, whites calmly going about their business engaged in a manhunt played as sport.

The final injustice was, as has often been the case, that the events of the three days have been largely forgotten, ignored or hidden from the annals of US history and, where reported, incorrectly, presented as a race riot.

The **Father of Gospel** music **Thomas A. Dorsey** was born on this day 1899. While on the road he received word that his wife Nettie had died in childbirth. The baby died the following day. Distraught Dorsey wrote his most famous song 'Take My Hand, Precious Lord' a few days later, in 1932.

Dorsey started out in the blues as a composer and arranger. He toured with **Ma Rainey** playing the piano and arranging her material. After 1929 Dorsey only played gospel but never lost the influence of the blues. He wrote close to 3,000 songs including 'Peace in the Valley'. He stopped recording in 1934 but continued to be fully involved in the industry. Thomas A Dorsey died aged ninety-four on January 23rd 1993. His work would open doors for **Albertina Walker, Dorothy Norwood, The Clark Sisters, Shirley Caesar, Clara Ward, Walter** and **Tramaine Hawkins** just to name a few of the greats in the genre of gospel music. legacy See **Mahalia Jackson**, January 25th, **James Cleveland**, December 5th, **Andrea Crouch** below.

Shirley Caesar   Kirk Franklin   Clara Ward   and   Dorothy Norwood.

Blues songwriter **Willie Dixon** would write and co-write over 500 songs creating Chicago blues out of the Chess label. His work would be covered by contemporaries **Muddy Waters, Howlin' Wolf, Bo Diddley** and **Little Walter.** The British groups of the 1960s such as the Rolling Stones would cite Dixon's work as a major influence as observed by their cover of 'Little Red Rooster'. Willie Dixon was born **on this day** in 1915 and died on January 29th 1992.

Born into royalty, **on this day** in 1921, in what was Bechuanaland, later Botswana, **Sir Seretse Khama** would be the first president of independent Botswana. His marriage to a white English woman in 1948, Ruth Williams Khama would cause diplomatic problems in both countries. The story was captured in the 2016 film *A United Love*.

Sir Seretse Khama.

Khama returned to his homeland, a private citizen, founding the Democratic Party in 1962. In 1965 he became the county's prime minister. Khama helped negotiate independence for Botswana from Britain in 1966. That same year he was knighted. Sir Seretse Khama died on July 13th 1980. He was president from 1966 to 1980. Lady Ruth Khama, born 1923, died on 22nd May 2002 in Botswana.

Contemporary Christian music songwriter and singer **Andraé Crouch,** and his Twin sister **Sandra** were born **on this day** in 1942. He would dominate the Christian music scene in the 1970s and 1980s. His vocal arrangements would be employed by Michael Jackson in 'Man in the Mirror'. His songs: 'Take me Back', 'Jesus Is the Answer', 'Soon and Very Soon' and 'It Won't be Long' became standards within both the black and white church. Crouch adopted many contemporary styles, his music, although never traditionally Gospel nonetheless bridged the gap between the traditional Black Gospel sound and what would become known as Praise and Worship. Andrae Crouch died on January 8th 2015. See **Mahalia Jackson**, January 31st, **James Cleveland**, December 5th, **Mavis Staples**, July 10th, and **Thomas A. Dorsey** above.

Somalia independence from Britain and Italy took place **on this day** in 1960. The President of the United Republic of Somalia **Aden Abdullah Osman Daar** served from 1960–1967. The country's first Prime Minister was **Abdirashid Ali Shamarke.**

Somalian girl.

Athlete **Carl Lewis** was born **on this day** in 1961. He won nine Olympic golds and one silver in the 1980s and 1990s specialising in the 100m, 200m, four by 100m relay and the long jump. At the 1984 Los Angeles's Olympics Lewis won four golds, only the third person to do so in track and field after Alvin Kraenzlein in 1900 and **Jesse Owens** in 1936. Carl Lewis won ten World Championship medals including 8 golds in his career from 1979 to 1996. He had a winning streak of sixty-five consecutive victories in the long jump over a decade of competition. His indoor long jump record set in 1984 still stands at the time of writing thirty-six years later in 2020. Carl Lewis ran below 10 sec for the 100m fifteen times and below 20 sec for the 200m ten times.

Carl Lewis.

Rwanda and **Burundi** celebrated their independence **on this day** in 1962 from Belgium. Rwanda split from Burundi with **Gregoire Kayibanda** as president from 1963–1973. President **Juvenal Habyarimana** took control as president **from** 1973–1994. **Burundi** had a constitutional monarchy under King **Mwami Mwambusta IV**. Hutu **Pierre Ngendandumwe** served as the newly independent country's first **prime** minister. Neither country would find immediate stability or peace in independence.

Women from Rwanda and Burundi

Jamaican 'Crown Prince of Reggae' **Dennis Brown** was born in Kingston on February 1st 1957. A singer and songwriter Brown recorded prolifically releasing over seventy-five albums. He worked with many of his contemporaries including **Gregory Isaacs**, **Horace Andy, Mutabaruka, Beres Hammond, Freddie McGregor, Maxi Priest, Shabba Ranks, Beanie Man, Sly** and **Robbie** just to name a few.

Brown's most productive collaborations were with the producer **Niney 'the Observer' Holness.** As a teenager he recorded 'Money in my Pocket' with Holness. Brown would have numerous hits including: 'Revolution', 'Cheater', 'Too Much Information', 'Here I Come', 'Your Love Got a Hold On Me', 'How Could I Leave', 'Oh Girl', 'Wolf and Leopards', 'No More Will I Roam', 'Sitting and Watching' and 'Get Myself Together'.

Dennis Brown had respiratory problems that had been exacerbated by his addiction to drugs, cocaine in particular. He collapsed and was taken to hospital in Jamaica but weak from the drug abuse died aged forty-two **on this day** in 1999. See **Bob Marley** February 6th, **Jimmy Cliff** April 1st, **Desmond Dekker** May 25th, and **Toots Hibbert** September 11th

Soul singer Luther Vandross

Grammy award soul singer and songwriter **Luther Vandross** born April 20th 1951 died **on this day** in 2005. He was fifty-four. Vandross' silky smooth soul voice won him thirty-three Grammy nominations and eight Grammy Awards. He released thirteen studio albums and fifty-nine singles.

July 2nd:

The history of what would become the Democratic Republic of the Congo (DRC) and Belgium has been an uneasy and often brutal one. When **Patrice Lumumba** was murdered, along with **Joseph Okito** and **Maurice Mpolo,** the world looked on aghast in horror.

Patrice Lumumba was born **on this day** in 1925 from the small Congolese ethnic group of the Batetela. Lumumba showed early political interest writing essays and poetry for local journals. Involved with trade unions he went on a group tour of Belgium in 1956. On his return he was arrested and accused of embezzlement from the Post Office. Lumumba served twelve months in prison and was fined. The experience did not deter him from politics. On release, along with others, Lumumba launched the Congolese National Movement (MNC) in October 1958, the first national Congolese political party. The following year he attended the first All-African People's Conference held in Accra Ghana, December 1958. Lumumba returned with clear nationalist and pan-African goals.

Recognising the rise of nationalism and calls for independence, the Belgian government planned for local elections for December 1959. The MNC, fearing the election was about the Belgians installing a puppet government, refused to participate. Earlier in the year in October Belgian authorities clashed in the town of Stanleyville leaving thirty dead. Lumumba was arrested and charged with inciting riots. With a change of mind, the MNC entered the election and won a landslide with 90per cent of the vote.

In January 1960, the Belgian government held a round table conference to discuss independence. It was agreed that new elections would be held in May which the MNC won. Lumumba merged as the leading nationalist politician. The colonialist power attempted to stop him but failed, Lumumba was asked to form the new independent government on June 24th 1960.

Immediately a power struggle ensued as the mineral rich area of Katanga declared separation led by **Moise Tshombe.** The Belgian army used the opportunity to return to the newly independent country appearing to undermine the inexperienced government of Lumumba. A call was put to the United Nations requesting assistance. The UN was largely ineffective appearing condescending and rather assertive. Feeling let down and with nowhere to turn, Lumumba asked for help from the Soviet Union. The Western alliance, in the middle of the cold war, in horror turned a blind eye and deaf ears to the plight of Lumumba's government.

President **Kasavubu** dismissed Lumumba's government. While the legality of Kasavubu's actions were being investigated the army led by **Col Joseph Mubuto,** later President of Zaire, seized power. The UN recognised Kasavubu's government. Placed under house arrest Lumumba was captured as he attempted to flee. On a flight to Lubumbashi on January 17 1961 with Okito and Mpolo, the three were severely beaten by their captors. On arrival the three were beaten again before being executed by firing squad under Belgian command. Their bodies were buried in a shallow grave but ordered, by the Belgians, to be dug up. They were then hacked to pieces and either dissolved in acid or burned by fire. The deaths were only officially announced on February 13th 1961.

One can only speculate what would have happened in the Democratic Republic of the Congo had the country been supported through the process of independence rather than being seen as a land to plunder and exploit.

The siege of Salvador in Bahia Brazil ended **on this day** 1823. During the Brazilian War of Independence 1839. The siege started 2nd March 1822 lasting through to 2nd July 1832. The Brazilians and Portuguese suffered 3,250 dead with close to 1,000 wounded.

Aaron E Henry, activist and politician was born **on this day** 1922. He was a founding member of the Regional Council of Negro Leadership in 1951. He was the head of the NAACP chapter in Mississippi from 1960–1993.

Henry was arrested some thirty-eight times. On one occasion he was chained to the back of a refuse (garbage) truck and taken to prison in Clarksdale. In the early 1980s Henry was elected to a seat in the Mississippi legislature holding the seat until 1996.
Aaron E. Henry died on May 19th 1997.

Award-winning playwright **Ed Bullins** was born **on this day** in 1932. A prolific dramatist of black theatre in the 1960s. He was briefly the Minister of Culture for the Black Panther Party. Popular plays include *The Fabulous Miss Marie, Storyville, In the New England Winter, The Electric Nigger* and *Clara's Ole Man.*

July 3rd:

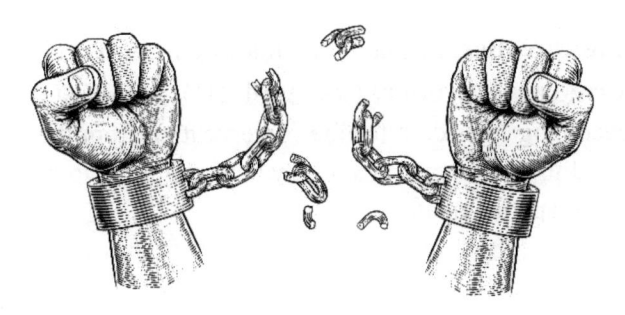

On this day in 1848 following a peaceful slave uprising on the island of St Croix, part of what today is the US Virgin Islands including St Thomas and St John, **slavery** was **abolished** in the Dutch West Indies **(US Virgin Islands).**

There had been a slave uprising on St John in 1733 which led to the slaves governing the island for six months before the rebellion was quashed with the assistance of the French. When news reached the island of St Croix that the French had abolished slavery on their West Indian islands in 1848 nine thousand slaves staged a non-violent rebellion. They demanded, eventually getting, their emancipation from the Governor of the island Peter Von Scholten.

Each year on July 3rd the islands celebrate commemorating 'V I Emancipation Day' as an official bank holiday.

John Smith Hurt was born **on this day** in 1893. Commonly known as country blues singer and guitarist **Mississippi John Hurt.** He started recording in the 1920s and was rediscovered as part of the American folk revival of the 1960s. He died on November 2nd 1966.

Bermudan born actor **Earl Cameron** along with **Cy Grant** (see November 8th) did more than any other actor to break the colour bar in British TV and film. He represented the black character in forty films, TV series and dramas.

Cameron's debut was in the 1951 film noir *Pool of London*. It was the first major British production to look at the question of interrelationships. He would appear in James Bond's *Thunderball* in 1965, act alongside Sir Laurence Olivier in the 1962 *Term of Trial* and appeared in *The Queen* (2006). On TV, Earl Cameron was in *The Prisoner* and *Danger Man* as well as numerous dramas and made for TV films. Earl Cameron died aged 102 **on this day** in 2020.

John Swan was Bermudan premier from 1982–1995. He resigned following his failure to convince Bermudans to vote for independence from Great Britain following the 1995 referendum.

Swan, a property developer and politician, transformed the island with major development projects, international trade and politics. He established Bermuda as an offshore financial centre having skilfully negotiated the Tax Treaty with the United States in 1985.
John Swan was born **on this day** in 1935.

Puerto Rican, salsa legend, **Cheo Feliciano** was born **on this day** in 1935. His deep baritone voice was unusual for a salsa singer. The performer was a talented percussionist and composer. Feliciano enjoyed a fifty-year career that embraced both salsa and bolero.

'Baby Doc', Jean-Claude Duvalier, was born **on this day** in 1951. Following the death of his father, the dictator **Papa Doc Francois Duvalier,** (see April 21st). Jean-Claude became the then youngest president aged nineteen, becoming 'president for life'. Intervention from the United States urged reforms. Although Jean-Claude moved to a moderate position, when compared to his father, he still made all the major political and top judicial appointments.

Like father like son!

Following a popular uprising Baby Doc left Haiti, with his wife Michelle Bennett, seeking sanctuary in France. The French resisted calls to extradite the former 'president for life'. Baby Doc returned on his own volition, after twenty-five years in exile, in January 2011 following the devastating earthquake that hit Haiti in 2010.

Jean-Claude Duvalier was taken in for questioning concerning corruption and embezzlement but was soon released. He proved uncooperative with the legal procedure. Duvalier refused to attend hearings looking at violations of human rights and abuses. Duvalier died October 4th 2014 before he could be brought to justice.

On this day in 1966 **racial violence** erupted in **Omaha, Nebraska**. The ingredients are all too familiar; an area that still had some Jim Crow laws in place, segregated policies employed by businesses, limited job opportunities for the black population and discriminatory housing policies, all ignited by police brutality killing young black people fleeing from the scene of a crime.

July 4th:

Founded as the Tuskegee Normal School, the **Tuskegee Institute** would become one of the great black American education establishments. Today the university offers about forty bachelor's degree programmes and around seventeen master's courses. Close to 75per cent of all black veterinarians in the US graduated from Tuskegee's School of Veterinary Medicine. The school would also become the base for the famous **Tuskegee airmen** flight training programme.

The Normal School was established by former slave and local black leader **Lewis Adams** and former slave owner **George W. Campbell**. Campbell had a commitment to providing education to the local black population. The two were able to negotiate the legal and political provision to establish a school. When seeking a principal twenty-five-year-old **Booker T. Washington** was recommended. He would lead the institute from its opening **on this day** 1881 to his death aged fifty-nine in 1915.

Washington opened the school in a rundown room with thirty adult students. The initial aim was to train teachers to go out into the black community of Alabama. It was the students that constructed the buildings, produced their food and provided most of their basic provisions. The skills learned and developed were part of the experience taking their expertise out into the community.

With close to 3,000 students today the university has an illustrious history. It provided the platform for Booker T. Washington to be the most influential black American of his time. Scientist **George Washington Carver** worked out of the institute. The establishment was designed and landscaped by **Robert Robinson Taylor** who was the first black man to graduate from the prestigious Massachusetts Institute of Technology. He worked in conjunction with **David Williston** who was the first professionally trained black American landscape architect.

Graduate Robert Robinson Taylor

On March 31st 1817 the state legislature for New York officially planned to end the legality of slavery. This took place **on this day** in 1827. New York became the first state to abolish slavery.

July 5th:

Tom Mboya (Thomas Joseph Odhiambo Mboya) born on August 15th 1930 was murdered **on this day** in 1969. One of the founding fathers of the Republic of Kenya, Mboya's work went beyond the confines of his beloved country. A member of the Lou people, Mboya was a pan-Africanist. He was elected by **Kwame Nkrumah**, in 1958 aged twenty-eight, as the conference chair at the first All-African Conference held in Accra, Ghana.

He would call for a conference to be held in Lagos, Nigeria in 1959, to form the first All-African labour organisation.

Tom Mboya's political career started out with the trade union movement. He was a key nationalist during the period of the Mau Mau uprising from 1952–1960. During that period Mboya was the general secretary of the Kenyan Federation of Labour. His position was unusual as pre-1960 no African national organisations were permitted under colonial rule. Elected as a workers' candidate onto the legislative council in 1957, Mboya was one of just eight African members on the council. That same year he helped form the Kenyan independence movement within the council and the People's Convention party, in Nairobi.

Working with the US President Kennedy and civil rights activist **Martin Luther King Jr,** Mboya helped to found the African-American Student Foundation raising money and providing transportation for East African students to study in the USA. In 1960 Tom Mboya became the first Kenyan to appear on the cover of *TIME* magazine. The same year he was a founding member of the Kenyan African National Union.

In the coalition government, before independence, Mboya served as the minister of labour. He was heavily involved in the independence talks that took place at Lancaster House in 1963.

Following independence on 12th December 1963 Tom Mboya served as minister of justice and constitutional affairs. From 1964–69 Mboya was minister for economic planning and development. He promoted a strong capitalist mixed economy. Many felt that Mboya's position under-mined African socialism which made him enemies. Shot by **Nahashon Njoroge** on this day 1969, Mboya's death caused anger on the streets with many believing it was a political assassination. Njoroge died on November 8th without revealing why he murdered the politician. A statue now stands where Tom Mboya fell.

Cape Verde celebrated its independence **on this day** 1975 from Portugal. **Aristides Pereira** served as the country's first president from 1975–91. The prime minister, 1975–91 was Pedro Pires who went on to serve as president from 2001–2011.

Aristides Pereira

Dr Martin Griffiths was appointed the first National Health Service (NHS) Clinical Director for Violence Reduction on June 20th 2019. He is, at the time of writing, the consultant vascular and trauma surgeon and lead surgeon at Barts Health NHS Trust in London. **On this day** in 2018 the NHS celebrated its seventieth anniversary. Griffith was selected as a 'Hero Doctor' for his lifesaving work focusing on stab and gun victims and his campaigning in British classrooms.

Martin Griffiths was motivated to specialise in trauma surgery following a knife attack and the death of a younger family member. The *Independent on Sunday* selected Griffith in 2014 for its 'happy list'. His team helped to reduce the number of victims returning to hospital from gun and knife related crime from 45per cent to less than 1per cent. He was appointed as the first Ambassador to the Mary Seacole Trust in 2018.

July 6th:

Canadian born **Viola Desmond** was born **on this day** in 1914. Her case, having been convicted for non-payment of tax for sitting in the more expensive white section of the cinema, would launch Canada's modern Civil Rights Movement.

Desmond's car had broken down in New Glasgow, Nova Scotia, November 8th 1949. She had been informed that it would not be returned to her until the following day. With no option than to stay overnight, Desmond ventured to the Roseland Theatre to watch *The Dark Mirror* that evening. She purchased a ticket but being near-sighted moved to a seat where she could see better. When asked to move it clicked that the theatre had a whites' only section. Desmond refused to move and was unceremoniously dragged from the cinema hurting her hip. She faced over twelve hours in the police cell and was fined $20 for having failed to pay the government tax of 1 cent on the more expensive ticket in the whites' only section.

Returning home Viola spoke to her husband about her experience. He told her to let the issue go. Having spoken to **William Pearly Oliver,** who worked at her local church and journalist and activist **Carrie Best** it was decided to appeal against the conviction. Oliver was central to the formation of four of Nova Scotia's key black Civil Rights organisations in the twentieth century. As the case had been about tax evasion and not one of civil rights Desmond lost her appeal but became famous for her stand.

Viola Desmond had trained as a beautician having to travel to Montreal, Atlantic City and New York where she attended **Madam C. J. Walker's** (see December 23rd) school. Returning to her home in Halifax she set up her beauty salon. She later opened her own school training black beauticians to work and provide employment in the community. Desmond also produced and marketed her own beauty products.

Following the cinema incident, case and appeal, Viola Desmond closed her businesses in Halifax and moved to Montreal eventually settling in New York City. She died aged fifty on February 7th 1965 and was buried at Camp Hill Cemetery, Halifax, Nova Scotia.

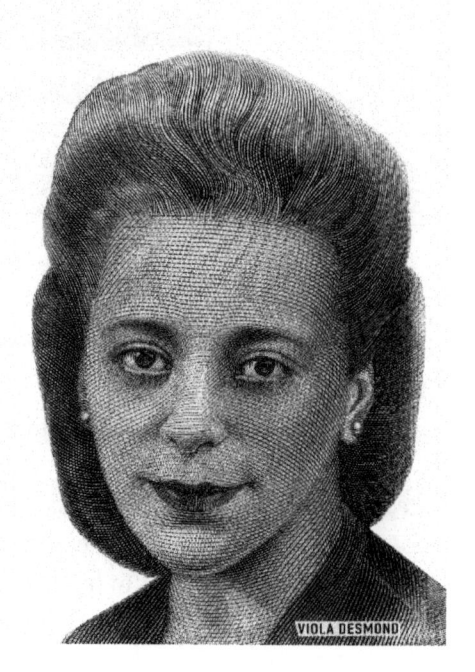

Viola Desmond

Viola Desmond was posthumously pardoned in 2010 becoming the first Canadian to receive the honour. She also became the first woman to appear alone on a Canadian bank note when she was illustrated on the $10 note in 2018.

The Nigerian Civil War, Biafran War or the **Biafran Nigerian War** started **on this day** in 1967. It was a conflict that would lead to the death of over a million people. More Biafrans died from starvation than from bullets or bombs. The images of starvation brought to the world's attention what was happening on the west coast of Africa.

Nigerian independence, October 1st 1960, had been followed by political and social unrest and turmoil. There had been political coups, retaliations, and the mass movement of the Igbo people. When senior Nigerian officers, many Igbo, were involved in the 1966 coup and the killing of the much loved and revered politician **Ahmadou Bello,** (see June 12th) the Igbo people, fearing and facing reprisals returned to their ancestral homeland.

Feeling marginalised and under attack Biafra declared independence from Nigeria. This was followed by war in July 1967 with the Biafrans led by **Lt Colonel Odumegwu Ojukwu** (1933–2011) fighting the Nigerian government of **General Yakubu Gowan.** The Nigerian forces were well equipped and supported by the British and the Soviets while the Biafrans started out with no modern weapons, a largely untrained army but received support from the French and Israel.

By October, the Biafran capital Enugu had fallen. In May 1968, the Nigerians had captured the oil rich Port Harcourt. The following year the newly established Biafran capital of Umuahia had been captured. January 1970 saw Ojukwu flee, forced into exile, seeking sanctuary in the Ivory Coast. That same month the Biafran forces surrendered on 15th January 1970.

Odumegwu Ojukwu would eventually receive a full pardon and return after thirteen years in 1982 to Nigeria. He died in November 2011 and was given a full military burial. The ceremony was attended by the then President Goodwill Jonathan.

The Nigerian forces described starvation as a weapon of war. As with any conflict it has proven difficult to heal the pain and division. There have been accusations of genocide while smaller ethnic groups in the Biafran area were attacked by both sides. Since the war – fifty years – there has not been an Igbo president.

The African country of **Malawi** gained independence from Britain **on this day** in 1964. Independence ushered in three decades of the autocratic rule of **Hastings Kamuzu Banda.** See November 25th

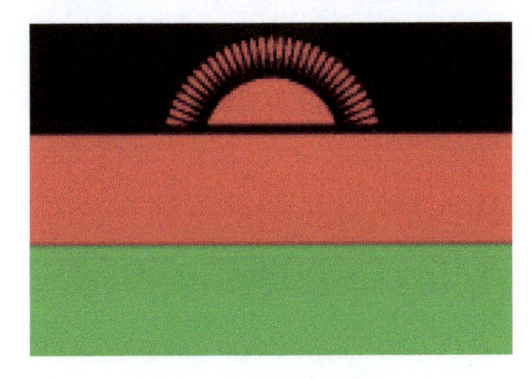

Malawi national flag.

The Comoros islands gained their independence **on this day** in 1975 from France. Granted autonomous rule in 1961, a referendum on independence was held on December 22nd, 1974. France had planned for the transfer of power to take place in 1978, the Comoros unilaterally announced independence for July 6th 1975. **Ahmed Abdallah Abderemane** served as the first president but was removed in a coup d'état by **Said Mohamed Jaffer** on August 3rd 1975. Jaffer in turn was ousted by **Ali Soilihi** in 1976. Political instability continued with the mercenary **Bob Denard** seizing power before returning Abderemane becoming president on October 25th 1978. He remained in power through to his death on November 26th 1989.

A Comoros Woman.

Allan Boesak published ***Black Theology and Black Power*** **on this day** in 1980. It followed the black theology presented by **James H. Cone** in 1969.

Boesak born on February 23rd 1946, cleric, politician and prominent former anti-apartheid activist also wrote: *Farewell to Innocence: A Socio-Ethical Study on Black Theology and Black Power* (1977), *The Finger of God: Sermons on Faith and Socio-Political Responsibility* (1982), *Black and Reformed: Apartheid, Liberation, and the Calvinist Tradition* (1984), *The Tenderness of Conscience: African Renaissance and the Spirituality of Politics* (2005), and *Dare We Speak of Hope?: Searching for a Language of Life in Faith and Politics* in 2014.

Black Theology.

Boesak served as president of the World Alliance of Reformed Churches, 1982–1991. One of his greatest achievements was to get the Alliance to declare apartheid a heresy resulting in white South African churches being suspended.

Convicted of fraud Allan Boesak served one year of the three-year sentence before being pardoned by President **Thabo Mbeki** in 2005. He was reinstated as a clergyman.

July 7th:

On this day in 1801 **Toussaint L'Ouverture** introduced a **new constitution** to the **Republic of Haiti.** The constitution was made up of seventy-seven articles under thirteen sections. Catholicism was the official religion, L'Ouverture did not embrace the Voodoo religion. Although the freedom of all was written into the constitution, workers were tied to their employment to ensure productivity and a strong economy. Toussaint L'Ouverture was the leader of the revolution that started in January 1st 1791 and ended on May 6th 1802. He served as the Lieutenant Governor of Saint Domingue from 1797 to July 7th 1801.

From July 7th 1801 to May 6th 1802 L'Ouverture was Governor General for life. He held office for a total of 1 year and 125 days.

The **Solomon Islands** gained independence **on this day** in 1978 from Great Britain. The first Minister was **Peter Kenilorea** (1943–2016). The island's first law graduate was **Frank Kabui** born April 20th 1946. He graduated in 1975.

The Island's national flag.

July 8th:

I would often hear how R&B came out of the blues, gospel and jazz but I could never identify the link. Who was the missing link? I had even greater problems finding the missing link between the three aforementioned genres and rock'n'roll. Then I heard **Louis Jordan and His Tympany Five.** All became clear and obvious, listening to his saxophone, the sound of jive, swing and that vocalisation opened the doors to new musical styles.

Louis Jordan emerged from the jazz and swing era. He worked with the **Chick Webb** orchestra with the young **Ella Fitzgerald** for two years from 1936–8. By the early 1940s he was one of the most popular recording artists who appealed and sold to both the black and white audience. From 1942 with 'I'm Gonna Leave You on the Outskirts of Town' to Weak Minded Blues in 1951 Jordan had fifty-seven R&B hits with Decca. He received equal billing with the likes of **Louis Armstrong,** Bing Cosby and Ella Fitzgerald.

Louis Jordan's popularity led to appearances in films: *Follow the Boys* (1944), *Meet Miss Bobby Socks* (1944), *Caledonia* (1945), *Swing Parade* (1946), *Beware* (1946), *Look Out, Sister* (1947) and *Reet, Petite, and Gone* in 1947. Jordan's popularity saw him spend 113 weeks at the top of the R&B charts.

Chuck Berry (see March 18th)**, Ray Charles** (see September 23rd) and Bill Hayley are just a few who state Jordan and His Tympany Five as a major influence. Ray Charles would sign Jordan recording him on his label from 1962–4. Jordan would record with Quincy Jones, 1956–7.

Louis Jordan fell out of fashion but continued to produce music at its best. By the time of his death February 4th 1975 his fame and knowledge of his influence had faded. With the success of **Clarke Peters'** musical homage to Jordan; *Five Guys Named Moe* a new audience discovered Louis Jordan and His Tympany Five. The musical was a major hit, first performed on 14th December 1990, enthralling audiences in London's West End and on Broadway in New York City.

Clarke Peters.

His Tympany Five was a strange name as there were usually six and no one played the tympany (kettle drums). Louis Jordan was born **on this day** in 1908. Many argue that 'Saturday Night Fish Fry' (1949) could be called the first rock and roll recording. Jordan was inducted into the Blues Hall of Fame in 1985 and the Rock and Roll Hall of Fame in 1987. He received a Lifetime Grammy Award in 2018. Jordan released 125 singles and had eighteen number 1s on the R&B charts. His hit *'Cho Cho Boogie'* spent eighteen weeks at the top spot.

Louis Jordan died from a heart attack and is buried in Mt Olive Cemetery in St Louis Missouri, he was sixty-six.

Tennis legend **Serena Williams,** born September 26th 1981, became world number one for the first time **on this day** in 2002. The casual observer would be wrong to believe that Williams was all about power, bulldozing her way through opponents. Serena Williams's skill, touch and match play have been underrated by commentators treating the tennis player as nothing more than a powerhouse out hitting the opposition.

The pre-eminent female tennis player of her age, winning twenty-three grand slams since her first slam victory at the US Open in 1999. At the time of writing, Williams is second only to Margaret Court in grand slam victories. Since becoming world number one she has spent a total of 319 weeks in the top spot, third after Steffi Graf and Martina Navratilova. Serena Williams has had to dig deep throughout her career. Her head to heads against many opponents demonstrates that Williams has never taken victory for granted. Serena record v Jennifer Capriati reads 10 wins and 7 loses. Serena v Martina Hingis 7 - 6, Serena v Justine Henin 8 - 6, Serena v Elena Dementieva 7 - 5, Serena v Venus Williams 14 - 11. The head-to-head matchups demonstrate Williams's resilience over a long period against a variety of opponents. One looks at previous tennis match ups: Sampras v Agassi, Borg v McEnroe and Navratilova v Evert. Serena has had to battle against a wider variety of opposition.

Physically, although a powerful presence on court, Serena has amazingly maintained her athleticism. She does not possess the typical or ideal body type for the game. It is to her credit that she has been able to play at the top of the game maintaining the physical atheism.

Serena Williams has won more grand slams in the modern era than any other female player. She has won all four slams consecutively twice in 2002/3 and again in 2014/15. With her sister Venus, Serena has won fourteen doubles grand slams. The sisters held four consecutive slam doubles titles in 2009/10.

Serena has also won two mixed doubles grand slams. She has won four Olympic golds, one in the singles and three in the doubles. She has a record, in the modern era, of thirteen grand slams on hard courts, seven Australian Open titles and equalled Chris Evert's record of six US Open titles. Serena Williams has lost ten grand slam finals. All figures correct to 2020. See **Althea Gibson**, May 26th, **Arthur Ashe** July 10th, **Yannick Noah** May 18th and **Yvonne Goolagong Crawley** July 1st.

July 9th:

On this day in 1860 **the slave schooner Clotilda**, crammed with 109 captured Africans, arrived in Mobile, Alabama to unload its human cargo. The importation of enslaved people into the USA had been banned in 1808. Profits in the cotton trade and the rise in the cost of buying slaves had led to calls for the import ban to be lifted. Local landowner in the area of Mobile, Timothy Meaher made a bet of $1,000 that he could sneak a shipload of human cargo into the States right under the noses of the authorities. It was a bet that he won.

The Clotilda would be the last known slave ship to enter America. Of the original 110 Africans that left the west coast of the continent on May 24th, one died on the six-week journey. The Clotilda was torched to hide the crime and the Africans, originally purchased for $9,000 in gold, were sold. They would have expected to have sold for close to $200,000 in 1860.

SLAVE AUCTION AT RICHMOND, VIRGINIA.

Zora Neal Hurston (see January 28th) interviewed **Cudjoe Lewis,** one of the last survivors from the ship, in 1927. His account was published in Hurston's **'Barracoon'** which was finally published in 2018. After the abolition of slavery in the USA survivors from the Clotilda unable to fund a return to their homeland bought an area north of Mobile and called it Africatown. Sylviane Diouf's book *Dreams of Africa in Alabama* (2017), documents the Clotilda story. With the discovery of the Clotilda burnt-out wreck there has been renewed interest in the ship and its story.

John Augustus Tolton was born, a commodity to be bought and sold on April 1st 1854. His father ran away to freedom to fight for the Unionist Army during the American Civil War. He died in battle. In 1862 the remainder of the Tolton family were able to escape, no longer someone's property but free to become somebody. Through the fog of racism and the brutality of the times, John Tolton was taken under the wing of Father McGirr who was able to enrol his young charge to receive an education. Witnessing Tolton's faith it was clear where his vocation lay. McGirr and others secured passage to Rome where Tolton trained at the seminary. No American seminary would accept a black man.

In his six years in Italy, Tolton is said to have become fluent in German, Italian, Latin, Greek and several African dialects as well as having become an accomplished musician. At the age of thirty-one he was ordained a priest on April 24th 1886. He returned to America as the first, publicly known, black priest (see **James Augustine Healy** August 6th & **Patrick Francis Healy**, holding his first Mass at St Boniface Church in Quincy, Illinois. Father Tolton became the pastor of St Joseph Catholic Church and school in Quincy. He was popular attracting white members, usually of German and Irish descent. The undercurrent of racism was never far away and drove competition and resentment. Father Tolton took a position in Chicago in 1889. He was able to secure funding to build the St Monica Church holding Mass there on the South side of the city in 1893. Often called 'Good Father Gus' Father Tolton died unexpectedly aged forty-three **on this day** in 1897. He is buried in Quincy, Illinois in the United States. See the first African American cardinal **Wilton Daniel Gregory** December 7th.

Govan Archibald Mvuyelwa Mbeki was born **on this day** in 1910. He joined the South African political freedom party the African National Congress (ANC) in 1935. He rose through the ranks to become the national chairman in 1956. Mbeki was arrested and put on trial as part of the infamous **Rivonia** case. Accused of plotting to overthrow the government he was given a life sentence and imprisoned on Robben Island.

While on Robben Island Mbeki produced the manuscripts for *South Africa: The Peasants' Revolt* were smuggled out. It's believed the manuscripts were written on toilet paper and taken to London where the book was published in 1964.

Mbeki was released from prison in 1981. Returning to politics he won a seat in the first all-race parliament in 1994. In 1999 the proud father Govan Mbeki saw his son **Thabo Mbeki** sworn in as President of South Africa.

Govan Mbeki the anti-apartheid activist, former leader of the ANC and the South African Communist Party died on August 30th 2001.

David Mandessi Diop was the angry young voice of Negritude literature. His voice through poetry promoted an independent Africa and condemned colonialism. He was described as the voice of the people without a voice. See **Aime Cesaire** June 26th and **Leopold Senghor** October 9th.

The Senegalese poet was born **on this day** in 1927. Influenced by **Aime Cesaire,** (see June 26th) his sole collection of poems *Coups de Pilon* (1956), was posthumously published in English as *Hammer Blows* in 1975, translated and edited by Simon Mondo and Frank Jones.

David Diop was seen as the most talented of the French West African poets that were emerging in the 1950s. The poems were a protest against European cultural values and the suffering of his people through the slave trade and colonialism. He called for a revolution. David Diop died before his ideas and ideals could reach maturity or be seen to unfold. He died aged thirty-one in a plane crash on August 29th 1960. See **Alioune Diop** January 10th.

The country of **South Sudan** was formed **on this day** in 2011.

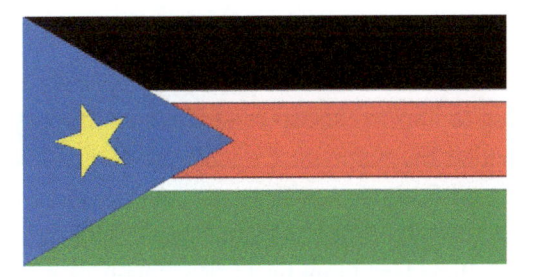

South Sudan's national flag.

July 10th:

Steve McQueen's 2013 Oscar-winning film *12 Years A Slave* was based on the life and times of **Solomon Northup.** Born **on this day** in 1807, Northup wrote about his experiences in the 1853 autobiography: *12 Years a Slave: Narrative of Solomon Northup, citizen of New York, kidnapped in Washington City in 1841 and rescued in 1853, from a cotton plantation near the Red River in Louisiana.*

Northrup was born free. Drugged and left unconscious he awoke shackled and held in an underground cell. He was abducted and taken to Richmond, Virginia then shipped to New Orleans and sold into slavery. It would take Solomon Northrup twelve years, experiencing the whip, attempts to lynch him and witnessing others whipped to death and lynched before he was able to regain and experience his freedom. He married Anne Hampton in 1828. The couple and their children were reunited in 1853 and granted freedom on January 4th.

Mary McLeod Bethune was born **on this day** in 1875. Called 'the female Booker T. Washington'. *Ebony* magazine, in July 1949, called Bethune *'the first lady of negro America'*. She was known as the first lady of the black struggle fighting to improve the lives of black Americans.

Mary McLeod Bethune founded the National Council for Negro Women in 1935. She acted as its president through to 1949. McLeod Bethune was also vice president of the National Association for the Advancement of Colored People 1946 to 1955. and established its journal *Aframerica Women's Journal*. She was appointed to work with President Franklin D. Roosevelt as a national advisor. They worked to create the Federal Council on Negro Affairs dubbed the 'black cabinet'.

Bethune the education champion opened a private school for black students in Florida. Today the school in Daytona Beach is called Bethune-Cookman University. Bethune was the only black female delegate on the United States team that helped to create the United Nations Charter. Mary McLeod Bethune was president of numerous black women's organisations. She died aged seventy-nine from heart failure on May 18th 1955. (See May 18th)

Mary McLeod Bethune.

Cuban poet **Nicolas Guillen** was born **on this day** in 1902. He would be remembered as the national poet of Cuba. Seen as one of the leading figures of the Afro-Cuban movement in the 1920s and 1930s, his poetry captured social unrest and protest.

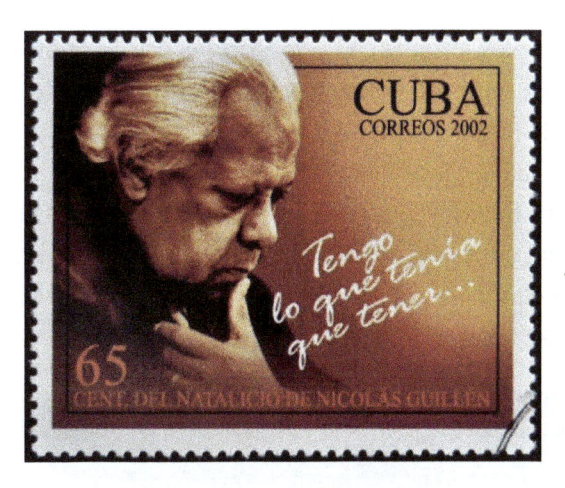

Cuban poet Nicolas Guillen.

Nicolas Guillen's early poetry looked at the daily lives of the poor. He became more politically outspoken in his work, calling out oppression. Guillen fought on the Republican side during the Spanish Civil War. On his return to Cuba, as a communist and critic of Batista's government in the 1950s, he was arrested several times and eventually went into exile. Guillen supported Fidel Castro in 1959. He became the director of Cuba's Union of Writers and Artists and was a member of the Central Committee of the Cuban Communist Party.

Nicolas Guillen died aged eighty-seven on July 16th 1989 suffering from Parkinson Disease.

One of the founding fathers of modern Nigeria, **Samuel Ladoke Akintola** was born **on this day** 1910. He held a number of government offices; as minister of labour and holding positions in health, communication and aviation. Akintola was a victim of the turbulent political history of Nigeria caught up in the 1966 coup. He died on January 15th of 1966.

David Dinkins was the first, and to date, the only black person to hold the office of Mayor in New York City. He was the 106th mayor of the city holding office from 1990–1993. David Dinkins was born **on this day** in 1927.

David Dinkins

Gospel singer, part of **The Staples singers, Mavis Staples** was born **on this day** in 1939. In the world of gospel music Mavis Staples with her father **Roebuck 'Pop' Staples** (1914–2000), sister **Cleotha** (1934–2013) and sister **Pervis** (1935-) were rare in being able to crossover to the wider world of secular music while losing none of their traditional beliefs or sound. With hits such as 'I'll Take You There', 'Respect Yourself', 'If You're Ready (Come Go with Me)' and 'Let's Do It Again', Mavis Staples was embraced by the public beyond the world of traditional gospel. Staples joined the rarefied world of **Sister Rosetta Tharpe, Mahalia Jackson** (see January 31st), **Edwin Hawkins** with 'Oh, Happy Day' and later **Kirk Franklin** as gospel artists with successful cross over careers.

Mavis Staple

Tennis player **Arthur Ashe** was born **on this day** in 1943. He would become the first black male player to win the US Grand Slam, as an amateur, in 1968, and the French Open Grand Slam title in 1970. He will probably be best remembered for winning Wimbledon against Jimmy Conners in 1975. He still remains the only black male player to have won Wimbledon forty-five years after his triumph. Ashe won the junior national titles in the US in 1960 and 1961. He became the first black player to be part of the US Davis Cup team in 1963. And the first black man to be ranked world number one.

Ashe was never comfortable having black expectations on his shoulders or having to be a spokesperson for the black community, neither did he shy away from being a representative and a role model. Arthur Ashe spoke out against apartheid and pushed to create inner city tennis initiatives. Ashe retired in 1980. He wrote three volumes looking at the achievements and struggles of African American athletes: *A Hard Road to Glory* in 1988.

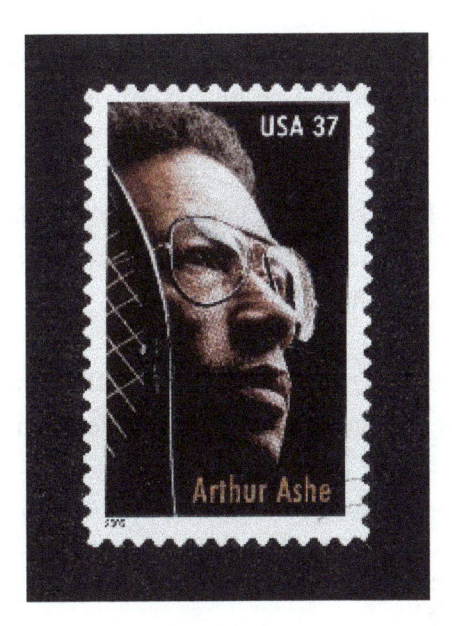

Arthur Ashe.

Ashe had had numerous health issues. In 1979 he had a quadruple heart bypass operation, which was repeated in 1983. Following paralysis in his right arm, Ashe had brain surgery. A biopsy revealed that Arthur Ashe had AIDS contracted from a blood transfusion following his 1983 operation. In 1992 he revealed his condition to the world and used his position to raise awareness about HIV/AIDS.

Arthur Ashe married **Jeanne Moutoussamy** in 1977. Their wedding was presided over by **Andrew Young,** the first black man appointed as the US Ambassador to the United Nations. The couple remained together until Arthur's death aged forty-nine on February 6th 1993. For tennis connections see **Althea Gibson** May 26th, **Yannick Noah** May 18th, **Serena Williams** July 8th, and **Yvonne Goolagong Crawley** July 1st.

On this day in 1951 **Randolph Turpin,** of Britain, shocked the boxing world by beating **Sugar Ray Robinson** of the USA (see May 3rd). Turpin (1928–1966) became Britain's first black world boxing champion, winning the middleweight title.

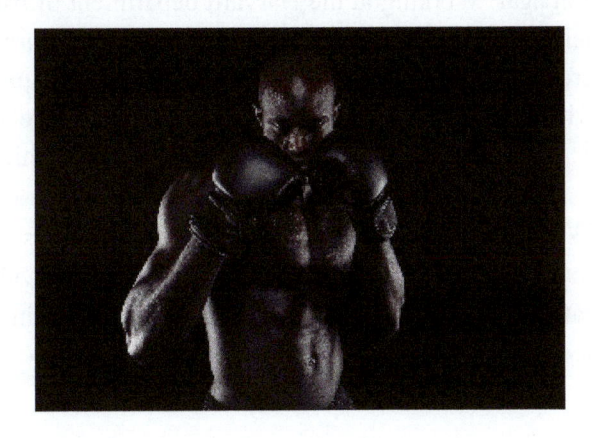

On this day in 1973 the sun set, after 300 years, ending British rule in the **Bahamas** as the islands celebrated independence. **Lynden Pindling** (see August 26th) considered the Father of the Nation led the Bahamas to majority rule on January 10th 1967. He served as Prime Minister from 1969–1992.

Pioneering black actor **Erroll John** was born in Port of Spain, Trinidad and Tobago, on December 20th 1924. John was one of the early presence of black actors on the stage, screen and on British TV. He died **on this day** in 1988. See **Earl Cameron** July 3rd.

Dr Mandisa Greene was appointed president of the British Royal College of Veterinary Surgeons (RCVS) **on this day** in 2020. She became the first black president in a profession where diversity is in the minority.

Jane Hinton, 1919–2003, and **Alfreda Johnson Webb,** 1923–1992, were the first two African American women Doctors of Veterinary Medicine graduating in 1949. They also became the first two black women members of the Veterinary Medicine Association in the USA. Before qualifying as a vet Hinton co-developed the Mueller-Hinton agar. Working at the Harvard department of bacteriology and immunology alongside John Howard Mueller, the pair discovered the properties of a culture medium where bacteria can thrive. This particular agar proved useful in testing bacterial susceptibility to antibiotics. Mueller and Hinton discovered that the starch within the agar helped to aid bacterial growth preventing bacterial toxins from interfering with antibiotic testing. The medium isolated neisseria which causes gonorrhoea and meningococcal meningitis.

Jane Hinton's father, **William Augustus Hinton,** 1883–1959, was the first African American professor at Harvard University. He developed a test for syphilis that was widely employed by US health authorities. With the publication of the 1936 *Syphilis and Its Treatment*, Hinton became the first African American to publish a medical textbook.

July 11th:

The updated reading, below, of a letter from **Queen Elizabeth I's Privy Council** has raised questions implying that the Queen wanted **all black people expelled from Britain**. Although some have appeared to reach that conclusion, the actions that followed would dispute a wholesale expulsion, questioning the premature conclusion of a mass deportation. Nonetheless the letter, one of two, raises many questions.

"An open letter to the Lord Mayor of London and the Aldermen and his brethren, and to all other mayors, sheriffs, etc. Her majesty, understanding that there are of late divers blackmoors brought into this realm, of which kind of people there are already here too many, considering how God hath blessed this land with great increase of people of our own nation as any country in the world, whereof many for want of service and means to set them on work fall to idleness and to great extremity. Her Majesty's pleasure therefore is that those kind of people should be sent forth of the land, and for that purpose there is direction given to this bearer Edward Banes to take of those blackmoors that in this last voyage under Sir Thomas Baskerville were brought into this realm the number of ten, to be transported by him out of the realm. Wherein we require you to be aiding and assisting unto him as he shall have occasion, and thereof not to fail."

The forerunner to the National Association for the Advancement of Colored People (NAACP), **the Niagara Movement** was organised in 1905. Twenty-nine delegates met at the Erie Beach hotel **on this day** through to the 13th July, at Fort Erie, Ontario, Canada. The group led by **William Monroe Trotter** and **W. E. B. Du Bois** met to form a national activist group opposing segregation, Jim Crow laws and disenfranchisement. They wanted to fight policies of accommodation and conciliation believed to be promoted by **Booker T. Washington.** The Niagara Movement pushed for both free and compulsory education for all and equal treatment for all under the law. Although short-lived, the Movement provided the foundation and blueprint for the NAACP formally established in 1910.

Following the success of the Brown v The Board of Education decision, (see May 17th) in 1954, there was an organised fight back. White supremacist, unapologetic racists, were horrified at the thought that schools could and would be integrated.

On this day in 1954 white residents of Indianola, Mississippi formed the first **White Citizens' Council.** The aim of the council was to defend the white way of life. They organised carrying out massive resistance to any form of racial integration. Although separate to groups such as the KKK the council's membership frequently overlapped. The day that the Brown decision was made public was called 'Black Monday'.

The manifestation of white supremacy and terrorism.

A year later there were over 250 white citizen councils with over 60,000 members located in thirty States. By 1957 the council membership had risen to 250,000, reflecting the deep-seated racial divide and hatred felt by many whites. White supremacy was defended using social pressure and economic means. When seventeen black parents signed a petition to desegregate schools in South Carolina, an area with fifty-five councils, within two weeks the seventeen parents were either fired or evicted from their farms. In Yazoo County, Mississippi, fifty-three black residents signed a NAACP petition. The council published the names of the fifty-three in a full-page newspaper advert. The signatories faced harassment, some were fired, and others had their credit cancelled. All fifty-three removed their names and the NAACP branch in Yazoo was forced to close. The white citizen council was so effective in its intimidation that in five deep south states, with a population of close to one and a half million black school children, no one attended a mixed, desegregated school until the 1960s. The white citizen council aligned with groups such as the Ku Klux Klan demonstrate the lengths many whites were and are prepared to go to maintain their privilege, distort history, and to challenge and disobey laws. The council also shows what black people have had to face, and continue to face, and how largely peaceful and dignified the community has been in its activism and struggle for civil rights. Facing Nazi-like opposition, many white supremacist groups proudly associate themselves with Nazism, wearing Nazi symbols. It is a testament to the resilience of many in the black community who have been able to progress and hold their heads high.

To Kill a Mockingbird **Nelle Harper Lee's** (1926–2016) classic was published **on this day** in 1960. The fictional story highlighted racial injustice faced by black defendants in a judicial system blighted by bigotry, prejudice and stereotypes.

July 12th:

One of the foremost experts in sickle cell anaemia, **Felix Konotey-Ahulu** was born **on this day** in 1930. The Ghanaian doctor, scientist and distinguished professor taught Human Genetics at the University of Cape Coast in Ghana.

Konotey-Ahulu was listed in The One Hundred Greatest Africans of All Time. When he read about his listing in the New African (Aug/Sept 2004) Konotey-Ahulu wrote an impassioned argument why his place should be taken by **James Emman Kwegyir Aggrey** (see July 30th). His Article on Aggrey appeared in a later issue of the *New African*.

Felix Konotey-Ahulu has written over 200 publications, some peer review papers are seen as definitive in their field. He has promoted ways to read African languages and dialects to spread medical and scientific knowledge beyond the use of English and other European languages. The doctor has been the recipient of numerous awards recognising the value of his work.

Bill Cosby was the TV father of the nation. In *The Crosby Show* he avoided negative stereotypes projecting a new acceptable professional middle-class image of the black family into the homes of America. His fall would be as shocking as his spectacular and meteoric rise.

Born **on this day** in 1937 Cosby the comedian, actor and producer rose to national and international prominence. He first appeared on TV in 1965 on *The Tonight Show with Johnny Carson*. The series *I Spy* (1965–68) was the first American series to provide a platform starring a black actor. Through the 1960s and 1970s Cosby appeared in a variety of shows providing a vehicle for his comedic talents; *Bill Cosby Specials*, *The Bill Cosby Show*, *The New Bill Cosby Show* and the cartoon *Fat Albert and the Cosby Kids* all showcased the comedian providing a positive wholesome image.

NBC's *The Cosby Show* (1984–1992) captured the heart of the nation with his easy going, family friendly in-offensive manner. The hit show catapulted Cosby into the nation's homes and consciousness. He opened doors for fellow black actors and became an icon representing all that was aspirational and good about the community. Cosby presented an image to be proud of. As important was that Cosby was embraced by the white audience. His comedy records won him eight Grammy Awards. The 1986 book *Fatherhood* built on Cosby's cultivated reliable image. He promoted education as the way forward for African Americans and challenged the excessive use of the 'N' word employed by Hip-hop artists.

Bill Cosby.

The cultural icon and pride of the black community fell from his entertainment perch following years of speculation and eventual accusation of drugging female victims and sexual assaults. Over fifty women came forward. In 2018 Bill Cosby was sentenced to 3–10 years in prison. His legal team would challenge the conviction. On June 30th 2021 after having served two years Prisoner 6387 Cosby was released from incarceration on a legal technicality aged 83.

Sao Tome and Principe celebrated independence **on this day** in 1975 from Portugal. The country proudly recalls **Rei Amador's** uprising and fight for freedom in 1595.

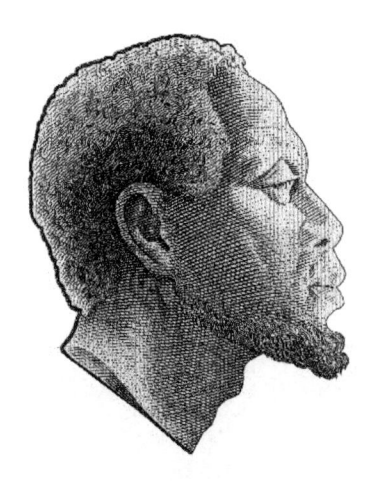

Rei Amador

Brazilian clarinettist, saxophonist and trumpeter **Paulo Moura** was born July 15th 1932. Moura combined classical training and popular music in his compositions and performances. He helped bossa nova reach an international audience. In 2000 Paulo Moura became the first Brazilian musician to win an instrumentalist Latin Grammy Award for 'Pixinguinha'. Moura became a professional musician aged fourteen. His first recording was an interpretation of Niccolò Paganini's 'Moto Perpetuo'. He went on to serve as the lead clarinettist at the Municipal Theatre Orchestra in Rio de Janeiro. In his recording career Moura played alongside **Nat King Cole, Ella Fitzgerald** and **Sergio Mendes.** He toured the world and appeared in several films.

Paulo Moura served two years as the director of the Museum of Image and Sound in Rio. He died **on this day** in 2010.

Zimbabwean poet, novelist and essayist **Chenjerai Hove** was born on Feb 9th 1956. Along with **Dambudzo Marechera, Yvonne Vera** and **Charles Mungoshi,** Hove is seen as one of the founding fathers of Modern Zimbabwean literature. His most famous book *Bones* was published in 1988. The 2002 essays *Papaver Finish* were critical of **Robert Mugabe's** government and politicians. He deplored the downward spiral of Zimbabwean political society and called for the *'empty talk'* to stop. Writing in English and Shona the poet went into exile in 2001, living in France, the USA and Norway.

Chenjerai Hove died aged fifty-nine from liver failure **on this day** in 2015. The quote below captures Hove's eloquence when addressing the populist political right-wing nationalist politics experienced during the first twenty years of the twenty-first century.

"*....in an interview in London in 2007 with the academic Ranka P*rimorac, he said: "For me. Even… financial [and] economic corruption begins with the corruption of language. Look at people talking about 'American Interests', or Mugabe talking about 'sovereignty' and 'patriotism'. All of a sudden there is a new definition of patriotism. Suddenly, some of us who are critical of the system are no longer patriots or nationalists. Of course, the person who is in political power is in charge of defining who is a patriot, who is a nationalist and what is sovereignty. All of a sudden, these words are being given a new meaning. So, the corruption of language, for me, psychologically and emotionally, is the beginning of a multiplicity of other corruption."

www.theguardian.com >books > jul > chenjerai-hove

July 13th:

Peter Jackson was born on July 3rd 1861 in St Croix, US Virgin Island. His parents were from Jamaica. He would become the Australian heavyweight boxing champion winning the title in 1886, knocking out Tom Lees in round thirty.

Moving to San Francisco in the USA, Jackson won the world 'coloured' heavyweight championship beating **'Old Chocolate' Godfrey'** on May 12th 1888. Travelling to Britain, Jackson fought for and won the British Empire title (later the British Commonwealth title), beating Jem Smith in the second round in 1882. Jackson repeatedly requested to fight John L. Sullivan for the heavyweight championship of the world. Sullivan continuously refused citing the colour bar, arguing that no black fighter should be able to become champion in the prized division of the heavyweight in boxing. At the height of his powers and at the top of his game Jackson was refused the chance to fight for the sports top prize.

When **Jack Johnson** (see March 31st) became the first black heavyweight champion he took the time to go on a pilgrimage to Jackson's grave to pay his respects. Peter Jackson died **on this day** in 1901 from tuberculosis in Queensland Australia. He was buried at Toowrong Cemetery with the words on his grave reading *"He was a man"*. Jackson had fifty-two career fights winning forty-two with thirty by knockout.

Born Yoruba in Nigeria, **on this day** in 1934, **Wole Soyinka** playwright, novelist, poet, essayist and political activist has spent much of his life challenging the abuse of power by colonialist and then by African tyrants, dictators, in particular military leaders.

In 1989 the playwright became the first black African recipient of the coveted Nobel Prize for Literature. Having graduated from Leeds University in England, 1958, Soyinka returned to Nigeria. His first major play was used as part of Nigeria's independence celebrations, *A Dance of the Forest* was performed in 1960 and published in 1963.

Wole Soyinka.

The Lion and Jewel performed in 1959 mocked the pomposity of Westernised school teachers. The 1960 production of The *Trials of Brother Jero* criticised preachers who grew fat on the backs of their simplistic credulous parishioners. Soyinka never shied away from showing his disregard for African authoritarian leadership and disillusionment with much of Nigerian society.

From 1960–64 Soyinka was co-editor of the important literary journal 'Black Orpheus'. He went on to teach literature at a variety of Nigerian universities. Following the Nobel Prize Soyinka was offered work in British and American universities. He became sought after as a speaker giving the Reith Lecture in 2004; *Climate of Fear.* Many of his lectures have been published. Wole Soyinka has written numerous novels including *The Interpreters* (1965), and *Seasons of Anomy* in 1973. Soyinka's poetry includes *Idanre and Other Poems* (1967), and *Poems from Prison* (1969). The latter was written while Soyinka was in solitary imprisoned from 1967–69. Soyinka had protested against the Nigerian/Biafran Civil War. *The Man Died* is the writer's account, in prose, of his arrest and twenty-two months in prison.

Wole Soyinka's work continued to address Africa's ills and Western culpability Resulting in him spending time in exile. Soyinka had been given the death sentence in absentia while in exile by the Nigerian military government. With new civilian leadership the activist author was able to return to his homeland in 1999. He has never denied his political involvement having formed, headed and participated in several political parties. In 2010 Wole Soyinka founded the Democratic Front a People's Federation where he served as the party chairman.

July 14th:

Born a freeman on October 7th 1821 **William Still** would nonetheless have a deep-rooted understanding and insight into the world experienced by enslaved people. His father **Levine Steel** purchased his freedom in 1798, but his wife **Sydney** had to run away twice before gaining her freedom. On the first occasion Sydney was captured with her four children and returned to life as a slave. The next time Still's mother escaped with her two girls, leaving the two boys behind. The boys would be sold on by slavers from Mississippi. Running away to New Jersey the Steels changed their name to Still. Sydney changed her name to Charity. The couple had fourteen more children, William being the youngest.

William Still.

The self-taught William moved to Philadelphia in 1844, aged twenty-three. He was employed by the Pennsylvania Anti-Slavery Society starting out as a janitor involved in a range of practical work. Becoming an active member of the Society, Still rose to become chair of the committee formed to help freedom seeking runaways in 1850. William Still worked on the Underground Railroad, a network of stations where escaped people could seek refuge while they made their way to freedom. Safe houses, places of sanctuary and safety were important stops for frightened and vulnerable runaways. The escaped people would travel along routes known as lines that networked through fourteen northern states helping many former enslaved people to make it to the promised land of Canada. Workers on the Underground were known as conductors and their charges were referred to as packages or freight.

William Still meticulously recorded and interviewed the lives of all who passed through Philadelphia knowing his record keeping would help to reunite families. His work earned him the title of Father of the Underground railroad. On one occasion listening to the story and experience of one person he realised it was his older brother Peter. Peter was reunited with his mother forty-two years after she was forced to leave her two boys behind. Unfortunately, the other son had been whipped to death after his wife had been out without the proper paperwork and permission.

Still's records provided the most detailed accounts and witness statement of the life of an enslaved captive. The horrors faced and harrowing experiences of those desperate to gain freedom and their humanity was meticulously written down. The information was kept secret until the abolition of slavery in 1865. The Fugitive Slave Act of 1850 allowed bounty hunters to track down slaves who had escaped north. Still chaired a group to challenge the 1850 Act in a bid to keep former slaves safe and free from abduction. In 1855 he travelled to Canada to see for himself how former slaves were adjusting to their new lives.

With the Civil War over and slavery abolished, William Still published his records and interviews in *The Underground Rail Road Records* in 1872. The success of the book led to the title of Father of the Underground Railroad. The book contains first-hand accounts of people detailing their heroic sacrifice, bravery and suffering. It also showed how in Philadelphia the abolitionist movement was largely black led. In the third edition, published in 1883, William added a mini autobiography.

As early as 1859 Still was looking at how to desegregate the city's public transport system. After eight years of constant pressure and lobbying Pennsylvania passed legislation desegregating the public transport system.

William Still married **Letitia George** in 1847. They couple had four children. William died from heart problems **on this day** in 1902. He was buried at Eden cemetery in Collingdale Pennsylvania, the oldest black-owned cemetery in the United States.

Estimates have between 40–100,000 people escaped enslavement via the Underground Railroad. Still is said to have helped 800 people to freedom and recorded the stories of 649 in his book. **Wesley Harris** was one such character, one of many people worthy of researching and discovery.

The story of fugitive Wesley Harris.

Born **on this day** in 1917 Nigerian painter and sculpture **Ben Enwonwu** would arguably be the most influential African artist of the twentieth century. He came to prominence in the 1950s having studied in England at Goldsmiths College, London, in 1944, Ruskin College in Oxford, 1944–46, and at Slade College of Art, London, from 1946–48. Enwonwu worked at universities in Nigeria and in the USA. He was commissioned to produce a sculpture of Queen Elizabeth II in 1956. The artist was also a writer and critic. He died on February 5th 1994.

Born November 9th 1923 **Alice Coachman** would become the first black female American athlete to win an Olympic gold medal. Setting a record of 6ft 6 1/8 inches in the high jump at the London Games, Coachman took the top medal. She died **on this day** in 2014.

July 15th:

The Universal Negro Improvement Association (UNIA) and African Communities League was formed **on this day** in 1914 in Jamaica by **Marcus Garvey** (see August 17th).

The UNIA experienced rapid growth after Garvey moved to New York in March 1916. The first New York division was formed with thirteen members in 1918. By 1920 the UNIA had over 1,900 divisions worldwide. The urban black working-class communities in the northern industrial towns and cities of the US embraced the UNIA's aims to promote racial pride, create economic self-sufficiency and the formation of an independent black nation in Africa. Garvey's vision had international appeal with divisions in more than forty countries including: Cuba, Costa Rica, Nicaragua, Ecuador, Venezuela, Ghana and Nigeria.

The first convention, held in 1920 in New York's Madison Square Gardens with 20,000 members in attendance lasted a month long. The UNIA's slogan was 'Africa for Africans, at home and abroad.' The motto was 'One God! One Aim! One Destiny.' The convention became a spectacle with marching bands and uniformed delegates parading through the city. 'The Declaration of Rights of the Negro People of the World' was drafted. The red, black and green flag was voted as the official flag of the African race. The same colours would be adopted by other black nationalist groups in the 1960s. The official anthem was 'Ethiopia thou Land of Our Fathers.'

With the deportation of Marcus Garvey from the USA to Jamaica and the second President **George Weston,** schisms appeared, and splinter groups were formed. The National Association for the Advancement of Colored People (NAACP) with W. E. B. Du Bois as their spokesperson were critical of Garvey and the UNIA. The purpose of the UNIA was to be a vehicle uniting the peoples of African descent. After the hay days of the 1920s the UNIA was never the force it had once been.

July 16th:

Born **on this day** 1862 into slavery during the American Civil War **Ida B. Wells** would lead a crusade against the crime of lynching, fight against segregation in schools and become a spokesperson for universal suffrage.

Ida B. Wells was posthumously awarded the Pulitzer Prize special citation 'For her outstanding, courageous reporting on the horrific and vicious violence against African Americans during the era of lynching' as illustrated May 4th in the Announcement of the 2020 Pulitzer Prize winners. Following the murder by lynching of three friends Wells started her anti-lynching crusade. Writing for the part owned Memphis 'Free Speech and Headlight' newspaper Wells tackled the evil of lynching. This resulted in the office and printing equipment being ransacked and destroyed. Undeterred Wells became a staff worker at the New York Age. During that period, she travelled speaking in numerous US cities on lynching. She travelled to Britain in 1893 and again in 1894 lecturing on lynching and suffrage. Her pamphlet 'Southern Horrors: Lynch Laws in All Its Phases' (1892), exposed the lies behind lynching. Southern whites had argued that lynching was reserved for black criminals. Wells demonstrated that lynching had little to do with crime. The noose was used to threaten black people that dared to challenge the white economic system or who dared to question white supremacy. *A Red Record* was published in 1895, it was a detailed expose of lynching.

From 1898-1902 Ida B. Wells served as the secretary of the National Afro American Council. In 1910 Wells co-founded and became the first president of the Negro Fellowship League. The organisation assisted southern blacks who had migrated to the northern states. Chicago's Alpha Suffrage Club founded by Wells in 1910, became the first black woman's suffrage group. Ida B. Wells was also a founding member of the National Association for the Advancement of Colored People. As a former teacher Wells challenged the promotion of segregated schools and employed the support of Jane Addams. Together both are credited with the failure of segregation becoming an official position in Chicago.

Ida B. Wells

Wells started her autobiography in 1928. She never got the opportunity to complete the work. It was published posthumously in 1970 under the title *Crusade for Justice*. Ida B. Wells died on March 25th 1931, aged sixty-eight, from kidney failure. She married attorney Ferdinand L. Barnett on June 27th 1895. From that date on she was officially called Ida B. Well-Barnett. The couple had six children. She is buried in the Oakwood Cemetery in Chicago.

Assata Shakur (JoAnne Deborah Byron) under normal circumstances would be simply viewed as a criminal involved in bank robberies, shootings and drug deals. Her story as a Black Panther and a member of the Black Liberation Army being part of the Black Power Movement places her as a political activist involved in a revolutionary struggle. When the FBI effectively declared war on the movement, adopting a policy of shoot outs, revolutionaries such as Shakur found themselves on the frontline.

Assata Shakur became the subject of a manhunt in May 1973. She faced numerous allegations covering the period 1971 to 1973 and would be in and out of court. When state trooper Werner Foerster was killed in a shootout in 1973, Shakur was captured having been shot in both arms and her shoulder. She was sentenced to life in 1977. While serving time at Clinton Correctional Facility for Women Shakur escaped in 1979. She eventually surfaced in Cuba in 1984 and was given political asylum. Shakur and the Cuban government have successfully resisted every attempt to legally extradite her.

Assata Shakur has been on the FBI Most Wanted Terrorist list since 2013. *Assata: An Autobiography* was published in 1987.

Celia Cruz the **Queen of Salsa**, and the **Queen of Latin music**, was born in Cuba October 21st 1925. Joining the Sonora Matancera Orchestra in 1950 as the lead vocalist, she would have an unrivalled fifteen years appearing with the band in five films and as the headline act at Havana's Tropicana Club. While with Matancera, Cruz recorded in a number of styles including guaracha, rumba and bolero.

With the 1959 revolution Cruz left Cuba for Mexico before settling in the USA. Recording with Tito Puente brought Cruz to the attention of a wider audience. She would win three Grammy awards and four Latin Grammy awards.

Her career took off gaining international attention when she started singing salsa. She recorded thirty-seven studio albums plus numerous live albums and collaborations. Twenty-three of her albums went gold. Her hits include: 'Juancito' (1956), 'Bemba Colora' (1966), 'Guantanamera' (1967), 'Quimbara' (1974),

'Toro Mata Cucula' (1983), 'Usted Abuso' (1999), 'Rie y Llora' (2003) and 'La Negra Tiene Tumbao' from Celia Cruz's fifty-ninth album.

Celia Cruz returned to perform in Cuba. She married Pedro Knight on July 14th 1962, they stayed together for forty-one years. They had no children and were described as inseparable. Celia Cruz died **on this day** in 2003 aged seventy-seven from complications following surgery on a brain tumour. She is buried in Woodlawn Cemetery in New York.

Celia Cruz.

July 17th:

Cudjoe Lewis born **Oluale Kossola,** 1841, was the third to last survivor of the last known slave ship to arrive in the USA **the Clotilda** (see July 9th). His story was recorded by **Emma Langdon Roche,** famous for her 1914 publication 'Historic Sketches of the South', and by **Zora Neale Hurston.** For many years it was believed that Kossola represented the last known enslaved person to arrive into the USA as part of the transatlantic slave trade. Research has since uncovered **Redoshi** who died in 1937 and **Matilda McCrear** who lived through to 1940. **Oluale Kossola** died **on this day** in 1935. He had lived in, with others he helped to found, the historic district of **Africatown** near Mobile, Alabama. Africatown was a self-contained black community. Kossola is buried at the Plateau Cemetery in Africatown. He had five sons and one daughter with his common law wife **Abilene** (Celia), she was also on the Clotilda. Abilene died in 1905.

Born **on this day** in 1939, **Lawrence Thomas Guyot** would challenge systemic racism and champion the cause of the Civil Rights Movement. He was imprisoned and beaten on numerous occasions for registering black people to vote. Spending time in Parchman Farm, Mississippi State Penitentiary, Guyot recalled the police officers burning his testicle with sticks. Although elected as the chairperson of the Mississippi Freedom Democratic Party he was unable to attend the Democratic National Convention as he had been placed in prison.

Lawrence Guyot was an original member of the Student Nonviolent Coordinating Committee (SNCC) and with the Congress of Racial Equality (CORE) he directed the Freedom Summer Project in Hattiesburg in 1964 Mississippi. In 1966 Guyot ran for Congress, unsuccessfully, as an anti-war candidate.

He continued to be involved with the Civil Rights campaigns working on a variety of programmes producing educational material and promoting initiatives and projects to assist and engage young people. Guyot would be a regular on Fox News defending the Movement against critical hosts engaging in heated debate over the history of the Civil Rights Movement. Guyot appeared in the 1987 award-winning documentary *Eyes on the Prize*.

Lawrence Thomas Guyot, attorney, died on November 23rd 2012. He had heart complications and was a diabetic, he was survived by his wife of forty-seven years Monica Klein Guyot and their son and daughter.

On this day in 1954 the Brooklyn Dodgers baseball team playing against the Milwaukee Braves, put out the first majority black team.

Eric Garner, aged forty-three, was suffocated by police in New York City. He was held in an illegal choke hold. His pleas that he could not breathe were ignored. Garner died **on this day** in 2014.

Eric Garner's mother.

July 18th:

He was the first Brazilian football superstar and the first Brazilian black sporting hero. **Arthur Friedenreich** was of mixed heritage; his father of European descent and his mother of African origin. Friedenreich would be known as the original 'Black' Pearl. He was born **on this day** in 1892.

Friedenreich would be the top scorer in the Sao Paulo League in 1912, a feat that he would repeat a further eight times. In 1917 he joined Club Athletico Paulistano. He stayed at the club for twelve years winning the city league title six times and being the top scorer for his team on six occasions.

Brazil had played their top XI on a couple of previous occasions, but it was not until 1914 v Exeter City (the British team) that Brazil officially recorded its first National XI. Friedenreich made his international debut as Brazil won 2-0. He would play twenty-two times for his country.

Following racist comments in the Argentinian press calling the non-white players monkeys the Brazilian officials chose to send an all-white team to the Copa America in 1917. The following year the South American Cup was held in Brazil. The final was played between the host and Uruguay. After extended extra time Arthur Friedenreich scored the only goal. He gained instant celebrity as Brazil lifted its first Copa America in 1918.

Legends of football

Friedenreich's celebrity helped to mould Brazilians' perception of themselves as a multicultural community. Change was neither certain or complete; Friedenreich felt the need to straighten his hair, dress and act in a white manner to be accepted. Many non-white players would powder their faces and bodies to make them appear whiter. To-date, 2020, the Brazilian Football Confederation has not had a black president.

Touring Europe, playing seven games in France, two in Switzerland and one in Portugal, Friedenreich's team C A Paulistano won nine of their ten matches. Paulistano beat the French national team 7-2 returning to Brazil receiving a hero's welcome. Arthur Friedenreich played in Brazil's first professional fixture Santos v Sao Paulo where his team won 5-1 in 1933.

Friedenreich retired in 1935 aged forty-three. His goal-scoring record was said to be second to none, but official records do not exist to verify his exploits. He died, age seventy-seven on September 6th 1969, in relative obscurity and with little money, having had to pay for his medical treatment. See **Pele** June 21st and **Ronaldo** September 18th.

Mamadou Moustapha Dia's place in the pantheon of Senegal's independence pioneers and leaders is secure. He was a protege of **Leopold Sedar Senghor** working closely with Senegal's president. Dia would serve as the country's prime minister from 1959–62.

The Prime Minister and President clashed and fell out with Dia's involvement in the 1962 attempted coup. Mamadou Dia was sentenced to life imprisonment but pardoned in 1974 and given official amnesty in 1976. Dia wrote several books including *'Réflexions sur l'économie de l'Afrique noire'* in 1960 and *The African Nations and World Solidarity* in 1961.

Mamadou Moustapha Dia was born **on this day** 1910 and died aged ninety-eight on January 25th in 2009.

South African anti-apartheid activist and hero of the liberation struggle **Adelaide 'Mama' Tambo** was born **on this day** in 1929. She married former ANC leader **Oliver Tambo** (see April 24th) in 1956. The couple went into exile in 1960 and remained together until Oliver's death in 1998. They had three children who Mama Tambo looked after while she worked as a nurse in England.

The family returned to South Africa in 1990. Adelaide Tambo served in South Africa as an elected politician from 1994–99 following the country's first democratically multi-racial election.

Nelson Mandela (Part 3, see February 11th and June 12th) was inaugurated as South African President in Pretoria on May 10th 1994. The African National Congress (ANC) captured 63per cent of the vote taking seven provinces, Inkatha and the National Party won one province each. The seventy-three-year-old Mandela was sworn in as the President.

The Government of National Unity inherited a population of 40 million with 33per cent unemployed and half the population living below the poverty line. Two million children were not receiving an education, 33per cent of South Africans were illiterate, 23 million lacked adequate electricity and adequate sanitation and twelve million lacked access to clean water. The country's finances were in a mess having to pay off enormous debts.

The election date of April 27th 1994 had been set. Having been released from Victor Verster Prison on February 11th 1990 holding **Winnie Mandela**'s hand (see 26th September), the path would be a difficult one to tread. F. W. de Klerk came to power following P. W. Botha's stroke and him stepping down. The political wind of change was blowing strong as the Berlin Wall fell in late 1989.

Mandela embarked on an important tour of Africa, Europe and America meeting world leaders, business leaders and celebrities. His first job was to unify the ANC. In 1991 Mandela replaced an ailing **Oliver Tambo** (see April 24th) as the ANC president. Political tension and rivalry broke out with thousands being killed. Supporters of Chief Buthelezi's Zulu led Inkatha, supported by elements of de Klerk's National Party, were threatening a civil war. The three party leaders signed a peace accord in September 1991. The violence decreased but did not end. Mandela and de Klerk were joint recipients of the Nobel Peace Prize in 1993.

With the 1994 election over Mandela sought to create the Rainbow Nation. He wanted to avoid a massive brain and investment drain convincing white South Africans that they had nothing to fear. At the same time the new ANC executive was more militant and demanding greater change. Mandela released his autobiography *Long Walk to Freedom* in 1993. As president he donated a third of his wages to the Nelson Mandela Children's Fund that he founded in 1995.

The symbolism of Mandela presenting the Rugby World Cup to the South African winning team captain Francois Pienaar went a long way to making white South Africans feel comfortable.

In his one, and only term, in office Mandela's government saw welfare spending increase by 13per cent 1996/7, 13per cent in 1997/8 and 7per cent 1998/9. Free healthcare was provided to all children under 6 and to pregnant women in 1994. By 1999 three million new people were connected to the telephone network. One and a half million extra children were receiving an education. Two million people had been connected to the electricity grid. Three million gained access to clean water. Seven hundred and fifty thousand new homes were built providing homes to almost 3 million people.

December 1997 saw Nelson Mandela step down as President of the ANC. March 29th 1999 saw Mandela deliver his farewell speech to Parliament. On leaving office he still retained an 80per cent approval rate for his presidency.

Statesman Nelson Mandela.

On release from prison Nelson had stood by his wife Winnie who was accused and convicted of kidnap and assault. Winnie received a six-year prison sentence, June 1991, which was reduced to two years on appeal. She had also had an affair with Dali Mpofu. Winnie Mandela's story is one that has to be taken into the context of the times and what she lived through. Nelson announced his separation from Winnie on April 13th 1992. The Truth and Reconciliation Commission was set up in 1996 and ran through to 2003 chaired by **Desmond Tutu** (see October 7th). It was established to address the hurt, the pain and the injustice of the apartheid era while seeking to ensure that there was no revenge and punitive justice. Crime statistics had risen while Mandela was president, he failed to address accusations of corruption and the concerns of HIV/AIDS. Out of office Mandela found his voice and stood up speaking out about HIV/AIDS.

Mandela married **Graca Machel** (see October 17th) in 1998. Nelson Mandela had six children. He died at the age of ninety-five on December 5th 2013. He had been suffering from a prolonged respiratory infection. Nelson Mandela International Day is celebrated **on this day**.

On this day in 1890 **George Washington Williams** wrote an open letter to King Leopold II of Belgium over the situation and conditions in the Congo (see Oct 16th for the full story).

Hosea Kutako, born in 1870, would die **on this day** 1970 aged 100. He is viewed as the father of Namibian nationalism. Chief Kutako fought as a commander in the German-Herero War (anti-colonial wars) of 1904. Along with the white British Anglican priest Rev Michael Scott, he submitted numerous petitions to the United Nations in the 1950s and 1960s pressing for an end to South African colonialism and Namibian independence. Kutako is one of Namibia's nine National Heroes (see Jan 6th)

Chief Hosea Kutako

July 19th:

Food pioneering inventor **Joseph Lee** was born **on this day** in 1849. Patent 504 533 on June 4th 1995 was for Lee's breadcrumb making machine. The machine was quickly adopted in commercial kitchens across the United States. Lee went on to patent a breadmaking machine which proved to be 75per cent more efficient than employing bakers. Joseph Lee changed the food industry in a simple but effective way. He was able to sell his inventions while retaining shares. Lee died on June 11th in 1905.

Harlem Renaissance poet, journalist, essayist, diarist, playwright and activist **Alice Ruth Moore** was born **on this day** in 1875. Better known as **Alice Dunbar Nelson**, she married poet **Paul Laurence Dunbar** (see February 9th) in 1898. A prolific writer, many of her politically challenging works looking at racism were not published in her lifetime. She wrote about the colour line. In the autobiographical *Brass Ankles Speak* Dunbar addressed the awkward existence she experienced as a mixed heritage person never fully at home or accepted in either white or black culture. Dunbar wrote about black soldiers placing their lives on the line fighting for their country only to return to the States to experience the threat of lynching. She supported the failed Dyer Anti-Lynching Bill in 1924. Dunbar wrote frequently about the role of black women in the workforce. She was an activist for women's suffrage.

Alice Dunbar Nelson's diary from 1921 and 1926–31 was published in 1984. An important work as her's was one of only two female black diaries published from a black woman born in the nineteenth century.

Dunbar married on two further occasions husband two being Doctor Arthur Callis in 1910 and husband number three poet and Civil Rights activist Robert J Nelson in 1916. She died on September 18th 1935.

Senegalese Sufi **Ahmadou Bamba** was believed to have been born in 1853. He spent thirty-three years in exile, living in Gabon (1895–1902) and Mauritania (1903–1907), on trial and under house arrest before the French authorities discovered his pacifist teachings and that he taught one should engage in a personal struggle against negative instincts. Bamba founded the Mouride Brotherhood in 1883.

He founded the spiritual city of Touba in 1887. Bamba is recognised as one of Senegal's greatest spiritual leaders. Only one photograph, taken in 1913, survives. The image has become iconic appearing throughout the country.

Ahmadou Bamba died **on this day** in 1927.

Touba Senegal.

Basketball player **Teresa Edwards** was born **on this day** in 1964. She would be listed at No 22 by Sports Illustrated, in 2000, as one of the top 100 Greatest Female Athletes. From 1981–2000 Edwards led the US basketball team to fourteen gold medals in 18 major international tournaments including four Olympic golds. She is the most decorated US national team basketball player, being both the youngest and oldest basketball gold medallist. See **Michael Jordan** February 17th and **Kobe Bryant** January 26th.

Ugandan poet, novelist and social anthropologist **Okot p'Bitek** was born on 7th June 1931. The 1966 epic poem *'Song of Lawino'* propelled p'Bitek onto the international stage receiving acclaim for his work. The poem was about a rural traditional wife whose university educated husband had embraced urban life, western culture and values leaving Ugandan Acholi tradition behind. *Song of Lawino*, a scathing criticism of the elite political classes, is recognised as a masterpiece of world literature. In the 1970 *'Song of Ocol'* by p'Bitek gave the husband his right of reply. *'Two Songs'* written in 1971 is the third major work of poetry produced by p'Bitek.

Okot p'Bitek was critical of much of western anthropology. He rejected simplistic terms as 'primitive' and 'savage' as offensive, misleading and unhelpful. Categorising groups as belonging to 'tribes' and examining African religions and philosophies through a western, colonial and Christian prism were challenged by Okot p'Bitek.

With the arrival of **Idi Amin** p'Bitek spent time in exile. He died **on this day** in 1982.

Acclaimed award-winning actor, **Sotigui Kouyate,** was born **on this day** 1936, in Mali to Guinean parents. He was taken to Burkina Faso as a toddler. Kouyate worked closely with Peter Brook demonstrating an extraordinary range as an actor appearing in eighteen films. He died on April 17 in 2010 aged seventy-three.

July 20th:

British born **John Kent,** the son of a slave, was born in Longtown, Cumberland in 1805. Kent would serve as a police constable in Maryport for the Carlisle city police for seven years from 26th October 1837 through to December 1844.

John Kent is the earliest black police officer recorded in England. For many years it was believed that **Norwell Roberts** (see 23rd October) was the first black police officer serving in the Metropolitan police force in the 1960s. Kent was sacked after turning up intoxicated to work. He then served as a bailiff for the local magistrate's court, then as the parish constable in Longtown before working on the railway. Known as 'Black Kent' his name was used to strike fear in misbehaved children when he was on patrol. John Kent died on this day in 1888. (See **Robert Branford** May 6th and **Sislin Fay Allen** Feb 1st.)

Toni Morrison described the writer **Henry Dumas** as

"... a genius, an absolute genius. I wish he were around now to help us straighten out the mess." Toni Morrison, April 24th 1983.

Black American Literature Forum Vol. 22, No. 2, Henry Dumas Issue (Summer, 1988), pp. 310-312 (3 pages) Published By: African American Review (St. Louis University)

Dumas was a Civil Rights activist who was part of the Black Power movement. His works were published posthumously following his death when he was shot in the chest by a New York City transport policeman at the age of thirty-three. The details of Dumas' death remain unclear as there were no witness statements and the files on his case have since gone missing.

Collections of his poetry include: 'Play Ebony, Play Ivory' (1974), 'Knees of a Natural Man: The Selected Poetry of Henry Dumas' in 1989. His short stories include 'Goodbye Sweetwater: New and Selected Stories', (1988), and 'Echo Tree: The Collected Short Fiction of Henry Dumas' in 2003. He often wrote about the clashes between black and white culture.

Henry Dumas married Loretta Panton in 1955. The couple had two children.

Eighteen months before the much-publicised **Greensboro Sit-ins** (see February 1st and January 3rd), **Ronald W. Walters** led a lesser-known sit-in. **The Dockum Drug Store Sit-in** organised by Walters led to the desegregation of drug stores in Wichita, Kansas. Walters would go on to manage and act as consultant for **Rev Jesse Jackson's** two presidential bids. He wrote hundreds of articles and seven books and was a regular political pundit and commentator for CNN on American television. Ronald W. Walters was born **on this day** in 1938. He died September 10th in 2010.

July 21st:

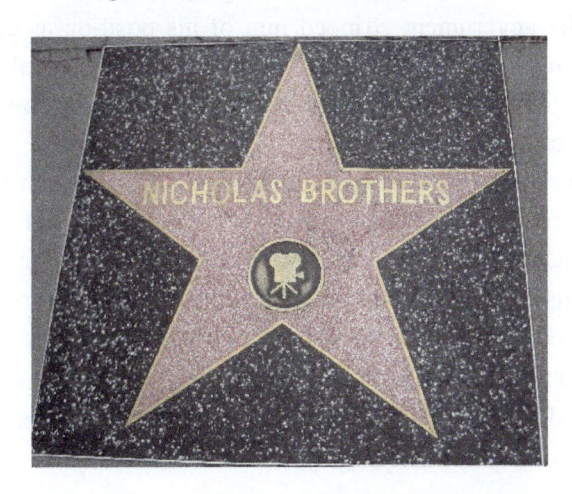

The 20th Century Fox production ***Stormy Weather*** was a showcase for black entertainers released **on this day** in 1943. Starring the tap dancer **Bill Robinson** (see May 25th) with the singer and Civil Rights activist **Lena Horn** (see, June 30th). Supporting actors & performers included the **Nicholas Brothers; Fayard** born October 28th 1914 died January 24th 2006 and **Harold** born March 17th 1921 and died July 3rd 2000, performing their classic mind-blowing acrobatic and athletically choreographed, 'Jumpin' Jive'. Many, including Fred Astaire, Gene Kelly, Mikhail Baryshnikov and Michael Jackson place the brothers amongst the best, if not the best. **Cab Calloway,** and **Fats Domino** both appear as themselves and then there is **Arthur Dooley Wilson,** he of 'Play it again, Sam' in Casablanca. The same year MGM released the classic *Cabin in the Sky* on April 9th.

Chief Albert Luthuli was born in, what is today, Zimbabwe in 1898. Following his father's death, the young Luthuli returned to his parental home in South Africa

When he was ten. Albert Luthuli married **Nokukhanya Bhengu**, a fellow teacher, in 1927. He was active in local politics, but activism was not a priority. When asked to take on a chieftainship in 1935 he reluctantly accepted the position which paid less than what he was earning as a teacher.

With the election win of the South African Nationalist Party in 1948 everything was to change for the worse. In the mid-1950s Luthuli joined the African National Congress (ANC). A year later he was elected to the Natives Representatives Council. He protested against police and troops action crushing an African miners' strike leaving eight dead and hundreds injured.

The ANC joined forces with the South African Indian Congress to oppose the new apartheid regime embarking on what became known as the Defiance Campaign. The protests led to over 8,000 people being sent to prison. Luthuli was given the option to either resign his position as chief or resign from the ANC. He chose neither option. The government stripped him of his position as chief in 1952. This enhanced Luthuli's reputation. That same year he was elected as the president general of the ANC, aged fifty-four. Luthuli toured the country giving speeches, holding meetings, visiting towns and villages. In 1954 he suffered a stroke and a heart attack.

One hundred and fifty-six people, including Luthuli, were charged with treason in Dec 1956. After a long trial with a lack of any credible evidence, Luthuli and the remaining defendants were released in 1957. On his release he called for a stay-at-home strike. Albert Luthuli's calls for disruption were met, in 1959, with him being confined to his rural neighbourhood and banned by the government from any gatherings for the next five years and charged with promoting racial hostility.

Following the 1960 **Sharpeville Massacre,** see March 21st, Luthuli called for a period of national mourning and publicly burned his pass. His defiant action received another prison sentence but being too ill to spend time in jail Luthuli paid a fine instead.

The government allowed the Nobel Prize recipient, Luthuli and his wife, to travel to Norway's capital Oslo to receive the award for his nonviolent action against the discriminatory policies of the National Party. He became the first black African recipient of the prize in 1961. Luthuli returned to South Africa and an ANC that had changed. Nonviolence was a tactic of the past. Within weeks the militant arm of the ANC, Umkhonto we Sizwe, was formed attacking numerous installations across the country. It is not clear how much Luthuli knew about the actions, but research suggests that he knew nothing.

Albert Luthuli returned to his enforced isolation. Viewed as an honoured elder statesman working on his autobiography, he met visitors vetted by the authorities. While on a customary walk Luthuli was hit by a train. He died **on this day** in 1967.

Why did it take so long for the British Broadcasting Corporation to end *The Black and White Minstrel Show*? The show appeared as a regular feature on the BBC first in 1958. Although there were numerous complaints about the offensive imagery, in the 1960s, the television show was getting audience figures of 16 million. The spin off stage show, packed audiences in breaking box office records. Blackface, for many was accepted and normal. Indeed, the BBC defended the show describing it as a proud part of British stage tradition.

Chief accountant Barrie Thorne was a dissenting voice in the corporation. He sent a memo to the Director-General's chief assistant. In the memo, which is held at the BBC's Written Archive Centre, Thorne questions the suitability of the show being aired.

"The BBC says that the Black and White Minstrels is 'a traditional show enjoyed by millions for what it offers in good-hearted family entertainment'. I think it was George Melly's comment that the same was said of throwing Christians to the lions."

The reply from the BBC defended the *Minstrel Show* turning the tables on those who found it offensive replying…

"People who are already racially prejudiced are more likely to be exacerbated by the protest itself than the object of the protest. The best advice that could be given to coloured people by their friends would be: "on this issue, we can see your point, but in your own best interests, for Heaven's sake shut up. You are wasting valuable ammunition on a comparatively insignificant target".

The BBC had been warned five years earlier by Thorne as he wrote a memo in 1962 to the Director of Television, Kenneth Adam…

"The Uncle Tom attitude of the show in this day and age is a disgrace and an insult to coloured people everywhere."

Adam dismissed the warning. In May of 1967, the Campaign Against Racial Discrimination presented a petition of 200 signatures calling for the end of the show. Although the call was ignored with the change of viewing tastes the end of *The Black and White Minstrel Show* was nigh. **On this day** in 1978 the last Minstrel show was aired on the BBC and one would imagine on all British TV full stop.

July 22nd:

White abolitionist **Cassius Marcellus Clay** was born in the American South on October 19th in 1810. The anti-slavery campaigner opened the newspaper the *True American* in Lexington, Kentucky in 1845 to spread the message to end slavery. A fierce individual Clay was prepared to fight for his beliefs. The doors to the newspaper's office were strengthened with sheet iron. Two brass cannons lay behind the folding doors loaded and ready. The workforce was armed and ready for an attack. A trap door in the roof offered a quick escape. Clay even had a keg of gunpowder at the ready to explode and blow up the office if required.

Clay had been inspired and influenced by the white anti-slavery leader **William Lloyd Garrison** (see December 10th). All the preparation and defence failed to protect the offices of The True American which were ransacked by a group while Clay was ill with typhoid. Cassius Clay was involved in numerous altercations and even had a duel in 1845. He avoided being shot but gouged out the eye of his opponent, cut off an ear and then split his face with a bowie knife. Clay later successfully sued the group that sacked his office.

Clay fought in the Mexican War but was captured in 1847, serving eighteen months as a prisoner. His abolitionist views led him to join the newly founded Republican Party in 1856 where he became associated with Abraham Lincoln. As the ambassador to Russia, where he served for seven years, Clay helped to negotiate the purchase of Alaska in 1867.

The unconventional emancipationist divorced in 1878. His wife Mary Jane (Warfield) Clay called it a day after forty-five years of marriage. She was fed up of his extra marital affairs. They were married in 1833 and had ten children; six lived through to adulthood. At the age of eighty-four in 1894 Clay married fifteen-year-old Dora Richardson, resisting all efforts by the authorities to seize the teenager. The marriage lasted for three years. Known as the 'Lion of Whitehall' Clay lived as if under siege. He was declared insane before he died **on this day** in 1903.

Born **on this day** in 1923 **Chief Anthony Enahoro** would present the 1953 motion for self-rule in Nigeria envisaging Nigerian independence. Although limited in its success the call sped up the process and galvanised support leading to the country's independence in 1960.

Accused of involvement in a coup and threatened with detention Enahoro fled Nigeria via Ghana before settling in England. Calls for his extradition became known as the 'Enahoro Affair' as the British government struggled with compliance to the 1881 Fugitive Offenders Act v human rights abuses. Enahoro was extradited and put on trial accused of treasonable felony. He was given a seven-year sentence which was reduced on appeal. He wrote his autobiography *Fugitive Offender* in 1965 and was released from prison in 1966. The prominent anti-colonialist and pro-democracy activist called for unity during the civil war, 1967–70.

Chief Anthony Enahoro's involvement in Nigerian politics would always be problematic as he fought and became caught up in the volatile post-colonial world of independent Nigeria.

He died aged eighty-seven on the 15th December in 2010.

Reluctant Civil Rights activist and campaigner **Mildred Loving** was born **on this day** in 1939. Her marriage to **Richard Perry Loving** would lead to challenges in court going all the way to the United States Supreme Court. Mildred, a black woman, fell in love with Richard, a white man. The couple decided to marry following eighteen-year-old Mildred getting pregnant. Virginia's Racial Integrity Act of 1924 meant that it was impossible to have an inter-racial marriage in the state. The couple travelled to Washington DC for the ceremony before returning to Caroline County, Virginia.

Only a few weeks later, following a tip off, Sheriff Garnett Brooks with two deputies caught the couple in bed and arrested both. Richard spent the night in prison. His pregnant wife spent a few more days in jail. The couple pled guilty for violating Virginia's law and were given a one-year suspended sentence on the condition that they left the state and would not return for the next twenty-five years together.

Richard and Mildred relocated to the city living in Washington DC. Mildred was never comfortable living in the city. They returned to Virginia individually to visit family and friends and even dared clandestinely returning together several times. When their son was involved in a car accident Mildred had had enough of city life and wished to return to her home in Caroline County.

In despair she wrote to the then Attorney General Robert Kennedy who directed Mrs Loving to the American Civil Liberties Union (ACLU). The union decided to take up Loving's case. Initially they appealed to Judge Leon M Bazile to overturn his original decision on appeal. He was not for moving replying in January 1965:

"Almighty God created the races, white, black, yellow, Malay and red, and he placed them on separate continents... And but for the interference with his arrangement there would be no cause for such marriages. The fact that he separated the races shows that he did not intend for the races to mix."
https://www.biography.com/activist/mildred-loving

Ruth Negga and Joel Edgerton appear in the 2016 *Loving*

ACLU representatives Bernard S. Cohen and Philip J Hirschkop took the appeal to the Virginian state supreme court who upheld the original ruling. Oral arguments were presented to the US Supreme Court on April 10th 1967. The high court agreed unanimously in favour of Mr and Mrs Loving in Loving v Virginia on June 12th in 1967.

The couple were free to live as husband and wife in their native Virginia. The Supreme Court judgement also ended similar discriminatory marriage laws that were still in existence in other states. Richard Loving died when a drunk driver smashed into his car on 29th June 1975. He was forty-one; born October 29th 1933. Mildred was in the car she lost the sight in her right eye in the accident. Born **on this day** in 1939, Mildred and her husband were shy people who never wanted to engage in the battle they were forced to fight. Mildred Loving died of pneumonia aged sixty-eight on May 2nd in 2008. She rarely gave interviews.

A made for TV film *Mr and Mrs Loving* (1996), revived interest in their story. In 2004 *Virginia Hasn't Always Been for Lovers* by Phyl Newbeck was published. The documentary film *The Loving Story* by Nancy Buirski came out in 2011. The film simply called *Loving* came out in 2016 with Ruth Negga and Joel Edgerton

Australian activist **Joyce Clague** born **on this day** in 1938. The Aboriginal Yaegi elder campaigned for the rights of indigenous Australians. When she received the Member of the Order of the British Empire (MBE) she renamed the honour **M**ore **B**lack than **E**ver. Clague wrote *Good News to the Poor* (1981), a challenge to the Church to be more affirmative. She collaborated on the *Aboriginal Studies Kit* (1984), and wrote in *1993 Staying to the End*.

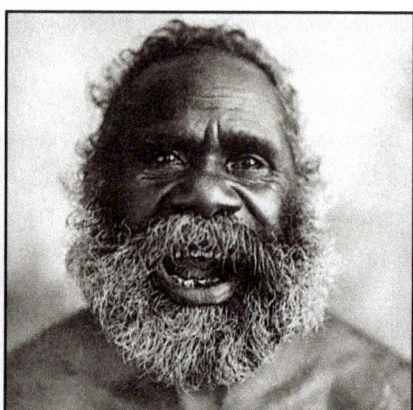

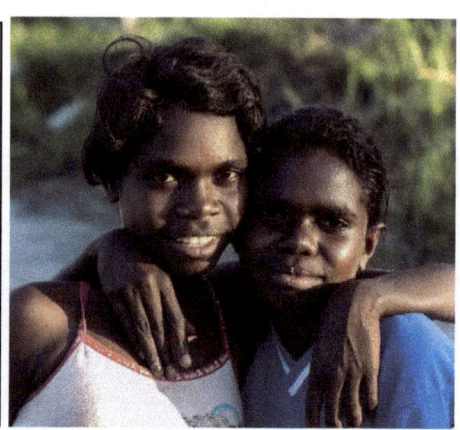

July 23rd:

Charlotte Forten Grimke's fame would grow after her death with the publication of the five volumes of her diaries. They provide a unique insight into the daily life of a black woman living in America from the mid-nineteenth century. The volumes covered the periods 1854–64 and 1885–92.

Charlotte Forten was born free on August 17th 1837. Her father was a freeman who ran a successful sail making business. Forten joined the Salem female Anti-Slavery Society. Many in her family were active in the Abolitionist Movement. In 1892 she was a founding member of the Coloured Women's League in Washington DC. Forten assisted in the formation of the National Association of Coloured Women in 1896. The societies promoted the best interest of and sought unity within the black community.

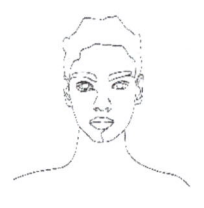

Charlotte Forten trained as a teacher, volunteering her services teaching former enslaved people in a government-run project known as the Port Royal Experiment. Following the illness of a close friend and the death of her father, Forten left after two years. She wrote about her experiences in an essay 'Life on the Sea Islands' which was published in the *Atlantic Monthly* in two parts coming out in the May and June issue in 1864. Forten continued her association with education, recruiting and training teachers to teach former enslaved people.

In 1878 the forty-one-year-old Forten married the mixed heritage twenty-eight-year-old Francis James Grimke who was from an influential and prominent family. Together the couple continued their activism. Charlotte Forten Grimke died **on this day** in 1914.

The first **Pan African Conference** was held **on this day** at Westminster Hall (now Caxton Hall) in London in 1900. The conference would be the first time that black people from all corners of the world would gather to discuss and improve the conditions of their people, to assert their rights and to organise, playing an equal part on the world stage. **Sylvester Williams** (see February 15th), a Trinidadian barrister, had organised the **African Association** September 24th 1897. He organised the London conference establishing Pan Africanism. Over thirty delegates including **Bishop Alexander Walters** of the AME Zion Church who chaired, **Samuel Coleridge Taylor** (see August 15th), **John Archer** (see June 8th) and **W. E. B. Du Bois** (see February 23rd and April 18th) attended. The delegates were mainly from Britain and the West Indies with some from Africa and the USA.

Walters opened the conference with a speech titled 'The Trials and Tribulations of the Coloured Race of America'. Du Bois drafted a letter to world leaders 'Address to the Nations of the World'. The appeal was for European leaders to take the moral high ground and politically oppose racism and oppression. A call was made to grant colonised countries the right to self-governance and a demand to greater political and civil rights for black Americans. It was at the conference that the phrase "The problem of the twentieth century is the problem of the colour-line" was heard. The line would be adopted by Du Bois in his seminal work *The Souls of Black Folk*.

Williams's African Association was absorbed into the Pan African Association. In September 1900, an appeal was written to Queen Victoria on behalf of her black subjects in South Africa and Rhodesia. She responded in the affirmative promising to investigate abuses and conditions experienced by black people in both countries.

Gibson Kente born **on this day** in 1932 would be called the father of black theatre in South Africa. He introduced musical theatre to the impoverished townships. The playwright produced twenty-three plays and TV dramas between 1963-1992. He announced that he had contracted HIV/AIDS and died November 7th in 2004.

William V. S. Tubman often called the father of modern Liberia was born on November 29th 1895. Tubman would serve as Liberia's 19th President. Liberia was Africa's first republic formed in 1847 retaining its independence during the European colonial scramble for Africa.

William V. S. Tubman.

Tubman studied law and passed the bar examination aged twenty-three. He would be appointed associate justice of the Supreme Court of Liberia from 1937 to 1943. Some argue that the appointment was to keep Tubman away from running for the top job.

Tubman won election to the Liberian Senate aged thirty-five. He ran for the presidency winning the election on May 4th in 1943, aged forty-eight. His inauguration took place on January 3rd 1944. That year he became the first African leader invited to the White House by President F. D. Roosevelt, along with his predecessor **Edwin Barclay.**

William Tubman would oversee Liberia's golden age. Economically the country thrived. Tubman was able to attract foreign investment. During the 1950s the country had the second highest rate of growth. By the time of Tubman's death Liberia had the world's largest rubber industry and was the third largest exporter of iron ore. Tubman oversaw the unification of the country allowing the indigenous population opportunity to participate fully in government. The elite Americo-Liberians had dominated politics since their arrival following their emancipation. He opened suffrage to females of twenty-one and older and gave women property rights. His government established a nationwide public school system.

Following the Pan African Conference held in Liberia's capital Monrovia in 1961, Tubman helped to found the African Union.

All the progress came at a price. Tubman's style was increasingly autocratic, he offered jobs and political positions to friends and family and kept power within his dominant True Whig Party. William Tubman held office for a record twenty-seven years from 1944 to his death **on this day** in 1971. It was only a matter of time following Tubman's death that the political stress and strains would appear.

July 24th:

Acclaimed Shakespearian actor **Ira F. Aldridge** was born **on this day** in 1807. As a teenager he performed at the Grove Theatre in New York City, the first theatre in America that catered for and was managed by black people.

Experiencing racist limitations in the work and where he could perform the young Aldridge left the United States arriving in Liverpool, England aged seventeen in 1824. The following year Aldridge was playing Othello at Covent Garden's Theatre Royal. He received positive reviews although one commentator felt uneasy seeing a black man touch a white woman on stage. Touring Europe, in 1852 opportunities opened up for Aldridge playing King Lear, Macbeth, Richard III, Shylock and Othello to rave reviews. So successful was Aldridge on the European stage after 1853 most of his work was on the continent.

Ira Aldridge became an English citizen in 1863. Earning £60 a show he was one of the highest paid actors of his age and recognised as one of the great exponents of Shakespeare. He died while appearing in Poland on August 7th 1867 and is buried in his tomb in Stary Cmentarz, Poland.

Charles S Johnson would serve as the first black president at the historic Fisk University from 1946 to 1956. The sociologist was born **on this day** in 1893.

Johnson served in France for the US Army during World War I. He founded and edited the journal of black life 'Opportunity' 1923–28. 'Opportunity' was a major voice during and as part of the Harlem Renaissance. Johnson spent his life advocating for racial equality and civil rights for blacks and other ethnic minorities in America. He was accused by W. E. B. Du Bois as being too conservative; he was pragmatic, not revolutionary, in his approach to achieving his aims.

Charles Johnson wrote numerous books including: *The Negro in American Civilization*, (1930), *The Negro College Graduate* (1936) and *Patterns of Negro Segregation* published in 1943. He was the first black man to serve as vice-president of the American Sociological Society appointed in 1937.

Charles Johnson died unexpectedly of a heart attack. He had been travelling by train when he had a heart attack on the station platform at Louisville, Kentucky. He died aged sixty-three on October 27th 1956.

Mary Church Terrell was born September 23rd in 1863. She would become a champion of racial equality and promote women's suffrage. Her parents had been born into slavery, but her father had gone on to run a successful business becoming a rare black millionaire in the American South. Terrell received a good education earning a bachelor's and a master's degree. She became a teacher and married a fellow teacher Robert Heberton Terrell in 1891.

Although conscientious, for a black person, issues of racism and prejudice was an everyday occurrence. It was the murder by lynching of an old friend **Thomas Moss** that launched Terrel's activism. Moss had been killed by white men who felt threatened by his business success. Terrell joined forces with **Ida B. Wells** (see July 16th) anti-lynching campaign. In 1896 Terrell helped to find the National Association of Coloured Women (NACW). The association adopted Terrell's words and policy "Lifting up as we climb." She was a firm believer in the power of education creating a racial uplift for the whole black community. Terrell served as president of the NACW from 1896–1901. In her position of leadership Mary Terrell travelled extensively networking with like-minded organisations, black and white, writing and delivering talks. It was at this time she embraced women's suffrage.

Terrell was one of the founders and charter members of the National Association for the Advancement of Colored People in 1909. Her 1940 autobiography explained, as its title suggested, *A Coloured Woman in a White World*. Terrell became the first black member of the hitherto all white American Association of University Women. At eighty-six she was not ready to put her feet up and retire. Involved in a lawsuit against John R. Thompson restaurant who had refused to serve Terrell and friends in 1950. The case was resolved by the Supreme Court that concluded that segregated facilities were unconstitutional in Washington DC on June 8th 1953.

Mary Church Terrell died aged ninety **on this day** in 1954. She lived long enough to hear the historic Brown v Board of Education decision (see May 17th).

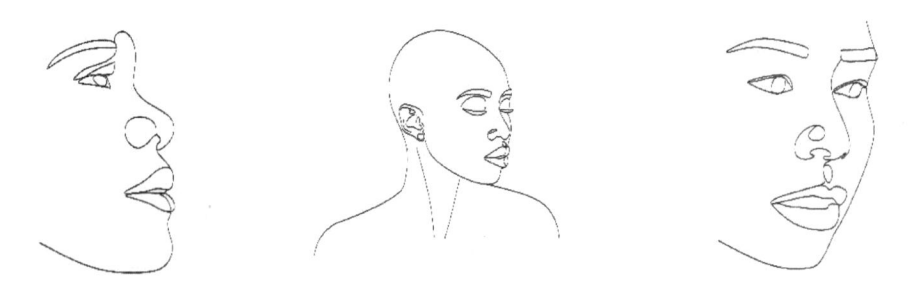

Ghanaian President **John Evans Atta Mills** was born on July 22nd 1944. He studied at the London School of Economics and Political Studies and then at the School of Oriental and African studies School of Law.

Mills was Ghanaian president from 2009 to 2012. His administration oversaw a period of austerity that started with the government. He reduced the number of ministers from eighty-seven to seventy-three. The immediate effect was to reduce costs by an estimated $4 million a year. Two aeroplanes had been ordered for the president's official use. Mills cancelled both. He cut back on advisors and expensive bureaucracy. In his short term in office Ghana's inflation entered single digits, the lowest that the country had seen in forty-two years. Prudent fiscal monetary policies led to the Ghanaian currency stabilizing. In 2011 Ghana's economy was the second fastest growing economy in the world. In the first half of the year growth was at 20.5per cent. At the end of the year growth was still spectacular at 14.4per cent. The budget deficit was reduced to 2per cent of GDP in 2012 from what had been 14.5 just four years earlier in 2008. Both domestic and foreign investment confidence grew. It was at this time Ghana was judged the best place for doing business in West Africa.

Oil production had started in 2010. The profits from the oil helped to fund programmes presented by Mills' government. Free school uniforms were provided for deprived communities along with 100,000 laptops and IT notebooks. More than 23 million free exercise books were distributed. School feeding programmes were expanded to include more than 230 extra schools. The administration paid in full the cost of tuition fees for all teachers pursuing further studies through distance learning. Of 4,320 Under Tree Schools were reduced by 1,700 as a school building programme was put in place. Additional funding was given to science teaching. Two new universities were opened by the Mills administration the University of Health and Allied Sciences and the University of Energy & Natural Resources.

Health policy and funding was addressed; buildings were improved, and several polyclinics were built. The National Ambulance Service was scaled up and improved. Cocoa farmers saw their highest revenue as production hit a record high.

Coverage of electricity was increased from 54per cent to 72per cent placing Ghana at third behind Mauritania and South Africa in sub-Saharan Africa.

John Evans Atta Mills died aged sixty-eight **on this day** in 2012. Few were aware that he had been suffering from throat cancer. But it was not the cancer that killed Mills. He died of a massive haemorrhagic stroke resulting from a brain aneurysm. One can only imagine how Ghana would have developed had Mills served a second term as president.

July 25th:

Marie Weston Chapman abolitionist and lieutenant to the revolutionary **William Lloyd Garrison** (see December 10th), was born **on this day** in 1806.

In 1830 Marie married Henry Grafton Chapman. As an abolitionist Chapman wanted an immediate end to slavery. Her campaigning was direct and unapologetic. When a crowd threatened to break up an abolitionist meeting Chapman is said to have stood up and said, *"If this is the last bulwark of freedom, we may as well die here as anywhere."* Chapman helped Garrison run the Massachusetts Slavery Society and to edit the campaigning paper 'The Liberator'.

Songs of the Free and Hymns of Christian Freedom was a collection published by Chapman in 1936. May 1838 saw Chapman addressing the Anti-Slavery Convention of American Women in Philadelphia. The mob that threatened to break up the meeting returned the following day and burned down the hall.

'Right and Wrong in Massachusetts' was a pamphlet written by Chapman in 1839 looking at the divisions between various abolitionists groups laying the blame at their attitude to women's rights. She edited the anti-slavery journal 'The Non-Resistant' from 1839–1842. Marie Chapman was placed in charge of fundraising. She wrote 'How Can I Help to Abolish Slavery' published in 1855.

Chapman lived briefly in Haiti and France but always had her finger on the pulse on what was going on in the movement. Following the Emancipation Proclamation (see January 1st) and the official end of slavery, Marie Chapman retired taking a back seat from 1863. She died on July 12th in 1885, knowing that her years of campaigning had a sense of victory.

Actor **Woody Strode** was born **on this day** in 1914. He would best be remembered for his Oscar nominated role in the film Spartacus.

Strode appeared in seventy films. In *Black Jesus*, the 1968 Italian-directed production, he starred in a film based on the story of Congolese leader **Patrice Lumumba** (see July 2nd). Before acting Strode was an athlete specialising as a decathlete, he was also one of four that integrated US football. Woody Strode died from lung cancer on December 31st 1994. He is buried at Riverside National Cemetery in Riverside, California.

Vincent G. Harding was one of many to remind the reader that the Emancipation Proclamation was not the victory hoped for or the end of the struggle. Born **on this day** in 1931, in the 1960s Harding was a Civil Rights activist in the United States working with the Southern Freedom Movement. It was during this time that he became a friend, associate and speech writer for Dr Martin Luther King Jr. Harding would become the first Director of the M. L. King Centre in Atlanta, Georgia. He worked on the ground-breaking award-winning documentary series *Eyes on the Prize'*.

Vincent Harding wrote numerous essays and nine books including: Hope and History: Why We Must Share the Story of the Movement (1990), There is a River: The Black Struggle for Freedom in America (1981) and Martin Luther King: The Inconvenient Hero published in 1996. Harding taught at Spelman College.

Working with and co-founder of The Veterans of Hope Project, the experiences of veterans of campaigns for social change were recorded and catalogued sharing the wisdom of elder activists.
Vincent G Harding died aged eighty-two on May 19th in 2014.

Champion boxer **Vernon Forrest** born January 12th 1971 had a seventeen-year professional career from 1992–2009. He held the IBF Welterweight crown in 2001, was the WBC Welterweight champion 2002–3 and held the WBC light Middleweight title from 2007–2009. With incredible hand speed he was nicknamed the Viper.

January 26th 2002 with a professional record of 30-0 Forrest faced Welterweight champion Shane Mosley whose record was thirty-eight fights and no losses. Forrest upset the odds that night taking the title. He won the rematch a year later on January 25th 2003. He was named Boxer of the Year 2002 by the Ring Magazine and the Boxing Writers Association of America. Forrest's career record reads forty-four fights, forty-one wins, 29 by knockout with three defeats.

While at a service station pumping up his tyre, Forrest had a gun pushed into his face and was ordered to hand over his watch and jewellery. The boxer gave chase but lost the gunman. He ran into another person but on seeing he was not the one who had robbed him Forrest started to make his way back to his vehicle. It was **on that day** in 2009 that seven bullets entered Vernon Forrest from behind, killing the boxer. The other person was Charman Sinkfield (30), who was working with the original gunman DeMario Ware (20). There was a third person in the gang Jquante Crews (25). Sinkfield was given a full life term without parole. The other two were given life sentences.

In 1997 Vernon Forrest had set up a charity Destiny's Child Inc a non-profit organisation that provided group homes and assistance to mentally challenged adults.

July 26th:

History of the Grain Coast, an area on the West coast of Africa identified as the country of **Liberia** goes back beyond the formation and independence of the country **on this day** in 1847. This entry will nonetheless focus on the history of what became the **Republic of Liberia.**

Some abolitionists in the United States of America looked to Africa as a haven for free blacks and emancipated enslaved peoples. Many slave owners in the Southern States supported the idea of free blacks returning to Africa. They feared free black people stirring up trouble among the enslaved people so backed calls for a homeland in Africa. Indeed, one of the main drivers behind the desire to create a land for free blacks was Ralph Randolph Gurley (May 26th 1797 – July 30th 1872). He advocated the separation of the races. It was Gurley who named the new land Liberia and is seen as one of the founding fathers.

The American Colonization Society (ACS) was formed in 1816 by Robert Finley to encourage and support the emigration of free black people to have the opportunity to make their home in Africa. The foundation of Liberia was established on January 7th 1822. The country declared its independence on January 26th in 1847. Independent Liberia would not be officially recognised by the United States until 1863.

Life was difficult for the settlers who had the highest recorded mortality rate of any group. Of the 4,571 emigrants who arrived from 1820–1843 only 1,819 survived. The settlement programme was full of controversy from the beginning with ideological differences among free African Americans, between abolitionists and the uneasy coalition of slave owners and abolitionists. Funding was a continuous and important concern.

The new arrivals known as Americo-Liberians set about taking control and governing. Little effort was made to integrate with the indigenous population. Americo-Liberians made up 2per cent of the population but were 100per cent of the qualified voters. From the 1860s Liberia was a minority ruled one party (the True Whig Party) state. English is the official language in a country that has twenty different languages spoken by the various ethnic groups.

Joseph Jenkins Roberts (March 15th 1809 – February 24th 1876) was elected the first president following independence from 1849–1856 and served as the seventh president from 1872–1876. **William Tubman** (see July 23rd) is recognised as the father of modern Liberia.

Joseph Jenkins Roberts

Considered one of the best exponents and performers of Caribbean music in Columbia **Joe Arroyo's** position is represented by a 3-metre-high statue that stands in the city of Cartagena.

Joe Arroyo, born November 1st 1955, had a career from 1969 to 2011. He mixed music from the African diaspora of the region including salsa, cumbia, porro, soca, konpa and zouk. His output included 'Rebellion',

'La Noche', 'Tania', 'El Ausente', and 'En Barranquilla'. Arroyo died **on this day** in 2011 from multi-organ failure. He was fifty-five.

July 27th:

South African Zulu singer **Simon 'Mahlathini' Nkabinde,** known as the Lion of Soweto, was born November 30th in 1937. As a boy he would sing in choirs and at weddings. When his voice broke, his parents suspected witchcraft. He developed a deep base, basso-profundo groan and became a prominent exponent of the style. Mahlathini translates as forest.

Nkabinde promoted rural Zulu roots style of music called Mbaqanga (jive) which he performed in the 1960s. He recorded with a female backing band known as Mahotella Queens and the backing band the Makgona Tsohle Band. They recorded and appeared live between 1964 and 1971. The partnership was reformed from 1983–1999.

Nkabinde's music in South Africa was no-longer as popular in the 1980s as it had been in the previous two decades. Paul Simon's Graceland album opened South African music up to an international audience. Dressed in traditional Zulu chief regalia, Nkabinde's performances attracted attention in Europe and America. He played at Wembley Stadium in 1988 as part of the Nelson Mandela seventieth birthday celebrations.

Simon Nkabinde died of diabetes related problems **on this day** in 1999. The Mahotella Queens and the Makgona Tsohle Band continued to perform, keeping the music of the Lion of Soweto alive.

July 28th:

The history of Australian indigenous people has not made for comfortable reading. Aboriginal life has been the story of struggle and survival. They were treated by the law as non-citizens in the land of their forebears and of their birth. Landscape artist **Albert Namatjira** born **on this day** 1902 would gain international recognition and fame. As an Aboriginal belonging to the Western Arrernte people the path as an artist would prove unpredictable.

In 1934 at the age of thirty-two, under the guidance of artist Rex Battarbee, Namatjira began to take his art seriously. The landscape watercolours produced, although western in style, contained many elements of traditional culture and symbolic artistic references. His first solo exhibition was held in Melbourne in 1938. Later shows were sold out in Adelaide and Sydney. By 1944 Namatjira was included in Australia's Who's Who? He was awarded the Queen's Coronation Medal in 1953 and met Queen Elizabeth II in Canberra in 1954.

As an Aboriginal life was never going to be straight forward. The Arrernte, a nomadic people, had a custom of sharing wealth. Albert Namatjira was supporting close to 600 people. In a bid to provide finances the artist chose to lease a cattle-station but having no ancestral claim to the land that had been earmarked for ex-servicemen, the lease was turned down. Namatjira purchased land to build a house but the sale was fraudulent as the floodplain near Alice Springs was unsuitable for building. Namatjira was forced to live in a shanty in a place called Morris Soak in relative poverty. The conditions of his lifestyle led to a public outcry.

In an attempt to give Namatjira the rights required to survive he became the first Northern Territory Aboriginal to no longer be a ward of the state. In 1957 he was given limited Australian citizenship which afforded him the right to vote, limited rights to buy land and the legal right to buy alcohol.

Albert Namatjira

Alcohol would cause its own problem. Albert Namatjira left a bottle of rum on the front seat of his car. When Fay Iowa was murdered Namatjira was held responsible for having left the alcohol in his car giving illegal access to Aborigines. He was initially sentenced to six months' imprisonment but served two months at Papunya Nature Reserve after public concerns were raised.

Albert Namatjira died in Aug 1959 from heart disease complicated by pneumonia. He had married aged eighteen to Ilkalita (Rubina) a Kukatja woman. The couple had five sons and three daughters. Part of the copyright to Namatjira's work was sold in return for royalties purchased by John Brackenberg in 1957 depriving the Namatjira family of their inheritance. The deal was seen as exploitative. It was in 2017 following the assistance of philanthropist Dick Smith that the rights were returned to the Albert Namatjira Trust.

Congolese singer **Papa Wendo (Antoine Wendo Kolosoy)** known as the father of Congolese Rumba (Soukous) was born April 25th in 1925. He laid the foundations of Congolese rumba combining local traditional songs, which Wendo learned working on the river meeting different communities, with Afro-Cuban rhythms.

'Marie-Louise' was a major hit in 1948. Wendo was arrested and accused of the music having supernatural satanic powers. Briefly imprisoned when he was released his fame exploded.

Papa Wendo was a personal friend of **Patrice Lumumba** (see July 2nd). Following his friend's death and the rise of dictators, Wendo stopped performing for the next three decades. He had a late revival in the 1990s with albums such as 'Nani akolela Wendo?' (1993), 'Marie Louise' (1999), and 'Amber' in 2002.

Papa Wendo was the subject of the documentary film *On the Rumba River* in 2007. He died **on this day** in 2008.

Mamadou Doudou N'Diaye Rose was declared a 'Living Human Treasure' by UNESCO in 2006 for preserving traditional rhythms and culture. The Senegalese percussionist's instrument was the traditional Sabar drum. He was known as the mathematician of rhythm. He composed numerous pieces often celebrating important occasions in the nation's history. He was a friend and favourite of the Senegalese president and poe**t Leopold Sedar Senghor.**

In 1960 Rose was appointed the drum major and first head of the Senegalese National Ballet. He toured with the Doudou N'Diaye Rose Orchestra in the 1970s and collaborated with **Miles Davis, Dizzy Gillespie**. the Rolling Stones and Peter Gabriel appearing on Gabriel's 1989 album 'Passion' and the 1992 album 'Us'.

Rose founded a percussion school in Dakar. His extended family made up the bulk of the group called the Drummers of West Africa. They successfully toured Europe, Japan and the USA. He even put together a rare female drumming group called the Rosettes. Their success helped to break down sexual barriers.

Rose was from a traditional griot family born **on this day** in 1930. It was said that **Josephine Baker** had told him that he would one day be a great drummer. The small figure would conduct fifty drummers and eighty singers, creating a multi-layered rhythm. He died aged eighty-five on August 19th in 2015, leaving behind four wives and forty-two children.

July 29th:

Author of the 1945 classic 'If He Hollers Let Him Go' and the nine book black detective series 'Harlem Detectives', **Chester Himes** was born **on this day** in 1909. In 1928 following an armed robbery Himes was sentenced to hard labour for 20–25 years and sent to Ohio Penitentiary. Finding his ability to write, his works were first published in 1931 in various magazines including *Esquire* in 1934. The writing afforded Himes respect in the prison, keeping him out of trouble and away from violence.

In 1930 Himes experienced a prison fire. He wrote about the event in *Cast the First Stone* which was re-published as *Yesterday Will Make You Cry* in 1998. He was released on parole to his mother in April 1936. Soon after he met **Langston Hughes** (see May 22nd) who was able to point Chester Himes in the right direction and provide important contacts.

Chester Himes wrote *If He Hollers Let Him Go* followed by *The Lonely Crusade* in 1947 about the experiences of black migrants travelling north from the Southern States. Having worked in Los Angeles and Hollywood, Himes left for France. He wrote about all that he, as a black man, had faced growing up in the American South and having been imprisoned, but it was the racism in Hollywood that left him bitter and angry.

In France Himes quickly became part of the Bohemian set mixing with **James Baldwin,** the cartoonist **Oliver Harrington, Richard Wright, Malcolm X,** poet **Yolande Cornelia, Nikki Giovanni,** author of 1926's *Nigger Heaven* and Harlem Renaissance patron **Carl Van Vechten** and black social protest novelist **William Gardener Smith.**

Chester Himes had a stroke in 1959. Although married to Jean Johnson in 1937, the couple separated in 1952. He met journalist Lesley Packard who would take care of the ailing Himes as well as doing a lot of the behind the scenes work with his writing. The couple eventually married in 1978. Life was not always easy for the interracial couple. They moved to Spain in 1969. The crime series Harlem Detective earned Himes the title of the Father of black American crime writing.

Chester Himes died from Parkinson's disease on November 12th 1984 in Spain. He is buried at Benissa Cemetery. Several biographies have been written about the novelist; Edward Margolies and Michael Fabre's 1997 *The Several Lives of Chester Himes*. *Chester Himes: A Life* (2000) by James Sallis and the 2017 *Chester B. Himes: A Biography* by Lawrence P. Jackson.

Samuel E. K. Mqhayi, called the father of Xhosa poetry, was born in South Africa on December 1st 1875. He helped to codify Xhosa grammar and standardise Xhosa orthography (the conventional spelling system of a language).

Mqhayi assisted in editing several Xhosa language journals. His first book, which has been lost, was *U-Samson*, based on the biblical Samson. *The Lawsuit of the Twins* (1914), was a defence of Xhosa law when in front of European administrations. Mqhayi's *Songs of Joy and Lullabies* (1927), became the first collection of Xhosa poems to be published.

Samuel Mqhayi's autobiography *Mqhayi of the Mountain of Beauty* was published in 1939. As an imbongi, a Xhosa praise poet who performs ceremonial activities at important events, Mqhayi captured many traditions and the daily life of the Xhosa people in his works. Much of his poetry in nationalistic and patriotic in nature and critical of foreign colonial powers.

Samuel E. K. Mqhayi died **on this day** in 1945 and is buried in Berlin near King William's Town. The grave is listed as a heritage site.

Lawyer and judge **Matthew James Perry Jr's** work in South Carolina's court transformed civil rights for black people in the state. Born August 3rd 1921, Perry worked tirelessly to advance the legal status of black people.

Edwards v South Carolina in 1963 upheld the right for blacks to engage in protest marches while receiving full legal protection.

Perry became an activist when he saw Italian prisoners of war comfortably, naturally, and happily eating with white American soldiers, something that was denied to black American soldiers subjected to segregation policies. Matthew Perry's legal efforts led to the official desegregation of South Carolina's public schools, state parks, beaches, hospitals, restaurants and Clemson, South Carolina University with the admission of **Harvey Gantt** and the University of South Carolina with the admissions of **James Solomon** and **Henri Monteith.**

President Gerald Ford appointed Perry to the US Military Courts of Appeal in 1976. President Jimmy Carter named Perry South Carolina's first black federal district court judge in 1979. He married Hallie Bacote in 1948. Matthew James Perry Jr died on July 29th in 2011 aged eighty-nine.

July 30th:

James Varick established the black-led denomination of the African Methodist Episcopal Zion Church (AME-Zion) in 1799. It was never as successful as **Richard Allen's,** (see March 26th), African Methodist Episcopal Church (AME) but its importance in American black history is undeniable. Future members would include **Frederick Douglass** (see February 14th), **Harriet Tubman** (see September 17th) **Sojourner Truth** (see November 26th) and **Paul Robeson** (see April 9th). AME-Zion became known as the Freedom Church fighting and preaching to emancipate its membership from spiritual, social and economic chains.

AME-Zion was formed to allow the black congregation total freedom from the religious restrictions that existed within the white led Methodist Church at the time. August 11th 1820 saw the decision to break from the white leadership and to be separate from Allen's AME church. **Abraham Thompson** and Varick were elected as elders on September 13th 1820. Thompson, Varick and **Leven Smith** were ordained supervisors of the Church on June 17th 1822. **On this day** in 1822 James Varick became AME-Zion's first bishop.

Varick was the co-founder of *Freedom's Journal* America's oldest black newspaper in 1827. Having celebrated July 4th rejoicing in the abolition of slavery in New York, James Varick died a few days later on July 22nd.

American artist **Betye Saar** was born **on this day** in 1926. She was part of the Black Arts Movement in the 1970s challenging racial stereotypes and politicising artwork. Saar studied various forms of printmaking and etching but found her artistic calling in 1968 developing an interest in three-dimensional work known as assemblage. Saar would incorporate items in the work that added to the aesthetic with symbolic and cultural meaning.

The recycled objects and items reflected recycled emotions and feelings. She wants the viewer to see her anger with segregation and racism that existed and exists in America.

Betye Saar

James Emman Kwegyir Aggrey born in the Gold Coast (Ghana) on October 18th 1875, would be regarded as the **'Father of African Education'**.

At the age of twenty-three, on July 30th 1927, Aggrey sailed to the United States for further academic studies. He graduated in 1902 with three degrees, speaking several languages including English, German, French, ancient and modern Greek and Latin as well as his African mother tongues. The following year Aggrey was ordained a minister in the African Methodist Episcopal Zion Church. He married the native Virginian Rosebud 'Rose' Douglas in 1905. The couple had four children. Further studies saw Aggrey awarded a doctorate degree in theology doctor of divinity in 1912, and a doctorate in osteopathy (osteopathic medicine) in 1914.

Heading the Phelps-Stokes Commission looking into the educational needs of Africa, Dr Aggrey visited ten countries in 1920 and 1921 including the Gold Coast, Liberia, Cameroon, Belgian Congo, Sierra Leone,

Angola and South Africa, emphasising the importance of education. Aggrey pioneered co-educational education at the Achimota College in the Gold Coast arguing that female education educated the nation.

Dr Aggrey faced racial opposition but spoke eloquently using the black and white keys of a piano to demonstrate the power of individuality and more so the power of unity. He spoke passionately wanting his people to be good Africans not poor imitations of Europeans.

A second Phelps-Stokes Commission trip to the African continent in 1924 saw Aggrey found the Achimota School. He served as the vice principal from 1925–27. Back in the USA James Emman Kwegyir Aggrey fell ill with meningococcal meningitis. The fifty-two-year-old doctor died **on this day** July 30th 1927. He is buried in Oakdale Cemetery in Salisbury, North Carolina.

British decathlete **Daley Thompson** was born on this day in 1958. As a junior he set a British junior record of 6,685 points. After taking silver at the European Championships in 1978 Thompson would go undefeated for the next nine years. He won nineteen decathlons, including twelve in a row.

Thompson set the first of his four world records in 1980 with 8,622 points. At the Moscow Olympics that same year he won his first Olympic gold medal. The year 1982 saw Thompson set two further world records. At the Helsinki World Championships in 1983 Thompson took gold. The following year at the Los Angeles Olympics he successfully defended his title, winning gold in 1984. He was only the second person to do so after Bob Mathias in 1948 and 1952. Daley Thompson's Olympic points score was adjusted for technical reasons in 1985 giving him his fourth world record with 8,847 points. In addition to the successes listed above Daley Thompson won two European Championships and three Commonwealth gold medals. Two black British athletes worthy of mention performed in the heptathlon, **Denise Lewis**,

born 27th August 27th 1972. She became the first European to win the Olympic heptathlon at Sydney in 2000. **Jessica Ennis-Hill** born January 28th 1986 was the 2012 Olympic heptathlon gold medallist, three times World Champion, 2009, 2011 and 2015 and European Champion in 2010. See **Linford Christie** August 1st and **Mo Farah** March 23rd.

July 31st:

Some sources cite July 30th, others say the 31st, **on this day** in 1863 the General **Order No 252** was given. Commonly known as **'an eye for an eye'**. American President Abraham Lincoln warned the Confederacy that for every black prisoner shot that a Confederate prisoner would be executed. The order went on to say that for every black person sold on into slavery in the deep South a Unionist prisoner would be given a life sentence of hard labour.

Whether the order resolved any problems or was enacted effectively is doubtful. Some Confederates continued to kill black rebels and still sold people into slavery.

One of the big six American Civil Rights leaders **Whitney Young Jr** was born **on this day** in 1921. He came to attention elected as the executive director of the National Urban League in 1961 serving as its head through to 1971. The ten years under Young's leadership saw the League's chapters rise from sixty to ninety-eight. It was a period that redirected the league's focus from black middle class concerns to that of the urban black family, while seeing an additional move towards the national Civil Rights movement.

Young drove the demand for black people to receive equal opportunities in the workplace and in government. He was at the forefront of workplace racial integration and black economic empowerment placing blacks in hitherto white only positions. Young advocated for a domestic 'Marshall Plan', although this did not succeed it is believed to have influenced the Democrat administration's 1963–69 poverty programmes. Whitney Young was a close advisor to both President Kennedy and President Johnson. He is seen as co-author of Johnson's 'War on Poverty'. As the executive director Young connected the League to white political and business leaders towards ending racial economic disparity, addressing racial problems, while building a bridge with younger militant black groups.

Young is credited with persuading white corporate America and major foundations to aid the Civil Rights movement and support self-help programmes for jobs, housing, education and families. At his behest, the League was a co-sponsor of the historic 1963 March on Washington.

Whitney Young Jr.

Following a visit to Vietnam, Young established a veterans' affairs department at the League. Attending a conference in Nigeria to enhance Afro-American understanding, Whitney Young drowned whilst swimming on March 11th 1971, he was forty-nine.

Young wrote *To Be Equal* in 1964 and *Beyond Racism: Building an Open Society* published in 1969. Whitney Young has been the subject of several biographies and a PBS documentary.

Of Aboriginal heritage belonging to the Wiradjuri people of New South Wales in Australia tennis player **Evonne Goolagong Cawley** was born **on this day** in 1951. She would win Wimbledon in 1971 and 1980, the French Open in 1971 and the Australian title in 1974, 1975, 1976 and 1978. For tennis connections see **Althea Gibson** May 26th, **Arthur Ashe** July 10th, **Yannick Noah**, May 19th and **Serena Williams** July 8th.

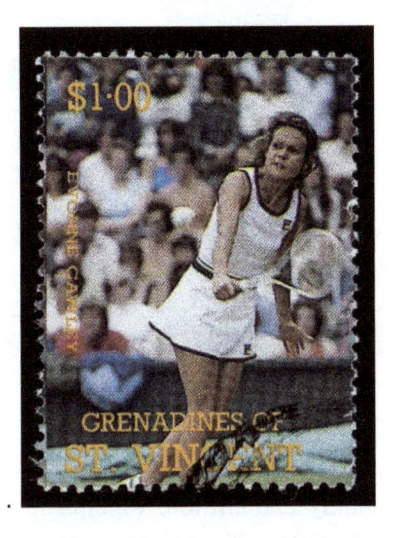

Evonne Goolagong Cawley.

Aug 1st:

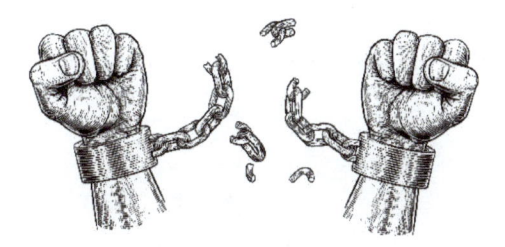

The Slavery Abolition Act received Royal Assent on August 28th 1933. The Act took effect a year later **on this day** in 1834. The Act was to emancipate an estimated 800,000 enslaved people in the British Empire apart from those who lived in territories that were in the possession of the East India Company Ceylon (Sri Lanka) and Saint Helena.

Children six and under would be freed immediately. Enslaved people aged seven and above would be required to work for free for their former masters as apprentices for a further six years. As William Wilberforce had argued, freeing the slaves would be a disaster, believing that they required training and education to equip them for their new life. All enslaved people were eventually freed following further legislation that came into force **on this day** in 1838.

Emancipation cost the British economy £20 million, 40per cent of the national budget. The loan would take 182 years to repay, finally paid off in 2015. The freed people received no financial support. Momentum to end slavery had been growing. Economically the triangular Atlantic trade was no longer making the profit it once did. The abolition of the slave trade, in the British Empire, in 1807 had been all about economic prudence. Ships that had a human cargo were left useless, covered and infused with human excrement, vomit, blood and food waste putting the vessel out of

Outside the British Houses of Parliament stands the Buxton Memorial commemorating the end of slavery in the British Empire.

action, unable to have a quick turnaround for trade. Slave revolts such as the Baptist Wars in Jamaica 1831 frightened parliament. The Abolitionist Movement was growing. In 1833 petitions collected 1.3 million signatures opposing the slavery. Religious arguments and Christian teaching on the slavery trade were pushing back against the trade challenging its morality.

The son of former slaves **Benjamin Mays** would receive fifty-six honorary degrees, quite an achievement for a black man who grew up in the Jim Crow segregated south of the USA. Born **on this day** 1894 Mays would be fifty-one before he could vote, in the land of the free, in 1945. Described as the school master of the revolution, Dr Mays was appointed president of Morehouse College, a position he would hold for twenty-seven years from 1940–1967. Former student Martin Luther King described Mays as his spiritual mentor and intellectual father.

Mays is credited with laying the intellectual foundation of the American Civil Rights Movement referenced in his nine books including *The Negro Church* (1933), *The Negro God* (1938), *Disturbed About Man* (1969) and in his autobiography *Born to Rebel* published in 1971.

Benjamin Mays gave the benediction ending the programme at the historic 'March on Washington' in 1963 and gave the eulogy at Martin Luther King's funeral in 1968. He died, aged eighty-nine, on March 28th 1984.

Born **on this day** in 1918 **T. J. Jemison** would become the leader of America's largest black led Christian denomination the National Baptist Convention from 1982–1994. The Civil Rights struggle was an issue that Jemison had been aware of from a young age. In 1945 he formed the local chapter of the National Association for the Advancement of Colored People in Staunton Virginia. He became the pastor of the Mount Zion Baptist Church in Baton Rouge in 1949.

His first major political and legal battle came challenging the Jim Crow segregationist attitude embedded in the public bus system. Sick and tired of the humiliation having seats reserved for whites and seats at the back for blacks, the black community organised a boycott that lasted eight days demanding a first come first served policy. Following limited success Jemison took the case to the courts and won desegregating the public transport system. When Dr Martin Luther King's Montgomery Improvement Association embarked on their year-long bus boycott 1955–6 Jemison was contacted for advice and was able to provide support.

T. J. Jemison was a founder member of Dr King's Southern Christian Leadership Conference civil rights movement and served on its executive board. Theodore Judson Jemison died aged ninety-five on November 13th in 2013.

Born **on this day** in 1932 Aboriginal **Lowitja O'Donoghue** would rise from humble beginnings to be voted 'Australian of the Year' in 1984. Aged two she became part of Australia's stolen generation, although she prefers to say that she was removed and not stolen. It would be thirty-three years before she would see her Aboriginal Yankunytjatjara mother again. Having been raised in a children's home and given a white education O'Donoghue found that the door to her chosen profession as a nurse was firmly closed. Joining the Aborigine Advancement League, she fought to overcome institutional racism, finally becoming the first Aboriginal trained nurse in 1954 at Adelaide Hospital. Over the following decade O'Donoghue rose to the position of ward sister.

Following a trip to India, O'Donoghue joined the South Australian Public Service as an Aboriginal liaison and welfare officer in 1962. She would hold a variety of administrative positions joining the Department of Aboriginal Affairs in 1967 and being appointed regional director at the Adelaide office. The year 1970 saw O'Donoghue become the first female appointed a regional director of an Australian federal department. As a member of the Aboriginal Legal Rights Movement 1971–72 Lowitja O'Donoghue was continuously at the forefront fighting for representation and a full voice for Aboriginal rights. In 1976 she became the first Aboriginal woman to receive the Order of Australia (OA). The following year she was elected chair of the National Conference formed to express Aboriginal views.

O'Donoghue has spent a lifetime working in health, housing, community development and fighting for land rights. She became the first Aboriginal Australian to address the United Nations General Assembly in December 1992. Lowitja O'Donoghue was named a 'National Living Treasure' in 1998.

On this day, the former French colony of Dahomey now **Benin** gained its independence in 1960. Formerly Dahomey, **Hubert Maga** (1916–2000) served as the Premier 1959–1960, and President from August 1960–1963. **King Behanzin** is one of the country's celebrated resistant leaders and rulers who campaigned from1844 to1906

Elderly woman from Benin.

On this day 1984 at the Barcelona Olympics 100m sprinter **Linford Christie** won gold. In doing so the Jamaican-born British sprinter became the oldest man to claim the title aged thirty-two and 121 days.

Christie was born April 2nd 1960. He would become the third British athlete to take Olympic gold in the 100m after Harold Abrahams and Allan Wells, and only the fifth European. He was the first European to break the 10 second barrier, a feat that he achieved on nine occasions. 1993 saw Christie become the first man to hold the Olympic title, the World Championship, the European Championship and the Commonwealth Games 100m titles all at the same time. That same year he was voted BBC Sports Personality of the Year. In 1990 Linford Christie was awarded the MBE and in 1998 he was given an OBE. The end of his athletic career was blighted by allegations of drug taking and receiving a two-year ban by the IAAF of World Athletics. **Colin Jackson** born on February 18th 1967 a contemporary of Christie, specialised in the 110 high hurdles. He was two times World Champion, and undefeated in the European

Championships for twelve years. His world record of 12.91 stood for over a decade and his indoor 60m record stood for twenty-six years. See also Mo Farah March 23rd and Daly Thompson July 30th.

Record-breaking British hurdler.

Aug 2nd:

American writer, playwright, novelist, essayist, poet and activist **James Baldwin** was born **on this day** in 1924. A social observer, he was one of the great voices of the Civil Rights movement. His work mirrored black aspiration, disappointments and coping strategies, often reflecting on his own life experiences as in the semi-autobiographical *Go Tell It on the Mountain*. The 1953 novel looked at Baldwin's relationship with his stepfather and the role of religion in the black community.

Baldwin never knew the name of his biological father. He was raised, from the age of three, by his Baptist minister stepfather who he called and saw as his father.

His father died on July 29th, 1943 on the same day his eighth sibling was born. Life was precarious; money tight, work a necessity taking precedence over education and all the time facing racism.

James Baldwin moved to France in 1948. From there he was able to have a better perspective of his and the black situation in America. Following *Go Tell It on the Mountain* he published his second novel *Giovanni's Room* in 1956. It looked at an American in Paris and the life of a homosexual with all its complexities and complications. Baldwin never hid his sexuality, believing sexuality was more fluid than the frequently presented binary choice. He would return to issues of sexuality in later writings such as the 1978 *Just Above My Head*.

Another Country (1962) examined interracial relationships, as with homosexuality, both topics were considered taboo in most of conservative America. Baldwin explored the psychological implications of racism for both the oppressed and the oppressor. He successfully ventured into being a playwright with 1954's *Amen Corner*. The play explored the world of Pentecostal Christianity in the black American community.

It was as an essayist that Baldwin's stature rose. His prodigious output captured the black experience in America. *Notes of a Native Son* (1955), *Nobody Knows My Name: More Notes of a Native Son* (1961) and *The Fire Next Time*, published in 1963, were million sellers. They were both commercial and critical successes. *The Fire Next Time* saw Baldwin talking to white America, showing his audience how they were seen through the eyes of the black community. In educating white America Baldwin skilfully removed layer after layer of protection used to shield the white American, preserving their sense of nationalistic pride, white supremacy and white privilege. As each layer was removed Baldwin revealed the truth about the painstakingly curated myth that was America - The Land of the Free and the American Dream. He uncovered the uncomfortable truth; the reality of white American history while shining a light on the pain and challenges of being black. Baldwin was critical, analytical yet persuasive and unwavering as he wrote about the black experience facing racism in America. Prophetic warnings ran through his work, yet there was room for cautious hope and optimism.

James Baldwin appeared on the cover of *TIME* magazine in 1963. The following year he wrote the Broadway play *Blues for Mr Charlie* loosely based on the death of **Emmitt Till** in 1955 (see August 28th). He continued to write and teach through the 1970s and 1980s. The award-winning and acclaimed documentary *I Am Not Your Negro* (2016), based on the unfinished and unreleased *Remember This House* and *If Beale Street Could Talk* (1974), showed James Baldwin's continuing relevance. He died aged sixty-three from stomach cancer in France on December 1st 1987. James Baldwin is buried in Ferncliff Cemetery in Hartsdale near New York City.

Olufela Olusegun Oludotun Ransome-Kuti popularly known as **Fela Kuti** was a pioneer of Afrobeat, a mixture of traditional Yoruba music blended with Afro-Cuban influences and black American music such as funk and jazz. The multi-instrumentalist, composer and bandleader was born October 15th 1938 in Nigeria. Kuti named the music Afrobeat following a visit to Ghana in 1967. Visiting the USA in 1969 he spent ten months in Los Angeles. It was at this time he was introduced to the Black Power Movement by Sandra Smith adding a new layer of influences. Before returning to Nigeria, he released 'The 69 Los Angeles Sessions'.

Returning to Nigeria, Kuti renamed his band Afrika 70 and changed the focus of the lyrics from love songs to a greater emphasis on social and political issues. Kuti became increasingly outspoken against Nigeria's military junta. He formed a commune called Kalakuta Republic made up of a recording studio and accommodation for all connected to the band, situated in the suburbs of Lagos. He would later declare the commune independent, eventually making himself president. Kuti also opened a nightclub at the Empire Hotel originally called the Afro Spot before changing the name to Afrika Shrine. The commune and club were viewed by the authorities as political centres undermining the government. Nigerian officials raided the commune on numerous occasions, Fela Kuti would be arrested an estimated 200 times. The record 'Zombie' (1977) criticised the Nigerian soldiers as having no mind and no thoughts of their own, acting like zombies, blindly obeying outrageous orders. Such numbers were popular, especially with the poor in the country.

The Head of State General Obasanjo, an old classmate of Kuti, ordered

Fela Kuti.

the commune to be raided and raised to the ground. Hundreds of soldiers beat, raped and killed the occupants. Kuti's mother was thrown from an upstairs window and died from her injuries and Kuti was almost beaten to death. Facing trumped up charges Fela Kuti spent two years in prison from 1984 but nothing stopped his activism and outspoken lyrics. 'ITT' (International Thief Thief) released in 1979 attacked multi-national companies that exploited Africa and Africans. 'VIP' (Vagabond In Power) from the same year, called for the masses to rise up.

Fela Kuti became increasingly interested in ancient Yoruba deities. His behaviour became increasingly erratic reflected in album tracks that would last for more than twenty minutes. In 1978 he married twenty-seven wives, divorcing them in 1986, claiming that no man should own a woman. The cover of his 1989 album depicted images of Margaret Thatcher and Ronald Reagan as blood-sucking vampires.

Fela Kuti's last recording was 'Condom Scallywag and Scatter', critical of condoms as un-African. He claimed that AIDS was a white man's disease. Ironically Fela Kuti died from AIDS-related issues **on this day** in 1997, he was fifty-eight. Kuti left behind seven children and about fifty albums.

Co-produced by Jay-Z, the 2008 musical 'Fela' proved a major hit on the Broadway stage before successfully transferring to London. Fela Kuti posthumously gained the international recognition that he failed to achieve during his lifetime.

Aug 3rd:

On this day in 1936 athlete **Jesse Owens** ran into the history books at the Berlin Olympics. Over the next five days more history would be made as Owens took gold in the long jump on Aug 4th, gold in the 200m on Aug 5th and gold in the 4x100 relay on Aug 9th. The haul of 4 golds in track and field would not be repeated for forty-eight years until **Carl Lewis** (see July 1st) achieved the feat at the 1984 Los Angeles Olympic Games.

Born on September 12th 1913 **James Cleveland Owens** was left with the name Jesse after a teacher hearing Owens call himself J C misheard Jesse and the name stuck.

At the National High School Championships, Chicago, 1933 Owens equalled the 100-yard dash record with 9.4 seconds. He equalled the long jump record at 24 ft 9 ½ in. At Ohio State University running for the 'Buckeye' track team Owens's record-breaking achievement earned him the nickname of the 'Buckeye Bullet'. Described as the greatest forty-five minutes in athletic history, May 25th 1935 saw Owens set three world records and equal a fourth. In the long jump his distance of 26 ft 8½ in would stand for twenty-five years. Owens also set records in the 220 hurdles and 220 yards sprint. It is likely in breaking the sprint and hurdle records at 220 yards he also broke the record for the 200m in both events. He equalled the 100-yard dash record on that day.

Berlin had been awarded the Olympic Games in 1931. Hitler came to power two years later. Concerns had been raised about the racial politics of Hitler's Nazi regime but there was no boycott. Before the competition took place Owens was met by Adi Dassler of Adidas and persuaded to wear their shoes. This made Jesse Owens the first black American to be sponsored. Rumour has it that after winning gold Owens was snubbed by the Fuhrer. Hitler had been greeting German winners but when instructed that he would either have to greet all competitors or none. Hitler chose to greet none. Owens and others spoke of Hitler saluting Owens' achievements. One witness even reported seeing the pair shake hands. What was more disconcerting for Owens was on his return to the USA President F. D. Roosevelt neither invited the multiple gold medallist to the White House nor bothered to send the athlete a telegram of congratulations.

Jesse Owens.

Owens received a ticker tape parade through the streets of Manhattan and was greeted by New York mayor Fiorello LaGuardia. At the reception held in his honour at the Waldorf Astoria, Owens was not allowed to enter through the front and had to take the freight lift to his reception. Such racial humiliation, bias and mistreatment was not new to the athlete. He never received a scholarship to study in spite of his achievements and had to work to pay for his tuition and trained when, where and how he could. Even at the University Games, although Owens was the team captain, he and other black athletes were not allowed to stay in the dormitories provided for the white athletes. Eating on the road was a continuous problem. At the 1936 Olympic Games in Germany black and white American athletes shared the same accommodation.

Jesse Owens married his childhood sweetheart **Minnie Ruth Solomon** on July 5th 1935. They would remain together until Jesse's death. They had three daughters. Money was always an issue, Owens turned professional, deciding to cash in on his Olympic success, but promotional opportunities quickly dried up and as a professional Owens was barred from appearing for his country. The former champion took on numerous jobs to make ends meet famously racing horses. From 1942–46 Owens worked for the Ford Motor Company in Detroit.

He initially spoke out against the raised clenched fist salute by Tommy Smith and John Carlos in 1968 but admitted a few years later that he had got that call wrong. After years of struggle having been left out in the cold and ignored by the Athletics Association, Jesse Owens was slowly brought back into the fold. He received honours and recognition in the late 1960s and the 1970s.

Brothers Jackie and Mack Robinson.

Jesse Owens had lung cancer. He'd been a smoker for thirty-five years. He died on March 31st 1980, age sixty-six. Jesse Owens is buried at Oak Woods Cemetery in Chicago.

Eighteen black athletes participated as part of team USA in the 1936 Berlin Olympics. They brought home fourteen medals; eight were gold. **Archie Williams** took gold and **James LuValle** bronze in the 400m. **Mack Robinson** (older brother to baseball's Jackie Robinson) came second to Owens in the 200m. **Ralph Metcalfe** came in second in the 100m and won gold in the 4x100m relay. **Cornelius Johnson** won gold and **Dave Albritton** silver in the high jump. **Fritz Pollard** came in third with a bronze in the 110m high hurdles. All the African American athletes attempted to overcome obstacles in their pursuit of sporting excellence. Some had their hopes crushed by the team selectors never getting their chance as happened to **Louis Stokes** and boxer **Howell King**. All faced racism, closed doors, and limited opportunities when they returned home to the land of the free.

South African political leader **Davidson Don Tengo Jabavu** would be a prominent educationist and politician in the first half of the twentieth century. His father **John Tengo Jabavu** founded and edited the first South African black-owned Bantu language newspaper in 1884 called *Black Opinion*. John was also a co-founder of the South African Native College later called the University of Fort Hare. His son Davidson Jabavu travelled to Britain studying in London, Birmingham and Wales. He returned to South Africa in 1914 and became the first black professor at Fort Hare staying there for more than thirty years.

Jabavu was actively involved in establishing organisations to ensure black political support, agitation and union involvement. He founded the Black Teachers Association, was president of the Cape African Teachers Association and the South African Native Teachers Federation. Jabavu founded the South African Native Farmers Association advocating for better farming methods. He was also a founding member of the South African Institute of Race Relations. In 1936 Jabavu became the first president of the All-African Convention opposing segregation policies. As president of the Cape Voters Convention Jabavu fought for the retention of African voting rights in the 1920s and 30s.

Davidson Don Tengo Jabavu wrote *Black Problem* (1920) and *The Segregation Fallacy and Other Papers* in 1928. He died at the age of seventy-three **on this day** in 1959.

Niger celebrates its independence from France **on this day** in 1960. December 18th 1958 marks the official founding of the Republic of Niger. Between December 1958 and 1960 the country remained a semi-autonomous region being part of the larger French Community. On July 11th 1960 the French agreed to full independence. Hamani Diori was elected president by the National Assembly. Riddled with corruption and eventually removed in a coup. Dior had attained a level of respect on the African

Young woman of Niger.

international political stage. **Hamani Diori** became independent Niger's first president from 1960–74. He was born on June 6th 1916. Diori died April 23rd 1989.

South Africa's most popular and outspoken reggae singer/songwriter **Lucky Philip Dube** was born **on this day** in 1964. The singer's lyrics were critical of apartheid and of post-apartheid administrations as well as denouncing excess alcohol and drugs. Lucky was given his name after his mother had had several failed attempts to have a child. He sang in Zulu, Afrikaans and English releasing his first album in 1984. He toured and appeared with Peter Gabriel, Sting and Sinéad O'Connor. At Reggae Sunsplash in Jamaica 1991 Dube was the only artist asked to come back on stage and perform a twenty-five-minute encore.

Lucky Philip Dube was attacked and murdered by three gunmen in what appeared to be a carjacking. Shot and injured Dube drove his car into a tree. He died on October 18th in 2007.

Aug 4th:

Few artists can claim the status, respect, longevity and influence that has been accorded to the jazz legend **Louis Armstrong.** His recordings on the Okeh label with the Armstrong Hot Five and The Hot Seven (1925–28) are recognised for their influence and importance in jazz and music in general. He transformed jazz from being an ensemble product to a soloist art. Armstrong emerged as a famous musician, singer and composer playing on tracks such as 'Cornet Chop Suey' and 'Potato Head Blues'. His vocal performances popularised the scat style of vocal improvisation. It is unclear whether Armstrong created scat, but he made the style his own and popularised it with the 1926 track *'Heebie Jeebies'*. His transformative singing and phrasing would influence all who followed including Bing Crosby, **Billie Holiday**, (see April 7th) Frank Sinatra and **Ella Fitzgerald** (see April 25th).

Born **on this day** in 1901 in New Orleans, the child Louis Armstrong would experience extreme poverty. The area he lived in was so rough it was nicknamed 'The Battlefield'. Aged ten or eleven he had to leave school to find work, never being educated beyond the fifth grade. Firing his father's gun in the air celebrating New Year in 1912 the young Armstrong was arrested and spent the next two years in the Coloured Waifs School, a correctional facility for juvenile delinquents. It was at the school Armstrong learned to play the cornet.

Armstrong's talents were recognised by the leading cornet player in New Orleans at the time **Joe 'King' Oliver.** Oliver took the young musician under his wing and mentored him. By 1918 Louis Armstrong was good enough to replace Oliver in the city's top band The Kid Ory Band. Armstrong would play on the Mississippi River boats meeting jazz pioneers such as the great Bix Beiderbecke. In 1922 Oliver sent for his protege to join him in Chicago to play second coronet in Oliver's Creole Jazz Band. Louis Armstrong made his first recording demonstrating his solo ability on April 5th 1923 on 'Chimes Blues'. He would also back other artists such as **Bessie Smith** (see September 26th) and **Ma Rainey** (see April 26th). Armstrong married Lillian Hardin in 1924. It was at her suggestion that he left King Oliver and moved to New York to play with **Fletcher Henderson's** band. Armstrong's playing style introduced swing to what is considered one of the early jazz big bands. Armstrong was now playing the trumpet having moved on from the smaller compact coronet.

Recording with the Hot Five and the Hot Seven Armstrong hit a rich vein demonstrating his innovative style on close to sixty recordings. He paired with pianist **Earl 'Father' Hines** (see December 28th) in 1928 producing recordings such as 'Weather Bird' and 'West End Blues'. Moving to New York Louis Armstrong performed in *Connie's Hot Chocolate* a show based on Fats Waller's music (see December 15th). He also started to record popular songs such as 'I Can't Give You Anything but Love', 'Star Dust' and 'Body and Soul'.

Armstrong was able to break through the colour bar appearing in Hollywood productions, although he rarely received the roles reflecting his stature. *Swing That Music* (1936) Armstrong's autobiography was the first of its kind for a black jazz artist. He also published *Satchmo: My Life in New Orleans* in 1954.

Louis Armstrong toured England in 1932 and Europe in 1933. In 1937 the trumpet player became the first black man to host a nationally sponsored radio show. Mr and Mrs Armstrong (his fourth wife) moved to live in Corona Queens in New York. The house 34–36 on 107th street would be the couple's home through to Louis' death. Today the property is the Louis Armstrong House Museum. It was declared a National Historic Landmark in 1977.

Recordings in the 1940s and 1950s such as 'Blueberry Hill' (1949), 'That Lucky Old Sun' (1949), 'La Vie En Rose' (1950), 'C'est si bon' (1950), 'A Kiss to Build a Dream On' (1951), 'I Got Ideas' (1951) and 'Mack the Knife' in 1955 helped to spread Armstrong's popularity. The albums 'Louis

Armstrong plays W C Handy', 1954 and 'Satch plays Fats' in 1955 continued to extend Armstrong's appeal and critical acclaim.

The rise of bebop with musicians such as **Dizzy Gillespie** (see October 21st), **Charlie Parker** (see August 29th), **John Coltrane** (see September 23rd) and **Miles Davis** (see September 28th) appeared to make Armstrong old-fashioned and yesterday's man. The bebop crowd saw themselves as artists while Armstrong was an entertainer smiling and performing for his audience. With Armstrong's failure to speak out on civil rights and racial issues he faced criticism from a younger and increasingly militant generation. He spoke out angrily, being critical of both governor Orville Faubus and President Eisenhower over their failures with the Little Rock Nine (see September 5th) incident in 1957.

Louis Armstrong's touring continued across the world. He was followed by journalist and presenter Edward Murrow who filmed performances producing the 1957 documentary *Satchmo the Great*. The gruelling schedule took its toll in 1959 when Armstrong had his first heart attack performing in Italy. It was not long before he returned to his punishing 300 shows a year. The 1960s saw three untypical yet commercially successful recordings: *Hello Dolly* (1964), *What a Wonderful World* (1967) and the James Bond Theme 'We Have All the Time in the World' (1969). *What a Wonderful World* received little promotion in the USA but became an international hit.

Kidney and heart problems forced Armstrong to stop performing, although he continued to practice. He returned to the stage in 1970 but following a two-week spell at the Waldorf-Astoria in New York Louis Armstrong had another heart attack. He died in his sleep on July 6th in 1971 aged sixty-nine. Although married four times Armstrong never had any children, although letters reveal that he saw Sharon Preston-Folta as his daughter, apparently conceived following an affair. No DNA test has ever been carried out, but Sharon does look similar to Louis. Clarence Armstrong, 1915–1998, the son of Louis' cousin who died giving birth was adopted by Louis. Clarence was adopted at the of age three following a head injury that left him disabled. Clarence lived with Louis Armstrong all his life.

Idi Amin (see January 25th) announces that all 50,000 **Asians to be expelled** from Uganda **on this day** in 1972.

Haitian-born **Michaelle Jean** was appointed Canada's first black Governor General **on this day** in 2005. Born in Port a Prince September 6th 1957, Jean was the Governor General from September 27th 2005 to October 1st 2010.

Part Two starts with Obama's election win in 2009. (See Jan 21st for Part 1 and January 17th for Michelle Obama.) **Barack Obama** was born **on this day** in 1961. There was a mind-blowing, dreamlike celebration, people – black people in particular – were stunned, amazed seeing the first man of African heritage entering the White House. Few who saw the coverage can forget the image of Civil Rights champion **Jesse Jackson** (see October 8th) with tears of joy, pain and history running down his face, capturing the intensity of the moment. The enormity of Obama's inauguration, the 44th President of the USA, was inescapable.

Having inherited a damaged economy, major wars and a country drowning with guns Obama faced an immediate uphill struggle that would only get harder as the Republicans doubled down opposing everything that was Obama as a matter of principle. The irony was their opposition was so planned, open and unwavering one is left asking the question, were there any principles? The extract below is illuminating:

The Party of No: New Details on the GOP Plot to Obstruct Obama
By Michael Grunwald Aug. 23, 2012

Vice President Biden told me that during the transition, he was warned not to expect any bipartisan cooperation on major votes. "I spoke to seven different Republican Senators who said, 'Joe, I'm not going to be able to help you on anything" he recalled. His informants said McConnell had demanded unified resistance. "The way it was characterized to me was 'For the next two years, we can't let you succeed in anything. That's our ticket to coming back" Biden said. The Vice President said he hasn't even told Obama who his sources were, but Bob Bennett of Utah and Arlen Specter of Pennsylvania both confirmed they had conversations with Biden along those lines.

Interviewed on Fox News by Sean Hannity December 2019, Mitch McConnell boasted and laughed admitting that he had been successful in his attempts to block Obama for two years. This failed to prevent the election to the Supreme Court of the first woman of Hispanic heritage Sonia Sotomayor August 6th 2009 and a year later Elena Kagan. For the first time in its history the Supreme Court would have three sitting females at the same time.

Nine years before in 2010 McConnell speaking to the National Journal October 23rd declared "The single most important thing we want to achieve is for President Obama to be a one term president."

In an article for Politico 'The GOPs no compromise pledge', 10/28/2010 by Andy Barr he quotes Republican John Boehner *"We're going to do everything – and I mean everything we can do – to kill it, stop it, slow it down, whatever we can"* with regards to Obama's agenda. There was to be no honeymoon period in office. Plotting to obstruct President Obama had taken place before his inauguration.

President Barrack Obama.

Obama expanded hate crime to address threats faced by the LGBT community (October 8th 2009). The ban on people with HIV entering the USA was lifted, (October 30th 2009) allowing people to visit friends, family and to receive treatment. Gay and lesbian people were no longer required to hide their identity in the military (December 22nd 2010). In 2016 the Pentagon ended its policy preventing transgender people from openly serving in the military. In challenging these civil rights issues Obama became the first president to call for full equality for the gay community in America, January 12th 2013.

Obama had to grow the American economy and tackle unemployment. Unemployment went from 10 per cent in 2009 to 6.3 per cent in 2014. Economic growth rose from 1.6per cent in 2009 to 2.9per cent growth in 2010. The economy under Obama had grown faster than any of the original NATO members by a wider margin since the end of World War II. His economic stimulus passed in July 2010 was the most wide-ranging and sweeping since Roosevelt's New Deal of 1933–39.

The environment was under review as the Democratic administration looked to the future for a greener, sustainable environment policy. Health care reform presented numerous challenges as Obama looked to provide a comprehensive system to ensure all had suitable coverage. 'Obamacare' would remain controversial with few, outside of the States, able to understand the opposition to a universal health care system.

The President challenged the epidemic of guns in the country and the resulting senseless killings. Many, especially right leaning National Rifle Association sponsored groups, demanded that their 2nd Amendment rights remain untouched. Murders at Sandy Hook School where twenty children and six adults were killed, the gunman killed his mother earlier in the day and eventually took his own life, December 14th 2013 and in Orlando, Florida when a gunman shot and killed forty-nine people in and around the Pulse Nightclub injuring fifty, June 12th 2016, failed to slow the sale of high-powered weapons. Many onlookers around the world were, and are, left stunned and shaking their heads in despair unable to make sense of the American love affair with military-style weapons. Nonetheless President Obama pressed ahead experiencing constant push backs in his attempts to control the sale of semi-automatic weapons.

The Dream Act: Development, Relief and Education for Alien Minors attempted to address the issue of immigration offering children, who had arrived into the USA, aged sixteen and under, citizenship.

June 2009 saw Obama visit Egypt to reach out to Muslims around the world. He had to navigate conflicts in Iraq, Afghanistan, Syria and the implications of the Arab Spring. May 1st 2011 saw the announcement of Al Qaeda leader Osama bin Laden's death.

President Obama's second term in office saw him win in 2012 taking 332 v 206 of the electoral votes. There was a drive to normalize relations with Cuba sixty years after the 1959 Castro Revolution.

Concerns were raised over the continuous deaths of predominantly young black men at the hands of, often, white police officers.

Obama's hands had been tied; his political options limited. He left office unaffected by any personal or political scandals. His personal approval ratings and popularity, as with the first lady, remained high. He remained in Washington following the end of his tenure so that his daughter could complete her schooling. He promised to stay out of politics unless systemic racism grew, or if there were obstacles to voting rights, or if there were efforts to silence the press or peaceful protests.

Obama's legacy, in the writer's opinion, is one where the ire of the right has been unleashed. The anger of white supremacists has grown as they felt their god given, natural, white privilege being threatened. Obama's election mirrored emancipation. Following the Civil War in 1865 the period of Reconstruction was a golden period, albeit all too brief. People failed to see the birth of the Ku Klux Klan that followed. They failed to see the rewriting of history producing a sympathetic and romantic narrative of the Confederate South illustrated in *The Birth of a Nation* and *Gone with The Wind*. When Johnson signed the Civil Rights Acts of 1964 and 1968 his administration was followed by the election of the right-wing republican Richard Nixon. Few had anticipated that Obama's immediate legacy would be a boost for racism and a right-wing backlash culminating with the election of the self-proclaimed disrupter, the 45th President Donald Trump. Trump promised to row back on all that his predecessor had achieved. There was a clear and determined effort to besmirch Obama and his legacy. Barack Obama remains popular but many on the right paint a critical, uncomplimentary picture driven by their need to blame someone, a drive often fuelled by racism.

Aug 5th:

When England's King George IV was crowned at Westminster Abbey on July 19th 1821 there were eighteen ushers, all bare-knuckle boxers. Among the eighteen was a fifty-seven-year-old black boxer called **Bill Richmond.** His story starts in slavery. He was born **on this day** in 1763. He fought during the American War of Independence for the British. Richmond was taken under the wing of Hugh Percy the Earl of Northumberland. Percy persuaded the Rev Richard Charlton to release his possession. In England, 1778, the Earl provided Richmond with an education and an apprenticeship as a cabinet maker.

Bill Richmond married a local girl called Mary on June 29th 1791. The couple would have four children. Living in London, Richmond found himself acting as bodyguard to the boxing-loving young rake Thomas Pitt Lord Camelford. When Pitt died in a duel, March 11th 1804, Richmond decided to put his pugilist skills to making money. Known as the 'Black Terror' it was not long before Richmond's fame was gaining him recognition. He was popular, introducing fast footwork and dancing round the ring, being too small to stand and trade blows. It was his size that led to his defeat against English boxing champion Tom Cribb in 1805.

Richmond's ring career was brief but spectacular. He started boxing aged forty-one, fought nineteen bareknuckle contests with seventeen victories. Age meant that Richmond had to retire already in his sixties. He bought a pub and opened a gym for professionals and amateurs in the pugilistic art. He trained several luminaries in British society including John Neal, Lord Byron, William Hazlitt and Piers Eagan. It is from Eagan's writings that we learn a great deal about Bill Richmond.

While training English gentlemen and nobility Richmond also trained prize fighters. **Tom Molineaux,** March 23rd 1884–August 4th 1818, a former slave was part of Richmond's stable. He fought Cribb in 1810. The controversial first fight was marred by the white mob embarrassed by their hero Cribb being beaten by a black man or angry that they were going to lose their investment. The crowd entered the ring and broke Molineaux's fingers. Cribb was also allegedly given an illegal thirty second count. The record books show a Cribb victory. Molineaux was totally outclassed in the rematch, 1811, failing to train and having a drink problem.

Richmond fell into debt following losses from gambling and had to sell his pub. He would never regain his wealth and would be frequently found drinking in the pub of his old adversary and now good friend Tom Cribb. The first black British sports star died on December 28th 1829 aged sixty-six. His wife died destitute in the workhouse.

Formerly **Upper Volta, Burkina Faso** gained independence from France **on this day** 1960. The first leader of the independent Upper Volta was **Maurice Yameogo** who served from 1959–1966. Burkina Faso means 'Land of Incorruptible People' the name was adopted in 1984. Le **Moro Naba Kougri** was the country's last king. **Princess Guimbe Quattara** is one of the country's heroic national figures**.**

Young woman of Burkina Faso   King Moro Naba   Princess Guimbe

Legal powerhouse workhorse **Oliver W. Hill** was an attorney in Virginia, USA. With his legal partner **Spotswood W Robinson,** they put together a team, often working with the NAACP, filing more cases in Virginia than had been filed in the whole of the segregation era in all Southern States combined. There were often as many as seventy-five cases pending at any one time. Hill worked closely with **Thurgood Marshall** (see January 24th) including on the ground-breaking 1954 Supreme Court ruling Brown V Board of Education (see May 17th). Oliver Hill was born May 1st 1907 and died at the age of 100 **on this day** in 2007.

Abdulrahman Mohamed Babu was a Marxist revolutionary. The left wing, pan Africanist champion was born in Zanzibar on Sept 22nd1924. He would be recognised as one of Africa's foremost thinkers and analysts. A leader of the anti-colonialist struggle he visited China in 1959. His ideas lay the foundation for the Zanzibar Revolution of 1964. A few months later Zanzibar and Tanganyika united as Tanzania. The US had feared Zanzibar would become the 'African Cuba' spreading communism throughout East Africa.

Babu was a cabinet minister in **Julius Nyerere**'s (see April 13th) government. Following the assassination of Zanzibar's President Sheikh **Abeid Amani Karume**, Babu with thirty-four others was sentenced to death for their alleged involvement. Babu was imprisoned for six years from 1972–78. He was given amnesty by Nyerere. He spent most of his life living and working in London effectively in exile. Abdulrahman Mohamed Babu died **on this day** in 1996 aged seventy-two. He published *African Socialism or Socialist Africa?* in 1981.

Abeid Amani Karume.

Aug 6th:

Faustin-Elie Soulouque was a career officer and general in the Haitian army. He was chosen as president, March 1st 1847 – August 28th 1849, believed to be dull, ignorant and malleable, seen as perfect to play the role of a puppet leader.

The massacre of mulattoes on April 16th 1848 in Port-au-Prince the capital and the ousting of those who believed they had been pulling Soulouque's strings in 1849 opened a new era for the new emperor. As emperor, August 29th 1849 – January 15th 1859, Soulouque attempted to take the eastern side of the island in 1849, 1850, 1855 and 1856. Each incursion failed. To consolidate power, he attempted to establish a Haitian nobility, creating four princes of the empire, fifty-nine dukes, two marques, ninety-nine counts, 215 barons along with hereditary chevaliers and lesser nobles.

The emperor was deposed in the revolution of 1858 in Haiti led by General Fabre Geffrard who defeated the Imperial Army. Soulouque abdicated on January 15th 1859 and went into exile traveling on board a British warship, arriving in Kingston, Jamaica where he stayed for several years.

Faustin-Elie Soulouque was permitted to return to Haiti and died **on this day** in 1867.

David Walker's father was a slave, but his mother was a free black woman. When Walker was born in 1796 or 1797, he too was free like his mother. He received an education and travelled throughout the country before settling in Boston. Although free Walker was badly affected by the racial treatment he saw and received.

In 1829 he produced a series of abolitionist pamphlets 'Appeal to the Coloured Citizens of the World'. The seventy pages revealed the abuses and inequalities of slavery. They called for enslaved people to fight for their immediate freedom and for individuals to act according to religious and political principals. Many Southern States were so appalled by Walker's writings that legislation was passed banning the distribution of such material and preventing slaves from learning to read and write. The governor of Georgia placed a $10,000 reward on Walker's head.

David Walker had opened a successful second-hand clothing shop in Boston. He concealed copies of the 'Appeal' in the pockets of garments sold, often to sailors who would knowingly, or unknowingly, distribute pamphlets around the country. The 'Appeal' was also given out to sympathetic black sailors.

Warned to escape to Canada for his own safety Walker refused to leave Boston. He was found dead. The community began to speculate that he had been poisoned but the truth was that he probably died from tuberculosis **on this day** in 1830. His daughter Lydia had died from tuberculosis a week before on July 31st. David Walker was only thirty-three but his influence on the Abolitionist Movement was immense. The 'Appeal' was reprinted and continued to be distributed after his death.

Jamaica gained independence **on this day** in 1962 from Britain. The first prime minister of the independent country was **William Alexander Clarke Bustamante** born 24th February 1884. He died **on this day** in 1977, twenty-five years to the day after Jamaica celebrated its independence.

Jamaica

Forbes Burnham would serve as the Prime Minister of British Guiana 1964–1980 and as Guyana's president 1980–1985. Born February 20th 1923 in Georgetown, British Guiana. He studied law in London in 1947. Returning to Guiana he formed the People's Progressive Party (PPP) in 1950 with the left-wing labour leader Cheddi Jagan. The PPP would win elections in 1957 and 1961.

British concern over the left leaning PPP led to political interference as the newly elected government was suspended. The British and American security services wishing to secure their business interests, in this period of Cold War diplomacy, actively undermined the PPP's position. The constitution was changed in 1964 to give Burnham's 'moderate' People's Congress a chance to gain power. The Congress was formed in 1955 following a split from Jagan and the PPP. The People's Congress came to power through a coalition with a small right-wing party. In May 26th 1966 Forbes Burnham became the newly independent Guyana's first prime minister.

The West provided investment, often with demanding interest rates, while retaining ownership of companies in Guyana. When Burnham turned to Cuba and the Soviets in 1970, he declared Guyana a Co-operative Republic. From 1971 to 1976 there was extensive nationalization with private shares in the economy reduced to 10per cent. The constitution was changed in 1980 giving Burnham presidential powers. As the West doubled down on Guyana with tariffs and political interference and pressure the economy went into stagnation. He loaned land to the cult leader Jim Jones who paid $2 million for 4,000 acres in 1974. With the economic deterioration and Burnham's increasingly authoritarian behaviour many left the country as economic and some as political emigrants.

Forbes Burnham died in office of heart failure while undergoing throat surgery **on this day** in 1985.

Aug 7th:

Ralph Bunche born **on this day** in 1904 would become the first black recipient of the Nobel Peace Prize in 1950. He was part of President Roosevelt's 'Black Cabinet'. He refused a position as assistant secretary of state offered by President Truman largely due to the segregated housing that existed in Washington DC.

Bunche neither founded nor led any major Civil Rights organisations but frequently used his position to speak out. He eloquently argued that there was no scientific, biological or anthropological basis for racial prejudice. He believed that whites had to demonstrate that democracy was colour blind and believed that segregation and democracy were incompatible. He would later be involved in the 1963 March on Washington and the March to Selma.

Ralph Bunch.

Ralph Bunche was appointed by the UN Secretary General, Trygve Lie, to be in charge of the Department of Trusteeship in 1946. His role was to address the problems and needs of people who had yet to attain self-government. The following year Bunche sat on the UN Special Committee on Palestine. Partition plans for the area had been dropped with rising tension and conflict in 1948. Count Folke Bernadotte was appointed to mediate between the Israelis and the Arabs. Bunch was the chief aide. When Bernadotte was assassinated on September 17th 1948 Bunche took over the Count's roll. After eleven months of continuous and intense negotiations Bunche was able to secure signatures for an armistice agreement between Israel and the Arab States.

Bunche returned to America given a ticker tape welcome in New York City. He received the Nobel Peace Prize in 1950. Bunche would continue working for the United Nations, as the Secretary-General Dan Hammarskjold's trouble-shooter. He worked on the peaceful deployment of atomic energy, was involved in the Suez Crisis, Cyprus between the Greeks and Turks, and the Congo.

Ralph Bunche retired in 1971 due to ill health. He died that same year December 9th aged sixty-seven. He is buried at Woodlawn Cemetery in the Bronx in New York City.

Two times Olympic marathon champion and twice world record holder **Abebe Bikila** was born **on this day** 1932. A soldier in the 5th Infantry Regiment of the Imperial Guard who guarded and protected the Emperor of Ethiopia.

Bikila entered the Rome Olympics in 1960, largely unknown. Running barefoot he took gold in the then record time of 2hrs 15 mins 16.2 sec becoming the first black African to win an Olympic gold. In the 1964 Tokyo Games Bikila became the first person to successfully defend their marathon title with another record-breaking run of 2hrs 12mins and 11.2 sec, on this occasion he had running shoes. Abebe Bikila ran in sixteen marathons winning twelve. He failed to complete his last two races due to injury.

Paralysed in a car accident on March 22nd 1969 Bikila was left a paraplegic and would never walk again. Receiving treatment in England Bikila took part in the 1970 Stoke Mandeville Games, a precursor to the Paralympics. He entered archery and table tennis. The following year in Norway he competed in both sports, but it was in the cross-country sleigh riding that he took gold.

Abebe Bikila died from a cerebral haemorrhage on October 25th 1973 age forty-one.

Côte d'Ivoire (Ivory Coast) gained independence **on this day** in 1960 from France. **Felix Houphouet-Boigny** was the first president 1960–1993.

A young Cote d'Ivoire woman

Aug 8th:

Henry the Navigator's captain Nuno Tristao returned from Africa to Portugal with a human cargo of fourteen Africans in 1443. The prospect of a lucrative trade in humans led to a fleet of six ships led by **Lancarote de Freitas** sailing to the Bay of Arguin, Mauritania. Freitas returned to Lagos, Portugal with 235 enslaved Africans **on this day** in 1444. This was **the first recorded large shipment and sale of African captives in Europe**. (See birth of slavery in America August 20th.)

Slaver Nuno Tristao   and   Henry The Navigator

The infamous image of commercially enslaved people in transit.

Aug 9th:

This day is the annual **World Indigenous Peoples' Day.** The UN uses the day focusing on projects worldwide and addressing the needs of indigenous people who number 370–500 million. International Year of Indigenous Languages in 2019 recognised the threat and possible loss of linguistic diversity. Of the estimated 7,000 languages spoken 2,680 spoken by indigenous groups are under threat. The loss of mother tongues across the globe threatens cultural diversity and history. World Indigenous Peoples Day celebrates diversity, achievements and the contributions made by people, often marginalised, across the world.

The United Nations, Education, Scientific and Cultural Organisation (UNESCO) helps to support and address the challenges faced by indigenous people. UNESCO recognises the cultural and biological diversity such people bring to the table.

Aug 10th:

Canaan, New Hampshire in the United States is the setting for one of the hundreds of stories witnessing the white population rising up and unapologetically attacking members of black communities. There are too many such events to mention all. I have attempted to provide a few examples to illustrate the unfounded fear, the unwarranted anger, racism and cruelty employed by many in the white communities throughout the United States in their attempt to subjugate the black citizen. The uprisings harmed the chances of harmony & peace.

Noyes Academy, named after Samuel Noyes, was established in March 1835 by abolitionists, with a roll call of twenty-eight white and seventeen black students. The school hoped to provide an uplift, educating young black people as well as females. Many in the white community disliked the arrival of so many black students from out of town, traveling in to receive an education. **On this day** in 1835 some 300 whites gathered to raise the school to the ground. In its place they built the white only Canaan Union Academy.

Joe Gans born November 25th 1874 (unofficial) was a lightweight boxer described by the Ring Magazine founder and editor Nat Fleischer, as the greatest fighter of his division.

Monte D. Cox (Cox's Corner) in the article; "*Joe Gan's The Old Master…. 'He Could Lick Them All On Their Best Day"* quotes:

"John L. Sullivan, former heavyweight champion of the world said, (*St. Louis Post Dispatch*, Sep. 2 1906), "*I never liked a negro as a fighting man…but Gans is the greatest lightweight the ring ever saw. He could lick them all on their best day. Gans is easily the fastest and cleverest man of his weight in the world. He can hit like a mule kicking with either hand."*

As a black man Gans was frequently forced to fight and carry white opponents for the full distance. In many of the thirteen draws, he was considered to have won, he was cheated by racism and betting syndicates. Beating Frank Erne May 12th 1902 Gans became the World Lightweight Champion. He held the title from 1902–1908. There were fifteen title defence titles with nine by knockout. His boxing score card reads 131 wins (eighty-eight by KO) nine losses with thirteen draws.

Joe Gans died **on this day** 1910 from tuberculosis. His position in boxing history is best summarised in the words of his contemporaries, many of whom were equally considered greats in the world of boxing. **Sam Langford** described Gans as the greatest boxer of all time. Benny Leonard idolised Gans. Bob Fitzsimmons thought Gans the cleverest boxer he'd seen. Abe Attell saw Gans as the greatest lightweight to enter the ring. Recognition from one's contemporaries is praise indeed as is praise across the colour line from Sullivan, Leonard, Fitzsimmons and Attell.

'Crazy Blues' recorded **on this day** 1920 became the first blues recording by a black female artist. The featured vocalist was **Mamie Smith** May 26th 1891 – September 16th 1946.

Influential and award-winning songwriter, musician, producer, composer and performer **Isaac Hayes** was born August 2nd 1942. Pioneer of southern soul music and a major force behind the Stax label Hayes, with **David Porter,** he was behind major hits such as **Sam and Dave**'s 'Soul Man' (1967).

Isaac Hayes experienced success as a solo artist with albums such as 1969's 'Hot Buttered Soul' and 'Black Moses' in 1971. In 1972 he became the third black person after **Hattie McDaniel** (see June 10th) and **Sidney Poitier** (see February 20th) to win an Oscar for Best Original Song for the 'Theme from *Shaft*'. The previous year saw the release of the blaxploitation film *Shaft* starring **Richard Roundtree.** Both the film and the soundtrack were box office hits.

Composer Isaac Hayes.

As one of the voices on the animation *South Park* from 1998 to 2006, Isaac Hayes was introduced to a new generation. It was reported, and later confirmed, that Hayes had had a stroke early in 2006. Ten days before his sixty-sixth birthday Hayes' unresponsive body was found. He had another stroke, dying **on this day** in 2008. Isaac Hayes is buried in Memorial Park Cemetery in Memphis, Tennessee.

Aug 11th:

Abolitionist Thaddeus Stevens.

Thaddeus Stevens was a white Republican whose political stance earned him the title as a radical Republican. He was known for his fierce determination and opposition to slavery and discrimination against the black population. Born April 4th 1792 Stevens sought to secure the rights of blacks during the Reconstruction Period that followed the Civil War. He was involved in the process, later reversed, providing freedmen with 40 acres and a mule. Through the Bureau of Refugees, Freedmen and Abandoned Lands 1865–1872 Stevens helped freedmen receive an education, clothing and fuel. Legal advice, usually relating to family issues and new employment contracts, was provided as was help to locate lost family members.

When Thaddeus Stevens died **on this day** in 1868, aged seventy-six, his pallbearers were both black and white as were those in his military guard of honour. He is buried in Shreiner-Concord Cemetery which at the time permitted both blacks and whites to be buried together. Thaddeus Stevens's position in American history has slowly been revived as initially he was simply criticised as hating white people. Now he is seen as a pioneer of civil rights and freedoms.

African American author **Alex Hayley** was born **on this day** in 1921. His first book was the ghost written: ***The Autobiography of Malcolm X*** published in 1965, following fifty in-depth interviews with Mr X.

It was the phenomenon ***Roots*** that propelled Hayley to national and international prominence. The 1976 book followed Hayley's genealogy from 1767 Gambia and the enslavement of Kunta Kinte through seven generations. The TV series of the same name aired in 1977. It was an extraordinary success with 130 million viewers. The book would be written in thirty-seven languages. Hayley received a special Pulitzer Prize for *Roots* that same year.

ABC produced '*Roots: The Next Generation*' in 1979. Haley admitted that all in *Roots* was not factual and that there were fictional elements. He was also forced to settle out of court a complaint of plagiarism made by Harold Courlander and his book *The African*. Alex Hayley died aged seventy on February 10th 1992.

Born May 12th 1930 South African poet **Mazisi Kunene** is most famous for his 1979 epic poem 'Emperor Shaka the Great', a history of the Zulu leader. 'Anthem of the Decades' (1981) is another prominent work.

Kunene went into exile, escaping the apartheid regime and arriving in Britain in 1959. Kunene was named the **poet laureate of Africa** by UNESCO in 1993 and became South Africa's first poet laureate in 2005. Mazisi Kunene died **on this day** in 2006 of cancer. The same year the Mazisi Kunene Foundation was set up to promote his work and to promote indigenous African literature.

Chad gained independence from France **on this day** in 1960. **Francois Tombalbaye** had acted as the colonial prime minister for the year before independence. He was the first president of independent Chad from 1960 to April 13th 1975.

Young woman of Chad.

It was the largest urban riot of the Civil Rights era. The **Watts Riots** started **on this day** in 1965, lasting for six days. When brothers **Marquette** and **Ronald Frye** were pulled over, suspected of driving while intoxicated, their subsequent arrests were resisted and drew attention from the gathering crowd. When their stepmother, **Rena**, arrived on the scene she too was arrested. The crowd was growing and becoming agitated. **Joyce Ann Gaines** was arrested, accused of spitting at a police officer. Tensions were high. The following day Rena, who had been released from custody on bail, along with Marquette and Ronald**,** called for calm along with church leaders, government officials and the NAACP. The community were angry living in the segregated city of Los Angeles. The Watts district had experienced years of deprivation and neglect. Unemployment was high as were the number of gangs and the crime rate. The police department Chief William H. Parker refused to replace white officers with their black colleagues. As the riots continued, he accused the rioters of acting like monkeys at the zoo.

Shops were being looted, burning of buildings and cars continued. Firefighters were attacked preventing them from attending the devastation. Snipers were shooting police. The riots covered 50 square miles when 14,000 National Guards were deployed, and a nightly curfew put in place.

The riots were the result of dissatisfaction with living conditions and a lack of opportunity leading to a sense of hopelessness. Young black men, in particular, were angry at what they perceived as continuously being harassed by the police. The six days left thirty-four, mainly black, people dead. There were over 1,000 injured, almost 4,000 arrests with 1,000 buildings affected resulting in $40 million worth of damage.

Little changed in the neighbourhood. The authorities blamed outside agitators and elements such as the Nation of Islam for starting the riots. They failed to recognise the genuine grievances of the black community and struggled to understand the pent-up frustration and anger. All would be repeated in 1992 following the Rodney King incident (see March 3rd and May 1st).

Aug 12th:

He would declare himself the Mahdi (the guided one) on June 29th 1881. The Sudanese religious reformer and military leader **Mohammed Ahmed** was born **on this day** 1844.

Raised as a Muslim following Sunni orthodox Islam, Ahmed joined the Samaniyya order in 1861. He quickly gathered pupils drawn to his retreat on Abe Island 175 miles south of Khartoum. Ahmad believed that Allah had selected him as the messianic Mahdi. His fame went beyond the hermitage and his disciples. Sudan had been ruled by the Turco-Egyptian regime from 1820. Many across the country saw the rulers as aliens, immoral and corrupt.

Ahmed (Al-Mahdi) was able to unite all the factions that existed in Sudan to oppose and overthrow the Egyptian rulers. His puritanical Islam saw it as a duty to restore rejuvenate and purify the faith. To do so they had to battle the immorality and corruption that came with the alien powers. With confusion and instability in Egypt the Mahdists experienced a series of military victories. On January 26th 1885 the capital Khartoum fell. Ahmed's theocratic kingdom was formed. It was a rare victory for an African country expelling a foreign power in the nineteenth century. A new capital was established at Omdurman.

Mohammed Ahmed died from suspected typhus on June 22nd 1885 but the kingdom he established lasted a further thirteen years through to 1898. Ahmed was a nationalistic leader, the precursor of Sudanese nationalism who liberated the country ushering in the modern Sudan while changing the perception and course of African history.

Tiyo Soga, one of Africa's pioneering intellectuals is recognised in developing early forms of black consciousness and black nationalism. Born in South Africa in 1829 Soga would be educated in Scotland, then returning to Scotland to study theology at Glasgow University, graduating aged twenty-seven. He was ordained December 10th 1856, admitted to the ministry in the United Presbyterian Church, becoming the first black South African minister in Scotland. He married Scottish woman Janet Burnside, the following year, before returning to South Africa. The couple, in particular Janet, would have to face continuous racism from both white and black people.

In 1857 Soga started his journal which would become the earliest such record by a black South African. The clergyman would collate local fables, folklore, proverbs, legends and produce historical records mapping out the genealogies of chiefs. His translation of John Bunyan's *Pilgrim's Progress* for the Xhosa people was second only to the Bible in its popularity and literary influence. Soga was also instrumental in working on the translation of the Bible into Xhosa although he did not live to see the work completed. He was also respected for writing hymns.

Tiyo Soga died of tuberculosis aged forty-two **on this day** in 1871. He and Janet had seven children. William and John followed their father into the ministry. Isabella and Francis were teachers at the mission. Kirkland studied law in Glasgow and returned to South Africa as the first black lawyer. He was also instrumental in the formation of the African National Congress. The fourth son Jotello Festiri Soga became the country's first black veterinary surgeon.

Born to Indian parents in South Africa, Muslim political activist, writer, anti-apartheid and social rights campaigner **Fatima Meer** was born **on this day** in 1928. A trusted friend to **Winnie** and **Nelson Mandela** her name would adorn the first authorised biography of Mandela *Higher Than Hope* (1990).

Along with **Kesavelu (Naidoo) Goonam**, Meer was elected as the first woman on the executive of the Natal Indian Congress in 1950. Following conflict and unrest between Africans and Indians in Durban in 1949, Meer established The Durban and District Women's League to build alliances between the two communities.

The National Party's rise to power in South Africa in 1948 and the implementation of apartheid saw Meer banned, in 1952, for three years under the Suppression of Communism Act. She was confined to the Durban area facing restrictions on who she could see with bans on any of her publications. Undeterred Meer was a founding member of the Federation of South African Women in April 17th 1954 leading anti- pass marches. The 1960s saw Meer organising and leading vigils against mass detentions. The 1970s saw her embrace **Steve Biko**'s (see September 12th) black consciousness ideology and the South African Student Movement.

Winnie Mandela and Fatima Meer founded the Black Women's Foundation in 1975. Meer became the organisation's first president. It would not be long before Mandela and Meer were locked up in solitary for six months for their political activities. After the Soweto uprising and massacres Meer was banned for five years in 1976. During this period, she survived two assassination attempts. The first saw her home petrol bombed and a friend shot. Her son Rashid was also forced into exile for his own safety. It would be twenty years before mother and son saw each other again.

Fatima Meer continued to organise and protest. She founded the Co-ordinating Committee of Black (Indian & Coloured Africans) Ratepayers Organisation to oppose injustices in black townships. The Phambili High School for African Students enrolling 3,000 pupils was a Meer project opened in 1986. Education was always important. Meer became the first woman of colour appointed to a white university in South Africa where she lectured in sociology at the University of Natal from 1956–1988.

Fatima Meer died aged eighty-one on March 13th in 2010.

Aug 13th:

When American figure skater **Debi Thomas** took bronze at the 1988 Calgary Winter Olympic Games her achievements made history. She became the first black person to medal at a Winter Olympics. Twelve years later at the 2002 Salt Lake City Winter Games **Vonetta Flowers** took gold as part of the US bobsleigh team. At the same games Canadian **Jarome Iginla** played in the hockey team that won gold. The USA four-man bobsleigh team that won silver in 2002 included black teammates **Randy Jones, Garrett Hines** and **Bill Schuffenhauer,** with fourth teammate Todd Hayes.

American speed skater **Shani Davis** born **on this day** 1982 would bring a new dimension to black athletes at the Winter Games and in winter sports. He won gold in the 1000m and silver in 1500m at the Turin Winter Olympics of 2006 repeating the feat at the 2010 Winter Games in Vancouver. He became the first black person to win an individual gold at the Winter Olympics and the first person to win back-to-back golds at 1000m.

Davis had not come out of nowhere to achieve success. In 2004 he won silver at the World All round Speed Skating Championships. He would go on to win gold in 2005 and 2006. In taking the top spot at 1000m in 2005 Davis broke the world record. He added the 1500m record in 2006.

Winning the World Sprint Championships in Moscow 2009 saw the speed skater become only the second man after Eric Heiden, to win both the Sprint and the World All round in their career. Shani Davis would collect six golds at the World Single Distance Championships for 1500m in 2004, 2007 & 2009. He took gold for 1000m in 2007, 2008 & 2011. Davis led the USA team to its first and only gold in the team pursuit at the 2011 World Championships. Shani Davis would win 10 overall World Cup Titles in the 1000m in 2006, 8, 9, 10 and 2012. With further titles at 1500m from 2008 to 2011. The 2013/14 season saw Davis with most points across all distances earning him the title of Grand World Cup Champion.

Born **on this day** in 1960 photographer **Lorna Simpson** would come to prominence in the 1980s using black and white images, often staged and offset against words. The conceptual multimedia works would frequently ask the viewer to look at and question the image, role and stereotypes surrounding the black woman.

The Central African Republic gained independence **on this day** in 1960 from the French. **David Dacko** would serve as the first president of the newly independent nation from Aug 14th 1960 to January 1st 1966. He would also serve as the third president from September 21st 1979 to September 1st 1981. Dacko ruled the republic as a one-party state. He was overthrown by **Jean-Bedel Bokassa** on the night of December 31st 1965. With the aid of the French Dacko seized back power, after thirteen years, on September 21st in 1979. Dacko would again be removed from power by General Andre Kolingba in September of 1981. David Dacko died on November 20th in 2003.

A Central African Republic woman.

Aug 14th:

Kenneth R. Manning's biography *Black Apollo of Science: The life of* **Ernest Everett Just** 1983, reminded the reader of a largely forgotten scientist. The biography recognised the struggles faced by black scientists such as Just. Manning revealed the racist attitudes held by an elite group of American scientists detailing the difficulties experienced and the social climate of the first half of twentieth century by black academics in the USA.

Biologist Ernest E. Just.

Ernest Everett Just the pioneering research biologist and educator was born **on this day** in 1883. He was a brilliant student. Aged fifteen he was certified to teach in any black school in South Carolina. Just pursued his studies graduating from Dartmouth College in 1907. As with most graduates of colour at the time options at white institutes were at best limited. Just joined the historical black establishment of Howard University, Washington, D.C., in 1910. Originally in the English Faculty, he moved to and took over the Biology Department teaching Physiology. He then formed the Zoology department becoming its first head.

While at Howard, Just was involved in research at the Marine Biological Laboratory in Woods Hole, Massachusetts. At the same time, he was studying for his PhD at Chicago University. He gained his PhD degree in experimental embryology in 1916.

Just worked on fertilization in invertebrates demonstrating that the egg surface and just beneath, ectoplasm, played an important role in the fertilization and the development of embryos. He identified that the sperm did not simply bore its way into the egg but was pulled in. Initially colleague and friend, Ernest. Just fell out with fellow scientist Jacques Loeb, who's findings and conclusions were being challenged and questioned by Just. The National Association for the Advancement of Colored People awarded Just its first Spingarn Medal in 1915 recognising the recipient's outstanding contribution to the black community.

Opportunities remained limited and funding scarce for the black scientist. Just moved to Europe where he continued research at the Stazione Zoologica in Naples, Italy. He published about seventy papers and two books: *Basic Methods for Experiments on Eggs of Marine Animals* and *The Biology of the Cell Surface*, both in 1939. The rise of Hitler and the Nazis threatened peace in Europe. Ernest Just was briefly locked up in a prisoner of war camp. He was released with the intervention of his German wife Ethel Highwarden and friends. He had been very ill in prison. Returning to the USA and resuming work at Howard in 1940 Just was diagnosed with pancreatic cancer.

Ernest Everett Just died on October 27th 1941. He is buried at the Lincoln Memorial Cemetery in Suitland, Maryland in the USA.

Kenneth R Manning resurrected Just's story and work from obscurity. The biography was a finalist for the Pulitzer Prize and won the Pfizer award and the Lunch Hampton Bostick Award. Today Just's important pioneering research in fertilization embryonic development and cytology, the study of individual cells, is recognised by the scientific community.

Writer, poet, speaker, social commentator and activist Australian Aboriginal of the Wiradjuri nation of central New South Wales, **Anita Heiss** was born **on this day** 1968. Verification of the exact day and month of birth has proven difficult.

She has written six novels plus children's literature. In 2007 she published a collection of poetry titled *I'm Not Racist but...* and *Am I Black Enough for You?* in 2012. Heiss edited *The Black Inc Anthology* (2018), featuring fifty-one contributors on the subject from the title "Growing Up Aboriginal in Australia".

Aug 15th:

Born **Omoba Aina** a Yoruba girl from West Africa would be known in British royal circles as **Sarah Forbes Bonetta.** Taken captive in war by **King Ghezo** of Dahomey the young Aina's parents were decapitated. We do not know what happened to her siblings.

Two years later royal naval Captain Frederick E Forbes arrived as an emissary of the British government. Acting as part of the West African Squadron, Forbes was attempting to address the question of slavery. For King Ghezo the trade was a major source of income. Forbes was able to persuade the king to give Aina into his custody. Before leaving West Africa Aina was christened Sarah Forbes Bonetta, named after the captain and his ship Bonetta.

On November 9th 1850, the seven-year-old Bonetta was presented to Queen Victoria. The queen sent her charge to be educated by the Church Missionary Society. In 1851 Bonetta returned to Africa attending the Female Institution in Freetown, Sierra Leone with the intention of becoming a missionary. She returned to England aged twelve where she was placed under the charge of Mr and Mrs Schoen for six years at Chatham. Her academic progress caught the attention of society keen to observe and scrutinise the capabilities of an African. Bonetta excelled in literature, arts and music. Her regal appearance and posture betrayed her suspected African royal heritage. Queen Victoria gave her charge an allowance; she became a regular visitor to Windsor Castle.

James Pinson Labulo Davies, a Yoruba businessman, proposed. Initially Bonetta showed little interest in marriage but with the Queen's insistence the couple were married on 14th Aug 1862. The newlyweds moved to West Africa, first to Sierra Leone before settling in Lagos. Their daughter Victoria was named after the Queen who was the baby's godmother. Bonetta Davies visited Queen Victoria with her daughter in 1867.

It was believed that the weather in England had been detrimental to Bonetta Davies's health, she was quite poorly and always had a cough. The family moved to Madeira where Sarah Forbes Bonetta Davies died from tuberculosis **on this day** in 1880, she was only thirty-seven. Queen Victoria gave her goddaughter an annuity and paid for Victoria's education at Cheltenham Ladies' College. They would remain in touch for the rest of their lives.

He described himself as an Anglo-African, the composer, conductor and political activist **Samuel Coleridge-Taylor** was born **on this day** 1875 in Holborn, London. The three cantatas based on Longfellow's trilogy; 'Hiawatha's Wedding' (1898), Death of Minnehaha (1899) and Hiawatha's Departure in 1900 would propel Coleridge-Taylor onto the classical music world stage. On the back of the cantatas the young composer toured the USA in 1904, 1906 and 1910. On the first occasion he was invited to the White House by President Theodore Roosevelt. White American musicians in New York referred to Coleridge-Taylor as the 'African Mahler', a somewhat confused compliment.

The fifteen-year-old Samuel Coleridge-Taylor studied at the Royal College of Music. His debut came with 'Ballade in A Minor' (1890) at the Three Choirs Gloucester Festival which he was recommended to attend by Edward Elgar.

The composer met in 1873, former director of the Jubilee Fisk Singers, **Frederick Loudin** who had introduced negro spirituals to Britain. Coleridge-Taylor showed an appreciation of music that had African roots embracing his heritage and incorporating it in his classical and concert compositions. He worked with poet **Paul Laurence Dunbar** (see February 9th) putting music to the poet's works in 'African Romances Op 17'. Coleridge-Taylor was politically active being the youngest delegate at the first Pan African Conference held in London (see July 23rd).

The composer made little money and struggled financially all his short life. To make ends meet, feeding and keeping a roof over his young family's head, Coleridge-Taylor was the professor of composition at the Trinity College of Music in London. He conducted many orchestras including the Handel Society.
Samuel Coleridge-Taylor married Jessie Walmisley who too had been a student at the Royal College of Music. They had a son Hiawatha (1900–1980) who continued to work on and preserve his father's music and Gwendolyn Avril who as a composer and conductor went by the professional name Avril Taylor-Coleridge (1903–1998). Samuel Coleridge-Taylor died from pneumonia on September 1st 1912 in Croydon, England aged thirty-seven. He is buried in the Bandon Hill Cemetery in Wallington, Surrey.

Born **on this day** 1976 the fourth prime minister of the Federal Democratic Republic of Ethiopia, **Abiya Ahmed** would take office on April 2nd 2018. The former military officer entered politics in 2010 in the Jimma region. He helped set up a 'Religious Forum for Peace' to address religious conflicts between Christians and Muslims. He stood up against illegal land grabs as the capital Addis Ababa looked to expand. Ahmed was required to take care of the one million Oromo people displaced from the Somali region following the 2017 unrest. As the Oromo Democratic Party Secretariat, he was prepared to reach out crossing ethnic and religious lines to create an alliance between the 66 million Oromo and Amhara groups.

Abiya Ahmed gained a bachelor's degree in computer engineering. He would become head of cyber security. He studied for his master's degree in transformational leadership, in 2011, from Addis Ababa and London's Greenwich University and would earn a second master's in business administration in 2013. His doctorate in 2017 was from the Institute for Peace and Security Studies at Addis Ababa University.

Abiya Ahmed.

Following the resignation of Prime Minister **Hailemariam Desalegn,** and the ensuing political instability, Abiya Ahmed emerged as the prime minister in 2018. He immediately set on a radical series of initiatives and reforms. Thousands of opposition political prisoners accused of terrorism were released. The new prime minister announced the amending of outdated anti-terrorism laws May 30th 2018. He announced the early lifting of the state of emergency on June 1st. Many accused him of doing too much too fast. Hardliners opposed the reforms. Ahmed proceeded with prison releases and pardons meeting with former leaders accused of terrorism. He was able to sign a peace deal looking at ending thirty years of conflict in the Ogaden region. He reached out to the Eritrean government meeting with its leader **Isaias Afwerki** ending twenty years of border conflict.

Recognising Abiya Ahmed's efforts to create stability in the region the Nobel Committee named the Ethiopian prime minister the Nobel Peace Prize recipient for 2019. Although the area continues to be volatile, Abiya Ahmed has mediated between Eritrea and Djibouti, Kenya and Somalia and within Sudan's civil conflict. Ahmed survived an attempt on his life when grenades were thrown in his direction at a political rally in June 2018 killing two and injuring many others. The following June reports of an attempted coup in the Amhara region surfaced where several high- ranking officials were killed.

The region continues to be volatile. Question rage over who are the guilty partners? Can peace be maintained and was awarding Ahmed the peace prize a premature move? The story remains live.

The **Republic of Congo** was established on 28th November 1958. The country gained independence from France **on this day** in 1960. **Patrice Lumumba** (see July 2nd) was the country's short-lived independent leader.

Aug 16th:

Wallace Thurman's home, 267 West 139th Street, Harlem, was referred to as '*Niggeratti Manor*'. It was a place where the black literary elite, the avantgarde of the Harlem Renaissance, regularly gathered. The editor, critic, playwright, novelist, poet and screenwriter was born **on this day** in 1902.

He arrived in Harlem in 1925, at the start of the second half of the Renaissance. His first novel *Blacker the Berry: A Novel of Negro Life* (1929) exposed prejudice within the black community. Such a work was part of Thurman's 'immoral independence'. The gatherings at his home were viewed as a place where the establishment could be challenged. *Infants of Spring* (1932) was a satire that continued the critical assault on, as he saw it, overrated creative figures, black socialists, who wrote for political purposes rather than focusing on their literary development. Thurman argued that too many black writers wrote to satisfy the black middle class and their white patrons.

The play 'Harlem',1929 was a popular, if not a critical, success. Written with white associate William Rapp, 'Harlem' debuted at the Apollo Theatre on February 20th 1929. Following the limited critical and commercial success of "The Intern", 1932, Thurman wrote two Hollywood screenplays: *Tomorrow's Children* and *High School Girl*, both in 1934.

A heavy drinker and suffering from tuberculosis, Wallace Thurman died on December 22nd in 1934. He was thirty-two.

The modernist, post-colonial Nigerian poet **Christopher Okigbo** was born **on this day** in 1932. Famous for his works *Heavensgate* (1962), *Limits* (1964), *Silences* 1962–65' (1966) and posthumously *Collected Poems* published in 1986.

Okigbo was active working with fellow writers among the community of writers and artists in Nigeria. Awarded the Langston Hughes Award for African Poetry at the Festival of Black African Arts in Dakar, Okigbo refused the accolade arguing that poetry should have no colour and should simply be judged as good or bad. He opposed negritude as a romantic pursuit of the mystique of blackness.

Okigbo was the assistant librarian at the University of Nigeria in Nsukka. He founded the African Authors Association with **Wole Soyinka** (see July 13th) and **Chinua Achebe** (see June 13th) and belonged to the Mbari Writers and Artist Club in Ibadan.

With Achebe, Okigbo founded the short-lived Citadel Press. He was the manager for Cambridge University Press of West Africa.

Fighting in the Biafra-Nigerian war as a major, Christopher Okigbo was killed in 1967.

Born in Trinidad **on this day** 1939, British journalist and broadcaster **Sir Trevor McDonald** would be a pioneering authoritative black voice and face, on British TV, delivering the news to the nation. He initially worked for the BBC World Service in 1969 but would find his home with the commercial broadcaster ITN (International Television News) in 1973. He would anchor the Channel 4 news programme before presenting the *10 O'clock News* on ITV. Receiving an OBE in 1992 and knighted in 1999 these acknowledged and reflected the fact that McDonald had become, what is lovingly referred to, as a national treasure. Trevor McDonald hosted the current affairs show *Tonight* as well as having made numerous documentaries. He has been married twice and has two sons and a daughter.

Sir Trevor McDonald.

Last survivor of the Harlem Renaissance **Dorothy West** died **on this day** 1998 aged ninety-one. She mixed with **Langston Hughes** (see May 22nd), who she asked to marry, **Countee Cullen** (see January 9th), **Claude Mckay, Wallace Thurman** (see August 16th) and briefly roomed with **Zora Neal Hurston.** (See Jan 28th.)

Born into one of Boston's wealthiest black families on August 29th 1924, West was intensely proud of her father's, born into slavery, rise from poverty. She was published by the *Boston Post* aged fourteen. The seventeen-year-old West would tie with the already established Hurston in a writing competition organised by the National Urban League in 1926. Her first novel *Living is Easy* went against the established norm of 'broke black' preferring to look at 'posh black'. It was this anomaly that appeared to result in West's work being overlooked. It was believed that the public had no appetite for stories of the chauffeur driven, privately schooled, black bourgeoisie.

It would take the urging of Martha's Vineyard neighbour Jackie Onassis to persuade Dorothy West to write a second novel. *The Wedding* was published in 1995 and immediately televised by **Oprah Winfrey**'s (see November 20th) Harpo Productions. West wrote many short stories. Published in 1995 was *The Richer, The Poorer: Stories, Sketches and Reminiscences*.

Dorothy West died aged ninety-one **on this day** in 1998. *The Dorothy West, Martha's Vineyard Stories, Essays and Reminiscences* was published posthumously in 2001.

Nigerian doctor and playwright **James Ene Henshaw** was born August 29th 1924. He is credited with bringing authentic African drama written and performed by Africans to the stage. He desired to create plays that would resonate in their familiarity and settings for the West African audience and reader. Henshaw's *This Is Our Chance* (1956) is believed to be the first full-length play by an African in the English language and recognised as a classic of African literature. He was one of the first Africans published outside of Africa.

Often accused of being simple in nature, Henshaw's plays were written for young people, to be performed in schools and colleges. His skill was to produce adult themes for a young audience to read, watch and enjoy. Common themes looked at the socio-cultural realities of pre-colonial Africa, tradition versus modernism, the struggle and corruption for and in power often coupled to the declining morality in newly independent societies.

Henshaw had his finger on the pulse capturing West African society at the time and reflecting the evolving post-colonial society. *Enough is Enough* (1976), about the Biafran-Nigerian Civil War, was the last of the pioneering African's work to be published. He continued to write up to his death **on this day** in 2017 aged ninety-two.

Aug 17th:

Born **on this day** in 1887 the Jamaican black nationalist **Marcus Garvey** would inspire millions with his grand parades, philosophy, rhetoric and the formation of the United Negro Improvement Association UNIA (see July 15th). Garvey would go on to inspire the Nation of Islam, **Malcolm X, Stokely Carmichael** and the **Rastafarian** movement. The pan-Africanist leader read Booker T. Washington while studying philosophy and law at Birkbeck College, London 1912–1914.

Returning to Jamaica, Garvey launched the UNIA, but it was not until he moved to the USA in 1916 that the organisation took off. Urban black communities throughout the North East of the United States embraced Garvey's philosophy of black pride and separatism towards establishing an independent Black African nation. It would be the belief in racial purity and the policy of separate but equal that would lead to conflict with the National Association for the Advancement of Colored People (NAACP).

Marcus Garvey.

W. E. B. Du Bois (see February 23rd**)** and **A. Philip Randolph** (April 15th) felt that integration and establishing civil rights in the USA was the way forward. When Garvey met with the KKK, sharing separatist ideals many felt that he had crossed the line.

The UNIA model 1919–1926 proved effective, Garvey established the Black Star Liner Company, having purchased their first ship re-named the *SS Frederick Douglass*. There was a chain of restaurants, laundries, grocery stores, hotels, a printing press and the Negro Factories Cooperation providing stock and aiming to produce everything a nation would require.

The UNIA's paper 'Negro World' taught about black heroes and the wonderous splendours of Africa and the need for the black community to be economically self-sufficient. Garvey's philosophy is best summarized in his words:

"We must canonize our own saints, create our own martyrs, and elevate to positions of fame and honour, black men and women who have made their distinct contributions to our racial history ... I am the equal of any white man; I want you to feel the same way."
David Van Leeuwen 'Marcus Garvey and the Universal Negro Improvement Association'

Marcus Garvey was targeted by J. Edgar Hoover through his Bureau of Investigation, the forerunner of the FBI. It's believed that Hoover hired the first black FBI agent to infiltrate Garvey's UNIA. On June 23rd 1923 Garvey, and others, was indicted for mail fraud, accused of illegally selling stock for the Black Star

Liner. Garvey served two years of the five-year sentence. In 1927 his sentence was commuted by President Calvin Coolidge when Garvey was deported back to Jamaica.

Speaking at the League of Nations in Geneva, Switzerland, 1928, Garvey addressed his audience on issues of race and abuse. Back in Jamaica he formed the People's Political Party, but he was never again to have the political and social influence that he had in the early 1920s. In 1935 Garvey moved to London where he lived until his death, aged fifty-two, on June 10th 1940, from complications following two strokes. Marcus Garvey was buried at St Mary's Roman Catholic cemetery in Kensal Green. On November 13th 1964 his body was exhumed and repatriated to Jamaica where he was laid beneath the Marcus Garvey Memorial in the National Heroes Park in the capital Kingston.

John Francis Leslie (Jack Leslie) would have the 'dubious' honour of being the first person of colour to be selected to play for the English national side. His skills and goal scoring exploits, first at Barking Town, in the London League, where he scored 250 goals, and then as a professional at Plymouth Argyle went before him. Leslie scored 134 goals with 384 appearances making him The Pilgrims fourth highest scorer. His record caught the attention of The Football Association.

Called into the manager's office Leslie was informed by his boss Bob Jack that he'd been selected to play for the national team. No Plymouth player before, or since, has had such an honour. Word spread through the town, there was a buzz of excitement then all went silent. The FA had discovered that the goal scorer had a Jamaican father. October 6th 1925 Leslie was officially named as one of two reserves. When an injury offered an opening, the FA picked Billy Walker of Aston Villa for his one and only England appearance. Although placed as one of two reserves Leslie never pulled on an England jersey. This all occurred fifty-three years before **Viv Anderson** (see November 29th) had the honour of being the first black man selected to play for England against Czech opposition.

After retiring from the game in 1935 John Leslie had a variety of jobs until Ron Greenwood of West Ham, and later England, employed the former player as a boot boy cleaning the boots of Geoff Hurst, Bobby Moore, Harry Redknapp, and Trevor Brooking. He died in 1988, an exact date unknown. One can only wonder why the Football Association with the talk of 'Kick It (racism) Out' has not respectfully found the exact date and cause of death.

On this day in 1960 **Gabon** gained independence from France becoming an independent republic. The country had two parties, but it was felt that was too divisive for such a small country. Elections in 1961 led to **Leon M'Ba,** born in 1902, becoming president to his death aged sixty-five in 1967. He had served as prime minister from 1959–1961. The former opposition leader **Jean-Hilaire Aubame** was appointed as the foreign minister.

A woman from Gabon.

South African **Ruth First,** wife of **Joe Slovo** (see May 23rd), member of the communist party, investigative journalist looking at conditions of labour, bus boycotts, slum life and the women's anti-pass campaign, was born on May 4th 1925.

First was a ferocious anti-apartheid campaigner. The couple's house became a centre for political activity where First focused on ideas to drive social action.

While studying First met fellow student Nelson Mandela. It was at this time that the young white student, already politically astute, helped to found the Federation of Progressive Students and where she served as the secretary to the Young Communist League. In 1949 First married Joe Slovo. The couple would have three daughters. Ruth First had a brilliant mind which she used to expose the harsh reality of life under apartheid in her investigative journalism.

Viewed as an enemy of the state the family home was regularly raided. First and her husband were charged with treason, along with over 100 others as part of the Treason Trial 1956–61. For over four years First faced harassment before the trial ended with acquittals for all concerned. Following the massacre at Sharpeville (see March 21st) First was banned from being quoted, published or attending meetings. In 1963 First was arrested, detained and held in solitary confinement for 117 days. The experience left her close to suicide and is captured in First's book *117 Days* (1965), outlining the torture of sensory deprivation and the interrogation by South African forces attempting to break her down and extract any useful information.

On release the family fled living in exile in London. First would live and work in the capital for the next fourteen years, being active in the British anti-apartheid movement and lecturing at various universities and institutions.

Ruth First accepted the position as director of research at the Centre of African Studies on November 1978 in Mozambique. The following year while working in her office attending the mail, a parcel bomb exploded. Ruth First was assassinated **on this day** in 1982 by the South African security services. Her daughter Gillian Slovo in her memoir *Every Secret Thing: My Family, My Country* (1997) recounts life in the family home growing up with her politically activist parents. The screenplay written by Shawn Slovo for the 1988 film *A World Apart* is loosely based on Ruth First and the Slovo family. Shawn also wrote the film *Catch a Fire* (2006), where her mother Ruth appears, acted by Robyn Slovo who was also one of the film's producers.

Aug 18th:

Namibia's second president since independence **Hifikepunye Pohamba** was born **on this day** 1935 in South West Africa (present-day Namibia). Inextricably linked to the fortunes of the South West African People's Organisation (SWAPO), which Pohamba co-founded aged twenty-four in 1960 and the struggle for Namibian independence, Pohamba would serve as the president of SWAPO from 2007-15. Before that he would face arrests, convictions, jail and exile.

Pohamba left his job as a miner to work full time with SWAPO. He was arrested in 1961 accused of political agitation, convicted, he received a public flogging. Soon after the painful humiliation Pohamba fled to present day Tanzania with the SWAPO leadership. He was arrested in Rhodesia again accused of political agitation in 1962 and given a two-month jail term then deported to Johannesburg where he was released later that year. Again, Pohamba was arrested and accused of illegally leaving South Africa. After spending four months in jail the future president would spend two years under house arrest. Pohamba moved to Zambia and in August 1964 opened the SWAPO offices there. He was able to return to South Africa with **Sam Nujoma** (see March 21st), the future first president of the newly independent Namibia.

Hifikepunye Pohamba would spend many years establishing links and consolidating SWAPO's position across the continent. He studied politics in the former Soviet Union. On Namibia's independence in 1990 and the election of Nujoma, Pohamba served in the administration as Minister in Home Affairs, Fisheries and Marine Resources. He oversaw land reform preferring a policy of persuasion rather than coercion. When Nujoma stepped down Pohamba was elected as president, sworn in on March 21st 2005. He immediately announced his cabinet which featured five women. He won a second term in office, re-elected in November 2009. On retiring in 2015 Pohamba was the recipient of the Ibrahim Prize for Achievement in African Leadership for 2014.

South Africa was **banned** from **The Olympics on this day** in 1964. The International Olympic Committee **barred** South Africa from the Tokyo Games because of the regime's apartheid laws.

Born on April 13th 1938 **Ola Rotimi** was Nigeria's complete theatrical dramatist: actor, theatre director, playwright, choreographer and designer. His plays would often have a huge cast with musicians, singers, dancers and acrobats as well as the actors.

Rotimi spent a good deal of time out of the country being educated and working in the USA. For political and reasons of personal safety he lived and worked in the United States and the Caribbean during the 1990s. His work examined Nigeria's history and ethnic traditions. In the 1968 play *The Gods Are Not to Blame*, a tragi-comedy, he looks at Nigeria's self-inflicted wounds. The 1969 play *Karunmi* anticipates the Biafran-Nigerian Civil War by looking at the Yoruba internecine wars from 1789 to 1880. "*Ovonramwen Nogbaisi*", (1971) reworks history by looking at the King of Benin not from the colonial viewpoint and the British expedition in 1897.

Rotimi wrote plays over a twenty-two-year period from *To Sir the Gods of Iron* in 1963 to 1985's *Hopes of the Living Dead*. Ola Rotimi died on this day 2000 aged sixty-one.

Dambudzo Marechera, Zimbabwean novelist, short story writer and poet was born in Rhodesia, June 4th 1952. He grew up in a racist and divided country ruled by the white minority government of Ian Smith. Expelled from the University of Rhodesia, Marechera would also be expelled from New College, Oxford in 1977. It was while in England that he wrote *The House of Hunger* (1978), the title describing his country. The book looked at lives disrupted and young disillusioned people living in a country under white rule. He would go on to produce *Black Sunlight* in 1980, *"Mindblast"* in 1984, was posthumously released. *The Black Insider* released in 1990, and the collection of poetry *Cemetery of Mind* in1992. *Scrapiron Blues,* published in 1994 is a collection of short stories, a play and a novella.

Dambudzo Marechera died aged thirty-five from an AIDS-related illness **on this day** in 1987. He lived an unsettled life even experiencing homelessness on his return to Zimbabwe in 1981. *The Guardian*'s 'A brief survey of the short story, part 54, Dambudzo Marechera' by Chris Power contains two quotes that illustrate the importance of the author: One from Doris Lessing who describes the young author's work *"like overhearing a scream"*. The same article quotes China Mieville describing Marechera's work: requiring: *"…sustained effort from the reader, so that the work is almost interactive – reading it is an active process of collaboration with the writer - and the metaphors are simultaneously so uncliched and so apt that he reinvigorates the language."*

Aug 19th:

Charles Bolden Jr born **on this day** in 1946 would become the first black Administrator of the National Aeronautics and Space Administration (NASA). As an astronaut Bolden made four space flights: January 12th 1986 for six days, March 24th to 29th 1990, March 24th to April 2nd 1992 and February 3rd to 11th 1994. During a thirty-four-year career in the Marine Corps Major General Bolden flew over a hundred missions during the Vietnam War from 1972–73. He retired from the Marines in 2003.

As the Administrator of NASA 2009–2017 Bolden oversaw the space shuttle programme and the use of private companies. It was on Bolden's watch that the rover 'Curiosity' landed on Mars in 2012. Bolden retired in 2017.

Zambian leader **Levy Mwanawasa** born on September 3rd 1948 would rise through the political ranks becoming Zambia's third president serving from January 2nd 2002 – August 19th 2008.

Mwanawasa was hospitalised for three months in 1991 following a road accident that killed an aid. The future president would be left with slurred speech. An investigation was set up to investigate a possible assassination attempt. As president, Mwanawasa moved to create national reconciliation appointing a number of the political opposition to his government. The president would publicly apologise for failing to address the poverty in Zambia January 2005. His efforts to tackle corruption led to foreign investment and economic growth at 6per cent a year. He developed the town of Livingstone near Victoria Falls to become a tourist hub. Surprisingly, the president sold off the Konkola Copper Mines to Vedanta for $25 m. The company had an asking price of $400 m. Within three months Vedanta made $25 m on their acquisition and were making $500 m a year in profit.

Levy Mwanawasa was one of the first African leaders to criticise Robert Mugabe's rule in Zimbabwe (see February 21st). Health issues dogged Mwanawasa for the last two years of his life. A series of strokes starting in 2006, followed by care and surgery in hospital led to premature stories of the president's death. Levy Mwanawasa died **on this day** in 2008.

Rev George Houser died **on this day** 2015. His passing marked the last surviving member of the original sixteen Freedom Riders from 1947. George Houser the son of missionaries was born June 2nd 1916.

Following the refusal of service at a restaurant in Chicago, Houser, **James Farmer** (see January 12th) and **Bernice Fisher** (1916–1966) founded the Congress of Racial Equality (CORE) in 1942. The congress would grow rapidly with chapters throughout the country numbering in the tens of thousands as a non-violent protest group. Houser served as CORE's first executive secretary.

While a student Houser joined the Fellowship of Reconciliation in 1938. The fellowship is a network of English-speaking, non-violent, religious organisations. Houser would be imprisoned in November 1940 as a conscientious objector just before America entered World War II.

When the US Supreme Court ruled that segregation on interstate transit was unconstitutional in Irene Morgan v Commonwealth of Virginia, 1946, Houser along with **Bayard Rustin** (see March 17th) hatched a plan to test the ruling with the Freedom Rides in what would be called 'The Journey of Reconciliation'. Sixteen men, eight black and eight white, were selected to ride the buses throughout the Southern States. The black men were instructed to sit at the front and the white volunteers to sit at the back. During April 1947, the riders travelled through fifteen cities in Virginia, North Carolina, Tennessee and Kentucky. They were frequently met with abuse, violence, beatings, blood was shed, and arrested. In North Carolina Rustin and fellow black rider **Andrew Johnson** were arrested and made to serve thirty days on a chain gang. This took place fourteen years before the Freedom Rides of 1961.

George Houser helped to found Americans for South African Resistance in 1952. He would serve as executive director of the American Committee in Africa in 1955 through to retirement in 1981. Houser would fight to end apartheid and colonial rule in Africa. He travelled to Africa on thirty occasions between 1954–2015 having close ties with leaders including Nelson Mandela, Walter Sisulu, Oliver Tambo, Amilcar Cabral, Julius Nyerere and Kwame Nkrumah.

George Houser wrote several books including *No One Can Stop the Rain: Glimpses of Africa's Liberation Struggle* (1989). George Houser the white Methodist minister. died **on this day** in 2015 aged ninety-nine.

American comic and campaigner **Dick Gregory** was born on October 12th 1932. Raised in extreme poverty he would joke that "we never ate off the floor. Any food that fell from the table never reached the ground". He recognised from a young age that if people were going to laugh anyway it's better, they laugh with him rather than at him. The pioneering satirist used humour as a force for civil rights in the 1960s. His biting brand of comedy attacked racial prejudice, poking fun at bigotry and racism in the United States. Gregory's act gained a crossover audience when he played at the Playboy Club in Chicago. He left his audience with a clearer understanding of the nation's shameful and embarrassing history. The comedian neither lectured nor scolded his audience, he chose wry observations to force the listener to look at America and laugh. The pioneering satirist used humour as a force for civil rights in the 1960s. Appearing on the *Tonight Show* Gregory persuaded the host, Jack Paar, to interview him on the sofa. Prior to that appearance black performers would do their thing and then leave the stage. Gregory opened doors for the likes of Bill Cosby (see July 12th) and Richard Prior (see December 1st). In 1962 Gregory demonstrated for black rights in Mississippi.

Dick Gregory.

He would be arrested on numerous occasions and have what he would describe his experience in a Birmingham jail in 1963 as the first beating that he had had in his life. Acting as peacemaker during the Watts riots in 1965 Los Angeles Gregory was shot in the leg. From the mid-1960s Dick Gregory moved away from the clubs, appearing on the college lecture circuit.

Initially a civil rights campaigner Gregory supported a wide range of issues. He would go on hunger strikes over the Vietnam War, police brutality, American Indian rights, apartheid, nuclear power, prison reform and the Equal Rights Amendment to the US Constitution, fighting for women's rights. Gregory, a vegetarian, also campaigned to improve the diet of black people in the States.

He married Lillian Smith in 1959. The couple had eleven children, one died in infancy. It was clear that Dick Gregory placed his family second behind the many issues that he championed. Gregory died of heart failure aged eighty-four **on this day** in 2017. (See **Richard Pryor** December 1st and **Eddie Murphy** April 3rd.)

Aug 20th:

Over 400 years of struggle begins.

On this day, or one very close, in 1619 the English ship, a 160-ton privateer the *White Lion* arrived at what was called Point Comfort in English North America. Point Comfort was named when English settlers arrived in 1607 seeking sanctuary and comfort. On board the *White Lion* were twenty Africans who had been taken from the Kingdom of Ndongo in present day Angola. They were being transported on board the Spanish ship the *Juan Bautista* to Mexico. The *White Lion*, with another privateer, the *Treasurer*, attacked and took the Africans.

Slave auction in Virginia.

Captain John Jope traded the Africans for food and supplies as indentured servants or slaves, it's not clear which, **thus begun 400 years of slavery in what would become The United States of America** at Fort Monroe, Hampton, Southern Virginia. A few days later the *Treasurer* arrived with the remaining Africans captured from Spanish ship the *Bautista*. See August 8th.

Ottobah Cugoano was baptised as **John Stuart on this day** in 1773 at St James' Church in Piccadilly London. Cugoano was an abolitionist, political activist and natural rights' philosopher campaigning for universal rights.

Close friends with **Olaudah Equiano** (see March 31st) and **Ignatius Sancho** (see December 14th), it is believed that Equiano helped Cugoano to write his autobiography *Thoughts and Sentiments on the Evil and Wicked Traffic of the Slavery and Commerce of the Human Species* in 1787. The pair travelled throughout the country on tour promoting their biographies. It was in his publication that Cugoano became the first African to publicly demand the emancipation of all slaves and the abolition of the slave trade. He argued that slaves had the natural right and moral duty to non-violently demonstrate opposition to their masters. He went further arguing that it is the duty of any man to get out of the hands of the enslaver. Cugoano wrote the most radical abolitionist text of the time. He questioned the concept of being civilised while having slaves, asking is slavery, robbery and murder no longer a crime? Cugoano sent copies of his book to King George III and Edmund Burke the Irish statesman and philosopher.

Born in present day Ghana, a Fanti, Ottobah Cugoano was kidnapped aged about thirteen and sold, as he wrote, for a gun, piece of cloth and some lead. Transported to Granada he witnessed the brutality of being enslaved. Captives were whipped for eating sugar cane. Many had their teeth knocked out to serve as an example to others and prevent them from eating further cane. Cugoano reports one person being flogged twenty-four times, having been seen in church on a Sunday when he should have been working. In 1772 the young slave was bought by an English merchant and taken to England. Following the Somersett Case (see June 22nd) Cugoano was given his freedom.

Ottobah Cugoano played an important role in establishing the freedom of Henry Demane in 1786. The following year he and Equiano founded the Sons of Africa, the first black British political organisation. The importance of the Sons of Africa's campaigning to end chattel slavery cannot be overstated. Beyond the names of many of the members there is little detail as to who the educated free African Sons were. On March 21st 1788 Equiano presented Queen Charlotte, wife of George III, a petition from the Sons of Africa.

Ottobah Cugoano disappeared from the records after 1791. It is believed that he died in his early thirties. A blue plaque was placed on Schomberg House in Pall Mall London, where he lived and worked as a servant for the artists Richard and Maria Cosway, in November 2020.

Boxing has had a mirky history with stories of The Mob fixing fights and issues of racism exemplified by the search for the great white hope. Promoter **Don King** with an amazing roster on his books and promoted by Don King Productions continued boxing's controversy King was born on this day 1931.

Behind the sport's most famous fights including the Rumble in the Jungle (1974) and the Thrilla in Manila (1975), Don King worked with boxing's biggest names: Muhammad Ali, George Foreman, Larry Holmes, Mike Tyson, Evader Holyfield, Wilfred Benitez, Roy Jones Jr, and Roberto Duran, to name just a few. Muhammad Ali, Larry Holmes, Mike Tyson, Lennox Lewis would all take out lawsuits against the promoter. All seven lawsuits against King would be settled out of court. Ali took out a lawsuit in 1982 accusing King of holding back $1.1 m in earnings. Larry Holmes accused King of cheating him out of $10 m. Tim Witherspoon claimed $25 m in damages from King. Mike Tyson sued King accusing the promoter of stealing $100 million.

Controversial boxing promoter Don King.

Don King has had a concerning relationship with the law. Shooting Hilary Brown in the back, King claimed self-defence accusing Brown of stealing from his illegal gambling establishment. King walked free as the judge ruled justified homicide. Thirteen years later King had to be dragged off thirty-four-year-old Samuel Garrett in 1966. He was said to have used a gun to beat his victim and to have stamped and kicked Garrett in the head. Pleading self-defence King was found guilty of the lesser charge of voluntary manslaughter, a murder committed in a fit of passion and rage, unable to control one's emotions. King served less than four years for beating to death his victim, accused of owing the promoter $600. In 1984 he was pardoned by Ohio Governor Jim Rhodes. In a strange twist to this unfortunate story Cleveland City Council chose to rename the road where Samuel Garrett was murdered 'Don King Way'.

Don King was involved in a charity benefit helping to provide much needed support for the Forest City Hospital. With Muhammad Ali present the event raised $85,000 ($500,000 in 2020). King took his usual cut of 85per cent. The hospital only saw $1,500. Boxers claimed that fights promoted by King were often rigged. Instantly recognisable with his distinctive signature hairstyle, King managed the 1984 Jackson's Victory Tour and bought and saved the weekly paper *Call and Post* in 1998. He continued to be a popular, influential figure and voice in the sport in his seventies and eighties.

Controversial Ethiopian leader Prime Minister **Meles Zenawi** swept into power aged thirty-six in 1991, his tanks rolled into the capital Addis Ababa. The West embraced Meles tasked with rebuilding a country broken by years of civil war and famines.

Meles Zenawi's government ushered in a period of transition creating a voluntary federation based on the various ethnic groups. This paved the way to Eritrea's independence on May 24th 1993. The Marxist-Leninist was a pragmatic democrat. He encouraged a free press and shunned emergency aid dependency, preferring long term development. To the outside world Ethiopia looked stable with double digit economic growth and improving education. Meles was viewed as a bastion against Islamists in Somalia. When his army led an assault against Al Shabaab the prime minister was praised as a stabilising influence in the Horn of Africa.

Meles Zenawi.

All was not as straightforward at home. Domestically Meles was increasingly authoritarian. Following the contested election of 2005 close to 200 protesters were killed as police and soldiers were ordered to open fire. Opposition media faced a crackdown and journalists were imprisoned. The West continued to overlook the prime minister's negatives in favour of the positives. In 2004 Meles helped to set up the Commission for Africa looking at poverty and famine on the continent.

Following illness Meles Zenawi died having contracted an infection. He died in hospital in Belgium on **this day** in 2012. Born May 8th 1955 Meles Zenawi was fifty-seven.

Born **on this day** in 1982 Cuban **Mijain Lopez** would win successive Olympic golds Beijing 2008, London 2012, Rio 2016 and the 2020 Tokyo Olympics in 2021. Lopez was the winner of five world titles: 2005, 2007, 2009 and 2010, taking silver in 2006 and 2011. He has won multiple golds at the Pan American Games including 2003, 2007 and 2011.

The Greco-Roman wrestler nick-named 'the Kid', ironically because of his size, fighting at 120 kgs and then at 130 kgs. Lopez is also nick-named 'the Terror' based on his performances.

The outstanding world beating athlete Mijain Lopez was named Cuba's top athlete in 2007 and 2010.

Aug 21st:

The Haitian Revolution started **on this day** in 1791. A series of organised slave uprisings involving French, British, Spanish and American interests. The revolution would lead to the creation of Haiti, formerly

Saint Domingue. The new independent country, reverting to its Arawak name, would be governed by former slaves. The revolution was the largest and most significant uprising of slaves since the failed effort of the Thracian gladiator Spartacus in the third Servile war against the Roman Republic.

The island of Hispaniola had been divided between the French Saint Domingue in the west and the Spanish Santo Domingo on the eastern side of the island. For the French the possession was an economic gold mine through the production of coffee and sugar. Saint Domingue was a country in miserable conflict with divisions between the different white inhabitants, the whites disliked and distrusted the mulattoes who reciprocated the hate while looking down on the freed blacks and even further down on the enslaved population. It was the slave population that bore the brunt of all the social, racial and class division and unrest.

The country had roughly 40,000 white inhabitants, 28,000 freed blacks and mulattoes and 452,000 black slaves. Two thirds of the slaves were born in Africa which often meant that they were more militant and less submissive. Conditions for the slaves were appalling with the death rate greater than the birth rate. Overwork, inadequate food, shelter, clothing and poor medical provision saw an annual decline in slave survival by two and five per cent, resulting in greater numbers of captured Africans being imported.

Toussaint Louverture.

Toussaint Louverture (see May 20th) emerged as the military genius that led the revolt. **Henri Christophe** (see October 6th) and **Jean Jacques Dessalines** (see September 20th) would see the revolution through to its natural conclusion. The US President Jefferson, who owned slaves on his Virginian plantation, refused to recognise independent Haiti fearing that the rebellion would inspire the enslaved population in America. It was not until 1862 that the US officially recognised Haiti.

Athletic superstar Jamaican **Usain Bolt** was born **on this day** in 1986. The eleven time World Champion, winner of nine Olympic golds having completed the triple triple, winning golds in three consecutive Olympic games – Beijing 2008, London 2012 and Rio 2016 – in the 100m, 200m and the 4 x 100m relay.

Usain Bolt, at the time of writing, 2020, holds the 100m record at 9.58, 200m at 19.19 and the 4 x 100m record with the Jamaican relay team at 36.84. He has run the three fastest times over 100m, holds five of the ten fastest times over 200m and with the Jamaican team has the seven fastest 4 x 100m relay times.

As a teenager Bolt won gold in the 200m, aged fifteen, becoming the youngest male junior world champion in any event. Aged sixteen Bolt set the Under 19 junior record for the event at 20.13 seconds. At seventeen the young athlete became the first teenager to run under 20 seconds at 19.93. Running the 100m in New York in 2008 Bolt set a new record for the distance with 9.72 seconds. All looked promising for the Beijing Olympics where Bolt set new records 100m = 9.69, 200m = 19.30 and 4 x 100m relay = 37.10. Bolt would later be stripped of the relay gold as a team member had a positive drugs test. The triple was repeated at the next two games. He won his final gold at Rio, Brazil the day before his thirtieth birthday.

Usain Bolt.

Usain Bolt's achievements at the Athletic World Championships were phenomenal from 2007 when he won silver over 200m. Two years later at Berlin, 2009, Bolt set the 100m record at 9.58 seconds, four days later he ran 200m in a new record time of 19.19 sec. At Daegu, South Korea Bolt false started in the 100m but took gold in the 200m and relay, 2011. In Moscow, 2013, he was back on form taking three golds repeated at the Beijing World Championships of 2015.

Few would dispute that Usain Bolt is the greatest sprint athlete as recognised in his memoirs co-written with Shaun Curtis in 2010 *My Story 9.58: The World's Fastest Man.* The expanded reissue released in 2012 is titled *The Fastest Man Alive: The True Story of Usain Bolt.* (See Shelly-Ann Frazer Price December 27th.)

Mario Pinto de Andrade the father of Angolan nationalism was a writer, historian, poet and politician. Born in what was the Portuguese colony of Angola, Andrade studied at the University of Lisbon where with **Agostinho Neto** (see Sept 10th) and **Amilcar Cabral** (see January 20th) he formed the Centre for African Studies. Later studying in Paris at the Sorbonne Andrade started to write anti-colonialist poetry and was an editor of the Presence Africaine 1955–58.

Working with Neto, Andrade attempted to unite the different groups within the Popular Movement for the Liberation of Angola, MPLA. Andrade was elected president, 1960, following Neto's arrest but stood down when Neto escaped detention while under house arrest in Portugal. Increasingly disillusioned by Neto's and the MPLA's increasing authoritarian style, Andrade split from the popular movement in 1974.

Angola achieved independence on November 11th 1975, Agostinho Neto was declared the country's first president. Andrade chose to live in exile, spending time in Cape Verde, Mozambique and Guinea-Bissau. In Guinea-Bissau he worked with his friend, now President Amilcar Cabral, in various government departments including the commissioner of culture. Andrade edited several anthologies of African poetry. He felt that his main contribution to Angolan independence was to document its history. Mario Pinto de Andrade was writing a major piece on Angolan nationalism, while living in Mozambique and France. Born **on this day** 1928, Andrade died aged sixty-two on August 26th in 1990.

Born **on this day** in 1939 **Festus Mogae** would serve as Botswana's third president from March 31st 1992 to April 1st 2008. His administration would see political stability and steady economic growth. Facing an HIV/AIDS pandemic across the continent, Mogae was one of the first African leaders to combat the stigma associated with the disease, putting into place progressive, comprehensive programmes to deal with HIV/AIDS. He left office with the prevalence of the disease decreasing. Mogae also challenged traditional and religious views concerning the LGBT community. As president he achieved gender parity in education.

The former economist worked in various government departments including the Financial Development Planning Ministry before moving to Washington DC in 1976, recruited by the International Monetary Fund, where he worked through to 1980. Returning to Botswana Mogae served as the governor of the Central Bank of Botswana before taking a political role in President Masire's government. He was appointed Masire's vice-president in 1992. That same year Mogae won election as Botswana's third president.

On August 5th 2008 the former leader launched the 'Champions for an HIV Free Generation in Africa' organisation. He would also be chair of the Council of Elders.

Festus Mogae has been the recipient of numerous awards and was the second person to receive the Ibrahim Prize for his economic work in the face of the HIV/AIDS pandemic and for tackling corrosive attitudes towards those with the disease.

Aug 22nd:

Born **on this day** 1917, the actual year of birth is disputed but 1917 is the most commonly featured date, **John Lee Hooker** would become one of the legends of the blues being an inspiration to artists such as the Rolling Stones and the Animals.

The young Hooker ran away from home aged fourteen, believed to never see his mother or stepfather again. Arriving in Memphis he played on Beale Street. The blues singing, songwriter and guitarist had early success with 'Boogie Chillen'' in 1948. It went on to

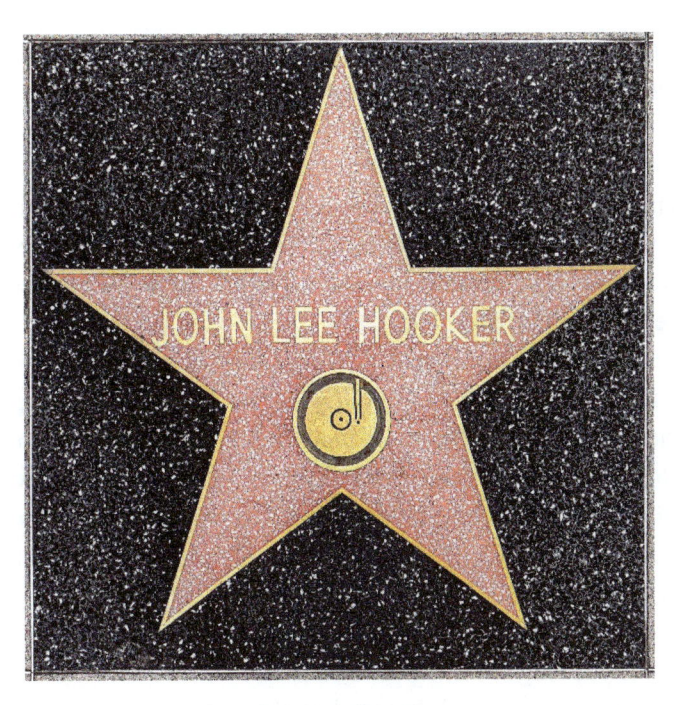

John Lee Hooker

become the biggest-selling race record of 1949. 'Crawling King Snake' (1948) and Weeping Willow (Boogie) (1949) established Hooker on the blues scene. To make money he would often record variations of the same song, paid upfront, with a variety of record labels, frequently using different names to avoid breaking his recording contract.

Touring Europe as part of the annual American Folk Blues Festival, John Lee Hooker came to the attention of a new audience. England discovered the 1956 recording of 'Dimples', making it a hit in the UK in the early 1960s. 'Boom Boom', recorded in 1962, would be Hooker's most recognisable track. He would appear in the 1980 film *The Blues Brothers* performing the hit. Hooker also had screen time in *The Colour Purple* in 1985.

John Lee Hooker collaborated with a variety of artists including Canned Heat, Steve Miller, Van Morrison, Carlos Santana, Los Lobos and Bonnie Raitt. The album 'The Healer', 1989 was a commercial and critical success as was 1997 Grammy-Award-winning 'Don't Look Back' and the 1998 album 'Best of Friends'.

John Lee Hooker died peacefully in his sleep on July 21st 2001. He was interned at the Chapel of Chimes in Oakland, California.

Huey P. Newton was born February 17th 1942. He co-founded the Black Panther Party for Self-Defence with **Bobby Seale** (see October 22nd) in 1966. Later called the **Black Panther Party** (see October 15th), Seale was the party chairman and Newton served as minister of defence. The party was formed following incidents of police brutality and acts of racism. Newton and Seale put together a ten-point programme to create self-reliance in the black community. Providing meals for children and clinics, and having a strong image, dressed in black and wearing berets the Panther Party quickly grew to 2,000 members and had chapters in many urban areas.

Nothing was straight forward with the iconic figure Huey P. Newton. He'd been convicted serving six months having repeatedly stabbed Odell Lee in 1964 with a steak knife.

Following a shootout in 1967, police officer John Frey was left dead while Newton and another officer were injured. In September 1968 Newton was convicted and sentenced to 2-15 years. Support for Newton to be released grew with marches and calls of 'Free Huey'. The original court decision was reversed in 1970 followed by two further trials, both ending with hung juries. There was no fourth trial and Newton was released. Newton's biographer Hugh Pearson claimed that while drunk Newton confessed to shooting Frey although the claim has never been corroborated.

Now free Newton accepted an invitation to China where he met the ambassadors to North Korea and Tanzania and a delegation from North Vietnam. Following the 'Free Huey' campaign Newton became the popular face of the Panthers and a leading figure in the Black Power movement of the 1960s.

Seventeen-year-old street worker Kathleen Smith was said to have called Newton 'baby', a term he had always hated. He was accused of shooting the sex worker who died three months later. At the same time, he was accused of assaulting his tailor Preston Callins, allegedly pistol-whipping his victim, again for using the term 'baby'. Newton faced a further allegation accused of being involved in the murder of Betty van Patter a white woman who was a bookkeeper for the Panthers. Fearing conviction Newton took the opportunity to flee the country hiding out in Cuba for three years.

On his return in 1977 Newton faced trial. In October of that year three panthers planned to kill Crystal Grey, a key prosecution witness in the Smith case. The attempted murder was bungled as the panthers entered the wrong house. One panther Louis Johnson was shot dead, and the two others fled. Flores Forbes made it to Las Vegas with the help of panther paramedic Nelson Malloy. In November Malloy was found in a shallow grave in the desert. He had been shot in the back and was paralysed from the waist down. Malloy said that orders from high up in the organisation had been given to kill him and Forbes leaving no witnesses to the attempted assassination of Grey. Malloy later pointed out Rollin Reid and Allen Lewis as his assailants. Huey Newton claimed no knowledge of any of the events.

The tailor Callins' testimony kept changing. In the end he said he had no idea who attacked him. Newton was sentenced for illegal possession of a firearm. Crystal Grey refused to testify. Following two trials and deadlock with the jury charges were dropped against Newton, there was no third trial.

While he had been in Cuba, Newton had been visited by cult leader Jim Jones who received the Panthers' leader's support. Newton's behaviour became increasingly erratic and unstable. He fell out with leaders within the party. Alcohol and drugs were a serious problem. **On this day** 1989 forty-seven-year-old Huey P. Newton was murdered by Tyrone Robinson in Oakland, California. Robinson claimed that he acted in self-defence. He was convicted of first-degree murder and given thirty-two years to life.

Huey P. Newton's ashes were interred at Evergreen Cemetery in Oakland, California.

Newton wrote *Revolutionary Suicide* (1973) with Hugh Pearson. Pearson would write Newton's biography *The Shadow of the Panther: Huey Newton and the Price of Black Power in America* in 1994.

Aug 23rd

Born **on this day** in 1954 the Nigerian computer scientist, **Philip Emeagwali's** work would make him one of the **fathers of the internet.**

Emeagwali's education was interrupted at the age of fourteen when he was drafted into the Biafran army during the Nigerian civil war. The man described by *TIME* magazine as the unsung hero of the internet, Emeagwali is said to have an IQ of 190. Despite his educational setbacks he would gain a Maths degree then a Masters in Ocean and Marine Engineering followed by a second master's degree in Applied Mathematics. The realisation of Emeagwali gifts became clear when he won the Institute of Electronics and Electrical Engineers' Gordon Bell Prize in 1989.

Philip Emeagwali won the prize after gaining access to the Connection Machine, a super-computer that no-one had effectively been able to utilise to its true potential. The Connection Machine was linked to 65,536 microprocessors. Emeagwali was able to link each microprocessor to another six neighbouring microprocessors creating the fastest computer able to make 3.1 billion calculations per second. Using his programme Emeagwali's formula accelerated the way that computers speak to each other using a parallel collaboration system. Nicknamed 'Calculus' as a schoolboy Emeagwali used the Connection Machine to accurately calculate the amount of oil in a simulated reservoir. The oil industry adopted Emeagwali's work as did search engines such as Yahoo.

Philip Emeagwali's programmes which he based on the cooperative interconnected community of bees in their hive are used in numerous fields such as predicting the weather and global warming.

Hurricane Katrina developed from a tropical depression **on this day** in 2005 over the Bahamas, to become the largest and the third strongest hurricane to make landfall in the United States. The devastation it wrought made it the costliest natural disaster in US history. As always, the poor, predominantly black population were hit hardest. In the years that followed the storm that broke the city levees, on August 29th 2005, it has been the black population that has failed to return to the city of New Orleans in particular the number of black, middle class citizens.

The Category 5 hurricane saw wind speeds of over 270 km per hour. The storm surge was up to 6 meters breaking over levees designed for a category 3 storm not the Category 5 of Katrina. The resulting death toll of over 1,800 affected seniors, blacks and the poor the most. Years after the storm hit, over 700 people are still reported missing. More than 80per cent of New Orleans was flooded resulting in excess of $100 billion worth of damage.

US President Bush was criticised over the slow response to the hurricane which left thousands homeless and hundreds clinging to rooftops waiting to be rescued.

Aug 24th:

Born **on this day** in 1759 **William Wilberforce** would become the most famous name in the British abolitionist movement. He became the MP for Hull in 1780 and would later represent Yorkshire. Wilberforce would be the parliamentary voice championing the end of the Transatlantic slave trade.

A close friend of the future British prime minister William Pitt the Younger, the pair met while at university. In 1784/5 Wilberforce converted to Evangelical Christianity later joining the Clapham Sect. All changed for the politician, now a social reformer and philanthropist. He was influenced by former slaver John Newton, abolitionists **Thomas Clarkson** (see March 28th) and **Granville Sharp** (see November 10th) becoming heavily involved in the anti-slave trade movement.

It would take over eighteen years of parliamentary campaigning introducing motions to the House of Commons to end the abhorrent trade. In 1789 Wilberforce introduced twelve resolutions against the trade. Supported by friends Edmund Burke, Charles Fox and Prime Minister William Pitt, the motion was defeated. In 1791 Wilberforce's motion was defeated 163 to 88 votes. The following year a petition signed by tens of thousands helped to drive the 1892 bill to where it was agreed that the abolition of the slave trade would be a gradual process. Little happened for the next fifteen years largely due to the Napoleonic wars. The bill to **abolish the slave trade** in the British West Indies was passed on **February 23rd** by 283 votes to 16 and became law on **March 25th in 1807**.

William Wilberforce   and   Former slaver John Newton

Wilberforce retired from politics in 1825 passing the parliamentary campaign on to Sir Thomas Fowell Buxton. As part of the Clapham Sect Wilberforce was involved in other campaigns for social change. Hannah More was a major influence on the MP. Outside of the abolitionist movement Wilberforce is most famous for his work with the Royal Society for the Prevention of Cruelty to Animals (RSPCA) which was founded in 1824.

William Wilberforce died on July 29th in 1833 he was seventy-three. Three days earlier the **Slavery Abolition Act was passed on July 26th 1833** the decisive move towards emancipation of enslaved people in the British Empire.

Nigerian businessman, politician and philanthropist, **Moshood Kashimawo Olawale Abiola** was born **on this day** in 1957 a Yoruba Muslim. Educated in Scotland, on a scholarship, Abiola studied at the University of Glasgow graduating in 1963. He graduated from the Institute of Chartered Accountants, also in Scotland, in 1965.

Returning to Nigeria Abiola had a rapid rise, working in a variety of areas before becoming the chief executive and chairman for Nigeria's International Telephone and Telegraph company (ITT). He amassed a personal fortune estimated to have been about $2 billion. Detractors would argue that the fortune was the result of cutting corners and using poor grade resources as the ITT system was often unreliable.

Moshood Abiola freely gave away a good deal of his wealth. He funded schools, mosques, churches, libraries and a variety of development projects across the country. It is said that he funded over 2,500 students through university.

Abiola was a popular public figure who supported liberation causes in southern Africa. He also sought international compensation for Africa, having suffered from the slave trade, colonialism and the exploitation of the continent's natural resources. After almost twenty years of military rule elections were held in Nigeria on June 12th 1993. International observers declared the elections to have been the most open, fairest and honest held in the country's brief history. Indications pointed to Abiola being the clear winner.

Before the winner was announced the military leader Gen Ibrahim Babangida annulled the election. The resulting political protest that followed led to Abiola being arrested and charged with treason by the new leader Gen Sani Abacha. Confined to solitary confinement, not allowed visits from family and friends, Abiola was kept in the political dark unable to access news. It was of great concern that the businessman was not permitted to have his own doctor. A delegation from the United States visited Abiola in prison. He was due to be released from custody after four years. Gen Abacha had died on June 8th. Abiola collapsed and died on July 7th 1998 of a heart attack. The sudden and unexpected death led to a number of conspiracy theories with long-time friend and supporter Wole Soyinka suspecting foul play and reports that Abacha's Chief of Security Officer Al-Mustapha saying that Abiola had been beaten to death. Medical checks reported that Abiola had a diseased heart and that a heart attack was the likely cause of death.

Dub poet, social commentator and activist **Linton Kwesi Johnson** was born **on this day** in 1952 in Jamaica. He arrived in England, living in London, when he was eleven. His work written in the unstandardised Jamaican patois captures the life of the Afro-Caribbean living in the UK. He provided social commentary covering events such as the Brixton riots of 1981 in the poem 'Di Great Insohreckshan' (1983), and criticising the controversial police policy through the anti-sus poem of 1979 'Sonny's Lettah'.

Kwesi Johnson's work was first published in the journal Race Today with his debut collection *Voices of the Living Dead* in 1977 and his second collection *Dread Beat an' Blood* (1975). In 1977 he received the Daw- Lewis Fellowship. That same year he was writer in residence for the London Borough of Lambeth. A meeting with Richard Branson in High Street Kensington saw the poet release his first album also titled 'Dread Beat an' Blood' in 1978. That year the poet was the subject of a documentary about his work. His third book *Ingland is a Bitch* was released in 1980. His record label LKJ Records was launched in 1981.

His poetry is unashamedly political. He sees the British Conservative party as not only the nasty party but as the anti-immigrant party, the party of the Windrush scandal and the 'hostile environment'.

Linton Kwesi Johnson's work has gained international recognition. He is only the second living poet and the first black poet to have his work published in the Penguin Modern Classic series with *Mi Revalueshanary Fren* in 2002 and 2006's *Linton Kwesi Johnson's Selected Poems*. Other album releases include 'Forces of Victory' (1979) and 'Bass Culture' in 1980. His work takes on a dynamic, allowing the written word to take on new life when performed against the reggae beat and the persuasive rhythm of Kwesi Johnson's spoken word.

On this day in 1972 **Rhodesia** (now Zimbabwe) was banned from **The Munich Olympics.** Four days before the games were due to begin Ian Smith's minority rule government found their country thrown out of the international competition.

Aug 25th:

With the infamous words written by KKK leader and segregationist speech writer Asa Earl Carter, Governor **George Wallace** spoke at his inauguration, 1963, proclaiming "segregation now, segregation tomorrow, segregation forever."

Born **on this day** in 1919 the Governor of Alabama Wallace would stand in front of the entrance to the University of Alabama blocking the entrance to black students; **Vivian Malone** (1942–2005) & **James Hood** (1942–2013) on June 11th 1963. Three months later he would attempt to prevent four black children enrolling at four separate elementary schools in Huntsville, Alabama. Intervention by a federal court in Birmingham ensured that **Sonnie Hereford IV** aged six became the first black child to integrate a primary or secondary school in Alabama on September 9th 1963. Hereford gained entry along with **David (Piggee) Osman** aged six, **John Anthony Brewin** and thirteen-year-old **Veronica Pearson.** Pearson had to wait a week to be admitted while the mindless mob outside the school dissipated.

Governor George Wallace was shot five times, leaving him paralyzed from the waist down, on March 15th 1972. The would-be assassin Arthur Bremer, twenty-one, was given a sixty-three-year prison sentence reduced to fifty-three years on appeal. He was released after thirty-five years on November 9th 2007 aged fifty-seven. Brewin had no political issue with Wallace; he shot the governor to gain notoriety.

Wallace would hold office for sixteen years; 1963–67, 1971–79, 1983–87. In his last term in office, he appointed a record number of black people to state positions including two black people as members of the same cabinet for the first time.

George Wallace in later life suffered from impaired hearing and Parkinson disease. He was always in pain due to the shooting. He died from septic shock having picked up an infection on September 13th 1998. He ran for president four times and failed four times but became an influential politician in the process.

Born **on this day** in 1949 singer songwriter **Salif Keita** would become Mali's most famous musical son. The descendant of Mali's thirteenth-century warrior King Sundiata, the founder of the Mali Empire, Keita grew up in relative poverty in the countryside far from the trappings of royalty. Called the golden voice of Africa it was out of necessity that Keita turned to music.

As a person with albinism Salif Keita was severely bullied at school. The condition which leaves a black person with a disfigured type of white skin meant that Keita had to stay out of the sun. His eyes and sight suffered but it was African tradition that created the greatest obstacles. Many believe albinism to be a sign of misfortune. Those with the illness are frequently ostracised, beaten or even killed. They are dismembered in the belief that their limbs have magical and medicinal powers. Keita was told that his desire to be a teacher was impossible, fearing that he would scare the children. Feeling that music was his only option the eighteen-year-old left his family and travelled to Bamako where he joined the Rail Band. He quickly established a reputation and was confidently able to leave Mali for Abidjan in Cote d'Ivoire where he joined the Ambassadors in 1973. Keita's family had looked down from their lofty noble ancestry at one of their number becoming a singer. Now famous, the performer was reconciled with his family.

In the early 1980s Salif Keita moved to Paris. The 1987 album *Soro,* received popular and critical acclaim. The following year saw Keita receive international exposure appearing at Wembley Stadium performing at Nelson Mandela's 70th birthday celebration. An estimated audience of 600 million in 67 different countries saw Keita on stage. Credited with creating afro-pop, Salif Keita was able to mix traditional African styles, in particular mande from Mali, with jazz, rhythm & blues and rock.

Returning to Mali and back in Bamako in 2001, Keita released the album 'Moffou' in 2002. He collaborated with a range of artists from the continent and further afield from Europe and the Americas. Salif Keita used his prominence to question politics and corruption arguing that corruption was endemic especially in Mali and Cameroon. The singer questioned whether democracy could work in Africa, as democracy requires understanding which is not possible with a poorly educated electorate coupled with corruption. Keita controversially believes Africa would fare better with a benevolent dictator who loved the country and its people putting them first rather than lining their own pockets. Keita has tirelessly campaigned to end the discrimination of people with albinism setting up foundations in Mali and the USA. Following his 2018 album 'Un Autre Blanc' (Another White) Salif Keita announced his retirement from recording.

Aug 26th:

Sudanese independence leader **Ismail al-Azhari** was born October 20th 1900. As prime minister 1954–56 on December 19th 1955 the Sudanese parliament adopted a declaration of independence. The country gained independence from Britain and Egypt on January 1st 1956. Appointed head of state 1965–1969 the president had limited power and would be removed from office in a coup. Ismail al-Azhari was admired for his ability to survive. He was loved and respected in the unstable, volatile world of Sudanese political uncertainty. Azhari died **on this day** in 1969.

Born on March 22nd 1930 **Sir Lynden Pindling,** knighted in 1983, would become the Bahamas first black prime minister under the colonial rule of the British. He would be re-elected five times from 1967–1992. Described as the founding father of the nation taking the Bahamas through independence from Britain on July 10th 1973. The father of the nation spoken of by his supporters as the black Moses formed the Progressive Liberal Party in 1953 advocating for the community. His administration oversaw a period of rapid economic growth and thriving tourism.

After losing the 1992 election Pindling graciously accepted defeat. Investigations claimed that the Bahamas had been used by Colombian drugs cartels and that there were several million in Pindling's bank account that could not be accounted for.

Sir Lynden Pindling retired from politics in 1997. He died of prostate cancer on August 26th in 2000.

Sir Lynden Pindling

Aug 27th:

Haile Selassie, I born July 23rd 1882 as **Tafari Makonnen,** would be Ethiopia's last Emperor. His full title was 'His Imperial Majesty Haile Selassie I, Conquering Lion of the Tribe of Judah, King of Kings and Elect of God'.

Following the death of **Menelik II**'s daughter **Zaudita** (Zewidita see April 29th) Tafari was crowned emperor of Ethiopia in a lavish ceremony attended by royalty, leaders and dignitaries from around the world in 1930. Tafari had established himself as a modernising influence. Following the death of Menelik II, Tafari was central to the downfall of his heir the Muslim leaning **Lij Yasin,** in 1916, who was out of favour with the country's political Christian elite. Tafari had already proven his worth as a modernising governor first in the Sidama region and then in the province of Harar. When Zaudita became the Empress in 1917 Ras Tafari was named the regent and heir apparent. The conservative Empress allowed or was forced to allow the day to day running of the country to her prince regent. In 1924 Ras Tafari travelled to Europe visiting

Rome, Paris and London. He was crowned (negus) King in 1928 and then Emperor following the Empress' death. Ras Tafari took the title Haile Selassie I (Might of the Trinity).

Haile Selassie.

In 1931 the emperor introduced the country's first written constitution limiting the power of parliament. Selassie became the government establishing schools, developing the police force and outlawing the feudal tax system.

Mussolini's Italian army invaded in 1935. Although the emperor led the resistance he was forced into exile, living in England in the city of Bath, from May 1936. The next month, on June 30th, Selassie spoke in Geneva in front of the League of Nations appealing for assistance. With help from the British and Ethiopian exiles in Sudan an offensive was launched in January 1941. The capital, Addis Ababa, was re-taken, and Haile Selassie was installed as emperor. With a new constitution in 1955 Selassie established his old powers and continued the process of modernisation. He had led Ethiopia into the pre-war League of Nations in 1923 and ensured that Ethiopia had a seat at the United Nations.

December 1960 saw a short-lived challenge to the emperor's authority from a dissident wing of the army. Selassie had a religious following in Jamaica. **Marcus Garvey** (see August 17th) had said:

"Look to Africa, when a black king shall be crowned for the day of deliverance is near."

The Rastafarians saw the emperor as the Messiah, God incarnate, believing that the foretelling of the black king was Selassie following his 1930 coronation. He travelled to Jamaica on one occasion on April 21st 1966. Land in Ethiopia was given to Rastafarians in 1948 to establish a community in the Rift Valley in Shashamane. Although a settlement was established it never truly thrived or integrated. Garvey had been critical of Selassie leaving his country during the Italian invasion and accused the emperor of having slaves. Slavery was not abolished in Ethiopia until 1942.

It is estimated that $35 million was spent celebrating the emperor's eightieth birthday while there was famine in the Wollo region and Tegray, 1972–74, said to have killed an estimated 200,000. Unemployment was on the increase and elements of the army were mutinying. Selassie was deposed by the army on September 12th 1974. Members of his family and high-ranking army officials were rounded up and imprisoned. On November 23rd sixty high-ranking army officials were executed by firing squad without trial. The provisional Marxist military government ruling the country is said to have ordered Haile Selassie to be strangled. In 1994 the courts ruled that the eighty-two-year-old emperor had been killed by strangulation.

Many Rastafarians refused to believe that their messiah was dead. His bones were discovered in 1992 under a concrete slab in the palace grounds. His remains would rest in a coffin in the Bhata Church for almost ten years before having an official burial in 2000 by the Eastern Orthodox Church.

Australian Aboriginal, community leader working to raise the status of indigenous people, **Gladys Elphick** was born **on this day** in 1904. Founding president (1964–73) of the Council of Aboriginal Women of South Australia, Elphick was involved in providing a social worker, setting up of sports clubs and arts & crafts groups, public speaking classes enabling women to express themselves and their needs, and a shelter and health care in Adelaide. From 1966–71 Elphick was a member of the South Australian Aboriginal Affairs Board. She was the founder of the Aboriginal Medical Services in 1977. Awarded an MBE, Gladys Elphick of Kaurna and Ngadjuri descent died on January 19th 1988 aged eighty-three.

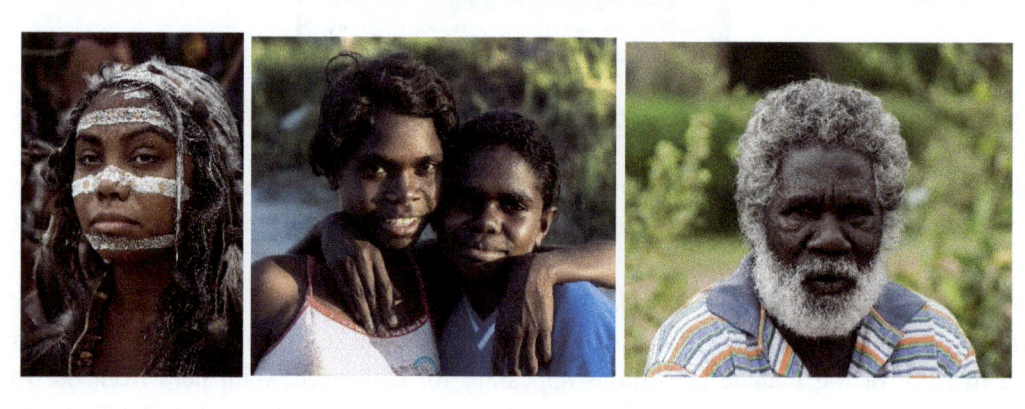

Aug 28th:

Dr Martin Luther King Jr (Part 3, see January 15th and April 4th).

With the refusal of **Rosa Parks** (see February 4th) to give up her seat on December 1st 1955, the wheels were set in motion and thus began the **Montgomery Bus Boycott**. Months earlier, in March, **Claudette Colvin's** case (see September 15th) was not considered watertight to provide a challenge to the city's segregated bus system. **E. D. Nixon** planned the boycott that would be led by a young, largely unknown, Baptist minister called Martin Luther King Jr. It is said that senior black leaders felt they had too much to lose so pushed King to the fore. Three hundred and sixty-five days later following the **Browder v Gayle** decision, affirmed by the U S Supreme Court on November 13th 1956, the protesters and King emerged victorious. The Baptist minister became the voice and face of the Civil Rights Movement. A battle had been won but if King had been under any illusions the bombing of his home on January 30th 1956 made it clear that the war would continue.

Urged by **Bayard Rustin** (see March 17th) and others, King founded the civil rights activist, nonviolent movement called the **Southern Christian Leadership Crusade** (SCLC). Rustin, King, **Ralph Abernathy** (see March 11th), **Ella Baker** (see December 13th), and **Fred Shuttleworth** (see October 15th) were all present at SCLC's birth.

In 1967 FBI head J. Edger Hoover would label the SCLC as a black nationalist hate group. The SCLC was the vehicle through which King planned marches, voting drives, desegregation policies and actions and fought for labour rights.

Signing copies of his book *Strive Towards Freedom* at Blumstein's Department Store in Harlem, King was stabbed by Izola Curry on September 20th 1958. It was said that the knife was so close to his aorta that if King had sneezed, he would have died. First aid by two police officers present, followed by a three-man surgery team saved King's life. Ms Curry's mental condition was such that it was agreed she was not fit to face trial.

Martin Luther King would be arrested twenty-nine times. On May 4th 1960 he was stopped and charged with driving without a valid licence. Although the charge lacked credibility King paid the fine not knowing that his lawyer had made a plea deal with a probation element attached. Later that year on October 19th, taking part in a sit-in at a restaurant in Rich's Department Store in Atlanta, King and other protesters were arrested. Unlike his fellow activists King was retained in custody due to the probation clause from May. On October 25th he was given a four-month sentence. The next day he was transferred to a maximum state security prison. The arrest and sentence gained nationwide coverage. Presidential candidate J. F. Kennedy called the democratic governor and urged his brother Robert to exert pressure on the authorities for King's release. John Kennedy called King's wife **Coretta** (see April 27th) offering sympathy and support. On King's release King Sr endorsed Kennedy who on November 8th 1960 won with a wafer-thin majority.

The black Civil Rights elders of Atlanta, including King, announced that the city had agreed to desegregation in the autumn of 1961. Many of the student activists were angry at the delay forcing King to speak passionately for unity within the movement.

Demonstrations had been planned to resist all forms of segregation in Albany, Georgia. King arrived December 15th 1961 and found himself rounded up as part of a mass arrest. Returning to court having made bail King was given a forty-five-day jail term or a $178 fine (about $1,500 in 2020). King chose jail. Three days later King was released. To avoid publicity the police chief Laurie Pritchard arranged the fine to be paid. It would later emerge that evangelist Billy Graham paid the fine.

Dr King could not continually live off the past glory of Montgomery. He and the SCLC needed public victories. Too often King was drawn into protests that he had little organisational control over. The city of Birmingham in Alabama offered King the chance to apply the tactic of nonviolent confrontation forcing the authorities to show their true colours. The aim would be to fill the jails highlighting injustice and abuse. When **James Bevel** recruited school children police chief Eugene "Bull" Connor obliged by attacking using high pressure water hoses and dogs. All was captured on film and relayed on the national and international news. King faced criticism but achieved a much-needed victory as Connor lost his job, segregation signs were removed, and the black community gained greater access to public spaces. While in the city King was arrested for the thirteenth time. In prison he penned his famous 'Letter from a Birmingham Jail', an eloquent defence on why the protesters could no longer wait. Walter Reuther, president of the United Auto Workers Union, paid King's and fellow protestors' bail of $160,000.

On this day in 1963 Luther King Jr delivered one of the great speeches in any language. Urged by **Mahalia Jackson** (see January 27th) to tell the audience about his dream, King moved from his script and spoke passionately, persuasively and with authority for seventeen minutes to the gathered 250,000 people, and an even greater TV audience. The speech and day would go down in history. Bayard Rustin was the key logistical and strategic organiser. Walter Reuther helped to mobilise demonstrators and the big six; **Roy Wilkins** of the NAACP, **Whitney Young** of the National Urban League, **A Philip Randolph** of the Brotherhood of Sleeping Car Porters, **John Lewis** of SNCC, **James Farmer** of CORE and **Martin Luther King Jr** of the SCLC, pooled their resources, expertise and experience. The day saw thousands march to desegregate all public schools, to campaign for a fair minimum wage and to demand meaningful Civil Rights legislation. Standing close to the podium where King gave the 'I Have A Dream' speech was twenty-six-year-old George Raveling. He made a simple request and was given Dr King's original typed script. The year 1964 saw landmark Civil Rights legislation. That same year Martin Luther King Jr received the Nobel Peace Prize on October 14th.

J. Edgar Hoover had been given permission to monitor King. The FBI and CIA recorded every phone call King made and bugged everywhere he stayed. The surveillance from 1963 to 1968 and constant threats against his life left King paranoid. In 1977 Judge John Lewis Smith ordered that certain tapes be kept from public access until 2027.

The plan to march from Selma to Montgomery, Alabama's state capital, to ensure voting rights would be captured in the 2014 Ava DuVernay film *Selma*. A local judge had issued an injunction preventing three or more protesters from gathering, identifying forty-one Civil Rights leaders. On January 2nd 1965 Dr King defied the injunction and publicly spoke at Brown Chapel. March 7th 1965 saw protestors leave from the chapel only to be attacked and beaten by the police and the racist mob on Edmund Pettus Bridge. The day became known as Bloody Sunday. King had been away on church duties but returned to lead another peaceful, dignified march only two days later. This time, after leading the protesters in prayer, he urged everyone to go home to avoid breaking the legal injunction and a repeat of the previous bloodbath. The march across the bridge and on to Montgomery went ahead as planned, led by King on March 25th. The great orator addressed the crowd from the steps of the state capital.

Speaking out against the Vietnam War and looking at the weaknesses of capitalism saw Martin Luther King attract wide criticism, lose support and gain more enemies. He was outspoken about the loss of life and the waste of money seeing inner city and rural poverty that disproportionately affected the black population. Calls to end economic injustice and discussions on the redistribution of wealth may have led to the assassination (see April 4th) of the Civil Rights icon. When letters and calls were sent to King's home for him or his wife to read the intent and threats were clear. People wanted the preacher out of the way.

Some have argued that King's dream turned into a nightmare. Some tried to foolishly pit King the pacifist against Malcolm X the militant, clearly misunderstanding and misrepresenting both. Some tried to pull King from his pedestal revealing his numerous extra marital affairs. All too often King the Christian is lost to King the activist. King, the political Civil Rights leader, has frequently left King the spiritual leader behind. Martin Luther King's light continues to shine brightly untarnished. He alone was able to hold the black community together in the city of Montgomery, facing legal and physical threats for over 350 days. He alone had to bear the weight of the expectant black community in the USA and abroad on his shoulders. He harnessed the power of oratory and championed the need for nonviolence and dignity when many understandably wanted to wage a bloody war. Dr Martin Luther King recognised the need to have a coalition when groups like the Nation of Islam were calling for separatism. King always said he would never reach forty; he died aged thirty-nine.

On this day in 1955 fourteen-year-old **Emmett Till** was brutally murdered. Exactly seven years later Martin Luther King Jr would announce his 'dream'. Till's murder shocked but did not surprise America. What could a teenager from Chicago have done to warrant such a death? Till had been visiting family in Money, Mississippi. He was aware of segregation having attended a segregated elementary school and had been warned by his mother about dangers in the South. Till is said to have been boasting that up north he had a white girlfriend. Disbelieving his claim Till was dared to speak to twenty-one-year-old Carolyn Bryant who stood behind the counter at the local store. She would later claim that the boy had flirted with her, used lewd suggestive language, whistled, even placed his hands on her waist and shouted "bye, baby" as he left the shop.

Mrs Bryant's husband had been out of town on business. Returning four days later, having been told of the incident, Roy Bryant and his half-brother J W Milam turned up with weapons at Till's great uncle **Moses Wright**'s home. Wright could do nothing to prevent Bryant and Milam abducting the boy. Four days later Till's body was found by a fisherman in the Tallahatchie River. Black witness **Willie Reed** would bravely report that he saw the two white men driving a pickup with three black men in the back, one being Emmett Till. He would add that he heard Till's cries and screams as he was being beaten up. Till had been beaten close to death, one eye gouged out, was shot in the head, then thrown into the river, his lifeless body weighed down. When he was found it was in such a mess the teenager could only be identified by Moses identifying a ring still on his finger.

The local authority sheriff Strider ordered Wright to have the body buried by night fall, but Till's mother **Mamie Bradley** demanded that her son's remains be returned to Chicago. In a courageous move Bradley ordered that her son's casket remain open so on-lookers at the funeral would see what had been done. Pictures captured by *Jet* magazine (see January 19th) shocked its readers. The images were picked up by other black publications and white papers revealing the ugly truth of racism in Jim Crow America.

Two weeks later Bryant and Milam faced trial in the county courthouse in Sumner, Mississippi. Each of the five days of the trial saw the building packed to its 280 capacity. It took the all-white, all-male jury less than an hour of deliberation to find the defendants not guilty. Questions had been raised over the identity of the body. Moses Wright bravely pointed out the two accused as having kidnapped Emmett Till. Both men had admitted to the abduction but claimed to have released their captive later that night. Reaction from the jury varied; some said that they knew Bryant and Milam were guilty, but no white man should go to prison or face the death penalty for killing a black man. Others said that they believed that the prosecution had failed to prove the body was Till's and that they even failed to prove that Till had been murdered. Only one juror is said to have called for the two to be found guilty, he later changed his decision.

The following year protected by the double jeopardy rule, where one cannot be tried twice, having been lawfully convicted or released for a crime, Bryant and Milam gave an interview to Look magazine's William Bradford Huie. He never asked any questions. The defence lawyers put all the questions to the pair who showing no remorse for what they had done pocketed the $3,600–$4,000 offered and admitted to the murder.

Emmett Till was born on July 25th 1941, fourteen short years later he would be brutally slain. One has to ask what possessed twenty-four-year-old Bryant and thirty-six-year-old Milam? Where did such outrage and anger come from? From where did the belief that they were justified in doing what they did stem? Why would a community from the sheriff to the jurors' act in such a way apparently believing the life of a black person is worthless, having no value, being a meaningless life? Why would anyone believe Emmett Till, and many like him before and since do not matter, that they do not count?

Milam died of spinal cancer December 30th 1980, aged sixty-one. Roy Bryant also succumbed to cancer dying on September 1st 1994, aged sixty-three. At the time of writing Carolyn Bryant is still alive aged eighty-six (2020). In an interview given to Tim Tyson, author of *The Blood of Emmett Till* (2017), Carolyn Bryant is said to have admitted that Till had not touched, threatened or harassed her and that nothing he did deserved what happened.

Mamie Bradley, Emmett's mother, lived to the age of eighty-one. She died of heart failure on January 6th 2003. Willie Reed traumatised by the events changed his name to Willie Louise moved to Chicago. His wife only found out about her husband's story from a relative. Uncle Moses died in his early eighties in 1973. He too moved for his own safety to Chicago. Emmett Till's body was laid to rest in Burr Oak Cemetery, Illinois, USA. His death remains a lasting testament to the ugly face and truth of racism and how those affected by the disease often lose any sense of reason, left ostracised from any understanding of the value of a life.

Rita Dove became America's first black and youngest poet laureate aged forty in 1993. Dove was born **on this day** in 1952. Prior to Dove was **Robert Hayden** August 4th 1913 – February 25th 1980. He acted in the same role under a different title from 1976–78.

Aug 29th:

When the famous New York City Jazz Club opened up as 'Birdland' December 15th 1949 it was cashing in on the fame of the alto saxophonist **Charlie Parker.** There are a couple of theories why Parker was nicknamed 'Yardbird' shortened to just 'Bird'; he either was seen as being as free as a bird, or while on the road he hit a bird while driving. Whatever the reason the name stuck.

Charlie Parker.

Charlie Parker was born **on this day** in 1920. The legendary pioneering jazz saxophonist and composer would be credited with creating, along with friend **Dizzy Gillespie** (see October 21st), a new sound and era in jazz called bebop. By the age of fifteen Parker's instrument of choice was the saxophone. He dropped out of school in 1935 to pursue his musical ambitions. The next four years saw Parker playing at a number of spots in Kansas before moving to New York City where he made his first recording in 1940. Dizzy Gillespie and pianist **Thelonious Monk** (see October 10th) saw Bird playing in the early 1940s. Parker would appear with **Earl Hines** (see December 28th) and later with **Billy Eckstine** while finding opportunities to play alongside Gillespie. It was at this time that the pair created a new complicated virtuoso style of playing free from the established melody, chord restrictions and accepted time keeping. Traditionalists in jazz struggled to understand the new form of expression which did not always adopt a melodic style.

Bird's health had suffered following a car crash aged sixteen. He became addicted to opiates having taken morphine for the pain, thus began his relationship with heroin. When heroin was unavailable Bird found that alcohol provided a useful substitute. In June 1946, the saxophonist suffered a nervous breakdown. He would spend over six months in hospital leaving in January 1947. Parker made his debut in Europe performing at the Paris International Jazz Festival in 1949.

His personal life remained chaotic. Following an arrest for possession of heroin in 1951 Bird found that he could not perform in New York's clubs as his cabaret card was removed. Even when the card was returned many venues refused to hire the erratic musician. Relationships and marriages were short-lived and when his daughter Pree died, aged three, things fell apart for Parker who attempted suicide twice that year – 1954 – by drinking iodine.

The musician and composer had a major effect on the world of music, famous for tracks such as 'Autumn In New York', 'Birds of Paradise', 'All the Things You Are', 'Grooving High', 'Summertime,' Parker's Mood' and 'Funky Blues'. He would be dead by the age of thirty-four. Charlie Parker died from pneumonia, a bleeding ulcer and the long-time effects of drug taking and alcoholism while at the Baroness Pannonica de Koenigswarter's apartment at the Stanhope Hotel in New York City, on March 12th 1955. She was the only person prepared to take him in. He is buried at the Lincoln Cemetery in Missouri.

Tensions had been growing in and around the area of Notting Hill in London. The racist, war time leader Oswald Mosely had leased an office for his Unionist Movement at Kensington Park Road. Nearby the White Defence League could be found operating out of 74 Princedale Road. Immigration from the West Indies into the area, already populated by a poor white community and slum housing, angered many locals. When nine Teddy Boys went on what they described as a "nigger hunting expedition" leaving five black men hospitalised, three seriously so, the scene was set for a bigger conflagration, **the Notting Hill Riot.**

Jamaican **Raymond Morrison** was seen arguing with his white Swedish wife Majbritt outside Latimer Road tube station **on this day** in 1958. A group of white people gathered to intervene. Fighting broke out. The following evening, with rumours that a white woman had been raped, saw mobs of up to 400 people rampaging through the streets of Notting Hill shouting "down with the niggers" and "go home you black bastards". The police were threatened with violence as bottles rained down. In the midst of the violence that continued through to September 5th and spread to Nottingham, the *Daily Mail*'s incendiary headline read "Should We Let Them Keep Coming In?"

Black youth fought back, throwing Molotov cocktails while wielding machetes and meat cleavers. One hundred and forty people were arrested, 108 charged – seventy-two white and thirty-six black. Thankfully, no one had been killed. Judge Salmon made an example of nine white defendants, sentencing each to four years with £500 to pay for their part in the riots.

Mosley stood for election in Kensington North and with few votes lost his deposit in 1959. The same year **Claudia Jones** (see January 30th) founded and held the first Notting Hill Carnival at St Pancras Town Hall.

Born **on the same day,** in the same year as the aforementioned Notting Hill Riots, was Lenworth Henry from Dudley, England. The comedian, actor, singer, writer, charity fundraiser, TV presenter and Chancellor of Birmingham University is better known as **Lenny Henry.** He would receive a CBE in 1999 and be knighted in 2015.

<u>Sir Lenny Henry.</u>

A young Henry, born to Jamaican parents, burst on the scene, winning the television talent show New Faces in 1975, telling jokes and performing impressions. As a young naive talent his earliest performances included tours with *The Black and White Minstrel Show* (see July 21st). He would regret the association and lack of guidance received relating to those early years. In 1976 Henry appeared in the comedy *The Fosters* (see April 9th) with **Norman Beaton.** From 1978–1981 Lenny appeared on the children's TV show *Tiswas*. Along with Tracey Ulman and David Copperfield, Henry starred in and wrote sketches in the comedy *Three of a Kind* (1981–1983).

The stand-up comic met Dawn French on the alternative comedy scene. They would be married from 1984 to 2010. Lenny Henry has continuously worked appearing on TV as a presenter, doing voiceovers for a number of different characters, acting in dramas and films while receiving positive reviews playing roles on stage, such as Shakespeare's *Othello* and starring in the theatre production of **August Wilson**'s *Fences*. Many of his characters 'Theophilus P. Wildebeest' and 'DJ Delbert Wilkins' would become permanent fixtures often appearing in *The Lenny Henry Show* which started in 1984 running on and off for almost twenty years. The six foot five performer would convincingly give impressions of Tina Turner, Michael Jackson and Prince.

In 1985 Lenny Henry co-founded Comic Relief, the charitable organisation aimed at raising funds for children's causes mainly focused on the needs in the African continent. Henry has used his position and celebrity to call for greater diversity in positions of power in the entertainment industry. He continues to remain a permanent fixture in British culture.

Aug 30th:

The 'scramble for Africa' (see Berlin Conference Feb 26th) saw Germany occupying territories in Tanzania, Rwanda, Burundi, parts of present-day Mozambique, Namibia, Cameroon and Togoland. To maintain control the Germans had a series of forts. They would often resort to extreme violence and repressive tactics. African kings that failed to comply would be killed.

Humiliating and demanding taxes were levied in 1898 and forced labour used to build roads and other projects. Local life was disrupted creating social turmoil with the men of the village forced to work away from home while the women took on traditional male roles. When the German colonial leader Karl Peters, known as 'Mikono wa Damu' ('man with blood on his hands'), ordered each village to produce its quota of cotton to export as a cash crop, many areas struggled for food self-sufficiency. Problems intensified following the drought of 1905 leading to widespread famine.

Kinjikitile Ngwale, a spirit medium from a folk Islamic and animist tradition, convinced a variety of ethnic groups that he had found sacred water, Maji Maji, that could repel German bullets. Armed with spears and arrows, dipped into the water, Ngwale led attacks on the German occupiers. The rebellion would last two years from 1905–07. The critical moment took place **on this day** in 1905 when several thousand Maji Maji warriors attacked, but failed to overrun, the German fort of Mahenge.

By 1907 between 180,000 and an estimated 300,000 Africans were dead. The uprising might have proven unsuccessful, but it illustrated Ngwale's ability to unite as many as twenty ethnic groups to fight a common enemy. The rebellion revealed the depths colonialist powers would plunge to retain control. Most victims died through famine caused by German farming demands, the drought of 1905 and the scorched earth policy ordered by Gustov Adolf von Gotzen governor of German East Africa.

Kinjikitile Ngwale died early in the conflict but his leadership would become the story of legend and inspire future generations.

One of the big six in the United States Civil Rights Movement **Roy Wilkins** would be called the senior statesman of the movement. Born **on this day** in 1901, Wilkins would work in journalism as a reporter before becoming the managing editor of the influential black community newspaper the *Kansas City Call*. It was while working at the paper Wilkins came to the attention of **Walter Francis White** who headed the National Association for the Advancement of Colored People (NAACP). White persuaded Wilkins to join the staff at the NAACP where he served as assistant secretary 1931–34.

One of the big six, Roy Wilkins.

When W. E. B. DuBois left the organisation in 1934, Wilkins took the role of editor at the NAACP's official publication *The Crisis*, 1934–49. One of Wilkins' first journalistic roles was to investigate and report on working conditions for Southern blacks in Mississippi River Levee Labour Camps. He would use The Crisis to advocate for anti-lynching legislation.

Roy Wilkins saw the NAACP's main role to agitate for equal rights and for change through the courts. He initially opposed nonviolent direct action believing that the courts and legislation would prove the best way forward. Following the Montgomery Bus Boycott, Wilkins offered the Montgomery Improvement Association, led by Martin Luther King, legal-council and financial support. He believed that it was NAACP lawyers that ultimately ended bus segregation in Montgomery following the Supreme Court decision: Brown V Gayle in 1956.

The NAACP legal team headed by **Thurgood Marshall** (see January 24th) would have many successes, none more important than Brown v Board of Education 1954 (see May 17th). Wilkins was at the heart of the activism leading to the Civil Rights Act of 1964 and the Voting Rights Act of 1965. He would go on to have the ears of President Johnson, Nixon, Ford and Carter. Wilkins would be critical of Nixon in his autobiography.

An early victory for Wilkins, at the NAACP, was securing credit for black businesses and organisations. Depositing funds in the black-owned Tri-State Bank allowed black individuals and groups a fair chance to gain credit. Having to seek credit from unsympathetic white institutions in Mississippi, where the White Citizens' Council imposed a credit squeeze, provided yet another hurdle to the already subjugated black community.

In 1950 Wilkins, along with A. Philip Randolph (see April 15th) of the Brotherhood of Sleeping Car Porters and Arnold Aronson from the National Jewish Community Relations Advisory Council founded the

Leadership Conference on Civil Rights, (LCCR). It remains America's oldest, largest and most diverse coalition promoting and protecting civil and human rights.

Roy Wilkins was a liberal who opposed communist sympathisers and separatist elements within the Civil Rights Movement. He would oppose the militancy of the black power movement but was persuaded to offer legal support to some militant groups. Wilkins and King often disagreed but events such as the March on Washington (see August 28th) showed how they were able to work together and cooperate. The pair would ensure that there were no public schisms. Roy Wilkins disagreed with King's critical comments concerning the Vietnam War. Wilkins believed that financially the black soldier had a lot to gain and that he would be seen as a patriot defending the country, fighting for equality at home and abroad. Wilkins helped to organise the March on Washington; he also addressed the 250,000 strong crowd. He participated in the Selma-Montgomery March 1965 and following the shooting of James Meredith took part in the 1966 March Against Fear.

Roy Wilkins retired in 1977 aged seventy-six. He died on September 8th in 1981 from kidney failure. His autobiography *Standing Fast: The Autobiography of Roy Wilkins* was published posthumously in 1982, co-written by Tom Mathews.

On this day in 1983 **Guion S Bluford** (see November 22nd) would become the first African American in space (see September 18th). Arnaldo Tamayo Mendez, a Cuban of African descent became the first black man in space in 1980.

Aug 31st:

Born **on this day** in 1935 baseball outfielder **Frank Robinson** would become the **first black manager of a major league baseball team**. Inducted into the baseball hall of fame in 1982, Robinson would be the only player to be named 'Most Valuable Player' in the National League, playing for the Cincinnati Reds in 1961 and then in the American League playing for the Baltimore Orioles in 1966. Robinson played for five teams from 1956–79. On retirement his 586 career home runs ranked at number four in Major League history.

As player/manager of Cleveland Indians Frank Robinson broke the managerial colour line, twenty-eight years after **Jackie Robinson** broke the players colour line (see April 15th).

Frank Robinson.

He would go on to manage the San Francisco Giants, Baltimore Orioles and Montreal/Washington Nationals. Frank Robinson died from bone cancer age eighty-three, on February 7th 2018. See **Marcenia Lyle Stone** November 2nd.

West Indian (WI) cricket captain **Clive Lloyd** was possibly the most successful leader of a national cricket team but certainly the most successful captain of any West Indian cricket team. The six foot five hard-hitting Guyanese batsman was born **on this day** in 1944.

Captaining the West Indian team from 1974–85, Lloyd saw the team win the first One Day World Cup in 1975 where the captain hit 100 in the final. The team would win again in 1979 before reaching a third final losing to India in 1983.

Clive Lloyd's team had thirty-six test victories with eleven wins in succession. He employed an unrivalled fast bowling line-up that included **Andy Roberts, Malcolm Marshall, Joel Garner** and **Michael Holding**. Lloyd was able to call on a world beating batting line up, that included **Gordon Greenidge, Desmond Haynes** and **Viv Richards** (see March 7th).

Sir Clive Lloyd was knighted in 2020. He made his test debut on December 13th 1966 facing India. 7,515 runs later, with a batting average of 46.67, including 19 x 100s & 39x 50s, with a top score of 242, he played his last test on Dec 30th in 1984 versus Australia. Lloyd played first class cricket for Lancashire in England where he scored what was the fastest first-class double 100, hitting 201 in 120 minutes in 1976. (For **Brian Lara** see May 2nd and **Learie Constantine** see March 26th.) **On this day** in 1968 cricketing history was made when **Sir Gary Sobers** (see February 2nd) hit 6 sixes in one over in 1968.

On this day 1962 **Trinidad and Tobago** gained independence from Britain. **Eric Williams** became the new country's first prime minister, 1956–1981.

Sept 1st:

When San Francisco 49er National Football League (NFL) quarterback **Colin Kaepernick** (born November 3rd 1987) **'took a knee'** along with teammate **Eric Reid,** (born December 10th 1991) they had the courage of their convictions, protesting against police brutality and for racial equality in the United States.

Colin Kaepernick.

For most non-American observers, it is difficult making sense of the country's obsession with their flag, the national anthem and the daily pledge of allegiance that was recited at the start of each school day. Such behaviour appears to be akin to the nationalism that took place during Mao's communist cultural revolution, or the obedience found in Stalin's USSR. For many the founding fathers have achieved a god-like status, a deification along the lines demanded by North Korea's Kim Jong-un or accorded to Japan's Emperor Hirohito. The constitution, for some treated as a holy text, used to rally patriots chanting "U-S-A". The 45th President of America Donald Trump capitalised on this, promising to "Make America Great Again" returning to a dream time when all was perfect and well, a time when America was the land of the free, where anyone could become president and the American Dream was alive. Kaepernick and Reid dared to question the Disney-like, historical representation of the nation taking a knee, while the anthem played at the start of the national game. What was more bemusing to the outsider was the reaction of many, including President Trump who suggested in September 2017 that anyone taking a knee should be fired. The outsider could understand consternation if players turned their back, or remained seated and talked amongst themselves while the anthem played, that would be disrespectful, but to take a knee seems to be quite reasonable, indeed respectful behaviour especially as a silent protest.

TAKING A KNEE

Colin Kaepernick initially remained seated during the anthem at a pre-season match on August 26th 2016. It was at the suggestion of ex-Green Beret **Nate Boyer** that Kaepernick and Reid take the knee. **On this day** in 2016 during the anthem in San Diego, playing against the Chargers, the pair knelt. Kaepernick also promised to donate $1 m to organisations fighting against police brutality and for racial equality.

The act drew comments and reactions. President Obama argued that it was a constitutional right to protest and that there was no legal requirement to stand during the anthem at a game. The first day of the NFL season September 11th saw other athletes take a knee. Reid and Kaepernick took the knee again on September 12th. Reactions to the action were divided. On January 1st 2017 Colin Kaepernick played his last game in the NFL. Frozen out from signing a new contact, after six seasons with the 49ers, Kaepernick took legal action before receiving an out of court settlement. Eric Read found a new team, The Carolina Panthers on September 26th 2018.

Owner of The Dallas Cowboys Jerry Jones in a show of solidarity and empathy took the knee with the team on September 25th 2017. Following the death of George Floyd on 25th May 2020 taking the knee took on renewed national and international significance.

Gambian poet, novelist and surgeon **Lenrie Peters** was born **on this day** in 1932. The pan-Africanist studied in England gaining his medical degree in 1959. From 1955-68 Peters worked for the BBC on African radio programmes.

Recognised as an original, intellectual poet, Peters is seen as one of the most important poets of the second half of the twentieth century in Western Africa. In 1965 he published his only novel *The Second Round*. The semi-autobiographical story followed a doctor returning to Freetown in Sierra Leone just to discover that all the important traditions have been lost and replaced by nothing of value. The doctor finds life unsettling in an unsettled country. His only source of solace is working in an isolated upcountry hospital.

Lenrie Peters published several collections: *Poems* (1964), *Satellites* (1967), *Katchikali* (1971), *Selected Poetry* (1981) and *A New Book of African Verse* in 1984.

Peters served as president of the Historic Commission of Monuments of the Gambia and was president of the board of directors of the National Library of the Gambia. Lenrie Peters died on May 27th 2009.

Sept 2nd:

Zambia became the first African country to extradite defendants to the International Criminal Tribunal for Rwanda (ICTR) following the arrest of Rwandan **Jean-Paul Akayesu** in October 1995.

The former teacher, school inspector, politician in the Republican Democratic Movement Party was the mayor of the Taba commune in Gitarama Region, one of Rwanda's twelve provinces. As mayor Akayesu was reportedly well liked and intelligent and had authority over the area's police.

Tutsis in the area suffered atrocities with many murdered, subjected to violence and threats, (see April 6th). Akayesu was accused of not only doing nothing to prevent Hutu attacks on Tutsis but was believed to have ordered house to house searches for Tutsis and to have supervised the murder of many victims. He was reported to have provided a death list of Tutsis to the Hutus.

Social worker and genocide survivor **Godelieve Mukasarasi** was charged with gathering evidence and putting together a case against Akayesu. She refused to be intimidated even after her husband and daughter were ambushed and killed in 1996. Mukasarasi would go on to fight as a rural development activist and set up SEVOTA an organisation to help women and children that survived the Rwanda genocide. Mukasarasi found four witnesses prepared to testify. Among many awards in recognition for her work and sacrifices, Godelieve Mukasarasi would win an International Woman of Courage Award in 2018.

American lawyer **Pierre-Richard Prosper** was the lead prosecutor. The defence argument stressed that Akayesu had nothing to do with the fifteen counts of genocide and crimes against humanity. The ICTR found Jean-Paul Akayesu guilty on nine accounts **on this day** 1998. He received life sentences on each account and is presently serving his sentence in Mali.

Kenyan leader **Daniel arap Moi** was groomed by former president **Jomo Kenyatta** (see December 12th). Moi would be Kenya's longest serving president from 1978–2002. He only stepped down, forced by the country's constitution. An autocratic dictatorial leader Moi ruled as a one-party state banning opposition parties until pressure from the West forced him to allow other political parties and to have democratic elections. Although Moi declared victory in the 1992 and 1997 elections both would be disputed and seen as fraudulent.

Moi appointed the respected environmental activist Richard Leakey to clean up the corruption. Moi would himself be criticised for his role in corruption and human rights abuses but never face charges.

Daniel arap Moi was initially supported by the West during the Cold War receiving financial support leading to economic growth in Kenya pre-1990. Born **on this day** in 1924 Daniel arap Moi died aged ninety-five on February 4th in 2020.

Sept 3rd:

The man who killed Jim Crow. Charles Hamilton Houston worked tirelessly challenging the legality of Jim Crow laws built on the Supreme Court's Plessy v Ferguson (1897) separate but equal ruling. Houston successfully argued in Gaines v Canada (1938) that if a state were to provide education for whites, then they had to provide a separate but equal facility for the black community. In establishing this duty Houston used law schools to demonstrate his argument. Law schools were

used as: 1) they were male-dominated so there would be little concern over the sexes meeting, mixing, having relationships and marrying. 2) Judges ruling might look more sympathetically on plaintiffs who were looking at a career in the law. 3) As students were older there would be no immediate fear of school children mixing and becoming used to each other leading to future miscegenation. Houston illustrated that to fully comply with 'separate but equal' would be costly. Parallel schools would have to be established and teachers receiving equal pay. His approach would eventually lead to the landmark decision of Brown v Board of Education (1954) (see May 17th) where **Thurgood Marshall** (see January 24th) applied Houston's argument demonstrating that Jim Crow applied the separate but failed to recognise the equal.

Houston fought as a first lieutenant in the US Infantry from 1917–19 during WORLD WAR I serving in France and Germany. It was the racism, hate and scorn faced from his white compatriots that led Houston to study law in order to defend those unable to fight back. The former teacher studied at Harvard Law School (1919–1922) earning a Bachelor of Law degree. In his final year Houston became the first black person to edit the Harvard Law Review. In 1923 he gained his Doctor of Law degree before studying civil law at the University of Madrid. In 1924 he was admitted to the bar in the District of Columbia. From 1935–40

Houston served as special legal counsel to the National Association for the Advancement of Colored People (NAACP). He would be involved in every legal challenge pursued by the NAACP from 1930–1950.

At Howard Law School faculty Houston would recruit students for the NAACP. The class of 1933 saw him mentor and enlist Thurgood Marshall and Oliver Hill. Howard University at the time was training close to a quarter of the country's black lawyers.

Charles Hamilton Houston challenged restrictive housing policies and all white juries. He remained largely unknown, to the wider public, only receiving deserved recognition posthumously. **Genna Rae McNeil**; *Groundwork: Charles Hamilton Houston and the struggle for Civil Rights*, published in 1983, demonstrates the importance of Houston's work. Born **on this day** in 1895 Houston died from a heart attack, aged fifty-four, on April 22 in 1950.

Aboriginal Australian indigenous artist **Emily Kame Kngwarreye** came to prominence in the last decade of her life. She had a short professional career as a painter which saw her become one of Australia's most significant contemporary artists. Kngwarreye's abstract art made up of dots and free flowing lines on batik cloth saw her being viewed as one of the most prominent and successful indigenous painters. Born in 1910, Kngwarreye belonged to the Utopia Community from the Northern Territory. She died **on this day** in 1996 aged eighty-five or eighty-six.

Sept 4th:

The Eusebio de Queiros Law was passed in Brazil **on this day** in 1850. Previous Acts to end the slave trade in Brazil had failed with little will to enforce legislation. The **Aberdeen Act** of 1884, permitted British war ships to stop and search Brazilian vessels, even in port, to look for illegally transported Africans. The Brazilian government disliking the British imposition felt compelled to take control. This led to a rush of Africans being seized and imported. One hundred and fifty thousand enslaved people arrived between 1847 and 1849. Brazil received between 3.5 and 5 million Africans from 1525–1851. As late as 1859 there was still a trickle of captives being imported. Queirós Law was effective finally leading to Brazil officially becoming the last western nation to end slavery in 1888. Rio de Janeiro had about 80,000 enslaved people making up just over 38 per cent of the population. The slave suppression law was named after Brazil's minister of justice 1848–1852. Queiros was born in 1812 and died May 7th 1868. See May 13th, November 7th & 20th on Brazil and slavery

---

He did not invent the telephone but worked closely with Alexander Graham Bell. He did not invent the light bulb but improved on it working closely with Thomas Edison. **Lewis H Latimer** was employed by Bell in 1876 to draft the required drawings for a patent for the telephone. Working with Edison's rival Hiram S. Maxim, Latimer along with Joseph V. Nichols held the patent for the electric lamp issued in 1881. He also held the 1885 patent for the process of manufacturing carbon, the filament used in incandescent light bulbs.

Latimer's parents, George and Rebecca, escaped enslavement in Virginia on October 4th 1842. On arriving in Massachusetts George was recognised and arrested on October 20th. Represented by **Frederick Douglass** (see February 14th) and **William Lloyd Garrison** (see Dec 10th) George would eventually be able to purchase his freedom. Following the Dred Scott v Sandford Supreme Court ruling of March 6th 1857, George was forced to flee, unable to prove that he was a freeman, and the family were split. The Dred Scott case, often cited as the Supreme Court's worse decision described as the Court's greatest self-inflicted wound. The 7 to 2 decision denied black people, free or enslaved, the right to citizenship arguing that when the word 'citizen' appears in the constitution it does not apply to black people. Latimer with his brothers was sent to a farm school and his sisters went to live with a family friend.

On September 16th 1863 Latimer joined the US Navy, honourably discharged on July 3rd in 1865. Working as an office boy at a patent law firm he quickly gained the required skills so that he was promoted to the position of head draftsman on a weekly salary of $20 by 1872.

With Charles Brown, Latimer co-patented an improved toilet system used for railroad cars in 1874. A couple of years later Bell employed Latimer to draft the drawings for the telephone in 1876. Having worked with Edison before 1885, Latimer qualified to become a member of the Edison Pioneers. He was the only black employee in the group of 100.

Latimer wrote *Incandescent Electric Lighting: A Practical Description of the Edison System* in 1890. Lewis Latimer believed like Booker T. Washington that technology and innovation could provide the black community with an up-lift towards progress but, equally recognised the structural problems that led to disenfranchise and disempower minorities.

Lewis H Latimer married Mary Wilson Lewis on November 15th 1873. The couple had two daughters. The inventor and draftsman was **born on this day** in 1848. He died aged eighty on December 11th 1928.

Sept 5th:

Elvis Presley topped the charts with 'All Shook Up'. **Sam Cooke** (see December 11th) romantically crooned 'You Send Me'. **Fats Domino** (see October 24th) sang about 'Blueberry Hill', and Jerry Lee Lewis excited the crowds with 'Whole Lotta Shakin' Going On'. For music 1957 was a great year in the United States. Unfortunately, 1957's America had another story, an ugly, raw story that revealed the ever-present fermenting bile of racism. A group of school children, teenagers, would be known as **the Little Rock Nine.**

The nine had been carefully selected to integrate Little Rock Central High. The school opened in 1927. The school in Little Rock, Arkansas, USA had a white roll of 1,900. It was getting ready to integrate black students. The state capital was to witness extraordinary scenes that would horrify the nation revealing the unmistakable truth of America's education apartheid.

Brown v Board of Education (see May 17th) Supreme Court decision had opened the door to school integration. The nine: **Thelma Mothershed,** 16 (see November 29th), **Minnijean Brown,** 16 (see September 11th), **Ernest Green,** 16 (see September 22), **Melba Pattillo,** 15 (see December 7th), **Gloria Ray,** 15 (see September 26th), **Terrence Roberts,** 16 (see December 3rd), **Jefferson Thomas,** 15 (see September 19th), **Elizabeth Eckford,** 15 (see October 4th) and **Carlotta Walls,** 14 (see December 18th) were selected for their attitude, aptitude and excellent grades. **Daisy Bates** (see November 4th) of the National Association for the Advancement of Colored People's (NAACP) selected the students. All knew that integration would pose problems. The teenagers were vetted, trained and counselled on what to expect and how to react in a hostile situation. No one could have guessed the intensity and anger of the opposition.

Two groups had been formed; the Capital Citizens Council and the Mother's League of Central High School to oppose integration. September 2nd 1957 Governor Orval Faubus announced that he had called in Arkansas' National Guard to ensure that there would be no violence and to maintain the peace, while blocking the nine from entry into school. The following morning the Mother's League held a service at sunrise to underpin their righteous opposition. That same day the federal judge Ronald Davies announced that desegregation would take place as planned for September 4th.

Daisy Bates had arranged to have the students driven to school. Elizabeth Eckford whose home did not have a telephone had not received the information. Arriving late and on her own, television cameras captured the lone teenager surrounded by a white mob shouting repeatedly "Nigger go home". Press pictures captured faces distorted by anger and twisted by rage. Out of the crowd a white woman escorted the fifteen-year-old

Eckford to safety but not before a woman had spat on the girl. The news coverage brought Little Rock, racism and segregation to the nation's attention.

Judge Davies started legal action against the governor while President Eisenhower tried privately to convince Faubus to remove the national guard and allow the nine entry into school. Under orders from Davies the guards were removed only to be replaced by the city police.

Following legal battles on September 23rd the nine finally made it into the school building. The ugly crowd turned on four black journalists attacking **James Hicks**, **Alex Wilson**, **Moses J. Newson** and **Earl Davy.** Alex Wilson, a former soldier who stood over six foot, fell to the ground having been struck on the back of his head by a rock wielding hooligan. He went on to develop a nervous disorder and died three years later, aged just fifty-one. The four were accused of acting as decoys allowing the teenagers to make it into the school through a side entrance. Evil like a mist descended as some in the crowd called to hang one of the nine. The chief of police was reported to enquire "How are you going to choose? Are you going to draw straws?" Recognising the urgency of the situation the nine were ordered into the basement and bundled into police cars. The drivers were given orders to drive and to not stop, the children instructed to keep their heads down, fearing a mass lynching.

Witnessing the brutal scenes in Little Rock unfold left Eisenhower with no choice. One thousand two hundred soldiers of the 101st Airborne Division entered the state capital to ensure the nine made it into school safely. The first day in school had been achieved. Day one would be the beginning of a school year like no other. Looking at the tumultuous academic year ahead for the pioneering nine see Sept 11th and Minnijean Brown. September 5th was chosen to recall this story honouring **Jefferson Thomas** who **died on this day** in 2010. At the time of writing Thomas is the only one of the courageous students to have passed sixty-three years after the event.

Sept 6th:

Jazz pioneer, cornet king of New Orleans and one of the founding fathers of jazz, Charles **'Buddy' Bolden** was born **on this day** in 1877. There are no recordings of his work. Bolden played by ear, improvising, leaving no written music. There is only one known photo of the illusive musician.

By 1895 Bolden was leading a band and is believed to have played with several outfits simultaneously through to 1907. Bolden mixed spirituals, blues and ragtime creating what we know as jazz.

Suffering from acute mental problems, probably exacerbated by alcohol, Buddy Bolden would be arrested on several occasions. Arrested on March 13th 1907 Bolden was committed to the state insane asylum in Jackson, La. He had been institutionalised for close to a decade before the term jazz was coined and before the first jazz recording was released. **Jelly Roll Morton** (see October 20th) and **Louis Armstrong** (see August 4th) spoke of his power as a musician. Although musically Bolden remains a mystery, the house he lived in for twenty years still survives, a ramshackled affair on 2309 First Street in New Orleans. Efforts have been made to preserve the site. Charles 'Buddy' Bolden died on November 4th in 1931.

Buddy Bolden.

Canadian born heavyweight boxer **Sam Langford** (March 4th 1883 – January 12th 1956) is described as **'the greatest fighter that nobody knows'.** He made his professional debut on April 11th 1902. Langford is said to have run away from home to get away from an abusive father. He would fight under the names 'The Boston Bone Crusher', 'Boston Terror' or the racially driven 'Boston Tar Baby'.

Aged fifteen, Langford won the amateur featherweight championship of Boston. His reputation as a fearsome puncher would mean that he would be arguably the best boxer to not be given the right to fight for or as a result to win a world title. He fought many champions either before or after they held the title but would not be given a fair chance to compete for a recognised title. **On this day** in 1919 Langford became the world-coloured heavyweight champion after **Jack Johnson** (see March 31st) became the official heavyweight champion. Johnson had already beaten Sam Langford in a fifteenth round decision when Langford weighed in at 156 lbs v Johnson's 185 lbs in 1906. Johnson always argued that a rematch was pointless as there was no money to be made. Many believed that now Langford had put on extra weight Johnson feared a re-match. Lanford was kept away from a title shot due to the colour bar that existed in the heavyweight division. Jack Dempsey would confess in his autobiography that Langford would have flattened him. Langford beat **Joe Gans** (see Aug 10th) the then world lightweight champion, and the first black world boxing champion, in a non-title fight, December 8th 1903. Langford fought **Joe Walcott** for the welterweight title. The verdict was a draw although many observers argued that the challenger had won having left the champion bleeding by round two and later forced to one knee. On August 15th 1911 Langford beat the former light heavyweight champion Jack O'Brien in round five.

Sam Langford would go on to fight until he was almost blind relying on inside fighting and using the ropes to make his way back to his corner. He retired aged forty-three. By the mid-1930s Langford was totally blind and had disappeared into obscurity living off charity from a foundation for the blind. Journalist Al Laney writing for the New York Herald Tribune tracked Langford down in 1944 asking what ever happened to the former boxer? His article resulted in boxing fans donating $10,000 to the former boxer who was able to live out his final years in comfort. Langford died in a private nursing home aged seventy-two.

Numerous names in the business rated Sam Langford highly. Fight manager Charley Rose saw him as the best heavyweight of all time. Dan Morgan who saw Langford fight said he would defeat Joe Louis in six or seven. Mike Silver, author of the Ring Boxing Almanac said Langford was possibly the greatest fighter that ever lived. Founder of *The Ring* magazine Nat Fleischer placed Langford in the top ten best heavyweights. Boxing trainer Teddy Atlas placed Langford as the fourth pound for pound greatest boxer of all time.

Swaziland gained its independence from Britain **on this day** in 1968. The landlocked country bordered by Mozambique and South Africa, slightly larger than Belgium, made King Sobhuza the head of state on independence. The new constitution made the king the absolute ruler. Swaziland changed its name to **Eswatini** (eSwatini) meaning place of Swazi. The country is governed by a prime minister who serves for a five-year term but cannot serve more than two consecutive terms

Local boy   The national flag   King Sobhuza

Born in Dominica on May 15th 1919 Mary **Eugenia Charles** would become the country's first female lawyer. She would go on to become the country's first and only female prime minister serving from 1980 to 1995. She was the first black female prime minister and the second female prime minister in the Caribbean after Lucina de Costa of the Dutch Antilles. Charles would be Dominica's longest serving politician. When she took office following the 1980 election where the conservative Dominican Freedom Party, which she co-founded in 1968, won seventeen of the twenty-one seats Charles simultaneously served as the foreign minister 1980–90, and as minister of finance 1980–95.

Operation Red Dog was an attempted coup in 1981. Drug dealers and key political figures wished to see the return of the former prime minister Patrick John to facilitate the trade, open a free port and create a centre for gambling. The FBI in New Orleans uncovered the plot of eight American and Canadian mercenaries, six with connections to white supremacists and KKK were employed in the failed coup.

Eugenia Charles appeared alongside US President Ronald Reagan supporting the US invasion of Grenada on 25th October 1983. Reports suggest that the Dominican government received millions of dollars for their stance, from the USA.

Having been the longest continuous serving female prime minister Charles oversaw a decrease in inflation from 30per cent to 5per cent. The country had a budget surplus. In July 1981 Dominica joined the Organisation of Eastern Caribbean States which Charles chaired in 1983.

Eugenia Charles was knighted, becoming a dame, in 1991. She retired in 1995. She travelled widely giving talks and was involved with former US president Jimmy Carter promoting human rights and observing elections. Charles died aged eighty-six from a pulmonary embolism, a blockage of an artery in the lungs **on this day** in 2005.

Sept 7th:

American artist **Jacob Lawrence** was born **on this day** in 1917. His work captured black life, in particular the 60-panel called 'The Migration Series' and historical works on Toussaint L'Ouverture, Harriet Tubman and Frederick Douglass.

Lawrence studied under Harlem Renaissance painter **Charles H. Alston.** The tutor introduced his student to many of the leading figures of the Renaissance.

At twenty-one Lawrence produced forty-one paintings capturing the Haitian revolutionary general **L'Ouverture** (see May 20th). He produced a series of thirty-one paintings of **Harriett Tubman** (see September 17th) from 1938–9 and thirty-two pieces on **Frederick Douglass** (see February 14th) from 1939–40. It was the Migration Series panels that brought Lawrence to national prominence. His works illustrated the great migration of black people from the rural South to the urban North as they travelled, seeking work, escaping poverty, injustice, and Jim Crow laws. From 1916–1970 six million migrated north. The twenty-three-year-old painter was part of the Cubist movement but got his style from the shapes and colours he found in Harlem and not from France. Lawrence's modernist style looked at everyday life in the black community. During World War II he continued to paint but although some of those paintings were exhibited all forty-eight works produced at that time were lost, blamed on the chaos and disorder following demobilisation.

Exhausted and overwhelmed by his success and the relative failure of friends and contemporaries led to Lawrence spending a year in hospital experiencing depression. While recovering Lawrence created the 'Hospital Series' in 1950. His next major work was the *Struggle: From the History of the American People*. The series showed scenes from 1775–1817. Four panels have been lost, two other panels were found, one in 2017 and another in 2020. The series had been purchased privately then broken up and sold as individual pieces.

Jacob Lawrence became one of the first nationally recognised black American artists. He would go on to capture the Civil Rights Movement in the 1960s and produce illustrations for books and eight screen prints in 1983 known as the Hiroshima Series. Lawrence wanted his paintings to be universally accessible to all people. He desired his work to be aesthetically clear and strong. The painter spent 16 years as a professor at the University of Washington. Jacob Lawrence painted close to the end of his life. He died on June 9th in 2007 aged eighty-two, survived by his wife Gwendolyn Knight, who died in 2005.

For generations of Jamaicans at home or living abroad **Miss Lou, Louis Bennett** was their voice. The poet took the dialect, the patois, to a higher respectable level using the language as an art form. Bennett gave expression to a people using a language that was theirs, capturing the joys, sorrows, the wit, religion and culture of Jamaica and Jamaicans.

Born **on this day** in 1919, Bennett won a scholarship becoming the first black person to study at London's prestigious Royal Academy of Dramatic Arts (RADA) in 1945. While in England she would perform at a variety of venues as well as work at the BBC on radio programmes Caribbean Carnival 1945–46 and West Indian Night in 1950.

Returning to Jamaica, Bennett taught folklore and drama at the University of the West Indies. Her status as a living legend was cemented with a series of radio monologues captured in 'Mis Lou's Views' from 1965 to 82. When she hosted the children's tv programme *Ring Ding* from 1970 to 82 she was able to speak directly to and for the country's children. Bennett was a cultural icon, the unofficial poet laureate. She always performed with humour appearing as everyone's loving mother and then grandmother.

Louise Bennett married Eric Winston Coverley in 1954. The couple had a son named Fabian and remained together until Eric's death in 2002. Louis Bennett-Coverley spent the last decade of her life in Ontario, Canada where she died aged eighty-six on July 26th 2006. Her body was repatriated to Jamaica and buried in the National Heroes Park in Kingston. Bennett the writer also appeared in two feature films: *Calypso* (1958) and *Club Paradise* in 1986.

Former soldier and journalist **Mobutu Sese Seko** seized power deposing President Kasavubu in 1965. Mobutu would remain in control changing the name of the Democratic Republic of Congo to Zaire in 1971 and changing his name from Joseph-Desire Mobutu to Mobuto Sese Seko Koko Ngbendu Wa Za Banga meaning 'The all-powerful warrior who, because of his endurance and inflexible will to win, will go from conquest to conquest, leaving fire in his wake'.

Mobutu found himself as the power broker taking Kasavubu's side over the Premier **Patrice Lumumba** (see July 2nd). It's not altogether clear how involved, if at all, Mobutu was in Lumumba's assassination. When Mobutu, the commander in chief, returned power to Kasavubu further political infighting, with the new premier Moise Tshombe, broke out. Mobutu seized the opportunity to take power in 1967. His totalitarian regime received support from the West during the cold war period. Mobutu was able to thwart attempted coups retaining a stranglehold on power. In 1977 he called on France for military assistance helping Zaire to defeat ethnic exiles supported by Angola. Mobutu proved adept at repelling internal opposition but struggled to create a growing or stable economy.

Mobuto Sese Seko.

The county's flag.

Corruption was endemic, mismanagement a chronic problem, the country's infrastructure was neglected while Mubuto amassed a personal fortune believed to be one of the richest men in the world. Economic exploitation, human rights violations, uncontrolled inflation and a rising national debt all took place while Mobutu was believed to have embezzled between $4 and $15 billion.

With the end of the Cold War Mobutu was forced to share power leading a coalition government. He continued to manoeuvre to ensure that he retained the reins of power. While seeking treatment for cancer in Switzerland Joseph Kabila was able to seize power in May 1997 ending Mobutu's thirty-two-year rule. Mobutu went into exile ending his days in Rabat, Morocco. He died from prostate cancer **on this day** in 1997, aged sixty-six.

Behind the headlines are the people. Less we forget the Democratic Republic of the Congo.

Senegalese President **Abdou Diouf** would serve as regional governor 1961–62, secretary general to the government 1964–65, and minister of planning and industry 1968–70. He was well prepared to take the position of prime minister from February 28th in 1970 serving under President Leopold Senghor (see October 9th). When Senghor retired the trained lawyer Diouf was constitutionally promoted to president.

Diouf looked for Senegal to cooperate with other African countries. The brief and loose Senegambia Confederation was formed 1982–89. The president would successfully chair the Organisation of African Unity (OUA) restoring its fragile reputation in 1982–83. He was given a second term in office from 1992 to 1993. Diouf would also serve as the chair of the Economic Community of West African States (ECOWAS).

In 1986 Diouf addressed HIV/AIDS providing a clear programme of safe sex education. Sex workers were required to be registered and Christian and Islamic leaders asked to promote awareness. Senegal was able to keep its infection rate down at 2per cent.

The 1993 election win by Diouf's Socialist Party faced criticism and trouble on the streets from opposition groups. Abdou Diouf stepped down from power after losing the 2000 election to Abdoulaye Wade. Three years later from January 1st 2003 to December 31st 2014 Diouf served as the executive secretariat of the International Organisation of La Francophonie uniting countries that speak French or share French culture.

Sept 8th:

Born under British rule in Basutoland, now Lesotho, on December 22nd 1876 **Thomas Mokopu Mofolo** was a pioneering African writer. Writing in the Sesotho language he's considered the greatest Basotho author. Creating western style novels in his mother tongue, Mofolo is ranked alongside Nobel laureates **Wole Soyinka** (see July 13th), Nadine Gordimer and Naguib Mahfouz.

The Traveller of the East published in 1907 was Mofolo's first novel. The fictional work follows a young African whose search for truth and virtue takes him to a foreign land where he discovers Christianity. It was translated into English in 1934. *Pitseng* (1910), Mofolo's second offering reveals a new Sotho consciousness, the author questions his missionary up-bringing. The Christian fable is critical of white people who have betrayed the promise of their religion. It was 'Chaka' completed in 1912, but published in 1925, that was to be Mofolo's masterpiece. The historical novel placed the Zulu hero in a pre-Christian Africa. The book's failure to condemn pagan and tribal customs created fear amongst the missionaries who believed that the story could inspire anti-Christian sentiment. Recognised as the earliest black African contribution to modern world literature the opposition to publish left Mofolo disillusioned. It was his last work. He left for South Africa working as a labour agent recruiting for the gold mines of the Transvaal and plantations of the Natal. In 1927 Mofolo bought a shop and in 1937 he acquired a farm. Following the Bantu Land Act Thomas Mofolo was evicted. Broken and sick he returned to Lesotho. Mofolo never recovered from a stroke suffered in 1941 and died **on this day** in 1948.

Actor and singer **Dorothy Dandridge** was the first black woman to be nominated for an Academy Award for Best Actress following the success of Otto Preminger's all-star black cast in 1954's ***Carmen Jones***. Born on November 9th 1922 Dorothy performed as part of the Dandridge Sisters from 1934 to 1940. Going solo performing at the Cotton Club and the New York City's Apollo Dandridge would return to music when stage and film options dried up.

Following the success of Carmen Jones, Dandridge became the first black woman to adorn the cover of Life Magazine on November 1st 1954. The following year Dandridge was the first black performer to open at the Empire Room at the Waldorf-Astoria Hotel in New York. Her performance opened the door for other black performers. Targeted by gossip columnist in the tabloid 'Confidential' Dandridge and Maureen O' Hara testified against the publication and its salacious gossiping accusations. Dandridge won a $10,000 out of court settlement.

Although seen as Hollywood first black sex symbol, described as the black Marilyn Monroe, Dandridge always felt that if she had been white, she would have gone a lot further. In 1957's *Island in the Sun* Dandridge acted alongside James Mason, Joan Fontaine, **Harry Belafonte** (see March 1st) and Joan Collins. Her role caused some controversy playing in an interracial affair with white actor John Justin. 1958's *Tamango* saw Dandridge's only on-screen interracial kiss opposite Curd Jurgens. She never got the breaks beyond 1959's *Porgy and Bess* opposite **Sidney Poitier** (see February 20th).

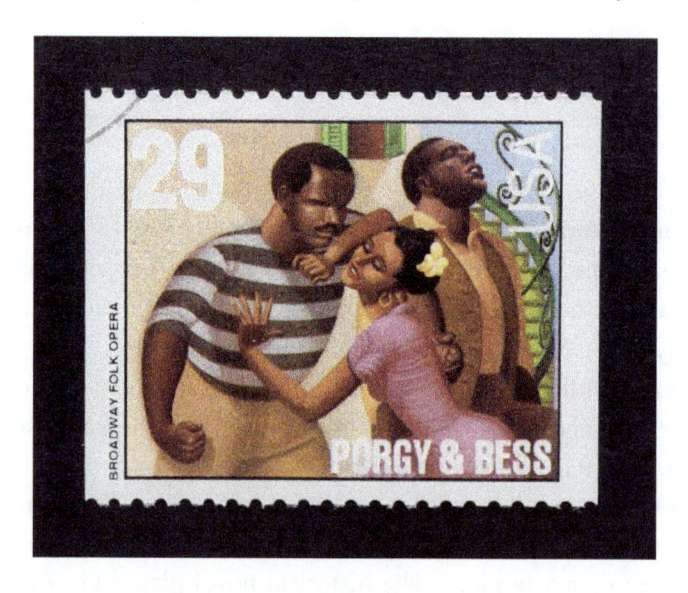

Porgy and Bess.

Dandridge's working life was not easy as a black woman of her time, trying to sustain a career in racially sensitive Hollywood. Her private life was tumultuous. She married, September 6th 1942, **Harold Nicholas**, one of the greatest dancing pairs. Dandridge suffered from having an inattentive womanising husband. When she went into labour, aged twenty, he left her stranded, away playing golf. Dandridge, wanting her husband by her side, delayed as long as possible before going to the hospital. The baby was delivered using forceps. Dandridge would understandably question the delay as her daughter Harolyn was born on September 2nd 1943 brain damaged. It is believed that her daughter died in 2003. Was it her fault that Harolyn could not speak and would never recognise her mother? Harold and Dorothy divorced in 1951. Dandridge had a four-year affair with married director, Preminger. Pregnant, the studio forced her to have an abortion in March of 1957. The affair ended when Dandridge realised Preminger was not going to leave his wife. Film work had dried up and relationships were a mess. Married for a second time on June 22 1959 to Jack Denison, the couple would divorce in 1962 with allegations of financial impropriety and domestic violence.

Financial problems added insult to injury, providing another layer of difficulties on top of dysfunctional relationships, raising Harolyn, and a stuttering film career. $150,000 was swindled from her by those managing her finances leaving Dandridge owing $139,000 in back taxes. The actor was forced to sell her Hollywood home and place her daughter into care.

Today Dandridge would probably have been diagnosed as suffering bi-polar disorder. Dorothy Dandridge's naked body was found lifeless at her apartment on 8495 Fountain Avenue, West Hollywood. She is recorded as having died from an overdose of the antidepressant Imipramine **on this day** in 1965, aged forty-two. HBO released the film *Introducing Dorothy Dandridge* in 1991.

Norman Rockwell's 1964 painting 'The Problem We All Live With' captured the scene; a little six-year-old black girl walking to school, shadowed by four US marshals, passing graffiti scrawled on the wall proclaiming 'nigger' and 'KKK'. That six-year-old elementary school girl was **Ruby Bridges.** Born **on this day** in 1954.

Ruby would find herself on the front-line of school desegregation. The local authority had insisted that if schools in New Orleans and Louisiana were to be integrated then the black students had to prove that academically they were able to keep up with their white contemporaries. Yet another hurdle to clear which six girls successfully did. Two of the six chose to remain at their school. Three, known as the McDonogh Three; **Leona Tate, Tessie Prevost** and **Gail Etienne** attended McDonough Elementary School. Within days, the three were the only pupils at the school as white parents withdrew their children in protest. For the next year and a half, the three girls at McDonogh nineteen attended lessons behind papered-over windows, even the water was turned off for fear of poisoning.

Ruby Bridges' father, Abon, had concerns over sending his daughter to William Frantz Elementary School. Her mother, Lucille had wanted her daughter to have the educational opportunities that she had never had. On November 14th 1960 escorted to school surrounded by US marshals Ruby and her mother walked. The first day was spent in the principal's office as chaos in and out of the school unfolded. White parents pulled their children from class. Crowds of white adults, holding obscene placards, shouted epithets and abuse as the six-year-old daily walked the gauntlet, for a year, facing the ugly racist onslaught. The marshals instructed their charge to look straight ahead so that she could not see the distorted rage on the protestors faces or read the placards. Ruby recalls that she never felt fear until one day she saw a black doll in a coffin. The marshals were amazed how their little girl never cried, not even whimpered; she just marched like a little soldier.

Only one teacher stepped up and stepped forward to teach Ruby. Bostonian Barbara Henry taught Ruby all year in a class of one. The little girl had to eat alone and frequently played alone if Ms Henry was not available. Child psychologist Robert Coles would meet with Ruby to closely monitor the school child and provide support. It later emerged that the well-dressed Ruby had received her lovely clothes from one of Coles relatives.

The Bridges family suffered for their courageous pioneering stand. Abon lost his job, the local grocery store where Lucille had shopped refused to serve her. Ruby's grandparents who had lived and worked as sharecroppers lost their home of twenty-five years. Eventually Abon and Lucille divorced.

Ruby as an adult worked as a travel agent, she married and had four sons. She would be reunited with Barbara Henry and both appeared together at speaking engagements. Psychologist Coles wrote *The Story of Ruby Bridges* (1995), based on their meetings. Ruby wrote *Through My Eyes* (1999) and a children's book of her experience *Ruby Bridges Goes to School: My True Story* in 2009. She established the Ruby Bridges Foundation in 1999 to promote tolerance aiming to create change through education. All the proceeds from Coles' book went to the Foundation.

See **Sarah Roberts** February 15th, **Little Rock Nine** September 5th and **Elizabeth Eckford** October 4th.

Sept 9th:

Born in Grenada **on this day** in 1937 former teacher **Jean Augustine** would become Canada's first black woman to serve in the federal cabinet, from 2002–2004, in the county's 135-year history. An immigrant from Grenada, Augustine became the first black woman elected to Canada's House of Commons as a member of parliament in 1993. The Liberal MP would win four consecutive elections before retiring in 2006.

Jean Augustine drove through the vote, winning by 305-0, designating February as Black History Month. Serving in a number of offices, Augustine was minister of multiculturalism and the status of women 2002–2004. She was voted three times as the chair for the National Women's Caucus and helped to pass legislation to protect disadvantaged low-income individuals.

Outside of the Commons, Augustine served as the national president of the Congress of Black Women of Canada and from 2007–2015 she was the Fairness Commissioner advocating for Canadians who hold foreign professional credentials. She never stood as a black woman but as a competent woman but showed black people, in particular females, what is possible.

Sept 10th:

US Republican politician, attorney and writer **John R. Lynch** was born **on this day** into slavery in 1847. He would be the first black person elected to be Speaker of the Mississippi House of Representatives, the first black person in that position in the country. Lynch was among the first generation of people of colour elected to the US House of Representatives serving from 1873–1877.

John Lynch wrote four books. The two most famous being *Coloured Americans: John R Lynch's Appeal to Them* and notably *The Facts of Reconstruction* published in 1913 outline the contribution made by the black population following the Civil War during the Reconstruction. Lynch as part of the great migration settled in Chicago and died in the city on November 2nd in 1939.

Hattie Cotton Elementary School opened on September 1st 1950 in East Nashville. Following the Brown v Board of Education Supreme Court decision in 1954 (see May 7th) Nashville looked to integrate its schools. The Nashville Plan was to integrate six city schools, one grade level per year starting in 1957.

Nineteen six-year-olds were selected to attend new, formerly, all white schools. On the first day four were turned away with administrative issues. Hattie Cotton admitted one black girl. Just after midnight an explosion at the school **on this day** shattered the night calm. Walls had collapsed and every window was shattered. Nine days later the school reopened without the little black girl who had been transferred to an all-black school in North Nashville.

No one was ever charged with detonating the thirteen sticks of dynamite. John Kasper (1929–1998) was suspected of having procured the explosives. The KKK member and segregationist was also connected to the bombing of synagogues and was convicted in 1958 for inciting a riot. FBI files refer to a terror cell of three being responsible for the **Hattie Cotton Elementary School bombing.**

Angolan independence leader and poet Antonio **Agostinho Neto** was born on September 17th 1922. Described as the **father of modern Angola** (see Andrade, August 21st) Neto became the first president of the independent People's Republic of Angola.

A qualified doctor, Neto led the Popular Movement for the Liberation of Angola (MPLA) leading the organisation during the War for Independence 1961–1974. Studying in Portugal, he would be arrested in 1951 for three months for separatist activities. He was arrested again in 1952 for joining the Portuguese Movement for Democratic Youth Unity. He would spend most of 1952 through to 1957 in custody.

Back in Angola the doctor was arrested in front of his patients at his surgery on June 8th 1960. The protests that followed saw the authorities open fire killing thirty and wounding 200. The incident became known as the Massacre of Icolo e Bengon. Placed in exile and then under house arrest, Neto was able to escape. He tried to seek assistance from President Kennedy's administration, but fearing Neto's left leaning sympathies and wishing to secure financial interest in Angola, help was denied. Neto turned to the Soviet Union and the Communist Bloc. He met with Che Guevara in 1965. Sharing an ideological outlook with Fidel Castro, Neto and the MPLA received much needed assistance from Cuba.

Angolan independence was achieved on November 11th 1975. The MPLA, one of four competing groups, had militarily secured the capital Luanda resulting in Agostinho Neto becoming the first president of the People's Republic of Angola. He was sworn in 1975 and remained president through to his death in 1979. Neto governed a one-party state and Marxism-Leninism became the official political position. Awarded the Lenin Peace Prize for 1975–6 that did not prevent an attempted, but failed, coup in 1977. The resulting retaliation saw thousands executed.

Neto the poet was at his most active from 1946–1960. He was part of a cultural movement that sought to rediscover indigenous Angolan culture.

Antonio Agostinho Neto died in Moscow from cancer **on this day** in 1979, he was fifty-six.

Agostinho Neto.

White librarian **Ruth Winifred Brown** came to prominence when, after thirty years working at Bartlesville public library in Oklahoma, she was dismissed on July 25th in 1950.

Brown had started her career as a librarian in 1919. She had always supported inclusivity believing that all should have access to and support from the library. Initially accused of promoting Communist literature. The city authorities employed McCarthyism arguing that Brown had been engaged in un-American activities. Many believed that it was Brown's desegregation activities that had led to her sacking.

Brown had attempted to invite black friends to her all-white church. She even dared, but failed, to have lunch in a segregated lunchroom but service was denied. It could have been plans to have an integrated children's story hour that forced Brown's dismissal.

Ruth Winifred Brown left Bartlesville to teach at an all-black school in Mississippi before moving on to Colorado where she worked as a librarian through to 1961. Brown died **on this day** in 1975. On March 11th in 2007 a bronze bust was unveiled of Ruth Brown at the library in Bartlesville. She never married but attempted to adopt two sisters but was refused as a single woman. When the eldest girl Mildred 'Holly' Holiday ran away from her abusive foster parents, at eighteen, she turned up at Brown's home. The younger sister Ellen also ran away to live with Brown who was eventually able to adopt.

Ballerina **Misty Copeland,** born **on this day** in 1982, became the first black female principal dancer on June 30th 2015 for the American Ballet Theatre in its seventy-five years.

Principal dancer Misty Copeland

Sept 11th:

Minnijean Brown, one of the **Little Rock Nine** (see September 5th) was the only one expelled from Central High. Only three of the nine graduated. It would be thirty years before Minnijean found herself able to speak about her experiences in 1957.

Born **on this day** in 1941 Minnijean was one of eighty black students who applied to attend Little Rock Central High. When it became clear that extra-curricular activities and clubs would be denied to the new students the numbers were reduced to nine. Having made it into school the nine would meet each morning at **Daisy Bates** (see November 4th) home. The students would have a military escort to school each and every day. Once in school each student was assigned a soldier who escorted the students from class to class. The cost of the protection is estimated to have cost $3.4 million. One could have built three Central Highs for $3.4 m.

Segregation in the South was so complete that the nine faced enormous hostility, harassment and bullying daily. Minnijean used the anger faced to create a sense of resolve, determination and courage not to give up or to give in. The daily insults were seen as a sadness, a sickness, where so many of the white students did not have the ability to think. The harsh reality meant that each of the nine had a spare set of clothing as spit, food and liquids thrown at them required they get changed. Daily the insults and name-calling never let up. So common was the situation that the nine stopped reporting incidents that were rarely addressed and often ignored. Being kicked, stepped on, having bruises and cuts on legs and feet, being body slammed against the wall occurred each day. **Melba Pattillo** (see Dec 7th) had acid thrown at her face. **Terrence Roberts** (see Dec 3rd) was kicked unconscious and **Jefferson Thomas,** (see Sept 19th) was beaten up in the basement.

There was a sense of physical isolation as the nine were placed in separate classes only meeting up at lunchtime. It was the mental isolation that created the greatest damage. Each in a bid to protect the others, the nine started keeping their horror stories from each other. Minnijean tried to keep the worse from her parents. The parents supported their brave sons and daughters as best as they could. Minnijean's father found that his work as a landscape gardener and a mason started to dry up. There were threatening calls to the home. Her mother and father were frequently called to go to the morgue to identify a body.

Walking in the cafeteria at lunchtime boys kept pushing the chairs into Minnijean's legs. Angry and in pain the girl dumped her food on a boy's head. She was suspended for six days. When she returned to school a boy threw his soup over her only to be suspended for two days. A gang of girls followed Minnijean kicking at her heels then throwing a bag full of metal locks at her head. In retaliation Minnijean called them 'white trash'. Her expulsion from Central High was met with printed coloured cards being distributed reading "one down eight to go".

Husband and wife psychologist Dr Kenneth and Dr Mamie Clark took Minnijean to live with them in New York City. The couple had been monitoring the nine providing vital support. Minnijean was taken aback by the crowd that greeted her on her arrival discovering that the nine had become nationally and internationally famous. She attended New Lincoln, a prestigious private school in Manhattan. She felt with the Clarks' that she was meeting New York's intelligentsia.

At the end of the academic year Governor Faubus held a referendum which saw 72per cent of Little Rock's voting public choose to close all schools rather than see further integration. It would take a year before NAACP legal challenges resolved the situation and the schools were opened. Minnijean Brown met Roy Trickey. The couple married in 1967 and would have six children. As a conscientious objector when called to fight in Vietnam, Roy and Minnijean, left to live in Canada. Minnijean Brown-Trickey worked as an anti-racist educator and environmental campaigner. She waited until her eldest was fifteen before she revealed her past to the family, choosing to show the family footage and coverage from 1957. It was following an appearance on *Oprah* in 1992 that many of her friends and associates first discovered that Minnijean was one of the nine. It was only after the group met, after thirty years, did each fully share what they had gone through.

Brown-Trickey worked for the Clinton administration from 1999-2001 as the deputy assistant secretary for work diversity. Seeing Trump supporters and the death of George Floyd left Minnijean asking was her experience a waste? Indeed, following white flight from the public school system schools in the US are more segregated in 2020 than they were in the early 1960s.

Kehinde Andrews wrote a piece titled 'Minnijean Brown-Trickey: the teenager who needed an armed guard to go to school' for *The Guardian* amended on 26th Nov 2020. I end this account with her own words from that piece.

"The US has two values: violence and segregation, and they do them both really well."

"I look at the photos of the nine of us, standing there, in contrast to those crazy people ... and what I say is that they threw away their dignity and it landed on us."

"Still photos cannot show how we are shaking in our boots, sandwiched between the Arkansas National Guard and a mob of crazy white people."

The 2011 BBC documentary *Reggae Got Soul: The Story of Toots and the Maytals*, showcased the influence **Toots Hibbert** had on Jamaican music and reggae in particular and the reverence fellow artists had for the man who would grace the world of music for close to sixty years.

Born in May Pen, Jamaica on December 8th 1942, by the age of eleven **Frederick Nathaniel Hibbert** was an orphan and had to go to live in Kingston with his brother. Toots formed the ska band the Maytals in 1961. The group consisted of Toots with **Raleigh Gordon** and **Jerry Mathias**. They released their first album in 1962 and would perform together until 1981. Toots the multi-instrumentalist, lead singer and songwriter, his voice often compared to soul legend Otis Redding, was at home singing reggae, soul, funk and country. The Maytals experienced major success on the island with songs winning Jamaica's National Popular song contest with 'Bam Bam' (1966), 'Sweet and Dandy' (1969), and 'Pomp and Pride' (1972).

In 1966 Toots spent eighteen months in jail for possession of marijuana. He said that he had been framed by those jealous of his success and never even smoked back then. His experience led to one of Toots most popular songs '*54-46 That's my Number*' released in 1968. Toots and the Maytals were reggae pioneers responsible for the first record cited as using the term reggae, '*Do the Reggay*' released in 1968 referring to a popular dance. their first reggae album was on Chris Blackwell's Island Records, 'Funky Kingston' released in 1972. That same year the group appeared in the film *The Harder They Come* performing 'Sweet and Dandy'. The soundtrack also contained their 1969 classic 'Pressure Drop'.

Although the original Maytals split in 1981, Toots continued to perform and collaborate. On stage in May 2013 at the River Rock Festival in Richmond, Virginia an audience member threw a bottle hitting the singer on the head. Months of shows had to be cancelled. When William C. Lewis was identified as having thrown the bottle, Toots wrote a letter, fearing that prison would ruin Lewis' life, asking for clemency. The judge gave Lewis a six-month prison sentence.

Toots was performing into his seventies. He died **on this day** in 2020 having tested positive for COVID and had been in an induced coma. He was survived by his wife of thirty-nine years and by seven of his eight children. He was seventy-seven. Reggae legend, **Peter Tosh** of the **Wailers** born October 19th 1944 died **on this day** in 1987. **Bunny Wailer** born April 10th 1947, died on March 2nd 2021, aged seventy-three. See **Bob Marley** February 6th. **Jimmy Cliff** April 1st, **Desmond Dekker** May 25th, and **Dennis Brown** July 1st.

Sept 12th:

Man's inhumanity to man is as old as history itself. The architects of South African apartheid Verwood, Vorster, Malan and Botha planned a system that would subject the majority black population to an inhumane existence. South Africa's Nationalist Party banned political opposition from the Communist Party, The Africa National Congress (ANC) and The Pan Africanist Congress (PAC).

By the late 1960s the Nationalist Party had been in power close to twenty years. They were creating a new, separate society with divided residential areas, even new 'countries', tribal homelands. Parallel, but certainly not equal, institutions such as schools and hospitals were promoted to ensure that blacks and whites were increasingly kept apart.

Steve Biko found himself at the heart of a political civil war engaged in a deadly cat and mouse struggle.

He had to navigate the crushing ideology of apartheid, to survive in a system that operated to disenfranchise a community leaving the majority black population demoralised, defeated and subservient. Born on December 18th 1946 Biko was thrown in at the deep end following his arrest with his older brother Khaya in 1963. Khaya was given a twenty-four-month sentence, with fifteen months suspended, which he served at Glamorgan jail. He was found guilty of belonging to the PAC military wing Poqo. The experience opened Steve Biko's political eyes. He returned to studying at Lovedale College but following a number of expulsions, including that of **Thabo Mbeki**, Biko was expelled after only three months.

Biko had been a member of the liberal, interracial, moderate National Union of South African Students but would go his separate way. Founding the South African Students Organisation (SASO) Biko believed that South African society needed to be rebuilt and restructured around the black majority. In doing so Biko joined in with the early throws of black consciousness promoting an inherent dignity and self-worth. Biko would become the most prominent spokesperson in the movement. The Black People's Convention was co-founded by Biko in 1972. The umbrella organisation looked to unite all the black conscious groups. Steve Biko quit his medical studies in 1972 getting involved in black community programmes (BCP).

March 1973 saw Biko and SASO banned, resulting in the restricting of associations, movements and public statements. Whenever a programme or an organisation moved to uplift the black community, the Nationalist Party would erect another hurdle restricting progress.

Increasingly recognised as a shrewd political activist Biko was continuously addressing audiences, mobilising activists, promoting black consciousness and involved in uplift programmes. Detained in 1975 for 137 days he was released having not been charged or put on trial. Already subjected to a banning order, the requirements of the new order were tightened in 1976. On August 27th of the same year Biko was arrested and held in solitary confinement for 101 days.

Whilst travelling the activist was stopped at a roadblock by South African authorities on August 18th 1977. Biko was arrested and jailed in Port Elizabeth. Chained and manacled, the detainee was kept in leg irons and left to lay naked in urine-soaked blankets at the Sanlam building of the Security Police. When ordered to stand Biko resisted and sat. Manhandled by Captain Siebert, Biko fought back. He was badly beaten on the 6th and 7th of Sept leaving him with a brain haemorrhage. Seen by one doctor the victim was given the all-clear. A second doctor raised concerns recommending that the patient be taken to hospital, but the police resisted. When a transfer to Pretoria, 740 miles away, was suggested the doctors showed no objection although Biko would lay naked in the back of a Land Rover frothing at the mouth and unable to speak in a vehicle without medical equipment.

Steve Biko was reported to have died **on this day** in 1977, he was just thirty. A local paper reported that this was one of twenty deaths in security police custody in the previous eighteen months. His death was the forty-sixth political murder in police custody from 1963–77. The official story put out was that Biko had died following a hunger strike. His burial on September 25th saw tens of thousands in attendance. The number of mourners would have been greater but for numerous roadblocks preventing free movement.

Steve Biko's death in custody became the first to have a public inquest. The purpose of the inquiry was to discover how Biko died but had no intention to apportion any blame or convictions. Biko wrote for SASO under the pseudonym Frank Talk under the heading *I Write What I Like*. The selected writings were first published in 1978.

Harry Burleigh, born December 12th 1866, would take African American (negro) spirituals to the classical concert stage. The acclaimed baritone vocalist and composer broke down racial barriers with his voice and talent.

Studying at the National Conservatory of Music in New York age twenty-six, Burleigh played the double bass in the orchestra. At the Conservatory he developed a friendship with the elder composer Antonin

Dvorak, introducing Dvorak to African American spirituals and plantation songs. These would influence some of Dvorak's most popular compositions and introduce the composer to Native American music too.

Burleigh became the first black person to be appointed soloist in 1894 at the all-white St George's Episcopal Church in New York. Although there had been racial opposition, he remained at St George's for fifty-two years, retiring in 1946 missing only one performance. The baritone was the first black singer to perform at Temple Emanu-El, a synagogue, from 1900–1925.

Harry Burleigh works include 'Saracen Songs' (1914), 'Ethiopia Saluting the Colours' (1915), 'Passionale' (1915), 'Five Songs of Laurence Hope' (1915), a collection 'Jubilee Songs of the USA' (1916), and his arrangement of 'Deep River' in 1917.

Harry Burleigh died from heart failure **on this day** in 1949, aged eighty-two. Although a lot of his music is out of print, Burleigh is seen as one of the most important American composers of the twentieth century.

Born **on this day** in 1973 **Tarana Burke** is an activist famous for using **Me Too!** aligning herself with other women who had similar experiences of sexual abuse in 2006. Burke wished to illustrate the pervasiveness of sexual abuse. Appropriated by actor Alyssa Milano, when women started to tweet about allegations of sexual abuses relating to Harvey Weinstein, **the MeToo Movement** took off. Burke was always supportive of **#metoo.**

Tarana Burke Me Too founder.

Tarana Burke started 'Just Be Inc' in 2003 focusing on the health, well-being and wholeness of young women of colour. Faced by traditional and social media, music and a pop culture that often attacks one's sense of worth, Just Be works to provide vital support needed by this vulnerable group.

Tarana Burke was '*TIME* Person of the Year' in 2017. At the time of writing, 2020, she is the senior director at Brooklyn-based Girls for Gender Equity creating opportunities for young women so they can live self-determined lives.

Sept 13th:

Prolific writer, philosopher, editor, heralded as the father, and chief interpreter, of the Harlem Renaissance, **Alain Locke** was born **on this day** in 1886. Arthur LeRoy Locke would adopt the name Alain aged sixteen.

Often cited as the dean and architect of the Harlem Renaissance, Locke's philosophical works were rarely for popular consumption. With the publication of *The New Negro* (1925), Locke provided a platform and a dignified voice. He edited the anthology of essays, poetry, plays and music with contributions from black and white artists including **Langston Hughes** (see May 22nd), **Zora Neal Hurston** (see January 28th), **Claude McKay** (see September 15th), **Countee Cullen** (see January 9th) and **James W. Johnson** (see June 17th). Locke wrote five entrees for the anthology. The' new negro' would become a term for those who were prepared to be outspoken. The Harlem Renaissance championed black intellectual writing and art during the 1920s and 1930s. Locke organised travelling art exhibitions and mentored Hughes, Cullen and Hurston.

In 1907 Locke became the first black Rhodes Scholar to go to Oxford University. It was not straightforward as some white American students refused to live in the same quarters or attend the same sessions as Locke. He eventually found a place at Hertford College where he studied through to 1910 before a further year at Berlin University.

Locke gained his PhD from Harvard in 1917. He taught philosophy at Howard University from 1912 to 1954. Close friends and associates knew Locke to be gay but he was aware of the legal and political implications if he were to go public about his sexuality.

Suffering from heart disease Locke died aged sixty-nine on June 9th 1957. His ashes were bizarrely kept in an almost casual manner for many years before they were eventually buried at the Congressional Cemetery in Washington DC fifty-seven years later on September 13th 2014. On his headstone Locke is described as 'the exponent of cultural pluralism'.

American sprint athlete **Michael Johnson,** born **on this day** 1967, dominated the 200 and 400m in his thirteen-year career through the 1990s. Anchoring the US relay 4 x 400 team he still holds (as of 2020) the record set in 1993 Stuttgart at 2:54.29. The four times Olympic gold winner and eight times World Champion gold medallist held the 200m world record set at the Atlanta 1996 Olympics at 19.32. In setting the record time Johnson was clocked running at 23 mph. In Seville 1999 he set the 400m world record at 43.18. At the Sydney Olympics Johnson became the first male athlete to successfully defend his 400m title.

He held the 300m record as well as the 400m indoor record. Michael Johnson still holds national records in the 200m, 300m and 400m.

Record-breaking Olympian Michael Johnson.

Born June 16th 1971 **Tupac Shakur** (**2Pac**) was one of his generation's most influential and gifted rappers. He was shot dead while sitting in his car waiting at traffic lights **on this day** in 1996. Shakur had a troubled life where life imitated art and art imitates life. The gangster rap lifestyle often glories in living close to the edge rubbing shoulders with criminals and street gangs arguing that the lyrics only represent the harsh realities of their lives. Tupac died aged twenty-five, often telling it like it is rather than telling it as it could be.

Tupac Shakur

Notorious B.I.G

On March 10th 1997 **Notorious B.I.G** (Christopher Wallace) age twenty-four was shot dead.

Sitting in his car at traffic lights in Los Angeles 2 Pac was gunned down. It is believed that a rift had taken place between East and West Coast performers six months earlier, when at lights seated in his car, **Tupac Shakur** was gunned down.

Sept 14th:

Cameroon writer and diplomat **Ferdinand Leopold Oyono** was born **on this day** in 1929. Oyono and fellow countryman and author, **Mongo Beti,** are seen as the forefathers of modern African identity.

Oyono wrote three books, the anti-colonialist activist novels, largely autobiographical, are considered classics of twentieth-century African literature. He wrote in French while studying in Paris. *Une Vie de Boy* (1956), translated as 'Houseboy' in 1966 tells the story of Toundi who turns away from traditional tribal values only to discover that the white colonialists, that he had been enthralled by, are only human and infallible. The book is praised for its straightforward language, realism and use of humour. Toundi discovers that none of the white, larger than life, characters rise above moral mediocrity.

Le Vieux Negre et al Médaille (1956) translated as 'The Old Man and the Medal' in 1967 tells the story of Meka who is rewarded with a medal for embracing French culture and rejecting his African tradition. Oyono is critical of his compatriots who let themselves be controlled, aspiring to European colonialist values and wearing western clothes often inappropriate in Africa. He portrays the white people as being insincere with their friendships, always wanting to control and be in charge. Meka eventually discovers the difference between sugary words and behaviour. Events teach the protagonist that even if he adopts French manners, they cannot shield him from the degrading restrictions of the indigenous code.

Oyono attempted to make his countrymen aware of the disastrous effects of colonialism. The third novel, *Chemin d'Europe* (1960), translated as 'Road to Europe' in 1989 continues the theme asking what price to pay for assimilation? The novels dissect the anatomy of the assimilationists' dream. How can one ever be good enough when faced with duplicitous colonial behaviour? Oyono is also critical of African tradition which proved weak allowing the colonialists in and then allowed the culture to be undermined. His writings showed that white people and culture could be mocked.

Oyono's, writing and acting career was brief. He ventured into the world of politics focusing on being a diplomat, representing his country at various levels. From 1961–62 Oyono was special envoy to Guinea, Mali, Senegal, and Morocco. He was the ambassador to Liberia, the Benelux countries and the European Common Market. As ambassador to France, he worked closely with Italy, Tunisia, Morocco and Algeria. From 1974–82 Oyono was Cameroon's permanent representative to the United Nations. He served as chairman of UNICEF from 1977–78 and was ambassador to the UK 1984–85.

Ferdinand Oyono returned to Cameroon from his globetrotting diplomacy to work in a variety of cabinet posts. He died having collapsed at the presidential palace, following a visit from the UN Secretary General Ban Ki Moon on June 10th 2010. Oyono was eighty.

Sept 15th:

The 16th Street Baptist Church bombing occurred **on this day** in 1963. It could be argued that white supremacist terrorism, on that morning, had stooped to an all-time low, but the deaths of four girls; **Addie Mae Collins,** 14 (born April 18th 1949), **Carol Denise McNair,** 11 (November 17th 1951), **Carole Robertson,** 14 (April 24th 1949) and **Cynthia Wesley,** 14 (April 30th 1949), although horrific, the four names are but a small part of a long list of atrocities suffered at the hands of warped white supremacists.

Nineteen sticks of dynamite had been secreted in the church building. Years later the niece, Elizabeth Cobb, of accused Robert Chambliss would say she heard her uncle claim that he had enough explosives to flatten Birmingham, Alabama. Threatening racist behaviour from white supremacists' groups like the KKK were so common the city of Birmingham had been nicknamed 'Bombingham' having had twenty-one separate bomb attacks against the city's beleaguered black community in the eight years prior to 1963.

All too often, and understandably so, the focus is placed on the dead. **Sarah Collins**, twelve-year-old sister of Addie Mae lost the sight in one eye having had twenty-one pieces of glass embedded in her face. Sarah was one of fourteen injured.

Later that morning **Virgil Ware,** 13, was shot in the face and chest by Larry Joe Sims, 16, accompanied by Michael Lee Farley, 16. The teenagers, unaware of the bombing, were returning from a supremacist meeting when they claimed the gun went off by accident killing Ware. Both were given two years' probation. Virgil Ware was buried by the roadside in an unidentified grave. On May 6th 2004 his remains were moved to an appropriate burial place and given a bronze marker following donations. That same day police officer Jack Parker shot **Johnny Robinson,** 16, in the back. He claimed he had only shot in the air as a warning. Forty-eight-year-old Parker was never charged with the murder. Only a few days later he would add his name to a petition to keep Birmingham's police force, like the firefighters, all white.

The explosion shook houses two blocks away from the church breaking many windows in neighbouring buildings. All but one of the church's stained-glass windows were shattered. A man was blown out of his vehicle. The girls' bodies were found piled on top of each other. One was decapitated, another was killed by a mortar embedded in her head. The explosion sent shock waves through the city, an alarmed country and onlooking world. A witness said the girls' bodies were propelled through the air like ragdolls. Before the bomb exploded **Carolyn Maull,** 14, took a warning call. She recalled hearing "three minutes". Less than a minute later the church was engulfed by a huge explosion.

Bobby Frank Cherry, Thomas Blanton, Robert Chambliss and Herman Frank Cash emerged as the main suspects by 1965. They were not charged due to a lack of physical evidence and the reluctance of witnesses to come forward. Alabama Attorney General Bill Baxley re-opened the case in 1976 which led to Chambliss, 73, being charged on September 26th 1977. On November 15th 1977 Chambliss was sentenced for first degree murder and given life imprisonment for the murder of Carol Denise McNair. He died in prison 1985, aged eighty-one.

Ku Klux Klan member Cash died in 1994 without being charged, aged seventy-five. New evidence led the FBI to reopen the case in July 1997. Blanton and Cherry were charged on May 16th 2000. A year later on May 1st 2001 Blanton was given four life sentences. He would be denied parole on Aug 3rd 2016 and died in prison on June 26th in 2020, aged eighty-two. May 22nd 2002 saw Cherry given four life sentences for his role in the bombing. He died in prison on November 8th 2004, aged seventy-four. The KKK members responsible for the events **on this day** in 1963 lived a combined total of 312 years and only served a total of twenty-nine years in prison. The four girls lived a brief total of fifty-three years.

The 16th Street Baptist Church was declared a national historic landmark on Feb 20th 2006. A bronze and steel statue of the girls was unveiled on September 14th in 2013 standing in Kelly Ingram Park, Birmingham, Alabama.

Jamaican poet and novelist **Claude McKay,** a key member of the Harlem Renaissance, was born **on this day** in 1889. He would use verse to celebrate everyday local life in rural Jamaica and poetry to protest economic inequalities. He was encouraged to write in the local dialect. In 1977 the Jamaican government named McKay, who took US citizenship in 1940, the country's national poet.

Claude McKay was not afraid to show his hatred of, and to challenge racism in his work. The 1919 poem 'If We Must Die' challenged the appalling events of the Red Summer of that same year where black Americans were being attacked and threatened across the States. McKay wrote two autobiographical books; *A Long Way Home* (1937) and *My Green Hills of Jamaica* published posthumously in 1979. His most famous novel was the award-winning *Home to Harlem* (1929) covering street life in the black centre of Manhattan. The depiction is an honest view of life in Harlem. McKay wrote *Banjo* (1929), which looked at how the French treated Sub-Saharan Africans and *Banana Bottom* in 1933.

McKay had always been drawn to Communism and even wrote glowingly of his stay in the Soviet Union. Towards the end of his life, he converted to Catholicism in 1944.

The writer died aged fifty-eight from a heart attack on May 22nd in 1948. Poetry published during his life included *Harlem Shadows*, Constab Ballads, *Songs of Jamaica* all in 1912 and *Gingertown* in 1932.

Claude McKay is buried in Calvary Cemetery in Queens, New York.

Sept 16th:

Born in Africa in 1778 and enslaved in what is today Guyana, **Quamina** was executed **on this day** in 1823. The enslaved population wanted better conditions, fed up of their servitude. The unrest led to the **Demerara slave uprising**, one of the largest of its kind.

Quamina

Quamina a senior church deacon who could read and write was not spared the humiliation of slavery. On one occasion he was beaten so badly that he was unable to work for six weeks. When his then wife Peggy was seriously ill, he was forced to continuously work only to eventually return home to find his wife dead. When word spread about the uprising Quamina urged his son John and other leaders to strike and not resort to violence.

The uprising started on August 18th 1823 and lasted two days. An estimated 10,000 rose up imprisoning many whites. Few were hurt but as is often the case the plantation owners sought revenge to make examples of the rebels. Hundreds were killed in skirmishes. Two hundred were beheaded. Quamina, who had called for restraint, was seen by the authorities as a ring-leader. He was captured and executed on September 16th 1823. His body was left hanging by the public roadside as a warning to others. Quamina's son John was sold and deported to St Lucia along with other ring leaders. Quamina is recognised as a Guyanese national hero.

Allan Glaisyer Minns born in the Bahamas in 1858 became the first mayor of African descent in Britain serving two one-year terms in Thetford Norfolk. Minns trained as a doctor at Guy's Hospital in London. He moved to Thetford to join his older brother, also a doctor.

Minns was elected to the town council in 1903. The following year, 1904, he was unanimously voted in for his first one-year term as mayor. Minns served a second term taking him through to 1906. His involvement in local politics saw Minns appointed as the chief magistrate for the borough. His son, Allan

Noel Minns, also a doctor, would serve as one of the few black officers in the British army during the Great War.

It had previously been believed, incorrectly, that **John Archer** (see June 8th) mayor of Battersea, the first black mayor in London, was Britain's first black mayor.

Papua New Guinea gained independence **on this day** in 1975 from Australia. **Sir Michael Somare** served as the county's first independence prime minister. He

Michael Somare. An elderly citizen of Papua New Guinea.

would dominate the political landscape serving as prime minister for seventeen years from 1975–80, 1982–85, and 2002–11. He retired in 2017.

Australian Aboriginal **Oodgeroo Noonuccal** was born on November 3rd 1929 christened **Kathleen Ruska.** She belonged to the Noonuccal people of Minjerribah (Stradbroke Island) part of South East Queensland.

The political activist, environmental campaigner, artist, educator and poet would be commonly recognised as **Kath Walker** following her marriage to Bruce Walker of the Gugingin people in 1942. Aged twenty-one, Noonuccal joined the Australian Women's Army Service. Two brothers had been captured by the Japanese in Singapore. Noonuccal would later say that at the time there were only two places where an Aboriginal could get an education, either in the army or in prison and she was not about to go to jail.

Joining the Communist Party Noonuccal found her political voice and developed her poetry. She became the first Aboriginal poet published in Australia, and the first Aboriginal woman published, for 1964's *We Are Going,* her first volume of poetry. She is respected as the first of the modern-day Aboriginal protest writers. Her unsophisticated accessible poetry is recognised and appreciated for the genuine accounts of Aboriginal loss, dispossession, outlining their plight yet signalling hope for the future. Her work includes *The Dawn is at Hand* (1966), *My People: A Kath Walker Collection* (1970), *Stradbroke Dream* (1972), which contains stories of the author's childhood and Aboriginal folktales.

Oodgeroo Noonuccal was active in the 1967 Referendum arguing for Aboriginal rights as citizens to be counted in the country's census and to not be treated as 'flora and fauna'. Visiting the Prime Minister Robert Menzies, he offered Noonuccal a glass of sherry only to be reminded by his guest that it was illegal to offer an Aboriginal alcohol. In the referendum the poet campaigned to abolish discriminatory anti-Aboriginal sections of the Australian Constitution. A win would allow the national government to legislate for Aboriginal rights rather than having six different sets of laws from six different states.

Returning to Minjerribah in 1971 Noonuccal opened a learning centre called 'Moongalba', the sitting down place, to teach about indigenous culture. Noonuccal received an MBE (Member of the British Empire) in 1970 but returned the award in 1987 to protest against the Australia Day bicentennial celebrations of 1987. Kath Walker changed her name that same year to Oodgeroo, meaning paperbark tree, and Noonuccal her tribe. She died aged seventy-two of cancer **on this day** in 1993.

'Rapper's Delight', released **on this day** in 1979, made music history becoming the first hip hop track to chart. Although not the first hip hop track, it was the first to reach a wider audience, and arguably the best track of the genre. Released to Chic's 'Good Times' **the Sugar Hill Gang** would see the single top the Canadian chart, go top three in the UK and make the top 40 in the United States.

On this day 1986 South Africa experienced **the Kinross goldmine disaster.** One hundred and seventy-seven miners were killed. It's believed that a welder's spark ignited an acetylene tank creating flames that spread through the tunnels, along the plastic that covered the wiring, and burned the polyurethane foam that covered the mine walls, used to keep walls dry. The toxic fumes spread through the mine choking its victims. Two hundred and thirty-five were injured and one missing. The wall covering used had already been banned in the UK and Australia. The mine owners were accused of negligence. A major strike and protests led to higher safety expectations. The 1986 disaster was the worst in South African history since 1946.

Sept 17th:

On this day in 1849, **Harriet Tubman,** known as Moses to those she led to safety, escaping to freedom. Born **Araminta Ross** she would take her mother's name Harriet Green later in life.

The young Harriet was hired out aged five as a nursemaid, where she experienced the cruelty of slavery. She would be whipped when the baby in her charge cried. Aged seven she was rented out, setting animal traps then later working as a field hand. Aged twelve Araminta was struck in the head by a 2lb weight. She had been caught getting involved between a fellow slave and an overseer. Failing to support the overseer's instructions, she was struck in the head. The incident left her with a broken skull, a scar and lifelong complications of headaches, seizures, and narcolepsy. Harriet would have vivid dreams and hallucinations often referring to these as visions. The list of infirmities made the young Harriet unattractive as a commercial property.

In 1840, her father, Benjamin Ross, aged forty-five, was set free. Unfortunately, his wife Harriet and their eight children were still enslaved as the new owner refused to recognise the previous owner's wishes expressed in his will. It was at this time Araminta adopted her mother's name becoming Harriet. Harriet met John Tubman, a free man, the couple married in 1844. The relationship was never harmonious or settled and was littered with a variety of problems.

Discovering plans to sell her younger brothers, Ben and Henry, led Harriet to organise an escape. **On this day 1849** Harriet travelled 90 miles along the Underground Railroad, a network of safe houses, making it to Pennsylvania. Fearing capture and its consequence with a bounty of $300 for their return, Ben and Henry voluntarily gave themselves up. Living in Philadelphia it was not long before Harriet felt the need to return to help others escape. Between 1850 and 1860 Harriet risked her freedom and life returning nineteen times to the South. The Fugitive Slave Act of 1850 demanded runaways travel further north, often to Canada before safety could be guaranteed. The Act legally encouraged hunters to capture runaways returning them to their former owners. Harriet would travel with a gun, not just for her own safety but also to drive on runaway slaves, who began to have doubts. She would drug babies and children to stop them crying and revealing their whereabouts. Her mother and brother Benjamin were led to freedom in 1857. Harriet encouraged her husband to move north but he remarried, content to live in Maryland. The activist and conductor on the Underground Railroad Harriet became friends and associates with many abolitionists of the day including **Frederick Douglass**, (see February 14th) **Thomas Garrett** and **Martha Coffin Wright** (see December 25th). In 1858 she met **John Brown** (see December 2nd) who she called a martyr. He would call her 'General Tubman'. She opened her own Underground Railroad network thrilled to have never lost a passenger. She led seventy people to freedom. Some figures argue that Harriet was responsible for 300 fugitives escaping.

The Civil War, 1861, saw Harriet recruited to assist escaped slaves stationed at Fort Monroe. She worked as a cook, nurse and did the laundry. Later in the conflict Harriet played an important role as a Unionist spy. She was able to scout, recording information, providing invaluable intelligence, mapping Confederate army positions and their supply routes. Harriet was employed to help fugitive slaves form the Black Union Regiment. She became the first woman in the American field of battle to lead an armed expedition guiding the Combahee River raid, liberating more than 700 in South Carolina.

After the war Tubman settled in New York marrying former slave and Civil War veteran **Nelson Davis** in 1869. Her former husband had died in 1867. Her home was an open affair offering comfort to anyone in need. She had to rely on loans and donations from family and friends while selling home grown produce to survive. The government took thirty years to pay Harriet for her work during the war. After repeated requests she eventually received a $20 monthly pension.

Harriet leant her name to the women's suffrage movement. Being illiterate never held her back. She would go on speaking tours promoting the vote for women. Nelson died of tuberculosis in 1888.

Land adjacent to Harriet's home was purchased leading to the establishment of the Harriet Tubman Home for Indigent and Coloured People on 23rd June 1908. Harriet would become a resident in 1911 following brain surgery to relieve the lifelong pain that she had in her head. Harriet Tubman died from pneumonia March 10th 1913. Some say she was ninety-three but with no record to confirm the date or year of her birth we may never know her exact age. Plans were announced for Tubman's image to appear on the $20 bill. At the time of writing little promised progress had been made.

Andrew 'Rube' Foster, born **on this day** in 1879, would be called **the father of black baseball.** Foster started playing at seventeen. The six foot four pitcher played for several teams including an integrated team in the semi-professional league in Michigan.

Baseball had a racial colour line following a 'gentleman's agreement'. By 1887 it was made clear that no black player should be signed. Creeping Jim Crow segregation spread like an infection through American sport and society. It was not until **Jackie Robinson's** signing (see April 15th) for the Brooklyn Dodgers in 1947 that the colour bar was finally broken.

Andrew 'Rube' Foster.

Foster gained the nickname Rube having out pitched the Philadelphia Athletic star pitcher Rube Waddell taking his name as a trophy. Pitching for the Cuban X-Giants, Foster came to prominence. His team won four of the seven-game series against the Philadelphia Giants in the Coloured Championship of the World in 1903. The 1905 season saw Foster total fifty-one victories out of fifty-five. As star pitcher and manager of the Leyland Giants he guided the team to a 110 to 10 victories with forty-eight consecutive wins in 1907.

The innovative strategist and aggressive management style saw continued success. In 1910 Foster acquired the Leyland Giants leading the team to a 123 to 6 record that season. The following year Foster formed the Chicago American Giants with business partner John Schorling. The Giants won the 'Negro League' in 1914, 1915 and 1917.

Rube Foster met with seven owners in Kansas City, Missouri, 1920 and the Negro National League (NNL) was formed. Under Foster's guidance, and as its first president, the NNL thrived. It proved to be the longest lasting of all the black baseball leagues from 1920 to 1930. His team the Chicago American Giants would win the NNL in 1920, 1921 and 1922.

Stress took its toll with Foster experiencing mental illness and being admitted to a mental hospital in Kankakee, Illinois in 1926. He died four years later on December 9th in 1930. He was elected to the Baseball Hall of Fame in 1981.

Sept 18th

Inspired by rock'n'roll and electric blues, **Jimi Hendrix** was born Johnny Allen Hendrix, November 27th 1942. His father changed his son's name to James Marshall Hendrix. He would be a, if not the, pioneering force in exploring the explosive possibilities of the electric guitar.

Given his first acoustic guitar in 1958, later that year Hendrix briefly played with The Velvetones. The next year he was given an electric guitar and started performing with The Rocking Kings. Enlisting in the US Army in 1960 Hendrix was discharged following an injury in a parachute jump. Hendrix's playing ability was respected as a session musician he played for **Ike and Tina Turner, The Isley Brothers,**

Sam Cooke (see December 11th) and **Little Richard** (see December 5th). Leaving Richards, Hendrix launched out to play at the front of the stage.

Guitar hero Jimi Hendrix

    Meeting bassist Chas Chandler of the Animals in New York City, 1965, Chandler signed Hendrix the following year. He changed Hendrix's stage name from Jimmy James to Jimi Hendrix and created a trio with Mitch Mitchell on drums and Noel Redding on bass forming The Jimi Hendrix Experience. The group took London by storm. Their first single 'Hey Joe' peaked at number 6 in the UK charts, 1967. Later that year they released their first album 'Are You Experienced?' Prominent tracks included 'Purple Haze' and 'Foxy Lady'.

    Hendrix's career took off in the United States when he performed 'Wild Thing' at the Monterey International Pop Festival in June of 1967. The second album 'Axis: Bold as Love' was released in 1968. Taking greater control of his music Hendrix built his studio, Electric Lady Studios, where the double album 'Electric Ladyland' was recorded. The critical and commercial success would be Hendrix's only number one album in the USA. Touring commitments saw The Jimi Hendrix Experience split. Hendrix headlined at Woodstock in Aug 1969 remembered for his rendition of the 'Star Spangled Banner', playing with an assortment of musicians making up the 'Gypsy Sun and Rainbows'. Four performances on December 31st and January 1st 1970 with the 'Band of Gypsies' resulted in an album release in 1970. From those performances 'Hendrix: Live at the Fillmore East' was released in 1999.

Jimi Hendrix headlined at the Isle of Wight Festival in 1970. The Jimi Hendrix Experience was reformed that same year with Mitchell and Billy Cox on bass. Recording material for the new double album 'Rays of the New Rising Sun' had started but would not be completed. After an amazing four years, Jimi Hendrix died **on this day** in 1970. The guitar icon had embraced blues, rock, jazz, R&B, psychedelia and ballads redefining popular music. He became part of the infamous '27 Club'. He spent his last hours with Monika Dannemann who said she awoke to find Hendrix breathing but unconscious. The ambulance was called at 11.18 a.m. arriving just 9 minutes later. Jimi Hendrix was pronounced dead at 12.45 by Dr John Bannister. It was concluded that the legendary self-taught musician had asphyxiated on his own vomit while intoxicated, having taken barbiturates.

Cuban pilot **Arnaldo Tamayo Mendez,** born January 29th 1942, became the **first person of African heritage to travel into space.** Following the Cuban Revolution Mendez joined the Cuban Air Force in 1960 and trained in the Soviet Union flying MiG-15s in 1961 and 1962. Returning home the newly qualified nineteen-year-old combat pilot flew twenty reconnaissance flights during the Cuban Missile Crisis.

Selected as part of the Soviet Union's interkosmos programme March 1st 1978, Mendez undertook two and a half years training as a guest cosmonaut. He travelled into space alongside Soviet Yury Romanenko on Soyuz 38. Docking with the Salyut 6 Space Station, Mendez became the first Cuban, first Latin American and first person of African descent into space. Scientific experiments were conducted during the eight days that saw the cosmonauts orbit the earth 124 times.

The political significance of Mendez's flight into space was important propaganda as the Soviets beat the USA in placing a man of colour into space. Mendez returned to Earth to be showered with honours receiving the Hero of the Republic of Cuba medal, named Hero of the Soviet Union and receiving the Order of Lenin. Mendez became a member of the Cuban legislature as a deputy in the National Assembly of People's Power in 1980. Mendez continued his career as a military officer rising to the rank of brigadier general.

For stories of black achievements in space see, Mae Carol Jenison (October 17th), Ronald McNair & Michael P Anderson (January 28th), Guion Bluford and Frederick D Gregory (November 22nd).

Arnaldo Tamayo Mendez.

Brazilian football superstar **Ronaldo Nazario,** "O Fenomeno" (the phenomenon), was born **on this day** in 1976. It took his father four days to register the birth leaving some to believe that Ronaldo was born on the 22nd September.

At seventeen, Ronaldo was the youngest player in the world beating Brazilian team of 1994, he never played at the tournament held in the USA. The 1998 FIFA World Cup in France saw Ronaldo win the Golden Boot as the tournament's top goal scorer. Four years later Ronaldo would grace the world's stage scoring twice for Brazil, the tournament's winners, in the final. He won the title and the Golden Boot, in Japan/South Korea, 2002. His fifteenth World Cup final goal in 2006, Germany, saw Ronaldo become the then highest goal scorer in World Cup history.

Making his international debut March 23rd 1994 Ronaldo played ninety-eight times and scored sixty-two goals for Brazil. He stands as his county's third highest goal scorer. In 1997 Brazil won the Copa America in Bolivia. Ronaldo was voted player of the tournament with five goals one behind the Golden Boot winner Mexico's Luis Hernandez. 1999's Copa America saw Brazil win the tournament for a sixth time in Paraguay. Ronald was the competitions' top scorer, along with Rivaldo, both with five goals.

The domestic game saw Ronaldo signed to PSV Eindhoven in 1994. Records and goals continued when he signed for a then record fee to Barcelona in 1996. That season he netted forty-seven times in forty-nine games leading the Catalonian side to the UEFA's Cup Winners Cup. At twenty-one, Ronaldo became the youngest recipient of the Ballon d'Or in 1997. He would repeat the feat in 2002.

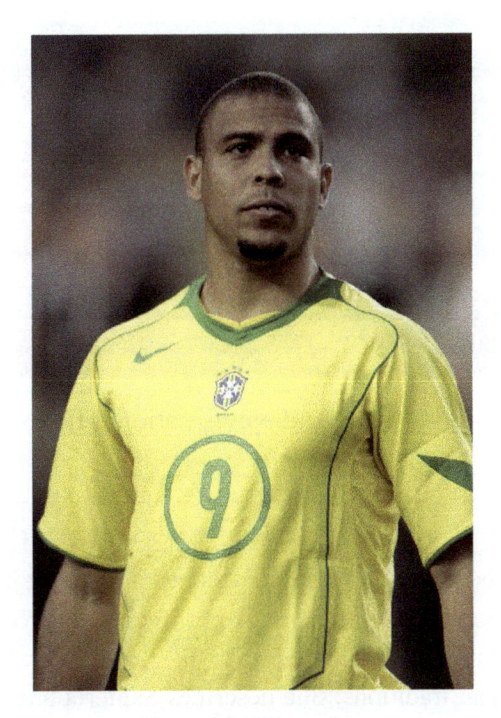

Ronaldo Nazario.

Contractual issues saw Ronaldo sign for Inter Milan for another record-breaking fee. That 1997/8 season saw him emerge as La Liga's top scorer with thirty-four goals in thirty-seven matches receiving the Golden Shoe as Europe's top goal scorer in the continent's top leagues. Ronaldo scored in Inter Milan's 3-0 victory over Lazio in the UEFA Cup final, 1998, where he was voted 'man of the match'. By twenty-three, Ronaldo had scored over 200 times for club and country. That year the Phenomenon was voted Serie A's Footballer of the Year.

Injuries became part of Ronaldo's story, first appearing against Lecce on November 21st 1999. He would be out of the game for almost three seasons after it appeared that his kneecap exploded. Fighting his way back to fitness, Ronaldo signed for Real Madrid in 2002 winning La Liga that year. He scored twenty-three times that season winning the Intercontinental Cup for Real versus Olimpia of Paraguay on December 3rd 2002. Ronaldo scored and was 'man of the match'. The 2003 Spanish Super Cup was lifted by Real Madrid with Renaldo scoring against Mallorca in the final. Ronaldo Nazario is recognised and respected as one of the greatest forwards and footballers of all time. He retired from playing in 2011 but continues to be involved in the game. See **Pele** June 21st and **Arthur Friedenreich** July 18th.

Sept 19th:

Saint Kitts and Nevis gained their independence **on this day** in 1983 from Britain. **Kennedy A. Simmonds** became prime minister in 1980. When the country gained independence, Simmonds was hailed as the Father of the Nation. He remained in power through to 1995. In 2004 the former prime minister became Sir Kennedy Simmonds. It was announced **on this day** in 2015 that Kennedy Simmonds would become a National Hero, the fifth person to be given the honour and the first living hero

Saint Kitts and Nevis national flag.

White Cuban **Lydia Cabrera** born May 20th 1900 developed an interest in ethnography focusing on Afro-Cuban people, their culture, customs and religions. A prolific writer producing over one hundred books, few available in English, Cabrera's most famous work *El Monte, The Wilderness* (1954), was the first ethnographic study of Afro-Cuban traditions. She describes Santeria and Ifa religious traditions from the African diaspora, of Yoruba origin, developed in Cuba between the 16th & 19th centuries. Cabrera also looked at Palo Monte originally found in Central Africa. Lydia Cabrera is credited with transforming Afro-Cuban oral narratives into literature. Her second publication *Por Que* ('Why'?) is a collection of twenty-eight short stories recording religious rituals and traditions. Cabrera collected folklore, often interviewing former enslaved people, providing a marginalised Afro-Cuban community with an identity, a history and respectability. She found a way of telling Cuban history through the stories of the Afro-Cubans and from their perspective.

Lydia Cabrera left Cuba after the revolution. Her extensive work and papers were left at the Cuban Heritage Collection at the University of Miami in Florida. Cabrera died **on this day** aged ninety-one in 1991.

One of the **Little Rock Nine** (see September 5th and 11th) **Jefferson Thomas** was born **on this day** in 1942. He would be one of only three from the nine to graduate from Central High in 1960. Thomas narrated the Academy Award-winning documentary *Nine from Little Rock* (1964). He would enlist in the army serving in Vietnam. After the war Thomas worked for Mobile Oil before becoming an accountant for the US Department of Defence. Jefferson Thomas was a Civil Rights activist regularly speaking at schools, colleges and universities. He was the first and, at the time of writing in 2020, the only member of the Nine to have died. Thomas died of pancreatic cancer aged sixty-seven on September 5th 2010. He is buried at Forest Lawn Memorial Park in Glendale, California.

Dancer **Arthur Mitchell** would become the first African American to be the principal dancer for a major American company. The charismatic ballet dancer experienced national & international recognition with the New York City Ballet. The premier of *Argon* (1957), a piece choreographed by George Balanchine, saw Mitchell dance with Diana Adams. Their performance was a critical success. Mitchell played the role of Puck from *A Midsummer Night's Dream* in 1962, again working with Balanchine. The performance reinforced Mitchell as one of the world's major stars of ballet.

The assassination of Dr Martin Luther King in 1968 led Arthur Mitchell to co-found, with Karel Shook, the Dance Theatre of Harlem, America's major black classical ballet company in 1969. He argued his major success would be to bring a black audience to the art and to present black dancers to a wider public. Arthur Mitchell, dancer and choreographer, died of heart failure aged eighty-four **on this day** in 2018.

Arthur Mitchell.

Sept 20th:

Believed to have been born **on this day** in 1758 **Jean-Jacques Dessalines** would be one of the main leaders instrumental in the founding of independent Haiti.

Born into slavery, Dessalines could not read or write but was a brilliant soldier and talented military leader. He joined with **Toussaint L'Ouverture** (see May 20th) fighting against the French with the Spanish on the island of Hispaniola (today Haiti and Dominican Republic). When France declared the end of slavery in 29th August 1794, in the French Caribbean, L'Ouverture and Dessalines turned to fighting the invading British and Spanish armies. The French Revolution allowed the independent fighters of Saint Domingue (Haiti) to seize control and declare independence in 1804.

L'Ouverture had been freed from enslavement in 1776. He led the initial slave uprising in 1791. It would lead to the only successful slave rebellion and the creation of the first modern black republic. L'Ouverture had tied himself closely with France copying many French political systems and cultural practices. He felt that he could diplomatically work with France. This alignment led to L'Ouverture's betrayal, capture and murder. Dessalines had been L'Ouverture's lieutenant. He spoke clearly to his soldiers and united the men. Having a distrust of the white colonists, and the French in particular, when Napoleon threatened to reinstate slavery, Dessalines had no option but to engage the French forces. The revolution that started in 1791 came to an end at the battle of Vertieres on 18th November 1803. Dessalines' forces defeated the French.

Jean Jacques Dessalines.

The following year a declaration of independence was published with Saint Domingue becoming Haiti, the original name used by the indigenous Taino people. Dessalines was the governor general from November 1803. He was declared emperor September 22nd 1804 and crowned Emperor Jacques I of Haiti in October of that year.

Declaring Haiti, a black nation, Dessalines distrusted the whites as former colonialists, slave owners and the enemy as represented by the French, British and Spanish forces faced over the previous decade. He took land owned by white people and made it illegal for them to own property. Fearing an uprising and allegiance with France, Dessalines killed between 3,000 to 5,000 white inhabitants in what is known as the Haitian Massacre of 1804. Jean-Jacques Dessalines' autocratic style saw many rebellions. An uprising of mulattos led by Alexandre Petion would lead to the emperor's capture and assassination on October 17th in 1806. The mutilated body was retrieved by **Dedee Bazile** (Defilee) and buried. The country's national anthem, 1903, was named La Dessalinienne in his honour. Unrest continued after Dessalines' death. Petion and **Henri Christophe** (see October 6th) eventually divided power between themselves.

One of nine Namibian national heroes, represented at Heroes Acre, opened on August 26th 2002, **Jacob Morenga** was born in 1875. The revolutionary figure is famed for leading a guerrilla resistance against the German colonists in what was called German South West Africa.

Morenga was able to unite the rival Herero Bantu ethnic group with the Namaqua, the largest of the Khoikhoi people. He was born to a Herero mother and a Nama father. Opposing German occupation Morenga set out with just 11 men. His tactical approach, amazing horsemanship and knowledge of the land saw military success in the period of insurrection from 1904–1908. The initial eleven rose to 300 fighters by 1905. Such was Morenga's success on the field of battle an emergency election was called in the German Reichstag, January 15th 1907, following heavy German losses.

Morenga was famed for his strategic thinking as his men lived off captured enemy supplies. Facing state of the art weapons and a modern army Jacob Morenga was eventually captured by South African police after more than fifty battles. The British forces imprisoned their captive but released him on the promise that he would not return to German South West Africa.

Morenga soon broke the agreement. He gathered the remnants of his fighting force to attack German troops and oppose German occupation. The tactical genius was nicknamed 'der schwarze Napoleon' (the black Napoleon) by his opponents. After the battle of Rooysvlei, Morenga was forced to flee seeking refuge in the Kalahari Desert. Tracked down by joint British and German forces the freedom fighter Jacob Morenga was shot and killed **on this day** in 1907. See Namibian heroes January 6th; Chief Mandume ya Ndemufayo.

Academic, doctor, diplomat, writer and poet **Dr Davidson Nicol** was born in Sierra Leone on September 14th 1924. He would become the first black African to graduate with a first-class honours from Cambridge University in 1946. He would be the first black African elected as a Fellow of a Cambridge College in 1957, the first in either Cambridge or Oxford. Nicol completed his PhD in 1958.

Davidson would make a breakthrough in medical science being the first to analyse the breakdown of insulin in the human body, leading to improved treatment in diabetes. Nicol wrote and lectured widely on medical topics.

Appointed as the first black African principal of Fourah Bay College in Freetown Sierra Leone, Nicol served from 1960–68. He was vice-chancellor of the University of Sierra Leone from 1966–68. Venturing into diplomacy Nicol was the permanent representative to the United Nations as his country's ambassador from 1969–71. He held a variety of positions at the UN from 1969–1980: executive director of the UN Institute for Training and Research, 1972–82 and president of the World Federation of UN Associations 1983–87.

As an author Dr Davidson Nicol published *Two African Tales* (1965) and *The Truly Married Woman and Other Stories* (1965). He wrote fiction under the name Abioseh Nicol. Two other notable works include *Africa, A Subjective View* (1965) and *Creative Women* in 1982. The doctor died on September 20th in 1994, aged seventy.

Ursula Burns was born to Panamanian immigrants in the United States **on this day** in 1958. She rose from humble beginnings becoming the **first black woman CEO of a Forbes 500 Company.** Burns won an internship at Xerox in 1980 and stayed with the company for the next thirty-six years. Xerox started in 1906, was a byword for photocopying but by the time Burns took over the helm, the company had seen better days and was now being left behind in the new twenty-first-century IT-led world.

Ursula Burns having worked her way up from the bottom, knew the organisation inside out, and was prepared to make important decisions to turn the company around. As CEO from 2009–2016 and Chairwoman of Xerox Corporation 2010–2017 she steered the hardware company towards a software future. In the process Xerox's fortunes were revived, 2015 generating $18 billion, with profits up. Forbes would name Burns as the county's fifth most powerful woman in business and place her at 22nd as the most powerful women in Tech. *Fortune* magazine ranked Burns, at one point, number 17 in a list of world's most powerful women.

Ursula Burns has served on numerous boards including Exxon Mobil, Uber and Veon. She was named executive chairman of Veon, the telecommunication provider based in Amsterdam. Burns served as Veon's CEO from 2018–2020.

Sept 21st:

As illustrated by the **Berlin Conference** (see February 26th), Africa was up for grabs. If land, resources and power could not be acquired 'legitimately' then other pressures were brought to bear. The son of the great Ngoni King Zwangendaba, **Mpezeni** was born in what is present day Zambia 1830. The warrior king's story is just one of numerous attempts to resist European control.

Mpezeni had been courted by Europeans wishing to acquire land and mineral concessions. The king had turned down several advances before reaching terms with the German, Karl Weise who then sold his 'rights' to the London based North Charterland Company (NCC), a subsidiary of the British South African Company. When Ngoni warriors attacked Weise and the NCC in a bid to reclaim their land and rights, the British military responded, forcing Mpezeni to surrender in 1898. In defeat the king was given the title of paramount. To this day his ancestors still retain the title Paramount Chief Mpezeni. Mpezeni died **on this day** in 1900.

Born in Martinique **on this day** in 1928, poet, novelist and theorist, **Edouard Glissant** is recognised as one of, if not, the most important theoretician and cultural thinkers from the Caribbean. Glissant is respected in the French and francophone world as one of the greatest thinkers and writers of his time.

He produced eight novels, nine volumes of poetry, one play and fifteen essays. His work reflected on colonialism, slavery, racism but also looked towards a bright future of cultural diversity where culture transcends the Caribbean to become a theory about living globally.

Glissant the poet had to become a philosopher, to distil insight, revealing the fluidity of relation. He desired to break down the emerging walls protecting particular genealogical groups, keeping others out. Glissant insisted that culture was not concrete but continuously transforming. His work was to destabilise and see difference as constructive when viewed as the result of solidarity and conciliation. Such transformative differences are to be celebrated, opening the previously closed doors to systems of discrimination, segregation and rejection. In Glissant's world mentality relation and difference have enormous energy out of which beauty and freedom can be found. The poet moved beyond postcolonial debates towards the possibilities of cultural plurality and globalisation.

Edouard Glissant was a contemporary of **Franz Fanon** (see Dec 6th). The pair studied together at Lycee Victor Schoelcher in Fort-de-France. **Aime Cesaire** (see June 26th) taught at Lycee, but it is not believed Glissant was in his classes. Glissant was influenced by Cesaire and helped to organise his political campaign when Cesaire stood as a communist at the 1945 French parliamentary elections. This period of his life is recounted in Glissant's first novel *La Lezarde* ('The Ripening') in 1958.

In Paris, at the Sorbonne in 1946, Glissant studied philosophy and history. He earned his PhD in ethnography at Musée de l'Homme. It was at this time that his first volume of poetry *Un Champ d'iles (A Field of Islands)* was published in 1956.

Glissant campaigned for independence for Martinique and for other overseas French colonies. He supported Algerian liberation during the Algerian War. His political activities saw French president Charles de Gaulle bar the poet from leaving France from 1961–65.

Returning to Martinique in 1965 Glissant would write two dark novels *Malemort* (*Violent Death*), 1975, a colonial history of Martinique through contemporary experiences. And *La Case du Commandeur (The Overseer's Hut)* in 1981 which follows the family history to discover identity and belonging. Both books were pessimistic and critical, the dark clouds of colonialism overshadow the narrative of personal experience. Other works of note include *Le Discours Antillais* (*Caribbean Discours*) in 1981, *Poetics of Relations* (1990) and *Tout-monde* (1993).

Edouard Glissant died on February 3rd 2011 aged eighty-two.

Ghanaian writer, poet and diplomat **Kofi Awoonor** died **on this day** in 2013, a victim of the Kenyan terrorist attack that took place at the Westgate Shopping Mall in Nairobi. Awoonor was one of sixty-seven murdered that day. His son, Afetsi was one of a hundred and seventy-five injured from the attack. Awoonor had been attending the four-day literary Storymoja Hay Festival.

Kofi Awoonor gained his MA from the University College London in 1970. While in England he wrote plays for BBC radio. He completed his PhD in the USA at Stony Brook University in 1972. While in the United States Awoonor wrote *This Earth, My Brother* a poem about exile and a spiritual return home, looking at a mythical world through the lens of the Ewe people. The Ewe people of West Africa are largely found in Ghana and Togo. Awoonor wrote *Night of My Blood* using traditional Ewe song to lament the loss of cultural and ancestral shrines and gods dazzled by the great cathedrals of western culture. Both books were published in 1971.

Awoonor returned to Ghana in 1975 taking the post as head of English at the University of Cape Coast. He was arrested, accused of being involved in a coup to oust the military government. Arrested and imprisoned without trial Kofi Awoonor wrote *The Home by the Sea* (1976), about his experience in prison that year.

The writer became involved in politics serving as Ghana's ambassador to Brazil, 1984-88, and ambassador to Cuba 1990–94. As Ghana's permanent representative to the United Nations Awoonor headed the Committee against Apartheid. As an Elder and a prominent citizen Kofi Awoonor served on the Council of State advising the president from 2009-2013. Born on March 13th 1935 Awoonor died aged seventy-eight.

Indigenous activist, Aboriginal **Dr Evelyn Ruth Scott** was born in 1935. She became active in politics, fighting for improved treatment for the Aboriginal community in education, employment, housing and health. She was active in the 1967 Constitution Referendum where 90per cent voted to give Aboriginals full citizenship.

Scott joined the Federal Council for the Advancement of Aborigines and Torres Strait Islanders (FCAATSI) in 1971. She became an executive vice president and was central to the organisation being indigenously controlled by 1973. She was chair of the Council for Aboriginal Reconciliation from 1997–2000.

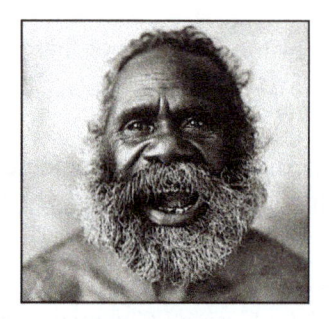

Evelyn Scott promoted greater involvement from the Aboriginal community to have their voices heard concerning the land and sea. She was a passionate campaigner for the preservation of the Great Barrier Reef. Dr Evelyn Scott the indigenous rights, trailblazing, activist died aged eighty-one, **on this day** in 2017.

Belize gained its independence **on this day** 1981 from Britain. **Dame Elmira Gordon** became the country's first governor general. George Price was the first prime minister.

Belize national flag.

Sept 22nd:

Brazilian classical composer, music teacher, organist and priest **Jose Mauricio Nunes Garcia** was born **on this day** 1765. He would write Brazil's first opera *Le Due Genelle* (*The Two Twins*) in 1817.

Jose Mauricio's grandparents were slaves. A natural talent, by the age of twelve he was teaching music. At sixteen, 1783, the teenager composed his first piece 'Tota pulchra Es Maria'. Jose Mauricio would write an estimated five hundred pieces but only 240 have survived. He wrote the 'Funeral Symphony' (1790) for a royal visit.

Jose Mauricio was ordained a priest in 1792. That same year he entered the Brotherhood of São Pedro dos Clérigos in Rio de Janeiro. He became a public music instructor in 1795. The 90s was a productive period of composition. As the chapel master, 1797, Jose Mauricio wrote for religious feasts, marriages and to celebrate births. 'Te Deum' (1798) was written for the birth of the Portuguese Prince D Pedro.

The priest embraced Brazilian popular music and folk style into his liturgical compositions. His requiem mass in honour of dead priests was composed in 1799 as were the Christmas martins. Two overtures *Tempest* and *Zemira* represented a change in musical direction, both were composed in 1803.

Although Jose Mauricio is credited as the first to conduct Mozart's Requiem, in Brazil, and was knighted in 1809, he still faced and suffered racial intolerance. Some felt offended being led by one considered as racially inferior. Internal politics and rivalry saw Jose Mauricio removed from his position as chapel master in 1811. The following year he lost his position as the organist.

His mother and the Queen of Portugal died on the same day, March 20th 1816. This led the composer to produce two of his most famous works 'Requiem Mass; Missa de Mortos' and 'Oficio dos Defuntos'.

Although a priest, as was customary and accepted, he married Severiana Rose de Castro. The couple had six children. He continued to compose, his last work being 'St Celia Mass' in 1826. Financial pressures are believed to have taken their toll on his health. Jose Mauricio died on March 20th 1816. His 'Funeral Symphony", which he had composed forty years earlier was played at his funeral. The classical composing priest was commemorated on a Brazilian stamp in 1973.

One of Africa's most famous and enduring names; **Shaka Zulu** was born in July 1784. **Sigidi kaSenzangakhona** (Shaka) was born to Senzangakhona, a chieftain of the Zulus, and Nandi, an orphaned princess, who belonged to a neighbouring clan, the Langeni. The parents separated when Shaka was six. The couple had violated Zulu custom, making Shaka illegitimate. He grew up fatherless and bullied, living with his mother with the Langeni, before the two were despised and driven out in 1802. Mother and son sought shelter with the Dletsheni, a sub clan of the powerful Mthethwa. Shaka continued to be shunned and bullied, experiences that would shape his future thinking and behaviour.

At the age of twenty-three, the Mthethwa paramount chieftain Dingiswayo called for young men to serve in his army. Shaka thrived in his new environment serving brilliantly for six years. When his father Senzangakhona died in 1816, Shaka was released to take over the Zulus, a small group numbering less than 1,500. The Zulus were the smallest of more than 800 Eastern Nguni-Bantu clans.

Cultural icon with restaurant named after Shaka.

Turning the insignificant clan into a fighting machine and creating the foundations of an empire have defined Shaka. When Dingiswayo was murdered in 1817, Shaka was unfettered to embark on his quest for power. Ambiguity and controversy surrounds Shaka Zulu. He ruled with an iron fist. Opposition was met with death. He revolutionised the army, weapons, shields and introduced a system of regiments adopting new military tactics. Within a year, local small clans had been defeated. Survivors were absorbed into the Zulus and strengthened his army. Shaka was brutal, seeking out those who had bullied him, leaving their bodies impaled on stakes. Conflict was a process of extermination. By 1823 whole areas were left depopulated and tribal patterns in tatters. The Zulu fighting machine quadrupled in size. The resulting chaos caused havoc in the region. Clans fleeing the Zulus seeking new land spread the carnage further inland. The time known as 'Mfecane' (crushing) in the first half of the nineteenth century left two million dead. The Afrikaans Boer Great Trek from the mid-1830s to early 1840s saw 12,000–14,000 Europeans settle. There were no groups to challenge their march occupying the land. Henry Francis Fynn and Nathaniel Isaacs learned to speak Zulu. A lot of what we know about Nguni and Shaka come from their writings.

When Nandi died in 1827 it unleashed a reign of terror born out of Shaka's grief. Pregnant women and their husbands were killed, cows with calves were slaughtered. No crops were planted that year and milk was not permitted to be consumed. It is estimated that Shaka saw 7,000 murdered. The increasingly despotic behaviour led to Dingane and Mhlangana, Shaka' half-brothers, to assassinate the irrational Zulu leader.

The powerful image of a strong, empire building African leader spoke volumes to a colonised and displaced people. He became an iconic figure having left the legacy of Zulus as all conquering, having built an empire. The truth is far more complicated. It reveals a land depopulated, tribal structures and traditions left in tatters and the road open for the Africaans to establish a foothold in southern Africa.

Born **on this day** in 1928 Pastor **James Lawson** was the tactical bedrock behind the non-violent protest of the Civil Rights Movement. In India as a Methodist missionary Lawson discovered Mohandas Gandhi's Satyagraha (truth force). Returning to the USA in 1955 he met **Dr Martin Luther King** (See January 15th, April 4th and August 28th) who urged Lawson to move to the South. In 1958 Lawson was living in Nashville. He would train Civil Rights' students including **Diane Nash** (May 15th), **James Bevel** (see December 19th) and **John Lewis** (see February 21st). His students were at the Nashville sit-ins from February 13th to May 10th in 1960. He was arrested after the Woolworth's sit-ins in Greensboro (see January 3rd). Lawson's activities resulted in him being expelled from Vanderbilt University. The university would apologise in 2006. Lawson taught there from 2006 to 2009.

James Lawson, in the middle, being recognised for his Civil Rights work.

James Lawson developed strategies for the Freedom Riders. Entering a 'whites only' restroom in Jackson, the Riders were arrested. Lawson and the group refused the NAACP's offer to pay bail. At the trial all twenty-seven were found guilty and jailed. It was only with the intervention of Attorney General Robert Kennedy that all were released. President J. F. Kennedy ordered that passengers could sit and rest anywhere in September 1961.

Lawson moved to Memphis where he served as pastor of the Centenary Memphis Church. Following the death of two sanitation workers who had been crushed, workers went on strike. Lawson was called to act as chairman on the strike committee. He called on support from Dr King, who delivered his famous 'Mountain Top' speech on April 3rd 1968 and who was assassinated the following day.

Moving to Los Angeles in 1974 Lawson served as the pastor at Holman United Methodist Church. He officially retired in 1999 but continued to be active. He supported Palestinian and immigrants' rights and trained students in non-violent direct action.

Born into royalty belonging to the Nigerian Adesida dynasty **King Sunny Ade** also wears the musical crown as King of Juju. The pioneering multi-instrumentalist, singer/songwriter developed a dance inspired hybrid of Western pop, rock and roll, with traditional African music fused with Yoruba vocals. Ade is a major influence and one of the earliest performers from Africa to go international. Born **on this day** in 1946, Ade formed his own band, in 1963, The Green Spots. He changed the name to The African Beats in 1974. Success made it possible for Ade to set up his own record label. By 1977 Nigerian journalists were calling Ade 'King of Juju'.

Promoted as the African **Bob Marley** (see Feb 6th), Ade signed to Island Records in 1982 but only released three albums. In 1996 he signed for a subsidiary of Atlantic Records again he released three albums.

Notable long play recordings include 'Sound Vibrations', (1977), 'Royal Sound' (1979), 'Juju Music' (1982) and 'Synchro System' released in 1983.

Little Rock Nine's Ernest Green (see September 5th and 11th) was the first of only three students from the nine to graduate. After completing his schooling at Central High Governor Faubus closed all schools. In order to stop integration, Forbus received unanimous support, preferring that no child could attend school rather than have integration.

An anonymous donor enabled Green to attend Michigan State University. It later transpired that the donor was the president of Michigan State College, John A Hannah. Green earned his BA degree in 1962 and his master's degree in sociology in 1964. He was involved in employment law and worked to promote educational and work opportunities and has served on numerous boards. Ernest Green was born **on this day** in 1941. He made history graduating from Little Rock Central High on May 27th 1958.

The national flag of Mali.   A young woman from Mali.

On this day in 1960 **Mali** gained its independence from France. The Sudanese Republic and Senegal formed the Federation of Mali in 1959. The socialist **Modibo Keita** served as the new country's first president. Born on June 4th 1915 Modibo Keita was an African socialist and Pan Africanist and served as president from July 20th 1960–1968. He would die in prison on May 16th 1977, having spent the last eight years incarcerated.

Born **on this day** 1966 in Tanzania to Ghanaian parents, having lived in Egypt, Yemen and Lebanon with his diplomatic father, internationally renowned architect **David Adjaye** came to live in England at the age of nine. The British Ghanaian, Adjaye, is responsible for numerous structures around the world houses, museums, places of worship, retail and offices.

This entry will focus on one of Adjaye's proposed projects, the National Cathedral of Ghana. The $100 million plan was unveiled by Adjaye Associates in March 2018. The Cathedral will be the centre piece celebrating sixty years of Ghana's independence. The religious centre will provide seating for 5,000 with accommodation in additional chapels and a baptistery. Plans include a museum dedicated to the bible as well as a school for music and an art gallery. The design draws inspiration adopting art and culture from the varied ethnic groups found in Ghana.

For David Adjaye's most iconic project, to date, go to September 24th to read about the National Museum of African American History and Culture found in Washington DC.

Sept 23rd:

Musical giant **Ray Charles** was born **on this day** in 1930. Given the monikers 'The Genius' and 'Brother Ray' the legend would become one of the fathers of modern popular music and a soul music pioneer.

At the age of five Ray witnessed his four-year-old brother drown in his mother's laundry tub. A year later Ray's eyesight was affected by glaucoma. He would be blind by the age of seven. His father died when the boy was only ten and his mother died of cancer when her son was fifteen. Attending the St Augustine School for the Deaf and the Blind, 1937–45, Ray was able to develop his interest in music playing the piano, saxophone, clarinet, trumpet and organ.

Music genius Ray Charles.

Making his way in the world Charles started playing with various groups. He met his lifelong friend **Quincy Jones** when he was sixteen. His first recording *'Confession Blues'* came in 1949 playing with The McSon Trio. Ray Charles recognising that he was not **Nat King Cole** (see March 17th) set out to find his own sound. Over the years Charles would embrace blues, gospel, jazz, R&B, country and rock creating pan American music. The distinct style would lead to thirty-seven Grammy Award nominations, receiving seventeen Grammy Awards plus a Lifetime Achievement Award. Charles became the only artist to win Grammy Awards in four consecutive years 1960–63. He won ten Grammys with cover versions.

The 1950s saw Charles release a string of hits 'Mess Around' (1952), 'It Should Have Been Me' (1953), 'I've Got a Woman' (1954), 'What I'd Say' (1959), 'Night Time Is) the Right Time' (1959) and 'Let the Good Times Roll' (1959).

From the birth of the Billboard Hot 100 in 1958 to 1990 Charles had eighty hits. Moving to ABC Paramount in 1960 he became the first major artist to negotiate ownership of his material. That year he bought an aeroplane large enough to transport his backing group The Raelettes and his full orchestra on tour. The hits continued in the 1960s with 'Georgia on My Mind' (1960). The song spoke romantically of the state at a time when there was unbridled racism, segregation and the rise of the Civil Rights Movement. 'Hit the Road Jack' (1961), 'Unchain My Heart' (1961), 'I Can't Stop Loving You' (1962), 'Busted' (1963) and 'Crying Time' in 1965. During the decade Charles successfully put his soulful interpretation onto country music recording thirty-three country songs,1962–66, following the ground-breaking 1962 album 'Modern Sounds in Country and Western Music'.

Brother Ray performed at the 'A Salute to Freedom' concert in 1963 raising funds for the historical March on Washington (see August 28th).

Charles became the first major artist to build and own a state-of-the-art recording studio in 1965. Releasing sixty albums he was the only vocalist to have Billboard hits in seven different decades, while recording award-winning material in 6 different decades. His autobiography written with David Ritz *Brother Ray: Ray Charles' Own Story* was published in 1978. He appeared in twelve films including 1980s *The Blue Brothers*. He sang on the charity single 'We Are the World' in 1985.

Ray Charles received recognition and awards from around the world and continued to be active in numerous civil rights programmes. Charles collaborated with numerous artists. He had a heroin addiction which started in the 1960s and was arrested for possession in 1965. He died on June 10th 2004 aged seventy-three. Charles was survived by his long-time friend, manager, producer and promoter, since 1958, **Joe Adams.** Adams, a former Tuskegee airman in World War II, appeared in more than twenty-five films notably playing the boxer Husky Miller in Carmen Jones. Twice divorced Ray Charles left behind twelve sons and daughters. That same year the biopic *Ray* was released gaining an Academy Award for Best Actor for **Jaime Foxx** in his portrayal of Ray Charles.

Saxophonist, band leader, composer and icon of twentieth-century jazz **John Coltrane** was born **on this day**, a year before Ray Charles, in 1929. Working with **Miles Davis** (see September 28th)**, Dizzy Gillespie** (see October 21st) and **Thelonious Monk,** Coltrane absorbed ideas and techniques. Moving from clarinet to alto saxophone, tenor saxophone and then soprano saxophone Coltrane's style was continuously developing and evolving.

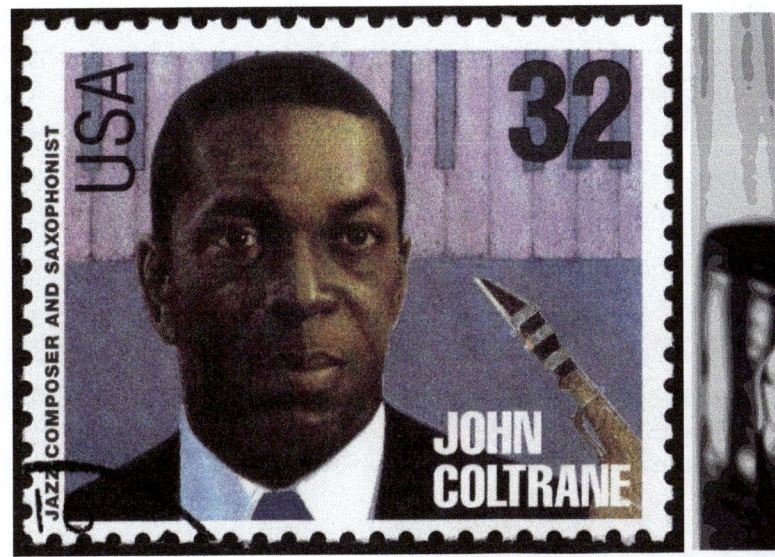

Saxophonist John Coltrane.

Seeing **Charlie Parker** (see August 29th) perform June 5th 1945 confirmed to the young musician where he wanted to be. Coltrane embraced bebop's fast snapping and popping style with its complex rapid chord progressions and changes.

He made his first recording playing solo with Gillespie on 'We Love to Boogie' in 1951. It was working with Davis that thrust Coltrane to jazz prominence playing in the Miles Davis Quintet from 1955–57. The 'First Great Quintet' recorded a marathon session in 1956 producing 'Cockin with the Miles Davis Quintet' (1957), 'Relaxin with the Miles Davis Quartet' (1958), 'Workin with Miles Davis Quartet' (1960), and 'Steaming with the Miles Davis Quartet' in 1961. In 1951 Coltrane started taking heroin, he was drinking too. The quartet split when Davis sacked the saxophonist. After going through cold turkey, kicking his addiction, Coltrane returned to work with Davis, 1958–60, including 1959s 'A Kind of Blue' album.

'A Kind of Blue' was a complete contrast to Coltrane's first album as a band leader with Atlantic Records 'Giant Steps' (1959), where he played all his own compositions. The album saw some of the most difficult chord progressions recorded. Coltrane's improvisations, virtuosity and dexterity saw his play speed up. The cascading of notes reflected Coltrane's increasing attraction with chord progressions.

John Coltrane recorded continuously leaving behind a body of work that perfectly documented his musical evolution. He recorded over fifty albums including classics: 'Blue Train' (1957), 'My Favourite Things' (1960), and 1964's 'A Love Supreme'.

Later avant-garde work inspired by Indian and African sounds and rhythms moved Coltrane towards free jazz. His last work reflected an increasing spiritual content. The music was challenging often leaving his audience and critics divided. The new sounds and style were not easy on the ear and was a challenge to comprehend. Technically Coltrane produced a sound with clear definition and full body. He could move smoothly from note to note with no discernible breaks.

John Coltrane died from liver cancer aged forty. He was survived by his second wife, pianist, Alice, one daughter and three sons.

Industrial product designer **Charles Harrison** was born **on this day** in 1931. As a freelance designer working for Sears, Roebuck and Company in 1958 he modified the View Master (Model F) to create the popular children's toy. He had been told that Sears had an unwritten policy of not hiring black people. When employed Harrison broke the colour bar, in 1961, becoming part of the twenty-person product design team. Harrison rose to lead the design team and became Sears' first black executive. He remained with the company for thirty-two years.

The View Master.

In 1966 Harrison gave the world the plastic rubbish (garbage) bin. The design was an immediate success. For the product designer aesthetics were important but never at the expense of function. He wanted to design items that made life easier and did not require instructions. When he retired in 1993 Harrison was the last industrial designer at Sears. He was credited with over 600 products including: riding lawn mowers, hedge clippers, wheelbarrows, toasters, stoves, blenders, fondue pots, coffee percolators, see through measuring jugs, steam irons, sewing machines, cordless electric shavers, portable hair dryers, portable turntables, domestic power tools and hearing aids. Harrison was committed to the average consumer.

Teaching at the School of Art, Institute of Chicago and Columbia University, Harrison never limited the cost of his students' designs rather focusing on quality. Harrison became the first black person honoured with the Cooper-Hewitt National Design Museum Lifetime Achievement Award in 2008. He wrote *A Life of Design,*' published in 2006.

Charles "Chuck" Harrison died at the age of eighty-seven on November 19th in 2018.

Largely forgotten, Trinidadian Malcolm Ivan Meredith Nurse was born in 1902. He would be more familiar as **George Padmore** the revolutionary anti-colonialist, communist, and Pan-Africanist was the thread that connected likeminded individuals and groups in Africa, the Caribbean, North America, Europe and Asia. In the mid-1920s Nurse travelled to the USA studying at Fisk University, New York University and Howard University in Washington DC. While in the States he joined the Communist Party in 1927 and changed his name to George Padmore providing articles for the Daily Worker.

Living in the Soviet Union, Moscow, Padmore organised the first International Conference of Negro Workers. He was invited to head the Negro Bureau of the Red International of Labour Unions. During this period, he was elected to the city council. The energetic activist and writer moved to Hamburg in Germany at this time he edited the *Negro Worker*. With the rise of Nazism and a falling out with official Soviet policy Padmore moved to London, England. Wherever Padmore settled he continued to write for a variety of left-wing newspapers. In 1936 he published *How Britain Rules Africa.* The following year, *Africa and World Peace* was published. Padmore connected with fellow activists, known for his orchestrating skills and as an expert strategist. In 1937 he founded the International African Service Bureau. Joining forces with others the Pan-African Federation was formed. It would be responsible for organising the fifth Pan-African Conference. In attendance at the Manchester 1945 Conference were **W. E. B. DuBois** (see February 23rd) and **Kwame Nkrumah** (see January 2nd).

The socialist Padmore wrote *Pan-Africanism or Communism?* in 1957. That same year he moved to Ghana where he acted as the newly elected independent leader Kwame Nkrumah's personal advisor on African affairs. It appears that Padmore was finding life difficult in Ghana and was about to leave. Suffering from failing health George Padmore returned to England for medical attention. He died **on this day** in 1959 from cirrhosis of the liver. His ashes were buried at Christiansborg Castle in Ghana on October 4th 1959.

Sept 24th:

Fighting for freedom.

Poet, novelist, journalist, speaker, abolitionist and suffragist, **Francis Ellen Watkins Harper** was born **on this day** in 1825. With the publication of 'Two Offers' she became the first African American woman to publish a short story. Her novel *Iola Leroy* (1892), was one of the earliest novels published by a black woman. It dealt with issues of education, interracial relationships, abolition, the reconstruction, and being accepted into different racial groups. *Poems on Miscellaneous Subjects* (1854) saw sales of 12,000 copies in its first four years and would have twenty reprints in Harper's lifetime. The poems focused on Christianity, slavery and women.

In 1858, ninety-seven years before Rosa Parks, Harper refused to give up her seat on a segregated trolley car in Philadelphia, refusing to sit in the coloured section. That same year she published one of her most famous and moving poems *Bury Me in a Free Land*. A prolific writer Harper would be the most successful black American poet before **Paul Laurence Dunbar** (see February 9th). She published her first book of poetry when she was twenty.

In 1852 Harper lived with **William Still's** family (see July 14th). It was at this time, closely connected to the slave escape route, the underground railway, that Harper started writing anti-slavery literature. She joined the American Anti-Slavery Society in 1853 becoming a public speaker and political activist traveling the country. Harper served as the superintendent of the coloured section of Philadelphia's Women's Christian Temperance Society in 1886. She helped to found the National Association of Coloured Women in 1896 for which Harper served as vice president. (See **Mary Terrell** July 24th.)

Francis Harper died on February 11th in 1911 at the age of eighty-five.

American sociologist **E. Franklin Frazier** provided insight into problems faced and how these affected the black community. It proved difficult for Frazier to find a publisher for one of his earliest works *The Pathology of Racism* (1927). When the book was published it led to Frazier receiving death threats and being released from his employment. Frazier concluded in the book that southern whites acted in an insane manner when it came to the question of race. White people who were normally level-headed, reasonable, rational, law abiding and civil when faced with the issue of colour, would behave abnormally with issues of dissociation, thinking in a delusional manner and becoming paranoid. Just as the lunatic grabs hold of every fact supporting their delusion the white southerner seizes on myths and rumour to support his twisted view of the black man. Frazer argued that this type put certain questions beyond discussion and would rather fight than debate. Southern whites were driven mad by the 'negro complex'.

Frazier published eight books, eighty-nine articles and produced eighteen chapters in books edited by others. His works looked at the historical forces and influences that affected the development of the African American family. He mapped the dynamics of social change and race relations. Key books include: *The Negro Family in Chicago* (1932), *The Negro Family in the United States* (1939), *The Negro Youth at the Crossways* (1940) and 1957's *Race and Culture Contacts in the Modern World*. *Black Bourgeoisie* published in French in 1955, then in English in 1957, was controversial. Frazier critically accused the black middle class of not doing enough, distracted by their desire to gain acceptance by the white community.

Frazier helped to draft UNESCO's 'The Race Question' in 1950. 'The Race Question' was an attempt to clarify what we know and understand scientifically about race and to produce a moral condemnation of racism. It was revised in 1951, 1967 and 1968.

Franklin Frazier became the first black president of the American Association in 1948. Frazier died on May 17th 1962 aged sixty-seven.

On this day in 1988 Canadian Jamaican sprinter **Ben Johnson** won the 100m. He would later be disqualified from the record-breaking run and charged with taking performance enhancing drugs. Johnson born December 30th 1961 ran 9.79 on that day. See March 5th.

David Adjaye's (see September 22nd) architectural masterpiece; the **National Museum of African American History and Culture** (NMAAHC) located at 1400 Constitution Ave, NW, Washington DC. 20560 opened **on this day** in 2016. Years of lobbying and planning resulted in an Act of Congress in 2003 establishing the museum.

Four hundred thousand square feet over 10 floors, five below ground, house 40,000 objects. The NMAAHC is part of the Smithsonian family of museums.

Guinea Bissau gained independence **on this day** in 1973 from Portugal, recognised September 10 1974.

A woman from Guinea Bissau.

Sept 25th:

Antonio Aurelio Goncalves was born **on this day** in 1901 in the capital Mindelo on the island of Sao Vicente, Cape Verde.

The Portuguese African novelist, critic and teacher would spend twenty-two years away from home being educated and working in Lisbon, Portugal. He returned to the place of his birth in 1939 teaching history and philosophy. As a writer Goncalves, popularly known as **Nho Roque,** was important in addressing the position of women on the Cape Verde islands where emigration saw the loss of many men and a society in constant flux.

Prodiga (The Prodigal Daughter), 1956, looks at a wayward daughter who leaves home and has an affair before returning to the fold. *O Enterro de Nhá Candinha Sena* (The Burial of Mrs Candinha Sena), 1957, follows the narrator looking back at their childhood and the relationship they had with a childless woman of great personality and kindness. *Noite de vento* (Night of Wind), 1970 looks at a black woman following her desires. *Virgens Loucas* (Crazy Virgins), 1971, again the main protagonists are female. Giving Cape Verdean women a central place in his work placed Nho Roque at the vanguard of such literature on the islands.

Sixteen-year-old student **Barbara Rose Johns,** on April 23rd 1951, led the all-black student body of Robert Russa Moton High School on strike. Plans ensured the principal was off site, downtown dealing with students who were supposedly being disruptive. This was not true and just a distraction. With the principal out of the way a forged note instructed teachers to gather the student body for an emergency assembly. Left alone as instructed Johns was able to address the gathering of 450 students.

Johns spoke of the poor conditions; the school built for 200 now accommodated more than twice that number. The buildings were poorly heated, students often sat in class with coats on. When it rained water would pour through leaky roofs. On occasions students sat beneath umbrellas in class. There were no science laboratories, and any equipment was old and in poor condition. The school had no gymnasium, cafeteria or lockers. Johns demanded a new facility be built with improved conditions. The students went on strike as the all-white school board had repeatedly failed to adequately upgrade the building.

The strike received support from the NAACP who took legal action in the case Davis v Prince Edward County. The case became one of five that formed the ground-breaking **Brown v The Board of Education** 1954 (see May 17th). Davis was the only student-led case. The strike is often cited as having given birth to the modern Civil Rights movement in the USA.

All black schools in Virginia's Prince Edward's County were closed for the next five years. The KKK burned a cross in Johns' front yard. She had to move to Alabama for her own safety, living with an uncle, to continue her education. Completing her studies Barbara Rose Johns became a librarian married William Powell and had five children. As I type plans are in place to replace a statue of the Confederate general Robert E. Lee with one of Johns placed in the National Statuary Hall in the county's capital. Barbara Rose Johns died from bone cancer **on this day** in 1991.

On this day in 1957 troops escorted the **Little Rock Nine** into school (see September 5th and 11th).

On this day 1977 Steve Biko's funeral was attended by 15,000 mourners (see September 12th).

Sept 26th:

Born April 5th 1894, blues singer and songwriter, **Bessie Smith** would be declared Queen of the Blues by Columbia Records' publicity department, only to be upgraded by the popular press to **'Empress of the Blues'**.

When **Mamie Smith** (no relation) recorded 'Crazy Blues'' on August 10th 1920 she showed that there was a market for black female blues artists. Bessie Smith knew poverty well and lost both parents when a child. She met **Ma Rainey** (see April 26th) aged sixteen. Rainey would say she taught Smith some valuable lessons but there is no evidence to substantiate this.

Smith hit the ground running with her recording career. She started recording on February 15th 1923. 'Cemetery Blues' was issued on September 26th 1923. After ten months at Columbia, Smith had sold 2 million records. Over the next four years she would sell 6 million records. She recorded 160 records for Columbia. Sales were huge but Bessie Smith was only paid a flat fee per record receiving no royalties. She made her money touring and performing. She recorded with talented artists including a young **Louis Armstrong** (see August 4th), **Fletcher Henderson** and **Coleman Hawkins.**

Bessie Smith's rough, course, untamed manner surprised the music purist but was a hit with the listening public. Her first commercial success had previously been released by other artists. When Smith recorded 'Down Hearted Blues' (1923), it sold 780,000 copies. The recording of *'Cake Walking Babies'* on May 5th 1925 saw Smith's first electric recording showing off the true power of her voice. On the road Smith's popularity meant that she was the highest paid black entertainer of her day. She purchased a 72 ft long railroad car to go on tour. She was a headliner in the black vaudeville circuit, but also had crossover appeal appearing on radio.

Like the lyrics in her songs Smith appeared fearless, independent and enjoying sexual freedom. She let the world know that she, nor other working-class women, had to alter their behaviour to gain acceptance and respectability. Bessie Smith sang about issues people understood and related to. She sang about the troubles people knew well. Her performances were compared to the drama created by an evangelical preacher whipping up the congregation into a frenzy. Her vocals were described as one wishing to get something out and bring it to the surface. Bessie Smith's songs spoke of female emancipation, sexual freedom, the right to party and drink in an oppressive, depressing working class setting, alcohol, social issues, the penal system and the death penalty.

Smith made her last recordings with John Hammond on the Okeh label on November 24th 1933. She received $37.50 per track without royalties. The final recordings demonstrated how her contralto vocals had adapted to the swing era.

Richard Morgan, Smith's partner was at the wheel traveling on Route 61 when the couple were involved in a car accident, **on this day** in 1937. Dr Hugh Smith (no relation) found Bessie laying in the middle of the road. He believed that she had lost half a pint of blood and could see that her right arm was almost severed below the elbow. The singer had also sustained minor head injuries. Dr Smith would later attribute Bessie's death to severe and extensive crush injuries. Morgan emerged unscathed. The doctor instructed his friend, Henry Broughton, to find a phone and call for an ambulance. By the time Broughton had returned, twenty-five minutes later, Bessie was in a state of shock. Dr Smith and Broughton decided to take Bessie to hospital. They had moved the singer to the side of the road and were clearing the back seat to take Bessie to nearby Clarkson. Hearing a vehicle approaching at speed, Dr Smith flashed his car lights but was unable to avoid a collision as the speeding car smashed into the doctor's car, sending it colliding it into Morgan's vehicle. The couple in the car received life-changing injuries. As the chaos and carnage unfolded two ambulances arrived, one from the local black hospital and one for the local white hospital. A passing truck driver had called for the second 'white' ambulance. On arrival at the hospital Smith's arm was amputated but her life could not be saved. She never regained consciousness and died later that morning. It was Hammond, who would later manage **Billie Holiday** (see April 7th)**,** who erroneously put out the story that Smith died because the segregated white hospital refused to accept the singer.

Bessie Smith lay in an unmarked grave for over thirty years. On August 7th 1970 a headstone was erected, paid for by the singer Janis Joplin and Bessie's long-time friend Juanita Green. Janis Joplin's untimely death would occur just two months later.

Bessie Smith's popular hits included: 'Take me for a Buggy Ride', 'Jail-House Blues', 'Gimme a Pigfoot (and a Bottle of Beer)', 'Work House blues', 'Send Me to the 'Lectric Chair', 'Poor Man's Blues', 'Washwoman's Blues' and 'Sing Sing Prison Blues.' Bessie Smith was forty-three when she died.

Winnie Madikizela Mandela was born **on this day** in 1936. Described by her supporters as the 'Mother of the Nation', seen by some as a controversial character; found guilty of gross violations of human rights and later of fraud, Winnie Madikizela-Mandela is a complex figure. Her life cannot be reduced to taking sides or of broad-brush strokes comparing wrongs & rights. She was a person (a victim) of her time, a turbulent vicious time of discrimination and apartheid.

Winnie was the first black medical social worker at the Baragwanath Hospital in Johannesburg. Fieldwork experience confirmed the harsh reality of life faced by most black people in South Africa. In 1957 Winnie, twenty-two, met the married **Nelson Mandela** (see February 11th, June 12th, and July 18th). A year later, in June 1958, the couple were married. They had two daughters Zenani and Zindzi. The marriage would last thirty-eight years but Nelson would spend most of that time in prison from 1962–1990.

Winnie was closely monitored by the South African security services and frequently harassed by the authorities under the Suppression of Terrorism Act. On May 12th 1969 Winnie was arrested, spending the next seventeen months (491 days) in solitary confinement. Questioned and tortured, Winnie says that the experience hardened her. Following the massacre in **Soweto** in 1976 (see June 16th) Winnie was forced to relocate to the border town of Brandfort. Living in enforced exile, 1977–85, alienated and under house arrest left Winnie heartbroken. Police beatings left her with a back injury and in constant pain. She became addicted to painkillers and turned to alcohol.

A radical uncompromising Winnie emerged. Threatened, beaten and continuously harassed, this Winnie was a political radical. She believed the best form of defence was attack. She had reached her own Umkhonto we Sizwe (Spear of the Nation) moment. Wearing military fatigues Winnie cut an imposing figure. She returned to Johannesburg in1985 showing defiance of her exile and house arrest. Surrounded, initially for protection, by bodyguards known as the 'Mandela Football Club', Winnie refused to criticise punishment dished out to blacks, found to be collaborating with the apartheid regime. She condoned the practice of 'necklacing' where a tyre placed around the victim's neck would be set on fire. Winnie would be associated with at least fifteen killings and directly with the beating of four youths and the abduction and death of **Stompie Seipie (Moeketsei)** (14) in 1984. **Abu Baker Asvat**'s (46) death, January 27th 1989 is connected to orders, allegedly, from Winnie. In the middle of this period during 1988 Winnie's home, in Soweto, was firebombed and burned down by students angry at her actions and that of the Mandela Football Club thugs. She was convicted and given a six-year sentence, after appeal reduced to a fine. The South African Truth and Reconciliation Commission found Winnie guilty of gross violations of human rights in 1997.

Nelson Mandela, released from prison in 1990, stood by Winnie throughout the trial but the couple separated in 1992 and would divorce in 1996. The allegations, scandals, trials, convictions and radical politics failed to dent Winnie's grass roots popularity. She was elected president of the African National Congress (ANC) Women's League in 1993. When her, then still legal, husband became the country's first black president in 1994, Winnie was elected and served in government as the Deputy Minister of Arts, Culture, Science and Technology. Ousted by President Mandela for political differences and allegations of illegal behaviour in 1995 failed to prevent Winnie's re-election in 1999. In 2003 the troubled politician was convicted of fraud, later overturned as Winnie was determined to have made no personal financial gain from the action.

Winnie Madikizela-Mandela remained an iconic figure representing the struggle against apartheid through to the end of her life. In 2013 she visited her former husband before he died. She was recognised by the South African government with the Silver Order of Luthuli (see July 21st) for her role in the liberation struggle in 2016. When Winnie died on April 2nd 2018, she was given a state funeral at Orlando Stadium in Soweto on April 14th. The TV movie *Mrs Mandela* (2010), starring **Sophie Okonedo** and the 2011 film *Winnie*, with **Jennifer Hudson**, attempted to recognise the events and forces that shaped her behaviour, beliefs, actions and ultimately her life.

One of the **Little Rock Nine**; **Gloria Ray** was born **on this day** 1942. Daughter to Harvey C and Julia Miller Ray, Gloria was one of three children. At the age of fifteen she faced the anger and indignation witnessing faces screwed up and distorted by racial hatred as she attempted to enter Little Rock High (see Sept 5th).

Ray would go on to graduate earning a BA degree in Chemistry and Mathematics from the Illinois Institute of Technology in 1965. The following year she married Krister Karlmark. Gloria Ray Karlmark would teach in the public school system before moving on to Information Technology as a systems analyst and a technical writer. The Little Rock Nine survivor at the time of writing resides between Sweden and The Netherlands.

Sept 27th:

Faith Bandler was a campaigner for Aboriginal rights in Australia and for people from the South Sea Islands. Born **on this day** in 1918, her father was abducted from Ambrym Island, Vanuatu aged thirteen in 1883 and forced into slave labour. In 1977 Bandler published *Wacvie*, an account of her father's experiences and life in Queensland.

During World War II Faith and her sister worked on fruit farms. On being discharged in 1945 Bandler started to campaign for equal pay between the white and the indigenous workers. The year 1956 saw Bandler become a full-time activist emerging as a great public speaker and co-founder of the Sydney based Aboriginal-Australian Fellowship. The following year the Federal Council for Aboriginal Advancement was formed (FCAA, later FCAATSI). As its general secretary Bandler led the campaign for a constitutional referendum organising hundreds of public meetings and presenting numerous petitions. The 1967 referendum won important recognition for the first people of Australia. Bandler would write two histories of the 1967 referendum.

As a prominent member of the Women's Electoral Lobby, founded in 1972, Bandler applied pressure for fair and equal treatment focusing on Aboriginal women. After writing about her father, Bandler wrote *Welou, My Brother* (1984) about the life her brother faced living in New South Wales, Australia.

Later in life she turned her attention to the needs and the plight of the descendants of South Sea Islanders founding the National Commission for Australian South Sea Islanders in 1975. Described as the forgotten Australians, thousands were abducted and transported to work on Australia's sugar plantations from 1863–1904. Many then faced the indignity of mass expulsion in the early 1900s as the New Commonwealth of Australia pursued a policy to make Australia a white country. Faith Bandler died on February 13th 2015, one of Australia's most recognised citizens.

Born **on this day** in 1936, television host and creator of the iconic music and dance programme *Soul Train*, **Don Cornelius** would lead a fast, action pact life. Hosting 'Soul Train' from 1971–1993 Cornelius was able to take his creation to national syndication. He provided a platform for black performers to display their talent without having to pander to a cross over audience. The cut-throat industry saw Cornelius having to ward off pretenders to his throne. He too was not averse to sharp practises to stay afloat and in control. Cornelius sold *Soul Train* in 2008.

Soul Train's Don Cornelius.

In 1982, following a twenty-one-hour operation on his brain, Cornelius started having seizures which would continue for the next fifteen years, this led to drugs and alcohol problems. Believed to be suffering from the early onset of dementia or Alzheimer's, Don Cornelius shot himself in the head and died on February 1st 2012.

Born **on this day** in 1953, to Windrush Generation immigrants from Jamaica, **Diane Abbott** would become Britain's first female member of parliament of African descent, elected to the House of Commons in 1987 (see June 11th). She is the longest serving black MP in the Commons, representing Hackney North & Stoke Newington in London. Before becoming an MP Abbott worked at the Home Office as a civil servant, 1976–80, Thames TV and *TV-am* reporter, 1980–84, press officer for the Greater London Council and councillor for Westminster City Council, 1982–86.

On the left of the Labour party Abbott opposed Prime Minister Tony Blair's incursion into the Iraq War and proposals for the introduction of ID cards. She was a member of the Labour Party Black Section,1983–93, a caucus made up of Africans, Caribbeans and Asians.

Abbott failed in her attempt to become leader of the party but was appointed to the shadow cabinet, by the eventual winner Ed Miliband, as Minister of Public Health. She supported Jeremy Corbyn's bid for leadership of the Labour party in 2015. She was made Secretary for International Development, 2015–16. In June of 2016 Abbott was made Shadow Health Secretary. October of the same year saw her as Shadow Home Secretary. On October 2nd 2019 Abbott became the first black MP to stand at the dispatch box substituting for Corbyn at Prime Minister's Questions facing the first Secretary of State Dominic Raab.

Diane Abbott failed in her bid to be selected as Labour's candidate for London Mayor. She opposed Britain leaving the European Union and highlighted the Windrush scandal where immigrants, largely of Caribbean heritage, were illegally targeted by a hostile political Conservative policy deporting British citizens to countries they did not know. Abbott spoke out against Britain's support of Saudi Arabia involved in a devastating war against Yemen. Often controversial Diane Abbott stood down from front bench politics on April 5th in 2020.

Sept 28th:

Australian Aboriginal polymath, orator, evangelical activist **David Unaipon** was born **on this day** in 1872.

Obsessed with rotary motion and its possibilities Unaipon patented a shearing handpiece that improved on the clippers' rotational action adopting a more efficient lateral motion. By 1944 Unaipon had submitted numerous applications for patents but without finance was unable to follow through on his inventions, applications and ideas. This did not stop him being described as 'Australia's Leonardo' during his lifetime and repeated in a Guardian newspaper headline on Friday 5th October 2018. He appears on the Australian $50 note with his mechanical shearer.

With the publication of *Hurgarrda* (1927), Unaipon became the first Aboriginal author to be published with stories of Aboriginal myths and legends. Researching and collecting stories between 1924-25 Unaipon submitted thirty-one chapters in five volumes to Angus and Robertson in 1926 for publication. He even, at his own expense, included a photograph. Why we have no idea, the publishers sold the manuscript to Adelaide doctor and amateur anthropologist William Ramsey Smith who had the bound volumes published in London as *Myths and Legends of Australian Aborigines*. Smith appeared to know Unaipon, considered a friend, but did not acknowledge the Aboriginal in the book. It would not be until 2001 that Unaipon's name would appear on the work. Although a great public speaker there are no records of Unaipon questioning how and why his work was effectively stolen. David Unaipon had other books published; '*Kinie Ger – The Native Cat*' (1928), and '*Native Legends*' (1929). He published poems in the 1930s, more legends in the 1950s and 1960s. Two autobiographies were written: '*My Life Story*', (1951) and '*Leaves of Memory*' in 1953.

David Unaipon.

By the 1920s David Unaipon was the most famous Aboriginal in Australia. He was involved in inquiries and commissions contributing to the Royal Commission and Inquiries into Aboriginal Welfare and Treatment, 1926, and involved in the Bleakley Inquiry, 1928/9 into Aboriginal welfare. He stood as a political advocate for equality, as a spokesperson for his people. In 1934 Unaipon called for the Commonwealth to take control of Aboriginal affairs and called for the then South Australia Chief Protector of Aborigines, Mark Wilson, to be replaced by a board.

David Unaipon from the Ngarrindjeri people travelled and spoke widely. He died, aged ninety-four, on February 7th in 1967. The local preacher, inventor and author is buried in Point McLeary Cemetery.

There is **Louis Armstrong**, (see August 4th), **Duke Ellington** (May 24th), **Charlie Parker** (August 29th) and then there's **Miles Davis.** Davis was born May 26th in 1926. The revered trumpeter, bandleader and composer would be a major influence and innovator in the world of jazz and in the wider world of music for six decades.

Miles Davis' contribution and influence started in the mid-1940s when he dropped out of New York's Juilliard School of Music to play, making his professional debut, with his idol and bebop icon Charlie Parker, 1944–48. It was not long before Davis became the front man in his own band. The 1950s saw Davis working with **Dizzy Gillespie** (see October 21st), **Thelonious Monk** (see October 10th), **Cannonball Adderley** and **Sonny Rollins.** The decade saw Davis struggle with drug addiction. The resulting behaviour would see his behaviour as hedonistic, erratic, confrontational and often unreliable. In *Miles*, his 1989 autobiography written with Quincy Troupe, Davis is open about his troubled life.

| Miles Davis | Herbie Hancock. |

Appearing at the Newport Jazz Festival, 1955, offered Davis the opportunity to show that he was back on track. A series of albums were released: 'Round Midnight' (1957), 'Birth of the Cool' (1957), 'Miles Ahead' (1957), 'Porgy and Bess' (1958), 'Milestones' (1958), 'Kind of Blue' (1959), and 'Sketches of Spain' in 1960. The period saw Davis collaborate with arranger and conductor Gil Evans and **John Coltrane** (see September 23rd). 'Birth of the Cool' was recorded over three sessions in 1949–50. Davis had developed 'cool jazz', a lighter style, a relaxed tempo with soft tones. This juxtaposed with the often, frenetic chord changes of the popular bebop. He explored the trumpet's middle register. The outcome was melodic and lyrical with deliberate pacing. 'Kind of Blue' resonated with the buying public who could understand the simplicity of his style. The album would sell over 5 million copies in the US.

The 1960s saw Davis moving forward, having an ear for future sounds and would pursue that music. The trumpeter embraced free jazz and fusion. He introduced a young **Herbie Hancock** and worked with Chick Corea. Landmark albums were released including 'Seven Steps to Heaven' (1963), and 'Bitches Brew' in 1969. Davis experimented with rock and the electrification of his sound. He was pushing barriers in jazz as psychedelia was doing in rock. He employed James Brown's 'On the one' and the work and style of Sly and the Family Stone. Critics were not always complimentary, finding the material difficult to understand.

Davis spent a large part of the 1970s out of the spotlight. He had a car accident in 1972, and from 1975–80, tired with health, drugs and alcohol problems, he battled his personal demons.

Miles Davis reappeared in 1981 with his fusion of jazz, rock and funk. He toured to the end, often playing with his back to the audience while walking around the stage. The music was important, not the performer or the performance. Moving music on is what mattered not simply falling back on past successes. How much of that is true is hard to tell. Was Miles Davis being indulgent and, as his autobiography suggested, awkward? Davis married three times; Francis Taylor Davis 1959 – 68, Betty Davis 1968 – 1969 and Cicely Tyson 1981 – 89.

Davis died **on this day** in 1991, he was sixty-five. He had been admitted to hospital but went into a coma and was placed on life support. The support was turned off on 28th September 1991. His death was put down to a combination of a stroke, caused by a bleed on the brain, pneumonia and respiratory failure. Miles Davis was buried at Woodlawn Cemetery in the Bronx, New York.

Famed for her first novel in 1982, *The Women of Brewster Place*, author **Gloria Naylor** was born on January 25th 1950. Reading **Toni Morrison**'s (see February 18th) *The Bluest Eye* opened Naylor up to a hitherto unknown world of African American female literature. Her novel looked at the world of seven women set in an urban neighbourhood that had seen better days. The interconnecting stories follow the women in their daily lives, struggles and deferred love and relationships. The TV mini-series, 1989, *Women of Brewster Place* starred **Oprah Winfrey** (see November 20th), **Cicely Tyson** and **Robin Givens**.

Actor Cicely Tyson

Naylor would cover poverty, racism, homophobia, discrimination faced by women, and how the African American community is socially divided and stratified. Other popular books include *Linden Hills* (1985), *Mama Day* (1988) and *Men of Brewster Place* in 1999. Gloria Naylor, the American novelist died of a heart attack aged sixty-six **on this day** in 2016.

On this day in 2020 **Victoire Tomegah Dogbe**, aged sixty, took office as the first female prime minister of the West African country of Togo. Born December 23rd 1959, Dogbe has had over a decade of experience in Togolese politics.

Sept 29th:

Samora Machel, born **on this day** in 1933, became the first president of independent Mozambique. Growing up he saw his parents forced to grow cotton, having to accept lower prices for their crop and finally forced off the land to make room for Portuguese colonists.

Trained as a nurse, working in the profession for ten years, Machel protested the disparity in wages between his black and white colleagues. Fearing that the authorities were after him, he joined Mozambique's Liberation Front Frelimo (see June 25th), making his way to Dar es Salaam in Tanzania. Machel was sent to Algeria for military training. Back in Kongwa, Tanzania he led his own military training camp. Michel became a key commander in Frelimo following the launch of its war of independence on September 25th 1964. By 1966 he was head of the army after the death of Frelimo's first military leader **Filipe Samuel Magaia**. When **Eduardo Mondlane** was assassinated, February 3rd 1969, Machel emerged as Frelimo's leader.

Demoralised from fighting three protracted African wars led the Portuguese army to a bloodless coup, on April 25th 1974, overthrowing Prime Minister Marcelo Caetano.

Independence was agreed on September 7th 1974 and celebrated on June 25th 1975. Samora Machel's Marxist government set about nationalising industries and institutions. Land, health and education were nationalised. Private schools and clinics were abolished. Rented property was nationalised.

Trouble on its borders with white minority ruled Rhodesia (now Zimbabwe) and South Africa caused instability. The Mozambique National Resistance (renamo) supported by the white, minority led, neighbours engaged in a civil war starting in 1977. The bitter conflict would see human rights violations on both sides and not end until 1999. Samora Michel signed the Nkomati Accord with South Africa in 1984, an attempt to create some military and economic stability.

Samora Moises Machel.

Returning from Zambia flying to Mozambique, October 19th 1986, the President's aeroplane crashed. Samora Michel was killed aged fifty-three. Fingers pointed at South Africa's involvement. **Graca Simbine** (see October 17th), Michel's widow testified in front of South Africa's Truth and Reconciliation Commission placing suspicion at South Africa's door. Simbine married **Nelson Mandela** on July 18th 1998.

Sept 30th:

One of the finest operatic sopranos of her day, **Jessye Norman** was born September 15th 1945. She would challenge numerous rules in the Eurocentric world of opera, breaking out from the established roles expected of black female singers such as Bizet's exotic Carmen. Norman entered the world of opera winning Germany's ARD International Music Competition, the country's largest and prestigious international classical music competition in Munich 1968. The win led to a contract with the Deutsche Opera Berlin performing at Germany's second largest opera house in the home of the Berlin State Ballet.

Norman made her debut in 1969 as Elizabeth in Richard Wagner's *Tannhauser* in Berlin. This was followed by playing *Aida* in the city. She moved to Milan for La Scala and made her Covent Garden debut in 1972 playing Cassandra in Hector Berlioz's *Les Troyens* ('The Trojans'). Jessye Norman established herself as one of the highest paid performers as her reputation grew. It would not be until 1982 that she made her American debut performing with the Opera Company of Philadelphia.

Soprano Jessye Norman.

Norman toured continuously performing recitals from the great classical composers. Her recording career reflected her success on stage. Norman won a Grammy Award for Best Classical Vocal Solo in 1984. She won Grammys in 1989, 1990, 1999 and a Lifetime Achievement Award in 2006. Norman's performances were regularly televised.

Jessye Norman had a deep love of spirituals and was proud of collaborations with fellow black artists celebrating and commemorating black history. She acknowledged the path paved by predecessors such as **Marion Anderson** (see January 7th). Aware of prejudice and racism Norman recalls sitting on a 'white only' bench at a station platform, as a five-year-old, to the displeasure of her parents. Norman later kept a journal where she recorded all incidents of casual racism, she experienced but stopped the record when the process became too depressingly sad.

Jessye Norman performed at President Ronald Reagan's second inauguration in 1985. She would repeat the honour for President Clinton's second inauguration in 1997. She sang at Queen Elizabeth II's sixtieth birthday celebration in 1986 and was in France to celebrate the 200th anniversary of the French Revolution, singing the national anthem 'La Marseillaise', on July 14th 1989. Her international reputation took the soprano to Leningrad (St Petersburg) in Russia to perform at the 150th birthday Gala in 1990. Atlanta was the scene for Norman's performance at the city's Olympic opening ceremony in 1996. Following the terrorist attacks, September 11th 2001, in New York, Norman sang 'America the Beautiful' at the site of the Twin Towers, March 11th 2002, in a memorial for the victims of 9/11.

Working with the Rachel Longstreet Foundation, The Jessye Norman School of Arts was established in 2003. Essential in the early years of fundraising Norman was active in providing a free programme of tuition for disadvantaged students in Augusta, Georgia. Her memoir *Stand Up and Struggle* was published in 2014. Norman criticised many attacks on President Obama as fuelled by hidden racism pointing at the Republican Party.

Jessye Norman died **on this day** in 2019, she was seventy-four. The medical report said her death was caused by septic shock and multi organ failure from complications related to a 2015 spinal injury.

Journalist, essayist, writer and political commentator, **Ta-Nehisi Coates,** was born **on this day** in 1975. *The Beautiful Struggle: A Father, Two Sons and an Unlikely Road to Manhood* was written in 2008. The coming-of-age memoir looks at how the author's father, W. Paul Coates a former Black Panther and founder of the Black Classic Press publishers in 1978, influenced him. *The Beautiful Struggle* also looks at absent fathers in the black community, surviving the presence of street crime and navigating the education system.

Coates' essay 'Fear of a Black President' earned him a National Magazine Award in 2013. The following year he won a National Magazine Award for his essay looking at 'The Case for Reparation'.

Between the World and Me: Notes on the first 150 of America, published in 2015, won Coates the National Book Award for Non-Fiction. Set in Baltimore, the story is in the form of a letter written by a father to his teenage son about the realities of being black in America. Symbolism and feelings are explored against the background of the fear of street crime and violence with the rise of the crack cocaine epidemic to bring history alive.

The years 2016–2018 saw Coates writing the Black Panther Marvel Comic stories. Following on from the award-winning 'Fear of a Black President', Coates published a series of essays contained in *We Were Eight Years in Power: An American Tragedy*. The essays look at opposition to President Obama and obstacles placed in his path while comparing his time in office to the Reconstruction Era, 1863–77, that followed the American Civil War, 1861–65.

Ta-Nehisi Coates's first novel *The Water Dancer* (2019), is set in a period of slavery. The main protagonist, Hiram Walker, has a photographic memory but has no recollection of his mother. Almost drowned, Walker is saved by a mysterious force and acquires powers. Through conduction he's able to transport people. Folding the Earth like a cloth allows Walker to travel supernaturally along waterways.

Coates started working with Taylor Branch, in 2019, from Branch's three volume history of Martin Luther King. The pair look to release a series produced by Oprah Winfrey and aired on HBO focusing on Dr King and the Civil Rights Movement from 1965–68.

Botswana gained independence from Britain **on this day** in 1966. The country's first president **Seretse Khama** died in office in 1980. The country's national anthem was composed by **Dr Kgalemang Tumedisco Motsete.**

A young woman from Botswana.   and   Anthem composer Dr Motsete.

Oct 1st:

The History of Mary Prince: A West Indian Slave (1831) made its author the first black woman to be published in the UK. The book provided a window into the world of, and experiences faced by, enslaved people in the Caribbean and was adopted by the Anti-Slavery Society (1823–38).

Born into slavery in Bermuda **on this day** in 1788, Mary Prince would be separated from her family and sold four times. Beaten, sexually abused, finding herself working in harsh conditions, extracting salt, all had a detrimental effect on her health. She suffered badly from rheumatism.

In December 1826 Mary Prince married Daniel James. James had been able to purchase his freedom. In 1828 Prince travelled to England with her owners. Attempts were made to gain her freedom, but her owner would neither free her nor allow her to purchase her liberty. They hired Prince out and she ended up working for Thomas Pringle, the secretary of the Anti-Slavery Society (1823–38). Prince could read but it was Pringle who wrote the autobiography. The authenticity of the account made the book an immediate success. It was reprinted twice in its first year.

The History of Mary Prince clearly added ammunition to the abolitionists' cause. Prince became the first woman to present an anti-slavery petition to Parliament. Slavery was abolished in 1833 and come into law on August 28th 1834. We know nothing of Mary Prince's life after 1833. Did she remain in England? Did she return to Antigua to live with her husband? Did James travel to England?

Senegalese superstar, singer, composer, songwriter, businessman and politician **Youssou N'Dour** was born **on this day** in 1959. A traditional griot, N'Dour would develop the popular dance music known as mbalax.

The album 'Wommat' and the single '7 Seconds' with Neneh Cherry, 1994, saw N'Dour gain international recognition. In 2006 he played the role **Olaudah Equiano** (see March 31st) in the film *Amazing Grace*. He was the subject of the award-winning film by Pierre-Yves Borgeaud *Return to Goree* (2007), tracing the lives of enslaved people and how they developed jazz. Elizabeth Chai Vasarhelyi directed the documentary film *Youssou N'Dour: I Bring What I Love* (2008). It followed the release of his album 'Egypt' and N'Dour's attempt to promote a more tolerant understanding of Islam leading him to embrace Sufism.

Youssou N'Dour.

Following a failed attempt to run for president (it was said that he did not collect enough signatures to be on the ballot) Youssou N'Dour served as Senegal's minister of culture and tourism 2012–13.

On this day in 1960 **Nigeria** celebrated its **independence** from the British. Journalist Flora Shaw (Lady Lugard) suggested the name *Nigeria* on January 8th 1897. A British protectorate since 1901, colonisation ended in 1960. **Abubakar Tafawa Balewa (**born **on this day** in 1912) served as the country's prime minister from 1957. Elections in 1959 provided no majority and Balewa continued as prime minister. **Nnamdi Azikiwe** was the president, 1963–66 a largely ceremonial position for the prominent nationalist figure, even after Nigeria became a republic **on this day** in 1963.

Abubakar Tafawa Balewa.   and   A young Nigerian woman.

FIFA World Player of the Year 1995, winner of the Ballon d'Or 1995, top scorer in the UEFA Champion League 1995, African Player of the Year 1996 **George Weah,** born **on this day** 1966, had the football world at his feet. Brought to Europe by Arsene Wenger to Monaco, Weah scored fifty-seven goals for the team winning the French Cup in 1991. At Paris Saint Germain he won the Ligue 1 in 1994 and reached the semi-finals in the European Cup in 1995. Weah spent four seasons at AC Milan topping Serie A in 1996 and 1999. Towards the end of his eighteen-year professional career Weah had brief spells at Chelsea, lifting the FA Cup, Manchester City and Marseille. On the international stage George Weah had seventy-five caps and scored eighteen goals for Liberia, his country's team that he coached and financially kept afloat. Weah had campaigned to end the brutal civil war that had waged in his homeland. His interest in politics led to the formation of the party Congress for Democratic Change and running for the presidency in 2005. His foray into politics was unsuccessful, losing to **Ellen Johnson Sirleaf** (see Oct 29th). Weah ran for vice-president in 2011 again losing to Sirleaf. In 2014 the former footballer won election to the Liberian senate comprehensively defeating Sirleaf's son.

Three years later in 2017 George Weah was elected president of Liberia, sworn in on January 22nd 2018. His election would see the first transfer of power between two democratically elected leaders in Liberia since 1944.

Black History Month in Britain was first celebrated on this day 1987. Working for the Greater London Council (GLC) as special projects coordinator saw Ghanaian political refugee **Akyaaba Addai-Sebo** act as the nucleus to creating this time of celebration and education.

Addai-Sebo was born and raised in Ghana. He moved to the USA to continue his education. He was impressed by Black History Month held in February in the United States. The idea had evolved from Negro History Week founded in 1926, by Carter G. Woolston (see December 19th). Addai-Sebo established a radio programme called *African Roots, American Fruits*. Fleeing persecution from the **Jerry Rawlins** (see June 4th) regime, Addai-Sebo and his wife Nana Akua Owusu settled in London. Addai-Sebo was employed by the GLC as the project's coordinator, he was also chair of the African Refugees Housing Action Group and later would be operations manager at the Notting Hill Carnival.

Black History Month October in the UK.

Now living in Ghana, Akyaaba Addai-Sebo credits the establishment of Black History Month to a group effort at the Greater London Council.

Oct 2nd:

Born **on this day** in 1937, social justice lawyer and activist **Johnnie L. Cochran** is best remembered for getting his client, **O. J. Simpson** (see October 3rd)**,** acquitted in 1995. To focus on the 'case of the century' would be inappropriate in reflecting the work, career, courtroom tactician, determination and brilliance of Cochran.

Johnnie L. Cochran graduated from law school in 1962 and was admitted to the bar in 1963. Recognised as a defence advocate, he has worked on both sides of justice. Early in his career Cochran called out police brutality, excessive force, murder and sexual abuse. Early victories were difficult to come by, but the setbacks reinforced Cochran's determination to challenge a corrupt system that he saw as systemically racist. He lost the case of **Leonard Deadwyler**, shot dead by police 1966. He failed to win defending Black Panther **Geronimo Pratt** accused of murder, in the early 1970s. Decades later the case would be reviewed, as evidence emerged suggesting that the FBI had falsely and illegally framed Pratt. He had always declared his innocence, having an alibi demonstrating that he was not at the scene of the murder. Pratt was finally acquitted and freed in 1997. **Ron Settle** had been found hanging in his cell. Suicide was the medical conclusion. Cochran was able to demonstrate that Settle had been choked to death in a police-hold. Cochran has won over $40 million for his non-celebrity clients in his campaign for social justice. He would later recall being stopped by police, told to get out of his Rolls Royce with his two daughters, facing guns pointed at his person. It was only when they saw his district attorney card that the officers apologetically backed off. Cochran recognised the danger faced if he were seen to react in an "aggressive" manner.

Cochran proudly oversaw ten offices of his law firm 'Cochran, Cherry, Givens & Smith' located throughout the country. He was chair of the Upper Manhattan Empowerment Zone, a publicly funded agency operating in Harlem, Washington Heights and Inwood, seeking to economically develop the areas.

The philanthropic lawyer established The Johnnie L. Cochran Sr scholarship for African American men at the University of California Los Angeles. He published his memoir *Journey to Justice* in 1996. Cochran's activism saw him threaten to take a case to court representing clients who had started smoking under the age of eighteen in 2001. He argued that the cigarette companies had illegally and irresponsibly purposely targeted the age group through advertising. He was able to reach an out of court settlement, 2000, against Coca Cola accused of unequal wages against African Americans. A similar action was threatened against the pharmaceutical giant Johnson & Johnson. Legal action was proposed against the National Football League's (NFL) failure to hire more ethnic minority coaches.

For many Cochran is the man that led the team that skilfully and controversially, led to O. J. Simpson's acquittal. Simpson was accused of the murder of Nicole Brown Simpson and her friend Ronald Goldman. He is also the representative that defended former NFL player **Jim Brown** in 1985, *Diff'rent Strokes* actor **Todd Bridges** (1989), musician **Sean Coombes** (2001), former heavyweight boxer **Riddick Bowe**, athlete **Marion Jones**, hip hop artist **Snoop Dogg** and singer **Michael Jackson** (see February 28th).

NFL star Jim Brown.

In December of 2003 Johnnie Cochran was diagnosed with a brain tumour. He was operated on in 2004 but died from complications on March 29th in 2005, aged sixty-seven. His funeral was attended by his father and former clients Michael Jackson and O. J. Simpson.

With political instability and eventual collapse of the government in France, **Sekou Toure** emerged as the President. **Guinea** gained its **independence on this day,** in 1958. Ahmed Sekou Toure was born January 9th 1922. A dictator, he held power with an iron fist in Guinea for twenty-four years, he died on March 26th 1984.

Ahmed Sekou Toure.

Born April 27th 1945 American playwright **August Wilson** chronicled black American life throughout the twentieth century in ten plays known as *The Pittsburgh Cycle*. Described as the 'theatre poet of black America', Wilson produced material beyond the ten-play cycle. Influences included **Ed Bullins, James Baldwin** and **Amiri Baraka** (formerly **LeRoi James**).

August Wilson.

Each of the ten plays is set in a separate decade in the century. The first play in the series 'Jitney' (1982), set in the 1970s is located in a rundown taxi cab station in Pittsburgh. The second play, written in 1984, *Ma Rainey's Black Bottom* is set in the 1920s. Wilson was not going to be orderly or sequential in the writing and release of the plays. Each play stands alone but there are repeated themes, settings and character types. In 2020 the film *Ma Rainey's Black Bottom* was released. The Pulitzer Prize and Tony Award-winning *Fences,* 1982, was the third play in the cycle. Set in the 1950s it follows the life of a refuse collector and his family. The 2016 film *Fences* directed by and starring **Denzel Washington** was nominated for four Oscars winning Best Supporting Actor that year for **Viola Davis.** Wilson's rich vein of artistic and critical success continued with, 1986's *Joe Turner's Come and Gone* set in a boarding house in the 1910s. *The Piano Lesson* (1987), set in the 1930s won the Pulitzer Prize for Drama in 1990. *Two Trains Coming* (1990), is set in the 1960s. *Seven Guitars* (1995) takes the audience to the 1940s. *King Hedley II* (1999) feels contemporary set in the 1980s. *Gem of the Ocean* (2003) goes back to the start of the twentieth century. *Radio Golf* (2005), the final instalment appropriately focuses on the 1990s.

The Goodman Theatre in Chicago put on all the plays from 1986–2007. The Denver Centre Theatre Company achieved the same feat with Israel Hicks producing all ten plays from 1990 to 2009.

Three times married August Wilson was diagnosed with liver cancer in June 2005. He died from the illness **on this day** in 2005, age sixty. He was survived by his third wife Constanza Romero and two daughters. Laid to rest at Greenwood Cemetery, Pittsburgh. Wilson's home,1727 Bedford Ave, Pittsburgh was declared a historical landmark by the state on May 30th 2007. No. 1727 was placed on the National Register of Historic Places and declared a place of historic designation 2013.

Following Wilson's death, the ten plays also known as the 'Century Cycle' were also called 'August Wilson's Century Cycle' or 'The American Century Cycle'. Geva Theatre Centre in Rochester New York presented all ten plays, 2007–11 as the 'August Wilson's American Century'.

English playwright **Roy Williams** deserves a mention and entry. From his first production *The No Boys Cricket Club* in 1996 Williams has been an award-winning fixture in the British theatre. His plays include: *Clubland*, 2001, *Sing Yer Heat Out for the Lads,* 2002, *Fall Out,* 2003, *Baby Girl,* 2007 and *Sucker Punch in 2010.* He has written for Television and radio.

Oct 3rd:

Born **on this day** in 1954, Alfred Charles Sharpton Jr is commonly known as the **Rev Al Sharpton.** The Civil Rights activist, Baptist minister and talk show host has had a colourful, often controversial career campaigning for justice and equality for the black community in the USA. An extract from an article by Ron Kampeas best summarises Sharpton who vocalises concerns about conditions experienced by the black community in America. He has often mis-spoke or spoken without always thinking, facing criticism. Here he receives guidance from **Coretta Scott-King** (see April 29th).

Campaigner Rev Al Sharpton

"Al, the purpose of our movement has never been to just get civil rights for us, it's to protect and stand for civil and human rights for everyone."

"Sometimes you are tempted to speak to the applause of the crowd rather than the heights of the cause, and you will say cheap things to get cheap applause rather than do higher things to raise the nation higher."
Al Sharpton admits to using 'cheap' rhetoric about Jews BY RON KAMPEAS MAY 20, 2019 2:25 PM

Sharpton was appointed by **Jesse Jackson** (see October 8th) in 1969 as the youth director for the New York City branch of Operation Breadbasket to improve economic conditions within black communities across the United States. Aged sixteen in 1971, Sharpton established the National Youth Movement to fight the devastating increased use of drugs in the community while raising money for impoverished children in the inner cities. Black congresswoman **Shirley Chisholm**'s (see November 5th) presidential campaign, in 1972, saw Sharpton as her youth director. From 1973– 1980 Al Sharpton was **James Brown's** (see May 3rd) tour manager.

Sharpton found himself drawn into activism becoming the voice for many in the black community. He led protests and marches facing racism and threats campaigning for justice. He raised concerns, challenging a system that often felt corrupt, a system that appeared to fail, or suitably address, black concerns. His caseload included the Bernhard Goetz NYC Subway shootings in 1984 and the Howard Beach incident where three black men were assaulted. One young man was killed fleeing the scene hit by a passing motorist. The Bensonhurst beatings of four black teenagers and murder of sixteen-year-old **Yusuf Hawkins** in 1989. The police shooting of the unarmed twenty-three-year-old Guinean immigrant **Amadou Diallo** 44 times in 1999 came to Sharpton's attention, as did **Ousmane Zongo's** death in 2002 and **Sean Bell's** death in 2006. **Tanya McDowell** charged with larceny served five years for giving a false address to get her child into kindergarten was another case that Sharpton championed. When Sharpton arrived in the UK his presence fuelled media attention resulting in a legal appeal releasing what were known as the 'Cardiff 3'.

Image used at a protest march.

Travon Martin, killed by George Zimmerman in 2012, and **Eric Garner** choked to death by police in July 2014 were part of Sharpton's caseload. Sharpton survived an assassination attempt, January 12th 1991, when a knife was plunged into his chest by Michael Riccardi. Sharpton requested leniency for his assailant who was given a five-to-fifteen-year sentence. Riccardi served ten years and was released on January 8th 2001.

The campaigns generated publicity turning the Reverend into a national figure. Sharpton founded the National Action Network in 1991 New York. The not-for-profit organisation was created to improve voter education, while providing a service to those living in poverty. Small businesses receive support. Affirmative action was promoted and there was a drive for reparations following the period of enslavement.

Sharpton has continued to take on injustice wherever it is found. He stood up for an end to public money to maintain the Thomas Jefferson Memorial in Washington DC, citing the founding father as having 600 slaves and six children, in a non-consenting relationship, with his slave Sally Hemings.

August 28th 2017, the fifty-fourth anniversary of the 'I Have a Dream' speech, saw Sharpton organise and lead a multi-faith march on Washington. Thousands of religious leaders marched in a unified moral rebuke to President Donald Trump. He calls for equal treatment for gays and lesbians, supporting same-sex marriage, and has promised to root out homophobia from the Black church.

Al Sharpton wrote his autobiography with Nick Chiles, *Go and Tell Pharaoh* (1996). He has written three other books: *Al on America, The Rejected Stone: Al Sharpton and the Path to American Leadership* and *Rise Up: Confronting a Country at the Crossroad* (2020). He gave the eulogy at **George Floyd**'s (see May 25th) funeral. He has run for political office, unsuccessfully, it is not clear whether political ambition is about gaining a platform or to seek office. He hosts a daily radio show 'Keeping it Real', and hosts on MSNBC's cable channel, a one-hour political talk show which started on August 29th 2011.

Billed as **'the trial of the century'**, one must never forget that at the heart of the case, against former National Football League (NFL) legend **O. J. Simpson,** were the victims… the brutal murder of Nicole Brown and her friend Ronald Goldman. Unfortunately, it is in the opinion of the writer, that one should neither forget over one hundred years of injustice faced by African Americans in the legal system and decades of abuse experienced at the hands of police departments across the States.

On **this day** in 1995, a majority black jury – eight women (one white, one Hispanic) four men, (one white and one Hispanic) – acquitted Simpson of the double murder. Polls taken of the Los Angeles County residents revealed that most African Americans thought justice had been served by the not guilty verdict. **Malcolm X** (see February 21st) controversially spoke of "chickens coming home to roost" following President Kennedy's assassination. Was Simpson's acquittal one such moment? Was it ugly payback for the hundreds of not guilty verdicts following lynchings and deaths at the hands of overzealous policing in the black community?

Orenthal James Simpson was born on July 9th 1947. Before turning professional he played for USC Trojans setting National Collegiate Athletic Association records and lifting the Heiman trophy in 1968. He played for the Buffalo Bills from 1969–1977. Nicknamed 'The Juice', for five successive seasons, 1972–76, he topped 1,000 yards rushing leading the NFL in that category four times. In 1973 Simpson became the first man to rush more than 2,000 yards in a single season. He would record an average of 143.1 yards per game in a single season. A record at the time Simpson had twenty-three touchdowns in 1975. He rushed 273 yards against the Detroit Lions in 1976. O. J. Simpson retired after eleven seasons in 1979.

Infamous O. J. Simpson.

A career in the media, advertising, broadcasting, TV and movies opened up. The former halfback was able to cash in on his fame appearing in the 'Naked Gun' films. He married Marguerite L. Whitely on June 24th 1967. The couple had a son and two daughters. One daughter drowned, just before her second birthday, at home in a swimming pool incident. The couple divorced that same year, in 1979.

Simpson had already been involved with, the then teenage, Nicole Brown. The pair married in 1985. It was not long before complaints of domestic violence and abuse emerged. O. J. Simpson pleaded no contest when formally accused of spousal battery. Nicole filed for divorce in 1992.

Two years later in Brentwood, Los Angeles, Nicole's body, along with friend Ronald Goldman, was found. Both had been stabbed multiple times and were found dead at the bloody crime scene on June 12th 1994. Simpson, the only suspect, was ordered to surrender for 11 a.m. on June 17th. What happened appeared on national TV as police vehicles and a helicopter followed, in a slow convoy, a white Ford Bronco with Simpson sat in the back. The suspect gave himself up at his mansion in Brentwood. In his possession he had a gun, passport, $9,000 in cash and a disguise. The trial started on January 24th 1995 and ended **on this day** that year. Over 100 million tuned in to hear the verdict that astounded and split the nation, largely on racial grounds (see October 2nd Johnnie Cochran).

O. J. Simpson then faced a civil trial and on February 5th 1997 he was found liable for the wrongful deaths of Brown and Goldman and ordered to pay $33.5 m in damages. Simpson moved to Florida living in Miami where one's property cannot be seized to pay court costs. In 2000 Simpson was allegedly involved in a road rage incident. He was acquitted in October 2001.

In October 2008 Simpson was convicted on twelve accounts of armed robbery and kidnapping, along with accomplice Clarence 'C. J.' Stewart. On December 5th 2008 he was imprisoned for up to thirty-three years. The convicted felon served his sentence at the Lovelock Correctional Centre in Lovelock Nevada. He was paroled on October 1st 2017.

Orenthal James Simpson remains a controversial character. He has difficulty keeping out of public view and continues to express a desire to put the record straight concerning Brown and Goldman.

Val McCalla was born **on this day,** in Jamaica, in 1943. The accountant and bookkeeper joined the RAF with dreams of becoming a pilot. A perforated eardrum meant that flying an aeroplane was out of the question.

After the RAF, McCalla worked at several jobs before launching *The Voice* newspaper from his apartment at the Notting Hill Carnival in 1982. The weekly paper quickly established itself as the mouthpiece for the Afro-Caribbean population. Within eight years circulation topped 53,000. McCalla became a media entrepreneur launching *Pride*, *Chic* and the *Weekly Journal*. The black media pioneer Val McCalla died, age fifty-eight, from liver failure on August 22nd 2002. He is buried in Seaford in East Sussex, England.

Oct 4th:

Consent was not an issue in 1951. **Henrietta Lacks** was unaware that her cells were taken, having no knowledge that they would be harvested for use in medical research. Born Loretta Pleasant on August 1st 1920, she had been admitted to the John Hopkins Hospital in Baltimore, Maryland suffering from an aggressive form of cervical cancer, in January 1951. The mother of five, and wife to Day Lacks, would die **on this day** in 1951. She was thirty-one.

Unknown to Henrietta Lacks and her family, cells had been taken to look at how her cancer could be treated. It was discovered that the cells had an amazing ability to survive beyond the normal few days in the laboratory. The cells called HeLa reproduced at a rapid rate and were described as an immortalised human cell line. Cells from the original biopsy were passed on to other research centres and soon became the workhorse for cell related investigative medical research. The cells were used by Jones Salk in the polio vaccine in 1954. They were the first to be successfully cloned in 1955. Used to investigate; cancer, immunology, infectious diseases and in vitro fertilization, the HeLa cells are directly connected to almost 11,000 patents and have been used researching the COVID vaccine.

Henrietta Lacks' immediate family and descendants only discovered the connection of the HeLa cell line in 1975. No one ever gave consent and there had never been any form of financial settlement. The descendants were horrified when Henrietta Lacks name, medical records and even the DNA sequence of a strain of the HeLa cell was published by research companies in March 2013. What should have been protected by medical confidentiality and privacy laws became public knowledge. The online genome data was removed while an agreement was made between the family and the US National Institute of Health.

Rebecca Skloot who had written a book about Lacks set up the Henrietta Lacks Foundation. Grants are awarded to descendants and anyone whose body parts have been used without their consent for research.

The Lacks family seek to have acknowledged that Henrietta was an African American woman who lived and breathed, was married, had a family and whose life should be recognised. The question of consent is about an individual and one's rights.

One of the **Little Rock Nine** (see October 5th and 11th), **Elizabeth Eckford** is remembered for the ordeal she went through, as a fifteen-year-old black girl, facing an angry mob of malicious racist whites. She was alone, hearing calls to "lynch her, lynch her" and someone shouting "drag her over this tree! Let's take care of that nigger." From the mob came the familiar chant "2, 4, 6, 8 we ain't gonna integrate". A fellow teenager, a white girl, Hazel Bryan is pictured. Her face twisted and contorted with anger, possessed by rage shouting, "go home nigger, go back to Africa". Less than a hundred years after the abolition of slavery in the United States was the white mob ignorant of how and why so many black people had come to be in America?

Moments earlier Eckford had bravely taken public transport, alone. She had expected to meet up with the other eight black student pioneers, in their bid to break the colour bar at Little Rock Central High School. Her family didn't have a phone. Eckford had not been informed of the last-minute change to arrangements. The teenager arrived and made her way to the front of the school. She could see the National Guard at the entrance, students, white students, were being allowed in. Somehow Eckford found the courage and determination to make her way forward. Her path was blocked by a bayonet pointing guard. The fifteen-year-old tried to squeeze through but again with bayonets pointed the girl's entrance was denied. Distraught, Elizabeth Eckford made her way to the bus stop followed by the taunting crowd. Sitting on a bench reporter Benjamin Fine, he had a fifteen-year-old daughter, sat by the crying, yet dignified Eckford. He told the girl "Don't let them see you cry". Threatened, scared and harassed, Eckford was rescued by Grace Lorch, a white woman, who stepped forward to escort the girl on the bus.

Over sixty years later Elizabeth Eckford would write about that day and her life in the autobiography *The Worst First Day: Bullied While Desegregating Little Rock High School* (2018). In adulthood she went on to earn a BA degree in history from Central State University in Wilberforce, Ohio. Eckford went on to spend five years in the army first as a pay clerk and then as an information specialist and writing for army news publications. She became the first black person to hold a non-janitorial job at a bank in St Louis in 1958. Eckford went on to a variety of jobs ranging from waitress, teacher, welfare worker to probation officer.

Hazel Bryant and Elizabeth Eckford met up in 1963. Bryant had undergone a huge transformation and had been on her own journey of conversion and reconciliation. The pair shared a platform in 1998 and have attempted to stay in touch and remain friends. Both have history, both have had to deal with the psychological damage and fall out from that infamous day and the months and years that followed.

On January 1st 2003 Elizabeth's son Erin, 26, was shot and killed by police in Little Rock. The officer was cleared of any misconduct. In her eightieth year Elizabeth Eckford continues to speak on civil rights. (See **Sarah Roberts** February 15th, and **Ruby Bridges** September 8th.)

Lesotho gained independence **on this day** in 1966. Formerly Basutoland, Lesotho gained independence from Britain.

The national flag   A young Basutoland woman

Oct 5th:

Born March 8th 1922, **Fred Lee Robinson,** the famed civil rights leader would be best known as **Fred Shuttlesworth.** He adopted his stepfather's surname.

The activist minister was pastor at the Bethel Baptist Church in Birmingham, Alabama from 1953–61. The National Association for the Advancement of Colored People (NAACP) had been banned in 1955 by circuit judge Walter B. Jones at the urging of Alabama's attorney general John Patterson. To fill the void and continue protests Shuttlesworth formed the Alabama Christian Movement for Human Rights (ACMHR) in 1956. Shuttlesworth served as president through to 1969.

Fred Shuttlesworth was one of the founders of the Southern Christian Leadership Conference (SCLC) in 1957. He served as SCLC's secretary (1958–70) working closely with **Dr Martin Luther King** coordinating the black church leadership's response to civil rights issues.

Shuttlesworth survived his home being bombed and destroyed on Christmas Day 1956. Sixteen sticks of dynamite had been placed under his bedroom window. Attempting to desegregate John Herbert Philips High School enrolling his daughter, Shuttlesworth and his wife Ruby were viciously attacked by a gang of KKK members. The mob wielded whips, chains, baseball bats, knives and knuckle dusters. Ruby was stabbed in the hips. One of the assailants was Bobby Frank Cherry who would, six years later, be involved in the evil attack on the 16th Street Baptist Church bombing, killing the four little girls and injuring many others (see September 15th). A couple of years later a bomb would be found and removed from his Bethel church while Shuttlesworth was present.

Undeterred Fred Shuttlesworth took part in the lunch counter sit-ins in 1960 and 1961. That same year he joined forces with the Congress of Racial Equality (CORE) assisting with the organisation of the Freedom Rides. When riders were brutally attacked, beaten, nearly killed and hospitalised in Birmingham and Anniston, May 4th 1961, the pastor provided sanctuary in his church. The resilient riders attempted to continue on their journey, but no driver was willing to take on the challenge following the firebombing of the previous bus. Attorney General Robert Kennedy had given Shuttlesworth his personal number. Arrangements were made to fly the Freedom Riders out to safety.

The 1963 campaign in Birmingham, Alabama saw the Civil Rights Movement seeking confrontation to expose the criminal behaviour of the city authorities. Police chief Bull Conner arrested dozens of children, he turned high powered water hoses on defenceless children and set police dogs on non-violent protesters. Shuttlesworth was hospitalised after being slammed against a brick wall, hit by water from a high-powered hose. The visibility of the protest in Birmingham was a key factor in the passing of the 1964 Civil Rights Act.

The Bethel Church minister helped to organise the Selma to Montgomery march in 1965 which was instrumental in the passing of the Voting Rights Act that same year.

The pastor moved to Cincinnati, Ohio, 1961 where he founded the Greater New Light Baptist Church in 1966. Civil rights work continued. The Shuttlesworth Housing Foundation was set up in 1988 providing ways for low-income groups to purchase their own homes. Andrew M Manis wrote Shuttlesworth's biography *A Fire You Can't Put Out* was published in 1999.

The retired Shuttlesworth moved back to Birmingham in 2007. In honour of their illustrious son the airport was named Birmingham-Shuttlesworth International Airport on October 27th 2008. Fred Shuttlesworth died **on this day** in 2011; he was eighty-nine. Flags were lowered on state buildings, at the order of Alabama Governor Robert Bentley, until Shuttlesworth was laid to rest at the Oak Hill Cemetery, Birmingham.

Neil deGrasse Tyson, if not the most famous scientist in America, is the most famous astrophysicist in the USA. Tyson's strength has been to popularise science and space, opening up ideas to a mass audience who see a black face at the heart of the scientific community. Astrophysicists apply the methods and principles of physics to study astronomical objects and similar phenomena.

Astrophysicist Neil deGrasse Tyson

His mother was a gerontologist, the study of ageing, looking at social, cultural and psychological aspects while exploring its cognitive and biological side. His father was a sociologist looking at patterns of social behaviour, interactions and relationships. Science was in the Tyson home. At the age of nine Neil visited the Hayden Planetarium in New York. The boy was hooked. By the age of fifteen the teenager became a minor celebrity in the field giving lectures on astronomy. Studying at Harvard, Tyson majored in physics and gained his degree in 1980. He earned his MA in astronomy in 1983 and a PhD in astrophysics in 1991.

That same nine-year-old boy achieved his childhood ambition joining the staff at the Hayden Planetarium in 1994. The following year he was the acting director, becoming director in 1996. Tyson oversaw a $210 million reconstruction project which was completed in 2000. The planetary scientist helped people to understand the scientific study of planets and the moon and the process that formed them.

Neil deGrasse Tyson has written numerous books, essays and periodicals including: *The Sky Is Not the Limit: Adventures of an Urban Astrophysicist*, his autobiography in 2000. *Astrophysics for People in a Hurry* in 2017 and *Letters from an Astrophysicist* in 2019. Tyson embraced the mediums of radio and television to promote science. He hosted a four-part series *Origins* in 2004. The years 2006 to 2011 saw Tyson host the TV series NOVA scienceNOW. Since 2009 the science communicator has hosted the weekly radio show 'Star Talk'. The TV format of the radio show appeared on the National Geographic Channel in 2015. Neil deGrasse Tyson also hosted the television series *Cosmos: A Space Odyssey*.

Maggie Aderin-Pocock is a Black British scientist famous for promoting physics and space science in the UK. She co-hosted the long running programme *Sky at Night* in 2014. Aderin-Peacock was born to Nigerian parents in London on March 9th 1968.

Oct 6th:

Out of **the Haitian revolution** (see July 7th), the uprising led by **Toussaint L'Ouverture** (see May 20th) and his lieutenant **Jean Jacques Dessalines** (September 20th), emerged the military general, then president and eventually **King Henri I of Haiti, Henri Christophe.**

The King of Haiti.

Christophe was born into slavery, **on this day in** 1762, probably on the island of St Kitts or Grenada. By his early twenties he was living in San Domingue (Haiti). He purchased his freedom. When the uprising occurred in 1791, Christophe, although free, sided with the enslaved population and fought alongside L'Ouverture. He quickly rose through the ranks and was appointed a general. Alongside Dessalines he was L'Ouverture's trusted lieutenant. By 1802 Christophe was fighting a guerrilla war in the mountains. He eventually surrendered to the French commander, Charles Leclerc, on the understanding that he would receive a pardon, retain his military rank and that his fighters would serve in the French army. Eventually the other revolutionary forces followed Christophe's example. The truce did not last long. L'Ouverture was deported to France and assassinated.

Christophe joined forces with Dessalines who declared independence for Haiti January 1st 1804. Internal division and politics led to Dessalines's assassination on October 17th 1806, he was forty-eight. Henri Christophe became president on Feb 17th 1807. Internal struggles continued as Christophe maintained control in the north of the island while **Alexandre Sabes Petion** supported by **Jean-Pierre Boyer** controlled the South. On March 26th 1811 Christophe declared himself King Henri I of Haiti. The self-proclaimed monarch set about creating a hereditary noble system with four princes, eight dukes, twenty-two counts, forty barons and fourteen knights. He had six chateaux, eight palaces and the fortress Citadelle Laferriere built. Many of Christophe's constructions would be designated UNESCO world heritage sites in 1982. Catholicism was declared the national religion, schools and hospitals were built. A new monetary system was introduced and Henri's code, a legal system was adopted. The king was forward thinking but oversaw a harsh feudal system which was resented by the general population. Facing continuous threats from France, Spain, England, America and the South of the island, when the monarch had a debilitating stroke, in August 1820, his hold on power was threatened by riots. On October 8th 1820 Henri I of Haiti shot himself, with a silver bullet. Ten days later his heir, his son, was assassinated. In 1821 the northern kingdom became part of the Haitian Republic united by Jean-Pierre Boyer.

Born **on this day** in 1917 to sharecroppers in Mississippi, USA, **Fannie Lou Hamer** endured an early life of poverty, hard work, racism and uncertainty faced by many black people in the South. At the age of eight she witnessed the lynching of **Joe Pullman.**

Hamer would be drawn into civil rights campaigning for the black population to gain the right to vote. She was forty-four when she discovered that she had the right to vote. A group of seventeen attempted to register to vote, August 31st 1962, in Indianapolis, Mississippi. On their way home their bus was stopped. The driver was fined $100 on the trumped-up charge for his bus being too yellow. Hamer would lose her job, sacked by the cotton plantation owner B. D. Marlow, the family were kicked off the land. With no home and few possessions, the Hamer's moved to Ruleville in Mississippi. Intimidation was common. Of the 450,000 black people who could vote only 5per cent in the state of Mississippi were registered by the early 1960s.

Hamer had been sterilised without consent. The practise was so common in the state, for black women, it was known as 'Mississippi appendectomy'. Hamer had attended the North Sunflower County Hospital to remove a tumour. She would later surmise that six out of ten black women left the hospital with their tubes tied. Married to Perry 'Pop' Hamer in 1945, the couple would adopt two daughters.

On one voter registration drive, June 9th 1963, a few women sat in a whites' only section at a bus station. The women were arrested and viciously beaten. Two black men were forced to beat Fannie Lou Hamer until they were exhausted. She was left with lifelong injuries a blood clot in her eye, damage to her kidney and an injury to her leg. She would always walk with a limp. On their release the beaten women heard that **Medgar Evers** had been assassinated (see June 12th).

The Freedom Summer of 1964 saw a major drive recruiting volunteers to register black voters. The Student Non-Violent Coordinating Committee (SNCC) was behind the push. That same year Fannie Lou Hamer formed the Mississippi Freedom Democratic Party (MFDP) an integrated delegation made up of sixty-four black and four white delegates. Hamer served as the vice chair. The MFDP openly challenged the legality of the all-white delegation from Mississippi at the Democrat Convention. President Johnson, embarrassed by the challenge, felt it was politically astute to give a televised address just as Hamer stood to speak at the convention. What she said, the personal statement, delivered with passion and dignity made the evening news. Hamer, Victoria Grey, and Annie Devine became the first black women to stand in the House of Congress and protest. Hamer became nationally recognised and would be invited to speak across the country. Their actions were part of a concerted drive that led to the Voters Rights Act of 1965 on August 6th.

Fannie Lou Hamer promoted a 'pig bank' initiative in 1968. Free pigs were given to black farmers to breed and sell. The following year in her attempt to continue providing economic support for beleaguered black farmers the Freedom Farm Cooperative (FFC) was formed. Donors provided finances to help black farmers buy land to farm collectively. Hamer purchased 640 acres, launched a co-op store, boutique and developed a sewing enterprise assisting small black businesses. The FFC continued through to the mid-1970s.

The National Women's Political Caucus was formed with the help and drive of Hamer in 1971. She was directly responsible for ensuring that 200 low-income homes were built in Ruleville.

Fannie Lou Hamer had been threatened, arrested, beaten, shot at. The powerful and passionate speaker stood up for civil rights and the poor, seeking greater economic opportunities. She died from breast cancer, aged fifty-nine, on March 14th 1977. She is buried in Ruleville where a memorial garden exists in her name.

Born December 25th in 1918, to a Sudanese mother, **Anwar Sadat** would serve as the third president of Egypt. During the Second World War Sadat plotted with the Germans to remove the British from the country. His actions saw him arrested and imprisoned in 1942. Sadat escaped two years later, only to be re-arrested and held in custody, accused of being involved in the plot assassinating the pro-British Amin Othman. He was acquitted in 1948.

Anwar Sadat joined the future president, Gamal Abdel Nasser's Free Officers Organisation. He participated in the 1952-armed coup against the Egyptian monarch King Farouk and supported Nasser's election for president in 1956. Sadat served as vice president 1964–66 and again 1969–71. On Nasser's death Sadat became the acting president September 28th 1972 and became president on October 15th that year.

As the president, Anwar Sadat had an open-door policy (infitah). He looked to develop the Egyptian economy through decentralising and diversification, promoting and attracting trade while inviting foreign investment. Inflation and social inequality rose leading to food riots in January 1977. Diplomatic ties reached an all-time low with the Soviet Union seeing many Soviet technicians expelled from Egypt in 1972. The following year in October Sadat and the Syrians launched an attack on Israel. The Arab-Israeli War saw the

Anwar Sadat.

Israelis recapture the Sinai Peninsula but at a heavy cost of lives and equipment. Sadat was proclaimed a hero as the first Arab leader to capture land from Israel.

November 19th-20th 1977 saw the historic visit by Sadat to Israel for peace talks. Sadat ignored opposition from fellow Arab leaders and the Soviets. The United States' President Carter mediated what became the Camp David Accords of September 17th 1978. The progress to peace saw Sadat and Israel's Menachem Begin awarded the Nobel Peace Prize that year. The Peace Treaty was signed on March 26th in 1979, the first between Israel and an Arab country.

Viewed as a hero and a progressive on the world stage, Sadat suppressed public dissent jailing more than 1,500 protesters across the political spectrum at home. While inspecting the military, on Armed Forces Day commemorating the Arab-Israeli war of 1973, members of the Egyptian Islamic Jihad assassinated the sixty-two-year-old Anwar Sadat. He died **on this day** in 1981.

Oct 7th:

Born **on this day** 1897 to parents born into slavery, **Elijah Poole** would be better recognised as **Elijah Muhammad.** It was the mysterious **Wallace D. Fard** (see February 26th) the founder of the Nation of Islam (NOI), who gave Poole his new name. Later Fard would be believed by his followers to be Allah. Muhammad first encountered Fard at Temple No 1 in Detroit. When Fard disappeared in 1934, Muhammad became the leader and seen by his followers as The Messenger of God, the last great messenger of Allah.

Elijah Muhammed arrived in Detroit as part of the great migration of African Americans from the South seeking economic hope in the North. He arrived with his wife, Clara Evans, and two children. The couple were married in 1919. As the Minister of Islam, Muhammad established the NOI's first newspaper *The Final Call to Islam* in 1934. He set up a school but in doing so fell foul, of the education authorities, accused of, and arrested for, contributing to the delinquency of a minor, not sending his child to a public school in Detroit.

Moving to Chicago Muhammad established Temple No 2. During the Second World War he was jailed from May 8th 1942–46 for avoiding the draft and advising his followers to do the same. He argued that at forty-five he was too old to serve in the army and that as a Muslim he was not going to fight for the white infidels.

Elijah Muhammad's message of separatism calling the black population the chosen of God chimed with many in the working-class community. Promoting pride and self-reliance saw the NOI grow. Criticised by **Thurgood Marshall** (see January 24th) as run by thugs from prison in 1959. The NOI was praised for creating economic solidarity, respect for women, reducing instances of adultery, improving diets, having a non-alcohol practice, lowering rates of crime and juvenile delinquency within its community.

Malcolm X (see January 21st) was taught and mentored by Muhammad. With the arrival of Mr X the NOI experienced huge growth. Teacher and pupil would later clash. Malcolm X would question Muhammad's fidelity concerned that his mentor had fathered children, committing adultery on numerous occasions. X also feared that the NOI was behaving like criminals following the shooting of Ronald Stokes in 1962. Muhammad criticised Malcolm X after he made un-diplomatic utterances concerning the assassination of President Kennedy. Malcolm X was given a ninety-day ban following his remarks.

It was Elijah Muhammad who gave the young boxer Cassius Clay the name Muhammad Ali. He mentored **Louis Farrakhan** who would eventually inherit the name and central beliefs of Muhammad and the leadership of the Nation of Islam. As a separatist Elijah Muhammad called white people 'blue-eyed devils.' He taught NOI members to live apart from the greater white society in the USA, instructing followers to not get involved in national politics. It was Dr C. Eric Lincoln who gave the NOI the name 'Black Muslims' in his book *The Black Muslims in America*. In his later years the 'Messenger of God' would appear more moderate promoting self-help and avoiding confrontation. He argued that the former slave master is no longer holding the black person back and that it is up to black people to get things for themselves.

Elijah Muhammad had suffered with a heart condition, diabetes, bronchitis, and asthma. He was admitted into hospital on January 30th. He died on February 25th in 1975 the day before Saviour's Day when the Nation of Islam celebrates Fard's birthday. Elijah Muhammad was seventy-seven. He was survived by six sons and two daughters. He left the Nation of Islam with restaurants, stores, a bank, a publishing company, possession of 15,000 acres of farmland, producing beef, eggs, poultry, milk, fruit, veg, all distributed by a fleet of trucks and air transport owned by the Nation of Islam.

Born **on this day** in 1931 **Desmond Mpilo Tutu** would become the voice of the voiceless black South African. The 1980s saw Tutu become an international activist, rivalling the popularity and recognition of Nelson Mandela, opposing the South African policy of apartheid. He famously was awarded the Nobel Peace Prize in 1984, having been nominated in 1981, 1982 and 1983. Desmond Tutu became a teacher in 1955 but after a couple of years turned his attention to Christianity, theology and the clergy. In 1962 Tutu moved to study at King's College in London where he gained his master's in theology in 1966. Tutu lovingly recalled racial freedom in the capital, asking police officers the time or direction without fear of arrest. He returned to South Africa, 1967–72, teaching at a variety of institutions before returning to England from 1972 to 1975.

Desmond Tutu.

Back in his homeland Tutu was appointed the first black dean of St Mary's Cathedral in Johannesburg, 1975. The following year he became Bishop of Lesotho serving from 1976 to 78.

As the General Secretary of the South African Council of Churches, Tutu had the platform to address the inequalities and injustices of apartheid. He had a simple four-point programme: 1) Equal civil rights for all. 2) Abolition of the hated pass laws. 3) Universal and common education. 4) An end to forced deportation to homelands.

Calls for international economic sanctions saw the government remove Tutu's passport. Tutu was appointed the first black bishop of Johannesburg serving between 1985–86. Another first saw the bishop become the black archbishop of Cape Town. Tutu now was the religious, spiritual and moral leader of South Africa's 1.6 million Anglicans. Emboldened Tutu continued to call for sanctions and international pressure on the apartheid white minority regime towards universal suffrage. Tutu's non-violent dignified stance led to him being awarded the Nobel Peace Prize. He was increasingly being respected as a unifying force among South Africa's freedom fighters and black political groups. He famously challenged the practice of necklacing as he removed a burning tyre from the neck of a hapless victim deemed a traitor. The action placed himself in immediate danger from the angry crowd as well as from the fire burning his hands.

With the release of Nelson Mandela and a new government Desmond Tutu promoted the 'Rainbow Nation' of South Africa. He was appointed the chair of the Truth and Reconciliation Commission investigating abuses during the apartheid era. The experience left the archbishop devastated, having to regularly call a halt to proceedings, crushed by witnesses recalling in harrowing detail the horrors faced, imprisonment, injuries, torture and death. Tutu wrote a memoir from that period *God Has a Dream: A Vision of Hope for Our Time* published in 2014.

Tutu oversaw the introduction of women priests. He spoke out supporting gay rights. He has been very critical on the Israeli-Palestinian situation, opposed the war in Iraq, and was critical of African National Congress South African presidents Thabo Mbeki and Jacob Zuma.

Although one of the international statesmen known as The Elders, Desmond Tutu retired from public life at seventy-nine, in 2010. He left behind numerous publications including *The Divine Intervention* (1982), *Hope and Suffering* (1983) and *No Future Without Forgiveness* published in 1999. Desmond Tutu died on 26th December in 2021

Oct 8th:

Dr Harold Moody was born **on this day** in 1882 in Kingston, Jamaica. The pioneering civil rights leader arrived in England in 1904 to study medicine at King's College London. He graduated top of his class in 1910 age twenty-eight.

Although suitably qualified Moody found it impossible to find employment. The racial colour bar saw the young physician barred from the traditional occupation of a doctor. After three years of failing to open doors, Moody opened his own practice in Peckham London in 1913. That same year he married nurse Olive Mable Tranter. The couple went on to have six children.

The post-war situation in Britain proved challenging for all, particularly for the black immigrant community. Dr Moody listened to the problems experienced by many in the community. He found himself writing to political leaders, trade unionists and civil servants. In 1921 the devout Christian was elected to the chair of the Coloured Missionary Society's board of directors.

As the chair and through his practice Dr Moody created a network of contacts including **Paul Robeson** (see April 9th)**, Jomo Kenyatta**(see December 12th)**, Una Marson** (see February 6th)**,** and writer and activist **C. L. R. James** (see January 4th). The League of Coloured People (see March 13th) was formed in 1931. The league (LCP) is often viewed as the first effective black pressure group in Britain. That same year the doctor became involved in the Coloured Men's Institute (CMI), a religious and social organisation set up by the Sri Lankan **Kamal Chunchie,** appalled by the treatment of black people, in 1926. The CMI became a social centre for the welfare of coloured sailors. In 1936 Dr Moody became the president of the London Christian Endeavour Federation. He used the platforms available to campaign on a variety of civil rights issues promoting racial equality. Black people were assisted in finding accommodation and securing employment. Moody raised concerns about working conditions in the Caribbean and fought for fair wages for oil workers in Trinidad. He challenged the discriminatory Coloured Seamen's Act of 1925 which provided benefits to white British sailors. He fought to restore citizenship to black sailors in Cardiff in 1936. During the Second World War Harold Moody lobbied for the rights of black servicemen and women in the British armed forces. In 1943 he was appointed to a government advisory committee on the welfare of non-Europeans.

Following a demanding speaking tour of the USA, Dr Harold Moody returned to England exhausted. The sixty-four-year-old died of influenza, at home, on April 24th1947. His home at 164 Queens Road in Peckham, London is identified and commemorated with an English Heritage blue plaque. David A. VAughan published the biography *Negro Victory: The Life of Dr Harold Moody* in 1950.

Ordained a Baptist minister in 1968, the **Rev Jesse Jackson** was born on this day in 1941. Christened Jesse Burns he took his stepfather's name in his teens.

As one of the Greenville 8, the group were arrested for disorderly conduct at a sit-in protesting the segregated library system. Jackson took part in the march from Selma, Alabama, in 1965, alongside Dr King and James Bevel (see December 19th). The young man's enthusiasm was noticed but his ambition and attention seeking behaviour raised concerns for King. Nonetheless King and Bevel appointed Jackson, in 1966, to establish the Southern Christian Leadership Conference (SCLC) branch for Operation Breadbasket in Chicago. Breadbasket aimed to create an economic arm to the SCLC providing a job placement agency. Jackson developed the operation to boycott businesses that discriminated against black people while encouraging the black consumer to buy from black-owned firms. Jackson would serve as the Operations national director from 1967 to 1971.

When Dr Martin Luther King was assassinated1968, Jackson's claims that he was the last to speak to Martin and that King died in his arms would prove controversial and disputed by others who had been present. Jackson was accused of using the SCLC for personal gain. Internal differences between Jackson and **Ralph Abernathy** led to Jackson's resignation in 1971. December 5th of that year Operation People United to Save Humanity (Operation PUSH), based in Chicago, was launched by Jackson. The decade ended with Jackson visiting South Africa and speaking out against apartheid in 1979. PUSH advocated liberal views while promoting self-help, voter registration, fair housing policies, the boycott of businesses that failed to employ black people and those that restricted business with black companies.

Jesse Jackson's international profile grew in the 1980s. His political presence developed as he criticised Israel over the plight of the Palestinians and campaigned for a homeland. The new decade saw the minister continue voter registration drives seeing **Harold Washington** becoming Chicago's first black mayor in April 1983. Seeking selection to run for president for the Democratic Party Jackson came third in the 1984/5 primaries and second in the 1987/8 run off to Michael Dukakis. His political presence ensured that issues of race were placed centre stage in the Democratic Party.

Jackson founded the National Rainbow Coalition in 1984, seeking equal rights for black people, women and the gay community. That same year Jackson travelled to Syria successfully negotiating the release of US navy pilot Lt. Robert Goodman. In June of 1984 he secured the release of twenty-two Americans that had been held in Cuba. In Iraq 20 Americans and several British hostages known as 'the human shield' were released after Jackson intervened in 1990. Former Yugoslavia was the scene for Jackson's negotiated release of three prisoners of war in 1999.

The Rainbow Coalition and PUSH were merged in 1996 as Rainbow/Push. President Clinton appointed Jesse Jackson special envoy to Africa in 1997 to promote human rights and democracy. That year he founded the Wall Street Project to increase opportunities for minorities in corporate America.

1989 Jackson meets Nicaraguan president Daniel Ortega.

Leo Felton and his girlfriend Erica Chase were convicted for their terrorist plot to rid America of what they described as "mud people", Asians, Blacks, Latinos and Jews. Jackson was one of their targets. Felton was sentenced to twenty-six years and ten months. A cloud of controversy, 2001, hung over the Baptist minister when it was revealed that he had a child out of wedlock. It was announced in 2017 that Jackson was suffering from Parkinson's disease. No longer the charismatic, dynamic, passionate speaker Jackson continues to speak out against injustice supporting the Black Lives Matter protests against police shootings. Images of Jesse Jackson's face bathed in tears became an iconic picture capturing the historic magnitude and emotion of the moment when President Barack Obama won the election.

African American journalist and newspaper owner the republican **John Willis Menard** was born April 3rd 1838. He would have been the first black man elected to the US Congress (House of Representatives). Electoral disputes saw Menard denied his seat by the House. Menard died **on this day** in 1893.

Artist, speaker, and writer **Faith Ringgold** born **on this day** in 1930. She is best remembered for her captivating and innovative quilt-based artwork, capturing her beliefs, civil rights and the black community.

Oct 9th:

The first president of independent Senegal **Leopold Sedar Senghor** was born **on this day** in 1906. The African statesman, poet, writer, intellectual, cultural theorist, and one of the founding figures of Negritude arrived in France in 1928 at the age of twenty-two.

Senghor described this period in France as "sixteen years of wandering" through to 1944. He qualified to teach and taught at the universities of Paris and Tours from 1935–45. Drafted into the French army in 1939, Senghor was captured in World War II by the Germans spending two years in the prison camps. It is said that he wrote some of his best poetry while imprisoned. He was released due to ill health. On release Senghor joined the French Resistance.

He married Ginette Eboue on September 12th 1946. The couple had two sons. That same year he was elected to the lower house in the French parliament, The National Assembly, becoming one of two Senegalese deputies. Senghor went on to found the Senegalese Democratic Bloc. He was re-elected in 1951 to the National Assembly.

Pushing for independence Senghor appealed to the French leader Charles de Gaulle for Senegalese independence. Although the path to independence was not straightforward Leopold Sedar Senghor was elected president on September 5th 1960. His prime minister Mamadou Dia promoted programmes for national development while the president was involved in foreign policy. The two clashed with Dia, accused of an attempted coup d'état in 1962. Dia was sentenced to life imprisonment but released in 1974.

Senghor pursued a policy of African socialism, with a democratic and humanistic approach. He avoided Marxism and anti-western rhetoric. The president attempted to work cooperatively with his African neighbours while retaining links with the French. He challenged corruption and inefficiencies. The Roman Catholic leader was able to unite the largely Muslim country. Belonging to the Serer people he effectively led the predominantly Wolof people of Senegal. Recognised as one of the continent's great intellectuals Senghor received his support from the peasants. Promoting Negritude and being passionate about African culture he nonetheless appreciated all that Western culture had to offer. The president looked to improve and modernise the country's agriculture. On March 22nd 1967 Senghor survived what appeared to be an assassination attempt. The would-be assassin Moustapha Lo was executed on June 15th that same year.

Leopold Sedar Senghor met **Aime Cesaire** while he was living in Paris. With **Leon Damas** from French Guiana, Cesaire and Senghor became the three founders and main proponents of Negritude. Negritude was influenced by the Harlem Renaissance. The literary, artistic and political theory was an expression of African experience developed by French speaking Africans and Caribbean's in Paris in the 1930s. Critical of western culture, negritude examined, reassessing and promoted African culture, creating an understanding of the continents, distinct characteristics, values and aesthetics. Senghor became negritude's main spokesperson. In 1947 he helped to establish the journal 'Presence Africaine' which published African writers. The following year he edited *The Anthology of French Language African Poetry*.

Senghor was able to balance writing and politics. Some of his works include: 'Chants d'ombre' (Songs of Shadows), 1945, 'Hosties noires' (Black Offerings), 1948, 'Ethiopiques', 1956, 'Nocturnes', 1961, 'Poemes', 1964, 'Elegies majeures' (Major Elegies), 1979. Senghor's collected poems were published in 'Oeuvre poetique' (Poetical Works) in 1990. He published his memoir, 'Ce que je crois: négritude Francité et civilisation de l'universel' (That Which I Believe: Negritude Frenchness, and Universal Civilisation) in 1988.

On retiring from politics, December 31st 1980, Senghor became the first African to freely step down from office. A French citizen since 1932 Senghor moved to France. He died at the age ninety-one on December 20th in 2001. He married a second time and had another son.

Uganda gained independence from Britain **on this day** in 1962. The early years of the newly independent country were shaped by **Milton Obote,** prime minister 1962– 70 and president 1966–71. Overthrown by **Idi Amin Dada** on January 25th in 1971 (see Jan 25th), Obote returned as president from 1980–85.

A young woman from Uganda   Milton Obote

Ruby Smith-Robinson, born on April 25th 1942, would be a brief but important voice in the Civil Rights Movement in particular with the Students Nonviolent Coordinating Committee (SNCC). Watching images of the Montgomery bus boycott on the evening news motivated the thirteen-year-old Ruby to a future in activism. As a student at Spelman College, she was involved in nonviolent demonstrations and one of the first at the lunch counter sit-ins in Atlanta.

In 1961 Ruby joined SNCC. Protesting against student arrests in Rock Hill, Carolina Ruby was arrested and served thirty days. As a Freedom Rider in1961, Ruby was viciously beaten on May 17th and then arrested charged with "inflammatory" traveling. She spent forty-five days at the Parchman State Prison.

Ruby Smith married Clifford Robinson in 1964. The couple had a child. Soon after giving birth, Ruby continued with her activism. She became the first and only woman executive secretary of SNCC in 1966 following **James Farmer** (see January 12th). Ruby clashed with and opposed **Stokely Carmichael's** (see June 29th) more aggressive militant policies. Diagnosed with leukaemia Ruby Robinson died the following year **on this day** 1967, she was twenty-six. Ruby is buried at South View Cemetery in Atlanta. Cynthia Fleming's biography *Soon We Will Not Cry* based on Rubye Robinson was published in 1998.

Oct 10th:

Allen Macon Bolling's exact date of birth is unclear. Sources agree on 1816 as the year, but there is little agreement as to the exact date of birth for Bolling. Some sources suggest August 4th 1816, most acknowledge we know little of his early life.

On January 1st 1844 Bolling officially changed his name to **Macon Bolling Allen.** Born free in the state of Indiana of mixed heritage, Allen moved to the anti-slave state of Maine where he worked as a clerk for abolitionist and lawyer General Samuel Fessenden. While a clerk Allen studied law. Anyone of good character could be admitted to the bar in Maine. Allen's application was rejected. As a black man he was not considered a citizen. On July 3rd 1844 he passed the bar exam and became the first recorded African American licensed to practise law. Unfortunately, few white clients were prepared to hire the black lawyer and there were few black people living in the state.

Moving to Boston in 1845 Allen, with partner Robert Morris Sr, opened the country's first African American law office. Allen was licensed by the state of Massachusetts on May 5th 1845. Two years later as a Justice of the Peace in 1847 Allen became the first African American to hold a judicial position in the United States.

After the Civil War the JP moved to Charleston and opened a legal office with William J. Whipper and Robert Brown. He was appointed judge in the Inferior Court of Charleston in 1874 and was elected as probate judge for Charleston County in South Carolina. Allen ended up working in the capitol Washington DC as a lawyer for the Land and Improvement Association.

As with the date of birth there appears to be disagreements as to Macon Bolling Allen's date of death. For entry in this publication acknowledging the pioneering advocate I have chosen **this day October 10th**. Other sources cite October 15th or even June 11th. All agree the year was 1894. Allen died at the age of seventy-eight.

One of the undisputed greats of music, let alone jazz. **Thelonious Monk's** compositions are second only to **Duke Ellington** (see May 24th) in jazz recording frequency. Monk composed over seventy numbers including: 'Round Midnight', 'Evidence', 'Ruby My Dear', 'Epistrophy', 'I Mean You', 'Misterioso', 'Well We Needn't', 'Ask Me Now', 'Think of One' and a tribute to his friend and one of jazz's great patrons 'Pannonica'. Monk is one of only five jazz musicians to appear on the cover of *TIME* magazine, the others being **Louis Armstrong** (Dee August 4th)**,** Duke Ellington**,** Dave Brubeck and **Wynton Marsalis**.

Thelonious Monk   Wynton Marsalis

Born **on this day** in 1917, he was one of the founders of the jazz style bebop. Monk never received the immediate recognition of **Charlie Parker** (see August 29th) and **Dizzy Gillespie** (see October 21st)**.** His deliberate style of piano appeared untutored and crude. At first listening, Monk's sparse use of notes and chordal clusters sounds as if he were playing the wrong keys. It felt as if he was out of step with the fashionable fast moving and complex bebop. His style was slow, angular and spacious. The timing and phrasing were both unusual, often played with a heavy-handed style. Monk, as with many of his contemporaries, explored and challenged possibilities seeing how the shape of music could be altered.

Thelonious Monk, famous for his idiosyncratic music was equally recognised for his unusual behaviour. In his distinctive hats, suits and sunglasses Monk would often stand up, leave his piano and dance in the middle of a performance, he was also known to get up, leave his own gig, and wander out of the club. His undiagnosed bi-polar manifested itself in misunderstood eccentric behaviour. Misdiagnosed and incorrectly medicated, poor medical advice and the resulting prescription drugs left him unable to function.

He could play a variety of styles, having one foot in the past, his musical hero was Coleman Hawkins. Financially Monk struggled to make ends meet to provide for his family. He lost his cabaret licence twice: Heroin was found on his person, Monk refused to tell the authorities that the drugs belonged to **Bud Powell.** Police in Delaware arrested the composer, seeing a black man, who was not a chauffeur, sitting in Baroness Pannonica de Koenigswarter's Bentley.

A complex set of circumstances; misdiagnosis, incorrect medication, financial pressures, performing and his bi-polar saw Monk withdraw into a world of silence for the last five years of his life in 1975. With failing health, he lived with the baroness, who with his wife Nellie, took care of him. He suffered a stroke on February 5th 1982 and died twelve days later in his wife's arms on February 17th 1982. He was survived by his wife Nellie Smith (they married in 1949 and had a son and daughter). Thelonious Monk is buried in Ferncliff Cemetery in Hartsdale, New York.

-

Nigerian writer, poet, journalist, television personality, environmental and political activist **Ken Saro-Wiwa** was born **on this day** in 1941. His campaign against the multinational oil companies degrading and polluting the land and waterways, decimating the wildlife, led to his execution.

Saro-Wiwa's 1985 novel *Songs in a Time of War* is about a woman returning from Britain to Nigeria following her studies. On the aeroplane she has a romance, and the reader gets to see where this will lead. The same year the author published the political satire *Sozaboy*, a novel about the Biafran Civil War, written in pidgin English it looks at political corruption in Nigeria. As a television presenter Saro-Wiwa would become a household celebrity with the TV comedy series *Basi and Company*. The 150 episodes, aired in the 1980s, were adapted from an earlier play by Saro-Wiwa called *Transistor Radio*.

Ken Saro-Wiwa devoted his time to full-time activism, in 1991, defending the half a million Ogoni people of Ogoniland in the Nigerian Delta, Nigeria. Saro-Wiwa set up the nonviolent Movement for the Survival of Ogoni People (MOSOP) acting as its president. The Royal Dutch Shell Oil Company struck oil in 1958, in the delta. Over $30b has been extracted, huge profits for the company and the government but leaving the Ogoni land polluted. Little profit was ploughed into the community and there has been limited local employment. Saro-Wiwa accused the multinational oil companies of exploiting the people. He was also an outspoken critic calling out corruption in the military-led Nigerian government.

Following a series of marches, mob violence left four Ogoni chiefs dead. The men had been brutally attacked and hacked to death. It is not clear how or why the march turned violent. Many point suspiciously at the arrival of government forces who appeared to expect trouble. Although the MOSOP president had been turned away from taking part in the march he was arrested and accused of being implicated in the murders.

A year in custody would pass before the trial came to court. Amnesty International accused the Nigerian government of crimes against humanity. Ogoni people fled into the African bush fleeing assaults, beatings, arrests, intimidation and rape. Amnesty called Saro-Wiwa a prisoner of conscience for his nonviolent activities. As the special military tribunal trial started in February 1995, the accused were finally able to meet with their legal team. In May Saro-Wiwa had a letter smuggled out highlighting the torture and threats that he had experienced.

Nine including the author were executed by hanging on November 10th 1995. The British Prime Minister John Major led the international condemnation calling the trial fraudulent, the verdict as bad, the sentence as unjust and as judicial murder. The following day Nigeria was suspended from the Commonwealth, they would not be readmitted for three years. The Nigerian government faced condemnation from individual countries and the United Nations.

Shell paid an out of court settlement, with a non-guilty clause, in 2009 to the Saro-Wiwa family and others of $15.5 m. The payment followed a lawsuit from 1996 and was reached weeks before going to court. Ken Saro-Wiwa was fifty-four. He did not hang alone. Eight others were hung on that day.

Oct 11th:

Jamaican national hero **Paul Bogle** spoke to the crowd in August of 1865. People had gathered angry at their petitions, raising concerns over social and economic hardships, being ignored. Bogle was a supporter of mixed heritage **George William Gordon** who had challenged the island's governor Edward Eyre. The governor continued to take the side of the rich, land owning plantocracy.

Paul Bogle, appointed deacon of Stony Gut Baptist church in 1864 led the peasants' protest for justice and fair treatment under the law. The people wanted access to land. Their legal challenges were being thwarted by the lower courts. Bogle led a delegation to the then capital Spanish Town, over forty miles away. The group was refused an audience with the governor. Returning to Stony Gut, Bogle attempted to establish a legal system appointing magistrates and court officials.

Paul Bogle   George William Gordon

Two men were arrested. Bogle and his supporters marched on Morant Bay, the local administrative town a couple of miles away. The protestors surrounded the court to disrupt proceedings of the pair on trial. The loud but peaceful protest led to skirmishes with the authorities and two people were killed. An arrest warrant was issued for Bogle.

Paul Bogle led a march of over 400 protestors on Morant Bay **on this day** in 1865. The group raided the police station seizing arms. The local council was holding a meeting in the courthouse at the time. The courthouse was set alight. The governors' representative and seventeen officials were killed in the uprising as well as seven of the protestors.

The following day soldiers arrived by ship and on foot to quell the revolt. The protestors held the area in St Thomas for two days. The fear was that the protest would spread across the island. Martial law was declared. The rebellion was brutally crushed. Over 400 were killed, most hung, 600 flogged and a 1,000 homes and small land holdings destroyed.

Critic of the governor, George William Gordon was arrested, charged with treason and complicity with the rioters and hanged on October 24th. Paul Bogle had fled to the hills but was captured by maroons. He was hanged, in the courthouse in Morant Bay, on October 24th 1865.

A commission to look into the events of the Morant Bay rebellion was established by the British who took control declaring Jamaica a crown colony. Change and improvements were not immediate' but Bogle's protest eventually led to better conditions.

Paul Bogle was named one of Jamaica's five national heroes in 1969 alongside: **Alexander Bustamante**, (see August 6th) **Marcus Garvey**, (see August 17th), George William Gordon, **Norman Manley**, **Nanny of the Maroons** and **Samuel Sharpe**, (see May 23rd).

Canadian born composer, organist, pianist, choral director, music professor, poet and essayist **Robert Nathanial Dett** was born **on this day** in 1882. The polymath was the first black person to graduate from Oberlin College in 1908. He would be the first black person given an honorary Doctor of Music degree from the Oberlin Conservatory in 1914.

Dett published about 100 compositions for piano, vocal and choral works. His main contribution was preserving, called at the time, negro folk music and spirituals. Inspired by the black British composer **Samuel Coleridge Taylor** (see August 15th), Dett saw negro folk music as a gift to the world. He explored the music in a collection of four essays; 'The Emancipation of Negro Music', 'The Development of Negro Secular Music', 'The Development of Negro Religious Music' and 'Negro Music of the Present' all contained 'Negro Music' winner of a prestigious literary Harvard University award in 1920. Dett collected spirituals in two compilations, one being 'The Dett Collection of Negro Spirituals' in 1936. He went on to develop interests in ancient Hebrew legends, Hindu poets and African chants.

Dett compositions include popular pieces such as: 'Dance Juba' (1913), 'Listen to the Lambs' (1914), 'Somebody's Knocking at Your Door' (1919), 'I'm So Glad Trouble Don't Last Always' (1919), 'Don't Be Weary, Traveller' (1920), and the choral works 'Chariot Jubilee' and 'The Ordering of Moses'.

In 1914 Dett took his forty-strong Hampton Singers to perform at Carnegie Hall and became the first black person to hold the position of director of music at the Hampton Institute in Virginia, 1926. The same year December 17th Dett's eighty-strong choir was invited to perform at the Library of Congress in Washington, D.C. Before leaving the United States for a six-week seven country tour of Europe the choir performed on the lawn of the White House for President Herbert Hoover in 1930.

Robert Dett married Helen Elsie Smith on December 27th 1916. She was the first black graduate at the Institute of Musical Art, later called the Juilliard School in New York.

Robert Nathanial Dett died of a heart attack while travelling on October 2nd 1943. He was buried at Niagara Falls, Ontario, Canada.

Cuban right-handed baseball pitcher **Orlando Hernandez** was born **on this day** in 1965. He would have a win-loss record of 129-47, the best winning percentage in Cuban League history. Hernandez won gold playing for his country at the 1992 Barcelona Olympics. He won gold with Cuba at the Baseball World Cup in 1988, 1990 and 1994.

Hernandez, defected to the USA in 1997, making his debut for the New York Yankees on June 3rd 1998. He helped the team to three successive World Series titles 1998–2000. In 1999 Hernandez was named Most Valuable Player in the American League Championship series. A move to the Chicago White Sox saw the pitcher help the team secure a World Series title in 2005. Orlando Hernandez was nicknamed "El Duque", "The Duke". He retired in 2011.

Oct 12th:

Kenyan political scientist, professor and writer on Africa and Islam **Ali Al'amin Mazrui** was born on 24th February 1933. His need for original thinking meant that Mazrui was able to hold seemingly paradoxical ideas uniting mutually exclusive theories. His unconventional thought process often saw him appear controversial.

The BBC/PBS nine-part series, hosted by Mazrui, *The African: A Triple Heritage* looked at how the continent had been affected by the foreign religions of Islam and Christianity. With the damaging effects of colonialism, it was difficult to identify anything that was authentically indigenously African. Mazrui raised eyebrows in the series arguing Africa needed its own nuclear ability to create world balance. He believed that without African nuclear capability the continent would always be the weaker partner on the military world stage.

Critical of capitalism and socialism, Mazrui spoke out against Marxism at a time when young independent African countries and their leadership were developing an 'African Socialism'. The professor would advocate what he called liberal socialism. He worked at the University of Makerere in Uganda. Speaking out against the Ugandan leader **Idi Amin** he was forced to flee. The outspoken academic could not find employment in his homeland of Kenya, refused an academic position during the rule of **Jomo Kenyatta**(see December 12th) and **Daniel Arap Moi.** He ended up working at the University of Michigan in the United States in 1984.

Influenced by Pan-Africanism, Mazrui took the idea forward towards what he called 'Afrabia', a merging Africa and the Arab nations. Mazrui was critical of the State of Israel in particular with the plight of the Palestinians.

In *Black Reparations in the Era of Globalisation* 2002, Mazrui attacked western cultural imperialism demanding that reparations were essential for the continent to move forward. The author and co-author of over twenty books argued in *Islam between Globalization and Counter Terrorism* (2006), which he co-edited, that terrorist philosophy had ensnared Islam. The professor defended political Islam and Sharia law but rejected terrorism and violence as legitimate options. He opposed the second Iraq War 2003–2011, opposed in general to European and US military interventions.

Ali Al 'amin Mazrui, died **on this day** in 2014. His body was repatriated to Kenya.

Oil rich **Equatorial Guinea,** on the west coast of Africa, gained independence from Spain **on this day** in 1968. **Francis Macias Nguema** was the new country's first president, his reign of terror ended in 1979. During his presidency, a third of his countrymen fled. Removed from power by **Teodoro Obiang Nguema Mbasogo,** (Africa's longest serving leader), Nguema remains one of the continent's most Brutal dictators.

The national flag.   F. M. Nguema.

Oct 13th:

Novelist, poet, historian, biographer, librarian, and archivist **Arna Bontemps** was born **on this day** in 1902. A member of the literary and arts Harlem Renaissance, it is said that Bontemps' first novel, *God Sends Sundays* (1931) marked the end of the Renaissance.

The prolific writer is best remembered for his work as a librarian. For two decades at Fisk University from 1936, in Nashville Tennessee, Bontemps established one of the great collections of black literature in the United States. The archive helped to shape modern African American literature and influenced black American culture, while preserving the heritage. Bontemps married Albertina Johnson in 1926, the couple had six children. Critical literary success did not equal financial security which led the author to become a librarian.

Bontemps wrote historical novels looking at the slave uprising of 1800 Virginia in *Black Thunder* and *Drums at Dark* (1939) set in **L'Ouverture**'s Haiti (see May 20th). He produced biographies covering **George Washington Carver** (see January 5th), **Frederick Douglass** (see February 14th) and **Booker T. Washington** (see April 5th). Other works included children's fiction and his 1963 volume of verse *Personals*, *The Harlem Renaissance Remembered* (1972), and *The Old South* (1973).

Arna Bontemps died of a heart attack, aged seventy-one, on June 4th 1973. He is buried at Greenwood Cemetery in Nashville, Tennessee.

Ethiopian **Abuna Basilios** born 1891 became the first patriarch of the newly autocephalous, (ecclesiastically independent) Ethiopian Orthodox Church. He was appointed and consecrated as abuna or primate on January 1st 1957. After negotiations with **Emperor Haile Selassie I** reforms were taking place within the Church. Since the fourth century the Ethiopian Church had been effectively governed by the Coptic Church in Alexandria, Egypt. The Egyptian ecclesiastic leadership appointed the primate of the Ethiopian Orthodox Church. By the 1940s independence was gained. The Ethiopian Church had complete indigenous leadership by 1954 and complete independence established in 1959. Basilios served as the first Ethiopian primate. He died **on this day** in 1970.

Born **Betty Johnson,** in multi-racial Tiger Bay, Cardiff, Wales to a Barbadian mother and Jamaican father in 1933, **Betty Campbell** would become the first black headteacher in Wales.

At school Betty was devastated, having expressed her desire to become a teacher, being told that her ambitions as a black female would be insurmountable. She would later recall just placing her head on her desk and crying. Her father had died in World War II, in 1942, when the ship Ocean Vanguard was torpedoed. Betty's mother struggled to make ends meet. Winning a scholarship to Lady Margaret High School for Girls in Cardiff provided the educational foundation that the student required for a better future. Getting pregnant at seventeen was a major setback. Betty married Robert Campbell in 1953. Already with two children (the couple would have four), Betty Campbell applied to the Teacher Training College in Cardiff in 1960. She was one of only six women enrolled in that first year.

When the opportunity arose for a position in Tiger Bay, now Bluetown, Campbell accepted the post at Mount Stuart Primary School. At the school for twenty-eight years, she became the first black headteacher in Wales in the 1970s.

Campbell introduced a template for teaching about black history, slavery and the system of apartheid in South Africa. The pioneering and inspirational multicultural education package was part of Campbell's efforts to enhance black spirit and culture. Betty Campbell was a councillor for Bluetown on Cardiff City Council 1991–1995 and on Cardiff Council, 1999–2004. In 2003 she received the national award of recognition, an MBE. Campbell served as a member of the Commission for the Racial Equality and was a member of the Home Office's Race Advisory Committee.

Betty Campbell died **on this day** in 2017, she was eighty-two. The BBC's Hidden Heroines Campaign, looking to redress the imbalance of statues to men, had a shortlist of five women candidates. On January 18th 2019 Betty Campbell won the public vote from the shortlisted five. Sculpture Eve Shepherd was selected to create the statue that will stand outside BBC Wales in Central Square, Cardiff.

Jamaican award-winning novelist **Marlon James** became the first from his country to win the Man Booker Prize on this day in 2015. Born in Jamaica on November 24th 1970, James's work known for its graphic violence and sex is compared to the filmmaker Quentin Tarantino. Influences include **Ben Okri** (see March 15th), **Bob Marley** (see February 6th) and **Peter Tosh**.

Marlon James won the Booker Prize for his 2014 *A Brief History of Seven Killings*. He published *John Crow's Devil* (2009), *The Book of Night Women* (2009), and *Black Leopard, Red Wolf* published in 2019.

Oct 14th:

Oscar Charleston played baseball during a time when the game in the USA was segregated. Born **on this day** in 1896 Charleston would be seen as an exceptional player. He was considered by many to be the best all-rounder in the Negro League. Stationed in the Philippines, Charleston was the only African American player in the Manila League playing in 1914. Returning to the USA Charleston signed for the local black club in Indianapolis Indiana called the ABC's. The team won the championship in 1916. Recognised for his speed with a strong throwing arm, in 1919 Charleston joined Chicago's American Giants but returned to the ABC's the following season playing in the newly-formed Negro National League. The 1921 season saw Charleston lead the league in doubles, triples and home runs. He stole thirty-five bases in 60 games and had a batting average of .434 that season. Charleston would have a lifetime batting average of .357.

The years 1932 to 38, saw Charleston as player manager for the Pittsburgh Crawfords. He retired from playing in 1941. As a manager he would guide the Indianapolis Clowns to a Negro World Championship. Oscar Charleston died on October 6th 1954. In 1976 he was inducted into the Baseball Hall of Fame.

White German scholar, linguist and ethnologist **Oswin Kohler** was born **on this day** in 1911. His life's work would be donated to the Institute of African Studies which he led from 1962 to his retirement in 1977 at the University of Cologne.

Kohler passed his Swahili translator exam 1943. He was appointed the government ethnologist in Southern Africa in 1995 where he first encountered the Khoisan people. The ethnologist was captivated by the Khoisan. He devoted himself to studying their endangered language, famed for the click sound used in their consonants, and their customs. Kohler engaged in field work creating a record of the Kxoe people found largely in Namibia and Angola. He produced an unparalleled and monumental study. Two volumes were published: *The World of the Kxoe Bushmen in Southern Africa: A Self-expression in Their Own Language* in 1989. The second volume *A Self-expression in Their Own Language: Basics of Life: Water Collecting and Hunting, Soil Cultivation and Husbandry* was published in 1991.

Kohler's research contained irretrievable cultural and historical testimonies from rapidly changing people. Kohler helped to revive ethnology looking at the diversity of human ways of life as an empirical and comparative social and cultural science.

Oswin Kohler died aged eighty-four on May 2nd in 1996. He is buried at the Melaten Cemetery in Cologne.

Nicknamed 'The Chameleon' leader of Benin for a total of twenty-nine years, **Mathieu Kerekou** was born on September 2nd 1933 in what was Dahomey.

The military officer came to power in a coup on October 26th 1972. Kerekou introduced a Marxist-Leninist one-party state overseeing the expansion of the state and nationalisation. The name of the country was changed from Dahomey to The People's Republic of Benin in 1975. Recorded as a period of relative political stability with liberal socialist economic policies, Kerekou had to navigate threats of coups, political opposition and economic challenges. The president survived. In true chameleon fashion he dropped the Marxist policies and introduced multi- party elections. Having lost the election in 1991 Kerekou stepped down from power. Benin became the first sub-Saharan African country returned from a dictatorship by popular discontent and agitation to a multi-party democracy. Mathieu Kerekou stepped back from the political arena and kept a dignified silence.

The former dictator was returned to power in a free and fair election in 1996. Controversy surrounded his re-election in 2001 but again 'the Chameleon' refrained from changing the constitution allowing a third time in office. Kerekou stepped down at the end of his tenure. Leaving office in 2006, as in 1991, the former president stepped back from politics. Suffering from ill health in 2014 he sought treatment in Paris. Poor health continued. Mathieu Kerekou died **on this day** in 2015; he was eighty-two.

Oct 15th:

On this day in 1966 two students at Merritt College founded the **Black Panther Party for Self-defence.** The name would be shortened to the **Black Panther Party** (BPP). Influenced by **Marcus Garvey**'s Universal Negro Improvement Association (see July 15th and August 17th), The Nation of Islam (see October 7th) **Malcolm X** (see February 21st) and **Stokely Carmichael** (see June 29th), the BPP grew out of the need to empower and protect the black urban community.

Huey P Newton (see August 22nd) and fellow student **Bobby Seale** (see October 22nd) formed the party to observe police behaviour, Copwatch, in the area of Oakland, California. Armed members would monitor police operations to ensure that the officers were not harassing and shooting members of the black community. The northern urban black community had experienced racial unrest, joblessness, issues of poor health, violence, repression, police victimisation and a feeling of helplessness, unable to create real change and improvement. Malcolm X had died a year earlier, something had to happen.

The Black Panther Party set up a series of community survival programmes, helped to provide education, testing for tuberculosis, legal aid, ambulances and transport facilities. The most significant and high-profile provision was the Free Breakfast for Children Programme rolled out in January 1969. The BBP had expanded to sixty-eight American cities in forty-eight states by 1970. Their influence extended beyond the USA with chapters as far afield as Australia, England and Algeria.

The sight of young black men upholding their 2nd Amendment rights to constitutionally bear arms was too much for many in authority. The Mulford Act was signed by California's governor Ronald Reagan in direct response to the BBP. The act repealed a law that had allowed the public to carry a loaded firearm. The Federal Bureau of Investigation Director J. Edgar Hoover turned his full attention and considerable power to destroy the BBP which he labelled communist. In 1969 he declared the party to be the greatest threat to internal security. COINTELPRO, a counter-intelligence programme was launched. The sole purpose of COINTELPRO was to destroy the Panther Party using surveillance to undermine the BPP's leadership, create misinformation, infiltrate, incriminate, assassinate, discredit, criminalise, harass, and sabotage by any means possible. The FBI's actions were so complete it was clear that war on the Panthers had been declared. Newton was imprisoned, **Eldridge Cleaver** (see May 1st) fled into exile, **Angela Davis**, although never a BPP member, became one of the FBI's most wanted. Most serious were the shootouts with police. Up and coming panther **Fred Hampton** (see December 4th) was murdered in 1969.

The resulting chaos saw the BPP leadership fall apart. Huey P. Newton's erratic drug fuelled behaviour created turmoil and disorder within the party. The leadership splintered. In the early 1970s membership declined. By 1980, what numbered at close to five thousand now saw less than fifty members. The decline of the self-help group that grew out of Copwatch had officially closed by 1982.

Oct 16th:

George Washington Williams enlisted to fight in the American Civil War for the Unionist army at the age of fourteen. He would be discharged, having a lung wound, in 1868. Born **on this day** in 1849, Williams would be described first and foremost as a historian, but he was much more. Ordained a Baptist minister in 1874, he worked in several churches before turning to politics. Williams served Cincinnati for a single term in the Ohio House of Representatives 1880–1881, he was the first black person to do so. After his stint as a politician Williams took up legal work as a lawyer. At the time he also wrote *History of the Negro Race in America from 1619–1880*, published in 1882. It would be the first historical work employing scientific and objective research while not being a voice for campaign, black apologetics or propaganda. Williams wrote *A History of the Negro Troops in the War of the Rebellion* (1888). He interviewed veterans and sourced newspaper accounts for his study.

On visiting the Congo in Africa Williams was appalled, witnessing the brutal exploitation of the people by the Belgian King Leopold II. Outrage compelled Williams to devote the rest of his life to publicising the cruelty faced by the people of the Congo. On July 8th 1890 Williams wrote an open letter to Leopold listing twelve areas of concern regarding atrocities. He concluded that all the crimes; deceit, fraud, robberies, arson, murder, slave raiding, the policy of cruelty and widespread avarice among the Belgian officials were all done in the King's name.

George Washington Williams returned to the seaside town of Blackpool to recover from illness experienced when he was in Africa. Williams died aged forty-one from tuberculosis and pleurisy on August 2nd 1891. He is buried in Layton cemetery in Blackpool, England (see Berlin Conference February 26th and Alice Seeley Harris May 10th).

The atmosphere was toxic; civil rights leader Dr Martin Luther King had been assassinated six months before the Mexico Summer Olympics of 1968. Many in the USA and around the world were left, shocked, bewildered and angry. Cities throughout the States were on fire and under curfew. Two months later Robert Kennedy was gunned down. America was at war in Vietnam and in chaos at home. **Harry Edwards** led the call for athletes, in particular black athletes, to boycott the summer games. Edwards founded the Olympic Project for Human Rights (OPHR). The proposed boycott made four demands: 1) The removal of South Africa and Rhodesia from the games. 2) Muhammad Ali to be reinstated as the heavy weight champion. 3) Avery Brundage to step down as president of the International Olympic Committee. 4) Hire more black assistant coaches. Only the first demand was conceded.

Tommy Smith had supported the boycott but agreed to run in Mexico 1968 along with his main rival **John Carlos.** The 200m final saw Smith, 24, take gold in a world record time of 19.83. He was the first person to officially run below 20 sec for the distance. His record stood for eleven years. Australian **Peter Norman** came in second with Carlos in bronze position.

The medal ceremony would become one of the great moments in Olympic history. The image captured by photographer John Dominis became and remains one of the great iconic and inspirational pictures from the games. Smith and Carlos strode out to receive their medals, shoeless, wearing black socks representing the poverty faced by many in black America. Carlos had forgotten his pair of gloves. On the podium as the United States anthem played Smith raised his right arm with a clenched black gloved fist, Carlos did the same with his right arm held aloft with heads bowed. All three athletes proudly wore OPHR badges. Norman had always been critical of his county's white Australia policy (see December 23rd). Carlos would say that leaving his tracksuit unzipped showed solidarity with blue collar workers. The beads he wore around his neck represented all those lynched and the victims of tarring and hanging who never had a prayer said for them. The shockwaves were immediate and in the US were seismic. The athletes left the stadium to boos. The president of the International Olympic Committee (IOC), American, Brundage was furious calling for Smith and Carlos to be suspended from the USA team and for them to be banned from the Olympic village. When the United States Olympic Committee refused to comply, Brundage threatened to ban the whole US track team. Smith and Carlos were expelled from the games.

Back in America the two athletes faced universal criticism from an outraged media. They and their families faced abuse and death threats. Any hope of a future in athletics looked slim for the former medallists. Peter Norman received criticism back in Australia. Although he had run the qualification time on several occasions, he was not picked for the 1972 Munich Olympics. When the games arrived in Sydney 2000, he was not invited to take part in any of the ceremonies. Norman (June 15th1942 – October 3rd 2006) died of a heart attack, aged sixty-four. Smith and Carlos were pallbearers at his funeral. In 2012 Australia belatedly apologised for Norman's treatment, calling his stand both heroic and humble.

Smith returned from the games and completed his BA in social science in 1969. He went on to earn his master's in social change. The seven times individual world record holder went on to play in the National Football League (NFL) for the Cincinnati Bengals. Over the years as the dust settled both Smith and Carlos received recognition and acceptance for what they did **on this day** in 1968. Tommy Smith was born on June 6th1944. John Carlos was born on June 5th 1945. Both men are regularly invited to talk about that moment and the iconic image. Smith's autobiography *Silent Gesture* was published in 2007. John Carlos's biography written with Dave Zinn, *The John Carlos Story: The Sport's Moment That Changed the World* was published in 2011. Carlos is quoted saying:

"It's great when an individual (goes) from the most hated individual in society and then becomes a formative icon in society," *"Then everyone wants to be attached to that history."*
   "You have to realize this: You can't ever sign a waiver to disregard the fact you're involved in the human race," ... *"How can you disassociate yourself from the issues of human rights?"*
Nancy Armour: USA Today (Updated 9.40PM EST Dec 14 2019)

   "I went up there as a dignified black man and said: 'What's going on is wrong,'" Carlos said.
David Davis *Smithsonian* Magazine Aug 2008

Oct 17th:

Philip Quaque born in the Gold Coast (Ghana) in 1741 would become the first African ordained in the Anglican church in 1765. Believed to be Fante in ethnic origin, Quaque is often the name given to one born on a Wednesday.

Quaque's education was sponsored by the Society for the Propagation of the Gospel (SPG). They sent him to England to receive an education. While studying he lost the ability to speak in his native tongue.

Back in the Gold Coast, 1766, the ordained Quaque arrived from England with his wife Catherine Blunt, both events took place in 1765. Quaque spent the next five decades promoting the Christian faith. The priest met with little success. Some white people disliked receiving instructions from a black man. Some Africans distrusted Quaque who used an interpreter while other locals and relatives disliked that he had a white wife. Baptisms and conversions were slow. By 1774 only fifty-two people had been baptised.

Philip Quaque's correspondence tells the reader a lot about what was happening in West Africa in relation to revolutions in America and France. Writing over fifty letters to London and North America, reporting on his missionary work, Quaque reveals his evolving attitude to the slave trade and slavery corresponding with abolitionists.

Philip Quaque died **on this day** in 1816 in the Cape Coast aged seventy-five.

Samuel Ringgold Ward, abolitionist, newspaper editor, labour leader, teacher, Congregationalist minister and public speaker was born **on this day** in 1817.

Ward and his parents escaped slavery in 1820. Educated in New York, Ward taught for a while at an all-black, school. In 1839 he joined the American Anti-Slavery Society as one of their agents. That same year he was ordained a minister. In South Butler, New York, Ward served as pastor to an all-white, congregation from 1841–1843. Known for his oratory as a public speaker he travelled through most of the northern states addressing the issue of slavery.

Frederick Douglass (see February 14th) and Ward established the first black labour union on June 13th 1850. The American League of Coloured Labourers was formed to protect employees from exploitation and unfair treatment and to provide financial provision for small businesses and create a black-owned bank. Ward was president and Douglass vice president.

The Slave Fugitive Act, 1850, saw escaped slaves being captured and returned to enslavement. Ward helped to rescue **William Henry** on October 1st 1851. In danger himself Ward fled to Canada where he continued to assist fugitive slaves. North of the border Ward continued his abolitionist work joining the Anti-Slavery Society of Canada and as an editor of campaigning newspapers. The fugitive pastor worked with and for **Mary Ann Shadd** (see June 5th), the first black woman publisher in North America and the first female publisher in Canada.

Samuel Ringgold Ward travelled to England in 1853, spending two years speaking and fundraising for the abolitionist movement. While in Britain Ward published his *Autobiography of a Fugitive Negro: His Anti-Slavery Labours in the United States, Canada and England* in 1855. From the sales Ward was able to retire to Jamaica where he settled working as a minister and farmer.

Samuel Ringgold Ward died in Jamaica in 1866. He was either forty-six or forty-seven.

Independence revolutionary, teacher, politician, activist and international stateswoman, **Graca Simbine Machel** was born **on this day** in 1945.

Revered for her tireless work, campaigning and pragmatism, Simbine had to cut her education short in Portugal having been under surveillance by the Portuguese secret police. The student fled to Switzerland fearing that her political agitation would land her in prison. While in Europe Simbine joined the Mozambique Marxist liberation movement group **FRELIMO** (see June 25th).

Back in Africa, Tanzania, Simbine helped to found headquarters for FRELIMO, storage facilities, supply routes and training camps, one run by the Soviets and one by the Chinese. Simbine underwent military training. It was at this time Graca Simbine met **Samora Machel** (see September 29th). She would marry the president of independent Mozambique in September 1975. The couple had two children. Simbine was stepmother to Machel's five children from his previous marriage. His former wife Josina died from leukaemia.

In the new independent government Simbine served as the minister of education from 1975–85. She fought for universal education increasing numbers in school from 40per cent to 90per cent for boys and 75per cent for girls. When her husband died, along with 33 other passengers, in a plane crash October 19th 1989, Simbine resigned her government position. She left a country with illiteracy levels reduced by 72per cent. Illiteracy had stood at 93per cent.

Free from the immediate concerns of government politics, Simbine threw herself into addressing the needs of a war-ravaged country. Mozambique had been engaged in a twenty-year conflict. The Marxist government had found itself embroiled in the Cold War East v West. Graca Simbine Machel found herself heading a variety of organisations looking at the cost of a war that had left schools in ruin, clinics dilapidated, a stagnant economy, one million refugees abroad, 750,000 children dead, 250,000 orphaned, many unregistered child soldiers and two million landmines across Mozambique.

As president of the Federation of Community Development, a non-profit organisation, grants are given out to strengthen communities, create social and economic justice to reconstruct the war-torn country. As chairperson of the National Organisation of Children of Mozambique, Simbine has placed orphans in village homes using families to rebuild a damaged society. The United Nations UNESCO appointed Simbine as chair of a commission looking into the impact of armed conflict on children. The report was published on November 11th 1996. Among its recommendations was the removal of landmines. It was stressed that the issue and removal of such mines should be part of any peace deal, and the cost of the removal should be shared by companies and countries that profited from their sale.

July 18th 1998 saw the former first lady of Mozambique marry South Africa's **Nelson Mandela.** As part of his eighty-ninth birthday, Mandela with Simbine and **Desmond Tutu** (see October 7th) announced the formation of the **Elders**, a group of respected elder statesmen and women internationally recognised and respected ex-politicians who could mediate and negotiate.

Graca Simbine Machel was awarded the 1992 Africa Prize, an annual award to an individual who has striven to contribute towards the eradication of hunger on the continent. In 1995 she received the Nansen Medal from the United Nations in recognition for her long-standing humanitarian work.

Mae C. Jemison, born **on this day** in 1956, became the first African American woman astronaut in space. She entered the history books on board the Shuttle Endeavour on September 12th 1992. Jemison spent a week in space: 190 hours, conducting a variety of experiments.

Astronaut Mae C. Jemison

Jemison earned her degree in chemical engineering in 1977 and graduated from medical school in 1981. Following a childhood ambition Jemison embarked on a career change and applied to the National Aeronautics and Space Administration (NASA) to become an astronaut. On June 4th 1987, a year after the shuttle Challenger disaster, Jemison was one of fifteen selected out of 2,000 applicants.
Jemison worked on the successful joint US-Japan space mission STS-47 going into space with six others.

With her feet back on earth Jemison has remained busy teaching, lecturing, and promoting research, development and marketing of advanced technologies. Mae Jemison wrote her memoirs for children *Find Where the Wind Goes*, published in 2001. Jemison has appeared in a variety of film and TV productions including *Star Trek, the Next Generation*, 1993 and *Star Trek, 30 Years and Beyond* in 1996. She built a dance studio and had choreographed performances featuring modern jazz and African dance.

For other firsts in space see **Arnaldo Tamayo Mendez** September 18th, **Guion Bluford** and **Frederick D. Gregory** November 22nd, **Ronald McNair and Michael Anderson** January 28th.

Oct 18th:

Born **Paulette Linda Williams on this day** in 1948, the African American author, playwright and poet would be known to the literary world as **Ntozake Shange.** Growing up, Shange's home was visited by **Miles Davis, Dizzy Gillespie** and **W. E. B. DuBois.**

Her writings contained black feminist themes acknowledging the double hit of existing in white, male orientated America. Other common themes included racial and sexual anger and black power.

For Coloured Girls Who Have Considered Suicide/When the Rainbow Is Enuf was the writer's breakthrough. Produced in 1975 the play premiered in 1976 being a hit off Broadway before a two-year Broadway run. The play appeared in theatres across the States. Based on twenty poems, the play shows the power of seven black women and their spiritual survival in the face of despair and pain. Each character is named after a different colour: Lady in Brown, Lady in Red. In 2010 the play was given the big screen treatment as *For Coloured Girls*.

A prolific writer, Ntozake Shange wrote fourteen plays, nineteen books of poetry, seven novels and five children's books. Her adaptation of Bertolt Brecht's 'Mother Courage' is set in the American Civil War following a black family, 1980, winning the Obie award in 1981. *Sassafras, Cypress and Indigo*, the 1982 novel, looks at the divergent lives of three sisters and their mother. The semi-autobiographical *Betsy Brown* (1985), follows a black girl who runs away from home. *Lilian: Resurrection of the Daughter* (1994) is a coming-of-age story. The main character Lilian Parnell, a black businesswoman in the American South is discovered through the voices of all those that know her.

Shange's poetry includes *Nappy Days* (1978), and *Ridin' the Moon in Texas* (1987). Books for children feature *Whitewash* (1997), *Daddy Says* (2003), and *Ellington Was Not a Street* published in 2004.

Following a series of strokes, 2004, Ntozake Shange was placed into support care in an assisted living facility. She died on October 27th in 2018, aged seventy.

African American boxer **Thomas 'Hitman' Hearns,** born **on this day** in 1958, became the first boxer to win four world titles at different weights in 1987. Hearns went on to win six world titles in five divisions welterweight, light middleweight, middleweight, super middleweight and light heavyweight. His achievements are more spectacular fighting during a golden age for boxing, facing many of the greats in the sport from 1977–2006. Hearns record stands at sixty-seven fights, sixty-one wins, forty-eight by KO, five losses and one draw. Hearns was one of the four Kings of the golden age of the Middleweight division, also known as the fabulous four, along with Roberto Duran, **Sugar Ray Leonard** and **Marvellous Marvin Hagler.** Leonard, born May 17th 1959, had forty professional fights with thirty-six wins, twenty-five through knockout. He was the first boxer to earn $100m in purses considered boxer of the decade for the 1980s. Two of his three defeats came when he was in his forties, having come out of retirement.

Thomas Hitman Hearns   Sugar Ray Leonard

Marvellous Marvin Hagler won forty-five of his fifty-six amateur bouts. He became the undisputed middleweight champion beating Alan Minter. Minter was recorded as saying *"No black man is going to take my title"*. In defeating Minter, Hagler faced boos, racial taunts and bottles thrown. He left the ring without lifting his belt. Hagler defended his title successfully twelve times from 1980 to 1987. His professional career saw the fighter win sixty-two fights with three losses and three draws. Hagler was born on 23rd May 1954 and died aged sixty-six on March 13th 2021.

Writer **Terry McMillan** hit literary gold with her third novel *Waiting to Exhale* in 1992. The novel was given the star movie treatment in 1995. *How Stella Got Her Groove Back* (1996) received similar attention and treatment appearing on the big screen in 1998. McMillan focused on middle class female protagonists. *A Day Late and a Dollar Short* (2001) was translated into a made for television movie in 2014.
Terry McMillan has produced eleven works up to the 2016 novel *I Almost Forgot About You.*

Oct 19th:

Baron Bill Morris of Handsworth was born Bill Morris **on this day** in 1938, in Jamaica. He followed his mother to England in 1954 and married Minetta, in 1957, they had two sons.
   As the General Secretary of the Transport and General Workers Union (TGWU), Morris became the first black leader of a major British trade union serving from 1992–2003. Bill Morris rose through the union ranks, joining the TGWU in 1958, becoming shop steward in 1962. He served on the Trade Unionist

Congress (TUC) General Executive Council (GEC), 1972–73. By 1985 Morris rose to the position of deputy general secretary of the TGWU, one of Britain's largest unions. Morris was elected general secretary in 1992 and re-elected in 1995. He remained in position through to his retirement **on this day** in 2003, Morris's sixty-fifth birthday.

Union leader Bill Morris

Bill Morris served as a member of the TUC General Council and Executive Committee from 1988–2003.

Following retirement Morris held a variety of positions including: non-executive director of the Bank of England, 1998. He served on the Royal Commission looking at the reform of the House of Lords, 1999–2000. And has been associated on a variety of levels with numerous educational establishments London's South Bank University, Universities of Northampton, Bedfordshire, Staffordshire and the University of Technology in Jamaica. Morris served as patron of the Refugee Council. He chaired the Morris Inquiry into professional standards in London's Metropolitan Police in 2004

Bill Morris was knighted in 2003. He sat in the House of Lords from 2009 to July 21st 2020.

African American actor **Juanita Moore** will be best remembered for playing the role of housemaid and mother Annie Johnson in the 1959 version of ***Imitation of Life.***

Moore, born **on this day** in 1914, was nominated for an Academy Award for Best Supporting Actress for her role as Johnson. She became the third black person in that category and only the fifth black person nominated in any Academy Award category. Moore was also a Golden Globe Award nominee in the same category.

Juanita Moore appeared in numerous cinema and television productions acting into her nineties. She died on January 1st in 2014, aged ninety-nine. Moore is buried at the Inglewood Cemetery, Inglewood, Los Angeles, California.

Oct 20th:

Jelly Roll Morton born **Ferdinand Joseph La Menthe, on this day** in 1890, would claim that he created jazz in 1902, although only twelve at the time. The prolific pioneering composer bridged the gap between ragtime and the modern jazz of the 1920s. He showed how an improvised style of music could retain its key characteristics after being written down. The pianist applied prearranged and semi orchestrated works with his bands, influencing the sound of early jazz. His 'Jelly Roll Blues' (1915) would be one of the earliest published jazz compositions. Morton is considered the first true composer of jazz and as a result remains a towering figure in the genre.

Jelly Roll Morton.

The name 'Jelly Roll' is rather crude terminology referring to female genitalia. The young Morton started performing in the red-light district of New Orleans in brothels. When his mother found out she disowned him for bringing disgrace to the family name.

Touring saw the bandleader help introduce blues and jazz to Chicago in 1910, New York City in 1911 and San Francisco in 1915. Morton travelled performing as far afield as Alaska, Vancouver and British Colombian. It was back in Chicago that, at the age of thirty-two, Morton's recording career started in 1923. He recorded thirteen piano solos the following year. As with many musicians at the time, Morton moved to New York in 1928. A fearless self-promoter, Morton faced considerable criticism from his contemporaries accused of bragging. Fed up reading how **W. C. Handy** (see November 16th) had created the music genre in a piece written by Mr Ripley in 'Believe It or Not', Morton considered Handy a mediocre musician who in his opinion had only written down other performers' music. Setting the record straight Morton wrote a letter that was printed in *Downbeat* magazine out of Chicago, August 1938, declaring that he had created jazz in 1902 in New Orleans 'the cradle of the music'.

However outlandish the claims it brought Morton to the attention of Alan Lomax from the Library of Congress. Lomax in a series of interviews – May 23rd, June 12th, December 14th, all in 1938 – produced

Mister Jelly Roll: The Fortunes of Jelly Roll Morton, New Orleans Creole and Inventor of Jazz. The book was published in 1950 appearing almost ten years after Morton's death.

While claims were being made and books written Morton's popularity, influence and perceived importance in the music had declined by 1930. He was eclipsed by the likes of **Duke Ellington** (see May 24th) and **Louis Armstrong** (see August 4th). It irked the composer, who had earned little money from his compositions and nothing in royalties, to hear his music being all the rage played by Benny Goodman. The 1930s saw the piano player become a jobbing musician. Little recording took place between 1930 and 1938. Morton moved to Washington DC in 1935 playing the piano and managing what was the Music Box, later the Blue Moon Inn and then the Jungle Inn. In 1938 Morton was stabbed. Taken to an exclusively white hospital the injured man was turned away having to make his way to a black hospital. Further delays and inadequate treatment meant the musician would never fully recover. Moving to California in 1940, Jelly Roll Morton fell ill with asthma and a heart condition. He died on July 10th in 1941, aged fifty. Morton is buried in Calvary Cemetery in Los Angeles. The fame and credit craved during his life came posthumously. Jelly Roll Morton's importance as a jazz pioneer and composer is universally acknowledged, heard in compositions including: 'Black Bottom Blues', 'Dead Man Blues', 'King Porter Stomp', 'Milenberg Joys', 'Wolverine Blues', 'Winin' Boy Blues', 'Don't Leave Me Here', 'Kansas City Stomp', 'Wild Man Blues' composed with Armstrong and Doctor Jazz, Morton's only vocal appearance.

Archibald Campbell Jordan, South African linguist, academic, teacher, literary historian and pioneer of African studies, was born Oct 30th in 1906.

Jordan gained his teacher's diploma in 1932 and his BA degree in 1934. He taught for ten years during which time he was elected president of the African Teachers Association and became fluent in the Southern Bantu language of Sotho. Jordan earned his master's degree in 1944. The thesis for his MA looked at the phonetic and grammatical structure of the Baca language, providing an early study into a non-standard Nguni language.

Ingqumbo Yemiyana, Jordan's 1940 novel looking at the tragic struggle between traditional western education and Xhosa culture and beliefs became a landmark in Xhosa tradition. The book would be published in English as *Wrath of the Ancestors* in 1980, Afrikaans in 1990 and in Dutch in 1999. Earlier in 1940 Jordan married Pricilla Phyllis Ntantala.

Jordan continued to research and study becoming the first black African to earn a doctorate at the University of Cape Town (UCT) in phonological and grammatical studies in 1956. He was appointed senior lecturer at UCT in 1946 a position he held through to 1961. Jordan lectured on African languages as well as Xhosa culture.

In 1961 Dr Jordan was offered the opportunity to tour colleges and universities in the USA but the South African government denied him a passport. Using an exit permit Jordan escaped to London before traveling to the USA where he settled in 1962 continuing his academic work at a variety of universities.

Jordan died in exile following a long illness **on this day** in 1968, he was 61. Posthumously his study of Xhosa literature was published in 1973. *Tales From Southern Africa* (1973) and *Towards an African Literature: The Emergence of Literary Form in Xhosa* also in 1973.

Kamala Harris born **on this day** 1964 became the first female and first person of African heritage to become vice president to President Joe Biden on January 20th 2021. Harris was elected to the Senate in

2016 becoming the second woman of African heritage and first of South Asian heritage to serve in the US Senate.

Oct 21st:

With his puffed cheeks, bent trumpet at a 45-degree angle, bebop horn rimmed glasses, black beret and goatee beard, trumpeter **Dizzy Gillespie** was instantly recognisable. The symbolic seminal pioneering figure of bebop jazz was born **on this day, John Birks Gillespie,** in 1917.

Gillespie bandleader, composer, arranger, singer and educator, wrote his work down keen to educate the next generation and to preserve the music. As a result, he allowed bebop to form the foundation of modern jazz. The name Dizzy came from his clowning around on stage. He also had the nickname 'Ambassador of Jazz'. Gillespie the singer was adept at scat.

As a trumpeter many argued that Dizzy was one of the greatest, second only to **Louis Armstrong** (see August 4th). Few were able to copy his style, yet he influenced all that followed. It would not be until **John Faddis** in the 1970s that someone was able to successfully imitate and be compared to him.

In 1939 Gillespie joined **Cab Calloway**'s band. At this time an early Gillespie composition 'Pickin' the Cabbage' was an early example introducing Latin infused jazz. Gillespie would go on to be one of the first jazz musicians to employ Afro-Cuban, Caribbean and Brazilian poly rhythms working with Cuban percussionist **Chano Pozo.** Dizzy composed: 'A Night in Tunisia', 'Manteca', 'Guachi Guaro', 'Cubano Be, Cubano Bop' in what he called 'Cubop'.

After Calloway, Dizzy Gillespie worked with many of the leading jazz performers and their bands from 1937–44, including **Ella Fitzgerald, Coleman Hawkins,** Benny Carter and **Duke Ellington** (see May 24th). The breakthrough came in 1945 when Gillespie recorded with fellow bebop legend and friend saxophonist **Charlie Parker** (see August 29th). Recordings such as *Show Nuff* and *Hot House*, introducing a new sound left many of the swing fans confused. It would be two years before bebop would become mainstream. From 1946–50 Gillespie had his own big band recognised as one of the great jazz bands.

Dizzy Gillespie bepop icon and pioneer   and   Percussionist Chano Pozo.

Dizzy Gillespie's song book would contain some of the finest works in jazz including: 'Oop Bop Sh' Bam', 'Salt Peanuts', 'Groovin' High', 'Johnny Come Lately', 'LeapFrog', 'My Melancholy Baby', 'Serenade to Sweden' and 'Sophisticated Lady'.

His memoir *To BE or Not to BOP: Memoirs of Dizzy Gillespie* written with Al Fraser was published in 1979. By this time his trumpet playing was not what it was but he continued to be revered and retained huge respect. The man who played the unusual looking trumpet, bent when someone either stepped or sat on the instrument in the 1950s, was quick to appreciate the new sound it made and how he could now be heard playing above the audience for those listening at the back. Dizzy Gillespie died on January 6th in 1993, aged seventy-five, from pancreatic cancer. He is buried in Flushing Cemetery, New York.

Oct 22nd:

The fight for freedom

James W. C. Pennington, historian, writer, minister, abolitionist, activist and orator, was born into slavery in 1807.

Pennington and his mother were given as a gift, by their master, to his son Frisby Tilghman when the boy was four. His father would eventually be bought resulting in, but not intended to reunite the enslaved family. Life for James was filled with fear, regularly abused, facing brutal irrational beatings. The child was sent to work and learn about being a stonemason, his younger brother was sent off to learn about pump making. The brothers would be separated from that time onwards. At the age of nineteen, on October 28th 1827, James ran away, leaving his parents and eleven siblings. He had witnessed his father's vicious whippings, accused of eyeballing a white master.

James was captured twice but claimed to be one of a group of slaves to be sold to Georgia because they had smallpox. The lie worked as the fugitive was released, eventually making it to Pennsylvania from Maryland.

Introduced to and given refuge by Quakers William and Phoebe Wright. The couple provided James with shelter and an education. It was at this time that James took the name Pennington after Isaac Pennington, a leading English Quaker.

Pennington headed off along the fugitive escape route of the Underground Railroad making it to New York City. He would become friends with leading abolitionists of the day including **William Lloyd Garrison** (see December 10th)**, Simeon Jocelyn** (he attempted to establish the first college for African Americans), and **Lewis Tappan**. Pennington became the first black student to attend Yale University although he had to sit at the back of the class and not ask any questions. Yale never awarded the student a degree, nonetheless Pennington would champion the need for black people to pursue education as far as they could.

James Pennington would be ordained a minister in the Congregational Church. He performed the marriage of the runaway **Frederick Douglass** (see February 14th) and **Anne Murray.** Increasingly politically active Pennington attended the Negro National Convention in Philadelphia in 1829. The Convention was set up by black leaders in Philadelphia to address hostilities, discrimination, exclusion and violence faced by their community. By 1853 Pennington served as the Convention's presiding officer. He was also involved in the founding of the American Anti-Slavery Society in 1833.

Jocelyn and Tappan helped in winning the case for the captured Mende people of the Amistad (see November 26th), 1839–41. Pennington set up what would become the American Missionary Society to raise funds for the thirty-five-year-old Mende who wished to return to Africa.

In 1841 Pennington published what was the first history of its kind ***The Origin and History of Coloured People.*** While attending the Second World Conference on Slavery, as an American delegate in London, England, Pennington wrote his autobiography, a slave narrative *The Fugitive Blacksmith* in 1849. Pennington spent two years in England touring, he travelled to Europe, speaking and preaching in white churches and raising funds for the abolitionist movement and was able to purchase his own freedom. He was in Scotland when the Fugitive Slave Act of 1850 was passed, threatening the liberty of any runaway former enslaved person. Fugitives could now be captured and returned to their former masters.

Back in New York, Pennington campaigned for **Elizabeth Jennings.** Jennings had been arrested in 1854, having rode in the white section of a streetcar. She won her case in February 1855. Jennings's attorney was a young Chester A. Arthur who would become the 21st President of the USA, 1881–85.

Although a pacifist from his days with the Quakers, Pennington helped to recruit black troops for the Unionist Army during the Civil War of 1861–65.

After the bitter conflict Pennington focused on his ministry working and serving as a pastor in a variety of churches. After a short illness James W. C. Pennington died **on this day** in 1870.

Founder of the **Black Panther Party for Self Defence** BPP (see October 15th), **Bobby Seale** was born **on this day** in 1936.

Seale met **Huey P. Newton** (see August 22nd) while the pair were at Merritt Community College in 1962. Seale was studying engineering and politics. Both students were influenced by **Malcolm X** (see February 21st). Seale became involved in the Afro American Association (AAA). In June 1966 he worked in the North Oakland Neighbourhood Anti-Poverty Centre. The programme helped Seale with his desire to teach Black American history to develop community pride, awareness and responsibility to others. It was at this time Seale met **Bobby Hutton,** the BPP's first member.

The Black Panther Party was set up to defend the black community from what was seen as a hostile, threatening, militarised police force. Seale wanted students to go out into the community to make a difference, resisting racism and classism, perpetuated by a corrupt capitalist system.

Seale's and Newton's 10-point programme in 'What We Want' called for an improved and fair legal system, an end to police brutality, improved job prospects and access to better housing. The programme demanded empowerment, a greater say and control over one's destiny.

The aims seemed reasonable but would be set against an angry FBI head, J Edgar Hoover. Hoover declared war on the Panthers vowing to destroy the organisation which he saw as the greatest threat to law and order in the country. By 1974 Seale would leave an embattled, bitter and disintegrating BPP.

Bobby Seale, the party national chairman was a last-minute replacement for **Eldridge Cleaver** (see May 11) to attend the Democratic convention. He had only been in Chicago for a couple of days during the National Convention of 1968. Anti-Vietnam demonstrations had taken place. Seale with seven others, initially called the Chicago 8, was arrested and charged with inciting riots. Although the evidence against Seale was slim, he was put on trial without access to his own legal representative. Denied his constitutional right to counsel, Seale continuously disrupted the proceedings. Judge Julius Hoffman ordered the defendant to be bound and gagged. Although the charges to incite riot were dropped, Seale was given a four-year prison sentence on sixteen accounts of contempt. The government suspended all charges against Bobby Seale who was released in 1972.

While serving his sentence Bobby Seale was put on trial accused of having ordered the torture and execution of BPP member Alex Rackley. Accused of being a police informant Rackley was kidnapped, tortured, allegedly confessing and after a kangaroo trial he was found dead in Middlefield, Connecticut. The 1970 trial became known as the New Haven Black Panther trial. George Sams Jr who it's believed killed Rackley turned informant and pointed the finger at Seale. The six-month trial ended with a hung jury. All charges against Seale were dropped.

While in prison Seale's wife became pregnant. The suspected would-be father, BPP member, Fred Bennett's mutilated body was found in what was believed to be a Panther hideout. The police had suspicions about Seale's involvement but did not pursue the case.

Bobby Seale ran for political office in Oakland as mayor in 1973. The bid saw him come second (out of nine candidates) to the eventual winner Mayor John Reading.

Spells of imprisonment and deaths saw the BPP fall into disarray. The leadership was at loggerheads, Newton's behaviour increasingly erratic involved in drugs. Eldridge Cleaver was abroad in exile. Rumour had it that Seale and Newton had a brutal fight leaving Seale requiring medical attention and having to go into hiding before he finally left the party in 1974. Seale denies that any such altercation ever took place.

Turning his back on a militant black empowerment ideology, Seale became more moderate in his activism. He continues to seek improvements for black communities, neighbourhoods and the environment. He travels widely on speaking tours. Bobby Seale returned to live in Oakland California in 2002. He has written several books including: *Seize the Time: The Story of the Black Panther Party and Huey P. Newton* written in 1968 and published in 1970. *A Lonely Rage: The Autobiography of Bobby Seale* (1978), and *Power to The People: The World of The Black Panthers* (2016), co-written with Stephen Shames.

Oct 23rd:

Years of unrest and animosity had raged between the Hutu and the Tutsis. When **Habyarimana's** (see April 6th) aeroplane crashed, 100 days of brutal murderous behaviour was unleashed, resulting in attempted genocide, massacring 800,000 Tutsis at the hands of the Hutu. An estimated one million would die in the resulting conflict centred on the African country of Rwanda.

Rising from the ashes **Paul Kagame** emerged as the benevolent dictator. Whether a benevolent dictator is an oxymoron is not in doubt. Is the term accurate? I would argue yes. Kagame commanded the Rwandan Patriotic Front (RPF) a Tutsi-based militia out of Uganda. His force of between ten and fourteen thousand intervened to end the slaughter. At the same time there was a reported massacre of the Hutu, by the RPF. The thirty-seven-year-old Kagame assumed the position of vice president and minister of defence.

Paul Kagame

It was clear who actually held the reins of power. Paul Kagame would officially be appointed president by the National Assembly in 2000 heading the transitional government. Many Hutu had fled to Zaire (now Democratic Republic of Congo). Hutu rebel attacks on Rwanda from across the border led to Kagame's forces to invade Zaire in 1996. The fighting escalated, Kagame was drawn into a wider conflict that became known as Africa's First World War. A peace accord was finally reached and signed in 2002.

The ethnic conflict of 1994, and the role of the media in fuelling the flames has seen Kagame avoid declaring himself a Tutsis. It could be argued that the internecine struggle has led the president to be cautious, if not dictatorial, with regards to political opposition. Human rights organisations have accused Paul Kagame of retaining the characteristics as leader of the militia; aggression, often uncontrolled violence resulting in murders, disappearances, politically motivated arrests, illegal arrests of opposition, critics and journalists from a critical media. His unhealthy relationship with the press has seen the suppression of freedom of information and the threatening journalists.

Allegations that the president and the RPF were involved in the shooting down of Habyarimana's plane led to diplomatic relationships between Rwanda and France to be severed. Rwanda launched an official inquiry into the crash. The 2007 conclusion pointed to Tutsis rebels who feared Habyarimana's peace negotiations with the Hutu.

Paul Kagame won the first multi-party election and was sworn into office on September 12th 2003, ending nine years of the transition government. He has won successive elections with impressive majorities of over 90per cent of the vote. Opposition has been scarce, and when present threatened and intimidated.

On the benevolent side while maintaining an iron grip on power, Paul Kagame has overseen economic and political stability. The president is revered by many and praised for pursuing selfless goals for the good of the country. Many young people praise him for getting things done. Umuganda is a policy where on the last Saturday of every month Rwandans have to give up time to help the country. The World Bank placed Rwanda at number twenty-nine out of 190 countries in its list of 'Doing Business'. It was second only to Mauritius on the continent in 2019. There has been consistent foreign investment in a country that is seen as stable and reliable. The Mara phone, Africa's first smartphone, is produced in the capital Kigali. Over 60per cent of law makers are women. On the environmental side plastic bags have been banned and the nation's capital is on course to have every house connected up to the sewage system by 2024. When threatened with COVID-19 Rwanda was the first sub-Saharan African country to lockdown including its borders. Only returning citizens, goods and cargo were permitted to enter. Even tourism and research relating to the gorilla population and other primates was put on hold.

The constitution allows Paul Kagame, born **on this day** in 1957, to remain in power through to 2034. His present term is due to end in 2024. Kagame has personally been involved in persecuting the hero of the 2004 film *Hotel Rwanda* Paul Rusesabagina. Observers argue that Kagame, jealous of the attention that Rusesabagina the hero of the book *An Ordinary Man the True Story Behind the Hotel Rwanda* has received, is behind the arrest trial and guilty verdict faced by Rusesabagina in September of 2021.

Norwell Roberts born **on this day** in 1946, in Anguilla, is often cited as the first black police officer to serve in London's Metropolitan Police. That honour goes to **Robert Branford** (see May 6th) recruited on September 24th 1838.

Robert's position is noteworthy as he was the first officer recruited post World War II. Refused on his first application Roberts was delighted to be accepted a year later to the force on his second attempt.

He enlisted on March 28th 1967 using his mother's maiden name, Roberts, fed up with all the mispronunciations and misspelling of his surname Gumbs. Norwell officially changed his name. Roberts joined the Met, aged twenty-one, on April 3rd 1967.

As the first black police officer in the Met and one of only five in the whole of the UK, Roberts became the poster boy receiving considerable media attention. In the American South, papers described him as "London's first negro cop". He appeared in the tabloids in cartoon form and was on the front cover of *Private Eye*. Being conspicuous did not mean that the young officer was embraced by the force or his colleagues. Roberts often ate alone, or on the beat at friendly stops in the community where he was offered a cup of tea, rather than face the hostile environment of the police canteen. Isolated, facing institutional prejudice, racial abuse, harassment and persecution Roberts felt ostracised. When he was introduced to his reporting sergeant, Roberts recalls being told "look you nigger, I'll see to it you never pass your probation". On one occasion on duty outside the Royal Opera House the officer heard "black cunt" shouted by a police officer from a passing police car. He saw colleagues laugh, as they drove off, leaving the humiliated Roberts to face the public. When he complained his concerns were dismissed. To his colleagues Norwell Roberts put on a brave face in private he admitted to crying.

Roberts arrived in England from Anguilla when he was nine. He, with his mother, settled in Bromley, Kent. In 1957 having passed the 11 Plus exam, Norwell's headteacher informed him that he would not be taking his place at the grammar school, as he had to learn English ways. The teenager Norwell did not have a positive relationship with his stepfather and left home when he was fifteen. He worked as a laboratory technician at Westfield College at the University of London.

Norwell Roberts remained in the force for thirty years. He recalls the racial barriers he faced by saying "in order to appreciate the present we have to revisit the uncomfortable past". He transferred to the Criminal Investigation Dept (CID) and became Detective Constable in 1977 working in the drugs squad. Roberts was the first black undercover officer. In 1985 he received a commendation for outstanding work for his part in the arrest of five contract killers. He was awarded the Queen's Police Medal for distinguished service in 1995. The medal was presented by Prince Charles at Buckingham Palace on March 15th 1996. On retiring Norwell Roberts worked in human resources promoting anti-discriminatory practices.

For more on black British police see **John Kent** (July 20th), and **Sislin Fay Allen** (February 1st).

Born in 1967 a Yuwallarai child raised in New South Wales Australia, **Kirsty Parker** taught herself to read and write after only one year of formal education. The journalist, Aboriginal activist and public policy advisor on indigenous affairs has held a variety of jobs championing first people's rights in Australia. Parker was co-chair, 2013–15, of the National Congress of Australia's First Peoples. From 2015–17 she was the chief executive officer of the National Centre of Indigenous Excellence. In August 2017 Parker became the director of Aboriginal Affairs and Reconciliation. She was also the third Aboriginal to serve on the Australia Press Council.

Kirsty Parker has been the recipient of numerous awards including Australian Peace Woman Award, in 2015, and **on this day** in 2018 the David Unaipon Award for her unpublished manuscript *The Making of Ruby Champion*. For **David Unaipon** see September 28th.

Oct 24th:

Quiet, unassuming and shy, **Fats Domino** was described by Elvis Presley as the true king of rock'n'roll. The piano playing singer never described what he did as rock'n'roll, yet he was a pioneer in the genre.

Alongside **Little Richard** (see December 5th) and **Chuck Berry** (see March 18th), Domino was one of the trio of black superstars of the music.

Born February 26th 1928, **Antoine Dominique Domino Jr,** would have early rhythm and blues hits starting with 1950s 'The Fat Man'. The track is said to have been the first rock'n'roll million seller. Domino would have 5 million sellers before his big breakthrough in 1955 with 'Ain't That a Shame'. The hits continued to flow selling over 100 million. Domino was one of the biggest selling artists of the 1950s. Between 1955 and 1960 he had eleven top 10 hits. In his career Domino saw thirty-five of his records in the US Billboard top 40. His catalogue included: Going Home (1952), Blueberry Hill, sold more than 5 million world-wide, 'I'm In Love Again', 'Blue Monday' and 'My Blue Heaven' were all released in 1956. That same year Domino appeared in the comedy film *The Girl Can't Help It*, alongside Little Richard and in the film *Shake, Rattle and Rock!*. Other notable hits include 'Walking to New Orleans' (1960) and 1961's 'Jambalaya'.

Fats Domino's style was disarming, simple, easy going. Some say his music reflected his innocence and essential goodness. He was able to cross over successfully appealing to a white audience. Alcohol, dancing and racial mixing led to four of Domino's concerts ending up in riots. Fats Domino recorded for the Imperial Records label through to 1963 releasing over sixty singles. Forty releases went top ten in the R&B charts.

With the British Invasion, headed by the Beatles, Domino's music was no longer fashionable. He continued to record and tour but never repeated the success of the late fifties. His last tour was in Europe in 1995. *Rolling Stone* magazine ranked Domino at No 25 in its 2004 '100 Greatest Artists of All Time'.

When Hurricane Katrina hit New Orleans in August 2005, reports circulated that Fats Domino had died. The singer survived Katrina by twelve years. Fats Domino died **on this day** in 2017, he was eighty-nine.

The Republic of Zambia gained its independence **on this day** in 1964 (formerly known as Northern Rhodesia). Kenneth Kaunda won the January 1964 election to become prime minister (see April 28th).

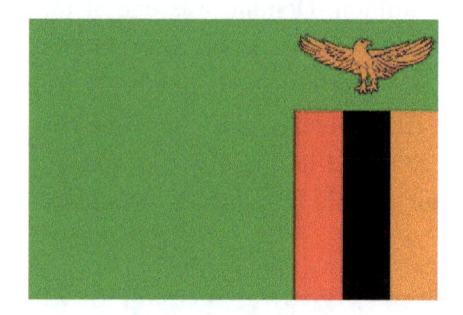

The national flag.

Oct 25th:

Born in Trinidad in July 1873, **Dr John Alcindor** would travel to Britain and study at Edinburgh University in 1893. He graduated in 1899 and worked in several London hospitals before setting up his own practice on Harrow Road, Paddington in 1913. Although fully qualified, Dr Alcindor's application to join the Royal Medical Army Corp in World War I was denied due to his colonial heritage. Undeterred, the doctor served with the British Red Cross during the conflict. He would be awarded a Red Cross Medal. Alcindor continued at his practice after the war and was the senior district medical officer in Paddington from 1921 through to his death.

John Alcindor was always politically active. He was involved in the first Pan African Conference held in London,1900, organised by **Henry Sylvester Williams,** (see February 15th) and took part in the 2nd and 3rd Congresses in 1921 and 1923. In 1921 Alcindor took the presidency of the African Progress Union (APU) after **John Archer** (see June 8th) stepped down. The union was an association of people from Africa, the West Indies, British Guiana, Honduras and America formed in 1918.

Dr John Alcindor married in 1911 and had three boys. He died **on this day** 1924, aged fifty-one. A Nubian Jak blue plaque marks the spot where his Harrow Road practice stood. The inscription on the plaque reads 'Physician, Pan-Africanist and World War I Hero'. Alcindor is basketball legend **Kareem Abdul-Jabbar's** great-uncle.

British novelist, essayist and professor, **Zadie Smith**, was born Sadie to a Jamaican mother and English father **on this day** in 1975. While in her final year at King's College, Cambridge, Smith completed her first novel *White Teeth*, published in 2000. It was an immediate critical, commercial and international award-winning success. Adapted for television in 2004.

The *Autograph Man* (2002), was shortlisted for the Man Booker Prize. *On Beauty was written in* 2005. *NW* published in 2012 is set in north-west London and was adapted by the BBC as a film shown in 2016. *The Embassy of Cambodia* was published in 2013 and *Swingtime* in 2016.

Zadie Smith has also worked with *Harper's Magazine* and the *New Yorker*. In America she taught non-fiction at Colombian School of the Arts and at New York University. Smith has published a collection of short stories: *Grand Union* in 2019. There have been three essay collections: *Changing My Mind* (2009), *Feel Free, a* collection of thirty-three essays from 2008–2017, published in 2018, and *Intimation: Six Essays* (2020).

Zadie Smith married Northern Irish novelist and poet Nicholas Laid in 2004. The couple have a son and daughter.

Operation Urgent Fury was the name given by the US military for the **Invasion of Grenada.** Supported by Jamaica, Barbados and the Organisation of Eastern Caribbean States (OESC) with the Dominican prime minister Eugenia Charles, chair of the OESC, the combined armies invaded **on this day** in 1983.

The invasion was ordered by President Ronald Reagan following the coup and execution of the island's former leader **Maurice Bishop** on October 19th. Thirteen to nineteen associates were killed alongside Bishop, his body has never been found. Reagan argued that the occupation was necessary to secure American lives, including the safety of 600 medical students, and for stability in the region. Both of the country's airports were secured as 1,900 troops landed by air in the South at Point Salines Airport and a combined helicopter and amphibian landing in the north at Pearls Airport. Soldiers from six Caribbean nations supported the American troops. Six hundred Cubans and thirty Soviets were arrested.

Maurice Bishop.

As the invasion force grew to over 7,000 the Grenadian force either surrendered or fled. Forty-five Grenadians fighters were killed, 358 injured. Twenty-four Cubans were killed, fifty-six wounded. Nineteen American soldiers were killed in combat, 116 wounded. Twenty-four civilians died, including eighteen when a mental hospital was attacked.

Britain's Prime Minister Margaret Thatcher was angry at the invasion of the former British colony and attempted to dissuade her American counterpart the day before. She was angry at not being informed of the impending military action. The Pentagon had supported Britain during the Falkland conflict and had expected Britain to reciprocate with regards to Grenada. The United Nations held a vote, October 28th, deploring the invasion with 108 to 9 agreeing with the UN motion. The US vetoed the motion.

With order restored elections were held in 1984 with the centre-left New National Party gaining the most votes and **Herbert A. Blaize** elected as the new prime minister. **Bernard Coard** and thirteen associates were arrested, tried and given the death penalty for their part in the coup and Bishop's execution. In 1991 the sentence was commuted to life imprisonment.

The date of the invasion is a national holiday and is celebrated as Thanksgiving Day.

Oct 26th:

A national icon in Mali, the last chancellor of the Islamic University of Sankore in Timbuktu, philosopher, author of over forty books and teacher

Ahmed Baba al-Massufi al-Timbukti was born **on this day** in 1556.

Exiled, accused of sedition, following the Moroccan invasion of Songhai. Ahmed Baba was a Berber who belonged to the federation of the Songhai people. The philosopher remained in exile in Morocco for twelve years returning to Timbuktu on April 12th 1608.

Ahmed Baba wrote several biographies including one on Muhammad, Abd al-Karim al-Maghhili an influential Muslim Berber responsible for converting the ruling class and the Tuareg people of west Africa to Islam. Ahmed Baba was critical of black Africans involved in the slave trade and warned against the wrong interpretation of the Curse of Ham found in Genesis 9: 20–27. The teacher controversially argued that the enslavement of non-believers, infidels or Kafir's was acceptable. Ahmed Baba considered knowledge more important than ethnic differences.

In Timbuktu it is the Muslim men, not the women, who cover their face.

Ahmed Baba al-Massufi died on April 22nd in 1627, he was seventy. The Timbuktu Institute of Higher Learning and Islamic Research with its library of 30,000 manuscripts is named in honour of Ahmed Baba as is a crater on Mercury. Muslim men in Timbuktu formerly cover their faces; women do not.

Benedict Wallet Vilakazi, born January 6th 1906, became the first black South African to earn a PhD in 1946 from Witwatersrand University in Johannesburg. His dissertation on Zulu poetry looking at oral tradition and Zulu and Xhosa languages led to his doctorate in literature.

Vilakazi earned his BA in 1934 from the University of South Africa and his MA in 1938 at Witwatersrand. The poet, novelist and educator, taught and studied Zulu languages and literature serving as a senior lecturer at Witwatersrand.

Benedict Vilakazi's first book of verse *Inkondlo KaZulu (Zulu National Song)* (1935), was the first western influenced poetry published in the Zulu language. The collection became the first in Witwatersrand's *Bantu Treasure Series*. The poet's second collection *Amal'eZulu (Zulu Treasures)* (1945), became the eighth volume in the *Bantu Treasures series*. The combined volumes were published in English as *Zulu Horizons* in 1962. Dr Vilakazi wrote three novels: *Nje nempela (Really and Truly)* (1933) was one of the first works of modern Zulu fiction. His best-known novel *Noma nini (Forever and Ever)* was published in 1935. The third novel *U-Dingiswayo KaJobe (Dingiswayo, Son of Jobe)* was published in 1939. Vilakazi worked on producing a Zulu-English dictionary.

Dr Benedict Vilakazi died from meningitis **on this day** in 1947. Vilakazi Street in Soweto is named after the poet. Both Nelson Mandela and Desmond Tutu lived on Vilakazi Street (see **Jordan** October 20th).

Born **on this day** in 1919, **Edward Brooke III** would become the first black person elected, by popular vote, to the United States Senate. He served two terms from 1967-1979. **Blanche K Bruce** and **Hiram R Revels** (see March 16th) were both elected to the Senate but by the Mississippi Legislature, not by popular election, in the 1870s.

Brooke served in the Second World War, from 1941, as an infantry officer He eventually rose to the rank of captain. In 1948 he opened up a law practice having gained two law degrees from Boston University. Elected as Massachusetts' Attorney General in 1963, Brookes became the first black person to hold that position in any state. He won the election with a landslide winning by more than half a million votes. As Attorney General, Brooke vigorously pursued corruption in official places.

Following Emancipation many former enslaved people moved north.

He wrote *The Challenge of Change: Crisis in Our Two-Party System* in 1966. The book focused on self-help as a path to address social ills in the United States. Standing in the Democratic state of Massachusetts, Brooke reversed the national trend by defeating Governor Endicott Peabody, gaining more votes than any other Republican across the country to become the senator.

Politically described as a centrist, Brooke disliked being pigeonholed seen as the African American. He opposed the expansion of the nuclear arsenal, shifted position over the Vietnam War. He promoted fair housing policies as realised in the 1968 Civil Rights Act, which he co-wrote. Brooke wanted the Republicans to put forward programmes to aid the cities and the poor. He also supported the legalisation of abortion. Following the Watergate scandal Brooke was the first Republican to call for President Richard Nixon's resignation.

Blanche K. Bruce.

Edward Brooke's political career survived a public divorce from Remigia Ferrari-Scacco. Years later broadcaster Barbara Walters revealed in her autobiography that she was having an affair with the senator at the time. Brooke's own memoir *Bridging the Divide* was published in 2007. The autobiography explored his experience of race and class as a Republican in a Democratic state.

After having breast cancer and a double mastectomy, Brooke campaigned to raise awareness of the cancer among men. Edward Brooke died at the age of ninety-five on January 3rd 2015. He is buried at Arlington National Cemetery.

Oct 27th:

Called the Father of African Humanism, a giant of modern African literature, editor, letter writer, 'Dean of African letters', essayists, writer of fiction and educationalist, **Ezekiel Mphahlele** was born on December 17th 1919 in South Africa. He would adopt the name **Es'kia**, dropping Ezekiel in 1977.

Mphahlele, one of the founding figures in modern African literature, reflected on his experiences in and outside of South Africa for a lot of his work. The South African classic, the autobiographical *Down Second Avenue* (1959), recounts Mphahlele's struggle to become a teacher and the setbacks faced in his profession. *Second Avenue* looks at the young man's development into an adult, facing the structures of apartheid.

Man Must Live was one of the first collections of short stories written by a black South African in English, published in 1947. The following year, 1948 saw the nationalist D F Milan elected as prime minister introducing the policy of apartheid. The Bantu Education Act was passed in 1953 and enacted on Jan 1st 1954. As a teacher and union member Mphahlele protested against the segregationist, inferior education system. He was arrested and placed in jail. On release Mphahlele was banned from teaching in any government-controlled school. In self-imposed exile for twenty years Mphahlele changed his South African passport for a British one.

In Nigeria, 1957–61, the writer launched two literary magazines and became friends with **Wole Soyinka** (see July 13th)**, Chinua Achebe** (see June 13th) and **Christopher Okigbo** (see August 16th). He co-edited the periodical *Black Orpheus*, (1960–64) and *Africa Today* in 1967. Mphahlele founded and directed the cultural centre Chemchemi for writers and artists (1963–65). On top of writing, he found time to work at the Congress of Cultural Freedom in Paris, living in France from 1961–63, as the director of the African programme.

The African Image (1962), a collection of essays, looked to address negritude and the African aesthetic. In 1969 Mphahlele was nominated for the Nobel Prize for Literature for the *Wanderer*.

Living in America between 1966–1977, Es'kia Mphahlele joined the University of Denver in Colorado earning his PhD in 1968. He also worked at the University of Pennsylvania.

The writer was never settled or comfortably happy in exile. He was critical of and disillusioned by African tyrants and what he described as "clowns leading independent Africa". He argued with what he saw as the patronising liberal racism found in America and was sceptical of African American literature. His views appeared in the autobiographical novel *The Wanderer* and *Voices in the Wilderness* (1972).

Fearing the prospect of dying away from home, Es'kia Mphahlele returned to South Africa in 1977, aged fifty-seven. It is at this time, immersed in the black consciousness movement wanting to be at the heart of the renaissance and understanding the thinking of his people, that Ezekiel changed his name to Es'kia. From 1983–87 Mphahlele was the head of the department of African literature at the University of Witwatersrand.

Mphahlele wrote numerous letters revealing what is described as African humanism. The author wrote over thirty short stories plus poems and novels. *Chirundu*, 1979, was based on his time in Lusaka in Zambia. *Afrika My Music* (1984) was Mphahlele's autobiography. A collection of essays and other writings are contained in *Es'kia* (2002) and *Es'kia Continued* (2004).

The writer, educationist and philosopher died **on this day** in 2008, aged eighty-eight.

Saint Vincent and the Grenadines gained associate statehood from Britain **on this day** in 1969. The Caribbean Windward Islands were the last to gain independence **on this day** in 1979. Independence followed a referendum under **Milton Cato** who served as the first prime minister of Saint Vincent.

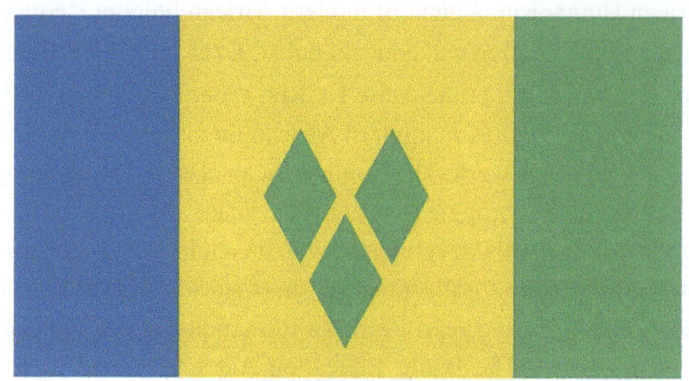

Saint Vincent and the Grenadines

The national flag.

Oct 28th:

Occasionally he would play out on the wing, but footballer **Arthur Wharton** was a goalkeeper. Born **on this day** 1865 in Jamestown (Accra), Gold Coast (Ghana) to a Ghanaian mother and a Grenadian father, Wharton would be recognised as the world's first professional mixed heritage player.

Arthur Wharton arrived in England to train as a Methodist missionary, at Cleveland College Darlington, at the age of nineteen in 1886. The young man soon forgot about his religious training and turned to sport. Running at the Amateur Athletic Association Championships, Stamford Bridge in London in 1886, Wharton equalled the world amateur record of 10 sec for the 100 yards, becoming the fastest man in Britain. He also set a cycling record time from Preston to Blackburn the following year.

Arthur Wharton signed for Darlington Football Club before joining Preston North End for the 1886-7 season. That season the club got to the FA Cup semi-finals. Wharton left to pursue his running career before returning to football playing at Rotherham for six years. Wharton's career was not remarkable, he never won a major competition, the league or received an international call up.

Arthur Wharton

The goalkeeper retired in 1902 at the age of thirty-six. He had a variety of jobs but died poor on December 12th 1930. Wharton was buried in an unmarked grave in Ellington Cemetery, Doncaster. In 1997 a memorial headstone was put up to remember the world's first professional black player and the first professional black player to play in the Football League.

Arthur Wharton was a pioneer in the black British game of football standing alongside **John Francis Leslie** (see August 17th), **Andrew Watson** (March 12th), **Walter Tull** (March 25th), **Tony Collins**

(March 19th), **Viv Anderson** (November 29th), **Laurie Cunningham** (March 8th), **Paul Ince** (June 9th) and **Mary Philips** (March 14th).

Known the world over as jazz singer **Cleo Laine,** Britain's very own queen of jazz, proudly wears the formal title **Dame Cleo Laine, Lady Dankworth.** She was born Clementine Dinah Bullock **on this day** 1927, to a Jamaican father and English mother, in Southall, London.

Cleo Laine appeared in the 1940 film *Thief of Bagdad* alongside her sister Sylvia and brother Alexander as street urchins. Her big break came when at twenty-four the young singer was hired as vocalist for the Johnny Dankworth Seven in 1951. She performed exclusively with the jazz group for seven years gaining a loyal following.

In 1958 Laine appeared on stage acting in *Flesh to a Tiger* a play set in Jamaica. Her acting career would go hand in hand with her singing. Cleo Laine appeared in *Valmouth* (1959), *A Time to Laugh* (1962), *Boots with Strawberry Jam* (1968), and *Show Boat* (1971). The singer/actor appeared in London's West End, and also on the BBC as a regular on the political news satire *That Was the Week That Was*. Laine married Johnny Dankworth in 1958. The couple remained together until Dankworth's death on February 6th 2010. Husband and wife opened The Stables in 1970. In the first year the venue hosted forty-seven concerts. Cleo Laine appeared on Broadway and in the USA in *A Little Night Music* and *The Merry Widow*. Laine received a Tony nomination for her role in *The Mystery of Edwin Drood,* and further success in 1989's *Into the Woods*. The early 1970s saw the singer famed for her scat improvisation and an almost four octave range, touring North America. She received the accolade of appearing on *The Muppet Show* in 1977. Cleo Laine was a regular touring Australia where she released six top 100 albums.

Cleo Laine would be the only performer to be nominated for Grammy Awards in the jazz, popular music and classical categories. She won a Grammy Award in 1986 for best female jazz vocal performance for the album *Cleo at Carnegie: The 10th Anniversary Concert* (1985). Laine duetted with **Ray Charles** (see September 23rd) on the *Porgy and Bess* album and appeared with Frank Sinatra at London's Royal Albert Hall for a week of performances in 1992.

The autobiography *Cleo* came out in 1994. A second book *You Can Sing If You Want* was published in 1997. That same year Cleo Laine was made a Dame in the New Year's Honours List. Her husband would later be knighted, they would become one of the few couples to receive separate honours.

Journalist and poet, **Rui de Noronha** of mixed Indian and African heritage was born **on this day** in 1909, in Mozambique. He influenced the next generation of writers, recognised as a founding figure in Mozambique writing. Noronha faced racial and colonial barriers. His collection of sixty poems *Sonetos* was published posthumously in 1946. Rui de Noronha died December 25th in 1943, he was thirty-four.

Oct 29th:

Nobel Peace Prize winner in 2011 for furthering women's rights, **Ellen Johnson Sirleaf** was born **on this day** in 1938. Johnson Sirleaf became **the first woman leader of an African country,** in Liberia as president from 2006–18. When she stood down the country saw the first peaceful democratic transition of power since 1944.

Ellen Johnson Sirleaf travelled to America to further her education, gaining her M A from Harvard University in public administration, 1971. Returning to Liberia, Johnson Sirleaf served as assistant minister of finance from 1972 to 73 under President **William Tolbert.** Following the military coup of 1980, and the execution of Tolbert, Johnson Sirleaf served as the finance minister from 1980 to 85 under the military dictatorship of **Samuel K Doe**. She clashed with both Tolbert and Doe. The minister would be arrested twice, narrowly escaping death, after criticising the dictatorship. She was given a ten-year sentence before being released and permitted to leave the country.

Ellen Johnson Sirleaf spent twelve years in exile, living in Kenya and the USA, working as an economist at several financial organisations including Citibank and the World Bank. Johnson Sirleaf served as the director of the Regional Bureau for Africa in the United Nations Development Programme, 1992–97.

Ellen Johnson Sirleaf.   Samuel K Doe

With the Unity Party the former exile returned to politics and ran for the presidency but came second to **Charles Taylor**. Again Johnson Sirleaf, accused of treason, found herself living in exile. The second Liberian Civil War 1999–2003 ended with Taylor himself going into exile. Johnson Sirleaf chaired the Commission on Good Governance in 2005. The Commission prepared the ground for and oversaw the domestic elections. Johnson Sirleaf ran for president promising to rebuild the country's battered infrastructure, to end the civil conflict, create unity and end corruption. Nicknamed the Iron Lady, Ellen Johnson Sirleaf was sworn in on Jan 16th2006 having defeated former footballer **George Weah** (see October 1st).

The president inherited a country with 80per cent unemployment and 15,000 UN peacekeepers. By 2010 Liberia's debt had been erased with the country attracting millions of dollars in foreign investment.

The Truth and Reconciliation Committee (TRC) was set up in 2006 to investigate corruption and to heal ethnic divisions. TRC accused the president of complicity having supported Charles Taylor early in the war. They recommended that Johnson Sirleaf be barred from political office for thirty years. Public and international support for the president saw her remain in politics and in office.

The Anti-Corruption Committee was established in 2008. Ellen Johnson Sirleaf would later be criticised for nepotism in 2012 with family members having important positions in government and state-run institutions. Seeking a second term in office Johnson Sirleaf faced a legal challenge. The 1986 constitution forbade anyone who had not been in the country for ten years from standing for election. The residency policy was overruled as it was agreed that exile and civil war had not been anticipated. When the president shared the Nobel Peace Prize with **Leymah Gbowee** (see February 1st) and Tawakkol Karman, days before the election, the Nobel committee was criticised for external interference. The twenty-fourth president was sworn in for her second term on January 16th 2012.

The Ebola virus of 2014 killed over 4,800 Liberians, leaving a devastated economy. In 2016 President Johnson Sirleaf became the first woman elected as chair of the Economic Community of West African States (ECOWAS), which was established on May 28th 1975. The president was expelled from her own Unity Party having supported George Weah as her successor and not her serving deputy Joseph Boakai. Ellen Johnson Sirleaf stepped down on January 22nd in 2018. She was awarded the Ibrahim Prize for Achievement in African Leadership that same year.

The former president has published several books. Her autobiography *This Child Will Be Great: Memoir of a Remarkable Life by Africa's First Woman President* was published in 2010.

Dancer, choreographer, and anthropologist **Pearl Primus** was born in Trinidad on November 29th 1919. Responsible for bringing African dance to a wider American audience, Primus was interested in her heritage and the African diaspora. Her proselytization of African dance along with the cultural expressions of dance from the impoverished black American South and the West Indies, helped to bring such performance and understanding to an American audience.

Pearl Primus travelled to research, study, codify and on occasion preserve dance. Her work brought an awareness of the richness, history and complexity of African and Caribbean dance. She died **on this day,** from diabetes aged seventy-four, in 1994.

Oct 30th:

Richard Arrington, born October 19th 1934, marked a seismic shift in racial politics in the city of Birmingham, Alabama. Infamous for its problematic racial divide and history, the elections held **on this day** in 1979 saw Arrington become the first African American mayor of Birmingham. It was a close-run affair with an estimated 10per cent of the white electorate crossing the colour divide, seeing Arrington defeat his white opponent lawyer, Frank Parsons.

Richard Arrington was subject to close scrutiny, but his popularity never waned. He served five terms in office before stepping down in 1999. Arrington appointed twenty-three of the city department's twenty-four heads in 1995. Birmingham now had twelve black and twelve white officers in place. During his tenure the city saw greater financial and service development at its centre. Recruitment of black people to both the police and fire departments improved.

On this day in 1991 **BET Holdings Inc,** parent company to Black Entertainment Television sold 4.2 million shares making it the first African American company to be listed on the New York Stock Exchange (NYSE). Founded by **Robert L Johnson,** 1979, the media company, part of the cable TV network, became the first black majority owned company on the NYSE.

Muhamad Ali v George Foreman clashed in the heavyweight title fight **Rumble in the Jungle, on this day** 1974 in Zaire (see February 25th). Heavyweight boxing champion George Foreman was born on January 10th in 1949. On November 5th 1994 Foreman became the oldest heavyweight champion at forty-five. He beat the formerly undefeated, 0 for 35, WBA champion, twenty-six-year-old Michael Moorer.

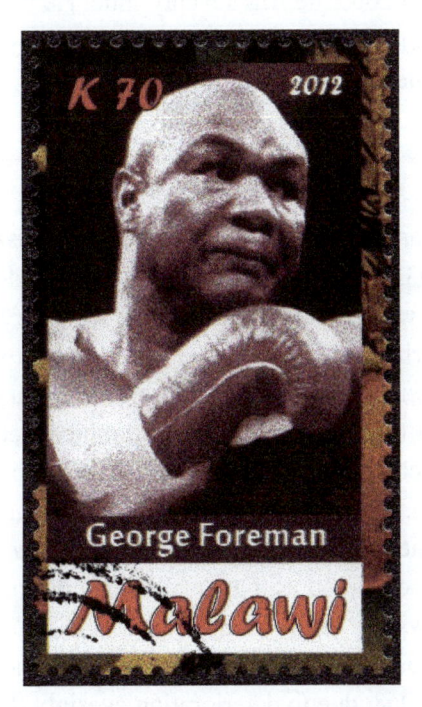

Heavyweight champion boxer George Foreman.

Oct 31st:

Peter Frayer, white author of the influential and ground-breaking *Staying Power: The History of Black British People in Britain* (1984) was a Marxist writer and journalist.

Born in Hull in February 1927, Frayer joined the Communist League in 1942. As a reporter at the Yorkshire Post he was dismissed in 1947 for refusing to leave the Communist Party which he had joined in 1945.

The left-wing journalist writing about the Hungarian Laszlo Rajk's confession and subsequent execution, 1949, started to become disillusioned with communism. Frayer's position was further challenged covering the Hungarian Revolution of 1956. He was disturbed by the heavy censorship of his reports by the Daily Worker, now the Morning Star, which he had joined in 1948. Peter Frayer filed his reports with the New Statesman. He published the book *Hungarian Tragedy* defending the revolution and was expelled from the Communist Party in 1956 for being critical of Soviet troops in Hungary and rejecting Stalinism.

The white English journalist covered the arrival of the *Empire Windrush* at Tilbury Docks in 1948 (see June 22). His experience sparked interest, sowing seeds leading to research covering, or uncovering, 2,000 years of black history going back to the Roman occupation in Britain. *Staying Power: The History of Black British People in Britain* revealed the black presence. Frayer's work made connections to named and unnamed characters, influences on politics, social institutions, traditions and cultural life.

Peter Frayer would write the sequel to *Staying Power*, *Black People in the British Empire*, 1988, examining the exploitation of the colonial system while placing the black experience at the heart of the narrative. *Aspects of British Black History* was published in 1993. *The Politics of Windrush* (1999), *Rhythms of Resistance, African Musical Heritage in Brazil* (2000), looks at how African music and rhythms affected the contemporary black music of Brazil and its wider influence on music world-wide. Frayer wrote a biography of the mixed heritage Chartist organiser *William Cuffay,* published in 2005.

Peter Frayer died **on this day** in 2006, he was seventy-nine. He was awarded the Knight's Cross of the Order of Merit of the Republic from the Hungarian president shortly before his death for his continued support for the freedom fight and the Hungarian Revolution.

Senegalese writer and politician, part of the negritude movement, **Ousmane Soce** was born **on this day** in 1911. With the novel *Karim* (1935), about an African at a crossroads, attempting to preserve his culture and tradition in an ever changing, westernised world. *Karim* won the West African Literary Grand Prize. Soce was one of his country's earliest novelists. As one of Senegal's first African students to obtain a scholarship to study in France, it was while in Paris studying veterinary medicine that Soce wrote his first and second novel *Mirages de Paris* (1937), a semi-autobiographical account of a tragic love story between a Senegalese student and his French girlfriend. Ousmane Soce wrote animal tales and historical legends based on Senegalese oral tradition: *Contes et Légendes d'Afrique noire, (Stories and legends of Black Africa)*, 1942. In 1956 Soce published a volume of poetry, *Rythmes du Khalam*.

As a politician the writer and poet served as mayor of Rufisque from 1936–45 and 1960–64. He held a variety of political positions. He was in the French Senate, 1946–52 and founded the Senegalese Union Movement in 1956. Soce was his country's ambassador to the USA and the delegate to the United Nations.

Ousmane Diop Soce retired in 1968, due to deteriorating eyesight. He died on October 27th in 1973.

Earl Lloyd, April 3rd 1928 – February 26th 2015, **broke the colour bar** in America's National Basketball Association (NBA). Playing for West Virginia State College, his team went undefeated in 1948. He was the second black player drafted into the NBA by the Washington Capitals; **Chuck Cooper** was the first for the Boston Celtics. **Nate 'Sweetwater' Clifton** was the first black player to actually sign an NBA contract. It just happened by order of play that Lloyd took to the court **on this day** in 1950, before Cooper and Clifton, becoming the first black person to play in the NBA. He scored six points in that first game. The black pioneers in the NBA faced some racial hostility but nothing compared to **Jackie Robinson** (see April 15th) in baseball (college basketball was already integrated).

Following active service in the Korean War Lloyd joined the Syracuse Nationals, 1952–58, winning the championship in 1955. With **Jim Tucker,** Lloyd became the first black person to play in a championship winning team. Lloyd's playing career ended with the Detroit Pistons, 1958-60. He played 560 games over nine seasons. Earl Lloyd became the first black assistant coach with the Pistons 1968–70, and the third black coach after **John McLendon** and **Bill Russell** (see January 8th). McLendon was the first professional sports coach in America in any sport.

Canadian **Arthur 'Art' Dorrington** born March 13th 1930, became the first black player to sign a contract for the New York Rangers ice hockey team in the National Hockey League (NHL), on November 16th 1950. Although signed to play he never took to the ice at the highest level. Dorrington died aged eighty-seven on December 29th in 2017. It was left to fellow Canadian **Willie O'Ree,** born October 15th 1935**,** to become the first black player in the NHL, breaking the colour bar, playing for the Boston Bruins. On January 18th 1958, the twenty-two-year-old O'Ree suited up to play for the Bruins v Montreal Canadians.

Maia Chaka became the second woman and the first black woman named to officiate at an NFL match, on March 5th 2021.

Empire Road was a pioneering black British television soap based on a multicultural road in Handsworth, Birmingham. Writer Guyana born **Michael Abbensetts,** 1938–2016, regarded as one of Britain's best black playwrights of his generation, was commissioned by the BBC to write the TV drama.

Empire Road ran for two series with fifteen episodes and starred **Norman Beaton, Rudolph Walker, Joseph Marcell, Corinne Skinner Carter** and **Wayne Laryea.** The ground-breaking soap first aired **on this day** in 1978. The final episode was shown on November 1st 1979. The theme tune recorded by the British reggae band Matumbi, was released as a single in 1978.

See Trix Worrell's ***Desmond's*** (January 5th), ***The Fosters*** (April 9th) two other important programmes in the history of black British television, and the first interracial kiss on British and American TV (see February 1st).

Nov 1st:

Eugene O'Neill's play *The Emperor Jones* premiered **on this day** in 1920. The powerful drama observes the key character Brutus Jones's rise and then descent into madness along the lines of Shakespeare's King Lear and Macbeth.

Some have been critical of *Emperor Jones's* failure to advance the position or image of the black man. They argue that the setting on an unnamed Caribbean Island where one can hear the drums as Jones wanders through the jungle is beset by negative stereotypes. **Paul Robeson** (see April 9th) played the lead on stage in the USA, UK and in the 1933 film. One cannot imagine the astute, politically aware actor and activist would be duped into playing and accepting backward stereotypes. The play is a product of its time but is also a priceless vehicle for any aspirational actor. With only eight scenes, six scenes 2-7, feature Jones on his own providing the performer a rare opportunity to investigate his character.

Emperor Jones follows train porter, (Pullman porter), Brutus Jones. Having committed murder Jones escapes prison and finds his way to a Caribbean Island. He convinces the locals that he has special powers leading to him being made emperor. When an assassination attempt fails Jones declares that only a silver bullet can kill him. The emperor's abuse of power and amassed wealth through heavy taxation leads to rumours of an uprising. Jones flees to the jungle where facing potential doom he is haunted by his past demons. The locals melt their silver coins, to produce the required bullets, while the sound of the drums get ever louder and closer.

A piece of its time O'Neill reflected on Haitian history, American involvement in Caribbean politics and his own drug driven hallucinations while prospecting for gold in Honduras in 1909.

On this day two important publications were first issued. **W. E. B. DuBois** (see February 23rd) published the **NAACP**'s monthly magazine *Crisis* in 1910. **John H. Johnson's** *Ebony* (see February 19th) appeared **on this day** in 1945.

Antigua and Barbuda gained independence **on this day** in 1981, ending over 350 years of British rule. The Caribbean islands became the 157th members of the United Nations and joined the Organisation of Eastern Caribbean States that same year. Prime Minister **Vere C. Bird** served from 1981 to 1994. He was succeeded by his son Lester 1994–2004.

The national flag.

With the release of **Nelson Mandela** and the legalisation of the African National Congress (ANC) the first all-race elections were held in South Africa on April 27th in 1994. Multi-racial democracy was tested again going to the polls in the first municipal, **multi-racial, elections on this day** in 1995. The ANC won 6,032 seats, with 58per cent, the National Party 1,814 seats, 18per cent, Inkatha Freedom Party 754 seats with 8.7per cent of the votes.

Nov 2nd:

The Mississippi Plan was a successful attempt by the Democrats, following the Civil War, during the reconstruction period, to disenfranchise the black vote. Republicans had won the state by 30,000 votes. The initial focus was on the 10 to 15per cent white vote that had remained with the Republicans. The Democrats made many white Republicans feel that their party was being taken over. The next stage was much more bold and unapologetically aggressive. Black lives were threatened. In the city of Vicksburg, it's estimated some 300 African Americans were killed and the black sheriff Peter Cosby was forced to flee, in August 1875. The situation was tense witnessing the rise of white militia and rifle clubs.

Former enslaved people get the vote November 1869

With the official launch of the Mississippi Plan **on this day** in 1875, the suppression of the black vote saw five majority black counties return only 12, 7, 4, 2 and 0 black votes. The Democrats saw a swing of 60,000 gaining a majority of 30,000.

Born July 17th 1921 **Marcenia Lyle Stone** would be popularly known in baseball as **Toni Stone.** In 1953 she would be signed to the Indianapolis Clowns. Stone became the first woman to play professional baseball alongside men. She played in what was previously the all-male negro league.

Toni Stone faced sexism from her teammates and the opposition. There was a good deal of hype over inclusion. Some accounts said she had signed for $12,000 a contract that was worth more than that of Jackie Robinson. She refused to play in a skirt wishing to be taken seriously. She could run 100 yards in 11 seconds and had a batting average of .243. Stone even got a hit off the legendary **Satchel Paige**, considered one of the all-time great pitchers. After fifty playing second base Stone was traded to the Kansas City Monarchs where she retired at the end of the 1954 season.

Having quit the game Stone spent time nursing her husband, forty years her senior, until he died in 1987. Toni Stone died **on this day** in 1996, aged seventy-five. See August 31st for Frank Robinson.

On this day in 1983 President Ronald Reagan signed into law **Martin Luther King Jr Day.** Introduced to Congress by Democrat Representative **John Conyers** and Republican Senator **Edward Brooke** (see October 26th) the bill would make King only the third person after George Washington and Christopher Columbus to have a national holiday in their name in the USA. Six million signatures later and the release of **Stevie Wonder's** (see May 13th) single 'Happy Birthday' political opinion shifted. Martin Luther King Day on the third Monday in January, was first observed on January 20th 1986.

<u>Democrat representative John Conyers</u>

Nov 3rd:

Saint Martin de Porres was beatified by Pope Gregory XVI on October 29th 1837. Over one hundred years later Pope John XXIII canonized Porres on May 6th 1962.

Martin was born on December 9th 1579 in Lima, Peru, to a Spanish nobleman Don Juan de Porres and a freed slave of African origin, Ana Velasquez. The family was soon abandoned by the father. Raised in poverty Martin had to navigate the twin difficulties of being illegitimate and a mulatto.

The young Porres sought training with a barber surgeon. It is not clear why, but the boy demonstrated extraordinary religious devotion, from a young age, that led to him seeking to be a volunteer with the Dominican order. Joining the full order for some one of mixed heritage was out of the question. Porres' devotion shone through and impressed. Doors were edged open. Accepting menial tasks, the boy was able to wear the habit and given accommodation with the religious community. Aged fifteen he was admitted to the Dominican Covenant of the Rosary in Lima. Porres' responsibilities grew, caring for the sick in the infirmary, doing laundry, working in the kitchen, performing general cleaning duties and distributing money to the poor as an almoner. In 1601 the young man became an obligate (lay monastic). He took vows as a member of the Third Order of Saint Dominic. At the age of twenty-four in 1603, Porres was permitted to profess religious vows going against tradition. By 1610 he was admitted as a Dominican. Ten years later, aged thirty-four, Porres was formally given the religious habit and assigned to the infirmary where he worked for the rest of his life. Working in the infirmary Porres displayed virtuous patience, caring for the sick regardless of ethnicity, wealth, standing or personal danger. Miraculous stories followed him in his desire to help others as he placed charity above everything else. In whatever he did the friar showed devotion and was in constant prayer, established a school, a hospital and an orphanage.

On his death people cut pieces of his habit off as holy relics. His spiritual service was legendary, fasting for long periods or only eating bread and having water, Porres stopped eating meat. His charitable work saw him provide 4,000 pesos for dowries allowing twenty-seven young women to marry. It is said that he was able to feed 160 daily as well as distributing money to the poor weekly. Saint Martin de Porres died **on this day** in 1659, he was fifty-nine

Saint Martin de Porres

Saint Martin is the patron saint of barbers, innkeepers, public health workers, for racial harmony and of mixed heritage people. His feast day is on November 3rd.

Born **on this day** in 1905, African American artist **Lois Mailou Jones** would enjoy a long, distinguished and influential career. By the age of eighteen she had her first solo exhibition. Jones became the first black student to graduate from the School of the Museum of Fine Arts in Boston.

The artist started out in textile design selling her work to department stores. When it was questioned whether a black woman could produce such amazing works, Jones turned to fine art where she could sign her paintings. Lois Mailou Jones worked at Howard University, Washington DC, from 1939–1977 influencing many generations. A major turning point came when attending the Académie Julian in Paris in 1937, Jones not only developed her expertise of painting landscapes but also discovered African art. Her love of the racial freedom she experienced in France meant that she lived as an expatriate in the country for many summers.

In 1953 she married the Haitian graphic designer Louis Vernigaud Pierre-Noel. Open to the bright colours and Haitian influences Jones met many of that country's artists all adding to her colour pallet.

Jones was commissioned by the United States Information Agency to act as a cultural ambassador to Africa. This saw the artist travel to eleven countries, lecturing, interviewing local artists and visiting museums. The decades that followed saw further exploration of Africa in her art.

A prolific artist, she had a long career. She was influenced by the Harlem Renaissance, her travels and people around her working on landscapes to African themed abstracts. She died, at the age of ninety-two, on June 9th 1998. Dr Charles Chapman wrote her biography *Lois Mailou Jones, A Life in Colour* in 2007. She is buried in Martha's Vineyard at Oak Bluff's Cemetery, USA.

The Caribbean Island of **Dominica** gained its **independence on this day** in 1978. The island had been in the possession of the Spanish, the French and then the British. A trophy of European conflict it saw little investment or development. Prime Minister Patrick John took office, but questionable business deals saw an interim government led by Oliver Seraphim take over in May 1979. The elections of 1980 saw the Caribbean's first female head of government with the Dominican Freedom Party winning a majority and **Eugenia Charles** becoming prime minister. The first year saw her survive two attempted coups. It was not a surprise following the coup in Grenada and assassination of **Maurice Bishop** (see October 25th) that, as the chairperson of the Organisation of East Caribbean States, Charles had endorsed the US invasion of Grenada.

The national flag.

Nov 4th:

Civil rights activist, journalist, and mentor to the **Little Rock Nine** (see September 5th) **Daisy Bates** was born, **Daisy Gaston,** on November 11th 1914. Gaston's mother Millie Riley was raped, killed and her body thrown into a millpond. Daisy was three at the time. Fearing that he would be killed, (the three white men suspected of the crime were not prosecuted) her father, Hezekiah Gaston fled. Daisy never saw her biological father again. The young girl was adopted, only finding out the truth of what had happened when she was eight. A cloud appeared and grew into a hatred of white people and injustice. On his deathbed her adopted father warned Daisy of the dangers of hate and how to channel her energy into using hate constructively.

Daisy married Lucius Christopher Bates on March 4th 1941; they had met when she was fifteen, started dating when she was seventeen, he was married at the time. The couple moved to Little Rock, Arkansas where they opened the weekly newspaper the *Arkansas State Press*. The first edition came out on March 4th 1941. The paper championed civil rights issues and was respected for being fearless and not afraid to highlight police abuse and brutality. The activism saw some white businesses pull vital financial advertising. Daisy would frequently edit and provide articles for the *Arkansas State Press*.

As president of the Arkansas chapter of the National Association for the Advancement of Colored People (NAACP), 1952, Daisy Bates led the protest against the slow nature of school integration. Little Rock school boards had agreed to a gradual (slow) policy of public-school integration in 1954. Bates had first-hand experience of the poor segregated schools, she argued for immediate integration. She would drive individual black students to register at white schools recording their rejection accompanied by a photographer.

Plans were announced to integrate Central High School in Little Rock. The opposition held rallies, took legal action, resorted to threats and acts of violence. Rocks and stones were thrown through the Bates' windows and bullets arrived in the post. After setbacks (see Elizabeth Eckford October 4th) the nine entered the school on September 25th 1957. Daisy Bates escorted the nine daily, kept the parents informed, and held press conferences with the students. She even joined the parent -teachers-association. The following year became known as 'the lost year'. All public schools in Arkansas, 1958–59, were closed to stall integration. The *Arkansas State Press* was forced to close on October 29th 1959 as white businesses withdrew all advertising.

The Bates moved to New York City where Daisy published her autobiography *The Long Shadow of Little Rock* in 1962. Moving to Washington, Daisy got involved working with the Democratic party on voter registration drives. With President L. B. Johnson, she participated in anti-poverty programmes.

Daisy Bates had a stroke in 1965, briefly returning to Little Rock. She continued to improve the social conditions within the local black communities. L. C. Bates died in 1980. The *Arkansas State Press* was resurrected in 1984. Daisy Bates died **on this day** in 1999, she was eighty-four. She is buried in the Haven of Rest, Little Rock, 7102 W. 12th Street. Daisy Bates always regretted the situation that Elizabeth Eckford found herself in, as a fifteen-year-old girl, all alone facing an angry mob of spitting and threatening white people calling to lynch her. Bates would apologise for her failure to protect Eckford.

Ophthalmologist, dealing with the diagnosis and treatment of eye disorders, **Patricia Bath** was born **on this day** in 1942. The invention of the Laserphaco Probe, in 1986, led to more precise and less painful cataract laser surgery. Bath became the first black, female doctor to receive a medical patent in 1988. Bath would achieve numerous firsts in her ground-breaking medical career.

From 1970–73, Patricia Bath became the first African American to complete her postgraduate training residency in ophthalmology, at New York University. A few years later in 1975 Bath became the first female faculty member in the department of ophthalmologist at the Jules Stein Eye Institute at UCLA.

Research by Bath confirmed that her black patients were twice as likely to suffer blindness and eight times more likely to develop glaucoma. Her findings led to the formation of community medical programmes. In 1976 Bath co-founded the American Institute for the Prevention of Blindness. The institute argues that eyesight is a basic right and seeks to protect, preserve and restore vision.

At UCLA Dr Bath founded the Ophthalmic Assistant Training Programme in 1978. She would be appointed its chair in 1983. Dr Bath oversaw the study and process of keratoprosthetics, the removal of diseased cataracts and their replacements with artificial ones, at UCLA.

Wishing to further her studies Dr Bath travelled and studied in England, France and Germany. She continued to develop innovative ideas using pulsing ultrasound to remove cataracts. In the USA Dr Bath had five patents to her name.

Doctor Patricia Bath died from complications related to cancer on May 30th in 2019, she was seventy-six.

Nov 5th:

On this day in 1968 **Shirley Chisholm** made United States political history by becoming the first black woman elected to the US Congress.

Born to an immigrant father from what was British Guiana (Guyana) and a mother from Barbados, on November 30th 1924. **Shirley Anita St Hill** would study to become a teacher gaining her BA in 1946 and MA in 1952.

Shirley married Conrad Chisholm in 1949, the couple divorced in 1977. Moving into politics Chisholm became the second black person elected to the New York State legislature serving there from 1965 to 1968. She stepped forward being elected to the House of Representatives, beating civil rights activist **James Farmer** (see Jan 12th) from the Congress of Racial Equality (CORE), Chisholm took 67per cent of the vote. The congresswoman served seven terms through to January 3rd 1983.

As a liberal Chisholm opposed weapons development. In her first speech on the floor in March 26th 1969, she made her opposition to the war in Vietnam clear. Shirley Chisholm was a founding member of the Congressional Black Caucus, Jan 1969, and the National Women's Political Caucus in 1971. The women's caucus sought to identify, recruit, train and endorse women running for political office. Chisholm supported the Equal Rights Amendment. First introduced to the Congress in 1923, the amendment was only approved by the US Senate in 1972. The Equal Rights Amendment was to ensure that gender did not determine one's legal rights. It was not ratified, failing to gain the 38 states required that would have made it the 27th Amendment to the Constitution. Chisholm supported legislation leading to abortion and the woman's right to choose.

Under the banner 'Unbought and Unbossed', also the title of her 1970 autobiography, Shirley Chisholm became the first woman to run for the Democratic nomination for president. She was the first woman to run for either the Democrats or Republicans. Chisholm gained 10per cent of the delegates with 152 votes before withdrawing in 1972. Chisholm wrote a second autobiography *The Good Fight* in 1973.

On retiring from front line politics Chisholm was busy on the lecture circuit but had time to co-found the National Political Congress of Black Women in 1983. President

Political champion and pioneer Shirley Chisholm.

Clinton attempted to entice the former congresswoman out of retirement, offering Chisholm the post of ambassador to Jamaica. She declined due to ill health.

Shirley Chisholm died on January 1st in 2005, she was eighty. Chisholm was laid to rest at Forest Lawn Cemetery in Buffalo, New York.

Nov 6th:

George Coleman Poage won bronze at the St Louis Olympic games 1904. It was the third Olympics but the first where an **African American won a medal.** Poage ran in the 220 yards and the 440 yards hurdles coming third thus becoming a double Olympic medallist.

George Poage was born **on this day** in 1880. He was the first black person to graduate from his school La Crosse High School in Wisconsin. He would go on to be the first black athlete to run for the University of Wisconsin's athletic team. The Olympic games in St Louis were controversial having segregated spectator sections. Poage never cashed in on his athletic achievements. After thirty years as a US postal worker, George Poage died at the age of eighty-two on April 11th 1962.

The accolade of the **first black Olympic gold medallist** goes to Haitian born **Constantin Henriquez de Zubiera.** Playing rugby for the French national team at the second Olympiad, 1900, in Paris, Zubiera picked up gold with the French beating the British team on October 28th.

Zubiera played rugby usually wearing No 8, on the wing or centre for Stade Francais winning the French Championship title in 1897, 1898 and 1901. Returning to Haiti Zubiera is credited with introducing football to the country in 1904 and scoring in their first international. By the 1950s Constantin Henriquez de Zubiera was a senator in Haiti. At the same 1900 Olympiad Zubiera was part of the silver medal-winning team in the tug of war.

Remembering great Olympians.

John Baxter Taylor Jr would be distinguished as the **first African American to win Olympic gold** at the London games of 1908. Running at the Shepherds Bush Stadium in the 1600m relay, the American team set a new record coming in first. Taylor also held records at the 440 and 660 yards.

The veterinary medical student graduated from the University of Pennsylvania in 1908. John Baxter Taylor Jr died from typhoid pneumonia five months after receiving gold and a month before his twenty-sixth birthday.

Special mention should be made of **Harry Francis Vincent Edward.** Running for Britain in the 100 and 200 metres at the 1920 Antwerp Olympic games he won bronze in both races. Edward became the first black British Olympian medallist. Born in Berlin April 15th 1895, Edwards died in Germany on July 8th 1973.

Jack Edward London born in British Guiana (Guyana) on Jan 13th 1905 won silver in the 100m and Bronze in the 4x100m relay at the 1928 Amsterdam Olympics running for Britain. London died on May 2nd 1966.

Alice Coachman dominated the national sport of the high jump. She won ten years of successive competitions at the American Amateur Athletic Union's outdoor championships from 1939–1948. One can only wonder what the record holder could have achieved had the 1940 and 1944 Olympics not been cancelled. At the 1948 games in London's White City Stadium, Coachman set a new record with her first jump winning gold, with 5 ft 6 ⅛ in. Born November 9th 1923, she died on July 14th 2014.

Ghanaian boxer **Ike Quartey** would have the distinction of being the first black African Olympic medallist. The light welterweight won silver at the 1960s Rome Olympics, five days before Ethiopian **Abebe Bikila** (see August 7th) won gold running barefoot in the marathon.

Born on February 12th 1984, Afro-Colombian **Caterine Ibargüen** became her country's first athlete in track and field to win an Olympic Gold in 2016. She competed in the triple jump.

Caterine Ibargüen.

Kenyan athlete, long distance runner **Paul Kipkoech** was born on January 6th 1963. He died March 13th 1995, aged thirty-two. He was the first Kenyan track athlete to win a gold medal-winning the 10,000 m in the 1987 World Championships in Rome.

The Mills Brothers were a jazz/pop vocal quartet who experienced amazing success over their fifty-year career. Their 1976 fiftieth anniversary celebration was hosted by Bing Cosby.

'Paper Doll' (the B side to 'I'll Be Around'*)* became their biggest hit with six million sales. 'Paper Doll' (1943) saw the Brothers become the first black act to get to No one on the American Billboard on this day 1943. With over 2,000 recordings, 50 million sales, and at least 36 gold records the Mills Brothers were also the first black act to have a network show on the radio in 1930.

The vocal group was made up of John Mills Jr, Herbert, Harry & Donald. Their father John Mills Sr started the group and initially performed with his sons. When John Mills Jr died in the 1930s, he was replaced by Bernard Addison on guitar and on occasion the group appeared with Gene Smith. Film appearances included: *The Big Broadcast* (1932), *Twenty Million Sweethearts* (1934) and *Broadway Gondolier* (1935). In 1934 the quartet became the first black act to give a Royal Command Performance for Britain's George V and Queen Mary at the Regal Theatre in London.

The Mills Brothers had their last hit with 'Cab Driver in' 1968. Their back catalogue includes: 'Tiger Rag', 'Goodbye Blues', 'Nobody's Sweetheart!', 'Ole Rocking Chair', 'Lazy River', 'How'm Doin', 'Lazy Bones', 'Sweet Sue', 'Sleepy Head', 'Lulu's Back In Town' and 'Bye Bye Blackbird'.

Nov 7th:

The Brazilian Slave Trade (see May 13th) officially started in 1533 when a request was made to import seventeen enslaved Africans. The trade became legal on March 29th 1559 authorised by Catherine of Austria, Regent of Portugal. By 1800 there were some two million enslaved people in Brazil. The trade saw approximately 38,000 people imported in 1806. Between 1821 and 1830 figures put it at 553,000 human beings sold into slavery.

With the independence of Brazil in 1822, the British hoped that there would be a gradual negotiated decline in the slave trade. The lifting of tariffs on sugar saw continued demand for enslaved workers. On November 23rd 1826 a British/Brazilian treaty was signed in Rio de Janeiro making it illegal for Brazilians to participate in the international slave trade. All enslaved people entering Brazil were declared to be free. This and later legislation was largely ignored and not enforced.

On this day in 1831 **Feijo's Law** was passed. Named after the priest who negotiated it, the law was a farce known as "para ingles ver", (merely for the English to see). The Brazilians showed little interest in enforcing a ban on the trade in Africans. The period 1831–1852 became recognised as the period of the contraband slave trade. Numbers of imported Africans between 1831 and 36 were put at 26,095. The numbers rose to 201,140 from 1836 to 1840.

Enslaved, statue found in Sao Paolo

The Aberdeen Act, named after the British foreign secretary Lord Aberdeen, passed in 1845 gave the British Royal Navy the power to board any Brazilian ship suspected of transporting captured Africans and to arrest the traders to be put on trial under British law. Prosecution numbers rose but so did the number of people being imported. A new trade act came into play in 1850 this time the Brazilians enforced the law. The decade saw a real decline in the cargo of human beings. The law of the free womb, 1871, granted freedom to children of enslaved mothers. The sexagenarian law freed any enslaved person over the age of sixty, Brazil saw the beginning of the end in 1888 of African slavery, (see the Golden Law May 13th, September 4th and November 20th).

Mixed heritage boatman **Francis McIntosh** was arrested, having refused to take part in supporting police officers who were in pursuit of two suspected sailors. When asked how long he would be in jail, charged with a breach of the peace, it is reported that McIntosh was told five years. Grabbing a knife, the twenty-six-year-old stabbed and killed one officer and severely injured another. Francis McIntosh escaped but was

Burning of McIntosh at St. Louis, in April, 1836,

quickly apprehended and returned to jail.

An angry mob of white citizens broke into the jail and took the terrified boatman to the edge of town where they chained him to a tree and set fire to wood placed around his legs. McIntosh begged to be shot but his pleading was ignored. An elderly African American was paid to ensure that the fire remained burning throughout the night. In the morning white boys arrived and threw stones to smash the victim's head. It is believed that Francis McIntosh survived twenty minutes in the flames.

Writing for the St Louis's *Observer,* **Elijah Parish Lovejoy** was blamed by Judge Lawless for inciting McIntosh's actions. Lovejoy, a white Presbyterian preacher, abolitionist and journalist, had been outspoken on a number of issues; Roman Catholicism, tobacco, alcohol and openly critical of slavery. Born November 7th 1837 Lovejoy settled in the slave state of Missouri, in St Louis in 1827. He became acquainted with abolitionists and members of the American Colonisation Society who sought to help freed slaves return to Africa. After a period of religious doubt Lovejoy became ordained in April of 1833.

The Mob attacking the Warehouse of Godfrey Gilman & Co. Alton Ill. on the Night of the 7th Nov. 1837.

Pro-slavery opponents and prominent men wrote and signed an open letter to Elijah Lovejoy, in 1835, asking him to tone down the nature of the *Observer*'s editorials. Lovejoy's refusal saw his printing press destroyed on three occasions and thrown into the Mississippi, forcing him to move to Alton, Illinois. The move was not enough. A mob of between twenty and thirty people attacked the newspaper's office. Elijah Lovejoy was shot five times while the warehouse was set ablaze. The mob threw the new printing press out of the window and smashed it to pieces. Thirty-four-year-old abolitionist Elijah Parish Lovejoy died **on this day** in 1837, defending freedom of speech.

For thirteen years **Helen Suzman** was the lone voice in the parliament in the House of Assembly of South Africa. The daughter of Jewish immigrants escaping the anti-Semitic prejudice and restrictions of eastern Europe, she was born **Helen Gavronsky, on this day** in 1917.

Helen married Dr Moses Suzman in 1937. Taking up politics Suzman entered parliament representing the United Party in 1953. Along with twelve like-minded MPs, Suzman formed the Progressive Party, a liberal, aggressively anti-apartheid party extending rights to all in South Africa. The 1961 elections saw Suzman the only party member to retain her seat. The English-speaking Jewish woman faced an often-hostile anti-Semitic sea of white, male dominated Afrikaners in the 160-member opposition. Undeterred Helen Suzman during her thirteen-year solo period made sixty-six speeches, moved twenty-six amendments and put 137 questions to the floor. She was a champion, an outspoken advocate for South Africa's majority non-white disenfranchised population.

Helen Suzman.

It was only after the 1974 election that Helen Suzman was joined by seven newly elected MPs in the renamed Progressive Federal Party. She used her parliamentary privilege to publish and release material to the press and to visit political prisoners, including **Mandela** and others on Robben Island. When invited she attended the funerals of black activists hoping that her presence would ensure that the police kept a dignified peaceful distance. An opponent of the death penalty and the banning of the Communist party Suzman was a constant thorn in the Nationals Party's side.

After thirty-six years Helen Suzman retired in 1989, but that was not the end. She sat as the president of the South African Institute of Race Relations from 1991 to 1993. On the Independent Electoral Commission, Helen and the team oversaw the first all-race democratic elections of 1994. Suzman was a member of the Human Rights Commission from 1995–1998. She proudly and deservedly stood by Nelson Mandela's side when he signed South Africa's new constitution in 1996.

The Helen Suzman Foundation was founded in 1993 to promote liberal democracy through developing public debate and research. The nation celebrated Suzman's 90th birthday **on this day** in 2007. Helen Suzman died in her sleep on January 1st 2009, she was ninety-one.

Nov 8th:

Cyril Ewart Lionel Grant became the first regular black person to appear on British TV in the 1960s BBC current affairs programme *Tonight*. Recognised by the name **Cy Grant** he had a career on stage, in theatre, cabaret, in concert, on radio, television, in films and as a writer.

Born **on this day** in Guyana in 1919, the twenty-two-year-old Grant came to England in 1941 to train in the RAF. Following huge losses during the Battle of Britain, over four hundred people were recruited from the West Indies to train and fight. Flight Lieutenant Grant flew as a navigator in the Avro Lancaster bomber as part of 103 Squadron. Returning from Germany on their third mission, Grant and the seven-man crew was shot down over the Netherlands. He parachuted safely with plans to make it to Spain. The conspicuous black man in occupied territory was soon captured and handed to the Germans by a Dutch police officer. He served the next two years in Stalag Luft III, a Luftwaffe run prisoner of war camp holding Western air force personnel. Stalag III would become famous as the camp featured in the 1963 film *The Great Escape.* Cy Grant was liberated by allied forces in 1945.

Cy Grant would eventually be reunited with Joost Klootwijk. At the age of eleven Klootwijk, saw Grant's Lancaster bomber shot down. He had always wondered what had happened to the crew. Sixty-five years later Grant and Klootwijk emotionally met up as part of a 2008 documentary film. Grant was taken aback by the respect given to him by Klootwijk. As a member of the RAF Grant felt that he, and other black recruits never received such respect in England. The former prisoner of war spoke about his experiences during the war in the 2011 documentary *Into the Wind*.

After the war Grant qualified as a barrister but found it impossible to find work at the bar. Turning to acting to make a living, his first role was on stage in *13th Death Street, Harlem* in 1950. Grant appeared in the film *Safari* (1955), set during the Kenyan Mau Mau uprising. Grant appeared alongside Victor Mature, Janet Leigh and **Earl Cameron** (see July 3rd). It would be the first of thirty-two film appearances over the next twenty years. In *Sea Wife* (1957), set in Jamaica, Grant starred alongside Richard Burton and Joan Collins. The 1958 film *Calypso* saw Grant play the romantic lead alongside Cary Grant and **Louise Bennett** (see September 7th). Other major films would include *Shaft in Africa* (1973), with **Richard Roundtree** and *At the Earth's Core* in 1974.

Cy Grant's television career was impressive; *For Members Only* (1955), his own series. *Man From the Sun*, a 1956 TV drama looked at the lives of West Indian immigrants in Britain following World War II. He was in the award-winning *Home of the Brave* (1957), and another award-winning series *Freedom Road* (1964), where Grant appeared with **Cleo Laine** (see October 28th) and **Madeline Bell.** Grant's appearances continued on radio, in cabaret, singing in concerts and releasing records. The big break came when he appeared as a regular on BBC's *Tonight* a current affairs news programme. Setting the news to calypso music Grant would sing and play the guitar. After two and a half years he left the show fearing that he would be typecast and thus trapped.

Cy Grant was performing at a time, alongside Earl Cameron, when there were very few roles for black people. You had major white actors blacking up to play Shakespeare's *Othello* and *Tarzan* still ruled the jungle. Grant was able to navigate the restrictive world of entertainment but never felt free to fully express himself and to play the roles that he felt he deserved. A hero of Grant was the politician, poet and philosopher **Aime Cesaire,** (see June 26th) the architect of negritude. Grant toured for two years – 1977/8 – in a one man show, performing Cesaire's epic poem *Notebook of a Return to the Native Land.* In 1973 the actor co-founded, with Zimbabwean **John Mapondera**, and was chair through to 1978 of the London based arts centre Drum. The centre produced black performances and linked up with similar projects in the United States.

Cy Grant wrote *Ring of Steel, Pan Sounds, and Symbols* in 1999, and the part memoir and part cultural negotiation; *Blackness and the Dreaming Soul* in 2007.

The man who acted alongside Roger Moore and Tony Curtis in *The Persuaders,* was the voice of Lieutenant Green in *Captain Scarlet and the Mysterons*, and who appeared in the BBC's *Blake's 7* died on February 13th in 2020. He was ninety years old.

Cy Grant appeared on BBC Four in *TV Black Pioneers* in 2007 and on BBC Radio 4's *Black Screen Britain* in 2009.

On May 11th 1938 the BBC broadcast Eugene O'Neill's ***Emperor Jones*** (November 1st) starring Guyanese-born actor **Richard Adams.** He became the first black actor to play a major part on British TV. He was the first black actor to appear in a Shakespearian role playing in *The Merchant of Venice* in 1947. He was active as an actor from 1935 to 60. See **Erroll John** July 10th.

Nov 9th:

Born **on this day** in 1961 **Jackie Kay** was appointed the 'makar', the national poet for Scotland. The child of a Scottish mother and Nigerian father, Jackie was adopted by Helen and John Kay.

Jackie Kay graduated from Stirling University in 1983 having studied English. Her first collection of poetry *The Adoption Papers* (1991) received immediate recognition winning the Saltire Society award for best first book and a Scottish Arts Council book award. The author used three voices to help the child discover their identity. The voice of the birth mother, the adoptive mother and the adopted child tease out the emotional depth and breadth of everyday experiences while revealing the transformative power of love.

The author of novels, short stories, works for radio, theatre, children's fiction and poetry has a wide range of work. Jackie Kay's first novel, *Trumpet*, won the Guardian Fiction prize. The book is based on trumpeter Billy Tipton, 1914–89, who self-identified as male. Only at his death was it revealed that the husband to five wives was actually female. Kay used *Trumpet* to explore the fluid nature of identification, how one can be reinvented and escape fixed categories? Kay, a black Scottish lesbian, returns to these themes in her writing.

The professor of creative writing at the University of Newcastle, and later chancellor of the University of Salford in 2014, published *Other Lovers* in 1993. The quest for identity pursued through colonial history and slavery, using the power of language influenced by Afro-Caribbeans'. *Off Colour* (1998) examined issues of health and illness. *Off Colour* contains a sequence of poems on **Bessie Smith** (see September 26th). *Bessie Smith* was a 1997 book by Kay. A former Radio 4 book of the week, Kay found in Smith a tempestuous pioneering woman who she could identify with, be inspired by and look up to.

A prolific, and somewhat fearless writer produced *Life Masks* (2005) after sitting for sculptor Michael Snowden. A bust of the poet laureate now resides in Edinburgh's business park. Other selected writings include *Darling New and Selected Poems* (2007) and *The Lamplighter* (2008), first broadcast on Radio 3 exploring the Atlantic slave trade. Collections of short stories: *Why You Stop Talking* (2002) and *Wish I Was Here*, (2006). *Red Cherry Red* (2007) is a poetry collection for children. It won the 2008 CLPE Poetry Award, (Centre for Literacy in Primary Education).

Jackie Kay was made an MBE in 2006 for services to literature.

Benjamin Banneker used his self-taught abilities to demonstrate what a black man could achieve and questioned the system of slavery as practiced in the United States. He was frustrated that everything that he accomplished was always about his colour and not simply about his work. Banneker received recognition and acknowledgment but always in the prism of his ethnicity and race.

Born **on this day** in 1731 Benjamin Banneker was a largely self-taught, free, black man. At the age of twenty-two he achieved local fame having made a fully working clock, that struck on the hour, out of wood. The timepiece was constructed using a pocket watch as a model and kept perfect time for the rest of Banneker's life. When the Ellicotts, a Quaker family, moved into the area they became friends with Banneker. Like most Quakers, the Ellicotts had progressive abolitionist views about slavery and race. In 1788 George Ellicott loaned his neighbour some astronomical books. The fifty-seven-year-old Banneker used the books to teach himself algebra, geometry, logarithms, trigonometry and astronomy. In 1789 Banneker predicted his first full eclipse. So accomplished was Banneker that he was employed by George's cousin, Andrew Ellicott, to assist in mapping out and surveying the new federal city that would be Washington DC in 1791. On July 16th 1790 Congress passed a residence act to establish a new federal city. Andrew was employed as a practical engineer. Although Banneker's work was universally recognised, that did not prevent enslaved people being used in sourcing and delivering the materials to build the capital, as well as participate in the construction.

That same year Benjamin Banneker produced a detailed almanac plotting planetary conjunctions, eclipses, weather forecasts, dates for farmers to plant and even tide tables. On August 19th 1791 with an accompanying letter, Banneker sent the then secretary of state Thomas Jefferson a handwritten version of his yet to be published almanac. The letter raised concerns about slavery and the apparent hypocrisy of Washington's and Jefferson's government's position with regards to servitude to the British while retaining a system that enslaved Africans. Jefferson had 600 slaves and was unmoved by the discourse but promised to send Banneker's papers to the esteemed mathematician and philosopher Marquis de Condorcet at the prestigious Académie des Sciences, Paris (founded in 1666). Banneker produced almanacs through to 1797.

Benjamin Banneker died on October 9th in 1806, he was seventy-four. On the day of his funeral his home burned to the ground destroying all his records and works, including the clock. Only the published almanacs, the handwritten copy sent to Jefferson and a journal survived. In 1977 a commemorative obelisk was erected close to Banneker's unmarked grave. A replica of his log cabin was constructed in Oella, Maryland in the Benjamin Banneker Historical Park in 2017. His statue resides in the Smithsonian's National Museum of African American History and Culture in Washington DC

Victor Hugo Green would be associated with his travel guide for black people in the United States. Commonly known as ***the Green Book,*** the full working title; ***The Negro Motorist Green Book*** was first published, by the then forty-four-year-old Green, in 1936. The fifteen-page booklet was not the first of its kind but was by far the most successful and longest lived, published annually through to 1966.

Victor Hugo Green dreamt of a time when travel for African Americans would be safe and easy. Until that time *the Green Book* provided an invaluable service. The black traveller, be it for business or pleasure, had to navigate where it was safe to eat and sleep. One had to be aware of 'Sundown towns', white, segregated, municipal neighbourhoods, districts or towns with signs that read "coloured people had to leave town by sunset". Such inhospitable conditions were not confined to the Jim Crow south but appeared through the United States. Indeed, travel in the north could be far more hazardous as there were no clear signs to warn the traveller what and where was off limits. A driver had to know which garages would repair their automobile and to be aware of racist police who would arbitrarily stop and arrest them.

Born in New York City **on this day** 1892, Green would work for the postal service. He married Alma S. Duke (1889–1978) on September 8th 1917. The couple lived at 580 St Nicholas Avenue in Harlem. Green served in the First World War from 1918–19. *The Green Book* was an immediate success. Motels and restaurants advertised themselves to the black traveller. In 1947 Green opened a travel agency.

Victor Hugo Green died, aged sixty-seven, on October 16th 1960. The travel guide continued to be published for six more years. With the Civil Rights Act of 1964 the publication saw the beginning of the end.

Nov 10th:

One of the central figures in the British abolitionist movement **Granville Sharp** devoted his life opposing not just to the conditions of slavery but challenging a system that he saw as evil. Along with Quakers such as **Anthony Benezet**, Sharp would argue that slavery was un-Christian.

Born in Durham, in the north of England, **on this day** in 1735 Granville Sharp's life took a new direction in 1765 when he and his brother, William, met and nursed Jonathan Strong. Strong had been severely beaten about the head with a pistol leaving him almost blind and struggling to walk. Thrown out on the street Strong received care from the brothers before being taken to St Bartholomew's Hospital in London. His injuries were so severe he stayed there for four months. Jonathan Strong had been bought in Barbados and taken to England by David Lisle who inflicted the pistol-whipping. Lisle sold Strong to James Kerr, a Jamaican plantation owner, for £30. Strong was apprehended by slave hunters who took their charge to be transported to the Caribbean. Sharp intervened and with the decision of the Lord Mayor secured Strong's freedom. Kerr returned time and time again to challenge the decision. Jonathan Strong never recovered and died at the age of twenty-five in 1770.

Granville Sharp recognised the need to have a law that would make it illegal for any enslaved person to be taken out of Britain against their will. He published the pamphlet 'A Representation of the injustice and dangerous tendencies of tolerating slavery in Britain' in 1769. The Somersett Case, or Somersett v Stewart (see June 22nd) 1772 came the closest with the Chief Justice William Mansfield in preventing an enslaved person being transported out of Britain against their will, although they were still not free.

Sharp was involved in the case of the slave ship the **Zong** (see December 22nd). The captain of the Zong threw more than 103 Africans overboard, one survived. The owners of the 'cargo' claimed insurance for their loss, £30 per head. Although their claim was rejected no-one was prosecuted for the massacre. The Atlantic slave trade was unbearably cruel. Twenty-three out of every one hundred on the ships of the Royal African Company died in transit, between 1680–1688. The Dolben Act 1788 was an attempt to improve conditions for the captives on board ship, but the Swede Carl Wadstrom living in England revealed in *Observations on the Slave Trade* (1794) that each male had 6 ft by 1 ft 4 in, a female's space was restricted to 5 ft by 1 ft 4 in and a child was afforded 4 ft 6 in by 1 ft.

Sharp co-founded with fellow Anglican **Thomas Clarkson** (see March 28th) The Society for the Effecting the Abolition of the Slave Trade. Of the twelve members, nine were Quakers and three Anglican. Better known as The Society for the Abolition of the Slave Trade, they persuaded **William Wilberforce** (see August 24th) to be their spokesperson in parliament. During the 1780s Granville Sharp supported the idea of settling former enslaved people in Sierra Leone. The promotion of the resettlement project has seen Sharp recognised as one of the country's founding fathers.

Granville Sharp never lived to see the end of slavery in the British Empire. He died on July 6th 1813. He is buried with his brother and sister in All Saints Fulham, Pryors Bank, Bishops Park, London SW6 3LA.

Mama Africa, Miriam Zenzi Makeba was born in South Africa on March 4th 1932. The name Zenzi comes from the Xhosa 'uzenzile' meaning 'you have no one to blame but yourself'. The Empress of African song, a legendary singer, outspoken critic of apartheid and civil rights activist became a statesman recognised across the world.

Makeba turned professional in 1954 joining the Manhattan Brothers. While they toured abroad Makeba would perform with the female vocal group the Skylarks. Their harmonies were new and trendsetting. With over 100 recordings the group's sound became influential. Makeba never saw any royalties from those recordings.

Miriam Makeba would be married five times. She had her daughter Bongi when she was seventeen in 1950. She would eventually accompany the Manhattan Brothers on their foreign tours. In 1959 Makeba played the lead in the popular South African musical *King Kong*, about a boxer. The role brought her to the attention of a white audience. That same year the singer achieved international recognition appearing in Lionel Rogosin's dramatized documentary *Come Back, Africa*. Makeba travelled to the Venice Film Festival, the film was an instant success. In London she met **Harry Belafonte,** (see March 1st). He would become Makeba's mentor when she arrived in New York and settled in the United States. The single 'Lovely Lies' was released in 1959 and became her first solo success, becoming the first South African artist to make the US Billboard top 100.

The new decade opened with the massacre at Sharpeville in March 21st 1960 and the death of Miriam Makeba's mother. The South African apartheid regime revoked the singer's passport. She was unable to attend her mother's funeral, thus began her thirty years in exile. In 1962 Mama Africa returned to the continent visiting Kenya. She addressed the United Nations Special Committee on apartheid calling for an arms embargo. Her records were banned in her homeland. Ethiopian Emperor Haile Selassie invited Makeba to perform at the inauguration of the Organisation of Africa Unity in Addis Ababa.

Meeting fellow countryman, trumpeter **Hugh Masekela** (see April 4th) the couple married in 1964. Her third marriage would only last a couple of years, but their professional relationship would last till death do us part. The Empress of African song would win a Grammy award with Harry Belafonte in 1966, in the Folk category for the album 'An Evening with Belafonte/Makeba'.

Miriam Makeba's politics developed beyond the issue of apartheid, embracing black consciousness and the black power movement. She met activist **Stokely Carmichael**, later **Kwame Touré,** and the couple married in 1967. Her popularity among many whites plummeted in the United States, her husband was seen as a political and racial revolutionary. The US cancelled her visa. The couple settled in Guinea she would divorce husband number four in 1978. With the death of her daughter Bongi in childbirth on March 17th 1985, Miriam Makeba suffered depression and moved to live in Belgium.

Miriam Makeba.

Miriam Makeba wrote her autobiography *Makeba: My Story* in 1988 with James Hall. A second autobiography came out in 2004: *The Miriam Makeba Story*.

With political changes in South Africa, Makeba returned to the country giving her first performance there in 1991. The internationally recognised artist was largely unknown to many young people in the country. The singer appeared in the 1992 film *Sarafina* and *Amandla! A Revolution in Four Part Harmony* in 2002, which looked at the black struggle during apartheid through music. She was invited to become a UN goodwill ambassador in 1999.

Performing alongside former husband Hugh Masekela and Paul Simon on the Graceland project all three were boycotted by anti-apartheid groups for their failure to follow the letter of the law over the boycott of South Africa. Miriam Makeba's activist credentials were not tarnished. She announced her retirement in 2005 but calls to perform enticed Makeba back on stage. She performed right to the end. She collapsed after performing her most famous track 'Pata Pata' on stage in Italy. She suffered a heart attack. Miriam Makeba died **on this day** in 2008, she was seventy-six.

She was famous for numerous songs including political numbers such as Soweto Blues (1977), following the Soweto massacre. *Lumumba*, 1970, *Malcolm X*, 1974. Notable albums include: 'Sangoma' ('Healing') in 1988, an album of healing chants. 'Eyes on Tomorrow' (1991), 'Homeland' (2000), 'The Queen of African Music' from 1987. Miriam Makeba sang traditional songs including: 'The Click Song/ Mbube' (1963) and 'Malaika'. The documentary film *Mama Africa*, by Finnish director Mika Kaurismaki was released in 2011.

Nov 11th:

The story of the **Nat Turner Rebellion** or the **Southampton Insurrection** would become the pro-slave South's worse nightmare. Accurate information is unclear, with the events being used to terrify the black population from ever thinking of rebelling, to dehumanise the character of Turner, ensuring that he was not viewed as a heroic martyr, or to legitimise the behaviour of the white mob and slave owners.

Nathanial 'Nat' Turner was born in Virginia on October 2nd in 1800. He was unusual having received a rudimentary education able to read and write. Within the local community of enslaved people, he was known for his oratory and devotion. Many called him the prophet, a role that Turner would embrace. He believed that he was called by God to lead his people, like Moses, out of bondage. When he was sold, for either the third or second time, to Joseph Travis he started to see signs. On February 12th 1831 an eclipse of the sun led Turner to believe that now was the time to rise-up. With four others, Turner chose July 4th as the time for his attack. Unfortunately, Turner was ill, and the assault could not proceed.

Discovery of Nat Turner.

The plan was for the group to march to the county seat of Jerusalem, now called Courthouse, where they hoped to capture the armoury. On their march they would kill all the white people they encountered freeing the enslaved people. Turner believed that the slaves would rally to his cause. The growing rebels would march to an area of marsh land called Dismal Swamp in the South east of Virginia where it would be difficult for anyone to attack them.

A new sign appeared on August 13th where the sun looked to be an unusual colour. The date was agreed. On August 21st, with seven trusted slaves, the rebellion began. The first to be attacked and killed were Jarvis and his family. The group marched killing between fifty-five and sixty-five white men, women, and children. The enslaved blacks did not respond as hoped indeed many tried to defend and protect their white owners. The rebels grew to a number of just over fifty, some accounts say as many as seventy-five. The group never made it to the armoury. White militia and state soldiers numbering close to 3,000 crushed the undisciplined insurrection. The response was immediate and revenge bloody. As many as 120 innocent black people free and enslaved were indiscriminately killed. The state executed fifty-six of the rebels.

Nat Turner remained at large for another six weeks before being captured on October 30th. He was put on trial and given the death sentence on November 5th. A few days later on the 11th Turner was hanged. Rumour has it that he was decapitated, and his body quartered. His skull and brain were sent off to be studied. The fat from his body was used to grease the wagon wheels and pieces of his skin were given out as souvenirs. The rebels were laid in unmarked graves.

What we know about Turner are from interviews that he gave to the lawyer Thomas Ruffin Grey. These were compiled in a pamphlet: 'The Confessions of Nat Turner: The Leader of the Late Insurrection in Southampton Virginia'. Myth and embellishment are believed to have surrounded what Grey wrote. The Pulitzer Prize-winning work by William Styron: *The Confessions of Nat Turner* (1967) raised questions of authenticity and accuracy.

The slave-owning, South were desperate to make an example of Nat Turner. They struggled to believe that their contented, but docile, slaves could be organised to commit such atrocities. Prohibitive legislation was passed preventing both free and enslaved blacks from being educated, there were restrictions on movement and gatherings. Sunday worship in the black churches had to have a white minister in attendance. Those against abolition stiffened their resolve, a position that was held through to the American Civil War (1861–65).

On this day in 1975 **Angola** celebrated independence from Portugal. The Angolan war of independence started in 1961 and ended in 1974. A coup in Lisbon saw the Portuguese army withdraw from Angola. Independence was not the solution as warring factions continued fighting. Angola was embroiled by civil war during the period 1975–2002. **Augostinho Neto** was the country's first independent leader.

A citizen of Angola.

Born **on this day** in 1978, Colombian **Paula Marcela Moreno Zapata** became the country's first African Colombian woman to have a government cabinet position. She was only the fourth person of African descent to be in the government cabinet and at twenty-nine the youngest person to serve at that level.

Appointed on June 1st 2007 Moreno, an engineer and professor, was Minister of Culture. She promoted the protection of indigenous languages, there are eighty different indigenous groups in Colombia. The ministry looked to build a new national library system and had a national monument commemorating the plight of tribesmen in the country's Amazon region. Moreno's work received numerous awards including being a recipient of the **Unita Blackwell** Award from the National Conference of Black Mayors of the United States recognising the minister as one of the most influential black leaders in the world (Unita Blackwell was the first African American female mayor, a civil rights activist, in the state of Mississippi). In 2011 Moreno was awarded the Order of the Aztec Eagle by the President of Mexico, Felipe de Jesús Calderón Hinojosa, for improving Colombian/Mexico relations. The year 2014 saw the BBC recognise the Colombian as one of the world's top 100 leaders.

Long time, member of ASWAD, Association for the Study of the Worldwide African Diaspora, Moreno founded Manos Visibles (Invisible Hands) in 2010. As its president the organisation promotes reconciliation through a reduction and end to political violence, working to end racial inequality and raising awareness of the problems faced by women and young people.

For other notable Colombians see: **Emilsen Manyoma** January 14th, **Piedad Córdoba** January 25th, **Carlota Perez** March 24th, and **Francia Marquez** April 23rd.

Nov 12th:

Sir John Hawkins was one of the heroic and famed sea dogs of the Elizabethan Age. Alongside Sir Francis Drake (his younger cousin), Sir Walter Raleigh and Sir Martin Frobisher, Hawkins was commissioned by Elizabeth I to upset Spanish trade ensuring England's dominance of the sea. Hawkins would be rewarded by being knighted, receiving his own coat of arms, he was the treasurer of the navy, 1578–1595. As such John Hawkins is seen as one of the founding fathers of England's naval tradition. Facing the Spanish Armada of 1588 John Hawkins was the vice-admiral of the fleet.

Sir John Hawkins's presence in this book is not due to his sea-fearing exploits. His entry concerns his position in consolidating England's role in the Atlantic slave trade. He was not the first person from Britain to trade in slaves, most notably Thomas Wyndham and John Locke preceded him in the 1550s. But Hawkins was able to demonstrate success in making profit from the trade and showing that the stranglehold by the Portuguese and Spanish could be broken.

In October 1562 Hawkins set sail with three ships the Solomon, Jonas, and Swallow for Sierra Leone. With 300 captured Africans the fleet headed for the Americas where the human cargo was traded for pearls, hides and sugar. Such was Hawkins's financial success he set the pattern that would become England's slave trade triangle. John Hawkins was given his own coat of arms featuring a slave.

On Hawkins's second voyage (1564–65), new investors, none less than the crown, got involved in the human trade. The investors saw a profit of 60per cent.

From 1564–1569, over three voyages, it is believed that Hawkins transported 1,200 Africans to Hispaniola (Haiti). On the voyages Hawkins was accompanied by Drake. All was literally not plane sailing the Spanish and Portuguese did not take it lightly seeing the English muscling in on their trade. Clashes would lead to conflict and the Armada.

Following an ill-fated expedition, another clash with the Spanish, Sir John Hawkins the chief architect of the Elizabethan navy died of illness at sea near Puerto Rico **on this day** in 1595. Sir Francis Drake would die of dysentery, a few months later on the same expedition at sea on January 28th 1596. It was the end of a sea fearing era.

Hawkins's role in the slave trade has led to a revision of his place in history. The city council in Plymouth, England have looked at changing the name of Sir John Hawkins Square. The name Jack Leslie Square (see August 17th) has been put forward. June 2006 at Independence Stadium in Bakau, Gambia saw descendent Andrew Hawkins apologise, symbolically wearing chains, with twenty others for slavery. The vice-president Isatou Njie-Saidy symbolically removed the chains in an act of reconciliation and forgiveness.

Prospects did not look good for the young **Wilma Rudolph.** The child suffered ill health with scarlet fever and polio. Having been told that she would probably never be able to walk, by the age of twelve, Rudolph was able to enjoy playing basketball discarding her leg brace and orthopaedic shoe. She would overcome her childhood physical disability, wearing a brace on her leg, to become an Olympic gold medallist.

Aged sixteen, at the Australian Summer Olympics in Melbourne 1956, Rudolph won the bronze medal in the 400m relay.

At the 1960 Rome Olympics, Wilma Rudolph, already the 200m record holder at 22.9 seconds, took gold in the 100m with the record equalling time of 11.3 sec. She won gold in the 200m and gold in the 4x 100m relay. The relay team set a world record of 44.4 sec in the semi-finals. Wilma Rudolph became the first American woman to win three golds in a single Olympics. She retired at the height of her game holding the record for the 100m and 200m in 1961.

Her autobiography *Wilma* was published in 1977. Wilma Rudolph born June 23rd 1940 died from a brain tumour and cancer of the throat, aged fifty-four, **on this day** in 1994.

Athlete Wilma Rudolph.

Nov 13th:

English abolitionist, journalist and poet **Edward Rushton** was born **on this day** in 1756. Experiences working on slave ships had a two-fold effect on the sailor: Attending to the medical needs of captured Africans, Rushton contracted a disease that left him blind. What he witnessed left him determined to oppose the slave trade. The prominent abolitionist based in Liverpool wrote to George Washington and Thomas

Paine inquiring why they failed to use their position and influence to challenge the imposition of slavery. He never received a reply.

Edward Rushton anonymously wrote four poems set in Jamaica. ***The West Indian Eclogues*** in 1787. The poems were designed to rouse moral indignation and outrage within the British public at the Atlantic slave trade. They are spoken by the enslaved Africans. Angry enslaved husbands were left defenceless having to watch the sexual abuse and rape of their wives by the white masters. Revenge was spoken of. Some critics argued that revenge should have not been voiced as there was the possibility of losing an otherwise sympathetic reader. At the time it was popular in French poetry to look at the French feudal system where the lords would take at will the virginity of the serf women. Rushton was criticised for supporting French republicanism, but he acknowledged the similarities between feudalism and the slave trade.

Rushton opened a school for the blind in Liverpool in 1791. Today the school is the longest continuously running establishment of its kind, in the world. It is now called The Royal School for the Blind. In 1782 Rushton married Isabelle Rain. After thirty-three years his eyesight was restored following an operation in 1807.

Edward Rushton died on November 22nd 1814. Other contemporary authors of anti-slavery literature of this type included Thomas Chatterton. On January 3rd 1770 he published *Three African Eclogues. The Slave, an American Eclogue*, 1783/84 was written by Hugh Mulligan. The Rev George Gregory also wrote an American eclogue as well as a biography on Chatterton.

Born in Somalia **on this day** in 1969 **Ayaan Hirsi Magan** would drop Magan and replace it with Ali, was raised a devout Muslim. The activist, feminist, writer, and former politician would argue that political Islam, radical Islam, is incompatible with Western freedoms and a democratic lifestyle. She would present the position that fundamentally Islam is incompatible with Western democratic values, in particular concerning woman's rights. Her father was a politician, jailed as a dissident, he fled his homeland living in exile in Saudi Arabia and Ethiopia before settling in Kenya, where his daughter grew up.

Ayaan Hirsi Ali.

Hirsi Magan underwent female genital mutilation, a custom that is still practised in many cultures. Plans were made for her to marry, against her will, a distant cousin in 1992. En route to Canada, Hirsi Magan sought political asylum as a refugee in the Netherlands. She changed her name to Hirsi Ali and her date of birth to avoid being tracked down by her family. Hirsi Ali studied political science at the state university of Leiden graduating with a master's degree in 2000.

Critical of the Dutch immigration system Hirsi Ali argued that Muslim enclaves were permitted to take root fearing that this could only lead to alienation and instability in the country. In 2003 she was elected to the House of Representatives for the liberal People's Party for Freedom and Democracy. Politically Hirsi Ali continued to challenge immigration policy while championing women's rights.

In 2004 Hirsi Ali collaborated on Theo van Gogh's film *Submission*. Islam was depicted as a religion that sanctioned the abuse of women. A few weeks after being aired on Dutch TV Gogh was murdered, shot and stabbed. A letter was pinned to his body by a knife calling for Hirsi Ali's death. Ironically, the murder and threats served only to validate the position taken by the film.

Questions were raised about the legitimacy of Hirsi Ali's citizenship, later to be dropped. She left her role as a politician in 2006. Promoting her book, *The Caged Virgin*, originally published in 2004, Hirsi Ali toured the United States. The book was critical of Western countries for their perceived collective failure to recognise, acknowledge and act on oppression, and suppression, of women in Islamic societies. As a US citizen, in 2013 Hirsi Ali continued to highlight what she saw as cultural and religious rationalised violence against women. The theme was picked up in her writings *Infidel* (2007), *Nomad* (2010), and *Heretic: Why Islam Needs a Reformation Now* published in 2015.

The conversation over the Muslim woman.

Her critics claim her views simply perpetuate ignorance of Islam and create a system where Muslim's face travel and immigration difficulties. She is accused of ignoring the work done by liberal Muslims on social cohesion, day to day improvements and championing women's rights within the faith. Hirsi Ali has to live with heightened security which underlines her belief that Islam is hostile to individual freedoms, free societies and religious tolerance.

The Philadelphia based Ayaan Hirsi Ali Foundation, (AHA), was established in 2007 to protect women in the West against militant Islam.

Nov 14th:

Signed on November 7th 1775, **Dunmore's Proclamation** was formerly ratified and proclaimed **on this day** in 1775. The proclamation focused on the words "and I do hereby further declare all indentured Servants, Negroes, or others, (appertaining to Rebels) free that are able and willing to bear Arms…"

The Scottish aristocrat John Murray the 4th Earl of Dunmore was the royal governor of the British colony of Virginia, 1771–1775. He hoped that the promise of freedom for the enslaved people of Virginia would swell numbers in his forces. The plan was to cause disruption in productivity resulting in the Virginian patriots looking to domestic concerns, fearing violent slave insurrections, rather than opposing the British. It is estimated that between 800 and 2,000 runaways joined Dunmore. Three hundred black men formed what was known as the Ethiopian Regiment. The Virginian Convention declared on December 13th that if any slave returned within ten days they would be pardoned. Failure to return after the amnesty would result in the death penalty without the benefit of the clergy. Patrols were doubled on land and water and slave meetings were restricted. Newspapers questioned Dunmore honesty accusing him of being a slave owner and threatening that he would sell the runaways into slavery in the West Indies.

The British force was decimated by disease, in particular smallpox. Military action was unsuccessful with half of the ships being destroyed and Dinmore's forces leaving with the healthiest 300 escaped former slaves. The short-term loss saw long term gains. Seeds of sympathy grew as the abolitionist movement took root in Britain. June 30th 1779 saw the ***Philipsburg Proclamation.*** This applied to all colonies in America and saw between 80,000 and 100,000 enslaved people escape. Issued by Sir Henry Clinton, escapees were not even required to sign up to the British army.

The path of political activity is rarely a smooth one. **Herbert Macauley,** often described as the founder of Nigerian nationalism, was born **on this day** in 1864. His father the Rev Thomas Babington Macauley was the founder of the first secondary school in Nigeria, CMS Grammar School. The school opened on June 6th 1856. His mother, Abigail Crowther, was the daughter of Samuel Ajayi Crowther (see June 29th).

Macauley, civil engineer, journalist, activist and musician, was one of Nigeria's first leaders opposed to British rule. Awarded a scholarship to study civil engineering in Britain, Macauley returned to Lagos three years later and was appointed a surveyor of Crown Lands. He resigned his position in 1898 critical of increasing European discrimination in the system. Reports suggest that Macauley was not averse to stretching the law, gaining contracts for himself and associates. Herbert Macauley set up as a private surveyor.

Increasingly Macauley found himself as a spokesperson opposing British rule. A regular contributor to the *Lagos Daily Times* he spoke out against British administrative expansion. In 1908 the surveyor exposed European corruption with railway finances. Arguing the legal case for the chiefs affected by the corruption, Macauley was able to secure compensation in 1919. Adopting the mantra 'no taxation without representation', as the leader of the Lagos auxiliary of the Antislavery and Aboriginal Protection Society, Macauley fought the expansion of taxation, the rise in water rates and land reform.

In 1921 Macauley travelled to London representing the King of Lagos, arguing that the British were eroding the power of traditional Nigerian leaders. Co-founding the Nigerian Daily News, Macauley found a new platform to challenge colonial authority.

Limited franchise was permitted in 1922. Elections for Lagos and Calabar, 1923, saw the formation of the Nigerian Democratic Party, (NDP) the first party of its kind in the country. The NDP would win all the allocated seats in the 1923, 1928 and 1933 elections.

Following the 1944 meeting of the Nigerian Union of Students, Macaulay and **Nnamdi Azikiwe** co-founded the National Council of Nigeria and Cameroon (NCNC), Nigeria's first national political party. A nationwide tour was planned but Herbert Macauley fell ill and died on May 7th 1946, he was eighty-one. Azikiwe would take over as president of the NCNC and become the first president of independent Nigeria 1960–66. Herbert Macauley is buried at Ikoyi Cemetery in Lagos.

Roberta Barkley Patterson was born in Townsville, Queensland, Australia on August 16th 1943. The poet, writer, activist and campaigner for human rights, civil rights and indigenous land rights would be recognised by the name **Roberta 'Bobbi' Sykes.** Raised by her white mother Rachel Patterson, Sykes would only find out later in life that her father was an African American soldier called Robert Barkley. From an early age Sykes controversially identified as Aboriginal.

The teenager left school at fourteen. She worked in a variety of jobs including as a shop assistant, nursing aid and took to the stage with the name of 'Opal Stone' appearing as a stripper at Kings Cross's 'Pink Pussycat' in Sydney where she moved to in 1971. At seventeen, Sykes was gang raped by four white men. When convicted one defendant shouted racial abuse, making light of the crime as she was only Aboriginal. It was at this time Sykes met and married Howard Sykes. The couple had a daughter. Sykes already had a son conceived in the pack rape. Howard and Bobbi separated in 1971.

The 1967 referendum in Australia sparked Syke's political interests. In July 1972 she was one of the founders of the Aboriginal tent embassy located on the green outside of Australia's Parliament House in Canberra. As the embassy's first secretary, Sykes was arrested. Her activism campaigning for indigenous land rights placed her under scrutiny from the Australian Security Intelligence Organisation, (ASIO), who regarded the poet as a national security risk. They would later hand the writer three volumes of security data compiled on her. The tent embassy continues to be active.

The writer, of ten books including two collections of poetry, used her pen to extend her activism and criticism of Australian society. As a journalist Sykes contributed numerous articles and pamphlets. Bobbi Sykes wrote her autobiography, originally in three parts *Snake Cradle* (1997), *Snake Dancing* (1998), and *Snake Circle* (2000). The complete work was published in 2001 under the title *Snake Dreaming: Autobiography of a Black Woman*. The first volume won numerous awards including: The National Biography Award (1998), the Nita B. Kibble Literary Award (1998), and the Age Book of the Year in 1997. Sykes was criticised for adopting the motif of the snake as she was not Aboriginal. In 1979 her first book of poetry; *Love Poetry and Other Revolutionary Acts* was published. Sykes went on to ghost write the autobiography of **Colleen Shirley Perry Smith** the indigenous Wiradjuri social worker and humanitarian activist for the health, welfare and justice of the Aboriginal people. She was warmly known as **Mum Shirl.**

Shirley Smith (Mum Shirl).

Attending Harvard University in the USA, 1979, the thirty-eight-year-old Bobbi Sykes graduated with a PhD in education in 1983, becoming the first black Australian to graduate from Harvard and the first black Australian to get a PhD from any American university.

Sykes was an advisor on Aboriginal health and education to the New South Wales (NSW) Health Commission, 1975–80. She would go on to be a consultant for several government departments including the NSW Department of Correction Services and the Royal Commission into Aboriginal Deaths in Custody. Bobbi Sykes received the Australian Humans Rights Medal in 1994 for her advocacy of civil and political rights for the indigenous population.

In 2002 the activist had a stroke. She was not found until the following day. **On this day** in 2010, sixty-seven-year-old Bobbi Sykes died. She never fully recovered from the stroke eight years earlier.

Nov 15th:

Politician, activist, educator, diplomat, abolitionist, and attorney **John Mercer Langston** was born on December 14th 1829. Langston would be involved in the African American struggle before, during and after the American Civil War.

He attended Oberlin College and graduated in 1849. Elected to the local office in Brownhelm Township in Ohio in 1855, Langston would go on to work in Oberlin in a variety of positions as well as serving on the board of education from 1865 to 67. He was believed to be the first African American to apply to law school, although denied, but still became the first black man admitted to the bar in Ohio in 1854. In Ohio Langston led the Anti-Slavery Society. As an abolitionist he would help runaways along the state section of the Underground Railway escaping to the north.

During the American Civil War (1861–1865), John Mercer Langston was appointed to recruit black soldiers to fight in the Union Army following the government approval and founding of the United States Coloured Troops. Langston would argue the case for voting rights for African Americans having fought and died for their country and democracy. During the war Langston helped form the National Equal Rights League. As the League's first president, he fought to abolish slavery, have equal rights for all under the law, supported racial unity and the right to vote.

After the war, Langston moved to Washington DC where he practised law. He established and became the first dean of the law school at Howard University, the first black law school of its kind in the United States. He went on to become the first president at the Virginia Normal and Collegiate Institution, established on March 6th 1882, (now known as Virginia State University). Langston was involved in the drafting of the Civil Rights Act of 1875. In 1877 he was appointed as the US minister to Haiti and the charge d'affaires to Santo Domingo (Dominican Republic) through to 1885. After a contested election John Mercer served as the Republican representative for Virginia for the U S House of Representatives. He became the first black man to serve in Congress for the state of Virginia and would be the only such person for the next one hundred years, September 23rd 1890 – March 1891.

The first seven black men voted into the senate, all republicans. From left to right. Hiram R. Revels, 1870, Mississippi. Benjamin S. Turner, 1871, Alabama. Robert C. DeLarge, 1871, South Carolina. Joseph T. Walls, 1871, Florida. Jefferson F. Long, 1871, Georgia. Joseph H. Rainey, 1870, South Carolina. Robert B. Elliot, 1871, South Carolina.

Joseph Hayne Rainey, elected from South Carolina in 1870, became the first black person to serve in the US House of Representatives and the second black person to serve in the Congress (see **Hiram Revels** March 16th).

John Mercer Langston, the great-uncle of poet and writer **Langston Hughes** (see May 22nd) died **on this day** in 1897, he was sixty-seven. He is buried in Woodlawn Cemetery, Washington DC.

Writer, essayist, lawyer, reporter, teacher and activist, **Charles Waddell Chesnutt** was born on June 20th 1858. Considered the first important African American writer of fiction, born to black parents, Chesnutt could pass as white. Both of his grandmothers were of mixed heritage which would always place limits on Chesnutt's ambitions and inform his work.

Charles W. Chesnutt.

His mother died when he was fourteen. He became a pupil teacher to aid the family income. Chesnutt lived in Fayetteville, North Carolina, where he taught, becoming the principal of the Fayetteville State Normal School for Negroes in 1877. The following year, aged twenty, Chesnutt married fellow teacher, Susan Perry. The couple would have four daughters. Moving to Cleveland, Ohio, Charles Chesnutt worked as an office clerk before becoming a court reporter. In 1887 he passed the Ohio state bar exams. He set up his own attorney-at-law firm and court reporting business. Now financially secure, Chesnutt had his first short story *Uncle Peter's House* published in 1885. Further works followed *Goophered Grapevine* appeared in the *Atlantic Monthly,* August 1887. Chesnutt used African American folklore and dialect to bring his characters to life. The story contained issues of race, prejudice, slavery and miscegenation. He became the first black person to be published in the *Atlantic* beginning a twenty-year association. *The Wife of His Youth and Other Stories of the Colour-line,* a collection of short stories followed in 1899.

The Conjure Woman (1899) was another collection of short stories. The critically acclaimed work showed clever slaves outmanoeuvring their masters. *The House of Cedars* (1900) was Chesnutt's first published novel. He tried to have *A Business Career* published. Written in 1890 the novel would only be published in 2005. *Cedars* was about siblings and mulattos, who could pass as white in the antebellum American South, the period from 1800 to the Civil War 1861.

Writing was financially successful Chesnutt closed his business to concentrate on literature. In 1899 he published a biography of **Frederick Douglass** (see February 14th). The second of his three novels *The Marrow of Tradition*, was published in 1901. Using stories from relatives and friends, the book is about the Wilmington Massacre of 1898 in North Carolina, whites rioted killing between sixty and 300 blacks. Businesses and homes were looted and destroyed, and the biracial government was ousted in the only coup d'état on American soil. The book was a financial failure requiring the author to return to his former business to support his family.

The third novel was *The Colonel's Dream* (1905). After the third and final novel Charles Chesnutt's, literary output focused on a few essays and letters.

In 1917 Chesnutt successfully lobbied to prevent the showing of the controversial KKK vehicle W. D. Griffiths' *Birth of a Nation* being shown in the state of Ohio. He focused on activism working with the National Association for the Advancement of Colored People and with **W. E. B. DuBois** (see February 23rd) and **Booker T. Washington** (see April 5th). Charles W Chesnutt died **on this day** in 1932, he was seventy-four. He is buried at Lake View Cemetery in Cleveland, Ohio.

Nov 16th:

Father of the blues

W. C. Handy (William Christopher) born **on this day** in 1873, titled his 1941 autobiography *Father of the Blues*. A radio episode of *Ripley's Believe it or Not* in 1938, described W. C. Handy as the father of jazz as well as the blues, to the annoyance of **Jelly Roll Morton** (see October 20th).

Handy left his home in Florence, Alabama in 1892. He never created either genre of music but was a key player in both integrating blues into ragtime. In publishing music, composing, recording and writing anthologies, W. C. Handy was instrumental in consolidating and popularising African American music from folk, blues, spirituals, and jazz music.

From an early age Handy demonstrated the ability to play a variety of instruments including the organ, piano and guitar but it was with the cornet and the trumpet where the young man excelled. For a brief period, 1900 to 1902, Handy was a teacher but the poor pay and the attraction of his true love; music and performing, drove him on to the road.

Memphis Blues was written in 1906 but published in 1912. *Yellow Dog Blues*, (1912) *St 'Louis Blues'* (1914), 'Beale Street Blues' (1916), and 'Loveless Blues' in 1921 were early but influential Handy compositions. When he struggled to get his music published Handy partnered with Harry Pace to form the Pace & Handy Music Company in 1912.

W. C. Handy was not satisfied at publishing and composing; he wanted to write, catalogue and record a written history and anthology of African American music. Blues An Anthology: Complete Words and Music of 53 Great Songs, was published in 1926, and Book of Negro Spirituals and Negro Authors and Composers of the United States, in 1938, and Unsung Americans Sung, was published in 1944. A Treasury of the Blues was written in 1949 containing the music of sixty-seven songs.

Handy married Elizabeth Price on July 19th 1896. The couple would have six children. At the age of eighty in 1954 after Elizabeth died, Handy married Irma Louis Logan. The composer was blind having fallen off a subway platform in 1943, the accident resulted in the loss of sight. In 1955 Handy had a stroke, leaving him in a wheelchair. Eight hundred people gathered to celebrate the Father of the Blues' 84th birthday at the Waldorf-Astoria Hotel. The composer, writer and occasional band leader died four months later from bronchial pneumonia on March 28th 1958.

One of **Dr Martin Luther King**'s inner circle (see January 15th), and his trusted lieutenant, **Hosea Williams** was born on January 5th in 1926. His blind teenage mother died in childbirth when Hosea was ten. He accidentally bumped into his father 'Blind' Willie Wiggins, but they had no relationship. He was raised by his maternal grandparents in Georgia in the USA. At thirteen Williams was threatened with lynching and had to escape, leaving home, having befriended a white girl.

During World War II Williams served in an all-black unit. Under attack in France, he was the sole survivor of thirteen in his group. Being transported by ambulance the vehicle was hit, again Williams was the only survivor. He spent thirteen months recovering in a British hospital.

Back in the United States Williams, dressed in his uniform, was seen taking a drink from a 'white's only' fountain at a bus station in Americus Georgia. The purple heart recipient was badly beaten by a gang of white thugs and left for dead. In the hospital they feared the patient would not survive. The only hospital prepared to take the black victim was an army veteran's hospital over 100 miles away. Williams spent eight weeks in recovery, at times wishing that Hitler had won the war, before being released.

Looking to rebuild his life Williams attended Morris Brown College in Atlanta where he gained a bachelor's degree and a master's degree from Atlanta University both in chemistry. From 1952–63 he worked for the US department of agriculture in Savannah, Georgia as a research chemist. It was at this time he joined the National Association for the Advancement of Colored People (NAACP). Observing his work and hearing of his reputation Dr King recruited Williams to join his civil rights organisation the Southern

Christian Leadership Conference (SCLC). By 1962 King had invited Williams to join the SCLC's executive board.

Williams taught non-violence to volunteers, led marches and became known as the organisation's battering ram. Although he was fierce in his commitment Hosea Williams was always non-violent. In St Augustine, Florida, protesting, he was arrested with his wife and two of their children. He would be arrested 124 times.

In 1964 he was voted SCLC's man of the year. Hosea Williams joined as a full time, paid, staff member at SCLC as the director of voter registration in 1964. Accompanying **John Lewis** (see February 21st) of the Students Nonviolent Coordinating Committee (SNCC), Hosea Williams led the Selma March to Montgomery. On March 7th 1965, the two civil rights leaders marched 600 protestors peacefully and orderly with dignity, two by two, across the Edmund Pettus Bridge, that spanned the Alabama river. As they attempted to leave Selma state troops, many on horseback, viciously attacked. Over fifty were hospitalised on what became known as 'Bloody Sunday'. Dr King would arrive three days later to lead the march.

Hosea Williams led the SCLC's Summer Community Organisation and Political Education Project overseeing a budget of half a million and heading several thousand volunteers later in 1965. Williams took part in the March Against Fear following the shooting of **James Meredith** (see June 6th). Reluctantly, urged by Dr King, Williams moved north to Chicago to run the voter registration drive in the city. He worked on SCLC's Poor People's Campaign and supported the Memphis Sanitation Workers Strike. He was with King when the civil rights leader was assassinated at the Lorraine Motel on April 4th 1968.

After Dr King's death, Williams became the executive director at SCLC from 1968 to 79. He left the organisation following internal differences. Elected to Georgia's General Assembly as a state of Georgia representative, Williams served from 1974–84. He resigned his position which was won by his wife Juanita Terry Williams. The couple married in 1951 and had four sons and four daughters. Williams would be elected to the Atlanta city council and serve as commissioner to Dekalb County.

In 1987 Williams led the largest civil rights march witnessed in Georgia, in Forsyth County. Twenty thousand marched 'Against Fear and Intimidation' including **Coretta Scott King** (see April 27th), **Jesse Jackson** (see October 18th), **Andrew Young** (see March 12th), **Ralph Abernathy** (see March 11th) and **Dick Gregory** (see August 19th). The marchers faced hundreds of KKK members and other white supremacist organisations.

Hosea Williams died from cancer aged seventy-four **on this day** in the year 2000. His wife Juanita died months earlier on August 23rd.

On this day Friday 2001, Nigeria's **Agbani Darego** was crowned **Miss World** becoming the first African woman to wear the crown. Agbani Darego was born on December 22nd 1982.

Josephine Hosten born October 31st 1947 became the first black woman and the first Canadian to win **Miss World.** Hosten was crowned on November 20th in 1970.

Vanessa Williams became the first black Miss America on Sept 17th 1984. She would be pressured into resigning following a controversy relating to *Penthouse* magazine on July 22nd 1984. As head judge of the 2016 competition Williams received a formal apology for what happened from the CEO Haskell. Vanessa Williams was born March 18th 1963.

Vanessa Williams.

Janelle Commissiong born June 15th in 1953 became the 26th Miss Universe. In doing so Commissiong was the **first black Miss Universe on this day** in 1977. Born to a Trinidadian father and Venezuelan mother, Commissiong became a politician in Trinidad.

On Wednesday March 26th 1999 Botswana model **Mpula Keneilwe Kwelagobe,** at nineteen, became the first African woman to be crowned **Miss Universe.** Born November 14th in 1979, Kwelagobe has used her win as a platform to address HIV/AIDS on the continent. She was appointed the United Nations goodwill ambassador to sub-Saharan Africa on HIV/AIDS in 2000.

Nov 17th:

Environmentalist and wildlife conservationist **Hammarskjöeld Simwinga,** often called **Hammer,** was born in Zambia **on this day** in 1964. The recipient of the Goldman Prize, the Nobel Prize for the environmental community, in 2007, that same year Hammer was listed in *TIME* magazine as one of their Heroes of the Environment.

The farm manager joined the North Luangwa Conservation Project (NLCP) in 1994. Founded by Dr Delia and Mark Owens in 1986, to stop the massacre of the elephant population by poachers after ivory in the North Luangwa National Park, an area covering 62,000 square kilometres. The Owens, two American zoologists, set up the conservation project. Africa had seen the slaughter of half of its 1.2 million elephants between 1979 and 1989. The population of elephants in the Luangwa Park had fallen from 17,000 to 1,300. All the black rhinos had been massacred as well as thousands of buffalos and antelope.

Luangwa National Park.

Community projects set up by the NLCP attempted to offer the poverty-stricken villagers an alternative to poaching and eating bush meat. 'Wildlife Clubs' cooperatives were provided with advice, basic goods, business loans and technical assistance. Small village general stores opened along with grinding mills offering work for book-keepers, and millers. Seed loans and transport helped to create an infrastructure for local commerce. The project was so successful it was closed down by corrupt government officials who had benefited financially from the illegal poaching. Their profits were hit hard. The government intervention saw NLCP closed, and the American founders warned to stay away. Their German funding came to an abrupt end.

Hammer Simwinga stood alone but kept the work going. He would walk twenty miles a day travelling from village to village establishing the new North Luangwa Wildlife Conservation and Community Development Programme (NLWCCDP). With funding from the British charity Harvest Hope and additional funds from the Owens', Hammer set out to protect the area's biodiversity and demonstrate that there were viable alternatives to poaching. Bee keeping and fish farming was developed. With innovative sustainable projects the local economy saw family income rise by 100per cent, food provision doubled, and diets improved. Greater income from agriculture saw the poaching of elephants fall by an extraordinary 98per cent. Micro lending, education, health programmes and the empowerment of women saw the area transformed becoming an exemplar to other similar regions throughout sub-Saharan Africa.

Hammer Simwinga brought advice on business management, sustainable farming and conservation education. Planting of hedgerows and use of natural manure and fertilizer have been part of a process that has helped to transform lives and an area once stricken with poverty while saving the wildlife.

Her work raged against the system, against the machine. Poet, novelist, essayist, activist **Audre Lorde** was born on February 18th 1934 in New York to immigrant parents from Grenada. Writing from experience and clear political aims, Lorde used the words black, lesbian, mother, warrior, to describe herself as a poet. Her first volume of poetry *The First Cities* was published in 1968. Lorde worked as the writer in residence at Tougaloo College in Mississippi that same year. She established her identity with themes of civil rights, feminism, classism, sexism, capitalism and heterosexism appearing in her writing. *Cables of Rage* (1970) contained expressions of her lesbianism and anger at personal social injustices.

The poetry volumes *From a Land Where Other People Live* (1973) and *New York Head Shop and Museum* (1974) were both more rhetorical and political. Lorde was producing powerful poems of protest, said to ring with passion, sincerity, perception and depth of feeling. Her work called for sexual and racial justice.

Coal (1976) was a compilation of her earlier work and the first by a major publisher. Many critics see *Black Unicorn*, 1978, as Lorde's finest work, where she starts to look ahead to Africa and at her role and the relationship between mother and daughter, using imagery and mythology. The mother/daughter theme runs through Lorde's novel *Zami: A New Spelling of My Name* published in 1982.

The Cancer Journals, 1980, has the writer reflecting on her fourteen-year battle with cancer and her mastectomy. The journals offered the opportunity to produce a feminist critique of the medical profession. *A Burst of Light* (1988), winner of a National Book Award in 1989, continues to look at the author's struggle with cancer.

As a feminist Lorde would challenge (white) traditional feminism, critical of its failure to understand and acknowledge black feminism. Audre Lorde saw all forms of oppression as interrelated. Her works intertwined feminist theory, race studies, queer theory with personal experiences and would be studied by students. *Sister Outsider: Essays & Speeches* (1984) has been a regular text in black studies, women's studies and queer theory.

With writer and activist **Barbara Smith** (see December 16th), Lorde opened a new publishing house; Kitchen Table: Women of Colour Press. In 1962 Audre Lorde married Edwin Rolling, a white gay man. The couple had a son and daughter before divorcing in 1970. The poet had two other relationships of significance; Frances Clayton was her romantic partner from 1968–1989, they stayed close for the rest of

Lorde's life. Dr Gloria I Joseph was Lorde's partner through to the end. Audre Lorde died aged fifty-eight **on this day** in 1992. She had been appointed the Poet Laureate to New York state the previous year. Just before her death the poet participated in an African naming ceremony taking the name **Gamba Adisa** meaning 'Warrior: she who makes her meaning known'.

The Collected Poems of Audre Lorde was published posthumously in 1997.

Nov 18th:

John Henry Clavell Smythe was born in Sierra Leone on June 13th in 1915. He received his emergency pilot's commission on May 14th 1943 to fly as a navigation office in the British Royal Air Force. After twenty-six successful missions Smythe's plane was shot down **on this day** over Nazi Germany in World War II. He served two years in a prison of war camp, Stalag I, before being rescued by the Russians receiving a hug and some vodka.

Back in England Flight Lieutenant Smythe joined the Colonial Office assisting demobilised RAF personnel from Africa and the Caribbean. Recognising that employment opportunities were limited back in the Caribbean he recommended that jobs could be found rebuilding war-torn Britain. It is Smythe's advice that led to the Windrush Generation.

Having successfully defended two men on court martial, a judge recommended that Smythe study law giving the flight lieutenant a letter of recommendation. Having qualified as a barrister John Smythe returned to Sierra Leone where he practiced as queen's counsel taking major cases. Smythe later became the attorney general. Visiting the United States Smythe was invited to the White House where President Kennedy and the former prisoner of war shared experiences. On one occasion at a function at the British ambassador's residence in Freetown John Smythe was talking to the German ambassador who declared that he shot down an enemy aeroplane on November 18th in 1943 in the same area where Smythe had been shot down. The pair hugged each other and shed a few tears. John Henry Clavell Smythe settled in England and died in 1996.

Cult leader of the Peoples Temple Church **Jim Jones** became infamous for the mass suicide and murders that took place **on this day** in **Jonestown,** Guyana in 1978. Over 900 bodies were found. Many had willingly taken flavoured Kool-Aid laced with cyanide. Those who had doubts were forced to drink the poisonous cocktail. Many investigative documentaries have been produced about the largest single number of deaths of Americans in a single case before September 11th 2001 and the destruction of the Twin Towers.

Most reports focused on the cult leader Jim Jones and the US Democrat representative Leo Joseph Ryan Jr and congresswoman Jackie Speier who had been shot and left for dead. Most interviews showed white survivors talking about their experience with the Temple, Jonestown and Jim Jones. Few reports covered the fact that almost 50per cent found dead on that fateful day were black women, and that black people made up between 75 and 80per cent of the church membership.

Jones established the Peoples Temple in Indianapolis in the 1950s. The church emphasised its multiracial civil rights credentials. The activist Peoples Temple became involved in social welfare programmes focusing on housing and healthcare in the African American community. Increasingly Jones promoted his rainbow family, his adopted black son was named Jim Jones Jr. The cult leader eventually started referring to himself as black. **Leslie Wagner Wilson**'s memoir *Slavery to Faith*, 2009, was the first black female survivor to write a book on her life in Jonestown. The 2004 essay collection *People's Temple and Black Religion* was edited by Pinn, Moore and Sawyer. Rebecca Moore lost family members in Guyana that day. The collection makes links between the massacre and the black liberation struggle. The church promoted integration. With the move to Guyana Jones used the theme of exodus and the promised land which resonated with many in the black community. African Americans had just participated in the country's largest mass migration from the South to the north. The move to Guyana taped into the exodus narrative. Jones promoted Jonestown as a racial utopia free from white supremacy. The novel *White Nights, Black Paradise* (2015) by the unapologetic black feminist and atheist **Sikivu Hutchinson** was the first of its kind to focus on black women in the Jamestown mass suicide and killings. Instead of heaven on earth Jonestown became hell with 909 dead.

The first **Music of Black Origin Awards** (MOBO) were held **on this day** in 1996. Founded by **Kanya King.** She was born in Kilburn, London to an Irish mother and Ghanaian father.

MOBO co-founder Kanya King.

Seeing that black music was struggling to get the recognition that it deserved, King re-mortgaged her home to fund the first award ceremony and to have the event televised. Carlton Television aired the show on November 21st. The MOBOs became an instant success with the best album award going to **Goldie** for *Timeless*. Best single to **Gabrielle** with *Give Me a Little More Time*. Best international act going to the **Fugees**, who also picked up best international single with *Killing Me Softly*. **Lionel Richie** was the first recipient of the lifetime achievement award. **Jazzie B** was awarded the outstanding contribution to black music award. The MOBO awards have grown in influence, relevance and respect but it has not been an easy journey.

Nov 19th:

Savion Glover is the pre-eminent exponent of tap dance of his generation. He worked with tap legends **Gregory Hines** and **Sammy Davis Jr,** (see May 16th). He played on Broadway and in films celebrating dance and the lives of tap dancing's most famous exponents such as **Bill 'Bojangles' Robinson'**, (see May 25th).

Born **on this day** in 1973 Glover started tap lessons aged seven, he could be described as a child prodigy, having the ability to pick up different styles and learn from past masters, like a sponge absorbing and learning from the best. Savion Glover created his own style that he describes as "young and funk" and "free form hard core". His tap is all about the beat, the rhythm, his pounding style is known as 'hitting'.

In 1984 Glover took the lead on Broadway in *The Tap Dance Kid*. A few years later in *Black and Blue*, 1989, he would be nominated for a Tony Award. That same year Glover appeared in the film *Tap*, working with Hines and Davis Jr.

<u>Glover & Hines.</u>

Savion Glover choreographed his first show at a festival held at the Apollo theatre in 1990. The dancer went on to play the young **Jelly Roll Morton** (see October 20th) in *Jelly's Last Jam* (1991), in Los Angeles before going on to Broadway. In 1996 *Bring in 'Da Noise, Bring in 'Da Funk* (1995) won four Tony Awards, including Best Choreographer for Glover. During the nineties the dancer was a regular on the children's show *Sesame Street* from 1990 to 1995. Choreographing the dance moves for the penguin character *Mumble* in the 2006 film *Happy Feet* saw Glover continue to spread tap to a younger audience.

Savion Glover has appeared in numerous films, on television, and on stage including *Bojangles* the 2001 biopic on Bill Robinson starring Gregory Hines. *Classical Savion* sees the dancer set his hoofing skills to classical music. In 2016 Glover choreographed the Broadway musical *Shuffle Along, or the Making of the*

Musical Sensation of 1921 and All That Followed for which he would receive another Tony Award nomination.

Clayton Bates was a tap-dancing phenomenon. Born in Fountain Inn, South Carolina on October 11th 1907, the five-year-old Bates was dancing on the streets receiving pennies and nickels. At the age of twelve, while working at a cotton mill, the young dancer lost his left leg and two fingers in a cotton gin accident. When his uncle returned from the First World War, he fashioned a wooden leg for his nephew. By the age of fifteen Bates was winning amateur dance competitions beating able-bodied competitors.

Clayton Bates appeared on segregated bills, in vaudeville shows, stage musicals, night clubs, television and in films. Although called **Clayton 'Peg Leg' Bates,** he was not a novelty act. As a tap dancer, Bates's abilities were as good as the best in the field. In 1936 and 1938 he played command performances for King George V and Queen Mary. He appeared on the popular Ed Sullivan show twenty-two times. Bates toured with **Louis Armstrong's** (see August 4th), first tour of Britain in the 1950s. Peg Leg Bates was the only black artist to perform on the vaudeville and entertainment *Tivoli Australian* circuit when he toured in 1938.

With his wife Alice, the couple opened the first black-owned resort in Ulster County in the Catskill Mountains. In the age of segregation Peg Leg Country Club attracted the who's who in the black entertainment world. When Alice died in 1987, Clayton Bates sold the country club.

Clayton Bates never forgot those who experienced suffering, performing for the troops in World War II and in hospitals. He officially retired in 1989. Clayton 'Peg Leg' Bates died aged ninety-one on December 8th in 1998. He was survived by his only daughter.

Nov 20th:

Celebrated as a hero known for his leadership qualities and courage **Zumbi dos Palmares,** was born free in 1655. In Brazil **on this day,** each year since the 1960s, Die de Consciencia Negra, black awareness day or black conscious day is celebrated. The day remembers the death of Zumbi fighting for his freedom on **this day** in 1695.

As a child Zumbi was kidnapped by the Portuguese who sold the boy to the priest Father Antonio Melo. The boy was baptised and given the name Francisco and taught Portuguese and Latin. At the age of fifteen, in 1670, Zumbi fled back to Quilombo. Quilombo dos Palmares was an independent settlement of eleven towns in the northeast of Brazil. At its height in the early 1600s the population stood at about 30,000. The area was seen as the promised land for escaped, enslaved people. It was run adopting traditional African politics and customs. The community survived on agriculture, gathering, fishing, trading and raiding local plantations. The area was surrounded by clay walls and palm trees with the three entrances defended by some 200 warriors. Quilombo had stood for over a hundred years as a beacon of freedom and independence. When **King Ganga Zumba** was offered the opportunity to become part of the wider Portuguese empire by the governor of Pernambuco, Pedro Almeida, in 1678, with the understanding that the people would be given their freedom he found the offer irresistible. Zumbi disagreed wondering how could one group of people be free while so many others in the country were enslaved captives? In 1694 Zumbi seized power, killing his uncle Ganga Zumba.

After eleven years in power the Portuguese under the command of Domingos Jorge Velho and Bernardo Vieire de Melo launched an all-out attack on Palmares. After forty-two days of fierce fighting the kingdom of Quilombo was defeated with the central settlement of Cerca do Macaco destroyed. **On this day** in 1695 Zumbi dos Palmares was killed. He was decapitated and his head was displayed on a spike to warn others against further resistance and to show that their leader was not a god or immortal. Brazil would be the last western country to abolish slavery. See May 13th, September 4th and November 7th on Brazil, and slavery.

Media mogul, television and film producer, actor, talk show host, author and philanthropic billionaire, **Oprah Gail Winfrey** was born on January 29th in 1954. **On this day** in 2013 she would be awarded the Presidential Medal of Freedom from President Obama.

Becoming a teenage mother at fourteen, her son Canaan was born and died in 1968, did not prevent Oprah from pursuing her education and a career. She would become the richest African American of the twentieth century, and the first black multi billionaire in North America. Many observers would say that on occasion Oprah was the most influential woman in the world.

In 1971, aged nineteen, Oprah became the co-anchor of the local evening news in Tennessee. She moved to Baltimore where in 1977 she hosted *People Are Talking Afterwards*, staying for eight years. Recruited to Chicago, in 1984, to host the morning show *AM Chicago,* her easy-going warm style attracted an ever-growing audience. Oprah's popular style revolutionised the talk show format, seeing the girl from Mississippi with a hit show, standing at number one in the ratings.

The *Oprah Winfrey Show* was launched in 1986 and would run for twenty-five years through to 2011. The programme initially appeared on 120 channels with an audience of 10 million in its first year. The show took $125 m of which Oprah was paid $30 m. With her own production company Harpo Productions (Oprah spelt backwards), the talk host took control of the show from ABC. By 2004 the Oprah Winfrey Show was on over 200 US tv stations and broadcast in 100 countries.

Oprah's Book Club had a significant effect on publishing. Featured authors, many previously unknown, would see their books appear on the bestseller lists. In 2018 Oprah interviewed the former First Lady **Michelle Obama** on memoir *Becoming,* (see Jan 17th). The successful monthly magazine *O: The Oprah Magazine* was launched in 2000. *O at Home* was launched in 2004 but folded in 2008.

Media mogul and chat show host Oprah Winfrey.

Oxygen Media was launched in 1999 providing programming for women on the internet and cable. Oprah Winfrey appeared in the Steven Spielberg film *The Color Purple* by **Toni Morrison** (see February 18th) in 1985. Oprah was nominated for an Oscar in the best supporting category. She would be a producer of the award-winning Broadway musical *The Color Purple* which ran from 2005–2008. Oprah co-produced the 2015 revival of the musical for which she won a Tony Award. Oprah appeared in the TV mini-series *The Women of Brewster Place* in 1989. Toni Morrison's *Beloved* starred Oprah and **Danny Glover** in 1998. Other notable appearances include in Lee Daniels' 2013 film *The Butler*, *Selma* in 2014, which she produced, and the 2017 HBO TV film *The Immortal Life of* **Henrietta Lacks** (see October 4th) for which she was the executive producer. Oprah Winfrey became the first female African American recipient of the Golden Globes' Cecil B. DeMille Lifetime Achievement Award in January of 2018.

Business Week named Oprah Winfrey the greatest African American philanthropist in US history. Her Angel Network sponsors domestic and international charitable projects. In 2007 the $40 million school for disadvantaged girls in South Africa, the Oprah Winfrey Leadership Academy for Girls in Henley on Klips, was opened. Her charity work, producing, writing, tv and film work are all too numerous to mention in this summary, not bad for a girl born into poverty in rural Mississippi.

Nov 21st:

Actor, playwright, producer, journalist, editor, publisher, historian, and African nationalist, the Sudanese Egyptian **Duse Mohamed Ali** was born in Egypt **on this day** in 1866.

Following the death of his father Ali returned to live in England where he had been studying. He embarked on an acting career writing and producing plays to positive reviews including *Othello* and the *Merchant of Venice* in Hull (1902). He wrote *The Jews Revenge* (1903), *A Daughter of Judah* (1906), *A Cleopatra Night* (1907), and *Lilly of Bermuda* in 1909. Acting and producing saw Ali tour Britain.

Living and working in London Ali set up the *African Times and Oriental Review,* out of 138 Fleet Street. The newspaper always struggled financially but acted as a voice for people of colour, developing a pan African ideology. A young **Marcus Garvey** (see August 17th) worked briefly with Ali and wrote for the paper's October 1913 issue. After the war publications seen as militant were censored and banned by the British in various parts of the Empire. Ali wrote *The Land of the Pharaohs* in 1911. Although he was criticised for the heavily plagiarised content having used works from; Wilfrid Scawen Blunt, Theodore Rothstein and the Earl of Cromer, the book gained wide recognition from many black communities, for its criticism of a speech given by the US President Theodore Roosevelt.

Duse Mohamed Ali was the vice president of the London-based Central Islamic Society. In 1915 funds were provided for widows and orphans of Indian Muslim soldiers. Ali also helped found the Anglo Ottoman Society.

In 1921 Ali left Britain, never to return, he arrived in the USA (New York) in 1921. He travelled the country acting, giving lectures, was involved in a variety of business ventures and briefly met up with and worked alongside Marcus Garvey. On September 3rd 1926 Ali received his naturalisation papers.

The year 1931 saw Duse Mohamed Ali living in Nigeria. In Lagos he was the editor of the *Lagos Times* and the *Nigerian Daily Times.* On July 3rd 1933 Ali established the weekly popular newspaper *The Comet.* Yet to hang up his performance shoes, he produced the play *Daughter of Pharaoh* in Lagos on October 30th 1932. The four times married Duse Mohamed Ali died, aged seventy-eight on June 25th 1945. It is said that 5,000 attended his funeral.

The case of the Scottsboro Boys publicly exposed the injustice, weakness and prejudice of the judicial system in the United States, in particular in the Southern Jim Crow states (see January 23rd for Part 1).

On this day in 2013 the Alabama Board of Pardon and Paroles granted posthumous pardons to **Charlie Weems, Andy Wright** and **Haywood Patterson** eighty-two years and eight months after their arrest.

Olen Montgomery was the only defendant who could write. He had hitched a ride on the train that fateful day, not knowing any of his eight co-defendants, to find work to get money to purchase a new pair of glasses. Montgomery was severely myopic and had a cataract in one eye. His glasses were broken that day, he would not get a replacement pair for another two years.

Clarence Norris was sentenced to the electric chair three times. He lost a finger in an accident working in the prison mills. He was paroled in 1944 but brought back to prison having broken his parole conditions. Released again in 1946. As with Montgomery he never knew his co-defendants before the incident. Norris was pardoned by Governor George Wallis October 25th 1976. His autobiography *The Last Scottsboro Boy* was published in 1979. Diagnosed with Alzheimer's disease Norris died January 23rd 1989 aged seventy-nine.

Haywood Patterson admitted to fighting on the day but denied rape. He was generally disliked by the other eight fellow prisoners and guards. His only solace being his knife. In February 1941, after being paid by a guard, a fellow convict stabbed Patterson 20 times. Amazingly Patterson survived. Patterson published his story *Scottsboro Boy* in June 1950. Patterson died of cancer (1952) one year into serving a 6-15-year sentence for manslaughter. Posthumously pardoned **on this day** in 2013.

Andy Wright was sentenced to ninety-nine years. He was assaulted by guards and prisoners spending time in the prison hospital. Fellow defendant Weems was stabbed in an attack meant for Wright. He was the last of the nine to leave jail. In 1951 he faced rape allegations; these were dismissed. Posthumously pardoned **on this day** in 2013.

Leroy Wright, believing his wife had cheated on him, he shot and killed her and then shot and killed himself in 1959.

Charles Weems's mother died in 1915 followed by six of his seven siblings in quick succession. His sick father sent Charles away to live with an aunt. While in prison Weems was admitted to hospital with tuberculosis. In March 1938 it was Weems who was mistakenly stabbed instead of Andy Wright.

Eugene Williams the youngest of the Scottsboro Boys was able to live what could be described as a stable life on his release.

Montgomery, **Roberson, Williams** and Leroy Wright had the charges of rape dropped and were released having spent six years in prison. All experienced the threat of lynching, hearing the angry mobs cry for blood. They faced the death penalty, the prejudice, demands and injustice of the legal system and the brutality of prison life. Uneducated, young and vulnerable all suffered, never again to find life easy. All were damaged by their experience and as damaged people, not being an excuse, some would go on to harm others.

Nov 22nd:

Born **On this day** in 1942, **Guion 'Guy' Bluford** became the first African American in space. On board the Space Shuttle Challenger mission STS-8, Bluford made history in the USA flying on Aug 30th and returning on September 5th in 1983 having orbited the earth ninety-eight times in a 145-hour mission. The former Vietnam veteran was decorated having flown 144 combat sorties. He retired from NASA in 1993 having flown into space on four missions totalling 688 hours. Bluford gained his master's degree and PhD both in aerospace engineering. In Jan 1978 he was one of thirty-five selected from 10,000 applicants to join the **N**ational **A**eronautics & **S**pace **A**dministration (NASA) team. In August 1979 he became an official astronaut.

Colonel Frederick D Gregory, born January 7th 1941, became the first African American to lead a space mission **on this day** in 1989. The former US Air Force pilot, military engineer and test pilot was selected as an astronaut in January 1987. He was the commander on board the Space Shuttle Discovery in the STS 33R mission, from November 22nd to the 27th, spending over 120 hours in space. He flew leading the mission on November 24th to December 1st in 1991 on board the Space Shuttle Atlantis. Having flown three space missions Gregory clocked up 456 hours in space.

For further historic black connections to space see **Arnaldo Tamayo Mendez,** the first person of African heritage in space, September 18th, **Mae Carol Jenison**, October 17th, **Ronald McNair & Michael P Anderson**, January 28th.

Nov 23rd:

In 2004 **Mary Seacole** was voted the greatest black Briton. **Mary Jane Grant** was born **on this day** in 1805 to a free black Jamaican mother and a white Scottish father in Jamaica.

The young Mary gained business skills working at her mother's boarding house, Blundell Hall where a range of practical items were sold, food served, and basic health care provided. It was her mother's experience of traditional herbal medicines that set Mary on the path as a doctress. Adopting traditional West African and Jamaican medical skills Mary Seacole gained experience caring for the sick. She frequently came into contact with soldiers in the garrisons on the island addressing their medical needs.

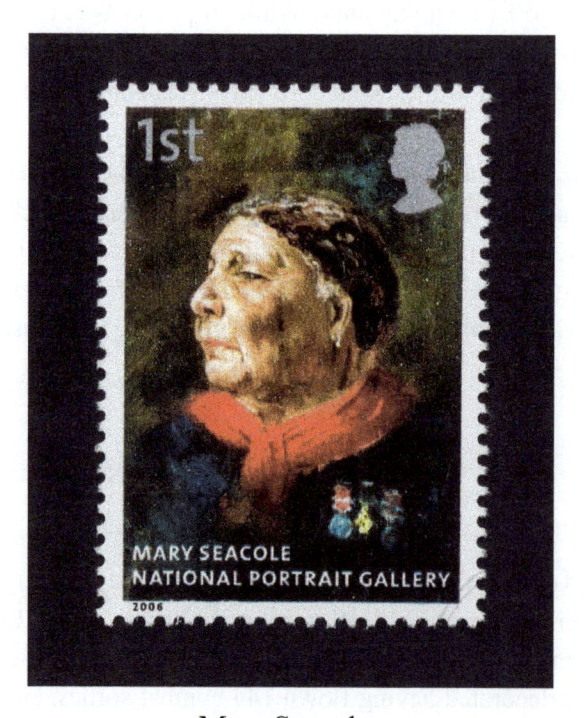

Mary Seacole.

Mary travelled to England with her patron when she was twelve. She returned alone staying for two years, aged sixteen, in 1821. Mary demonstrated independence from an early age. On her travels in 1825 Mary gained insight into local traditional medicines and practices in Haiti, Cuba, and the Bahamas. The mid-1840s proved to be a difficult time for the doctress. Mary married Edwin Horatio Hamilton Seacole on November 10th 1836. It's said that Edwin was the godson of Admiral Horatio Nelson but there is little evidence to support the claim. Fire destroyed their local hotel business on August 9th in 1843. The following year Edwin died in October 1844, a little while later her mother died leaving Seacole experiencing deep grief.

Visiting her brother in Panama her medical experience was put to the test dealing with an outbreak of cholera. Seacole caught the disease. Back in Jamaica Blundell Hall was rebuilt better than before. More a restaurant than a hotel, Seacole opened the British hotel which could feed up to fifty people. In 1853 Jamaica suffered an outbreak of yellow fever. Once again Seacole was called to help gaining invaluable knowledge and practical experience.

News reported that war had broken out between the Russians and French, British and Turks. Seacole wished to offer her services knowing many of the British soldiers that she had cared for in Jamaica. She arrived in England in 1854 and offered her services to the war office. Seacole felt that she was rejected due to her colour. Undeterred, and at her own expense, Seacole travelled to Balaclava on the Crimean Peninsula where, close to the front line, she set up her British hotel selling everything that soldiers would require while offering medical help. Mary Seacole brought hygiene, ventilation, warmth, hydration, nutrition and rest to her patients applying folk medicine. Soldiers flocked to the hotel. The doctress, often seen at the front, was affectionately called Mother Seacole. With the Crimean War (1853–1856) over, Mary Seacole returned to England. She was penniless having given away all that she had. In 1857 she wrote her travel memoirs, the first black woman to do so, *Wonderful Adventures of Mrs Seacole in Many Lands*. The success of the book, coupled with a four-day fundraising appeal organised by the soldiers, that same year, enabled Seacole to live the rest of her life being financially stable. The four-day gala on the Thames at Surrey Gardens saw 80,000, many veterans and their families, attend. Even Queen Victoria is said to have donated to help Seacole.

Mary Seacole died of apoplexy (bleeding in internal organs) on May 14th 1881, she was seventy-five. Her body was laid to rest at St Mary's Catholic cemetery, Harrow Road, Kensal Green, London. The grave was rediscovered, cleaned and reconsecrated on November 20th 1973.

After a hundred years in relative obscurity, largely forgotten, the name Mary Seacole has come to represent the heart of British black history. There were arguments that Seacole's story had been sacrificed to make way for Florence Nightingale. Was Seacole deemed too dark to represent the British narrative? The Conservative politician Michael Gove questioned the need for Seacole's inclusion in the English educational system.

On June 30th 2016 a statue of Mary Seacole was erected at St Thomas' Hospital in London. Some questioned the validity of the statue, arguing that Seacole was never part of the official British medical system, had no association with the hospital and as a doctress was not a nurse.

White writer, editor, speaker, educator and white anti-slavery crusader **Theodore Dwight Weld** was born **on this day** in the United States in 1803. He co-authored *American Slavery As It Is: Testimony of a Thousand Witnesses* in 1839 with his wife Angelina Grimke and her sister Sarah. The book would establish Weld as one of the architects of America's abolitionist movement in the 1830s and 1840s. *American Slavery* is said to have been the source material for **Harriet Beecher Stowe's** (see June 14th) 1852's *Uncle Tom's Cabin*. The two publications are viewed as the most influential on the American anti-slavery movement. Weld wrote numerous pamphlets, many anonymously. He published *The Bible Against Slavery* in 1837.

Travelling through slave states and reading **William Lloyd Garrison's** (see December 10th) abolitionist newspaper *The Liberator* and his book *Thoughts on African Colonisation* (1832) shaped Theodore Weld's views. In February 1834 Weld held eighteen public debates on the issue Abolition v Colonisation. The American Colonisation Society worked to assist freed black people in migrating to Africa but not to dismantle slavery. The public meetings were not debates; they were presentations on the horrors of slavery. Weld sought an immediate end to the slave system. That same year he became an agent for the American Anti-slavery Society recruiting and training. Beecher Stowe was probably his most famous recruit.

An impressive speaker, Weld temporarily lost his voice so turned to editing the New York City based abolitionist newspaper, *The Emancipator*, from 1836–40. It was during this period that he married Angelina, in 1838. The ceremony had two ministers, one white and one black. As a woman's rights activist Weld renounced any legal authority or power over his wife.

He became directly involved in politics working with the Liberty Party. The ani-slavery party was founded in the 1840s by **James Birney**, it would eventually lead to the establishment of the Republican Party in the 1850s. Weld lived in Washington DC from 1841 to 1843. He worked assisting John Quincy Adams petitioning Congress but fell foul, of the gag-rule which prevented certain issues from being discussed in Congress, one being slavery.

Theodore Weld and his wife moved to New Jersey where in 1854 they established a school for boys and girls of any race. This was repeated in Lexington, Massachusetts in 1864.

Theodore Dwight Weld died aged ninety-one on February 3rd in 1895 living to see the abolition of slavery in the USA.

Nov 24th:

It was the day after the initial massacre of November 23rd 1887 which had occurred in the city of Thibodaux, the parish seat of Lafourche, in Louisiana. **The Thibodaux Massacre** was one of the many dark periods of racially driven domestic terrorism in America. Official figures are hard to determine but it's agreed that between fifty and 100 were murdered and a total of 300 were either murdered, wounded or declared missing following the work of white vigilantes. For weeks afterwards bodies were being found in shallow graves.

Black sugar plantation workers had been agitating for increased pay. The hope was that workers supported by the country's largest and most powerful union The Knights of Labour, would see their pay rise from the famine wage of 45 cents a day to $1.25, for a twelve-hour day, or $1.00 a day plus a meal. Strikes had unsuccessfully taken place in 1874 when following a poor harvest and pressure from cheap West Indian imports the sugar growers wanted to impose lowering of pay. Further strikes took place in 1880 and 1883. The fight was not simply about improved wages. The White League, a white paramilitary group, one of numerous white supremacists organisations, was formed in 1874 to harass and intimidate Republicans who sympathised with black civil rights and to ultimately disenfranchise the black voter. The end of the Civil War, in 1865, saw gains for the black population with African Americans becoming legislators and sheriffs. The honeymoon period did not last long as the Reconstruction period saw the rise of white violence and lynching. When Republican Governor William Pitt Kellogg, showed sympathy for the plight of the black workers he lost his seat. It would be another 100 years before another Republican was elected in Louisiana.

White mobs terrorise black victims, often carried out with impunity.

Previous strikes had seen workers sacked, kicked off the land and arrested. November 22nd 1887 witnessed an estimated 10,000 farm workers go on strike led by people such as twenty-nine-year-old teacher **Junius Bailey, Hamp Keys** and **William Kennedy.** The situation turned violent in 1887 with Democrat newspapers falsely reporting black on white violence. White militia were formed armed with a hand cranked Gatling machine gun, a cannon was placed outside the local prison, and led by ex-Confederate General P. G. T. Beauregard. When the murder started it was indiscriminate with young, old, men and women being shot.

Republican District Judge Taylor Beattie, another ex-confederate and member of the white league, declared martial law with a 300-strong white militia sealing off Thibodaux. Local press continued to inflame the situation describing the black strike force as assassins ready to kill white women and children with their sharpened cane knives. Many black survivors escaped seeking refuge in the woods and nearby swamps.

The aftermath of the violence saw no federal inquiry, no convictions or punishment. One of the murderous mob, Andrew Price, won a seat in Congress the following year. It would not be until the 1930s that steps to unionise the black farm workers saw any progress. The brutal truth of the massacre was buried or distorted by inaccurate press coverage. It would take journalist and writer John DeSantis' dogged efforts investigating the events to reveal the truth behind the massacre culminating in his 2016 book, *The Thibodaux Massacre: Racial Violence and the 1887 Sugar Cane Labour Strike*.

White Australian anthropologist **William E. H. Stanner** was born **on this day** in 1905. Working extensively with the indigenous Australian community, Stanner helped found the Australian Institute of Aboriginal Studies (now the Australian Institute of Aboriginal and Torres Straits Islanders Studies) in Canberra.

The anthropologist would be invited by the Prime Minister Harold Holt, following the referendum of 1967, to form the Commonwealth Council for Aboriginal Affairs along with H. C. Coombs and Barrie Dexter. The council would advise on national policy. The referendum voted 91per cent, over all six states, to give the federal government the power to pass laws for the indigenous population and for Aboriginals to be officially counted in the county's census.

In 1932 Stanner received a grant from the Australian National Research Council. He spent 7 months in Aboriginal communities on the Daly River in the Northern Territory. Stanner rigorously documented details of transitional life while documenting historical change. Further research would focus on religion, ritual and social change.

While in England Stanner raised concerns over indigenous Issues in the *Illustrated London News* on October 24th in 1936. He would be publicly critical of the Australian government's Aboriginal policy on November 25th the following year.

Following the Second World War Stanner wrote a post-war report on the reconstruction of the South Pacific islands. The report was put together in the 1953 book *The South Sea in Transition*. A further series of articles from Oceania were published as *On Aboriginal Religion* in 1963. William Stanner became professor of anthropology and sociology at the Australian National University in 1964, remaining in post until 1971. He later became a member of the Commonwealth Council for Aboriginal Affairs, a position he held from 1967–1977.

In the Boyer Lectures, 1968, Stanner coined and popularised the term 'the Great Australian Silence'. The lectures titled *After the Dreaming* reflected on the silence in Australian history of the indigenous people. Stanner's work helped many Australians change thoughts on their country and Aboriginal culture. William Stanner was a founding member of the Aboriginal Treaty Committee in 1979. That same year he published *White Man's Got No Dreaming*.

William Edward Hanley Stanner died on October 8th in 1981, he was seventy-five.

Brazilian writer and leading figure of Symbolist poetry **João da Cruz e Souza** was born **on this day** in 1861 to former enslaved parents. Symbolist poetry represents absolute truths symbolically expressed through metaphorical language and images. The symbolist artist seeks to express individual emotional experiences through subtle and suggestive language.

Cruz e Souza was the director of the newspaper *Tribune Popular* in 1881, for which he wrote abolitionists articles. He had ambitions of becoming the attorney for Laguna, but he was not accepted because of his colour. Cruz e Souza wrote his earliest poetry in 1877. *Tropos e Fantasias* written with Virgilio Varzea was published in 1885.

The writer moved to Rio de Janeiro in 1890 where he was the archivist for the city's central railway. It was at this time he wrote his most famous works: *Missal*, a volume of poetic prose, *Broquei's* (Shields), and *Farois* (Beacons) all in 1893. *Farois* would be published posthumously in 1900. That same year saw the poet marry Gavita Goncalves. The couple had four children all would die early from tuberculosis. The suffering and death of his children, financial troubles and ill health affected Cruz e Souza's poetry alongside social concerns.

Unafraid to promote his blackness, contemporaries named Cruz e Souza 'cisne negro' (black swan), he was also referred to as the 'black Dante'. Joao da Cruz e Souza influenced those around him and would continue to do so for a generation. He died aged thirty-six, from tuberculosis, on March 19th in 1898.

Zimbabwean journalist and political activist **Willie Musarurwa** found himself in detention without trial from 1965–1974. He opposed the white minority government. Born **on this day** 1927, Musarurwa edited several newspapers including *African Weekly,* in 1958, the *African Daily News*, the *Bantu Mirror* and *African Parade*.

Willie Musarurwa supported **Joshua Nkomo's** (see June 19th) Zimbabwe African People's Union (ZAPU). In 1963 he became ZAPU's information and publicity secretary. After a decade in detention Musarurwa joined Nkomo in exile in Zambia. He represented Zimbabwe at all the independence talks including attendance in London in 1979.

Following independence Musarurwa was appointed as the first black editor of the highly respected *Zimbabwe Sunday Mail* in 1982. He would be dismissed in 1985 having been critical of Zimbabwean leader **Robert Mugabe** (see April 18th) and ZANU, Zimbabwe African National Union. Willie Musarurwa died of a heart attack aged sixty-two on April 3rd in 1990.

Nov 25th:

Autocratic and repressive leader of Malawi **Hastings Kamuzu Banda** led what was Nyasaland, to become independent Malawi in 1964. Banda is believed to have been born in 1898 but there is little evidence to confirm his date of birth.

At the University of Chicago, 1931, he gained his BA degree and at Meharry College in Tennessee, 1937 he earned his medical degree. Banda travelled to Scotland for further studies at Edinburgh University in 1941 before practicing medicine in northern England and London, between 1945 and 1953. Banda worked in Ghana from 1953-58. Returning home as president of the Nyasaland African Congress, Banda travelled the country making anti-federation speeches. He had opposed the Federation of Rhodesia and Nyasaland which existed from 1953–1963. A state of emergency in the country led to Banda's arrest, by the British, in March 1959. He was released in April 1960.

Hastings Kamuzu Banda.

General elections were held in August 1961 seeing Banda's Congress party win the majority of the votes. The year 1963 saw the end of the Federation and Banda became prime minister. The following year the country celebrated independence and was re-named Malawi. The new country and its leader would be intertwined. When Malawi became a republic. Banda became the president and would remain in power through to 1994. The republic became a one-party state, 1970, with Banda becoming the Malawi Congress party president for life, 1971. Banda was soon made Malawi president for life. What opposition there had been saw the increasingly autocratic leader receive western support because of his anti-Communist stance during the cold-war. He was criticised by fellow African leaders for continuing diplomatic relations with the apartheid, minority ruled South Africa. Human rights groups estimate that between 6,000 and 18,000 people were killed, tortured and imprisoned without trial as the president held on to power.

Internal and external pressure led to Hastings Banda agreeing to a referendum in 1993 on the question of having multi political parties. Banda lost and when open elections were held the following year, he lost his position of power, ending twenty years of control.

Hastings Kamuzu Banda died **on this day** in 1997 believed to have been either ninety-eight or ninety-nine.

One of the founders of the negritude movement, novelist, playwright, poet, and compiler of West African folktales, **Birago Diop** was born in Senegal on December 11th in 1906.

Diop trained as a veterinarian in Paris where he met like-minded Africans and Caribbeans, in the early days of the negritude movement. Negritude sought a unique and authentic black voice that would not simply be assimilated into the European narrative and culture. Back in Senegal in 1933, as the government's head of the cattle inspection service Diop's work took him throughout rural West Africa. On his travels he encountered elders and storytellers, known as griots within the Wolof community, hearing the legends and listening to the orally presented stories. Fellow writers in the negritude movement encouraged Diop to write down the folktales. Writing in French he recorded the tales of the Wolof people.

Les Contes d'Amadou Koumba, (Tales of Amadou Koumba) published in 1947, is a collection of short stories based on Senegalese folktales. It won the Grand Prix Littéraire de l'Afrique Occidentale Française. Diop wrote a second volume of short stories *Les Nouveaux Contes d'Amadou Koumba (The New Tales of Amadou Koumba).* Birago Diop became respected as an African renaissance man having helped to restore interest in African folktales.

Diop wrote his first volume of poetry in 1960 *Leurres et Lueurs (Lures* and Glimmers). That same year Senegal gained independence under the leadership of **Leopold Sedar Senghor** (see October 9th), who appointed Diop ambassador to Tunisia. He served from 1961 to 1965. Birago Diop's autobiography *La Plume Raboutee, (The Spliced Pen)* was published in 1978. Four further volumes of his autobiography were published in 1982, 1985, 1986 and 1989.

Birago Diop, one of Africa's outstanding Francophone writers, died aged eighty-three **on this day** in 1989. For exponents of negritude see **Aime Cesaire,** June 26th, **Leopold Senghor,** October 9th, **Ousmane Soce** on October 31st, **David Diop** July 9th, and **Abdoulaye Sadji** December 25th.

Suriname gained **independence** from the Netherlands **on this day** in 1975. The smallest independent country in South America. Prior to independence a third of the country's population emigrated to the Netherlands seeking security.

The country's first independent leader Johan Ferrer was overthrown in a military coup on February 25th in 1980. That same year saw counter coups in April and August. Further political instability continued with coups on March 15th 1981 and March 12th 1982. Settled times were far off seeing 10,000 Suriname's fleeing the country, escaping the civil war that lasted from 1986 to 1992.

A young woman of Surinam.

Nov 26th:

Born enslaved in 1779, the exact date of birth is unknown for **Isabella Baumfree** would become known as the outspoken advocate for the abolition of slavery. She promoted civil and woman's rights and campaigned for universal suffrage and the temperance evangelist. She would be commonly known as **Sojourner Truth.**

Aged nine, and called Bella, the enslaved girl was sold to John Neely for $100, along with some sheep. Her autobiography describes Neely as cruel and viciously beating the child. Truth would be sold three more times before being bought by John Dumont. The teenager fell in love with a fellow slave named Robert, with whom she had a child, but they were denied the right to marry. Truth was forced to marry an older slave called Thomas with whom she had a son and two daughters. She had another child having been raped by Dumont. After being promised her release, Dumont went back on his word. Truth escaped to freedom with her daughter Sophia in 1826. She sought refuge with Isaac and Maria Van Wagener. The Wagener's bought Truth's freedom for $20. On July 4th 1827 New York State declared all enslaved people free. This did not prevent John Dumont illegally selling Truth's son Peter south to Alabama. With Isaac and Maria, Truth sued Dumont and won. Peter was returned. Truth became the first black woman to successfully sue a white man in America.

In 1829 the former slave moved to New York City where, as a Christian she worked for the minister Elijah Pierson before moving to work with another minister Robert Matthews. Matthews would be accused of poisoning Pierson and Truth would be connected by association. Both were acquitted of murder although Matthews served time for lesser crimes.

In 1843 as a Christian evangelist Truth announced that the spirit had appointed her to preach the truth. It was at this time she changed her name to Sojourner Truth. As an itinerant preacher Sojourner Truth met abolitionist **William Lloyd Garrison** (see December 10th) and **Frederick Douglass** (see February 14th). Garrison encouraged Truth to give speeches on the evils of slavery.

Unable to read or write, Truth narrated her story to Olive Gilbert who produced the autobiography; *The Narrative of Sojourner Truth: A Northern Slave* in 1850. The book saw Truth financially stable while giving her national recognition. Truth used her platform to speak out on a variety of issues; women's suffrage, temperance and later prison reform, against capital punishment and on land rights for former enslaved people.

At a woman's convention in Ohio in 1851, Sojourner Truth gave her most famous speech *Ain't I A Woman?* The speech challenged racial and gender inequalities and inferiority. During the Civil War of 1861-65, Sojourner Truth encouraged black men to enlist in the Unionist cause. Working for the National Freedman's Relief Association, she organised supplies for black troops. Her efforts would see her meeting Abraham Lincoln in 1864. Following the conflict Truth assisted freed slaves find work to build new lives. She collected thousands of signatures and campaigned for former enslaved people to be given land rights.

Sojourner Truth died in the morning **of this day** in 1883. She was eighty-six. Her funeral was attended by almost a thousand people. Buried at Battle Creek's, Oak Hill cemetery in Michigan, Frederick Douglass gave the eulogy for Truth in Washington DC.

Contemporary African American artist **Kara Walker** is famous for her black on white paper cut out silhouettes. She has worked in several mediums as a painter, sculpture, printworker, installation artist and filmmaker. Walker explores identity, race, stereotypes, sexuality, gender, violence and history through her art employing humour and demanding the viewer to interact. Kara Walker was born **on this day** in 1969.

Nov 27th:

The nation was stunned. The news reported the stabbing of a boy, ten days before his eleventh birthday. **Damilola Taylor,** born in Lagos, Nigeria on December 7th 1989, had only arrived in London earlier in the year 2000. His sister Gbemi required treatment for severe epilepsy. All who knew Damilola described him as loving, personable, friendly and caring.

Walking home from Peckham library, London, Taylor was captured on closed circuit security cameras leaving at 16.51. Nearing the North Peckham Estate, at some point, the ten-year-old was stabbed in the left thigh, an artery was severed. Damilola made it to a nearby stairwell. Within thirty minutes he had almost bled to death. A workman following the trail of blood discovered the boy. Although still alive the paramedics were unable to save his life, Damilola died in the ambulance.

In 2002 four youths, two aged sixteen, faced charges at the Old Bailey. All four were acquitted. A key prosecution witness, who was fourteen, was ruled unreliable and two were found not guilty.

New DNA evidence emerged revealing Damilola's blood on trainers belonging to Daniel Preddie, who would have been twelve at the time of the ten-year-old's death, and on his brother Richard's sweatshirt cuff. Richard would have been thirteen at the time of the crime. This led to fresh arrests in 2005 of Daniel and Richard now sixteen and seventeen, along with a third accused, nineteen-year-old Hassan Jihad. The second trial started on January 24th 2006. On March 29th, the jury cleared Jihad of all charges but were unable to reach a verdict on the brothers.

A third trial took place on June 23rd 2006. After thirty-three days on trial, ending on August 9th, Ricky Gavin Preddie born in London in 1987, and Danny Charles Preddie, born in 1988 London, were convicted of manslaughter. The pair were sentenced to eight years in youth custody on October 9th 2006. The judge explained the sentence as both were young when the crime had been committed, the bottle used in the attack was found, the attack was not planned and that the brothers had no intention of killing Damilola.

Ricky was released on September 8th 2010 but violated his parole conditions being seen in Peckham and associating with gang members on March 13th. Recalled and imprisoned Ricky was released on January 25th 2012. Sixteen days later he was recalled again in February. Ricky was paroled in July 2012. Eight years later, driving while disqualified, Ricky drove a car at a policewoman leaving her with serious injuries. He was given a four-year sentence in 2020. Danny was released in 2011.

The torrid tale of gang violence in London in the first two decades of the twenty-first century witnessed a rise in gang violence and knife crime. In 2010 twenty-nine per cent of victims of gun crime were identified as black while the number was 24per cent for knife crime. In the twelve months to March 2017 over 12,000 knife crimes were recorded in London, most relating to violence and robberies. The Metropolitan Police force in London reported that 75per cent of victims were male and most under the age of twenty-five. One in five of all victims were described as black. Ninety per cent of all offenders were male with 62per cent coming from black and Asian ethnic minority groups (BAME). Almost half of non-domestic fatal knife attack victims were black males aged between fifteen and twenty-four. Forty-nine per cent of victims injured were aged twenty-four or younger, with 6 in 10 young male victims coming from Black and ethnic minority backgrounds. Almost half of the young male victims described themselves as black. Of the offenders over half of males under twenty-five described themselves as black. A horrifying story and accompanying data from one city. Any reader interested in the welfare of the black community should wonder and ask how and why we got here and how we can get out of such a violent and ugly situation?

Nov 28th:

Born on September 4th 1908, author **Richard Wright** had an uneasy childhood. His father left when he was only five. The family was forced to move between family members living in poverty, often with little to eat. Richard started school late unable to find decent clothing. By the age of twelve he had yet to complete a full year in school. Richard never completed his schooling. All this was set against the background of racism and prejudice of the Jim Crow South. The love of books and reading offered the young Wright an education and escape. Such was his appetite that he forged notes so that he could take books out, as a white co-worker, from the white's only public library in Memphis. Wright wrote his first play *The Voodoo of Hell's Half Acre* when he was fifteen but there are no existing copies.

A southern black newspaper published his first short story when he was sixteen.

In 1927 Richard Wright migrated north to Chicago. The time was one of economic depression for the country. Wright took a variety of jobs including sweeping streets and digging ditches. He joined the Communist party in 1932. To improve his chances of literary success Wright moved to New York City in 1937. The following year the critically acclaimed *Uncle Tom's Children* was published. The collection of four short stories told of lynchings in the American South. Winning a $500 prize from *Story Magazine* for *Uncle Tom's Children* led to a Guggenheim Fellowship for the author in 1939. *Native Son* (1940), built on Wright's literary success selling over 315,000 copies in just three months. The book would be translated into German, French, Czech, Italian and Dutch. *Native Son* tells the story of twenty-year-old Bigger Thomas who panics and accidentally kills a white woman fearing being found in her room. It would be the first book by an African American to be chosen as part of the Book of the Month Club. The following year the stage version of *Native Son* by Wright and Paul Green appeared on Broadway directed by Orson Welles. Richard Wright would play the lead role in the film version made in Argentina 1951.

Black Boy (1945), Wright's autobiography looks at his life of poverty and the racial violence faced growing up in the South. Wright described the experience as "dark and lonely as death". That year *Black Boy* was the fourth biggest selling non-fiction book in the USA.

Wright went to live in Mexico from 1940 to 1946 before disillusioned with communism and white America moving to live in France. He would only return briefly to the USA two times. Richard Wright continued to work producing *The Outsider,* 1953, considered America's first existential novel looking at a disintegrating society that is not ready to include the black man. Other works include the non-fiction *Black Power,* 1954, and *White Man, Listen,* 1957, based on a series of lectures given in Europe. *The Long Dream,* was published in 1958 and adapted as a play in 1960.

Richard Wright the novelist, poet, writer of short story and non-fiction died of a heart attack in Paris **on this day** 1960, he was fifty-two. He was interred in Le Pere Lachaise cemetery. Richard Wright's protest literature opened the gates for writers such as **James Baldwin** (August 2nd) and **Lorraine Hansberry** (May 19th) and is said to have helped change the landscape of race in America. The autobiographical *American Hunger* (1977), was published posthumously. It looked at his life having moved to Chicago. Unedited versions of *Native Son* and *Black Boy* including original extracts on race, sex and politics were published in 1991.

Berry Gordy Jr record executive, songwriter, music, TV and film producer was born **on this day** in 1929. He wrote or co-wrote 240 of Motown's estimated 15,000 songs. Before becoming a record producer, Gordy had been involved in penning hits such as **Jackie Wilson'**s 'Reet Petite' and 'Lonely Teardrops'. Urged by **Smokey Robinson** (see February 19th), **Gordy** used an $800 loan to establish Motown Records Corporation on January 12th in 1959, with the new label Tamla Records. Using his experience on the car assembly lines, Gordy produced a conveyor belt of artists and hits.

Berry Gordy and John Lewis.

Motown Records' home was at 2648 Grand Boulevard in Detroit. The company was incorporated on April 14th in 1960. **Barrett Strong'**s 'Money (That's What I Want)', co-written by Gordy with Janie Bradford, became the company's first hit in 1960. Success followed with **the Miracles '**Shop Around'. The 1960's smash became the label's first million seller reaching No 1 in the R&B charts and No 2 in the US Billboard pop charts. With the 1962 follow up 'You Really Got a Hold on Me', the Miracles became the label's first star act. The music flowed out of Studio A, a converted photography studio, at the back of the house. With the **Marvelettes** 'Please Mr Postman' (1961), the company had its first million seller. With a line-up of artists including; Mary Wells, **Marvin Gaye**, the Supremes, the Four Tops, the Temptations, **Gladys Knight and the Pips**, **Stevie Wonder**, **Michael Jackson** and the Jackson Five, Number 2648 became known as *Hitsville USA*.

Nothing was left to chance. Berry Gordy had a controlling eye for detail. The artistic development department worked on every area of presentation. The artists were schooled in how to talk, walk, sit, dance, dress and eat. The house band were an unrivalled outfit. One should watch Paul Justman's 2002 documentary *Standing in the Shadows of Motown,* about the Funk Brothers, handpicked by Gordy. Artists developed their song writing styles but at the heart of Motown were writers **Eddie** & **Brian Holland, Lamont Dozier, Norman Whitfield,** and Smokey Robinson**.**

The 1970s saw the company relocate to Los Angeles. Many wondered why Gordy would alter a successful formular? The decade saw Gordy move into film with success with *Lady Sings the Blues*, the 1972 biopic on **Billie Holiday** (see April 7th) starring **Diana Ross** and **Billy Dee Williams.** The pair featured in 1975's *Mahogany.* Ross acted alongside Michael Jackson in *The Wiz* (1978).

The 1980s celebrated over 100 Motown No 1s in the American Billboard 100. On June 28th 1988 Berry Gordy sold the company to media conglomerate MCA for $61 m. It was the most successful owned black record company and for several decades the most successful African American business. Polygram would later pay over $330 m for Motown's catalogue.

To Be Loved: The Music, the Magic, the Memories of Motown was Berry Gordy's autobiography (1994). He would write the book for *Motown: The Musical* which opened on Broadway in 2013 and in London's West End in 2016. Berry Gordy, now in his nineties, has five sons and three daughters.

Mauritania celebrates its **independence on this day** from France in 1960. The country's large nomadic population with it' capital Nouakchott, was governed by President **Moktar Ould Daddah.** A one-party state was established following Islamic socialism. Daddah, born December 25th 1925 maintained strong links with China.

The national flag.

He was deposed in a military coup in 1978. The desert country's first independent leader died on October 14th 2003.

Nov 29th:

Born on this day in 1908 Baptist minister, politician, and civil rights activists **Adam Clayton Powell,** would serve twelve terms in office from 1945 to 1971. Representing Harlem in New York City, the democrat

Powell was voted into the United States House of Representatives. The first black person elected to Congress from New York would be escorted on January 3rd 1945 into the House Chamber, on his first day, by **William Dawson** of Illinois. Dawson and Powell would be the only two black people in the House from 1945 to 1955.

Powell took over as the minister of the Abyssinian Baptist church in New York City, from his father. He inherited a church membership of 10,000 and built the congregation to 13,000. The 1930s saw Powell organise picket lines and mass meetings demanding reform in employment heading up the 'Don't Buy Where You Can't Work' campaign. Powell administered church sponsored relief programmes during the depression era providing clothing, food and temporary jobs for the thousands of Harlem's homeless and unemployed. Powell agitated for black people to be hired in restaurants, the Harlem Hospital and at the World Fair in 1939.

Aged 33 Adam Clayton Powell won a seat on the New York City council in 1941, the first African American to do so. He used his position and the weekly newspaper *The People's Voice,* which he edited 1941–45, to attack racial discrimination in the military.

Powell's first term in the House saw him introduce legislation to outlaw lynching and to end discrimination in the armed forces, housing, employment and transportation. His efforts earned him the title Mr Civil Rights. Continued efforts to prohibit federal funding to groups that advocated unequal treatment of black Americans became known as the Powell amendment. Eventually Powell's efforts were incorporated into the 1964 Civil Rights Act. Facing blatant racist opposition from the floor Powell called for an inquiry from the House Parliamentarian into the use of disparaging terms, pointing out southern Democrats such as the infamous John E Rankin. Rankin publicly declared that he did not wish to sit close to any black politician.

The Daughters of the American Revolution (DAR) had prevented the operatic contralto **Marian Anderson** (see January 7th) from performing to a mixed audience at Constitutional Hall in Washington DC in 1939. It took the intervention of the First Lady Eleanor Roosevelt to save the day opposing the racist DAR. When **Hazel Scott** (see June 11th), Powell's second wife, was barred from performing at Constitutional Hall by DAR, Powell hoped that the First Lady Bess Truman would step in. Nothing happened apart from Powell's protestations leading to his exile from the Truman White House.

Adam Clayton Powell urged the Eisenhower administration to support emerging African and Asian nations and oppose colonialism. He travelled with **Dr King** to celebrate Ghana's independence in 1958. On the House floor Powell gave speeches celebrating Ghana, Indonesia and Sierra Leone's independence.

As chairman of the committee on education and labour, 1961–67, the committee saw fifty measures approved including on minimum wages, training for the deaf, school lunches, vocational training and on student loans.

The flamboyant Powell made enemies. He faced a number of allegations of corruption in 1967 and was indicted for income tax evasion in 1958. The House voted to deprive Powell of his seat, but the activist was re-elected in 1968. The US Supreme Court declared the House decision to deprive Powell as unconstitutional. Ill health forced Powell to resign from frontline politics and from his church duties. He retired to Bimini Island in the Bahamas. Adam Clayton Powell died, aged sixty-three, on April 4th 1972 from acute prostatitis. He is buried in Flushing Cemetery in New York.

Born **on this day** in 1940 **Thelma Mothershed** would be best known as one of the **Little Rock Nine** (see September 5th). Mothershed, a junior, successfully navigated the abuse, threats and slurs to complete her year at Little Rock High School, 1957-8. When Governor Faubus closed all schools in what was called the Lost Year Mothershed did not allow restrictions, opposition and racism to stop her. She continued her education by correspondence graduating in 1959, receiving her diploma through the post.

Thelma Mothershed's determination shone through as she pursued her education gaining a BA degree in home economics from the Southern Illinois University of Carbondale in 1964. The following year Mothershed married Fred Wair. The couple had a son. Fred died aged sixty-five on May 25th in 2005. Thelma Mothershed-Wair earned her master's degree in guidance and counselling, in 1970 at the Southern Illinois University of Edwardsville. Two years later she gained an administrative certificate in education. Mothershed-Wair spent twenty-eight years teaching home economics in the East St Louis school system before retiring in 1994.

Thelma Mothershed-Wair worked at the St Clair County Jail Juvenile Detention Centre in Illinois. With the American Red Cross, the former school pioneer was an instructor in survival skills for women at the Second Chance Shelter for the Homeless.

On this day in 1978 English born **Viv Anderson** became the first black player, after 106 years of senior internationals, to play topflight football for his country. Born in Nottingham July 29th 1956, Anderson had made his debut for England under 21s earlier that year. Selected by manager Ron Greenwood, Anderson made history playing the first of his thirty matches wearing the three lion's shirt versus Czechoslovakia at Wembley in a 1-0 win friendly. With his third cap Anderson played a full competitive match versus Bulgaria. England won 2-0 in a qualifier for the European Cup in 1980. Viv Anderson along with **Laurie Cunningham, Cyril Regis** and later **John Barnes** paved the way for it to be commonplace to see black players wearing the national shirt.

Anderson played for ten years 1974–84 in Brian Clough's Nottingham Forest's team. They won promotion to the first division in 1977. The following season saw Forest lift the 1st Division title and win the league cup. They would win the league cup again in 1979 and appear in a third consecutive final losing to Wolverhampton Wanderers in 1980. Anderson's Forest team beat Malmo in 1979 to win the European Cup. They repeated the feat in 1980 beating Hamburger SV. The defender Viv Anderson played for Nottingham 328 times and scored fifteen goals.

Moving to Arsenal he played 120 games from 1984–87 scoring nine times. Next was Manchester United when Anderson became Sir Alex Ferguson's first signing, 1987–91. Anderson went on to play for Sheffield Wednesday, 1991–93 and was player manager for a season at Barnsley 1993–94.

He rarely faced racial abuse playing for England, putting that down to being a defender. But faced racist chants and missiles thrown at him on club level.

John Charles born September 9th 1944, made his debut for West ham United in 1963. He became the first black player to play for West Ham in Division One. Once again Ron Greenwood featured giving John Charles his first team debut on May 4th 1963. Selected for England Under 18's Charles became the first black player to represent England at any level. He went on to represent his country five times. John Charles retired from the professional game aged twenty-six. He died of cancer on August 17th in 2002 aged fifty-seven. For other black pioneers in the British football see **John Francis Leslie** (August 17th), **Andrew Watson** (March 12th), **Walter Tull** (March 25th), **Tony Collins** (March 19th), **Eddie Parris** (January 31st), **Paul Ince** (June 9th), **Mary Philips** (March 14th) and **Arthur Wharton** (October 28th).

Nov 30th:

The film *Shaft* (1971), directed by **Gordon Parks**, formed the foundation of the genre **Blaxploitation** films (see Van Peebles below). With the 1969 film *The Learning Tree, a* semi-autobiographical film from the book of the same name, Parks became the first African American to write, produce, and direct a film for a major studio with Warner Brothers. He followed *Shaft* with *Shaft Big Score* (1972), *The Super Cops* (1974), and *Leadbelly* in 1976 about the great blues performer (see January 20th).

Gordon Parks came to prominence as a photographer capturing images of the Jim Crow South, segregation, urban black life as well as fashion, sport and famous portraits. He worked for *Life* magazine from 1948–1972, and was voted Photographer of the Year in 1960 by the American Society of Magazine Photographers. Parks also wrote books on photography.

The photographer and filmmaker had further talents writing fifteen books including three memoirs: *A Choice of Weapons* (1966), *Voices in the Mirror* (1990) and *A Hungry Heart* in 2005. Parks wrote the screenplay for *The Learning Tree* and composed the soundtrack with Henry Bryant. Parks the musician composed and directed the ballet *Martin* (1989), a tribute to **Dr King**, assassinated in 1968.

The multifaceted Parks was the co-founder of the monthly magazine *Essence* in 1970. Born **on this day** in 1912, Gordon Parks died on March 7th in 2006. He was ninety-three.

Father and son Van Peebles.

Melvin Van Peebles was born August 21st 1932. Best known for the 1971 film *Sweet Sweetback's Baadasssss*. He self-financed the film with a little help from **Bill Cosby**, co-produced, wrote, edited, scored, directed and acted in the film which would launch the blaxploitation films of the early 1970s. He is the father of director and actor **Mario Van Peebles.** See film pioneer **Oscar Micheaux** January 2nd.

In 2020, at the age of seventy-one, the 97th Archbishop of York **John Sentamu** retired after being appointed Britain's first black archbishop fifteen years earlier. Born on 10th June 1949 near Kampala in Uganda, Sentamu studied law and became an advocate in the Supreme Court of Uganda. He was kicked, as he would describe like a human football, and beaten, left with severe internal injuries while in prison, having refused to find a family member of **Idi Amin** (see January 25th) not guilty. Such were Sentamu's injuries he was given the last rites by Keith Sutton, later bishop of Lichfield. After ninety days Sentamu was released. He married Margaret three weeks before being imprisoned in 1993. The following year Sentamu fled to Britain.

Settled in Britain Sentamu studied theology at Selwyn College, Cambridge gaining his PhD in 1984. Ordained in 1979, Sentamu would be consecrated as the bishop of Stepney on September 25th at St Paul's Cathedral by Archbishop George Carey. In 2002 he was appointed bishop of Birmingham. John Sentamu used his position to speak for the poor, a living wage, to invest in young people and opening up conversation about Jesus.

Sentamu faced racism, as bishop of Stepney in London he said that he had been stopped and searched by the police eight times, an experience not faced by any of his white contemporaries. He'd had excrement posted through his door and one woman refused to have him conduct the funeral for her husband because he was black. The archbishop was an advisor for the **Macpherson Inquiry** (see February 24th). He was the chairman of the inquiry into the murder of **Damilola Taylor** (see November 27th) in 2002.

A tent was set up in York Minster for a week of prayer drawing attention to the need for peace in the Middle East in 2006. The following year saw Sentamu on the BBC's *Andrew Marr Show,* on December 9th 2007, remove and cut to pieces his dog collar in protest against Zimbabwe's **Robert Mugabe** regime (see April 18th), and human rights abuses. When Mugabe resigned Sentamu started wearing his dog collar again.

The prime minister's office announced John Sentamu's translation as the 97th Archbishop of York on 17th June 2005. He was formally elected on the 21st and enthroned at York Minster **on this day** in 2005. The ceremony saw African music and dancing with Sentamu playing African drums. As Archbishop of York, Sentamu automatically took a seat in the House of Lords and would serve as an advisor to the Crown through the Privy Council of the United Kingdom. On his retirement in 2020 Sentamu was controversially left out of the first list of new peerages. The omission of what should have been automatic was criticised as a slight and an example of institutional racism, Sentamu's name appeared in the government's second list of peerages.

Barbados negotiated independence from Britain celebrating independence **on this day** in 1966. **Errol Barrow,** (1920–1987) was the country's first prime minister. He is listed as one of Barbados' ten national heroes. Queen Elizabeth II remained the monarch and Barbados joined the Commonwealth. On this day 2021 Barbados became a republic.

Errol Barrow.

Dec 1st:

Dancer, choreographer, director, producer, and activist **Alvin Ailey** was born in Texas on January 5th 1931. His family moved to Los Angeles when he was twelve, in 1942. It was at this time that the young Ailey was inspired having seen the Ballet Russe de Monte Carlo.

Alvin Ailey studied modern dance with Lester Horton in 1949 before joining Horton's dance company the following year. When Horton died in 1953, Ailey took over as the director of the Lester Horton Dance Theatre until it was dissolved in 1954. That same year saw Alvin Ailey move to New York City and make his debut on Broadway in Truman Capote's musical *House of Flowers*. He appeared in *The Carefree Tree* in 1955 and was the lead dancer in *Jamaica* (1957), alongside the star **Lena Horne.** Ailey continued to study dance under Martha Graham and acting with Stella Adler.

The Alvin Ailey Dance Theatre (AADT) was formed in 1958. It provided a haven for black performers while celebrating music of a black origin and revealing the universality of the black experience through music and dance.

The company debuted with *Blue Suit* (1958). *Blue Suit* drew on Ailey's southern experiences. The 1960s *Revelation* was Ailey's most celebrated work using blues, spirituals and gospel. With sponsorship from the US state department the AADT was able to tour the country and eventually the world. Alvin Ailey was the most famous choreographer out of the USA on the world's stage from 1960–1980, choreographing more than eighty ballets. Ailey stopped performing in the mid-sixties. *Masekela Language* (1969) saw the company explore the black experience in South Africa. The same year the Alvin Ailey Dance Centre was opened, now called the Ailey School.

Alvin Ailey was diagnosed with what we now call bipolar disorder in 1980. His work, after three decades, slowed. He died from an AIDS-related illness, aged fifty-eight, **on this day** 1989. The press release did not say that the cause of death was AIDS on Ailey's instructions to not cause his mother any embarrassment.

Rolling Stone magazine voted him the No 1 stand-up comedian topping their 50 best stand-up comics of all time in 2017. The US cable channel Comedy Central placed him top of the tree in their list of all-time greatest stand-up comedians in 2004. **Richard Pryor** was a comedian, actor and writer. He appeared in over thirty films from his 1967 debut *The Busy Body,* including *Lady Sings the Blues* (1972), *Car Wash* (1976), *The Muppet Movie* (1979), *Stir Crazy* (1980), *The Toy* (1982), *Superman III* (1983), *Brewster's Millions* (1985), *See No Evil, Speak No Evil* (1989), and *Harlem Nights* (1989).

Richard Pryor was born **on this day** in 1940. His observational, storytelling style proved infectiously popular and had a profound influence on his peers. The lovable self-destructive rogue showed his vulnerability on stage which led to Grammy award performances in 1974, 1975, 1976, 1981, and 1982. He posthumously received a Lifetime Achievement Award in 2006. Pryor's achievements were recognised with four Emmy nominations and with him winning in 1973 Emmy for Best Writing in Comedy/Variety, Variety or Music. The rich vein of success continued in 1974 when he won two American Academy of Humour Awards and a Writer's Guild of America Award. Pryor co-wrote the 1974 hit film *Blazing Saddles*.

Richard Pryor's life provided material for his shows, married seven times to five different women he had seven children by six different women. Heavy drinking and drugs took their toll on his relationships, behaviour and health. At the age of thirty-seven, Pryor had the first of three heart attacks. The second in 1990 would lead to a triple heart bypass operation in 1991. The diagnosis of multiple sclerosis, 1989, saw a major decline in the comic's health and put an end to his performances.

One can discover the master stand up at work, captured live in full-length movie shows: *Richard Pryor: Live and Smoking* (1971), *That Nigger's Crazy* (1974), *Is It Something I Said?* (1975), *Bicentennial Nigger* (*1976*), *Richard Pryor: Live in Concert* (1979), *Richard Pryor: Live on the Sunset Strip* (1982), and *Richard Pryor: Here and Now* in 1983.

He wrote his life story in *Pryor Convictions and Other Life Sentences* published in 1991. Pryor was raised living in a brothel run by his grandmother. His mother Gertrude L. Thomas was a prostitute and alcoholic who abandoned her child when he was ten. He was raised by a woman called Marie who would beat the boy regularly for the slightest thing. His father, LeRoy Pryor, was a boxer and hustler. Sexually abused at seven and excluded from school at fourteen, Richard's childhood was a forecast of potential troubles ahead. In the army, 1958–60, Pryor spent most of the time in an army prison in West Germany. He and other black soldiers had attacked a white colleague who appeared to behave in a racially insensitive manner while watching the racially charged film *Imitations of Life*.

The comedian was always nervous before taking to the stage. He started out with middle of the road material but would become famous pushing the boundaries when it came to the use of profanities and the word *nigger*. When hosting *Saturday Night Live* in 1975, the guest host was the cause of a few concerns with worries over whether he would use unacceptable language. Pryor, the first black person to host the show, caused no problems.

Real problems came when in 1980 Pryor, high on drugs, covered himself in rum and set himself on fire. Seen running down the road the comedian was treated for second- and third-degree burns. Multiple sclerosis saw Pryor using a mobility scooter and struggling to communicate. He died from his third heart attack on December 10th 2005, just nine days after his sixty-fifth birthday. See **Dick Gregory** August 19th and **Eddie Murphy** April 3rd.

Dec 2nd:

White abolitionist **John Brown** revered by his supporters as a martyr, some would argue a saint. He was the first man executed in the United States for treason. His actions and death can be directly linked to the American Civil War (1861–1865). Union soldiers marched singing *"John Brown's body…"*. They sang *"His truth still marches on…"*. The song led to the famous 'Battle Hymn of the Republic'. Witness to his execution was a pro-slave militia man John Wilkes Booth who would go on to assassinate Abraham Lincoln.

Brown and Sumner

John Brown struggled to provide for his family. He eventually settled in the black community of North Elba in New York. The land had been donated by white abolitionist and philanthropist **Gerrit Smith.** A series of events, skirmishes and attacks known as bleeding Kansas solidified Brown's opinion that American slavery could only be ended by force, pacifist thinking had failed to achieve its purpose. Brown believed that he had been called, appointed, by God to lead the uprising. The anti-slavery community of Lawrence was sacked, May 1st 1856, and one person killed by pro-slavery militia. The most prominent pro-slavery militia group was known as the Border Ruffians. On May 22nd, the pro-slavery Democrat Preston Brooks took his walking stick and attacked the anti-slave Senator **Charles Sumner** in the US Senate Chamber. In retaliation to all that happened, Brown and his supporters attacked and killed five men, dragging them from their homes and hacked them to death in what became known as the Pottawatomie massacre, May 24th 1856. A further skirmish took place on June 2nd, the battle of Black Jack. The opposing sides were fighting to decide whether Kansas would enter the Union as a slave state or a free state?

August 30th 1856 witnessed the battle of Osawatomie where five Free Staters were killed.

John Brown had declared in a speech in Ontario, Canada addressing an audience of black and white people, in 1858, that he was going to establish a free stronghold for escaped slaves in the mountains of Maryland and Virginia. A new constitution was drawn up for the proposed new United States. Brown was supported by an influential group known as the secret six: Gerrit Smith, **Samuel Gridley Howe, Franklin Benjamin Sanborn, George L. Sterns, Thomas Wentworth Higginson, and Theodore Parker**.

On October 16th 1859 John Brown led a group of sixteen whites and five black men raiding Harper's Ferry armoury in Virginia. The plan was to use the weapons seized to arm a slave uprising. Sixty hostages were taken, seven were killed and ten injured in the raid. Brown's hope that the enslaved population would rise up and form an army of emancipation failed to materialise.

Local militia with the US Marines led by Robert E. Lee killed ten of the rebels, including two of Brown's sons. The rest were either captured or forced to flee.

John Brown was put on trial. His passionate defence centred on the golden rule; Do unto others as you would have done to you. He equated the rule with the Declaration of Independence stating that all men are created equal. John Brown was found guilty of murder, slave insurrection and treason and hanged **on this day** 1859. He is buried in the John Brown Farm State, now a historic site in North Elba, New York.

Born into German governed Rwanda on May 15th 1912, **Alexis Kegame,** roman catholic priest, philosopher, linguist, historian, and poet would challenge the Belgian colonial attempts to impose European republican values on the country.

Employing ethnohistory, the study of indigenous peoples customs, and cultures through historical records, Kegame wrote *Inganji Karinga* (*The Victorious Drums*) *in 1943. It was* a history of ancient Rwanda. He studied indigenous philosophical systems as ethnophilosophy publishing *La Philosophie Bantu Comparee* (*The Bantu Philosophy Compared*) in 1976.

Researching Rwandan oral history, literature and traditions the priest wrote in both French and Kinyarwanda, an official language of Rwanda. Kinyarwanda was promoted by Kegame and is now recognised as one of the world's most orderly, complex and difficult languages. Kegame translated the Bible into Kinyarwanda.

Ordained in 1941 Alex Kegame was the editor of the Catholic newspaper *Kinyamateka* (*The Herald*) during the 1940s and 1950s. He became the first African to gain membership to the Institut Royal Colonial Belge (the Royal Academy for Overseas Sciences) in 1950. When he wrote *Le Code des Instructions Politiques de Rwanda,* 1952, he caught the attention of the Belgian authorities who felt threatened by his opposition to their colonial plans. The classic colonial policies of divide and rule challenged the established rule and traditions. The Tutsi monarchy had ruled since the eighteenth century. Kegame was sent away, out of the way, to Rome where he joined other students; Les Pretres Noirs developing their Christian understanding to create African nationalistic ideas.

Returning to Rwanda in 1958 as a teacher at the Catholic seminary Kagame became a prominent figure in the independence movement. He survived the Belgian intervention that led to the Hutu uprising, 1959–61 and saw the emergence of a Hutu dominated republic and an independent Rwanda on September 25th 1962.

Alex Kagame saw his works heavily censored; he was placed under house arrest advocating the Africanisation of Christianity in a bid to shake off the worst excesses of the white Christian missionary mentality. As a poet, Kagame's works include *Isoko y'Amajyambere (Sources of Progress) consisting of* 3 volumes from 1949–51. The epic poem *La Poésie dynastique au Rwanda (Dynastic Poems of Rwanda was published in* 1951. Kagame's master work a Christian epic *Umulirimbyi wa Nyili-ibiremwa* (*The Singer of the Lord of Creation) another* 3 volumes was published in 1950.

Visiting Nairobi in Kenya Alex Kegame died unexpectedly **on this day** in 1980.

Dec 3rd:

Born in Trinidad and Tobago on February 27th 1914, **Winifred Atwell** would become an unlikely piano superstar. Composing and playing ragtime, boogie woogie, music hall honky tonk, and classical piano, Atwell had a spectacular career. With *Let's Have Another Party,* she became the first black person to get to No 1 on the British charts **on this day** in 1954. Atwell would be the first British recording artist to have three million selling hits with 'Black and White Rag' (1952), 'Let's Have a Party' (1953), and 'Let's Have Another Party' (1954), which stayed at the top spot for five weeks.

Winifred Atwell was challenged to play boogie woogie back in Trinidad. She returned the next day having written 'Piarco Boogie', later titled 'Five Finger Boogie'. She trained in America then accepting a place at London's Royal Academy of Music, moving to England in 1946. Atwell played the piano to make ends meet while at the academy, before becoming the first female pianist to be awarded the academy's highest grading for musicianship.

It was the B side to 'Cross Hands Boogie' that led to nationwide recognition with 'Black and White Rag'. Written in 1908 by George Botsford 'Black and White' became a hit in 1952. The decade saw Atwell earning $10,000 a week. Her hands were insured by Lloyds of London for £40,000 with the stipulation that she did not wash the dishes. Atwell's hands saw her become the first and only holder of two gold discs and two silver discs for piano music. Her first No 1 hit was the first and only instrumental to make the top spot by a woman in the UK. Winifred Atwell sold over 20 million records having 11 top 10 hits in Britain.

Atwell is said to have played in every capital in Europe. She appeared in three Royal Variety performances. Success continued when she toured Australia in 1956. Although critical of racism, prejudice, injustice and the poverty faced by Australian Aboriginals the country embraced the pianist. Loved in Australia, Atwell had her own television special, 1960–61 and ended up living in Sydney in the 1970s. An appearance on the US TV *The Ed Sullivan Show* in 1956 should have opened up the country to her infectious talent. Concerns over how a black British sounding woman would be received in the segregated South meant that the show was never recorded. Nonetheless Atwell performed to over an estimated 20 million people in her career.

On commercial TV she had her own series in Britain; *Bernard Delfont Presents The Winifred Atwell Show* in 1956. She later moved to the BBC.

Atwell toured with two pianos, a grand and an old beaten up up-right bought from a junk shop for £2.50 known as "the other one". Both were slightly out of tune. The songwriter and lyricist Sir Richard Stilgoe ended up being the proud owner of "the other one". Former bus driver, singer Matt Monroe was discovered by Atwell who persuaded Decca Records to sign him.

Winifred Atwell married Lew Levisohn in 1946. The couple had no children and remained together until Lew's death in 1977. Atwell officially retired in 1980. She died from a heart attack following a major fire at her home, Winifred Atwell was sixty-nine. She was buried next to Lew at Gundurimba private cemetery in New South Wales, Australia.

Emile Ford born in St Lucia October 16th 1937 is often cited as the first black British person to have a million selling single, and the first British black male to top the UK charts with 'What Do You Want to Make Those Eyes at Me For?' in 1959. The song spent six weeks at number one in the UK charts. Ford devoted his time to creating the perfect sound acting as what he called a "sound scientist". He created pre-recorded backing tracks first used in 1960. They would be the forerunner of what would be Karaoke. Emile Ford died in London on April 11th 2016 he was seventy-six.

Little Rock Nine (see September 5th) **Terrence Robert**, was born December 3rd 1941. All nine were awarded the Congressional Gold Medal by President Bill Clinton in 1999. After completing that infamous year at Little Rock High School in Arkansas, 1957 to 58, Roberts had to complete his senior year at Los Angeles High School. Governor Faubus, in retaliation to attempts to desegregate schools in Arkansas, closed all public schools in the state for the school year 1958-59. It became known as the 'lost year'.

Terrence Roberts graduated with a BA degree in Sociology in 1967. He completed his master's in social welfare in 1970, and gained his PhD in psychology in 1976. Roberts put his mental survival down to his love of learning and education and the possibilities that they bring. He went on to have a distinguished career as a professor.

Looking back Robert's questioned how he and the other eight survived, what they went through and asked how did it even happen? As the CEO of Terrence Roberts Consulting, a management consulting firm, Terrence Roberts argued that the only way to create positive change is to treat each other as peers, as equals, not to look down or up to anyone but to look at each other at eye-to-eye level.

He was one of just over a dozen black scientists who worked on the American Manhattan Project that led to the atomic bomb and the end of the Second World War. Chemist **Ralph Gardiner,** born **on this day** in 1922, would add Chavis to his name in recognition of **John Chavis**, a distant relative, who was the first black person to graduate from Princeton in 1760. Ralph Gardiner-Chavis worked on the Manhattan Project from 1943–1947. He focused while at the University of Chicago on classified plutonium research critical to the development of the 'Fat Man' implosion bomb.

On leaving the programme Gardiner was unable to find employment as a scientist and spent the next two years waiting tables. He eventually found work as a research chemist with the Standard Oil Company in Cleveland, Ohio. In his twenty years with the company Gardiner-Chavis rose to become the project leader designing processes to refine gasoline. While at Standard he gained his masters in 1952 and his PhD in 1959, both in chemistry.

From 1968–1985 Gardiner-Chavis taught at Cleveland state university's chemistry department. Simultaneously he worked at the research lab at the private Molecular Technology Corp (MTC) where he was a pioneer developing hard plastics and researching catalysis and molecular technology. Ralph Gardiner-Chavis had 17 registered patents and numerous published scientific papers to his name. At MTC Gardiner-Chavis sat on the board of directors and was the vice president of research. He died at the age of ninety-five on March 27th in 2018.

Black scientists known to have worked on the Manhattan Project include **Lloyd Albert Quarterman, Edward A Russell, Moddie Taylor, Harold Delaney, Benjamin Scott, J. Earnest Wilkins, Jasper Jeffries, George Dewitt Turner, Cecil Goldsburg White, Sydney Oliver Thompson, William Jacob Knox** and **George Warren Reid.**

Dec 4th:

The Cook County Police Department described it as a shootout. It would later be described as an assassination. **Fred Hampton** was a rising star in the **Black Panther Party** (BPP see October 15th). He was the chair of the Illinois chapter of the BPP, and the deputy chair of the national party.

Born on August 30th 1948, the revolutionary socialist Fred Hampton caught the attention of the FBI. He co-founded the Rainbow Coalition on April 4th 1969 to end infighting between Chicago's street gangs and to work towards positive social change. The activist was viewed by J. Edgar Hoover's FBI as a radical threat. Under the programme COINTELPRO the FBI illegally attempted to undermine the BPP, Hampton and other civil rights groups. Employing illegal covert practices of misinformation, surveillance, infiltration, discrediting and disruption the FBI engaged in an all-out war against the Black Panther Party.

In the early hours, 0400 hrs of **this day** in 1969 with eight officers at the front and six at the rear, all hell broke out. Records show that **Mark Clark,** born June 26th 1947, was the first shot and killed. His gun went off as his body involuntarily convulsed shooting a bullet into the ceiling. Clark was twenty-two. Hampton was asleep beside his nine-month pregnant partner Deborah Jones. She was dragged from the bed and room. She later argued that Hampton had been drugged as he was sluggish, unable to gain full consciousness before being shot twice in the head. Fred Hampton was twenty-one. **Verlina Brewer, Ronald Satchel, Blair Anderson,** and **Brenda Harris** were seriously injured.

Five thousand attended Hampton's funeral. Eulogies were given by **Jesse Jackson** (see October 8th) and **Ralph Abernathy** (see March 11th). The following month in 1970 a coroner's inquiry ruled that the deaths were justifiable homicide. It would take more than a decade and the revelations of the FBI's COINTELPRO programme before a lawsuit was settled for $1.85 m in 1982. A third of the money was paid by the city of Chicago, Cook County and the federal government each. Hoover's tactics worked as the Black Panther Party fell apart. Projects aimed to improve the lives of those that lived in urban landscapes alongside crime, poverty, alcohol and drugs struggled to take root. The film *Judas and the Black Messiah* captures the time and the story.

Dec 5th:

Rock and Roll legend **Little Richard** was born **on this day** in 1932. The flamboyant, larger than life performer with his bouffant, pompadour hair, androgynous makeup and shrieking vocals set the template for the future of popular music. Lyrics that made no sense, such as the opening to his 1955 hit 'Tutti Frutti', ripped up the rule book and blew away the sophistication and order of crooners like Sinatra.

Little Richard would proudly wear the nicknames of *the Innovator, the Originator and the Architect of Rock and Roll.* Always one for self-promotion, Richard revelled in the knowledge that he influenced his contemporaries and then the next generation of musicians the Beatles, the Rolling Stones and Bob Dylan. **Jimi Hendrix** gained experience playing with Richard on tour, and how much of Richard did we see in **Prince?**

Rock and Roll legend Little Richard.   Inducted by Roberta Flack.

Little Richard followed up 'Tutti Frutti' with 'Long Tall Sally' in 1956. That year he released 'Slippin' and Slidin'', 'Rip it Up', 'Ready Teddy' and 'The Girl Can't Help It'. He appeared in the movies *Don't Knock the Rock* (1956) and *The Girl Can't Help It* in 1957. The hits continued with Lucille, 'She's Got It', 'Keep A-Knockin'', 'Jenny, Jenny', 'Miss Ann', and 'Send Me Some Lovin''.

Little Richard was born **Richard Wayne Penniman.** He left home in Macon, Georgia as his father accused him of being gay. His sexuality would be a point of interest throughout his life. At fifteen, already with the name Little Richard, the singer signed a record contract with RCA in 1951. He had been influenced by the church and the gospel music of performers like the indomitable **Sister Rosetta Tharpe**. Other influences included **Louis Jordan** (see July 8th) and a performer called **Esquerita.** One look at, and a listen to, Esquerita and it is clear where Richard got his image and piano style. Following 'Good Golly Miss Molly', 'True Fine Mama', and 'Baby Face', hits in 1958, Little Richard went into a self-imposed exile having found God. Musically all did not end as Richard made Christian enthused albums, the most famous being produced by **Quincy Jones;** 'King of the Gospel Singers' in 1962.

The hits would never return to what was happening in the late 1950s. Along with **Chuck Berry** (see March 18th) and **Fats Domino** (see October 24th), Richard opened up music to an integrated audience, although black patrons still had to often sit in the balcony. Richard undoubtedly had crossover appeal selling over 30 million records. His material was widely covered by his contemporaries. His music influenced R&B, soul and funk. The shrieking, full throated vocals and his energy led to him being described on stage as a force of nature that would be picked up by **James Brown (**see May 3rd) and rock groups.

Richard was comfortable with his sexuality but like his contemporary Jerry Lee Lewis, Richard felt that so much of his natural rock 'n' roll behaviour was at odds with his Christian faith. The documentary *Let the Good Times Roll* (1973), and the authorised biography *Quasar of Rock: The Life and Times of Little Richard*

(1984), by Charles White, offered insight into the man but he was often a bag of contradictions. Drugs took a hold of the singer who had been ordained a minister in 1970. He cleaned up his act after seeing cocaine kill his brother.

The singer, songwriter, musician and charismatic showman was inducted into the Rock and Roll Hall of Fame by **Roberta Flack,** at its opening in 1986, alongside Chuck Berry, James Brown, **Ray Charles** (see September 23rd), Fats Domino, and **Robert Johnson** (see May 8th)**.** He was awarded a Grammy Lifetime Achievement Award in 1993.

Poor health slowed Little Richard down. He had heart surgery in 2008 and a hip replacement operation the following year. His last recording is believed to have been on a tribute album to gospel singer Dottie Rambo in 2010.

Little Richard died aged eighty-seven on May 9th in 2020. He was interned at Oakwood University Memorial Gardens Cemetery at Huntsville in Alabama.

She was abducted aged about seven from West Africa (probably Senegal) and shipped to Boston. Sold off cheaply, the girl was believed to have a terminal illness and was seen as unfit for the slave markets in the American South or the West Indies.

Bought to work around the house, Susanna Wheatley wife of the tailor John Wheatley, the enslaved girl as was the custom took the name of her owners. **Phillis Wheatley**'s age was estimated by her teeth, her year of birth put at 1853. Although enslaved the girl was taught to read and write. She amazed the family learning Latin, Greek and science. She translated a tale from Ovid. Aged thirteen, Phillis had her first poem published and printed in the *Newport Mercury* on December 21st 1767. The poem 'On Messrs Hussey and Coffin', is based on a story of a miraculous saga of survival at sea.

Phillis Wheatley.

On May 8th 1771 Phillis set sail with the Wheatley's son John for England. On arrival in London the slave poet was met by numerous dignitaries: the abolitionist Earl of Dartmouth, poet and activist Baron George Lyttleton (soon to be Lord Mayor of London), Sir Brook Watson, philanthropist John Thornton and Benjamin Franklin. The bookseller Archibald Bell circulated the first edition of *Poems on Various Subjects, Religious and Moral* in 1773. Phillis became the first black woman from America to have her poetry published on September 1st 1773. She was only the third American woman to have her poetry published. A third of her poetry were elegies on the deaths of noted persons and friends.

Phillis then returned to America as Susanna Wheatley was gravely ill. The famous young poet accepted an invite and visited George Washington in March 1776. Phillis was severely affected by the deaths of Susanna Wheatley in 1774 and John Wheatley in 1778. Now free, Phillis lost her patrons, vital for publication. She married freed black man John Peter in 1778 but unable to have further work published she took work as a scullery maid in a boarding house. The couple lived in poverty. Her husband John was imprisoned for debt. Phillis Wheatley had three babies all died in infancy. She died in obscurity **on this day** in 1784, she was thirty-one.

South African teacher, political activist and dissident, known as 'The Professor' **Robert Sobukwe** was born **on this day** in 1925. While studying at Fort Hare University Sobukwe became interested in politics. With three other colleagues he launched the daily newspaper *Beware* in 1948. That same year he joined the African National Congress Youth League (ANCYL). December 1949 saw Sobukwe appointed as the national secretary of the ANCYL. Sobukwe met **Veronica Mathe** and the couple married in 1950. That same year Sobukwe started teaching. He was briefly suspended, having taken part in the Defiance Campaign opposing restrictions on indigenous education. The couple moved to Johannesburg in 1954 where Robert Sobukwe became a lecturer in African studies at the University of Witwatersrand. As editor of the *Africanist*, 1957, it became clear that Sobukwe was moving away from the liberal, multicultural position of the African National Congress. This led to the birth of the Pan Africanist Congress (PAC). At the inaugural congress, 4th-6th April 1959, Sobukwe was elected the first president of the PAC.

March 21st 1960 saw the launch of the PAC anti-pass laws campaign. All non-whites required a pass to travel in South Africa, even to and from work or school. That day Sobukwe resigned from the university with the plan to walk to the police station where he would give himself up for arrest in protest. Along the eight km walk he was joined by others. On arrival at Sharpeville police station all were arrested. This was followed by a gathering of five thousand protestors who when gathered were fired on, killing sixty-nine and wounding 180. For the **Sharpeville Massacre** see March 21st.

Robert Sobukwe was banished to what is now the north west province on March 25th 1960. The exile never happened as on May 4th Sobukwe was sentenced and imprisoned for three years for incitement. The defendant refused to recognise the court and declined an attorney and the right to appeal. On May 4th 1963, following the General Law Amendment Act, Sobukwe was subjected to prolonged detention. The Act gave the minister of justice power to prolong the detention of any political prisoners. This was only ever applied to Sobukwe who was transferred to Robben Island for six years of solitary confinement.

Imprisoned on the island, Robert Sobukwe obtained an economics degree by correspondence from the University of London, in 1964. The American organisation National Association for the Advancement of Colored People offered Sobukwe work, but the South African administration refused him permission to leave the country under the direction of John Vorster the minister of justice.

On release in May 1969, Robert Sobukwe was banished to Kimberly and placed under twelve hours a day house arrest. He was prohibited from any political activity. A further job offer came from the University of Wisconsin in the USA. Permission to leave the country was refused, again, for the dissident and his family in 1971.

Having studied law, Sobukwe established his own law firm in 1975. There was initial resistance from the apartheid government, but they relented allowing Sobukwe to represent clients in court. Newspapers were not permitted to quote any comments made by Sobukwe in court.

Diagnosed with lung cancer in 1977 the government made access to treatment and open support from visitors difficult. The former president of the PAC died from cancer on February 27th 1978. He was buried at Graaff-Reinet. Robert Sobukwe was fifty-three.

Born on this day in 1931, a child of the great depression, singer, arranger, music, composer and minister would emerge as the King of Gospel music. He worked under the tutelage of **Thomas A. Dorsey** (see July 1st) the Father of Gospel Music.

James Cleveland worked to maintain the traditional, while modernising the sound of gospel music. He worked with close friend **Aretha Franklin** (see March 25th) on the famed 'Amazing Grace' album with **Billy Preston** and gospel great **Albertina Walker** in the Caravans. Cleveland would collaborate with all the greats in the gospel industry. He produced numerous albums with choirs. Working with the Charles Ford Singers, Cleveland released five albums. He won four Grammy awards; 1975 'In the Ghetto', 1977 'Live at Carnegie Hall', 1981 Best Performance for 'Lord Let Me Be an Instrument', and two more Grammys in 1991 and 1999. James Cleveland was the first gospel artist to have a star on the Hollywood Walk of Fame.

A selection of the many songs recorded by James Cleveland include 'The Love of God' (1961), 'Peace Be Still' (1963), 'Lord Help Me to Hold Out' (1973), 'I Do His Will' (1972), 'I'd Love to Tell the Story' (1974), 'I Don't Feel No Ways Tired' (1975), 'Where is Your Faith?' (1981) and his version of the **Gladys Knight** (see May 28th) classic 'You're the Best Thing That Ever Happened to Me' in 1975.

James Cleveland died of congestive heart failure on February 9th 1991, he was fifty-nine. See **Andrea Crouch** July 1st, **Mahalia Jackson** January 31st, and **Sister Rosetta Tharpe**.

Dec 6th:

Frantz Fanon intellectual, social and political philosopher, psychiatrist, writer, Pan Africanist, was an original thinker whose legacy continues to be felt around the world. In his short life his writings challenged the preconceived colonial dominated thought process.

Born on 20th July on the Caribbean Island of Martinique in 1925, Fanon's experiences working in Algeria at the Blida-Joinville Hospital would lead to ground-breaking observations and conclusions. As the head of psychiatry Fanon noticed the effects of colonial violence on the human psyche.

Writing *Black Skin, White Masks* (1952), Fanon describes the affects and effects of anti-black racism. He notes that black people have to wear a white mask to get by in a white world, reminiscent of W. E. B. Du Bois' double consciousness. Fanon asks what are the foundations of anti-black racism? The book is an analysis on the effects of colonialism on racial consciousness? What are the psychosocial repercussions of colonialism on the colonised? Colonial dominance was only possible by reordering the world of the indigenous colonised people. A people who often only felt worth when wearing a white mask. Violence was viewed by Fanon as a tool of social control but just as importantly as a cathartic experience where the perpetrator saw violence as a potential sacrifice putting their lives on the line while being cruel to be kind.

Franz Fanon.

Frantz Fanon criticised post-colonial governments for failing to achieve true freedom from colonialism. The African political elite often failed to establish a new independent national consciousness continuing to wear the white mask of acceptability. The newly independent countries were led by mediocre politicians who oversaw the rise of corruption, ethnic division, racism and economic dependence.

Published in 1961 *Les Damnes de la Terre (The Wretched of the Earth)* helped to consolidate Fanon as an intellectual in the international decolonization movement. Diagnosed with cancer in 1960 Fanon travelled to the USA for medical treatment. He died from leukaemia **on this day** in 1961. Other works published include *A Dying Colonialism* (1959) and *Towards the African Revolution*. Fanon's original thinking highlighted how anti-black racism and consequently colonialism skewed rationality and reason, shaping the psychopathology of colonization and the social and cultural consequences of decolonisation.

As far as the constitution and the law were concerned the **13th Amendment**, passed by Congress on January 31st 1865, and ratified **on this day** in 1865, abolished the slave trade.

Former enslaved person Bob Lemmons.

The amendment was first proposed by Ohio Representative **James Mitchel Ashley** on December 14th in 1863. The amendment provides that *"Neither slave nor involuntary servitude, except as a punishment for a crime whereof the party shall have been duly convicted, shall exist within the United States or any place subject to their jurisdiction"*. With the abolition of slavery came push backs with the adoption of black codes, including legislation on segregation, separate but equal and Jim Crow laws. Intimidation from white supremacists such as the Ku Klux Klan and the use of lynching and voter repression were commonplace. The crime and convict clause in the amendment has been criticised with people of colour being over-represented in the penal system in the United States.

Dec 7th:

Felix Houphouet-Boigny was prime minister of the Ivory Coast (Côte d'Ivoire) from 1958-1960. He served as the West African country's president from November 2nd 1960. Ivory Coast gained independence from France on August 7th 1960. Houphouet-Boigny won elections unopposed, in the single party state, in 1965, 1970, 1975, 1980, 1985 and in 1990, when the country had its first multi-party state election.

Felix Houphouet-Boigny.

A political moderate, the Ivory Coast prospered economically under the majority of the president's thirty-three-year rule. Known for sound planning, close association with the West and France in particular, Houphouet-Boigny was a pragmatic politician adopting co-operation, consensus, and compromise while employing liberal free enterprise policies. Many Ivorians criticised the president's use of French personnel and technical expertise in the country at the expense of the country's citizens, but, as with the one-party state, opposition was limited while the economy prospered known as the Ivorian miracle.

African leaders such as **Kwame Nkrumah** (see January 2nd) of Ghana, and Guinea's **Sekou Touré** described Houphouet's policy as advancing neo-colonialism. When he recognised the **Biafran** leadership during the **Nigerian Civil War,** Houphouet lost support from Nigeria. On becoming president Houphouet proposed a meeting of French speaking African leaders to help end the Algerian war. In Oct 1960 representatives from twelve states met in the capital of the Congo, Brazzaville. All the countries represented were known for their pro-western position and belief in gradualism. Houphouet opposed any federations or alliances that would challenge the sovereignty of the Ivory Coast, but he supported the establishment of the Organisation for African Unity, created in 1963.

All appeared well on the domestic front with the 1970s witnessing the construction of roads, railways and hydroelectric power plants. Exports of coffee, cocoa, pineapples and palm oil rose. The president survived the economic challenges of the 1980s when cocoa and coffee prices plummeted. Questions of his successor were raised resulting in the introduction of a vice president. Violence and white-collar crime rose, but the president was able to hold the country's sixty plus ethnic groups together.

President Felix Houphouet-Boigny, known as the Sage of Africa and Grand Old Man of Africa moved the country's capital from Abidjan to Yamoussoukro where he faced severe criticism building the world's largest church; Basilica of Our Lady of Peace of Yamoussoukro at the cost of US$300 m.

The president was implicated in the ousting of Kwame Nkrumah in 1966, in the failed coup against Benin's **Mathieu Kerekou** in 1977, and was believed to have been involved in the coup that removed **Thomas Sankara** of Burkina Faso. At the time of his death Felix Houphouet-Boigny was the continent's longest serving leader, and the world's third longest serving leader after Cuba's Fidel Castro and North Korea's Kim Il-sung.

The president died from prostate cancer. He made arrangements for his life support to be turned off on **this day** in 1993, Ivory Coast's National Day. Believed to be eighty-eight, the date of birth October 18th 1905 cannot be verified. Following his death, the country experienced rapid economic decline, and a currency devaluation. A series of coups occurred between 1994 and 2002, when a civil war broke out.

One of the **Little Rock Nine** (see September 5th) **Melba Pattillo Beals** was born **on this day,** the day Pearl Harbour was attacked in 1947. Wishing to improve her education chances Pattillo enrolled at the all-white Central High School in Little Rock Arkansas, in May 1956. Aware of opposition to integration, Pattillo, and the other eight, still had no idea of the anger, threats and hostility that integration to Central High would unleash. It took President Dwight D. Eisenhower calling in the 101st Airborne Division to get the nine into school and ensure a degree of safety. Each day during the school year of 1957-8, the nine had a military escort to and from school. While at Central High each student had their own personal guard.

Pattillo completed the school year, but when Governor Faubus closed all state schools to halt integration she moved to Santa Rosa in California to complete her schooling. With the help of the National Association for the Advancement of Colored People, Pattillo attended and graduated from Montgomery High School. The experiences in front of the cameras, on the radio and talking to journalists throughout the Little Rock period drew Pattillo towards journalism. By the age of seventeen she was writing for major newspapers and magazines.

Melba Pattillo gained her BA degree from San Francisco State University and her master's in journalism from Columbia University. She married John Beals in 1961, the couple had a daughter, Kellie, but divorced in 1971. Pattillo adopted twins Matthew and Evans.

Using her diaries Melba Pattillo wrote about her time at Central High. She was the first of the nine to produce her memoirs in *Warriors Don't Cry: A Searing Memoir of the Battle to Integrate Little Rock's Central High* (1994). *White is a State of Mind* (1999) followed on from her experiences in Little Rock. The book examines how the teenager survived and healed after experiencing the anger and rage faced by the racist mob that called to lynch one of the nine.

Wilton Daniel Gregory was elevated to the position of cardinal on November 28th in 2020 by Pope Francis. Gregory became the first African American cardinal. His position means he will be one of the close advisors to the pope and one of some 120 cardinals who will appoint the next pontiff.

Born **on this day** in 1947 Gregory was ordained on May 9th 1973 and was consecrated on December 13th 1983. Appointed bishop of Belleville in Illinois on February 10th 1994 through to 2004. Gregory was installed as archbishop of Atlanta on January 7th 2005 serving through to 2019. He then took up the post of archbishop of Washington.

The archbishop made headlines criticising President Donald Trump's photoshoot, during Black Live Matter protests following the death of **George Floyd** (see May 25th). Trump stood outside the St John Paul II National Shrine, bible in hand, the archbishop of Washington spoke out at Trump's actions as a misuse and manipulation of religion, actions that violate religious principles that call to defend the rights of all people.

The archbishop of Washington's elevation to cardinal was largely welcomed by the LGBQT community who reflected positively on supportive, inclusive and understanding comments that Gregory has made. In 2001 Gregory became the first black president of the United States Conference of Catholic Bishops serving from 2001–2004. He had, prior to that appointment, been the vice president. The then bishop demonstrated compassion for the victims, and zero tolerance for the sex abusers, as he addressed the Church's handling of the sex abuse scandal.

Cardinal Gregory has written and spoken publicly addressing the death penalty, social justice and euthanasia/assisted suicide. See **John Augustine Tolton**, July 9th, the first known African American Roman Catholic priest.

Dec 8th:

White civil rights activist and union organiser **Bernice Fisher** was born **on this day** in 1916. She was one of the six co-founders of the Congress of Racial Equality (CORE). Called the godmother of the restaurant sit in technique, Fisher listed the rules to follow at demonstrations. CORE employed non-violent protest following Mahatma Gandhi's philosophies as codified by Krishnalal Shridharani in *War Without Violence.*

CORE was formed in Chicago 1942 concentrating on race relations. Fisher was working with the Fellowship of Reconciliation (FOR) which led to the establishment of CORE. Segregation was challenged in public places and accommodation. Fisher focused on integrating housing, on the repeal of laws against integrated neighbourhood and amusements in Chicago.

With the union Fisher organised female department store workers. Their wages were low, increases were restricted during the Second World War. The women were overworked, understaffed, not permitted to sit down and had irregular breaks. Observing her organisational skills, described as a nuts-and-bolts person, Fisher was invited to St Louis where she established a chapter of CORE. Her work in St Louis provided the template through the forties and fifties for the organisation.

A committed Christian, Bernice Fisher spent the last ten years of her short life working with the church. She died, aged forty-nine, in New York City and is buried at the Evergreens Cemetery in Brooklyn, Kings County, NYC.

In March 1942 the **Congress of Racial Equality** (CORE) was formed in Chicago.

The six key figures who co-founded the organisation were a mixed group of three black organisers **James Farmer** (see January 12th), **James R Robinson** who was the father of direct mail funding, keeping CORE financially afloat and **Bayard Rustin** (see March 17th). Rustin was not an official founder but worked closely with CORE from its conception. The three white co-founders were **George Houser,** he was essential in organising the first freedom rides with Rustin, **Homer Jack,** who participated in the first freedom rides in 1947, **Kenneth Earl Joe Guinn** and **Bernice Fisher.**

Born on June 6th 1934, **Roy Innis** was a civil rights activist and political figure. He was the national chairperson of the Congress of Racial Equality (CORE) from 1968 through to his death on January 6th in 2017.

British Labour Prime Minister Harold Wilson had promised Bristol bus boycott leader **Paul Stephenson,** (see May 6th), that there would be legislation on race relations if he were to lead the next government. With increased non-white immigration from the Caribbean, India and Pakistan to Britain, there were concerns with racist behaviour and attitudes coming from some in the white community.

The 1965 Race Relation Act followed the Labour government win in the 1964 election. The act outlawed discrimination in public places. It was now an offence to discriminate on colour of skin, race or ethnicity. Discriminatory adverts and notices were banned. The Race Relations Board and the National Committee for the Commonwealth Immigrants were formed. The 1965 Act gained royal assent on Nov 8th and became law **on this day** in 1965, but it did not apply to housing or to employment, two key contested areas.

The 1968 Race Relations Act included housing and employment. Days before the second reading of the 1968 Act Conservative **Enoch Powell** delivered his infamous Rivers of Blood Speech (see April 20th). The 1968 act promoted by the then home secretary James Callaghan failed to address issues relating to the police force.

The 1976 Race Relation Act defined discrimination to include indirect discrimination. The definition was seen as any practice that disadvantages a particular racial group. In 2000 there was an amendment to the Race Relation (amendment) Act bringing the police into the Act's scope. Public authorities now had a duty to actively promote race equality.

Dec 9th:

Author, editor, teacher, documentary filmmaker and social activist **Toni Cade Bambara,** was born **Miltona Mirkin Cade** in the USA on March 25th 1939. She worked to raise black consciousness and pride. As a writer Bambara believed that the artist's work should be determined by the community that they serve.

The author adopted the name Bambara in 1970, an ethnic group native to West Africa.

The Black Woman: An Anthology (1970) saw Bambara edit and contribute to the first feminist collection that focused on black women. Black female voices addressed issues that were not given pride of place in either the civil rights or women's movements. The anthology was followed by 1971's *Tales and Stories for Black Folks*. A notable short story is *Blues Ain't No Mockin Bird* (1971), looking at how a family's privacy is invaded by two white cameramen investigating the county's food stamp programme.

Gorilla, My Love (1972) is a collection of fifteen short stories written between 1960 and 1970. The collection has strong female leads and uses black urban street language. During the early 1970s Bambara visited Cuba and Vietnam looking at the political effectiveness of feminist movements, how they employed practical actions, towards deploying the lessons learned at community level in the United States. Her second collection of short stories *The Sea Birds Are Still Alive* (1977) looks at social change and community healing.

The importance of healing through tradition and folk medicines was further explored in Bambara's first novel *The Salt Eaters* (1980). The novel won the American Book Award in 1981. Wellness, healing and wholeness within the black community is at the heart of *The Salt Eaters*. Bambara was active in the black liberation movement and women's movement. Injustice and oppression were themes central to the author's writings and activity. She co-founded the Southern Collective of African American Writers in Atlanta. Although a feminist Bambara entertained the idea of neither manhood nor feminism but of blackhood.

Bambara moved from Atlanta to Philadelphia in 1985. She wrote numerous screen plays including *Bombing of Osage*. Bambara co-produced and narrated the documentary that looked at the attack on May 13th 1985. An army of five hundred state and city police officers attacked the community of MOVE, an anti-government, anti-technology and anti-corporation organisation, killing eleven including five children, destroying sixty-one homes, and leaving 250 homeless. Another screenplay written by Bambara was for *Tar Baby* based on the 1981 novel by Toni Morrison.

Considered Bambara's magnus opus *The Bones Are Not My Child* (1999) was published posthumously by close friend Toni Morrison. *The Bones* covers the story of how between 1979 and 1980 forty children disappeared in Atlanta.

Diagnosed with colon cancer in 1993, Toni Cade Bambara died **on this day** in 1995, she was fifty-six.

Photographer **Roy DeCarava** was born in New York City **on this day** in 1919. He grew up through the artistic period of the Harlem Renaissance. In the 1940s DeCarava turned to photography to inform his artwork. The photography took over, with the black and white images portraying black people through his poetic vision in a serious and artistic manner.

DeCarava had his first solo exhibition in 1950 at Forty Fourth Street Gallery in New York City. The artist became the first African American to win the Guggenheim Fellowship in 1952. This afforded the photographer to spend a year documenting life in Harlem. Collaborating with **Langston Hughes** (see May 22nd) the pair produced *The Sweet Flypaper of Life* (1955), a book of 140 photos with a narrative by Hughes. DeCarava published further books including *The Sound I Saw, Jazz Photographers* (1983) and *Roy DeCarava, A Retrospective* (1996).

DeCarava's pictures chronicled the greats of New York's jazz scene including **Duke Ellington**, **Billie Holliday** and **John Coltrane**. His works adorn album covers; **Miles Davis'** *Porgy and Bess*, **Mahalia Jackson's** *Bless This House*, **Big Bill Broonzy's** *Big Bill's Blues* and Carlos Montoya's *Flamenco Fire*.

A Van Der Zee photograph.

Roy DeCarava's work was the subject of twenty-five solo exhibitions. The photographer died on October 27th 2009 aged eighty-nine.

DeCarava followed in the footsteps of leading Harlem Renaissance photographer **James Van Der Zee** (June 29th 1886 – May 15th 1983). Van der Zee documented the period in New York City creating portraits of black New Yorkers.

British singer, songwriter, producer, arranger, and multi-instrumentalist **Joan Armatrading** was born **on this day** in St Kitts in 1950. After briefly living in Antigua the seven-year-old came to Britain to join her family in the Birmingham area.

Armatrading toured with the production of *Hair*, where she met the lyricist, Pam Nestor. The pair collaborated to release the debut album 'Whatever's for Us' in 1972. Later that year, November 28th, Armatrading appeared on John Peel's BBC Radio 1's show singing while playing guitar and piano. The following year, 1973, Armatrading was named Outstanding New Artist in Music Week. The same year her first single 'Lonely Lady' with lyric by Nestor, was released.

The release of the 1976 album 'Joan Armatrading' went top 20 and the single 'Love and Affection' went top 10 in the UK charts. Armatrading became the first black British female singer songwriter to gain international success. The late 1970s was a great time for the performer with live shows and appearing on US television in NBC's *Saturday Night Live* aired May 14th in 1977.

The independently-minded singer has always been determined to do her own thing. The fiercely private Armatrading has never been one for following trends, although there have been a number of hit singles, Armatrading was always an album performer. Her effortless eclectic style saw the songwriter becoming the first British female artist to debut at No 1 in the US Billboard Blues Chart and the first British female artist to be nominated for a Grammy Award in the blues category in 2007, for 'Into the Blues'. In 2012

Armatrading won the British Folk Festival Award, and the BBC Radio 2 Folk Award for Lifetime Achievement in 2016.

With over twenty album releases, Joan Armatrading frequently plays all instruments, writes all the songs and music as well as arranging and producing. Her skilful guitar playing is universally recognised.

Joan Armatrading composed the music for the Donmar Warehouse theatre's production of *The Tempest* which was performed in London and New York in 2016. The singer has been nominated for three Grammy Awards, and twice nominated for Brit Awards and has won an Ivor Novello Award for Outstanding Contemporary Song Collection in 1996. Joan Armatrading's singles include: 'Love and Affection' (1976), 'Down to Zero' (1976), 'Me Myself I' (1980), 'All the Way From America' (1980) and 'Drop The Pilot' (1983), her biggest-selling single in the United States.

On May 1st **Tanganyika** was granted full internal self-governance. **Tanzania** gained its independence **on this day** in 1961 from Britain. **Julius Nyerere** (see April 13th) was the country's first prime minister and then president. The socialist Nyerere turned the country into a one-party state in 1962.

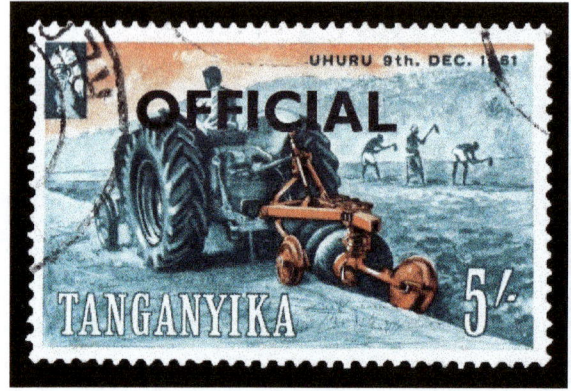

Uhuru 9th December 1961   A woman of Tanzania

Dec 10th:

William Lloyd Garrison was born **on this day** in 1805. By the age of twenty-five, the white activist had joined the anti-slavery movement. Unyielding and steadfast Garrison would fearlessly challenge what he saw as the sin of American slavery. Through the campaigning newspaper *The Liberator*, Garrison eloquently and passionately spoke up for the enslaved person.

In the opening edition of *The Liberator*, 1831, Garrison made his position clear:

"I do not wish to think, or speak, or write, with moderation…I am in earnest - I will not equivocate - I will not excuse - I will not retreat a single inch - and I WILL BE HEARD."

The journalist originally supported freed blacks being encouraged in a return to West Africa. Garrison soon realised that for many the proposal was just a ploy to have fewer free blacks in America so as not to tempt the enslaved population. Garrison took an extreme position demanding an immediate end to slavery believing that the country could accommodate and assimilate the freed people.

In 1832 Garrison founded the New England Anti-Slavery Society, the first of its kind in the country. The following year he helped organise the American Anti-Slavery Society. Although The Liberator was never widely read it and Garrison were influential in opposing slavery. He was also controversial. Garrison was a suffragist advocating women's rights which was a key issue with Garrison splitting from moderate abolitionists. He argued the campaign should be non-political and pacifist but also anarchist. The latter point argued the refusal to obey rules from a corrupt society. On one occasion he burned a copy of the constitution arguing that it was a pro-slavery document. Although a pacifist, through The Liberator John Brown's raid on Harpers Ferry (see December 2nd) to emancipate the slaves was hailed as a good thing. Garrison supported Abraham Lincoln in the Civil War and welcomed the Emancipation Proclamation of 1863.

Journalist and abolitionist William Lloyd Garrison.

When slavery was abolished and the 13th Amendment ratified (see December 6th) William Lloyd Garrison the abolitionist, crusading journalist and editor, the women's rights activist continued to fight for civil rights and reform but was no-longer on the front row. After 1,820 issues, the most uncompromising of all the abolitionist newspapers, The Liberator had its final publication in December 1865. Garrison never missed one issue. He resigned from the American Anti-slavery Society in May 1865 hoping that the organisation would be dissolved. Others believed that there was still work to be done especially in the South. The society continued for five more years until the Fifteenth Amendment to the United States Constitution gave the vote to black men.

After his wife Helen died on January 25th 1876, Garrison's health steadily declined. He died on May 24th in 1879. Flags in Boston flew at half-mast. He had black and white abolitionist friends as pallbearers. William Lloyd Garrison is buried at Forest Hills cemetery in Boston, USA, he was seventy-three.

Ray Charles (see September 23rd), **James Brown** (see May 3rd) and **Sam Cooke** (see December 11th) were the architects of what would be understood as soul music, but R&B and soul came together in the 1960s in the person of **Otis Redding.** Born September 9th 1941, Redding was the embodiment of all that was soul, he sang with emotion and power but was also sensitive and sincere. His live performances captivated the audience as the singer, songwriter and arranger gave everything to each word of each song. In the late 1950s Otis Redding was a backing singer in **Little Richard's** backing band the Upsetters. Redding had a minor hit with the single 'Shout Bamalama'. His real breakthrough came with the recording of self-penned 'These Arms of Mine' (1962). The debut album came a couple of years later 'Pain in My Heart' (1964). The album had four single releases the title track, 'These Arms of Mine', 'That's What My Heart Needs' and 'Security'.

During his brief career Redding recorded six albums: 'Pain in My Heart' (1964), 'The Great Otis Redding Sings Soul Ballads' (1965), 'Otis Blue/Otis Redding Sings Soul' (1965), 'Complete and Unbelievable: The Otis Redding Dictionary of Soul' (1966), and 'King and Queen' (1967) with **Carla Thomas.** Otis Blue was recorded in one day.

With his backing band **Steve Cooper,** co-writer and guitarist, **Donald 'Duck' Dunn** on bass, **Al Jackson** on drums and **Booker T. Jones** on keyboards **(Booker T. and the MG's)** the sound was tight. Redding's arrangements left nothing to chance. His performance at the Monterey Pop Festival reinforced what many already knew, he was the sound and voice of soul with the ability to cross over, undiluted, to a white audience. The future looked promising. The singer was earning $35,000 a week. In 1967 he earned $1 million.

On this day 1967, Otis Redding was on board a chartered plane when it crashed into Lake Monona in Wisconsin. All onboard apart from **Ben Cauley** of the Bar-Kays died. Four members of the **Bar-Keys** died **Jimmy King, Phalon Jones, Ronnie Caldwell** and **Carl Cunningham**, along with the valet Matthew Kelly and the pilot.

The eighteen-year-old Redding met fifteen-year-old **Zelma Atwood,** the couple had a son Dexter who was born in 1960. They got married a year later in August 1961 and would go on to have two daughters and another son.

'(Sittin' On) The Dock of the Bay', written with guitarist Steve Cooper, was recorded days before the singer's death on December 6th. The single went to the top of the charts and became the first album to posthumously reach No 1 in the UK. The six foot one Otis Redding was twenty-six when he died, more than 4,500 attended his funeral.

Dec 11th:

In memory of the **thirteen hanged on this day** 1917: **Sgt. William C. Nesbitt, Corp. Larsen J. Brown, Corp. James Wheatley, Corp. Jesse Moore, Corp. Charles W. Baltimore, Pvt. William Brackenridge, Pvt. Thomas C. Hawkins, Pvt. Carlos Snodgrass, Pvt. Ira B. Davis, Pvt. James Divine, Pvt. Frank Johnson, Pvt. Rosley. W. Young, and Pvt. Pat MacWharter.**

The thirteen were found guilty following riots/mutiny in Houston. A further thirteen were to be executed but an outcry led to only six being executed by hanging and sixty-three men given life sentences served in federal prisons. Of the 157 that faced charges, 110 African American soldiers were found guilty.

Segregation in the army.

There had been numerous incidents where the soldiers of the all-black 3rd Battalion of the 24th United States Infantry Regiment stationed at Camp Logan, just outside of Houston, had faced harassment from the local authorities. The soldiers had complained about being continuously stopped and arrested on trumped up charges. On August 23rd 1917 a black woman was dragged out of her home by white police officers and arrested for being drunk in public. Observing the scene, a black soldier questioned what was happening and he too was beaten and arrested. When MP Corporal Charles Baltimore heard of the incident, he investigated but he too was beaten and shot at as he ran for his life. Rumour reached the soldiers that Corporal Baltimore had been killed and that a white mob was fast approaching. The soldiers armed themselves and made their way into town.

The conflict that followed left sixteen white people dead including five policemen and four black soldiers. The three court martials that followed saw two white officers released but 110 African American soldiers found guilty. No white civilians were brought to trial.

Born on January 22nd 1931 **Sam Cooke** would be heralded by many as the king of soul. His early success in the genre as a singer, songwriter and businessman with a string of hits reaching a crossover audience in the late 1950s and early 1960s ensured his place shaping the sound of soul and reaching a pop audience.

Sam Cooke added the letter 'e' to his surname believing it looked distinctive, having a touch of class. Grounded in gospel music, the teenage Cooke formed the gospel quintet the Highway QCs based on the much-admired Soul Stirrers. At the age of nineteen Cooke had the opportunity to join the Soul Stirrers performing with the group for the next six years. Believing that he could reach a broader audience and achieve a lot more musically, Cooke set out on a solo career using the alias Dale Cook on the 1957 release 'Lovable'. Few who knew the successful gospel artist were fooled. Sam Cooke's distinctive sound shone through on the track. The stakes were high as it was frowned upon for a gospel singer to perform secular music.

The singer had made his move. Over the next eight years he would have twenty-nine top 40 hits on the US Billboard 100. The hits flowed with 'You Send Me', replacing Elvis Presley's 'Jailhouse Rock' at the top spot in 1957. Other hits included: 'Only Sixteen' (1958), 'Everybody loves to Cha Cha Cha' (1958), 'Chain Gang' (1960), 'Wonderful World' (1960), 'Sad Mood' (1960), 'Cupid' (1960), 'Twistin' the Night Away' (1962), 'Having A Party' (1962), 'Bring It On Home To Me' (1962), 'Tennessee Waltz' (1963) and 'Another Saturday Night', released in 1963.

Sam Cooke
January 22, 1931 – December 11, 1964

Gospel, R&B and soul pioneer.

Cooke was a shrewd businessman establishing his own publishing company in 1959. When he negotiated his contract with RCA the industry was amazed at the substantial advance received and that after thirty years the songwriter would have ownership of his master recordings. Cooke continued to build. He had his own record label SAR Records in 1961 signing the Valentinos (Bobby Womack and his brothers) and Jonnie Taylor.

The artist was ambitious, releasing eleven albums from 1958 with 'Sam Cooke', to 1964's 'Ain't That Good News'. During that period, he recorded two live albums: 'Sam Cooke at the Copa' (1964) and the 1963 recording 'Live at the Harlem Square Club' released in 1985. The *Harlem Square* performance previewed the direction of soul music. Cooke demonstrated a raw vocal side not the polished crossover material of hits like *Cupid*. Hearing Bob Dylan's 'Blowin' in the Wind', the songwriter asked why had a black man not written the song? In response he set about writing the politically conscious civil rights anthem 'A Change is Gonna Come'. The song would become his most famous.

The singer met Elisa Boyer at a bar in Los Angeles on December 11th 1964. The pair ended up at the Hacienda Motel. An altercation took place with Boyer leaving the scene, later calling the police. Cooke ended up arguing with the motel manager Bertha Franklin. As temperatures rose Franklin fatally shot the singer arguing she had done so in self-defence. Sam Cooke died **on this day** in 1964. It was concluded that his death was justifiable homicide, the family have never been comfortable with the conclusion and details concerning that fateful night.

Ray Charles (see September 23rd) and **Lou Rawls** sung at Cooke's funeral. The body of thirty-three-year-old Cooke was interred at Forest Lawn Memorial Park cemetery in Glendale, California. The singer had been married twice, first to Dolores Milligan Cooke. She died in a car accident, in 1959, the couple had divorced. Barbara Campbell Cooke survived her husband with their two daughters and a son. Sam Cooke had three other children outside of marriage.

Two posthumous studio albums were released, 'Shake' and 'Try a Little Love', both in 1965. **Kemp Power**'s 2013 play 'One Night in Miami' recalls the night of February 25th 1964, following boxer **Muhammad Ali**'s heavyweight triumph. Set in a hotel room Ali, athlete **Jim Brown**, activist **Malcolm**

X and Cooke discuss politics, life and the future. The film version was released in 2020. Sam Cooke's 'A Change is Gonna Come' was played at Malcolm X's funeral.

Jamaican evangelist Revd Dr **Oliver Augustus Lyseight** was born on this day in 1919. He joined the New Testament Church of God in Jamaica in 1939. Lyseight married Rose Goodson (1928–2020) on 11th June 1947. The couple would go on to have 7 children. Licenced as a minister in 1947, Lyseight arrived in England onboard the ship Britannica in Liverpool on November 8th 1951. Revd Lyseight held prayer meetings in a home on Faulkner Street, Wolverhampton. He found that many in the immigrant black community were missing the style of worship that they were familiar with back in the Caribbean. Some had also experienced racism among the white clergy and their congregations. The first official public service was held on Sunday 20th September in 1953 at the local YMCA on Stafford Road. With twenty-five members the church in Wolverhampton was officially established on 18th June 1955 along with Handsworth's forty members.

Oliver Lyseight tirelessly travelled the length and breadth of the country connecting with the growing immigrant West Indian community putting down roots and establishing churches. He was appointed the New Testament Church of God (NTCG) overseer in Britain, remaining in post for twenty-five years. Churches were organised into areas called districts with individual pastors and an overall district pastor. A calendar of district and national meetings were put into place. Huge gatherings, known as Conventions, took place twice a year, initially in Birmingham and Leicester. These conventions would witness the largest gatherings of people of Caribbean descent anywhere in the country outside of the Notting Hill Carnival.

On retiring as the national overseer, 1987, Revd Lyseight stepped down leaving eighty-seven churches, nine missions, 190 ministers, a church membership of 5,000 and assets of over £1 m. Oliver Lyseight died on Feb 26th 2006. He was 86. Today the largest black-led British denomination, the New Testament Church of God, proudly boasts 107 church branches, with an immediate membership of over 10,000 with an additional 20,000 adherents. In 2004 Pastor Lyseight was voted in at No 2 in the list of 100 Great Black Britons.

Dec 12th:

Born **on this day** 1897 or 1998 in what was British East Africa (Kenya), the young boy would be called **Kamau wa Ngengi** taking the name of his uncle. Raised in traditional Kikuyu culture Kamau would adopt the name **Jomo Kenyatta.** In Swahili, Jomo means *burning spear*, Kenyatta is a traditional beaded belt, the name translated as light of Kenya.

Following an illness, the young Kenyatta received good medical care from the Church of Scotland Mission. Impressed with his treatment, the boy left home to become a pupil, working to pay for his board at the Scotland Mission School in 1909. He disliked attempts to convert him to the Christian faith finding the tone patronising, dismissing traditional African culture and religion. Kenyatta was nonetheless baptised in August 1912. At the time he was apprenticed to the mission's carpenter.

Jomo Kenyatta.

When the opportunity arose, Kenyatta travelled to live and work in the busy, cosmopolitan Nairobi. He joined the East African Association (EAA) in 1921 formed by **Harry Thuku.** The previous year had seen the country become a British crown colony. The EAA fought to recover lost Kikuyu land. Africans had been dispossessed, with only white settlers being able to lease and own land. Overcrowded, native reserves were established. The EAA, under political pressure, folded and became the Kikuyu Central Association (KCA) in 1925. The KCA was formed by **James Beauttah** and **Joseph Kang'ethe.** By 1928 Kenyatta had risen to become KCA general secretary. That same year he opened the politically moderate monthly Kikuyu newspaper *Muiguithania* ('he who brings together').

Kenyatta travelled to London in 1929 seeking a meeting with the Secretary of State for Colonies to testify against proposals to unify Kenya, Uganda and Tanganyika (Tanzania). The audience was denied. In March 1930 Kenyatta wrote a letter to *The Times* of London outlining his concerns:

1) Africans require security with land holdings and there should be a return of land distributed to the European settlers.
2) Education facilities and provisions for the African should be improved.
3) Tax laws, in particular the 'hut tax', should be repealed. The 'hut tax' forced many women into prostitution.
4) The African should have political representation.
5) There should be respect and non-interference with traditional culture and customs.
6) If none of the above are accepted, then the logical conclusion would be a violent uprising which no one wants.

Jomo Kenyatta was ignored seeking another meeting in May 1931. The Carter Land Commission heard Kenyatta's appeals. The Commission's findings were published in 1934 offering to pay compensation for the loss of land but not to return confiscated farms. The White Highland Policy was to continue.

Looking to communism Kenyatta continued his studies in soviet Moscow before returning to England and the London School of Economics. It was at this time that Kenyatta wrote his thesis *Facing Mount Kenya*. The book on Kikuyu culture would be re-published in 1938. It celebrated many Kikuyu customs controversially including female circumcision.

With the arrival of the Second World War, Jomo spent fifteen years away from Kenya and grass roots political developments. He helped to organise the fifth and final Pan African Congress held in Manchester England, on Oct 15th to 19th in 1948. The congress called for independence across Africa and the Caribbean.

Kenyatta returned to Kenya in 1946 as the president of the Kenya African Union (KAU). As predicted in his letter to *The Times* violence erupted in 1952 with the Mau Mau uprising. Conflict continued through to 1959 when the state of emergency in the country was lifted on November 10th. The Mau Mau were brutally crushed and demonised in popular propaganda news coverage. Jomo Kenyatta was arrested on October 21st 1952 charged with directing the Mau Mau movement. On April 8th 1953, following a controversial trial, Kenyatta was sentenced to seven years in prison. While in detention the British conceded to the idea of 'one man one vote' in 1960. **Tom Mboya (**who would be assassinated in 1969) and **Oginga Odinga** (who would be held in detention) formed the Kenyan African National Union (KANU). In his absence they elected Jomo Kenyatta as the president of the political organisation. KANU refused to cooperate with the British until their president was released. Kenyatta declared that there would be room for the ordinary white citizen in an independent Kenya.

Released from detention on August 21st 1961, Kenyatta attended the Lancaster Conference in London in 1962 to negotiate constitutional terms for an independent Kenya. KANU won, dominating the elections of May 1963. **Kenya's independence** was celebrated **on this day;** December 12th 1963. Kenyatta served as the first prime minister 1963–64. A one-party state was established in 1964 with Kenyatta as president 1964–78. Successive constitutional amendments led to his greater autocratic control and rule. Kenyatta maintained an unusual balance where the country celebrated political and economic stability. He employed many from other ethnic groups in his government using his motto 'harambee' ('pulling together') but overall Kikuyu dominance remained. Disparity of wealth grew with Kenyatta's family. The Kikuyu had benefited from early land redistribution. An inner circle was known as the Kiambu Mafia. Power to arrest political opponents, holding them in detention without trial, was used effectively albeit infrequently.

Gross national product grew fivefold from 1971–1981. Kenya saw one of the best periods of economic growth on the continent with domestic exports thriving and foreign investment increasing. Kenyatta maintained a pro-British position. He published his memoir and speeches *Suffering Without Bitterness* in 1968.

In 1966 the president had his first heart attack, the second followed in 1977. To Jomo Kenyatta's credit he resisted calls for his successor to be another Kikuyu. His vice president, Daniel Arap Moi, from the Tugen sub-group of the Kalenjin people succeeded him. Jomo Kenyatta died on August 22nd 1978, he was either eighty or eighty-one.

Teacher, clergyman, and intellectual, nationalistic leader **Ndabaningi Sithole** was born July 21st 1920. He is often cited as the first black man in Rhodesia to express the philosophy underlying the black nationalist cause.

Following the publication of Sithole's *African Nationalism* in 1959 he was asked to join **Joshua Nkomo's** (see June 19th) newly-formed National Democratic Party (NDP). Sithole acted as the party treasurer. The NDP was banned in 1961. Sithole took the opportunity to help form the Zimbabwe African People's Union (ZAPU) but that party was also outlawed. The banning of militant political parties helped to add to the fractious nature of nationalistic politics and the infighting that disrupted the fight against white minority rule in Rhodesia.

Ndabaningi Sithole used Tanzania to broadcast revolutionary ideals into Rhodesia. Returning to Rhodesia in 1963 and backed by **Robert Mugabe** (see February 21st) Sithole formed the Zimbabwe African National Union (ZAPU). Arrested in November 1965, viewed as a disruptive militant, Sithole would not be freed from prison until December 1974. While incarcerated Mugabe took control of ZAPU adding the words Patriotic Front, the group now called ZANU-PF.

Arrested again, and taken into custody on March 4th 1975, upon release Sithole attended the meeting of the Organisation of African Unity in Dar-es-Salaam, Tanzania. Ndabaningi Sithole went on to serve in the government between 1978–79, as Rhodesia transitioned to Zimbabwe. Following the transfer of power Sithole fled the country to live in exile in the USA, in 1984. He feared assassination by Mugabe. He returned to Zimbabwe in 1992 and won a seat in parliament in 1995. He was arrested, this time, accused of conspiring to murder Mugabe. In 1997 Sithole was given a two-year sentence. Due to illness, he never served any of that time. He died in America **on this day** 2000 seeking medical care. Along with writing the book *African Nationalism*, Sithole also wrote a biography on **Obed Mutezo** published in 1972 and *Roots of a Revolution* in 1977.

Portia Simpson Miller served as Jamaica's first female prime minister from 2006–7 and again from 2012–16. Born **on this day** in 1945 Simpson married Errald Miller, adding his name to hers in 1998.

Miller became involved in politics at a local level with Kingston City Council representing the Trench Town area from 1974. Two years later she entered national politics with the People's National Party (PNP) in 1976 being elected to the House of Representatives. She was re-elected in 1980. The party sat out the 1983 general election, but Miller regained her seat in 1986.

In the PNP Michael Manley's government, Miller held her first cabinet position as Minister of Labour, Welfare and Sports in 1989. She would hold numerous positions remaining in the cabinet for the next seventeen years. Miller established the country's Sports Development Foundation in 1995 promoting Jamaican sporting excellence on the international stage. Miller was the PNP vice president from 1978–2006, and head of the party's Women's Movement from 1983–2006.

Following the resignation of prime minister P J Patterson, Miller was voted in as the party leader becoming Jamaica's first female prime minister. The PNP lost the general election in Sept 2007 to the Jamaica Labour Party (JLP). On December 29th 2011 the PNP and Miller won the general election convincingly. Portia Simpson Miller began her second term as prime minister serving through to March 2016.

Country singer **Charley Pride** was the genre's first African American singing superstar. When he appeared at the Grand Ole Opry in 1967 he was the first black performer to do so since harmonica blues player DeFord Bailey in 1941. Bailey was the first performer to appear on the Grand Ole Opry, the first to record in Nashville, 1928, and the first person to release a harmonica blues solo record.

Charley Pride was born on March 18th 1934. He gained a recording contract with RCA Victor and would go on to be the label's biggest seller, second only to Elvis Presley. Pride's first single was 1966's 'The Snakes Crawl at Night'. Audiences immediately gravitated to his baritone voice, his songs' clarity, simplicity and traditional content. Between 1966 and 1987 the singer released fifty-two singles that reached the country music charts top 10. Thirty of Pride's singles topped the country music charts, including eight No 1s between 1969–1971.

Charlie Pride was voted Country Music Entertainer of the Year in 1971 and Top Male Vocalist that same year, and again in 1972. He released forty-four studio albums. Later releases included Pride and Joy: A

Gospel Music Collection (2006), Choices (2011), and 'Music in my Heart' (2017). The three times Grammy Award-Winner also received a Lifetime Achievement Award in 2017.

Country singer Charlie Pride.

Charley Pride wrote his autobiography with Jim Henderson *Pride: The Charley Pride Story* in 1994. The singer died of COVID-related symptoms **on this day** in 2020. Major hits include: 'All I Have to Offer You (Is Me)' (1969), '(I'm So) Afraid of Losing You Again' (1969), 'I Can't Believe That You've Stopped Loving Me' (1970), 'Wonder Could I Love There Anymore' (1970), 'Kiss an Angel Good Morning' (1971), 'I'd Rather Love You' (1971), 'I'm Just Me' (1971), and 'Someone Loves You Honey' released in 1978.

Dec 13th:

One of the great civil rights leaders, and probably the most influential women civil rights activist in America, **Ella Jo Baker** was born **on this day** in 1903. Baker felt that true change had to be organic, built through grassroots activism.

During the Great Depression, living in New York City, Baker worked with the Young Negroes Cooperative League in 1931, and soon became its national director. The League's objective was for the community to pool resources to provide affordable goods and resources. In 1940 Baker joined the National Association for the Advancement of Colored People, (NAACP). She became a field secretary working in and travelling around the South organising new chapters, recruiting members and raising money and later was a national director of branches from 1943 to 1946. Baker was the NAACP's highest-ranking woman. She found the centralisation of leadership, and the cult of personality frustrating, wishing to empower local chapters to encourage grassroots development, embracing the young and women. She resigned her position in 1946.

'In Friendship' was co-founded by Baker to help raise money, from its New York base, for the civil rights movement in the South inspired by the Montgomery Bus Boycott of 1955. Working with **Dr Martin Luther King,** Baker applied her organisational skills to help get the Southern Christian Leadership Conference (SCLC) off the ground in 1957. She worked to encourage voter registration in a drive called Crusade for Citizenship. Again, she was frustrated feeling that King the great orator was too distant from the people. Baker was able to unify rival groups and competing personalities but struggled to get the SCLC, like the NAACP before, to work from the ground up rather than the established top-down model.

In 1960 Ella Baker left the SCLC and once again found herself at the heart of things helping to establish the Student Nonviolent Coordinating Committee (SNCC). She was given the Swahili nickname "Fundi" meaning one who teaches a craft to a new generation. Baker "the godmother of SNCC" encouraged participatory democracy adopting a collectivist model of leadership. With the SCLC she saw a model driven by the personality of Dr King based on the black church which had a predominantly female membership but a predominantly male leadership. As an adult advisor with SNCC Baker wanted to change things, utilising the young and encouraging female inclusion.

When SNCC moved towards the more militant and aggressive Black Power position, Baker took a backseat, largely for health reasons. She was not critical of the Black Power ideology; indeed, she saw the move as positive bringing much needed energy to the civil rights movement. Baker was intensely private, many had no idea she had been married for twenty years to T. J. Roberts, from 1938. The couple divorced in 1958.

In her career she worked closely with the movers and shakers of the movement:

W. E. B. DuBois, Thurgood Marshall, A. Philip Randolph, Diane Nash, Stokely Carmichael, Rosa Parks and **Bob Moses.** But she would prefer to be remembered for her associations and lifelong friendships made with civil rights workers throughout the United States who never became household names. Ella Josephine Baker died **on this day,** her eighty-third birthday. She is buried in Flushing Cemetery, Flushing, Queens County, New York.

Dec 14th:

Details of his birth remain disputed **Ignatius Sancho** records that he was born in Africa. Biographer Joseph Jekyll wrote *Life of Ignatius Sancho* published in 1782. He claims that Sancho was born onboard a slave ship midway across the Atlantic in 1729. The orphaned baby was sold into slavery. Aged two, Sancho arrived in England and was gifted to three sisters who lived in Greenwich, London. Sancho later wrote words to the effect that it was his misfortune to work in a house where ignorance was seen as the only and best way to ensure obedience.

Aged twenty, Sancho ran away to live and work at Montagu House in Greenwich. Befriended by John Montagu, the second Duke of Montagu, Ignatius Sancho was able to access the extensive library.

> IGNATIUS SANCHO
> c 1729 – 1780
>
> African man of letters,
> composer and
> opponent of slavery.
> Born on a slave ship he was
> encouraged to educate himself
> by John 2nd Duke of Montagu
> and served as butler
> to the Duchess
> here in Montague House.

The self-taught Sancho became a man of letters, a writer, composer, social reformer, abolitionist, and observer and commentator of life in eighteenth-century London. Employed at Montagu House, when the duke died Sancho served as the butler to Mary Montagu the Duchess until her death in 1751. He then was employed as a valet to George Montagu through to 1773. When the artist Thomas Gainsborough visited to paint the Duchess in 1768, he also painted a portrait of Sancho. On the Duchess's death Sancho received an annuity of £30 (£7,000 in 2020).

Ignatius Sancho married West Indian Anne Osborne in 1758. The couple had seven children and opened a grocery store in the Westminster area of London. Financially independent and a house owner Sancho qualified to vote which he did in 1774 and again in 1780, becoming the first black Briton to do so. Sancho published four collections of compositions: *Minuets, Cotillons and Country Dances by Ignatius Sancho* published in 1775. He was the first African to publish music in the European tradition. He also wrote a treatise *A Theory of Music and Songs, written in the 1770s*. Sancho already recognised in social circles corresponded widely and was known for his accounts and critiques of politics, economics, slavery and the slave trade. Sancho joined the British Abolitionist Movement and campaigned to end the trade and slavery, writing to editors of newspapers on the subject. Sancho became part of the intellectual black British community of the time and had read **Phillis Wheatley** (see December 5th). He was critical of British colonialism seeing it as morally destructive and demanded that British people dismiss any ideas of superiority over those that looked different.

Ignatius Sancho died **on this day** in 1780, he was either fifty or fifty-one. There is no recognised place of burial. He became the first black person to have an obituary printed in a British newspaper.

Ignatius Sancho's letters were published posthumously, *The Letters of the Late Ignatius Sancho, an African,* in 1782.

Dec 15th:

Fats Waller was one of the greats of jazz, developing modern jazz piano, popularising the Harlem stride style of playing that emerged from ragtime. He copyrighted over 400 songs, many with writing partner, poet **Andy Razaf.**

Fats Waller, jazz pianist, organist, composer, violinist, and singer was born on May 21st 1904. By the age of fifteen he was playing professional organ at the Lincoln theatre in Harlem. By eighteen, Waller was a recording artist. His first recordings took place in October 1922; 'Muscle Shoals Blues and Birmingham Blue'. His first composition for the automatic piano playing machine known as a piano roll was 'Got to Cool My Doggies Now', in 1922. Waller had his first composition 'Squeeze Me', published in 1924.

The piano player's popularity was demonstrated when in 1926 after a performance he was abducted by four gunmen and bundled into a waiting car. Arriving at the Hawthorne Inn, in Chicago, Waller discovered that he was the surprise guest. With a gun at his back Waller played for Al Capone the birthday boy. The composer wrote several Broadway musicals; *Keep Surfin'* (1928), *Hot Chocolate* (1929) and *Early to Bed,* the latter written with George Marion Jr, seeing Waller become the first African American to write a Broadway hit musical for a predominantly white audience. He toured the UK and Ireland in the 1930s, appearing on an early BBC television broadcast in September 1938.

The performer appeared in three films, the most famous being *Stormy Weather* with **Lena Horne** and **Bill 'Bojangles' Robinson** (see May 25th), in 1943. Famous for numerous compositions; 'Lennox Avenue Blues' (1927), 'I Can't Give You Anything but Love' (1928), 'Ain't Misbehavin'' (1929), 'Honeysuckle Rose' (1929), 'Blue Turning Grey Over' (1929), 'I've Got a Feeling I'm Falling' (1929), 'What Did I Do to Be So (Black and Blue)' (1929), and 'Jitterbug Waltz' in 1942.

Fats Waller died unexpectedly from bronchial pneumonia, aged thirty-nine, **on this day** in 1943. His funeral was attended by over 4,200 people at the Abyssinian Baptist Church in Harlem, **Adam Clayton Powell** (see November 29th) gave the eulogy. Waller's ashes were scattered over Harlem from an aeroplane.

Nigerian academic, poet and professor **Solomon Adeboye Babalola** was born on December 17th in 1929. He was educated in Nigeria, Ghana and gained his BA from Cambridge University in England and his PhD from the University of London.

With *Content and Form of Yoruba Ijala,* written in 1966, the professor of African languages and literature at the University of Lagos was credited with preserving African oral traditions. His work *Yoruba Ijala* recorded hunter's songs, chants used by hunters to entertain themselves and translated these into English.

Babalola collected, translated, and helped to preserve the oral poetry and folk tales, tradition in his country. The professor headed up research into African languages.

S. Adeboye Babalola died **on this day** in 2008.

Dec 16th:

Working alongside author **Audre Lorde** (see November 17th) **Barbara Smith** was at the forefront of the black feminist movement. With the Kitchen Table: Women of Colour Press established in 1980, Smith became the first US black publisher of books for women of colour promoting writers such as **Alice Walker** (see February 9th) and **Toni Morrison** (see February 18th).

Barbara Smith.

Born **on this day** in 1946, twin sister to Beverly, Barbara Smith was active in the 1960's civil rights movement. She gained her BA degree from Mount Holyoke College in 1969 and an MA from the University of Pittsburgh in 1971. With the Combahee River Collective, of 1974, Barbara with her sister Beverly and Demita Frazier produced the influential *Combahee River Collective statement*. This critiqued the idea of multiple forms of oppression, intersectional oppression, within the black community, racism in the feminist movement, heterosexism, and issues of class. Intersectional oppression recognised the over representation of lesbians being the victims of hate crime, fatal violence, harassment, homelessness and poor health care. Recognising the scale of the problem the socialist Smith coined the term 'Identity Politics' which provided a roadmap for black lesbians and feminists towards creative expression and political progress. She argued that intelligence was the only option afforded to the black woman as being a fool was too expensive. Smith teaches that feminists have to work to create real change. Smith recognised that neither the male dominated Civil Rights Movement, or the white dominated feminist movement had done enough to address the needs of the black woman, in particular the black lesbian woman.

Barbara Smith started teaching classes at Emerson College on black women in literature in 1973. Her essay 'Towards a Black Feminist Criticism' (1977), received a lot of positive attention. With the publishing company, Kitchen Table, Smith offered a platform for black female authors. She edited 'Home Girls: A Black Feminist Anthology (1983), integrating black lesbian voices with other black women. Kitchen Table: Women of Colour Press disbanded in 1992 following the death of Lorde.

Stonewall awarded the activist, educator and author an Award for Services to the Lesbian and Gay Community in 1994. Barbara Smith entered politics in 2005 elected to the city council with the Albany New York Common Council. In local office she focused her attention on addressing youth violence. That same year Smith was nominated for a Nobel Peace Prize.

Twin sister **Beverly Smith** is a prominent activist and author. Her essays on racism, feminism, identity politics and women's health have been published in the United States.

Dec 17th:

Cape Verdean singer **Cesaria Evora** gained international recognition in Europe, in particular in Poland, far beyond her West African origin. Born on Aug 17th 1941 Evora, commonly called **Cize** and recognised as the **Queen of Morna**, grew up on the Cape Verde Island of Sao Vicente. Her house was a centre for music where many Cape Verdean singers: Djo dEloy, Bana, Eddy Moreno, Luis Morais and Manuel de Novas would gather.

Evora sang at local bars in her hometown of Mindelo and would perform on cruise ships. She sang in Creole Portuguese, Cape Verdean folk songs which were often sorrowful and emotionally charged reflecting the island's history, its association with the slave trade, isolation and emigration. Usually accompanied by guitar, or piano, Evora also performed the up-tempo dance music *mornas e coladeras*. Her cousin Bana encouraged Evora to visit Paris, where the singer songwriter performed and recorded.

Queen of Morna Cesaria Evora.

Cesaria Evora's first commercially recorded album 'La Diva Aux Pieds Nus' *(The Barefoot Diva)* was released in 1988. With the 1992 release of 'Miss Perfumado' the singer toured Europe gaining wide popularity. The 1995 album 'Cesaria' saw her receive her first Grammy Award nomination. 'Cesaria' saw the artist win the KORA All African Music Awards in three categories: Best Artist of West Africa, Best Album and the Merit of the Jury Award. Evora won a second Jury Award in 2010.

The album 'Voz d'Amor' *(Voice of Love)*(2003), saw the Verdean become the first West African to go top ten in the Polish charts, and win the 2004 Grammy award in the World Music category. The tenth studio album 'Rogamar' (2006), charted in six European countries, again going top 10 in Poland.

Touring Australia in 2008 Cesaria Evora had a stroke. She recovered to release her eleventh and final studio album in 2009, 'Nha Sentimento'. The same year the singer was made a knightess of the French Legion of Honour, the first Cape Verdean to receive the honour. Evora's final performance took place in Lisbon on May 8th 2011. Two days later the songwriter had a heart attack and went through surgery. Cesaria Evora died from respiratory failure and hypertension **on this day**, seven months later, in 2011 aged seventy. She died in Sao Vicente. The main airport on the island is named after the singer where a statue was erected. Other legacies include a street name in Paris. She also appeared on a Cape Verdean stamp.

Dec 18th:

Born **on this day** in 1814 into a prominent white New England family, **Josephine Sophia White Griffing** would become an activist in the abolitionist and feminist movements. The campaigner married Charles Griffing when she was twenty in 1835. The couple moved to Ohio where they had five daughters, three survived through to adulthood.

Activity in the anti-slavery movement was immediate as the couple preached for the state to have no union with slave holders. The family home was used as a stop on the Underground Railway route assisting runaway slaves seeking freedom. From 1851–1855, Griffing was an employed agent of the Western Anti-slavery Society. She would travel on speaking tours and write abolitionist articles for newspapers such as the anti-slavery *Bugle of Salem*. During this time, as a founding member, Griffing was elected president of the Ohio Women's Rights Association. Josephine Griffing would later lecture on behalf of the Women's National Loyal League demanding immediate emancipation during the Civil War years from 1863–65.

Following the Civil War, Josephine moved with her daughters to Washington DC. It is not clear why she left her husband behind. Once in the capital she got to work helping the freed families that were descending on the city in their thousands seeking work, food, and shelter. Griffing lobbied for the creation of an official government body to provide support and give direction for the newly emancipated people. The Bureau of Refugees, Freedmen and Abandoned Lands was formed in 1865 and operated through to 1872. Although Griffing worked for the Bureau in 1865 and 1867 she never felt comfortable with the organisation's military structure and style of management. She argued that the Bureau was too impersonal and failed to meet the immediate needs to provide food, shelter and health provisions before finding employment. Nonetheless Griffing helped to maintain employment offices in Northern cities.

Josephine Griffing helped to found the American Equal Rights Association in 1866 and acted as its first vice president. The Association worked to create equal rights irrespective of race, sex, colour or class. The following year she founded and acted as president of the Universal Franchise Association of the District of Columbia. Two years later in 1869 Griffin joined the National Woman Suffrage Association when it was formed on May 15th of that year.

Records show that the fifty-seven-year-old Josephine Griffing died from consumption, (tuberculosis) on February 18th 1872. She is buried at Burrow Hill Cemetery, Hebron, Tolland County, Connecticut, USA.

Lord David Pitt, Baron Pitt of Hampstead was born October 3rd 1913 in Grenada. He won a scholarship to study at the University of Edinburgh, Scotland, graduating in 1938. That same year he returned to the West Indies setting up a medical practice in Trinidad.

While studying in the UK Pitt joined the British Labour party. In Trinidad he continued his political activity helping to found the socialist West Indian National Party, serving as the party president from 1943-47. The National Party advocated Trinidad independence and the formation of a West Indian Federation. Universal suffrage was granted to Trinidad and Tobago in 1945. The first elections were held in 1946.

Pitt travelled to England to campaign for independence, ending up settling in the country in 1947. He established a medical practice in Euston, London which ran for thirty years. A historical blue plaque identifies where his surgery once was.

Pitt was active fighting discrimination faced by the growing black immigrant population in the 1950s. He argued that it was not enough to believe that racism and discrimination is wrong. Such ideals had to be reflected and enshrined in the laws of the land. Pitt stood for election to parliament in 1959 becoming the first West Indian to do so. He faced death threats and racism in his failed bid but stood again in 1970. Although shaken he was not put off politics. Victory in 1961 saw David Pitt represent Hackney on the London County Council (LCC) later absorbed into the Greater London Council (GLC) in 1964. Pitt served as vice chair of the GLC 1969–70 and was the first black chair 1974–75.

Following the failed election bid of 1959, with the ferocious racism and discrimination Pitt founded the Campaign Against Racial Discrimination and served as its first and only chair. Prime minister Harold Wilson appointed Pitt to the House of Lords in 1975. He became the second black peer in the Lords after **Constantine Learie** (see March 26th). David Pitt would go on to be the longest serving black parliamentarian.

A pioneer in the anti-apartheid movement, his basement was used by the organisation but was attacked and set alight by opponents on March 4th 1961. Pitt also supported the Campaign for Nuclear Disarmament. He was criticised by some in the black community for his calls to recruit more black people into the armed forces. David Pitt worked tirelessly campaigning for the Race Relations Acts of 1968 and 1976 (see December 8th).

On February 3rd 1975, David Pitt became Lord Pitt of Hampstead in Greater London and of Hampstead in Grenada, where he was born. He would later say that his greatest achievement was being appointed president of the British Medical Association, 1985–1986. The Lord Pitt Foundation was established in 1983, his seventieth year. Pitt died at the age of eighty-one **on this day** in 1994. His body was repatriated and buried in Grenada.

One of the Little Rock Nine (see September 5th) she was only fourteen, the youngest. **Carlotta Walls LaNier** was born **on this day** in 1942. After facing hostilities, death threats, being spat at, the family home bombed on February 9th 1960, LaNier became the first black female to graduate from Little Rock Central High School in 1960. Her parents first discovered that their daughter had applied to attend the all-white, high school when the registration documents arrived in the mail.

Carlotta married Ira (Ike) LaNier in 1968. The couple had two children. The real estate businesswoman and mother continuously travelled the country talking about civil rights, opportunities, and her story. With the other eight, LaNier received the Congressional Gold Medal from President Bill Clinton in 1999.

Working with Lisa Frazier Page, Carlotta Walls LaNier told her story in *A Mighty Long Way: My Journey to Justice at Little Rock Central High School* (2009).

As president of the Little Rock Nine Foundation, LaNier works to promote equal opportunities, in particular in the field of education.

Benjamin O Davis Jr born **on this day** 1912 was a United States air general. He became the first black, four-star general appointed in retirement by President Bill Clinton on December 9th 1998. Junior's father **Benjamin O Davis Sr** made history becoming the first African American general in the United States Army.

Davis Jr earned his wings in 1942 and became the first black officer to fly an Army Air Corps aircraft solo. Promoted to lieutenant colonel in July 1942 Davis was named commander of the first all-black air unit the 99th Pursuit Squadron. Sent to North Africa, Tunisia the squadron saw combat on June 2nd 1943. Opposition to a fighting black unit led to accusations that the 99th were below par and not fit for service. An independent enquiry at Davis' behest revealed that with second rate aircraft the 99th were doing a sterling job and were no worse or better than their white counterparts.

Later that year in September Davis was deployed to command the 332nd Fighter Group. They would be known as the Tuskegee Airmen (see March 19th). After arriving in Italy, the 332nd flew 15,000 sorties, shot down 112 enemy planes and destroyed or damaged a further 273 on the ground with only a personal loss of 66 planes plus twenty-five bombers. In one night in Jan 1944 the squadron shot down 12 German planes. Davis flew 60 combat missions during the war.

On 16th July 1948 following President Harry S. Truman's executive order 9981, the forces were ordered to desegregate. With Davis's direction the Air Force was the first branch to be fully integrated. Davis became the first African American major general (two star) in 1959 and was promoted to lieutenant general in 1965 (three star).

Benjamin O. Davis Jr wrote his autobiography *Benjamin O. Davis Jr, American* 1991.

His wife Agatha died on March 10th 2002; she was ninety-four. Davis died a few months later on July 4th that same year. He was eighty-nine. The couple were buried at Arlington National Cemetery.

Benjamin O. Davis Sr

Roscoe Robinson Jr October 11th 1928 – July 22nd 1993 was the first African American four-star general in the United States Army in 1982. **Daniel 'Chappie' James** February 12th 1920 – February 25th 1978 became the first black, four-star general with the US Air Force on September 1st 1975.

Dec 19th:

His parents were enslaved people, when freedom came, they said it was the happiest day of their lives. Their son the historian, activist, educator and journalist, **Carter Godwin Woodson,** was born **on this day** 1875. Poverty meant that Carter Woodson was unable to attend school until he was twenty in 1895. Less than two years later he graduated in 1897 from Douglass High School. A career in teaching followed. Earning a BA degree in literature in 1903 was followed by Woodson going to the Philippines where he served as a school supervisor 1903–1907. With his PhD from Harvard University in 1912, Woodson became the second black graduate after **W. E. B. Dubois** (see February 23rd) to earn a doctorate from the prestigious university.

Recognising the limitations, bias and disinterest of the American History Association with regards to the black story, Woodson along with **William D. Hartgrove, George Cleveland Hall, Alexander L. Jackson** and **James E. Stamp,** founded the Association for the Study of Negro Life and History on September 15th 1915 in Chicago. The name of the association was altered in 1973 to the Association for the Study of African American Life and History (ASALH). As the president of ASALH, Woodson's mission was to address the cliches, traditional bias, distortions, and omissions of the black presence in history. In 1916 Woodson edited the association's quarterly publication: *The Journal of Negro History*. The important scholarly periodical continued through to 2001.

With the promotion and establishing of **Negro History Week** during the second week of February 1926 Woodson set the foundation for greater things to come. The week was used to look at, learn about, and promote the black contribution to history and civilization. The second week of February was chosen to coincide with the birthdays of Abraham Lincoln and **Frederick Douglass** (see February 14th). Black history month was first proposed at Kent State University in the USA in 1969 and adopted in 1970 from

January 2nd through to February 28th. The idea would go national and then international, taking root in the UK through **Akyaaba Addai-Sebo** (see October 1st) in 1987 and **Jean Augustine** (see September 9th) in Canada in 1996.

Carter Woodson founded and was the president of Associated Publishers. Recognising limited interest by established white owned publishers to bring black books to market, Associated Publishers focused on books looking at black life and culture. Woodson wrote *The Education of the Negro Prior to 1861* in 1915, *A Century of Negro Migration* in 1918, the celebrated *The Negro in Our History* in 1927, and *The History of the Negro Church* in 1927. When he died Woodson had been working on the projected six volume *Encyclopaedia African.*

Carter's sister **Bessie Woodson Yancey,** May 1882 – January 1st 1958, was a poet, teacher and activist. Probably her most famous work was *Echoes from the Hills* (1939). *The Hills* is recognised as the first work of Affrilachian for children. Affrilachian is a term coined in the 1990s by the writer **Frank X. Walker** focusing on the cultural contributions of African American artists, writers and musicians in the Appalachian region of the USA.

Woodson continued work as an academic. He was the dean of the College of Liberal Arts and head of the graduate faculty at Howard University, 1919–1920. From 1920–1922 he served as dean at the West Virginia State College Institute. Carter Woodson died unexpectedly of a heart attack on April 3rd 1950, he was seventy-four. Woodson is buried at the Lincoln Memorial cemetery, Suitland in Maryland, USA.

James Bevel, ordained Baptist minister and pastor at the Chestnut Grove Baptist Church was a leading figure in the voting rights drive and architect of the 1960s civil rights strategies.

Born on October 19th 1936 Bevel would be trained in Gandhian nonviolent tactics by **James Lawson** (see September 22nd) along with fellow students; **Diane Nash** (see May 15th)**, John Lewis** (see February 21st)**, Marion Barry,** and **Bernard Lafayette.** Bevel was a powerful, persuasive and inspirational preacher who would passionately connect faith to action. He was present at and helped to organise sit-ins in the early 1960s and was present at the meeting that led to the formation of the Student Nonviolent Coordinating Committee (SNCC). Bevel helped to organise the freedom rides of 1961. That same year he married Diane Nash. The couple would have two children but divorced in 1968.

Bevel left SNCC to join **Dr King**'s Southern Christian Leadership Conference in 1962, becoming the Mississippi field secretary. The following year it was Bevel that placed children on the frontline in what was known as the Birmingham Children's Crusade, 1963. Bevel's strategies to desegregate Birmingham gained international attention with the children facing Bull Conner's dogs, water hoses and seeing over 600 go to prison. Embedding the importance of nonviolence and discipline, Bevel employed the tactic during the Selma voting rights movement of 1963. He was responsible for the strategies behind the Selma to Montgomery march of that year. It was Bevel who suggested the SCLC call for and to join in the 1963 'March on Washington'. That same year he was appointed SCLC's national director of direct action and nonviolent action.

James Bevel moved to Chicago in 1965. With concerns over the USA's increasing involvement in the war in Vietnam, Bevel took the role as the national director of the Spring Mobilisation Committee to end the war. Bevel was present at the Lorraine Motel when Martin Luther King was assassinated. He would later fall out with SCLC who were critical of Bevel's increasingly erratic behaviour who would argue that

James Earl Ray (see June 10th) was not responsible for King's death and that he possessed evidence, although he never produced anything remotely incriminating.

James Bevel got involved in politics, as a Republican, but failed to get elected. He helped to organise the Million Man March in 1995. The new century saw Bevel's reputation tarnished. The ordained minister experienced a spectacular fall from grace. On trial in April 2008 accused of incest with one daughter and having sexually abused three others James Bevel was found guilty of unlawful fornication. He was given a fifteen-year sentence and fined $50,000. Released after seven months and awaiting his appeal James Bevel died of pancreatic cancer **on this day** in 2008. One of the central figures in the Civil Rights Movement he was seventy-two.

Dec 20th:

There have been numerous entries in this book that focused on the historical transatlantic slave trade, **Samuel Cotton's** life and work urgently reminds the reader of the insidious continuation of modern slavery. Born on January 24th 1947 and raised in New York City, Cotton dedicated his adult life to raising awareness among Americans to the existence of contemporary slavery and human rights abuses in Mauritania and Sudan.

Writing for the Brooklyn based African American newspaper *City Sun*, Cotton the journalist was sent to North Africa, in 1995, to investigate allegations of the enslavement of Africans in Mauritania and Sudan. Going undercover for twenty-eight days, Cotton interviewed enslaved and former enslaved people and spoke to local leaders of anti-slavery organisations. Cotton estimated that in Mauritania there were some 90,000 enslaved Africans. Samuel Cotton concluded that race was the driver and determining factor observing that it was darker Africa Muslims and Christians who were placed into bondage by their lighter skinned countrymen, usually of Arabic descent.

That same year Cotton organised the Coalition Against Slavery in Mauritania and Sudan (CASMAS), following an international conference on chattel slavery. In 1996 Samuel Cotton presented his findings to Congress before the Subcommittee on International Operations and Human Rights. The book and documentary film on Cotton's investigative work chronicling his abolitionist activity in the USA and Mauritania, *Silent Terror: A Journey into Contemporary African Slavery,* appeared in 1998. Samuel Cotton set up the Freedmen's Bureau to educate, feed, clothe and house former enslaved people in Mauritania.

Samuel Cotton was accused of being a puppet for Jews and seen by the Nation of Islam as hostile to their faith. He appeared on television and travelled the country, giving talks and being involved in debates, looking at contemporary slavery. He made it clear that he was neither opposed to Arabs or to Islam, just the enslavement of people.

The former journalist taught US social welfare policy at Columbia University School of Social Work. He had also worked with mentally ill criminals. Samuel Cotton died from a brain tumour **on this day** in 2003, he was aged fifty-six.

The injustice of modern slavery and child labour.

Amara Essy was born **on this day** in Côte d'Ivoire in 1944. Although a practicing Muslim he married a Roman Catholic, the couple have six children.

Essy's remarkable diplomatic career for Cote d'Ivoire started with Brazil in 1971. He has since held a variety of diplomatic, ambassadorial and special envoy positions working in Switzerland, Argentina, Cuba, Central African Republic, Madagascar, the Republic of Congo, Gabon and Angola.

Essy represented his country at the UN from 1973–75. In 1977 he was the president of the Group of 77, a non-aligned organisation of 134 less developed countries based in Geneva. Essy was elected as the vice-president of the United Nation General Assembly (1988–89) and its president (1994–95). Fluent in English, French and Portuguese the qualified lawyer was the president of the UN Security Council from 1990–91. **Kofi Anan** (see April 8th) chose the experienced Ivoirian, recognised for his negotiation and resolutions skills, to be the UN special envoy to the Central Republic of Africa.

Amara Essy served as the foreign minister for Cote d'Ivoire for ten years from 1990. The new century saw the diplomat and politician elected head of the Organisation of African Unity (OAU) in 2001. He oversaw the OAU's transition to the African Union, (AU). The AU had greater powers of intervention where it was deemed necessary to stop sovereign states from engaging in acts which violated human rights, to prevent crimes against humanity and genocide. Essy served as the AU's interim chairperson from 2002-2003. In 2009 he was appointed as the AU's special envoy to Madagascar. He continued to work as a member of the Global Leadership Foundation, a not-for-profit and non-government organisation composed of former heads of state and distinguished political leaders, assisting countries to develop proper governance and supporting democratic institutions.

Dec 21st:

There would appear to be some discrepancy as to the correct date of birth for the Ghanaian nationalist leader. Most articles say **J. B. Danquah** was born on December 18th in 1895, others say **on this day** in 1895.

Joseph Kwame Kyeretwie Boakye Danquah author, politician, scholar, and lawyer is described as one of the founding fathers of Ghana, the dean of Ghanaian nationalist politicians and the doyen of Gold

Coast politics. Having studied in Britain, Danquah became the first West African to obtain a Doctor of Philosophy degree from a British University in 1927.

On returning to what was called the Gold Coast he established a private legal practice. With the founding of the Times of West Africa he published the country's first daily newspaper in 1931. The moderate but elitist political party United Gold Coast Convention (UGCC) was co-founded by Danquah, becoming the colony's first political party. The UGCC stood for constitutional reform and campaigned for self-governance. The party would later split from the eventual independent Ghanaian president Kwame Nkrumah (see January 2nd) who formed the populist Convention People's Party (CPP). Ghana became the first of Britain's former African colonies to gain independence on March 6th in 1957. J. B. Danquah was the official opposition to Nkrumah and the CPP. Critical of the president, Danquah was accused of attempting to subvert the ruling CCP.

Key Ghanaian politicians with J. B. Danquah (bottom right).

He was imprisoned for a year in 1961 under the Preventative Detention Act. Released on June 22nd 1962, Danquah was elected president of the Ghanaian bar association that same year.

On January 8th 1964 Danquah was arrested again for allegedly plotting against the president and detained in Nsawam prison. J. B. Danquah suffered and died from a heart attack in detention on February 4th 1964. Among J. B. Danquah's most famous writings are *Gold Coast: Akan Laws and Customs and the Akim Abuakwa Constitution* (1928). *Akan Doctrine of God* (1944), was adopted by Protestant Christians to reclaim their African heritage. The author also wrote the play *The Third Woman* in 1943. Danquah lobbied for the creation of the University of Ghana established in 1948. The university is the oldest and largest of the country's thirteen national public universities.

I first came across this quote when reading **Desmond Tutu**. I do not know if he was the first or whether he borrowed it from another source, but the quote beautifully demonstrates the awkward relationship that Africa has had with missionaries and religion.

"When the missionaries came to Africa, they had the Bible, and we had the land. They said, 'Let us pray.' We closed our eyes. When we opened them, we had the Bible, and they had the land."

The Scottish missionary **Robert Moffat** was born **on this day** in 1795. Sent out to South Africa, with four others by the London Missionary Society on 18th December 1816, Moffat arrived on the continent at Cape Town in 1817. He would settle in Kuruman, 1825, southeast of the Kalahari Desert, spending the next fifty years working, preaching and travelling.

Moffat mastered Dutch and one of the main regional languages, Tswana. His linguistic skills were so remarkable that by 1830 he had translated the *Gospel of Luke* into Tswana. The New Testament's translation was completed by 1840, and the whole of the Bible by 1857. Moffat found time to produce a book of hymns in the Tswana language.

Committed to the mission Moffat was respected as a blacksmith and carpenter, he introduced agricultural methods and irrigation to the arid area. He married Mary Smith in 1819 in Cape Town. The couple would go on to have 10 children. Robert and Mary worked together establishing a thriving mission. They met their future son-in-law **David Livingstone** in 1840. His daughter married the famous missionary four years later.

Although dedicated and well meaning, Robert Moffat never truly embraced the African and failed to forge real friendships with the people. He, like Livingstone and later **Albert Schweitzer,** would be criticised for being too paternalistic. Moffat preached his final sermon on the continent in March 1870. Back in England Mary died in 1871. Moffat wrote *Missionary Labour and Scenes in South Africa* (1840), making him the most famous missionary of his age. He also wrote *Rivers of Water in a Dry Place* (1863). Robert Moffat continued to preach and travel throughout England raising funds for the London Missionary Society. He died on August 9th in 1883.

Schweitzer   Livingstone   and Moffat.

Dec 22nd:

The story of the slave ship **The Zong** would mark just one of numerous lows in the transatlantic slave trade. The ship's name *Zong* ironically means *Care* in Dutch. **On this day** in 1781, the ship arrived at the port on Black River in Jamaica. On board was the human cargo of 208 Africans.

The ship had set sail from Africa on August 18th 1781 with 442 captives. The crew of seventeen men was inadequate to meet the ship's sanitary requirements. The number of Africans numbered twice what a ship like the Zong would be expected to carry. Crossing the Atlantic saw the captain, and former ship surgeon Luke Collingwood incapacitated through illness. Collingwood would die three days after the ship landed at Black River. The captain's second in command, first mate James Kelsall had been suspended following an argument on November 14th. It was unclear who was in charge of the vessel. A navigational blunder saw the Zong pass Jamaica, which had been in sight, travelling a further 300 miles (480 km).

Conditions onboard saw illness, poor sanitation, and malnutrition resulting in the death of some crew and at least sixty Africans. Water and food provisions were running low. After consultation it was agreed to jettison some of the cargo. On November 29th fifty-four women and children were thrown through cabin windows to their death. December 1st saw forty-two men thrown overboard. Over the next few days, a further thirty-six people were jettisoned. Ten Africans committed suicide jumping to their deaths. In total 142 Africans were killed. When the slave ship arrived in Jamaica there were 208 Africans alive. Legally for purposes of insurance if any of the human cargo died on land then the £30 per head cover could not be claimed. If the African died from natural causes on route insurance claims could be challenged. 'General Average' was a law that argued that if a loss had to be made in order to secure the remaining cargo, then insurers were obliged to pay for that loss; if a ship is sinking and to ensure it remains afloat cargo has to be jettisoned that is considered General Average.

The surviving Africans were sold off at an average of £36 per person, totalling £7,488. The syndicate that owned the human cargo included Edward Wilson, George Case, James Aspinall and William, James & John Gregson. John Gregson was Mayor of Liverpool in 1762 and would be directly responsible for the shipment of 58,000 Africans into slavery. When the syndicate claimed insurance for their loss the insurance company refused to pay. The court case Gregson v Gilbert was heard on March 6th 1783. The ship's logbook had been lost, some fear that it had been destroyed. The jury found in favour of the slavers. The case received limited public attention. When news of the Zong reached England only one newspaper covered the story and that was eighteen months after the event.

Fresh evidence brought to light that there had been heavy rainfall and that water could have been collected and stored. The appeal case suggested that the captain and crew were at fault. The Africans were still determined to be cargo and therefore the insurers had to pay out. Witness to the original case, former slave **Olaudah Equiano** (see March 31st) contacted anti-slavery campaigner **Granville Sharp** (see Nov 10th). Sharp unsuccessfully pursued the crew through the courts but no-one was convicted for the massacre. Over the years the Zong became a cause celebre used by the abolitionist movement. It would be a further twenty years before the British abolished the slave trade on 25th March 1807 and eventually slavery in 1833.

Born **on this day** in 1960 to Haitian and Puerto Rican parents, American artist **Jean-Michel Basquiat** had a rock star feel and style about him as did his work. He started out as a graffiti artist influenced by punk, rap, street art, hip-hop culture and his experiences as a black man. The neo-expressionist street art was never going to be to everyone's liking. The abstract nature of his work, employing words and symbols, would not appeal to traditionalists or purists. But the power of his character, the energy of his youth, the contemporary images, the attacks on structures of power and the rage against systems of racism found in his canvases would connect with many in the world of art.

Basquiat elevated street art and graffiti, gaining wall space in New York's galleries. He moved from an underground graffiti artist into a painter. Basquiat's work captured the moment reflecting his hectic, somewhat hedonistic life. Jean-Michel Basquiat would be dead by twenty-seven from a heroin overdose. He, like his work, was a series of contradictions and dichotomies turning things inside out, juxtaposing wealth and poverty, integration, and segregation, pitting inner against outer.

Born December 22nd 1960 Basquiat died August 12th in 1988. At Sotheby's May 2017 his 1982 painting *Untitled* sold for $10.5 million a record, at the time, for an American artist.

Artist Jean Basquiat

Dec 23rd:

Self-made millionaire, some argue America's first certified, self-made female millionaire, **Sarah Breedlove** would become famous and rich as **Madam C. J. Walker** providing cosmetics and hair care products for black women.

Her parents and older siblings were all born into slavery. Born **on this day** in 1867 Sarah would be born free. Following the end of the Civil War life for many, especially the emancipated population, was hard. By the age of seven the girl was orphaned. The next few years saw the girl live with other family members finding work when and where she could.

Aged fourteen, in a bid to escape abuse and gain security, Sarah married Moses McWilliams in 1882. On June 16th 1885 she gave birth to her daughter A'Lelia. By the age of twenty Sarah would be widowed. Sarah Breedlove married a second time to John Davis in 1894. The marriage was short-lived, seeing the couple separate in around 1903.

Sarah's brothers were barbers and at the time, 1905, their sister was learning from them and the black hair entrepreneur **Annie Turnbo Malone.** The following year Sarah married **Charles J. Walker.** The couple worked together with Charles encouraging his wife to take the name Madam C. J. Walker. Walker and Malone fell out with Malone claiming, without any evidence, that Walker had stolen her hair formula. C. J. Walker had an amazing business mind recognising the need to have a brand and to connect with her clientele. She would go door to door communicating with black women. There were products on the market for the black woman but these were usually made by white companies who did not always appreciate the needs of their customers. C. J. Walker had lost her hair due to a scalp problem. She understood the needs of her people. Walker developed a pomade and other cosmetics, but it was producing her own lotions and promoting her products that made the essential difference. She trained women to go door to door and rewarded her workers accordingly. At the height of the Madam C. J. Walker Manufacturing Company, she was employing 3,000 people. The whole package became known as the 'Walker Method'. In 1908 the entrepreneur opened a factory and her beauty salon in Pittsburgh. Two years later and a move to Indianapolis C. J. Walker was making annual profits equal to several million dollars in today's money. C. J. did not just train her sales team she also trained the beauticians.

Business woman Madam C. J. Walker.

Following her divorce from Charles, 1912, C. J. travelled to South America and the Caribbean promoting the 'Walker *Method*' and her products. On returning to the United States, she moved to a townhouse in New York City. The residence became a centre for many in the up-and-coming Harlem Renaissance. Two years later in 1918 C. J. moved to Villa Lewaro, a home designed by the African American architect **Vertner Woodson Tandy** in Irvington-on-Hudson, twenty miles north of New York City. It would be designated a National Landmark in 1976.

C. J. Walker used her money on philanthropic ventures providing education scholarships, money to homes for the elderly, to the National Association for the Advancement of Colored People, and helping to finance the National Conference on Lynching, and gave money to the construction of a YMCA in Indianapolis in 1913. C. J. Walker died from hypertension on May 27th in 1919. She was fifty-one. C. J. Walker was buried in Woodlawn Cemetery in the Bronx, New York.

The Immigration Restriction Act came into law, assented, **on this day** in 1901. Australia became a federation in January 1901. The government of the first prime minister Edmund Barton immediately embarked on a white Australia policy. Drafted by Alfred Deakin, the country's second prime minister, the act required any selected migrant to pass a diction test in any European language of fifty words. If they failed, then entry was denied. After 1905 the test could be in any language. Entry could be denied if one was considered to be from an undesirable country, had a criminal record, considered morally unfit, or had medical issues such as an infectious or contagious disease.

The policy was clearly to keep the country white. For the following four decades Australia offered British people favourable entry to residency. The white Australia policy officially ended in 1958. All related laws were removed by 1975 with the passing of the Racial Discrimination Act.

Dec 24th:

Octavia V. R. Albert was born into slavery **on this day** 1853. With the end of the American Civil War and the Emancipation Proclamation she gained her freedom. Trained as a teacher, the twenty-one-year-old Octavia married fellow teacher **Dr Aristide E. P. Albert** in 1874. The couple had a daughter.

Dr Albert was ordained as a minister in the African Methodist Episcopal church in 1877. Octavia passionately believed teaching to be a Christian vocation. Over a period of fifteen years Octavia interviewed over a dozen former enslaved people recording their experiences, how they were affected by slavery, how they coped with freedom and how they adjusted to the new world following the war, emancipation and the eleven years of the Reconstruction period. She first met **Charlotte Brooks,** in 1879, the main focus of her interviews and work. There were others including **John** and **Lorendo Goodwin, Lizzie Beaufort, Colonel Douglass Wilson** and the female known only as **Hattie.**

Octavia Albert, the biographer who documented slavery in the United States, compiled her findings to tell their story to correct and create history. She wrote in the hope that all Christians would take responsibility for slavery, its lessons and legacy. She died on August 19th 1889. Her husband and daughter were able to get Octavia's life work published posthumously as *House of Bondage,* or *Charlotte Brooks and Other Slaves,* in 1890.

While Octavia V. R. Albert was compiling records from enslaved people, interviewing and chronicling their experiences about the post-civil war reconstruction period, white supremacist groups were forming. Knights of the White Camellia was launched in Louisiana 1867, there was also the White Brotherhood. But the most infamous, notorious and feared of all the white supremacist groups would be the **Ku Klux Klan.**

The KKK was founded **on this day** in 1865 by six former officers of the Confederate army Frank McCord, Richard Reed, John Lester, John Kennedy, J. Calvin Jones and James Crow. Whatever the original intentions of the KKK, the desire to oppose the political emancipation of the black population, to fight the perceived supportive liberal left policies of the Republican party and to re-establish white political and economic superiority was soon the clarion cry.

Ku Klux is derived from the Greek word kyklos meaning circle. Chapters of the KKK or Klan quickly formed throughout the South. The loosely organised groups were largely autonomous but acted with a unifying zeal to thwart what was viewed as radical reconstruction giving the black population voting, political and employment rights, towards achieving social equality. The group were instantly recognisable in their bazaar but threatening conical head covering, used to hide their identity, and flowing white dresses. Threatening behaviour was commonplace seeing the masked Klan attacking victims, usually black and at night under the cover of darkness. Ten per cent of the blacks voted for, winning elections in 1867 and sixty-eight were victims of violence with seven murdered. January 1871 saw 500 masked men attack the Union County Jail in South Carolina and lynch eight black prisoners. Lynching, burning of crosses, rallies, parades, marches and demonstrations were common and a constant source of intimidation. The KKK were successful in achieving their mission. By 1876 the entire South was under Democrat control.

Nathan Bedford Forrest was the first KKK national leader, the grand wizard, standing over the grand dragons, grand titans and grand cyclops. The look and names would sound and appear comical but with membership crossing class lines, and law enforcement either belonging to the Klan or refusing to act against it, and witnesses refusing to come forward and staying silent, the KKK got away with hundreds of murderous acts. Leading white citizens in the South remained silent giving their tacit approval to the Klan's actions. Psychological and sociological investigative work needed to have looked at what had happened to so many in the white community that led to the fears and rise of white supremacy?

The Republican federal government passed the Enforcement Acts of 1870 and 1871 contained three bills. Popularly known as the Klan Acts the three bills sought to protect African American rights to vote, hold office, serve on juries and have equal protection under the law. By 1870 the KKK was the main vehicle in the South for white resistance groups. They had proved to be successful in their immediate aims at suppressing the black population. They did not just have African Americans in their sights. The white supremacists saw and targeted immigrants, Jews, Roman Catholics, homosexuals, the far left and organised labour. They adopted a neo-confederate position, later taking neo-fascist and neo-Nazi ideologies onboard.

The Ku Klux Klan saw a revival in the 1910s and 1920s off the back of immigration, Thomas Dixon's *The Clansman* (1905), D. W. Griffith's 1915 *Birth of a Nation*, and the Bolshevik 1917 revolution. At its peak membership was as high as 4 million. By the 1940s the KKK disbanded having become largely irrelevant with a loss of membership following the Great Depression and the war years. The Civil Rights Movement of the 1950s and 1960s saw a resurgence and Klan numbers rise. There was an increase in threatening behaviour, killings, church, school, and homes were bombed. As with Klan crimes in the 1870s most murders saw no convictions. Where convictions did take place, they occurred decades after the events and were only due to the dogged efforts of a few determined individuals and organisations in their fight to get justice.

Dec 25th:

Jupiter Hammon is believed to be the first African American published. Born on October 17th 1711 into slavery to Henry Lloyd, Hammon spent his life enslaved working for four generations of the family.

An Evening Thought: Salvation by Christ, With Penitential Cries, was written **on this day** in 1760 and published in 1761. Hammon wrote eight published works all of a religious nature. His second published work came eighteen years later *An Address to Miss **Phillis Wheatley***. Wheatley (see December 5th), also enslaved at the time, had her book of poetry published in London in 1773. The pair never met. Other works of poetry and prose published by Hammon include *The Kind Master and the Dutiful Servant* (1778) and *A Poem for Children with Thoughts on Death* (1782).

Jupiter Hammond was respected within the black community and was permitted to preach to his enslaved brothers and sisters. Taught to read and write he worked for the Lloyd family business as a negotiator and bookkeeper. At the age of seventy-six and still not free, on September 24th 1786 Hammond delivered what would be known as the Hammon Address, *An Address to Negroes of the State of New York*. Hammon spoke of the hope that younger black enslaved people would be freed and that in heaven being black did not matter.

Although a valuable member of the Lloyd family estate, Jupiter Hammon was nonetheless enslaved for all his ninety-plus years. We have no records of when he died but research points to 1806. He was buried in an unmarked grave.

Abolitionist, feminist, close friend and supporter of **Harriet Tubman** (see September 17th) **Martha Coffin Wright** was born **on this day** in 1806. Her home at 192 Genesee Street, Auburn, New York became a staging post on the Underground Railroad sheltering fugitive slaves.

Martha C Wright.

Martha Coffin Wright co-signed the Declaration of Sentiments. Sixty-eight women and thirty-two men signed the document in 1848 at the first Woman's Rights Convention attended and supported by **Frederick Douglass** (see February 14th). The document sought to gain political, religious civil and social rights for women. Wright died in 1875 on January 4th. She is buried in Fort Hill cemetery Auburn.

The son of an imam who received his early education in Islamic schools **Abdoulaye Sadji** was one of the pioneers of **negritude** (see **Alioune Diop**, January 10th) the thought-provoking teaching and lifestyle that emerged between the world wars. Negritude looked to establishing an African identity amongst the French speaking Africans. It looked back at African traditions to inform its future avoiding assimilation and evolution based on western values. The ideas informed anti-colonial thinking and activity.

Abdoulaye Sadji was born in 1910. The teacher was one of the first Senegalese qualified to teach in the country's high schools. He became the second Senegalese to earn a bachelor's degree in 1932. Writing with the future president **Leopold Sedar Senghor** (see October 9th) Sadji produced *La Belle Histoire de Leuk-le Lièvre (The Splendid History of Leuk the Hare)* in 1953. The elementary school reading book became a classic collection of traditional stories from Africa.

Sadji wrote two novels: *Maimouna: Petite Fille Noire* in 1953, and *Nini Mulatresse du Senegal* in 1954. He also produced short stories, the best-known being *Tounka* (1952) and *Modou-Fatim* (1955). Abdoulaye Sadji's work often saw young women challenged by the changing face of their society, rural to urban, tradition being lost to an ever-creeping modernising westernised world. The women's experiences, hopes, challenges, doubts, and disillusions reflected that faced by the continent. The writer and teacher Abdoulaye

Sadji died **on this day** in 1961. For exponents of negritude see **Aime Cesaire,** June 26th, **Ousmane Soce** on October 31st, **David Diop** July 9th, and **Birago Diop** November 25th.

White Angolan multi-faceted figure **Joachim Dias Cordeiro Da Matta** was born **on this day** in 1857. He had a passion to discover the culture, tradition and history of his country being one of the first to promote autochthonous (native literature).

The self-taught poet, novelist, journalist, historian, folklorist, and philologist (the study of the history of language) and teacher lived during a period in the 1880s which saw a growth in Angolan literary activity. Although a lot of Matta's original papers and works were lost, *Delirios (Delirium) from* 1887 and individual verses from *Almanach de Lembrancas* survived along with his Kimbundu-Portuguese dictionary of 1893. Kimbundu is the second largest ethnolinguistic group in Angola. Matta is famous for having collected traditional proverbs; *Filosofia Popular em Proverbios Angolenses (Popular Philosophy in Angolan Proverbs) published in 1989.*

Joachim Matta developed a respect and knowledge for Kimbundu culture. He believed that to understand African history one has to cultivate literary and intellectual life. Metta investigated the history, legends, folklore and language of the country. His lost works include his many poems, two unpublished novels and *A Verdadeira Historia da Rainha Jinga (The True Story of Queen Jinga)* which documented the life of the seventeenth century Queen Mbundu who resisted Portuguese expansion.

Arlindo do Carmo Pires Barbeitos born December 24th 1940, is a white Angolan writer. Writing in Portuguese his work focuses on Angola's struggle for independence and the harmony between humans and nature. During the independence struggles Barbeitos taught at many of the political bases of the Popular Movement for the Liberation of Angola.

Barbeitos' poems include 'Angola Angolê Angolema' (1976), 'Nzoji' (Dreams) (1979), 'O rio: estórias de regresso' (The River Tales of Return) (1985), 'Fiapos de sonho' (Threads of Dreams) (1992) and 'Na Leveza do Luar Crescente' in 1998.

Dec 26th:

Adolphe Silvestre Felix Eboue was born **on this day** in French Guiana (Guyana). He rose through the pre independent French system becoming secretary general in 1932, and later acting governor of Martinique. He served as the secretary general from 1934 to 36, in French Sudan now Mali. Felix Eboue became the first black man in the French colonies to hold a high office post becoming the first black governor of Guadeloupe in 1936.

Felix Eboue.

On November 12th 1940 he was appointed governor of French Equatorial Africa (Chad).

With the fall of France to Nazi Germany and the rise of the Vichy government on August 26th 1940 Eboue declared his support for Charles de Gaulle. The future leader of France would reward Eboue by holding important talks, discussing post-war colonial reform, with Eboue at the capital Brazzaville in the Congo. Eboue had published *The New Indigenous Policy for French Equatorial Africa.* He argued for respect of African traditions, support for traditional leaders, help in developing existing social structures and an improvement in work conditions. Eboue also put forward the names of 200 Africans who he believed demonstrated education, ability and promise. While on leave in Egypt, Felix Eboue died unexpectedly, May 17th 1944, aged sixty. After his funeral, his ashes were interred at the Pantheon of Heroes in Paris, 1944 becoming the first black man to be accorded the honour. Eboue married **Eugenie Tell** (1889–1971). Their daughter **Ginette** married **Leopold Sedar Senghor** (see October 9th) in 1946.

Born **on this day** in 1918, the dedicated pan Africanist **Ntsu Mokhehle** would challenge foreign rule in landlocked Lesotho as a British protectorate. With the founding of the political party Basutoland African Congress (later called the Basutoland Congress Party, BCP) in 1959, Mokhehle as the party president brought modern politics to the country. From 1960 the BCP provided safety and refuge for political opponents to the brutal and oppressive apartheid regime in South Africa.

With the elections of 1965 and independence on October 4th 1966 Mokhehle became the official opposition leader to the Basutoland National Party (BNP) of **Chief Leabua Jonathan** having lost the election. The BCP won the 1970 general election but Leabua, considered to be a puppet of South Africa, refused to relinquish power. A state of emergency was declared, the constitution suspended and Mokhehle detained for two years. Sixteen years of exile followed with Ntsu Mokhehle living in Zambia and Botswana. After twenty-three years of successive dictatorships, Lesotho held democratic elections, in 1993.

Mokhehle's BCP won all sixty-five seats. Mokhehle became the first prime minister of a democratic Lesotho. Stability was short lived with **King Letsie III** dissolving the newly elected government in 1994.

King Letsie III   King Moshoeshoe II

The prime minister had refused to reinstate Letsie's father **King Moshoeshoe II** to power. Only after neighbouring Southern African countries intervened and the promise to restore the former king did Mokhehle's premiership continue. In May 1998, an ageing Mokhehle retired. The seventy-nine-year-old Ntsu Mokhehle died on January 7th 1999.

Harlem Renaissance short story writer, doctor and radiographer **Rudolph Fisher** was born on May 9th 1867. He graduated from Howard University having attended medical school in 1924. His first fiction appeared a year later in magazines. That same year he moved to New York City meeting with other renaissance luminaries such as **Langston Hughes, Nella Larsen, James Weldon Johnson, Walter White** and **Jessie Redmond Fauset.**

Often described as the most gifted short story writer of the Harlem Renaissance, Fisher was able to write of black people as people. He often looked at how migrant African Americans from the rural South featured arriving in the urban North. Fisher examined the relationship between whites and blacks in Harlem. *City of Refuge,* 1925 and *Vestiges,* both appear in **Alain Locke's** 1925 anthology *A New Negro: An Interpretation.* Further short stories include *The South Lingers On* (1925), *High Yaller* (1926), *Blades of Steel, Ringtail, Fire by Night, The Promised Land* and *The Backslider* all in 1927. Fisher's first novel *The Walls of Jericho,* was published in 1928 following a bet that the author could not bridge the divisions within the black community. The novel shows how African Americans can get ahead if they work together avoiding class and other divisions and distrust, created over centuries of oppression. *The Conjure Man Dies* (1932),

Fisher's second novel, would be the first detective crime mystery by a black American author that was not first serialised and was the first detective novel to have a full black cast.

Writing did not prevent Rudolph Fisher from publishing medical papers on his research into the effects of ultraviolet rays on viruses. He worked as the head researcher at Manhattan International Hospital and became superintendent of the International Hospital in Harlem in 1927. The medical practitioner opened a private practise as a radiologist with an X-ray laboratory in New York City.

Rudolph Fisher died aged thirty-seven **on this day** in 1934. It's believed that he suffered from too much exposure to radiation from his research and work. The author and doctor left behind his wife and son. He is buried in Woodlawn Cemetery in the Bronx, New York.

Poet, journalist, and activist **Dennis Brutus** was born in Salisbury in South Rhodesia (Harare, Zimbabwe) on November 28th 1924. The white campaigner was arguably the leading voice in getting South Africa suspended and later banned from the Olympic games in 1964. The country did not return to the games until 1992 after apartheid had been dismantled. Brutus had been active opposing discrimination in South African sport. He successfully opposed the West Indian cricket team's tour 1959. Attempts to meet with members of the Olympic committee saw the activist jailed for eighteen months. Later he would be arrested, in the process shot in the back, and given a further sixteen months (five in solitude), being placed in the cell next to Nelson Mandela on Robben Island.

While in prison Dennis Brutus's first collection of poetry *Sirens, Knuckles and Boots,* was published in Nigeria. When released in 1966 the poet left South Africa. Further writings were published; *Letters to Martha and Other Poems from a South African Prison* (1968) recorded his experiences, loneliness and misery as a political prisoner. Works included: *China Poems* (1975), *Salutes and Censures* (1982), *Airs and Tributes* (1986), *Still the Sirens* (1993), and *Leafdrift,* in 2005. Dennis Brutus is considered by some as the most important African poet after **Leopold Sedar Senghor** (see October 9th) and **Christopher Okigbo** (see August 16th).

The activist Dennis Brutus taught African literature as a professor at several American universities. The author died from prostate cancer **on this day** in 2009, aged eighty-five, in Cape Town.

Curtis Mayfield, singer, songwriter, producer, music entrepreneur, musician, social and political commentator was born on June 3rd 1942. The African American singer applied his gospel background with R&B to create a distinctive Chicago soul sound with **The Impressions.** The teenage Mayfield along with childhood friend Jerry Butler formed the group the Roosters who would become the commercial success: The Impressions. Their first chart hit was 1958's 'For Your Precious Love'. The track offered Butler the opportunity to go solo providing Mayfield with the chance to take centre stage and define the sound of the group.

The first Mayfield hit with the group was 'Gypsy Woman' in 1961. The decade saw the Impressions have fourteen top 10 hits, 1964 alone saw five top 20 releases. The group developed a distinctive sound with Mayfield's soft persuasive high falsetto. His guitar playing was influenced by playing the keyboards using only the black keys. 'People Get Ready' (1965) would go on to be recorded by over 100 artists. The track pointed the way for a socially conscious Mayfield. Black American music was dominated by dance music and love songs. Mayfield in the soul arena would lead the way producing material with a message. He would be called 'The Preacher' and 'The Reverend' but he saw himself first and foremost as an entertainer. The socially conscious themes were unmistakable.

The 1970s started with Curtis Mayfield going solo. With the rise of Blaxploitation movies and Mayfield writing the soundtrack to *SuperFly* (1972), the songwriter tackled the increase of drugs, crime, and poverty in African American communities. He saw the film as an advert promoting all that he despised but used the music to question the abuse with tracks: 'Freddie's Dead', 'Pusherman', 'Little Child Runnin' Wild' and 'Superfly'. Mayfield's music became a force for change. He produced message songs but did not shout and was never aggressive or angry. The singer cultivated a sound using gentleness, love and encouragement, giving him the nickname *the gentle genius*. The decade started with a string of socially conscious and commercially successful material: 'Move On Up' (1970), 'Don't Worry If There's a Hell Below, We're All Going to Go' (1970), 'Stone Junkie' (1971), 'Keep On Keepin' On' (1971), and ended with 'Trippin' Out' in 1980.

Curtis Mayfield wrote soundtracks and produced for other artists: Gladys Knight and the Pips performed for the film *Claudine* (1974), Aretha Franklin for the movie *Sparkle* (1976), the Staple Singers in *Let's Do It* (1975), and Mavis Staples in *A Piece of the Action* (1977). Within the music business Mayfield was a black capitalist recognising that owning the labels and producing and writing hits for numerous artists was both vital and necessary.

All literally came crashing down while onstage on August 13th 1990. A lighting rig fell on the singer at Wingate Field in Flatbush, Brooklyn, New York, trapping him and crushing his spinal cord in three places. Mayfield was left paralysed from the neck down. It would be years before the wheelchair bound Curtis Mayfield could perform. Against all the odds, singing one line at a time, laying on his back waiting to have enough oxygen to sing the next line, Mayfield recorded and released his final album; 'New World Order' (1996). He demonstrated that he had lost none of his music abilities. Two years before the industry honoured the performer with a Grammy Legend Award in 1994, then a Grammy Lifetime Achievement Award in

1995. It was the discovery of Mayfield and the sampling of his music by rappers and hip-hop music that resonated and spoke of his relevance.

Curtis Mayfield's health deteriorated. Suffering from type two diabetes, he had his right leg amputated in 1998 but the diabetes eventually led to the death of the gentle genius **on this day** in 1999. He was fifty-seven.

Dec 27th:

The Jamaican female sprinter over 60m, 100m, 200m and the 4x100m sprint relay, **Shelley- Ann Fraser-Pryce** has been the dominant athletic force of her generation. Born **on this day** in 1986 Fraser Pryce became the first Caribbean woman to win the 100m gold, at the 2008 Beijing Olympics. In 2012, in London, she became the third woman to successfully defend the 100m title. Injury before the Rio Olympics in 2016 saw the sprinter come in third but become the only female runner to medal at the distance in three successive Olympic games.

Fraser Pryce's personal best of 10.70 is the fourth equal fastest time over the 100m. She has clocked more than 50 sub 11 second times with 15 runs below 10.80, the most for any female sprinter.

Shelly-Ann Fraser Pryce.

Performing at the World Athletics Championships Shelly-Ann Fraser Pryce has won twelve medals, ten at gold and two at silver. She is the only runner to have four 100m golds winning in 2009, 2013, 2015 and 2019. Winning in 2019 at thirty-two she was the oldest female sprinter to do so and the first mother to take gold in the past twenty-four years. The year 2013 was a golden year for the athlete. She took gold in the 100m, 200m and 4x 100m relay. The following year she sprinted to gold in the indoor 60m becoming the first female to hold all four titles simultaneously.

Jamaican Shelly-Ann Fraser Pryce has won more 100m titles than any other woman. Winning gold in London 2012 in the 200m, in the time of 22.17sec, she became only the third woman to do the double having won the 100m a few days earlier. The sprinter was voted Woman Athlete of the Year in 2013 by the International Association of Athletics Federation. At the Tokyo Olympics in 2021 she gained silver running

10.74. Fraser-Pryce was beaten by **Elaine Thompson-Herah** who successfully defended her 100m & 200m title in Tokyo from the 2016 Rio Olympics. Thompson-Herah has since clocked 10.61 for the 100m second only to that by Florence Griffith-Joyner's 1988 mark of 10.49 sec. Elaine Thompson-Herah at 10.61 is the fastest woman alive. See Usain Bolt August 21st.

Dec 28th:

Born **on this day** in 1905, jazz pianist **Earl Hines** would be credited as the bridge between ragtime, the New Orleans piano playing of **Jelly Roll Morton** (see October 20th) and the stride piano of **Fats Waller** (see December 15th), taking the instrument towards a modern jazz sound, influencing bebop and masters of the keyboards such as **Thelonious Monk** (see October 10th), **Bud Powell** and **Oscar Peterson.**

Given the name Earl "**Fatha**" Hines the revolutionary piano stylist, band leader and composer was respected by his peers and influenced those that followed. Giving **Charlie Parker** (see August 29th) his big break, and that same year with **Dizzy Gillespie** (see October 21st) the pair joined Hines's big band. The seeds of bebop were planted and fertilised by Hines's piano playing.

Earl "Fatha" Hines made his earliest recordings at the beginning of the 1920s. By 1923 he had moved to Chicago. Duetting with **Lois B Deppe,** the pair are said to have been the first Africa American performers to appear on American radio in 1921 on KDKA radio. Hines teamed up with **Louis Armstrong** (see August 4th) in the mid-1920s. With Armstrong and his Hot Five, Hines and co cut iconic recordings including: 'West End Blues', 'Fireworks', 'Basin Street Blues', 'Muggles', 'Skip the Gutter', and 'Weather Bird'. Hines had developed what would be described as' trumpet style' piano. By 1928 Fatha had recorded his first ten piano solos including 'A Monday Date', 'Blues in the Third', and '57 Varieties'.

As a big band leader Hines stayed busy and at the top of the tree for twenty years. The man who was said to have the trickiest left hand in the business toured throughout the Depression, the musicians' strike of the early 1940s, and performed for the gangsters of Chicago. He worked with singers such as **Sarah Vaughan** and **Billy Eckstine.** With the rise of bebop and the decline of swing the great age of the big bands was over. Fatha Hines joined Louis Armstrong and His All Stars. After three years in 1951 the pair (a clash of egos) went their separate ways. On February 21st 1949 the trumpeter became the first jazz musician to appear on the cover of *TIME* magazine. The former band leader was not comfortable playing second fiddle.

Earl "Fatha" Hines looked at retirement but was persuaded otherwise. The 1960s saw a re-discovery of Hines. The decade saw him win numerous awards including in 1966 being elected as *DownBeat* magazine No 1 jazz pianist.

Hines recorded over 100 albums. He composed numerous material including 'You Can Depend on Me' (1931), 'Rosetta' (1933), 'Jelly Jelly' (1940) and 'Ev'rything Depends on You' in 1940. Rosetta has been covered by close to 200 artists. **Count Basie** (see April 26th) called Hines the greatest piano player. Hines played at **Duke Ellington's** (see May 24th) funeral. Aged seventy-nine, Earl "Fatha" Hines died on April 22nd in 1983. He is buried at Evergreen Cemetery in Oakland, California.

South African anti-apartheid campaigner, political activist and medical doctor **Mamphela Ramphele** was born **on this day** in 1947. The long-time partner of **Steve Biko** (see September 12th) the couple had a son and a daughter. Lerato died at two months and the son Hlumelo was born after his father's death. The couple met while at the University of Natal. Ramphele developed an interest in the Black Conscious Movement looking at black unity, rights, independence and opposing apartheid.

The activist Ramphele was charged under the Suppression of Communism Act, in 1974, for having banned literature and received a sentence of four and a half months. The following year Ramphele founded the Zanempilo Community Health Centre, one of the few private centres of its type in South Africa. Ramphele was involved in numerous community programmes and became the director of the Black Community Programme.

The oppressive apartheid regime placed Ramphele under a banning order where she was moved to Tzaneen in Northern Transvaal in April 1977. She remained under police surveillance until 1984. While banished Ramphele received visits from the MP **Helen Suzman** (see November 7th) and an Anglican priest called **Father Timothy Stanton.**

No longer a banned person Mamphela Ramphele was appointed vice-chancellor at the University of Cape Town, becoming the first black South African to hold that position in 1991. She joined the World Bank in Washington in 2000 and was responsible for human development. The South African was one of four managing directors. Ramphele was the first African to hold that position in the World Bank. She left the bank in 2004.

The political party Agang South Africa, (Agang is Sotho for 'build') was founded by Ramphele in 2013, to promote universal democracy, and an end to government corruption. With limited electoral success the party fell apart with party leader Ramphele announcing her retirement from party politics on July 8th 2014.

Mamphela Ramphele has written numerous books including *Uprooting Poverty: The South African Challenge* (1989), written with Francis Wilson, *Across Boundaries: The Journey of a South African Woman Leader* (1996), *Laying Ghosts to Rest: Dilemmas of the Transformation in South Africa* (2008), *Conversations with My Sons and Daughters* (2012) and *Socio-Economic and Democratic Freedom in South Africa* published in 2013.

African American actor **Denzel Washington** was ranked number one, greatest actor of the twentieth century, by the *New York Times* in 2020. Born **on this day** in 1954 Washington appeared in his first paid role as the real-life historical character **Matthias De Sousa** in a play about the founding of the colony of Maryland. His first screen appearance was in the 1981 comedy *Carbon Copy*. Playing the role of Dr Philip Chandler in the TV hospital drama *St Elsewhere* brought the actor into American homes weekly over six years from 1982.

Washington played a series of real-life characters on the big screen receiving critical acclaim for: *Cry Freedom* (1987) playing the South African activist **Steve Biko** (see September 12th), and ***Malcolm X*** in 1992 (see February 21st). Washington received a Best Actor, Academy nomination playing Malcolm X. In *The Hurricane*, 1999, the actor played the boxer **Rubin 'Hurricane' Carter.** He received another Best Actor nomination. He played the football coach **Herman Boone** in *Remember the Titans in* 2000. *The Great Debaters* in 2007 saw Washington play the poet and teacher **Melvin B. Tolson.** In *American Gangster* that same year he was the drug kingpin **Frank Lucas.**

Denzel Washington, up to 2020 has had nine Academy nominations, winning Best Actor for *Training Day* in 2001. With the win he became only the second male recipient of the Oscar after **Sidney Poitier** (see February 20th). Washington won the Best Supporting Actor in 1990, playing runaway slave in the American Civil War film; *Glory* in 1989. The actor has been nominated for ten Golden Globes taking three home for; *Glory, Training Day,* and winning the Cecil B. Demille Award. Denzel Washington has also appeared on stage winning a Tony in 2010 for **August Wilson's** *Fences* (see October 2nd). Washington would later direct the film version in 2016, receiving further Academy nominations, including as a director. *Fences* would be Washington's third directorial outing, the first being the biographical movie *Antwone Fisher* in 2002, followed by *The Great Debaters* in 2007.

He has co-starred in many movies including *Pelican Brief* (1993), *Philadelphia,* (1993), *Crimson Tide* (1995), *The Preacher's Wife* (1996), and *Courage Under Fire,* (1996). The popular lead actor demonstrated that there was room and an appetite for white audiences watching black male actors playing versatile roles, and not required to play stereotypes. Two other films of note early in Washington's career are collaborations with **Spike Lee** (see March 20th); *Mo Better Blues* (1990), and *Devil in a Blue Dress* in 1995.

Denzel Washington married Pauletta Pearson in 1983. The couple have four children.

Dec 29th:

Was she coerced or a willing victim? We will never know. What is not in doubt is that the South African, Khoikhoi woman sometimes called Saartjie, Sara or more familiarly **Sarah Baartman** was displayed as a freak and used in scientific racism reflecting the colonialist attitudes of the time. Baartman was born around 1789. Both parents died when she was relatively young. When her village was raided, and her husband killed. The Dutch settlers saw the Khoikhoi and the San people as little more than the missing link between apes and modern man. The enslavement of Africans and the subsequent dehumanisation of the African had been in place in one form or another for the previous two hundred years.

Baartman worked in Cape Town for the mixed heritage Peter Cesar as a washerwoman and nursemaid. She then worked for Peter's brother Hendrik as a wet nurse. At this time Hendrik and Baartman met Scott William Dunlop who frequently supplied animals and specimens back to Britain. He tried to persuade Baartman that she could make money as an exhibit back in England. Sarah Baartman declined the invitation. It would appear that Dunlop would not take no for an answer. Eventually Baartman said she would go if Hendrik agreed and accompanied her. Hendrik was in serious debt. Requiring finance, he moved from a position of doubt to agreeing to the venture.

The three, set sail from South Africa in 1810 arriving in Britain in November 1810 living in the wealthy district of St James, on Duke Street, London. It is believed that two African boys also lived at the address. They may have been illegally smuggled into the country. On November 24th 1810 Baartman was exhibited as the **Hottentot Venus** in the Egyptian Hall at Piccadilly Circus, London. The term Hottentot is now considered derogatory but at the time was the word used to describe people from a region of South Africa. Although part of a freakshow, this was not unusual for the time with bearded ladies, strongmen, giants and dwarfs being the order of the day. The lady's fashion of the time exaggerated the impression of extended buttocks. Nonetheless with the slave trade having been abolished in 1807 concerns were raised. **Zachary Macauley** supported by the abolitionist movement and the African Association took Baartman's case to court. Hendrik Cesar argued that Baartman had the right like any other in the circus to pursue a legitimate living. Baartman was questioned in Dutch for three hours declaring that she had not been coerced, was acting on her own freewill and had not been sexually abused. Although Hendrik was prevented from being present for the questioning Dunlop was there. We have no idea whether Sarah Baartman was intimidated by his presence. Following the trial and the resulting publicity Baartman was exhibited throughout England and Ireland.

It was at this time that one Henry Taylor came on the scene taking control of Sarah Baartman's future selling the woman on to French animal trainer S. Reaux. Baartman was on display at the Palais Royal in Paris for fifteen months. Although her resistance was low, she always insisted on remaining clothed. When artists and scientists wished to paint and examine her, she refused to appear naked.

Clothing issues aside, being the Hottentot Venus took its toll. Baartman was drinking. She died **on this day** in 1815. She was not yet thirty. It is unclear the cause of death, some suspect smallpox, others syphilis or pneumonia. Her brain and genitals were preserved, and a body cast made. Her bones with the cast and pickled items went on display. Her skull was stolen in 1827 but returned a few months later. When the Musée du l'Homme (Museum of Man) was opened in Paris 1937 her remains were put on display there. Protests led to Sarah Baartman's skeleton being removed in 1974. The body cast was removed two years later. Campaigners persuaded the French government to repatriate Baartman's remains. Sarah Baartman had a full funeral ceremony on August 9th 2002 returned home to South Africa.

Her story has been told in numerous books and in the 1998 documentary *The Life and Times of Sara Baartman* and the 2010 film *Black Venus*.

Dr Anderson Ruffin Abbott, born on April 7th 1837, became the first black person born in Canada to become a licenced medical practitioner. His parents had settled in Canada and prospered owning close to fifty properties. They were able to provide Anderson with a good education, seeing him graduate from the Toronto School of Medicine in 1857, becoming the first black student to do so. In 1861 Abbott received a license to practice from the Medical Board of Upper Canada.

Abbott applied to offer his medical services for the Union Army during the American Civil War. Although initially rejected, Abbott's persistence saw him become one of thirteen black surgeons to serve in the conflict. Abbott was one of those in attendance when the president Abraham Lincoln was shot. The former first lady Mary Todd Lincoln presented Abbott with the shawl that her husband wore on his first inauguration. Dr Abbott resigned from the Union Army in 1866.

Living in Canada Abbott set up his own medical practice. In 1871 he was admitted to the College of Physicians and Surgeons of Ontario. That same year, on Aug 9th the doctor married eighteen-year-old Mary-Ann Casey. The couple would have three daughters and two sons. As president of the Wilberforce Education Institute Dr Abbott fought racial segregation in schools from 1873–1880. The doctor was appointed coroner of Kent County in Ontario in 1874, being the first black man to hold that post. Working in the United States, in Chicago, Dr Abbott was appointed surgeon-in-chief, in 1894, at the Providence Hospital. Providence was the first hospital to train black nurses. In 1896 Dr Abbott served as the medical supervisor. A year later he was back working and living in Canada.

As one of Toronto's 273 Civil War veterans Abbott was elected as a member of the Grand Army of the Republic (GAR). He received and proudly wore the GAR fraternity badge and was referred to as Captain Abbott. In November 1892 Abbott was appointed as aide-de-camp on the staff of the Commanding Officer Department of New York. At the time this was the highest military honour bestowed on anyone of African descent in America or Canada.

When **Booker T. Washington** and **W. E. B. Du Bois** clashed over what was the best way forward for the black community, Dr Abbot sided with Du Bois arguing that access to higher education should never be compromised. Over the years the doctor wrote for a number of newspapers and magazines including: the *Chatham Planet, Coloured American Magazine,* the *Anglo-American Magazine* and the *New York Age*. He covered diverse subjects looking at black history, Darwinism, the Civil War, poetry, biology and medicine. Aged seventy-nine Captain Dr Anderson Abbott died **on this day** in 1913. He is buried at the historical Necropolis Cemetery in Toronto.

His grandparents had been enslaved. His parents moved to Los Angeles when their son was seven to escape segregation and the discrimination of Jim Crow laws. Growing up in the city and raised by a single parent, in his youth poverty was always at **Thomas Bradley's** door.

Born **on this day** in 1917 Bradley gained an athletic scholarship in 1956 to the University of California. The former classmate of **Jackie Robinson** (see April 15th) left UCLA without a degree and joined the Los Angeles police force (LAPD) in 1940. Bradley became one of 400 black officers alongside 4,000 whites. Serving for twenty-one years he reached the ceiling of lieutenant, the highest rank open to an African

American. It would not be until 1964 that black officers worked alongside their white counterparts. While at the LYPD, Bradley took a law degree, at South Western University in 1956, as his way out.

Thomas Bradley became involved in politics, as a democrat he became the first African American elected to the Los Angeles City Council in 1963. The city had been devastated by the Watts rebellion of 1965. In the shadow of the turmoil Bradley ran for city mayor in 1969, against Sam Yorty. His first attempt was unsuccessful having been cast as a radical and a militant. In 1973 Bradley ran again. This time he was able to secure enough votes forming a white coalition, in a city that in 1969 had a black population of 18per cent. Defeating Yorty in 1973, Bradley became the city's first and only (as of 2021) African American mayor. He would be re-elected four more times, serving from 1973 to 1993.

During Bradley's time as mayor the city's business and finance centre flourished seeing rapid expansion. The airport was developed, and the city gained a new skyline. Doors were opened for ethnic minorities, women and those with disabilities. Environmental issues were given priority and the city became a centre of diversity. During Bradley's tenure the city secured and hosted the 1984 Summer Olympics

Mayor Bradley was not without his critics. In 1989 he was fined in a civil case accused of receiving illegal consultant fees from firms winning contracts and doing city business. With the acquittal of four white police officers following their filmed attack on and beating of **Rodney King** (see March 3rd), Los Angeles witnessed five days of anger, protest and rioting leaving fifty dead, thousands injured, and the city seeing arson and looting in 1992. The mayor was criticised for his response.

With his decline in popularity Thomas Bradley did not stand for a sixth term. He had married Ethel Arnold on May 4th 1941. The couple had three daughters one died the day that she was born. Bradley had a heart attack while he was driving in March 1996. This was followed by an emergency triple bypass operation. The former mayor never fully recovered; he had a stroke which left him disabled down one side of his body. Thomas Bradley died on September 29th 1998. He was eighty.

Dec 30th:

Born in about 1811 **Adam Kok III** would be seen as the last in line of great leaders of the Griquas people. The chief from the Kok clan led the Griquas on a two-year trek from the area of Orange Free State to establish a new home known as Griqualand East.

A Griquas family in South Africa.

Adam Kok came to power in 1837 leading the Dutch speaking Griquas made up of former slaves of mixed Dutch and African heritage. The British recognised Kok III's sovereignty in 1848. As colonial expansion from the Dutch and the British encroached on traditional lands, Kok III accepted the British offer of new land on the eastern side of the Cape in 1861. The chief led the Griquas on a march that would see the loss of their cattle and horses through drought and enemy raids. Once settled in Griqualand East the Griquas established their life stock, traded and even had their own, but limited, currency. Although Adam Kok III's period in power was brief he was respected by his people.

The British seized political control in 1874 leaving the chief powerless. **On this day** in 1875 Adam Kok III died in a wagon accident.

To rise to politically leading a country one has to have certain characteristics, some admirable, others dubious. One has to be determined, focused. diligent, possess self-belief, in some cases hold on to a sense of entitlement and destiny. To remain in power one either does an amazing job winning the admiration and votes of the electorate or presides over a system of mis-information usually coupled with intimidation. If the illusion of democracy is to be maintained and power retained, at all cost, then opposition is not only out manoeuvred but crushed.

Born **on this day** in 1935 **Albert-Bernard Bongo** would convert to Islam and change his name to **El Hadj Omar Bongo Ondimba.** He served as Independent Gabon's second president following the death of his predecessor **Leon M'ba** in 1967. The former vice-president held a variety of political positions in M'ba's administration in the Gabonese Democratic Party (GDP). Under Bongo, Gabon had a standing army estimated at 10,000 combatants of which the president had a personal bodyguard of 1,500 soldiers.

For twenty-three years under Bongo, Gabon was ruled as a single party state with the president and the GDP holding power. External pressure forced the president to open up the country to a multi-party system in 1990. Bong had a controversial electoral victory in 1993. He was re-elected in 1998 and again in 2005. It is estimated that Bongo had amassed a personal fortune of $1 bn. When the Cuban leader Fidel Castro stepped down from power in 2008 Bongo became the longest serving non royal leader. At his death President Bongo had been in power for forty-two years. The people of oil rich Gabon saw few, if any, benefits. Only five kilometres of road was being laid a year in the country and at the time of Bongo's death, June 8th 2009, after four decades in power, Gabon had one of the world's highest levels of infant mortality.

Dec 31st:

Common in many black churches of Caribbean, American and African origin, the **Watch Night Services** in Black communities is familiar and practiced today. The origin can be traced back to gatherings **on this day** in 1862, also known as "Freedom's Eve."

On that night, Blacks in America came together in churches and private homes all across the nation, anxiously awaiting news that the Emancipation Proclamation, (see January 1st) actually had become law. At the stroke of midnight, January 1st 1863 was ushered in declaring all slaves in the Confederate States legally free.

The news was received by prayers, singing, praising God, shouts of joy as people raised their hands and fell to their knees and thanked God. In memory of emancipation the black community have gathered in churches annually on New Year's Eve praising God having brought them safely through another year.

Praying for a better tomorrow.

On June 29th, St Peter's Day, in 1864 **Samuel Ajayi Crowther** was ordained as the first African Anglican bishop. He was consecrated in Canterbury Cathedral by the Archbishop of Canterbury, Charles Langley. Crowther would later read the Lord's Prayer to Queen Victoria in Yoruba.

Ajayi had been captured and enslaved by Fulani and Yoruba Muslims aged twelve in 1821. He would be sold a few times before being purchased by Portuguese traders and taken on board bound for the transatlantic market. The ship was engaged by a British navy anti-slave vessel. All on board were released and taken to Sierra Leone. Baptised by John Raban on December 11th 1825, Ajayi took the name Samuel Crowther. He received schooling in missionary schools. In 1842 Crowther travelled to England to study at the Church Missionary College in London. He received holy orders and was ordained by the bishop of London, before returning to Africa in 1843. Crowther became active in spreading Christianity as a missionary amongst the Yoruba from 1843–1851. With the end of the slave trade in 1807, and slavery in 1833 in the British Empire, there was a drive for Christian conversion funded by well-meaning patrons back in Britain. Sierra Leone and Liberia, both set up for, and by freed slaves, provided the base for the missionary works.

Crowther was a recipient of the missionary movement and worked with the Christian Missionary Society (CMS). He found his mother and sister and converted both to Christianity. Crowther helped produce the bible in Yoruba having produced written grammar for Yoruba, Igbo and Nupe. The multi-linguist including Greek, Latin, English and Temne, spoken in Congo and Niger, had his work on Yoruba grammar published in 1852. He translated the Anglican Common Book of Prayer into Yoruba. Work on grammar and vocabulary in Nupe was published in 1864. The translation of the Bible was translated into Yoruba in the mid-1880s.

Visiting England in 1851 Crowther was able to influence and educate the government, church and public about Africa. The CMS sent Crowther out in 1857 to establish new missions on the River Niger he experienced both religious and political opposition. Later Crowther would establish dialogue between Christianity and Islam. Henry Venn of the CMS had the vision for African Christian autonomy creating self-governing, self-supporting and self-propagating African Churches. With this in mind Venn secured the appointment of Crowther as the Bishop of Western Africa beyond the Queen's dominions.

In Britain politics and racial issues caused problems. Some felt uneasy seeing Africans running their own affairs. With the death of Henry Venn, and Crowther now an old man, his mission and work was slowly dismantled. Crowther died, disillusioned, from a stroke **on this day** in 1891 in Lagos, where he was buried. Crowther married Asano, formerly Hassana which was her Islamic name. She too was believed to have been rescued from slavery on board the same ship where her future husband had been freed. His body was moved and laid to rest at the Cathedral Church of Christ in Lagos.

Index

Abba Dimi Mint **June 4**
Abbott Diane **Sept 27, June 11**
Abbott Dr Anderson Ruffin **Dec 29**
Abbensetts Michael **Oct 31**
Aberdeen Act **Sept 4, Nov 7**
Abernathy Ralph **March 11**
Abiola Moshood Kashimawo Olawale **Aug 24**
Abolition of slavery (GB) **March 25**
Abram Morris Berthold **June 19**
Accara **Feb 23**
Achebe Chinua **June 13**
Acosta Carlos **June 2**
Adam Lewis **July 4**
Adams Joe **Sept 23**
Adams Richard **Nov 8**
Addai-Sebo Akyaaba **Oct 1**
Adderley Cannonball **Sept 28**
Ade King Sunny **Sept 22**
Aderin-Pocock Maggie **Oct 5**
Adjaye David **Sept 22, Sept 24**
African Methodist Episcopal Church **March 26**
African National Congress **Jan 18**
Afwerki Isaias **Aug 15**
Agadez **June 22**
Aggrey James Emman Kwegyir **July 30**
Ahidjo President Ahmadou Babatoura **Jan 1**
Ahmed Abiya **Aug 15**
Ahmed Mohammed **Aug 12**
Ailey Alvin **Nov 8**
Akayesu Jean-Paul **Sept 2**
Akintola Samuel Ladoke **July 10**
al-Azhari Ismail **Aug 26**
Albert Octavia V R **Dec 24**
Albritton Dave **Aug 3**
Alcindor Dr John **Oct 25**
Aldridge Ira **July 24**
Alexander Crummell **May 6**
Alexander John Hanks **March 21**
Ali Ayaan Hirsi **Nov 13**
Ali Duse Mohamed **Nov 21**
Ali Muhammad **Feb 25, April 28**
Allen Macon Bolling **Oct 10**
Allen Richard **March 26**
Allen Sisley Fay **Feb 1**
All-race elections South Africa **Nov 1**

Amadi Elechi **June 29**
Amador Rei **July 12**
American Negro Theatre **June 5**
Amin Idi **Jan 25**
Amistad **Nov 26, Oct 22**
Amos Baroness Valerie **March 13**
Anderson Blair **Dec 4**
Anderson Charles 'Chief' **March 19**
Anderson Ivie **May 21**
Anderson Marian **Jan 7**
Anderson Michael P **Jan 28**
Anderson Regina M **May 21**
Anderson Viv **Nov 29**
Andrade Mario Pinto de **Aug 21**
Andrea Crouch **July 1**
Angelou Maya **May 28**
Angola **Nov 11**
Annan Kofi **April 8**
Anthony Michael **Feb 10**
Antigua and Barbuda **Nov 1**
Apollo Theatre **Jan 26**
Aptidon Hassan Gouled **June 27**
Archer John **June 8, July 23**
Armatrading Joan **Dec 9**
Armstrong Louis **Aug 4**
Arrington Richard **Oct 30**
Arroyo Joe **July 26**
Arroyo Martina **Jan 7**
Ashe Arthur **July 10**
Ashley James Mitchel **Dec 6**
Asian expelled Uganda **Aug 4**
Asvat Abu Baker **Sept 26**
Atlanta Compromise **Feb 23**
Attucks Crispus **March 5**
Attwood Zelma **Dec 10**
Atwell Winifred **Dec 3**
Augusta Georgia riots **May 12**
Augustine Jean **Sept 9**
Australian referendum **May 27**
Awolowo Chief Obafemi **May 9**
Awoonor Kofi **Sept 21**
Azikiwe Nnamdi **Oct 1**

Baartman Sarah **Dec 29**
Baba Ahmed **Oct 26**

Babalola Solomon Adeboye **Dec 15**
Babu Abdulrahman Mohamed **Aug 5**
Bahamas **July 10, Aug 26**
Bailey Junius **Nov 24**
Bailey Pearl **March 29**
Baker Ella **Dec 13, May 15**
Baker Josephine **April 12**
Baldwin James **Aug 2**
Balewa Abubakar Tafawa **Oct 1**
Bamba Ahmadou **July 19**
Bambaataa Afrika **April 17**
Bambara Toni Cade **Dec 9**
Banda Hastings K **Nov 25, July 6**
Bandler Faith **Sept 27**
Banks Tyra **May 22**
Banneker Benjamin **Nov 9**
Baptist church bombing **Sept 15**
Barbados **Nov 30**
Barbeitos Arlindo do Carmo Pires **Dec 25**
Barber Francis **Jan 13**
Bar-Keys **Dec 10**
Barnes John **Nov 29**
Barrow Errol **Nov 30**
Basie Count **April 26**
Basilios Abuna **Oct 13**
Basket James **Feb 20**
Basquiat Jean-Michel **Dec 22**
Bassey Shirley **Jan 8**
Bates Clayton **Nov 19**
Bates Daisy **Nov 4, Sept 5**
Bath Patricia **Nov 4**
Batson Brendon **March 8**
Bazile Dedee **Sept 20**
BBC Caribbean **Jan 5**
Beaton Norman **Jan 5, April 9, Oct 31**
Beauttah James **Dec 12**
Beckford Tyson **May 22**
Behanzin King **Aug 1**
Beharry Johnson **March 18**
Bekele Kenenisa **June 13**
Belafonte Harry **March 1**
Belize **Sept 21**
Bell Sean **Oct 3**
Bello Ahmadu **June 6, July 6**
Benin **Aug 1**
Bennett Louis **Sept 7**
Benson Mary **June 20**
Berbice slave up-rising **Feb 23**
Berlin Conference **Feb 26**

Berry Chuck **March 18**
Berry Halle **March 24**
Best Carrie **July 6**
BET Holdings **Oct 30**
Bethune Mary McLeod **July 10**
Beti Mongo **June 30, Sept 14**
Bevel James **Dec 19, Aug 28**
Biafran war **July 6**
Biassou George **May 20**
Bicknell John **June 5**
Bikila Abebe **Aug 7, Nov 6**
Biko Steve **Sept 12**
Biles Simone **March 14**
Bin Dooley **May 1**
Bird Vere Cornwall **June 28**
Birmingham Alabama riots **May 12**
Birney James **Nov 23**
Birth of European slavery **Aug 8**
Birth of slavery America **Aug 20**
Birth of Trans-Atlantic slavery **Jan 22**
Bishop Maurice **Oct 25**
Black & White Minstrels **July 21**
Black History Month (UK) **Oct 1**
Black Lives Matter **Jan 4**
Black Panther Party **Oct 15**
Black Theology **July 6**
Black Wall Street massacre **May 31**
Blackwell David Harold **April 24**
Blair Adrian **Feb 15**
Blair jr Ezell **Jan 3**
Blaize Herbert A **Oct 25**
Blake Robert **March 21**
Blake-Hannah Barbara **June 5**
Blaxploitation films **Nov 30**
Bluford Guion **Nov 22**
Blyden Edward **May 6**
Boateng Ozwald **Feb 28**
Boateng Paul **June 11**
Boesak Allan **July 6**
Bogle Paul **Oct 11**
Bokassa Jean-Bedel **Aug 13**
Bol Manute **June 19**
Bolden Buddy **Sept 6**
Bolden Jr Charles **Aug 19**
Bolt Usain **Aug 21**
Bond Horace Julian **Jan 14**
Bonds Margaret **March 14**
Bonetta Sarah Forbes **Aug 15**
Bongo Omar **Dec 30**

Bonner Neville **March 28**
Bontemps Arna **Oct 13**
Botswana **Sept 30**
Botswana & Homosexuality **June 11**
Bough Cecil Archibald **June 28**
Bowe Riddick **Oct 2**
Boyer Jean-Pierre **Oct 6**
Boyer Nate **Sept 1**
Boykin Edward **June 30**
Boykin Otis **March 13**
Brackenridge William **Dec 11**
Bradley Mamie **Aug 28**
Bradley Thomas **Dec 29**
Braithwaite E R **June 14**
Branford Robert **May 6**
Brathwaite Edward Kamau **May 11**
Brazilian slave trade **Nov 7**
Brewer Verlina **Dec 4**
Brewin John Anthony **Aug 25**
Bridges Ruby **Sept 8**
Bridges Todd **Oct 2**
Bridgewater George **Feb 29**
Britain rules Jamaica **May 12**
Brixton Riots **April 10**
Brooke Edward **Oct 26, Nov 2**
Brooks Gwendolyn **June 7, May 1**
Broonzy Big Bill **June 27, April 30**
Brown Bobby **Feb 11**
Brown H Rap **May 12**
Brown Henry 'Box' **June 15**
Brown James **Feb 11**
Brown Jim **Oct 2**
Brown John **Dec 2**
Brown Larsen L **Dec 11**
Brown Minnijean **Sept 11, Sept 5**
Brown Ruth Winifred **Sept 10**
Brown V Board of Education **May 17**
Brown William   **May 8**
Bruce Blanche K **Oct 26**
Brutus Dennis **Dec 26**
Bryant Kobe **Jan 26**
Bullard Eugene Jacques **March 19**
Bullins Ed **July 2**
Bumbry Grace **Jan 7**
Bunche Ralph **Aug 7**
Burke Tarana **Sept 12**
Burkina Faso **Aug 5**
Burleigh Harry **Sept 12**
Burnham Forbes **Aug 6**

Burns Ursula **Sept 20**
Burundi **July 1**
Bustamante Sir Alexander **Aug 6**
Buster Prince **April 1**
Buthelezi Mangosuthu **June 12**
Byrd Jr James **June 7**

C O R E **Dec 8**
Cabral Amilcar **Jan 20**
Cabrera Lydia **Sept 19**
Caesar Shirley **July 1**
Caetera Inter **June 18**
Caldwell Ronnie **Dec 10**
Calloway Cab **March 20**
Camejo Pedro **June 24**
Cameron Earl **July 3**
Cameroon **Jan 1**
Campbell Betty **Oct 13**
Campbell George W **July 4**
Campbell Naomi **May 22**
Cape Verde **July 9**
Carl Cunningham **Dec 10**
Carlos John **June 5, Oct 16**
Carmichael Stokely **June 29**
Carney William Harvey **March 21**
Carol Diahann **Feb 20**
Carver George Washington **Jan 5**
Cato Milton **Oct 27**
Cauley Ben **Dec 10**
Cawley Evonne Goolagong **July 31**
Celia Cruz **July 16**
Celikten Ahmet Ali **March 19**
Central African Republic **Aug 13**
Chad **Aug 11**
Chamberlain Wilt **Feb 17**
Chandler Owen **April 15**
Chaney James **June 21**
Chapman Marie Weston **July 25**
Charles Eugenia **Sept 6, Nov 3**
Charles John **Nov 29**
Charles Ray **Sept 23**
Charleston Oscar **Oct 14**
Chavis John **Dec 3**
Chenault Jr Marcus Wayne **June 30**
Chesnutt Charles W **Nov 15**
Cheswell Wentworth **April 10**
Chikerema James **June 24**
Chilembwe John **Feb 3**
Chisholm Shirley **Nov 5**

Christian Barbara **June 25**
Christie Linford **Aug 1**
Christophe Henri **Oct 6**
Chunchie Kamal **Oct 8**
Clague Joyce **July 22**
Clark Mark **Dec 4**
Clarke Austin **June 26**
Clarke Sisters **June 26**
Clarke William Robinson **March 19**
Clarkson Thomas **March 28 Nov 10**
Clay Marcellus Cassius **July 22**
Clayton Elias **June 15**
Cleaver Eldridge **May 1**
Cleaver Kathleen Neal **May 13**
Cleveland James **Dec 5**
Cliff Jimmy **April 1**
Clifton Lucille **June 25**
Clifton Nate 'Sweetwater' **Oct 31**
Clotilda slave ship **July 9, July 17**
Clutchette John **June 4**
Coachman Alice **July 14, Nov 6**
Coard Bernard **Oct 25**
Coates Ta-Nehisi **Sept 30**
Cochran Johnnie L **Oct 2**
Cochrane Kelso **May 17**
Code Noir **May 6**
Coffey Essie **Feb 25**
Cole Nat King **March 17**
Coleman Bessie **June 15**
Coleridge-Taylor Samuel **Aug 15**
Colfax Massacre **April 13**
Collins Aiden Mae **Sept 15**
Collins Bootsy **May 3**
Collins Sarah **Sept 15**
Collins Tony **March 19**
Colston Edward **June 7**
Coltrane John **Sept 23**
Colvin Claudette **March 2**
Commissiong Janelle **Nov 16**
Comoros Islands **July 6**
Cone James **July 6**
Congo Republic of **Aug 15**
Constantine Learie **March 26**
Conyers John **Feb 4, Nov 2**
Cooke Sam **Dec 11**
Coombes Sean **Oct 3**
Cooper Chuck **Oct 31**
Cooper Steve **Dec 10**
Copeland Misty **Sept 10**

Coppin Peter 'Kangushot' **March 31**
Corbitt Recy (Taylor) **Feb 4**
Cordoba Piedad **Jan 25**
Cornelia Yolande **July 29**
Cornelius Don **Sept 27**
Cosby Bill **July 12**
Cote d'Ivoire **Aug 7**
Cotton Samuel **Dec 20**
Courlander Harold **Aug 11**
Craft Ellen **Jan 29**
Craft William **Jan 29**
Crisis newspaper **Nov 1**
Crouch Sandra **July 1**
Crowder Henry **March 10**
Crowther Samuel Ajayi **Dec 31**
Cuban Race War **May 20**
Cudjoe of the Maroons **March 31**
Cuffy (Coffi) **Feb 23**
Cugoano Ottobah **Aug 20**
Cullen Countee **Jan 9**
Cullors Patrisse **Jan 4**
Cunard Nancy Clara **March 10**
Cunningham Laurie **March 8, Nov 29**

Daar Aden Abdullah **July 1**
Dacko David **Aug 13**
Daddah Moktar Ould **Nov 28**
Damas Leon **Oct 9**
Dandridge Dorothy **Sept 8**
Danquah J B **Dec 21**
Darego Agbani **Nov 16**
Davis Angela **June 4**
Davis Benjamin O **Dec 18**
Davis Ira B **Dec 11**
Davis Jr Sammy **May 16**
Davis Miles **Sept 28**
Davis Ossie **June 11**
Davis Shani **Aug 13**
Davis Viola **Oct 2**
Davy Earl **Sept 5**
Dawson William **March 13, Nov 29**
Day Thomas **June 5**
Dockum Sit-ins **July 20**
Deadwyler Leonard **Oct 2**
DeCarava Roy **Dec 9**
Dee Hezekiah **June 21**
Dee Ruby **June 11**
Dekker Desmond **May 25**
Delaney Harold **Dec 3**

Delany Martin Robinson **May 6, June 5**
Demerara Up-rising **Sept 16**
Denmark slave trade ban **Jan 1**
Denniston Oswald **May 24**
Deppe Lois B **Dec 28**
Deslondes Charles **Jan 8**
Desmond Viola **July 6**
Desmonds **Jan 5**
Dessalines Jean-Jacques **Sept 20**
Dett Robert Nathanial **Oct 11**
Dia Mamadou Moustapha **July 18**
Diallo Amadou **Oct 3**
Diddley Bo **July 1**
Dinkins David **July 10**
Diop Alioune **Jan 10**
Diop Birago **Nov 25**
Diop David **July 9**
Diori Hamani **Aug 3**
Diouf Abdou **Sept 7**
Diversas Dunn **June 18, Jan 22**
Dixon George **Jan 6**
Dixon Willie **July 1, April 30**
Djibouti **June 27**
Dobbs Dame Linda **Jan 3**
Doe Samuel K **Oct 29**
Dogbe Victoire Tomegah **Sept 28**
Dogg Snoop **Oct 2**
Dominica **Nov 3**
Dominican Republic **Feb 27**
Domino Fats **Oct 24, July 21**
Donald Jr Cleveland **June 6**
Dorrington Arthur 'Art' **Oct 31**
Dorsey Thomas A **July 1**
Douglas Aaron **Feb 2**
Douglas Gabby **March 14**
Douglass Frederick **Feb 14**
Dove Evelyn **Jan 11**
Dove Rita **Aug 28**
Dozier Lamont **Nov 28**
Dredd Harriett **March 6**
Dredd Sam **March 6**
Dredd Scott **March 6**
Drew Charles Richard **June 3**
Drumgo Fleeta **June 4**
Dube Lucky Philip **Aug 3**
DuBois W E B **Feb 23, April 18, July 23**
Dumas Henry **July 20**
Dunbar Paul Laurence **Feb 9**
Dunmore's Proclamation **Nov 14**

Dunn Donald 'Duck' **Dec 10**
Duvalier Francois 'Papa Doc' **April 22**
Duvalier Jean Claude 'Baby Doc' **July 3**
Dying Negro (The) **June 5**

East St Louis Massacre **July 1**
Ebony Magazine **Nov 1, Feb 19**
Eboue Felix **Dec 26**
Eckford Elizabeth **Sept 5, Oct 4**
Eckstine Billy **Aug 28, Dec 28**
Edgerton Joel **July 22**
Edwards Harry **Oct 16**
Edwards Teresa **July 19**
Elizabeth I (Queen) **July 11**
Ellington Duke **May 24**
Ellis Pee Wee **May 3**
Ellison Ralph Waldo **April 16**
Elphick Gladys **Aug 27**
el-Shabazz el-Hajj Malik **Feb 21**
Emancipation Proclamation **Jan 1**
Emeagwali Philip **Aug 23**
Emperor Jones (The) **Nov 1**
Empire Road **Oct 31**
Enahoro Chief Anthony **July 22**
Enforcement Acts (USA) **May 31**
Ennis -Hill Jessica **July 30**
Enwonwu Ben **July 14**
Equatorial Guinea **Oct 12**
Equiano Olaudah **March 31, March 24**
Eritrea **May 24**
Es'kia **Oct 27**
Esquerita **Dec 5**
Essy Amara **Dec 20**
Estenoz Evaristo **May 20**
Eswatini **Sept 6**
Etienne Gail **Sept 8**
Eusebio **Jan 25**
Evan Elgin **April 30**
Evers Medgar **June 12**
Evora Cesaria **Dec 15**
Eye for an Eye **July 31**

Faddis John **Oct 21**
Fanon Frantz **Dec 6, June 26**
Fanque Pablo **March 30**
Farah Sir Mo **March 23**
Fard Wallace D **Feb 26**
Farmer James **Jan 12**
Farrakhan Louis **June 23, Oct 7**

Feijo's Law **Nov 7**
Feliciano Cheo **July 3**
Ferguson Samuel D **June 24**
First Ruth **Aug 17**
Fisher Bernice **Dec 8, Aug 19**
Fisher Rudolph **Dec 26**
Fitzgerald Ella **April 25**
Flipper Henry Ossian **March 21, June 15**
Flowers Vonetta **Aug 13**
Floyd George **May 25**
Ford Emil **Dec 5**
Foreman George **Oct 30**
Forrest Vernon **July 25**
Foster Andrew 'Rube' **Sept 17**
Fosters (The) **April 9**
Freitas Lancarote de **Aug 8**
Franco Mariella **March 14**
Franklin Aretha **March 25**
Franklin Kirk **July 10**
Frayer Peter **Oct 31**
Frazier E Franklin **Sept 24**
Frazier Joe **Feb 25**
Freeman Bee **Jan 2**
Freeman Cathy **Feb 15**
Freeman Joseph **June 11**
Freeman Paul **Feb 29**
FRELIMO **June 25**
Friedenreich Arthur **July 18**
Frye Marquette **Aug 11**
Frye Ronald **Aug 11**

Gabon **Aug 17**
Gaines Joyce Ann **Aug 11**
Gambia **Feb 18**
Gans Joe **Aug 10**
Gantt Harvey **July 29**
Garcia Jose Mauricio Nunes **Sept 22**
Gardiner Ralph **Dec 3**
Garner Eric **July 17**
Garner Joel **Aug 31**
Garrett Thomas **Jan 25**
Garrison William Lloyds **Dec 10**
Garvey Marcus **Aug 17**
Garza Alicia **Jan 4**
Gates Henry Louis **March 15**
Gaye Marvin **April 1**
Gbowee Leymah **Feb 1**
George Houser **Aug 19, Dec 8**
Ghana **March 6**

Ghebreyesus Tedros Adhanom **March 3**
Ghezo King **Aug 15**
Gibson Althea **May 26**
Gill Gilberto **June 26**
Gillespie Dizzy **Oct 21**
Giovanni Nikki **July 29, June 7**
Givens Robin **Sept 28**
Glissant Edouard **Sept 11**
Glover Danny **Feb 9, Nov 20**
Glover Savion **Nov 19**
Goldberg Whoopi **Feb 9**
Golden Law **May 13**
Golliwog (The) **Feb 22**
Gomez Anderson **March 14**
Goncalves Antonio Aurelio **Sept 25**
Goodes Adam **Jan 8**
Goodman Andrew **June 21**
Gordon Dame Elmira **Sept 21**
Gordon George William **Oct 11**
Gordon Raleigh **Sept 11**
Gordon William J **March 18**
Gordy Berry **Nov 28**
Gowan General Yakubu **July 6**
Grant Bernie **June 11**
Grant Cy **Nov 8**
Green Earnest **Sept 22, Sept 5**
Greene Dr Mandisa **July 10**
Greenidge Gordon **Aug 31**
Greensboro four **Jan 3**
Greenwood Massacre **May 31**
Gregory Dick **Aug 19**
Gregory Frederick D **Nov 22**
Gregory Wilton Daniel **Dec 7**
Grenada **Feb 6**
Griffin John H **June 16**
Griffith-Joyner Florence **March 5**
Griffiths Dr Martin **July 5**
Griffiths Marcia **Feb 6**
Grimke Charlotte Forten **July 23**
Gueye Amadou Lamine **June 10**
Guillen Nicolas **July 10**
Guinea **Oct 2**
Guinea Bissau **Sept 24**
Guines Tata **June 30**
Guinn Kenneth E J **Dec 8**
Guyana **May 26**
Guyot Lawrence Thomas **July 17**
Gwala Harry **June 20**

Habyarimana President **April 6**
Hagler Marvin **Oct 18**
Haiti Independence **Jan 1**
Haitian Revolution **Aug 21**
Hall George Cleveland **Dec 19**
Hall William **March 18**
Hamer Fannie Lou **Oct 6**
Hamilton Lewis **Jan 7**
Hammon Jupiter **Dec 25**
Hammond John **May 8**
Hampton Fred **Dec 4, Oct 15**
Hancock Herbie **Sept 28**
Handy W C **Nov 16**
Hani Chris **June 28**
Hanley Ellery **March 27**
Hannett Leo **June 15**
Hansberry Lorraine **May 19**
Harding Vincent G **July 25**
Harper Francis E W **Sept 24**
Harrington Oliver **July 29**
Harris Alice Seeley **July 18, May 10**
Harris Barbara **June 12**
Harris Brenda **Dec 4**
Harris Kamala **Oct 20**
Harris Lynn E **June 20**
Harrison Charles **Sept 23**
Hartgrove William D **Dec 19**
Hastie William H **May 17**
Hattie Cotton school bombing **Sept 10**
Hawkins Coleman **May 24**
Hawkins Edwin **July 10**
Hawkins John **Nov 12**
Hawkins Thomas C **Dec 11**
Hawkins Tramaine **July 1**
Hawkins Walter **July 1**
Hawkins Yusuf **Oct 3**
Hayden Robert **Aug 28**
Hayes Isaac **Aug 10**
Hayes Roland **March 19**
Hayes Todd **Aug 13**
Hayley Alex **Aug 11, June 23**
Haynes Desmond **Aug 31**
Healy James Augustine **April 6**
Healy Patrick Francis **Feb 27**
Hearns Thomas 'Hitman' **Oct 18**
Heiss Anita **Aug 14**
Hendrix Jimi **Sept 18**
Henry Aaron E **July 2**
Henry Lenny **Aug 29**

Henry William **Oct 17**
Henshaw James Ene **Aug 16**
Henson Matthew **March 9**
Hereford IV Sonnie **Aug 25**
Hernandez Orlando **Oct 11**
Hibbert Toots **Sept 11**
Hicks James **Sept 5**
Higginson Thomas Wentworth **Dec 2**
Hill Oliver W **Aug 5**
Himes Chester **July 29**
Hines Earl 'Fatha' **Dec 28**
Hines Garrett **Aug 13**
Hines Gregory **Nov 19**
Hines Jim **March 5, June 20**
Hinton Jane **July 10**
Hinton William Augustine **July 10**
Hitimana Emmanuel **Feb 13**
Hobson Mellody **April 3**
Hodges Samuel **March 18**
Holding Michael **Aug 31**
Holiday Billie **April 7**
Holland Brian **Nov 28**
Holland Eddie **Nov 28**
Holman Moses C **June 27**
Holmes Larry **Feb 25**
Hood James **Aug 25**
Hood James **June 11**
Hooker John Lee **Aug 22**
Horne Lena **June 30**
Hose Sam **Feb 23**
Hosten Josephine **Nov 16**
Hottentot Venus **Dec 29**
Houphouet-Boigny Felix **Dec 7, Aug 7**
House Son **May 8**
Houston Charles Hamilton **Sept 3**
Houston Whitney **Feb 11**
Hove Chenjerai **July 12**
Howe Samuel Gridley **Dec 2**
Howell Leonard P **Feb 25**
Howlin Wolf **Jan 10**
Huddleston Trevor **April 20**
Hudson Rose **Jan 19**
Hughes Langston **May 22**
Huie Albert **June 28**
Hummingbirds Dixie **March 20, June 24**
Hundessa Hachalu **June 29**
Hurricane Katrina **Aug 23**
Hutton Bobby **May 1, May 13**

Ibarguen Caterine **Nov 6**
Iginla Jarome **Aug 13**
Iman **May 20**
Impressions (The) **Dec 26**
Ince Paul **June 9**
Indigenous Peoples' Day **Aug 9**
Interracial Kiss (TV) **Feb 1**
Isaacs Jerry **June 28**
Isandlwana battle of **Jan 22**
Italy annex's Ethiopia **May 9**
Ivonnet Pedro **May 20**

Jabavu Davidson Don Tengo **Aug 3**
Jabbar Kareem Abdul **June 25, Oct 25**
Jack Homer **Dec 8**
Jackson Al **Dec 10**
Jackson Alex A **Dec 19**
Jackson Brian **May 27**
Jackson Colin **Aug 1**
Jackson Elmer **June 15**
Jackson George **June 4**
Jackson Jesse **Oct 8**
Jackson Mahalia **Jan 31**
Jackson Maynard **June 23**
Jackson Michael **Feb 28, June 25**
Jackson Peter **July 13**
Jacobs Harriet A **Jan 11**
Jamaica **Aug 6**
James C L R **Jan 4**
James Jr Daniel 'Chappie' **March 19, Dec 18**
James Marlon **Oct 13**
Jay-Z **April 4**
Jean Michaelle **Aug 4**
Jeffries Jasper **Dec 3**
Jemison Mae Carol **Oct 17**
Jemison T J **Aug 1**
Jennings Elizabeth **Oct 22**
John Barbara Rose **Sept 25**
Johnson Andrew **Aug 19**
Johnson Ben **March 5, Sept 24**
Johnson Beverly **May 22**
Johnson Charles S **July 24**
Johnson Cornelius **Aug 3**
Johnson Frank **Dec 11**
Johnson Jack **March 31**
Johnson James Weldon **June 17**
Johnson John Harold **Jan 19**
Johnson Linton Kwesi **Aug 24**
Johnson Michael **Sept 13**

Johnson Robert **May 8**
Johnson Robert L **Oct 30**
Jones Booker T **Dec 10**
Jones Carmen **Sept 8**
Jones Claudia **Jan 30**
Jones Frederick McKinley **May 17**
Jones James Earl **March 31**
Jones Jim **Nov 18**
Jones Lois Mailou **Nov 3**
Jones Marion **Oct 3**
Jones Matilda Sissieretta **June 24**
Jones Phalon **Dec 10**
Jones Randy **Aug 13**
Joplin Scott **April 1**
Jordan Archibald Campbell **Oct 20**
Jordan Michael **Feb 17**
Jordon Louis **July 8**
Joycelyn Simeon **Oct 22**
Julian Percy Lavon **April 19**
Juneteenth **June 19**
Just Earnest Everett **Aug 14**

Kabila Laurent-Desire **Jan 16**
Kabui Frank **July 7**
Kadalie Clements **May 5**
Kaepernick Colin **Sept 1**
Kagame Alexis **Dec 2**
Kagame Paul **Oct 23**
Kang'ethe Joseph **Dec 12**
Karume Abeid Amani **Aug 5**
Kasavubu President **July 2**
Kaunda Kenneth **April 28**
Kay Jackie **Nov 9**
Keita Modibo **June 20, Sept 22**
Keita Salif **Aug 25**
Kenilorea Peter **July 7**
Kennedy William **Nov 24**
Kenneh-Mason Sheku **May 19**
Kent John **July 20**
Kente Gibson **July 23**
Kenya **Dec 12**
Kenyan Republic **June 1**
Kenyatta Jomo **Dec 12, June 1**
Kerekou Mathieu **Oct 14, Dec 7**
Keys Hemp **Nov 24**
Khama Seretse **July 1, Sept 30**
Khan Chaka **March 25**
Killens John **Jan 14**
King Albertina **June 30**

King BB **May 14**
King Don **Aug 20**
King Howell **Aug 3**
King Jimmy **Dec 10**
King Jr Martin Luther **Jan 15, April 4, Aug 28**
King Kanya **Nov 18**
King Leopold II **May 29**
King Letsie III **Dec 26**
King Moshoeshoe III **Dec 26**
King Rodney **March 3**
Kinross mine disaster **Sept 16**
Kipkoech Paul **Nov 6**
Kitchener Lord **Feb 11**
Knight Gladys **May 28**
Knight Joseph **Jan 15**
Knowles Beyonce **April 4**
Kohler Oswin **Oct 14**
Kok III Adam **Dec 30**
Konotey-Ahulu Felix **July 12**
Kossola Oluale **July 17**
Kougri Moro Naba **Aug 5**
Kouyate Sotigui **July 19**
Ku Klux Klan **Dec 24**
Kunene Mazisi **Aug 11**
Kunoth-Monks Rosalie **March 8**
Kutako Hosea **July 18**
Kuti Fela **Aug 2**
Kuzwayo Ellen **June 29**
Kwelagobe Mpula Keneilwe **Nov 16**

Lacks Henrietta **Oct 4**
Laine Cleo **Oct 28**
Lambede Anton **April 24, May 5**
Lamming George **June 8**
Langford Sam **Sept 6**
Langston John Mercer **Nov 15**
LaNier Carlotta Walls **Dec 18**
Lara Brian **May 2**
Latimer Lewis H **Sept 4**
Lawrence Jacob **Sept 7**
Lawrence Robert Henry **June 30**
Lawrence Stephen **April 22**
Lawson James **Sept 22, May 15**
Lead Belly **Jan 20**
League of Coloured Peoples **March 13**
Lee George W **Feb 4**
Lee Harper **May 1**
Lee Joseph **July 19**
Lee Spike **March 20**

Leonard Sugar Ray **Oct 18**
Leroy Wright **Nov 21**
Leslie John Francis **Aug 17**
Leslie Lynden **June 28**
Lesotho **Oct 4**
Levy Andrea **Feb 14**
Lewis Arthur **June 15**
Lewis Carl **July 1**
Lewis Cudjoe **July 17**
Lewis Denise **July 30**
Lewis John **Feb 21**
Lewis Lennox **May 8**
Liberia **July 26, July 23**
Lima Manuel dos Santos **June 28**
Liston Sonny **Feb 25**
Little Malcolm **Feb 21**
Little Rock Nine **Feb 21**
Livingston David **Dec 21**
Lloyd Clive **Aug 31**
Locke Alain **Sept 13**
Loguen Jermain Wesley **Feb 5**
Lopez Mijain **Aug 20**
Lorde Audre **Nov 17**
Los Angeles riots **May 1**
Loudin Frederick **Aug 15**
Louis Joe **June 22**
L'Ouverture Toussaint **May 20, July 7**
Lovejoy Elijah Parish **Nov 7**
Loving Mildred **July 22**
Loving Richard **July 22**
Lumumba Patrice **July 2**
Luthuli Albert **July 21**
LuValle James **Aug 3**
Luwum Archbishop **Feb 16, Feb 17**
Lynch John R **Sept 10**
Lynch Lorretta **May 21**
Lyseight Oliver A **Dec 11**

Maathai Wangari **April 1, June 5**
Macauley Herbert **Nov 14**
Maceo Antonio **May 20**
Machel Graca **Oct 17**
Machel Samora Moises **Sept 29, June 25**
Macpherson Report **Feb 24**
Macpherson Sir William **Feb 24**
Macaulay Zachary **Dec 29**
MacWharter Pat **Dec 11**
Madagascar **June 26**
Maga Hubert **Aug 1**

Maharero Samuel **Jan 6**
Makeba Miriam **Nov 10**
Makhubo Mybuyisa **March 8, June 16**
Malawi **July 6**
Mali **June 20, Sept 22**
Malone Annie Turnbo **Dec 23**
Malone Vivian **June 11, Aug 25**
Mandela Nelson **Feb 11, March 29, June 12, July 18**
Mandela Winnie **Sept 26, May 12**
Manley Edna **June 28**
Manley Norman **March 31**
Manning Kenneth R **Aug 14**
Manyoma Emilsen **Jan 14**
Mapondera John **Nov 8**
Marcell Joseph **Feb 22**
March on Washington **Aug 28**
Marechera Dambudzo **Aug 17**
Marechera Dambudzo **July 12**
Marie Laveau **June 15**
Markle Meghan **May 19**
Marley Bob **Feb 6**
Marley Rita **Feb 6**
Marquez Francis **April 23**
Marsalis Wynton **Oct 10**
Marshall Bobby **Jan 8**
Marshall Malcom **Aug 31**
Marshall Thurgood **Jan 24**
Marson Una **Feb 6**
Martin Luther King Day **Nov 2**
Martin Trayvon **Jan 4**
Masekela Hugh **March 4**
Mathias Jerry **Sept 11**
Matt Michael Ah **Feb 15**
Matta Joachim Dias Cordeiro da **Dec 25**
Matzeliger Jan Ernst **March 20**
Mau Mau **Dec 12**
Maull Carolyn **Sept 15**
Mauritania **Nov 28**
Mauritius **March 12**
Maxeke Charlotte **June 20**
Mayfield Curtis **Dec 26**
Mays Benjamin **Aug 1**
Mays Willie **May 4**
Maytals (The) **Sept 11**
Mayweather Jr Floyd **June 5**
Mazrui Ali Al'amin **Oct 12**
Mbasogo Teodoro O N **Oct 12**
Mbeki Govin **July 9**

Mbeki Thabo **June 18**
Mboya Tom **July 5, Dec 12**
McCain Franklin Eugene **Jan 3**
McCalla Val **Oct 3**
McCoy Elijah **May 2**
McCrear Matilda **July 17**
McDaniel Hattie **June 10**
McDonald Trevor **Aug 16**
McDowell Cleve **June 6**
McDowell Tanya **Oct 3**
McGhie Isaac **June 15**
McGrath Pat **June 11**
McIntosh Francis **Nov 7**
McKay Claude **Sept 15**
McLendon John **Oct 31**
Mcleod Don **May 1**
McMillan Terry **Oct 18**
McNair Carol Denise **Sept 15**
McNair Ronald E **Jan 28**
McNeil Joseph **Jan 3**
McNeil Genna Rae **Sept 3**
McQueen Butterfly **June 10**
McQueen Steve **July 10**
Mda Ashley **May 5**
Meer Fatima **Aug 12**
Menard John Willis **Oct 8**
Mendez Arnold Tamayo **Sept 18**
Meredith James **June 6**
Metcalfe Ralph **Aug 3**
Micheaux Oscar **Jan 2**
Middleton Delano **Feb 8**
Miller Doris **March 21**
Miller Portia Simpson **Dec 12**
Mills Brother **Nov 6**
Mills John Evans Atta **July 24**
Mingus Charlie **May 24**
Minns Allan Glaiyser **Sept 16**
Miracles (The) **Feb 19**
Mississippi Burning **June 21**
Mississippi John Hurt **July 3**
Mississippi Plan (The) **Nov 2**
Mitchell Arthur **Sept 16**
Mitchell Jerry **June 21**
Mitchell Jimmy **June 20**
Mckenna Clancy **May 1**
Mnangagwa President **April 18**
Mnyampala Mathias E **June 8**
MOBO **Nov 18**
Modjadji Rain Queens **June 28**

Moffat Robert **Dec 21**
Mofolo Thomas Mokopu **Sept 8**
Mogae Festus **Aug 21**
Moi Daniel arap **Sept 2**
Mokhehle Ntsu **Dec 26**
Molineaux Tom **Aug 4**
Mompati Ruth **May 12**
Mondelli Domenico **March 19**
Mondlane Eduardo **June 25**
Monk Thelonious **Oct 10**
Montgomery Olen **Nov 21**
Monteith Henri **July 29**
Moody Harold **Oct 8**
Moore Charles Eddie **June 21**
Moore Jesse **Dec 11**
Moore Juanita **Oct 19**
Moore Udine Smith **Feb 29**
Morenga Jacob **Sept 20, Jan 6**
Morgan Derrick **May 25, April 1**
Morgan Garrett **March 4**
Morgan Jr Charles **March 12**
Morris Bill **Oct 19**
Morris Robert **Feb 15**
Morrison Toni **Feb 18**
Morton Jelly Roll **Oct 20**
Moses Ed **May 4**
Moses Ethel **Jan 2**
Mothershed Thelma **Nov 29, Sept 5**
Motsetse Dr Kgalemang **Sept 30**
Moura Paula **July 12**
Mowatt Judy **Feb 6**
Mozambique **June 25**
Mpezeni **Sept 21**
Mphahlele Ezekiel **Oct 27**
Mpingana Nehale Lya **Jan 6**
Mpolo Maurice **July 2**
Mqhayi Samuel E K **July 29**
Mubuto Joseph **July 2**
Mugabe Robert **April 18, June 1**
Muhammad Elijah **Oct 7**
Mukarukaka Rosalie **Feb 13**
Mukasarasi Godelieve **Sept 2**
Mukwege Dr Dennis **March 1**
Mum Shirl **Nov 14**
Mungoshi Charles **July 12**
Mungunda Anna **Jan 6**
Munroe Carmen **Jan 5, April 9**
Murphy Eddie **April 3**
Musarurwa Willie **Nov 24**

Mutezo Obed **Dec 12**
Mutombo Dikembe **June 25**
Muzorewa Bishop **June 24, June 1**
Mwanawasa Levy **Aug 19**

N M of A A H & C **Sept 24**
N Y state ends slavery **July 4**
NAACP **Feb 12**
Nabuco Joaquim **May 13**
Naki Hamilton **May 29**
Namatjira Albert **July 28**
Namibia **March 21**
Namibia's national heroes **Jan 6**
Nanny of the Maroons **March 31**
Nash Diane **May 15**
Nash Johnny **Feb 6**
Native Lands Act (SA) **June 16**
Naylor Gloria **Sept 28**
Nazima Sam **March 8, June 16**
Ncube Sister Bernard **March 9**
Ndemufayo Chief Mandume ya **Jan 6**
Ndlovu Curnick **June 25**
Ndlovu Hastings **June 16**
N'Dour Youssou **Oct 1**
Negga Ruth **July 22**
Negritude **Dec 25, Oct 9, Jan 10, Oct 31**
Negro An Anthology **March 10**
Nelson Alice Dunbar **July 19**
Nesbitt William C **Dec 11**
Neto Agostinho **Sept 10, Nov 11, Aug 21**
New Cross Fire **Jan 18**
New Orleans transport **May 7**
Newson Moses J **Sept 5**
Newton Huey P **Aug 22**
Ngoombujarra David **June 27**
Nguema Francis Macias **Oct 12**
Nguvauva Kahimemua **Jan 6**
Ngwale Kinjikitile **Aug 30**
Niagara Movement (The) **Feb 23, July 11**
Nicholas Brothers **July 21**
Nichols Nichelle **Feb 1**
Nichols William **May 7**
Nicol Dr Davidson **Sept 20**
Niger **Aug 3**
Nigeria **Oct 1**
Nigerian Civil War **July 6**
Nixon Edgar D **Feb 4**
Nkabinde Simon 'Mahlathini' **July 27**
Nkadimeng John K **May 4**

Nkrumah Kwame **Jan 2**
Nkubito Alphonse-Marie **Feb 13**
Nkumo Joshua **June 1 & 19 April 18**
Noah Yannick **May 18**
Nolan Jimmy **May 3**
Noonuccal Oodgeroo **Sept 16**
Norman Jessye **Sept 30**
Norman Peter **Oct 16**
Njoroge Nahashon **July 5**
Noronha Rui de **Oct 28**
Norris Clarence **Jan 23, Nov 21**
Northup Solomon **July 10**
Norton Ken **Feb 25**
Norway bans slave trade **Jan 1**
Norwood Dorothy **July 1**
Notorious B I G **Sept 13**
Notting Hill Carnival **Jan 30**
Notting Hill Riots **Aug 29**
Noyes Academy destroyed **Aug 10**
Nsala **May 10**
Ntaryamira President C **April 6**
Nwapa Flora **Jan 13**
Nyandoro Chief Kunze **June 24**
Nyandoro George Bodzo **June 24**
Nyerere Julius **April 13**
Nzo Alfred Baphethuxolo **June 19**

O'Ree Willie **Oct 31**
Obama Barack **Jan 21, Aug 4**
Obama Michelle **Jan 17**
Obote Milton **June 3, Oct 9**
Obotseng Sister Christine **March 9**
Odinga Oginga **Dec 12**
O'Donoghue Lowitja **Aug 1**
Ojukwu Odumegwu **July 6**
Okello Tito **June 3**
Okigbo Christopher **Aug 16, June 13**
Okito Joseph **July 2**
Okonedo Sophie **Sept 26**
Okonjo-Iweala Dr Ngozi **March 3**
Okri Ben **March 15**
Olajuwon Hakeem **June 25**
Oliver Joe 'King' **Aug 4**
Oliver William Pearly **July 6**
Olympio Sylvanus **April 27**
Omaha Nebraska white violence **July 3**
O'Neil Eugene **Nov 1**
Operation Urgent Fury **Oct 25**
Orangeburg Massacre **Feb 8**

Organisation of African Unity **May 25**
Osman Aden Abdullah **June 8**
Osman David Piggee **Aug 25**
Ovington Mary White **Feb 12**
Owens Jesse **Aug 3**
Oyono Ferdinand Leopold **June 10**

Padmore George **Sept 23**
Paige Satchel **Nov 2**
Palmares Zumbi dos **Nov 20**
Pan African Conference **July 23**
Pan Africanism **May 6**
Papa Wemba **June 14**
Papa Wendo **July 28**
Papal Bull **Jan 8, June 18**
Papua New Guinea **Sept 16**
Parker Charlie **Aug 29**
Parker Kirsty **Oct 22**
Parker Maceo **May 3**
Parker Theodore **Dec 20**
Parks Gordon **Nov 30**
Parks Rosa **Feb 14**
Parris Eddie **Jan 31**
Pattillo Melba **Dec 7, Sept 5**
Paton Alan **Feb 20**
Patterson Hayward **Jan 23, Nov 21**
Patton Charley **April 28, May 8**
Peach Blair **April 23**
Pearson Veronica **Aug 25**
Pele **June 21**
Pennington James W C **Oct 22**
Pereira Aristides **July 5**
Perez Carlota **March 24**
Peris-Kneebone Nova **Feb 15**
Perkins John **Jan 27**
Perry Jr Matthew James **July 29**
Peters Clarke **July 8**
Peters Lenrie **Sept 1**
Petion Alexandre Sabes **Oct 16**
Philips Mary **March 14**
Pickett Bill **April 2**
Pieterson Antoinette **March 8**
Pieterson Hector **June 16, March 8**
Pilbara Strike **May 1**
Pinckney Leo **May 21**
Pindling Lynden **Aug 26**
Pitt Lord David **Dec 18**
Plaatje Solomon Tshekisho **June 19**
Plessy v Ferguson **May 18**

Poage George Coleman **Nov 6**
Pohamba Hifikepunye **Aug 18**
Poitier Sidney **Feb 20, June 14**
Pollard Frederick Douglass Fritz **Jan 8**
Pollard Fritz **Aug 3**
Poole Elijah **Oct 7**
Porres St Martin de **Nov 3**
Port Royal Jamaica **June 7**
Porter David **Aug 10**
Powell Adam Clayton **Nov 29**
Powell Bud **Oct 10**
Powell Enoch **April 20**
Powell Ozie **Jan 23**
Power Kemp **Dec 11**
Pratt Geronimo **Oct 2**
Preston Billy **Dec 5**
Prevost Tessie **Sept 8**
Price Florence **June 3**
Price Mary Leontyne **Feb 10**
Pride Charley **Dec 12**
Primus Pearl **Oct 29**
Prince Mary **Oct 1**
Prince Rogers Nelson **June 7**
Princess Makheala **June 28**
Prosper Pierre-Richard **Sept 2**
Pryor Richard **Dec 1**
Pullman Joe **Oct 6**

Quaque Philip **Oct 17**
Quamina **Sept 16**
Quarterman Lloyd Albert **Dec 3**
Quartey Ike **Nov 6**
Ouattara Princess Guimbi **Aug 5**
Queen Makobo Modjadji **June 28**
Queen Mokope Modjadi **June 28**
Queiros Eusebio de **Sept 4**

Race Relations Act (GB) **Dec 8**
Rainey Joseph Hayne **Nov 15**
Rainey Ma **April 26**
Ramphele Mamphela **Dec 28**
Randolph A Philip **April 15**
Rapper's Delight **Sept 16**
Rashard Phylicia **June 19**
Raveling George **Aug 28**
Rawlings Jerry **June 4**
Rawls Lou **Dec 11**
Ray Gloria **Sept 5, Sept 26**
Ray James Earl **June 10 & 8, April 4**

Razaf Andy **Dec 15**
Reboucas Andre **May 13**
Reckford Lloyd **Feb 1**
Rector Sarah **March 3**
Redding Otis **Dec 10**
Redoshi **July 17**
Reed Willie **Aug 28**
Regis Cyril **March 8, Nov 29**
Reid Gareth **April 22**
Reid George Warren **Dec 3**
Reid Vincent Albert **Jan 9**
Revels Hiram Rhodes **March 16**
Rhodesia minority rule ends **June 1**
Rhodesia Olympic ban **Aug 24**
Ribas Oscar **June 19**
Richard Little **Dec 5**
Richards Viv **March 7**
Richardson W H **June 18**
Richmond Bill **Aug 5**
Richmond David **Jan 3**
Riley Samantha **Feb 15**
Ringgold Faith **Oct 8**
Riots in Glasgow **Jan 23**
Rive Richard **June 4**
Roach Archie **Jan 8**
Roberson Willie **Jan 23**
Robert Shabaan bin **June 20**
Roberts Andy **Aug 31**
Roberts Ben F **Feb 15**
Roberts Francis **Feb 15**
Roberts George S 'Spanky' **March 19**
Roberts Joseph Jenkins **June 8, June 26**
Roberts Norwell **Oct 23**
Roberts Sarah **Feb 15**
Roberts Terrence **Sept 5, Dec 3**
Robertson Carole **Sept 15**
Robeson Paul **April 9**
Robinson Bill 'Bojangles' **May 25**
Robinson Frank **Aug 31**
Robinson Jackie **April 15**
Robinson James R **Dec 8**
Robinson Jo Ann **April 27**
Robinson Johnny **Sept 15**
Robinson Mack **Aug 3**
Robinson Rachell **April 15**
Robinson Roscoe **Dec 18**
Robinson Smokey **Feb 19**
Robinson Spotswood W **Aug 5**
Robinson Tyrone **Aug 22**

Roche Emma Langdon **July 17**
Rodney Walter **March 23**
Rogers Jimmy **April 30**
Rollins Sonny **Sept 28**
Romanus Pontifex **Jan 8, June 18**
Ronaldo **Sept 18**
Roque Nho **Sept 25**
Rose Doudou N'Diaye **July 28**
Ross Diana **April 1 & 7, Nov 28**
Rotimi Ola **Aug 17**
Roundtree Richard **Aug 9, Nov 8**
Rowland Dick **May 31**
Rrurrambu George **June 10**
Rudolph Wilma **Nov 12, June 23**
Rumble in the jungle **Oct 30**
Rushton Edward **Nov 13**
Russell Bill **Jan 8**
Russell Edward A **Dec 3**
Rustin Bayard **March 17, Aug 28**
Rwanda **July 1**

S W A P O **Aug 18**
Saar Betty **July 30**
Sadat Anwar **Oct 6**
Sadji Abdoulaye **Dec 25**
Saint George Joseph Bologne Chevalier de **June 10**
Sam Nujoma **Feb 9**
Sanborn Franklin Benjamin **Dec 2**
Sancho Ignatius **Dec 14**
Sankara Thomas **Dec 7**
Sao Tome/Principe **July 12**
Saro-Wiwa Ken **Oct 10**
Satchel Ronald **Dec 4**
Schuffenhauer Bill **Aug 13**
Schweitzer Albert **Dec 21**
Schwerner Michael **June 21**
Scott Benjamin **Dec 3**
Scott Dr Evelyn Ruth **Sept 20**
Scott Hazel D **June 11**
Scott-Heron Gil **May 27**
Scott-King Coretta **April 27**
Scottsboro Boys **Jan 23, Nov 21**
Scramble for Africa **Aug 30, Feb 26**
Seacole Mary **Nov 23**
Seale Bobby **Oct 22**
Seige of Salvador **July 2**
Seipie Stompie **Sept 26**
Seko Mobutu Sese **Sept 7**
Selassie Haile **Aug 22, Nov 2**

Sembene Ousmane **June 9**
Senegal **April 4**
Senghor Leopold Sedar **Oct 9**
Sentamu John (Bishop) **Nov 30**
Settle Ron **Oct 2**
Seychelles **June 29**
Shabazz Malcolm **June 23**
Shabazz Betty **June 23**
Shabazz Qubilah **June 23**
Shadd Mary Ann (Cary) **June 5, Oct 17**
Shaft (film) **Nov 30**
Shakur Assata **July 16**
Shakur Tupac **Sept 13**
Shange Ntozake **Oct 18**
Sharp Granville **Nov 10**
Sharpe Sam **May 23**
Sharpeville Massacre **March 21**
Sharpton Al **Oct 3**
Shavers Earnie **Feb 25**
Shuttlesworth Fred **Oct 5**
Sibomana Abbe Andre **Feb 13**
Sierra Leone **April 27**
Sifford Charlie **June 11**
Simbine Graca **Oct 17**
Simmons Kennedy A **Sept 19**
Simone Nina **April 21**
Simpson Lorna **Aug 13**
Simpson O J **Oct 2**
Sims Naomi Ruth **May 22**
Simwinga Hammerskjoeld **Nov 17**
Singleton John **Jan 6**
Sirleaf Ellen Johnson **Oct 29**
Sisulu Albertina **June 2**
Sisulu Walter **May 5**
Sithole Antoinette **March 8**
Sithole Edison **June 24**
Sithole Rev Ndabaningi **Dec 12, April 18**
Slovo Joe **May 23**
Smalls Robert **April 5**
Smith Barbara **Dec 16, Nov 18**
Smith Bessie **Sept 26**
Smith Beverly **Dec 16**
Smith Fanny Cochrane **Feb 24**
Smith Gerrit **Dec 2**
Smith Harry **Feb 8**
Smith Leven **July 30**
Smith Mamie **May 26, Aug 10**
Smith Tommy **Oct 16, June 5**
Smith William Gardener **July 29**

Smith Zadie **Oct 25**
Smith-Robinson Ruby **Oct 9**
Smythe John H C **Nov 18**
Snodgrass Carlos **Dec 11**
Sobers Garfield **Feb 2**
Sobukwe Robert **Dec 5**
Soce Ousmane **Oct 31**
Society of Surinam **May 21**
Soga Tiyo **Aug 12**
Soledad Brothers **June 4**
Solomon Islands **July 7**
Solomon James **July 29**
Somalia **July 1**
Somare Michael **Sept 16**
Somerset v Stewart **June 22**
Sons of Africa **March 31**
Soromenho Fernando de Castro **June 18**
Soul Train **Sept 27**
Soulouque Faustin-Ella **Aug 6**
Souls of Black Folk **April 18**
Sousa Matthias de **April 11**
South Africa Olympic ban **Aug 18**
South Sudan **July 9**
Souza Joao de Cruz e **Nov 24**
Sowande Fela **March 13**
Soweto Massacre **June 16**
Soyinka Wole **July 13**
Span Otis **April 30**
Spinks Leon **Feb 25**
St Kitts & Nevis **Sept 19**
St Vincent/Grenadines **Oct 27**
Stamp James E **Dec 19**
Stanner William E H **Nov 24**
Stanton Father Timothy **Dec 28**
Staples Mavis **July 10**
'Stay out' Boston schools **June 18**
Stephenson Paul **May 6**
Stepin Fetchit **May 30**
Sterns George L **Dec 2**
Stevens Thaddeus **Aug 11**
Stevenson Teofilo **June 11**
Still William **July 14**
Stinney George **June 16**
Stokes Louis **Aug 3**
Stone Marcenia Lyle **Nov 2**
Stormy Weather (film) **July 21**
Stowe Harriet Beecher **June 14**
Strayhorn Billy **May 24**
Strode Woody **July 25**

Stroman John **Feb 8**
Strong Barrett **Nov 28**
Stuart John **Aug 20**
Stuart John (Cugoano) **Aug 20**
Sudan **Jan 1**
Sugar Hill Gang **Sept 16**
Summer Donner **March 25**
Sumner Charles **Feb 15, Dec 2**
Surinam/Antilles end slavery **July 1**
Suriname **Nov 24**
Suzman Helen **Nov 7**
Swan John **July 3**
Swaziland **Sept 6**
Sykes Roberta 'Bobby' **Nov 14**
Sylvester-Williams Henry **Feb 15, July 23**

Tacky **April 7**
Taliaferro George **Jan 8**
Tambo Adelaide 'Mama' **July 18**
Tambo Oliver **April 24**
Tanganyika **Dec 9**
Tanna Laura **June 28**
Tansi Sony Lab'ou **June 5**
Tanzania **Dec 9**
Tappan Lewis **Oct 22**
Tate Leona **Sept 8**
Taylor Charles **Oct 29**
Taylor Damilola **Nov 27**
Taylor Jr John Baxter **Nov 6**
Taylor Moddie **Dec 3**
Taylor Robert Robinson **July 4**
Terrell Tammi **April 1**
Tharpe Sister Rosetta **March 20**
The Voice (newspaper) **Oct 3**
Thibodaux Massacre (The) **Nov 24**
Thirteenth Amendment **Dec 6**
Thomas Carla **Dec 10**
Thomas Debi **Aug 13**
Thomas Jefferson **Sept 19, Sept 5**
Thomas Stella **March 13**
Thompson Abraham **July 30**
Thompson Daley **July 30**
Thompson John **June 15**
Thompson Sydney Oliver **Dec 3**
Thuku Harry **Dec 12**
Thurman Wallace **Aug 16**
Till Emmett **Aug 28**
To Kill A Mockingbird **July 11**
Togo **April 27**

Tolbert William **Oct 29**
Tolson Melvin B **Dec 28**
Tolton John Augustus **July 9**
Tombalbaye Francois **Aug 11**
Tometi Opal **Jan 4**
Tosh Peter **Feb 6**
Toure Ahmed Sekou **Jan 25**
Toure Sekou **Oct 2**
Trevigne Paul **May 7**
Trinidad & Tobago **Aug 31**
Tristao Nuno **Aug 8**
Trotter William Munroe **July 11**
Truganini **Feb 24**
Truth Sojourner **Nov 26**
Tshilongo Lipumbu Ya **Jan 6**
Tsiranana Philibert (President) **June 26**
Tsvangirai Morgan **April 18**
Tubman Harriet **Sept 17**
Tubman William V S **July 23**
Tucker Ira B **June 24**
Tucker Jim **Oct 31**
Tucker Lorenzo **Jan 2**
Tucker William **Jan 3**
Tull Walter **March 25**
Tulsa white riots **May 31**
Ture Samori (Toure) **July 2**
Turner Charles Henry **Feb 3**
Turner George Dewitt **Dec 3**
Turner Nat **Nov 11**
Turpin Randolph **June 10, May 3**
Tyrrell Mary Church **July 24**
Tuskegee Airman **March 19**
Tuskegee Boycott **June 17**
Tuskegee Institute **July 4**
Tutu Desmond **Oct 7**
Tyson Cicely **Sept 28**
Tyson Mike **June 30**
Tyson Neil deGrasse **Oct 5**

Uganda **Oct 9**
Una Blasius To **Feb 2**
Unaipon David **Sept 28**
Underground Railroad **July 14**
Universal Negro Improvement Ass **July 15**
Upper Volta **Aug 5**
Upton Florence K **Feb 22**
US Virgin Islands abolish slavery **July 3**
USA ban slave imports **March 2**

Van Dee Zee James **Dec 9**
Van Peebles Mario **Nov 30**
Van Peebles Melvin **Nov 30**
Vandross Luther **July 1**
Varick James **July 30**
Vaughan Dorothy **Jan 28**
Vaughan Sarah **Dec 28, Jan 26, April 25**
Vechten Carl Van **July 29**
Vera Yvonne **July 12**
Vilakazi Benedict Wallet **Oct 26**
Voodoo Queen Laveau **June 15**

Wailer Bunny **Feb 6**
Walcott Derek **Jan 23**
Walcott Joe (Jersey) **Sept 6**
Walker Albertina **July 1**
Walker Alice **Feb 9**
Walker David **Aug 6**
Walker Frank X **Dec 19**
Walker George **June 27**
Walker Kara **Nov 26**
Walker Kath **Sept 16**
Walker Madam C J **Dec 23, July 6**
Wallace George **Aug 25**
Waller Fats **Dec 15**
Walls Carlotta **Dec 18, Sept 5**
Walter Bishop Alexander **July 23**
Walter Little **July 1**
Walters Ronald W **July 20**
Ward Clara **July 1**
Ward Samuel Ringgold **Oct 17, June 5**
Ware Virgil **Sept 15**
Warnock Raphael **Jan 5**
Washington Booker T **April 5, Jan 5, July 4**
Washington Denzel **Dec 28, Oct 2**
Washington Dinah **April 25**
Washington Fredi **May 25**
Washington Harold **Oct 8**
Washington Jesse **Feb 23**
Washington Kenny **Jan 7**
Watch Night Service **Dec 31**
Waters Muddy **April 30**
Watson Andrew **March 12**
Watts Riots **Aug 11**
We are the world **March 7**
Weah George **Oct 1, Oct 29**
Webb Alfreda Johnson **July 10**
Webb Chick **April 25**
Weems Charlie **Jan 23, Nov 21**

Weld Theodore D **Nov 23**
Wells Ida B **July 16**
Wells Mary **April 1**
Wesley Cynthia **Sept 15**
Wesley Fred **May 3**
West Dorothy **Aug 16**
West Dr James **Feb 10**
West Kanya **June 8**
Weston George **July 15**
Weston Kim **April 1**
Wharton Arthur **Oct 28**
Wheatley James **Dec 11**
White Cecil Goldsburg **Dec 3**
White Citizens' Council **July 11**
White Griffin Josephine Sophia **Dec 18**
White Portia May **June 24**
White Walter **July 1, Aug 30**
Whitfield Norman **Nov 28**
Wilberforce William **Aug 24**
Williston David **July 4**
Wilkins Earnest J **Dec 3**
Wilkins Roy **Aug 30**
William Cathay **March 21**
William Roberson **Nov 21**
Williams Archie **Aug 3**
Williams Billy Dee **Nov 28**
Williams Carmilla **Jan 7**
Williams Daniel Hale **Jan 18**
Williams Eric **Aug 31**
Williams Eugene **Jan 23, Nov 21**
Williams Francis **April 17**
Williams George Washington **Oct 16, July 18**
Williams Hosea **Nov 16**
Williams Paul Revere **Feb 18**
Williams Serena **July 8**
Williams Vanessa **Nov 16**
Wilson Alex **Sept 5**
Wilson Arthur Dooley **July 21**
Wilson August **Oct 2**
Wilson Jackie **Nov 28**
Wilson Leslie Wagner **Nov 18**
Wilson Margaret Bush **Jan 30**
Windrush Empire **June 22, March 30**
Windsor Harley **Feb 15**
Winfrey Oprah **Nov 20**
Winmar Nicky **April 17**
Wonder Stevie **May 13, Nov 2**
Woodfox Albert **Feb 19**
Woods Granville Tailer **Jan 30**

Woods Tiger **April 14**
Woods Wilfred (Bishop) **June 15**
Woodson Carter Goodwin **Dec 19**
Worrell Trix **Jan 5**
Wright Andrew **Jan 23, Nov 21**
Wright Andy **Nov 21**
Wright Leroy **Jan 23, Nov 21**
Wright Martha Coffin **Dec 25, Sept 17**
Wright Milton S J **March 11**
Wright Moses **Aug 28**
Wright Richard **Nov 28**

X Malcolm **Feb 21, June 23**

Yameogo Maurice **Aug 5**
Yancey Bessie Woodson **Dec 19**
Young Andrew **March 12**
Young Lester **April 7**
Young Rosley W **Dec 11**
Young Whitney **July 31**
Yunupingu Mandawuy **June 2**

Zambia **Oct 24**
Zapata Paula **Nov 11**
Zenawi Meles **Aug 20**
Zewditu Empress **April 29**
Zimbabwe **April 18**
Zong (The) **Dec 22, Nov 10**
Zong Ousmane **Oct 3**
Zubiera Constantine Henriquez de **Nov 6**
Zulu Shaka **Sept 22**

Lightning Source UK Ltd.
Milton Keynes UK
UKHW051436220922
409227UK00005B/79